D1480427

In Love and Struggle

In Love and Struggle

The Revolutionary Lives of
James and Grace Lee Boggs

Stephen M. Ward

The University of North Carolina Press
Chapel Hill

Library of Congress Cataloging-in-Publication Data

Names: Ward, Stephen M., 1970- author.
Title: In love and struggle : the revolutionary lives of James and
Grace Lee Boggs / Stephen M. Ward.
Other titles: Justice, power, and politics.
Description: Chapel Hill : University of North Carolina Press, [2016] | Series: Justice,
power, and politics | Includes bibliographical references and index.
Identifiers: LCCN 2015041272| ISBN 9780807835203 (cloth : alk. paper) |
ISBN 9781469617701 (ebook)
Subjects: LCSH: Boggs, James. | Boggs, Grace Lee. | African American political
activists—Michigan—Detroit—Biography. | African American radicals—
Michigan—Detroit—Biography. | Chinese American women—Michigan—
Detroit—Biography. | Political activists—Michigan—Detroit—Biography. | Civil
rights workers—Michigan—Detroit—Biography. | Black power—United States—
History—20th century. | Socialism—United States—History—20th century.
Classification: LCC F574.D49 A276 2016 | DDC 323.092/2—dc23 LC record available
at http://lccn.loc.gov/2015041272

For Mom, Sekai, and Chaney
Always

Contents

Acknowledgments

My life has been enriched through studying the ideas, activism, and partnership of James and Grace Lee Boggs. Of the many things I gained, one of the most important is a deeper respect and greater appreciation for the importance of community, the connections we have to each other, and the relationships that sustain us. One occasion stands out as my favorite illustration of this importance. In 1990, as James Boggs faced an uncertain future in his battle with cancer, fellow activists and friends of James and Grace Lee Boggs held a community celebration to honor the couple. After several people spoke in tribute and appreciation for the Boggses' decades of activism and mentorship, James Boggs delivered a moving speech thanking the assembled comrades but asking them not to lose sight of the larger community of which they all were a part. "I want to thank you for bringing us together in this kind of setting, because I think in this kind of setting we cannot just celebrate Grace and I," he insisted. "Let me tell you something, Grace and I in ourselves is nobody. It is only in relationship to other bodies and many somebodies that anybody is somebody. Let me tell you that. Don't get it in your cotton-picking mind that you are somebody in yourself." In that spirit, I offer these acknowledgements in sincere recognition of the many somebodies who have made me somebody and who have been part of the journey that produced this book.

Pride of place goes to my wife Sekai, and our beloved son Chaney, the two somebodies who are most responsible for making me feel like somebody. Sekai and Chaney travelled the journey of this book with me daily, and their love sustained me. Sekai and I started building our life together shortly before I began writing this book, and I cannot image completing this work without her love, companionship, and support. I have been working on this book Chaney's entire life, but I won't make any easy comparisons or use ready metaphors about the timing and intertwining of his young life and this book. As I think he knows, Chaney has a place all his own in my mind and in my heart. Together, Sekai and Chaney are my light and my joy, and I love them dearly. While it is only in these opening pages that their names appear, Sekai and Chaney have touched every page of this book.

My mother, Cheryl Ward, has also placed her distinctive mark on these pages. Her impact on me is so strong that it could not be otherwise. From my first days to the journey that produced this book, she has been the most consistent, and consistently loving presence in my life. Her generous and radiant spirit was a hallmark of my childhood, and she remains the most influential person in my life. These days she is known by several names and titles—among them Abuela, 'Buels, Ba, and Rev. Cheryl—reflecting the many lives she continues to touch. For me and my siblings, and now for my son and his cousins, my mother is our family's beacon of love. I thank her for everything, including for being my model of a loving and grounded human being.

My father, the late Michael Harold Ward, made his imprint on me, and by extension this book, well before I thought of writing it. From my earliest memory, he was there guiding, teaching, and inspiring. He taught me the joy of learning and made sure I was ready to say something intelligent at the dinner table. He also taught me the value of saying "I love you" everyday. In his last years, my father's wisdom and vision—and when I speak of my father here, I of course include his loving wife Tigi, for they were a beautiful team—helped me to grow in unexpected ways. My father passed away while I was writing this book. I carry his love and the enduring presence of his great intellect with me.

I want to also honor the other family members who set my foundation. This begins with the memory of my Grandmothers: June Ellen Springs Ward, Mary Howe Granberry, and June Fisher White. Though they were not here when I started writing this book, their love and labor made this work possible by instilling in me a sense of justice and a respect for knowledge. I recognize that they did a great deal for me—more, in fact, than I can ever know—while radiating love and faith in the future. Elijah Glenn Ward Sr. (Tio) and Adelaide Ward, are beloved elders, and they, along with my cousins, spread love through the family. Uncle Doug keeps my Dad's memory alive in word and deed, always reminding me of the pride and love that has flowed from generation to generation.

The other members of my family have also shared in the broader journey of writing this book. My brothers and sisters—Geoff, Toussaint, Tamiyah, Caryn, and Nisa—have been a constant source of support and encouragement. I want to thank Caryn in particular for her beautiful and uplifting spirit. She has inspired me over the years, teaching me to recognize and appreciate daytime in the nighttime. Geoff also deserves special mention. While he is my younger brother, he seems more like the big brother, and not only because he is taller than me. Growing up I marveled at how smart he was, and I have consistently learned from him. He is now making his mark as a scholar, and I am both proud of and inspired by his scholarship. My homeboys Desi Bryant and Damon Woodruff (Dez and Dub) can also be included as family. They may not pay much attention to the content of this book, but they are a significant part of the context in which it was written. They help me stay connected to the place that I still call home, even though I have now lived elsewhere for many years, and we are far removed from our days on Condon, Garth, and Sherbourne. Our friendship, along with the other homies Ramon Evans, Will Alexander, Dion Evans, and Toby Ferguson, has helped sustain me. No matter what may come, we will remain tight, like J. J., Papo, Cool Breeze, and Head.

I extend my deepest gratitude and appreciation to Grace Lee Boggs. She passed away on October 5, 2015, just as this book was coming to completion. While I am saddened that she did not get to see the book, I am thankful that I was able to get to know her during the last thirteen of her 100 years. Grace was quite obviously invaluable to this book. I learned a great deal from my many interviews and conversations with her, and she also shared various historical documents and other material related to her and Jimmy. She took me with her to meetings, speaking engagements, and other events, and she put me in touch with various activists and friends in Detroit and across the country. From the beginning of this project, Grace supported and encouraged me, but she never pushed me in one direction or another. She showed no interest in shaping the narrative or analysis of this book. Indeed, for many of those thirteen years, my interactions with Grace were not focused on my research or the book. Rather, they took place as I worked with her through the James and Grace Lee Boggs Center to Nurture Community Leadership (BCNCL) and in the context of ongoing grassroots political struggles in Detroit. As our relationship grew, Grace became a political and intellectual mentor to me, as she was for so many, and she brought me into a vibrant and inspiring community of activists, thinkers, and builders in Detroit. It is this, even more than her contributions to my research and this book, for which I am most thankful and appreciative.

The heart of this political community has been the Boggs Center, and I am especially grateful to be associated with it. I want to thank my fellow board members, past and present, with whom I have worked and from whom I have learned so much, including: Will Copeland, Myrtle Thompson Curtis, Wayne Curtis, Bernadette Dickerson, Richard Feldman, Michael

"Doc" Holbrook, Shea Howell, Scott Kurashige, Tawana Petty, Ron Scott, Kim Sherobbi, Larry Sparks, and Barbara Stachowski. Thank you to Alice Jennings and Carl Edwards for the vision and commitment that led to the founding of the Boggs Center.

I want to make special acknowledgement of Rich Feldman, or "Rick," as some of us call him. He has been an exemplary comrade and a warm friend, putting into practice the idea that caring human relationships can be the foundation of revolutionary change. Rick supported me throughout the process of writing this book, and I thank him for always being there to provide encouragement, talk through ideas, share material, read draft chapters, and offer suggestions. He has also inspired me with his political passion and untiring commitment to carrying out the work and vision of the Boggs Center.

That passion and commitment are matched by the brilliant Shea Howell, who also deserves special recognition. Over many years Shea has shared with me insights, recollections, and documents that helped me write the book. More importantly, I have admired and learned from Shea's activism, leadership, and intellect. From Field St. to Sutton, she is keeper of the flame. I also want to honor what I learned from Boggs Center member Ron Scott, who met the Boggses as a young radical during the Black Power movement and spent the rest of his life as a political activist, media maker, and community intellectual. During most of the years that I knew him, Ron described himself as a "transformational anthropologist," reflecting his commitment to theorizing and working toward human transformation as the essence of revolutionary change. Ron passed away at the end of November 2015, less than two months after Grace. His legacy of activism, particularly the work to create Peace Zones for Life, was an embodiment of the concept of Visionary Organizing that Grace urged during the final years of her life. I thank Rick, Shea, and Ron for teaching me about Jimmy and Grace, about the continuing development of revolutionary theory, and about the emerging possibilities for the transformation of Detroit.

An extended community of people in Detroit also nurtured me. A special thank you to Melba Boyd for her continued support and guidance. I was fortunate to meet Melba just as I began to simultaneously study the city's history and engage with its contemporary grassroots politics, allowing me to see the city through her perceptive eyes. She has been a wonderful mentor and friend, and she stands as a model of scholarly integrity. My study and engagement has been aided by supportive friends, colleagues, and mentors in Detroit such as Aneb Gloria House, Charles Simmons, David Goldberg, and Richard Levy; beautiful people and places like Janet Jones and the Source Booksellers; visionaries such as Julia Putnam, Amanda Rosman, and the James and Grace Lee Boggs School; creative artists such as Will See, Honeycomb, Jessica Care Moore, and Ill; and veteran activists who shared their time and insights (and photos), like Daniel Aldridge and Kenneth Snodgrass. The overlapping networks of people from whom I have learned about the history and especially the contemporary spirit of Detroit extends beyond the city to people across the country. Among them, a high power thanks goes to Matthew Birkhold. Matt's grasp of the Boggses' work and historical significance is extraordinary, and my long and frequent conversations with him helped to shape this book. Matt's own scholarship along with his efforts to develop the concept of visionary organizing will do much to interpret and extend the Boggses' legacy.

Unfortunately, I did not have the opportunity to meet James Boggs. He passed away in the summer of 1993, just before I began graduate school at the University of Texas that fall. It was there that I first learned of him and began reading his writings. That was the starting point for my interest, studying, and researching that became this book. My somewhat unorthodox path through graduate school began in the Department of Economics and ended in the Department of History. In Economics I had the good fortune of studying Marxism under the direction of Harry Cleaver, whose contributions to the tradition of Autonomous Marxism facilitated my initial encounter with the Boggses. I thank Harry for that, and for his crucial support during my short time in the economics department. In the Department of History, my good fortune multiplied as I benefitted from the guidance, intellect, and consistent support of Toyin Falola. From his independent study course that helped me see that I wanted to be a historian, to his wise counsel as I made my way to his department, to serving as my dissertation advisor, Toyin was there for me at every turn. The late Robin Kilson was an important influence and supported in the department. I learned great deal from Jim Sidbury as well. Juliet Walker took a faculty appointment in the department toward the end of my time there, and she graciously agreed to serve on my dissertation committee. Outside of the history department, Barbara Harlow was an also supportive and helpful.

I found an intellectual home in Center for African and African American Studies (CAAAS), and I offer a profound thank you to the center and those who made it what it was. The center nurtured, supported, and enriched my early scholarly development, including my initial thinking and research leading to this book. It pleases me to write that the center is now named after John L. Warfield, or "Doc" as most people knew him. Working with Doc during his final years was a formative part of my graduate school experience, and I will always remember him as a giving mentor and one of my first models of a community-oriented Black Studies scholar. The person who introduced me to Doc and brought me into the center became my closest friend at the University of Texas, the late Aime J. Ellis. Aime's passion for intellectual exchange and commitment to pushing the boundaries of Black Studies helped me to grow intellectually, and our friendship helped me to grow as a person. I still miss his brilliance and camaraderie. Among the other people who contributed to the nurturing environment of the center, Ted Gordon deserves recognition for provided crucial leadership for us graduate students who worked in the center, and Saheed Adejumobi for his refreshing combination of intellect and wit. The late Vincent Woodard, another friend gone much too soon, likewise made unique contributions to this rich environment and to my growth.

The ideas in this book also have a foundation in the political community in which I participated and from which I learned during my time at the University of Texas, and I would like to thank all of the people who helped build this community. This includes a series of organizations culminating in the Anti-Racist Organizing Committee and in several protest actions, including the "UT 10," all organized by undergraduate and graduate students. Key faculty allies and supporters included Ted Gordon and Bob Jensen.

I was able to complete my dissertation through a Pre-Doctoral Fellowship with the Center for the Study of African American Politics at the University of Rochester. For this wonderful opportunity I thank Fred Harris, the center's founding director and a gracious scholar. I also thank Valeria Sinclair-Chapman, Ghislaine Radegonde-Eison, Larry Hudson, and the Frederick Douglass Institute for African and African American Studies for their help and encouragement during my year there.

At the University of Michigan an honor role of friends and colleagues has supported me, and a few in particular stand out for special recognition. Charlie Bright has been there from the start. I *suspect* that he was the strongest supporter of my hiring; I *know* that he has been my strongest supporter since I arrived. The list of roles he has played for me includes mentor, colleague, collaborator, advocate, co-teacher, critical reader, friend and confidante. I have also benefitted from—and greatly appreciate—Charlie's years of engagement with the history of Detroit and labors to create meaningful pathways for students and others to learn from and with people in the city. I am thankful to travel the path he laid and follow the model he set. Julius Scott is another dear friend and valued colleague. I have learned and grown a great deal from my friendship with Julius—or Dr. J, as I like to call him. He keeps a low profile, but that cannot hide his brilliance, minimize his kindness, or undermine his generous spirit. To my mind he is the heart and soul of the Department of Afroamerican and African Studies (DAAS). Julius holds it down for DAAS like his namesake did for the Sixers. I have similar respect and appreciation for my man Larry Rowley and the friendship we have developed over the years. Indeed, Julius, Larry, and I have grown together through our passion for the practice and promise of Black History, our shared commitment to Black Studies, and our ongoing conversations (including our Jazz at Julius excursions, real and mythical). Larry's sharp intellect has pushed and inspired me, and our friendship helps me to be a better teacher and scholar.

There are several other colleagues at the University of Michigan that I am happy to thank for their roles in shaping my experience here and for their varied contributions to this book. A special thanks goes to Sherie Randolph, en excellent historian and even better friend. Her knowledge and insights have influenced and inspired me, and I always grow from our many conversations about the history we study, teach, and write. Matthew Countryman's mentorship, support, and critical eye have been indispensible. He guided and encouraged me from the beginning of this project, and he especially stepped in at crucial moments helping to ensure that this book came to be. Scott Kurashige told me about the position during my first visit to the Boggs Center in 2001, played a role in my hiring, and remained a steadfast colleague and comrade. Evans Young and Lester Monts provided support and guidance along the way. It has been a pleasure to work with Garrett Felber and Austin McCoy. They have helped to expand my thinking while writing this book, as it coincided with watching their development as emerging scholars and activists.

My joint appointment in the Department of Afroamerican and African Studies (DAAS) and the Residential College (RC) has made for a wonderful intellectual and institutional home, and I want to thank all of the people who make these two places special. Several friends and colleagues in DAAS and the RC have helped to sustain, drive, and support me. In DAAS, this begins with Elizabeth James, who has been a supportive friend from the very start and a stalwart for the department. I also thank other members of the DAAS community, including Faye Portis, Wayne High, Frieda Ekotto, Lori Hill, Martha Jones, Scott Ellsworth, Nesha Haniff, Robin Grice, Robin Means Coleman, Katherine Weathers, James Jackson, and Donald Sims. A special work of thanks goes to Angela Dillard and Tiya Miles, who were wonderfully supportive chairs and whose leadership helped to set DAAS on a solid course. To my good fortune, Angela also served as the Director of the RC, so I had the benefit of her stewardship and guidance in both units. I thank her for always looking out for me. Another person who makes the RC run, and makes it the special place we know it to be, is the amazing Jennifer Myers, and I thank her that and for consistently supporting me. Along with Jennifer, I thank Carl Abrego Charlie Murphy and the rest of the team in East Quad, as well as my Social Theory and Practice Colleagues. A big thank you goes to my Semester in Detroit colleagues Lolita Hernandez, Craig Regester and Alana Hoey Moore. Craig in particular has been there from the start, and I appreciate his support and comradeship throughout the time I have been writing this book.

It is a pleasure to recognize the friends and colleagues beyond my institution who have contributed to my scholarly growth and to this book. Cedric Johnson is a solid scholar and a solid friend, and I value him for both. He has been there for me along the long path of writing this book with his consistent support and encouragement, his critical eye, and timely conversations about the academy, contemporary black politics, our families, and the wider world. I shared a similar friendship with Ahmad Rahman, and I am the better for it. Ahmad passed away in September 2015, and I miss his presence and his smile and his "hey brother" greeting. A measure of appreciation goes to Robin Kelley for his support and his intellectual influence. Robin's scholarship has shaped my thinking and approach to the writing of history, and in this regard I am, of course, one of many. Indeed, a significant proportion of the works in this book's bibliography bear his intellectual imprint. This is a testament to his scholarly productivity and to his profound impact. Some of the other scholars who have also influenced my thinking, provided scholarly influence, encouraged me in this work, or served as mentors from afar include: Ernie Allen, Dan Berger, Martha Biondi, John Bracey, Pero Dagbovie, Elizabeth Hinton, Kwame Jeffries, Ollie Johnson, Clarence Lang, Donna Murch, Barbara Ransby, Jim Smethurst, Bill Strickland, Richard Thomas, Jeanne Theoharis, Akinyele Umoja, Derrick White, Fanon Che Wilkins, Rhonda Williams, and Komozi Woodard.

Several friends, colleagues, and mentors read early drafts and parts of this work, and I would like to thank them for their time, insights, and contributions to this book. Angela Dillard read an early book proposal and put me in touch with Bill Mullen and Jim Smethurst who also read it. Each of them gave me helpful feedback and guidance that propelled the project. Gina Morantz-Sanchez stepped in at a crucial time, reading my early material, helping to shape the project, and guiding me through the first stages of the publishing process. I would like to thank DAAS for holding a manuscript workshop, where I received great feedback and guidance from Matthew Countryman, Joe Trotter, Chris Phelps, and Angela Dillard, who served as the primary readers, as well as the other workshop participants, including Charlie Bright, Scott Kurashige, and Stephen Berrey. I received great feedback from close readings of draft chapters from Rick Feldman, Matt Birkhold, Frank Joyce, who each had unique insights informed by their familiarity with the Boggses. Beth Bates was extraordinary. She read multiple and successive draft, offering comments and suggestions that demonstrably made the work better at each step. I thank Beth for her thorough and careful reading and for the encouragement she gave along the way. At the very end of the writing process, I had the good fortune of working with Grey Osterud, and the book is surely better for it. Even in this short time, Grey's sharp eye and magical editing touch amazed me, and I see clearly why she garners such high praise.

I have long admired the work published by the University of North Carolina Press, and I now know something about the great effort put forward by those who make those books happen. Thank you to everyone at the press who helped to make this book. I was lucky to work with Sian Hunter during her last months with the press. Though it was only a short period of time, I am glad to have begun the process with such a knowledgeable and skilled editor. My good fortune continued as I travelled the rest of the road with Brandon Proia. Brandon has been a pleasure to work with not only because of his editorial skill but also his gracious manner. I must also thank him and his colleagues for an abundance of patience, which I surely (and perhaps sorely) tested. My appreciation also extends to Ashley Moore and Mikala Guyton at Westchester Publishing for their excellent work on the book, and to Laurie Prendergast for her sharp editorial eye and indexing. I thank Rhonda Y. Williams and Heather Ann Thompson for including this book in the Justice, Power, and Politics series and thereby allowing my work to sit in the company of the groundbreaking scholarship of Talitha LeFlouria, Dan Berger, and others.

These acknowledgments began with a departure from the convention of reserving for the end the naming of those closest to the author. Instead, I began there, opening my list of people to thank—the somebodies who make me somebody—with my wife Sekai, my son Chaney, and my mother Cheryl Ward. Now, I will in a sense revert to convention. I close by again recognizing and thanking Mom, Sekai, and Chaney. This book is dedicated to them, just as I am and forever will be.

A Note on Names

I have chosen to use the first names Grace and Jimmy throughout the book to avoid confusion or lack of clarity that may arise from using "Boggs" when referring to either of them. Furthermore, in my reference to James Boggs and C. L. R. James, I have avoided using the name James (except when using their full names), though friends and comrades did at times use "James" in reference to each man. In different periods of James Boggs's life, friends and comrades also called him Jim or Jimmy, while C. L. R. James also went by various names over the course of his life. During the 1950s, when the two men were in the same organization, members of the group generally referred to C. L. R. James as "Jimmie" and James Boggs as "Jim" (and in letters, where they often used a single initial as shorthand, they identified each man as "J"). However, after that period, and for the rest of his life, James Boggs was most often called Jimmy. Most of James Boggs's friends and comrades described in this book knew him as Jimmy, and that is the name by which he is most commonly known now. Therefore, for consistency and clarity throughout the text, I refer to James Boggs as "Jimmy" and C. L. R. James as "C. L. R."

Introduction

James and Grace Lee Boggs built a remarkable life together grounded in their shared commitment to making the next American revolution. By disposition and background, they were two very different people. They set out on disparate life trajectories and traveled distinct paths to radical politics, with little that would predict convergence. Yet, their paths crossed in the early 1950s. By that time, Grace and Jimmy had both become committed revolutionaries through participating in their respective spaces of radical politics over the preceding decade. As a couple, they reinforced the political project that each had come to separately and that emerged as the central objective of their partnered lives: apprehending the specific pathways for revolutionary transformation most appropriate for and unique to the historical moment in the United States. This shared commitment to conceptualizing a distinctly American revolution, in combination with their diverse backgrounds and experiences, allowed them to learn from each other and grow together in remarkable ways. From the beginning of their courtship in 1953 to his death in 1993, James and Grace Lee Boggs forged a unique and generative partnership sustained through their shared intellectual work and political activism.

Over these four decades, their conceptualization of revolutionary change continuously evolved. It was initially structured around a specific articulation of Marxist theory and organizational form, but by the early 1960s, the social and political struggle of African Americans, which had always been a component of their politics, overtook Marxism as their primary realm of political activity and theoretical reflection. The black struggle became the basis for their vision of an American revolution. As central and pivotal figures within a national network of black radicals during the 1950s and early 1960s, Jimmy and Grace helped develop the ideas and spaces of protest that led to the birth of the Black Power movement. Indeed, they did as much as nearly any other activist to lay the organizational and ideological groundwork for the emergence of Black Power in the middle of the 1960s. Their contributions to the Black Power movement grew from their quarter century of activism and theoretical work preceding it, and their participation in the movement further propelled their subsequent decades of political work, much of which focused on developing a vision for reconceptualizing and transforming postindustrial cities. These four decades of thinking, writing, and activism during the second half of the twentieth century produced an inimitable shared legacy of revolutionary thought and action for the twenty-first-century United States.

This book tells how they built this legacy. *In Love and Struggle* begins by uncovering the personal experiences and historical conditions under which each of them became a revolutionary thinker and activist. The book then narrates how their paths crossed, charts the beginning and early development of their partnership, and documents the first decade of their intellectual and political work together. Through its examination of the Boggses' activism, writings, ideas, and other movement-building activities from the 1940s to the early 1960s, *In Love and Struggle* shows that James and Grace Lee Boggs forged a continuous practice of political activism coupled with, informed by, and sustained through theoretical reflection. The pages that follow invite readers to contemplate both the practice and the products of this unique partnership.[1]

BY MOST MEASURES, James and Grace Lee Boggs made an unlikely pair. Born in 1915 in Providence, Rhode Island, to Chinese immigrants, Grace Chin Lee was raised in New York City and earned a Ph.D. in philosophy from Bryn Mawr College at the age of twenty-five. With dim prospects in academia as a Chinese American woman, she moved to Chicago, where she came of age politically by living in the black community and entering left-wing politics. James "Jimmy" Boggs was born in Marion Junction, Alabama, in 1919 and migrated to Detroit in search of employment in the auto industry following his high school graduation in 1937. In 1940, the year that Grace earned a Ph.D., Jimmy landed a job in a Chrysler auto plant, beginning a twenty-eight-year career as an autoworker and member of the United Auto Workers (UAW). Out of these divergent personal backgrounds and social experiences, Grace and Jimmy fashioned a unique brand of black radical politics by the early 1960s.

As an Asian American woman within black radical circles, Grace surely was anomalous, but this raised no significant concerns or barriers to her participation in various black organizations, struggles, and movements. While she never attempted to conceal her ethnic identity, Grace developed a political identity as a *black movement* activist—that is, an activist based in a black community and operating within black movements. Living with Jimmy in a black community in the 1950s and immersing herself in the social and political worlds of black Detroit, she solidified this political identity through her activism. By the early 1960s she was firmly situated within a network of activists building organizations, staging protests, and engaging in a range of grassroots political initiatives. By mid-decade, when the Black Power movement emerged, Grace was a fixture within black radical politics in Detroit and widely known in movement circles nationally.

Together, Jimmy and Grace helped to build a vibrant local black protest community in Detroit, the city that served not only as their home and political base, but also as a catalyst for new ideas about social change. They formulated their theories through grassroots activism in the context of—and at times directly in response to—the tremendous urban transformation experienced by the Motor City during the decades following World War II. Alongside their local efforts, the couple forged an ever-widening network of activists, artists, and intellectuals across the country, engaging multiple spaces of black activist politics. A diverse group of younger black activists from Detroit and across the country visited their eastside Detroit home—"the Boggses' University," as one of them labeled it.[2] Each received theoretical training, political education, and a sense of historical continuity between past and future struggles. Through their extraordinary partnership James and Grace Lee Boggs built several organizations, undertook innumerable local activist initiatives, produced an array of theoretical and political writings, and mentored a generation of activists.

In the course of their political work, Grace and Jimmy built a notable partnership of equals. They remained two very different people, not just in social background and individual life experiences, but also in their manner of intellectual engagement. But these differences proved generative throughout their four decades of collaboration, as they brought distinct and complementary strengths to their partnership that created the space for individual growth as well as learning from each other. At the core of this partnership sat their shared commitment to ideas and the melding of theory and practice.

"I believe ideas are life and death questions, and people ought to struggle over them," Jimmy said toward the end of his life.[3] He made this remark in the spring of 1993 during a presentation to a group of young activists in Detroit. His topic, "Think Dialectically, Not Biologically," urged his listeners to recognize changing social and political realities and avoid the narrow racial analysis that in today's academic parlance would be called essentialism. The theme was important to him. Two decades earlier, in 1974, he had delivered a speech with the same title. In its first iteration he explained to his audience that thinking dialectically meant being "ready to recognize that as reality changes, our ideas have to change so that we can project new, more advanced aspirations worth striving for. This is the only way to avoid becoming prisoners of ideas which were once progressive but have become reactionary, i.e. have turned into their opposite."[4]

Delivering this speech at the tail end of the Black Power movement, Jimmy cited experiences of the preceding two decades—the escalation and evolution of civil rights protest beginning in the 1950s followed by the rise and fall of Black Power—to emphasize the "very important dialectical principle" that "struggle is social practice and when you engage in social practice, you gain new insights."[5] This statement articulates the Boggses' understanding of the relationship between theory and practice; it emphasizes their belief in the dynamic interaction between events and thought, between historical circumstances and the life of the mind. Jimmy and Grace placed a high value on intellectual reflection, but always in conjunction with the practice and experience of struggle. From the original struggle, Jimmy explained, "you find out that there was much more involved than you had originally perceived to be the case when you began your struggle. Therefore you are faced with the need to raise your level of understanding, your level of conceptual knowledge. If you do not raise your level of understanding as the struggle expands and develops, then what began as a progressive struggle can turn into its opposite."[6]

These twin commitments—an adherence to the principle of dialectical thinking and an insistence on combining theoretical reflection with political practice—set the foundation for the Boggses' collaboration. Dialectical thinking gave them a theory of social and historical change. It also provided them a framework for recognizing the need to discard established ideas when new political circumstances and social realities had outstripped those ideas. The practice of combining theoretical reflection with political engagement helped them to anticipate new struggles, weather the vagaries of movement building, manage the distraction and discouragement of political splits, and maintain their remarkable longevity. Grace and Jimmy had come to revolutionary politics separately and independently when they met in the early 1950s, but their concept of revolutionary change and their understanding of what it meant to be a revolutionary continued to evolve as they lived, organized, theorized, and struggled together over the next four decades. From their combined and shared experiences with the labor movement, Marxism and the organized left, black radical politics, the Black Power movement, and community-based organizations in Detroit, Jimmy and Grace came to conceptualize their vocation as revolutionaries to be carried out in three fundamental steps: developing a philosophy of revolutionary change, then projecting a vision for change based on this philosophy and on the specific history and contemporary realities of our society, and finally, engaging in struggles to transform society in line with this vision. This framework encapsulates the driving dynamic of their forty year partnership.

In Love and Struggle examines the making of this partnership and offers a framework for assessing the Boggses' impact and legacy as thinkers, activists, and movement builders. The first part of the book traces their divergent backgrounds, describes their activist origins in separate political spaces at the beginning of the 1940s, and identifies the personal experiences and historical conditions under which each of them became a revolutionary thinker and activist. These chapters show how Grace and Jimmy followed parallel and ultimately convergent political paths during the 1940s, leading them to the same organization, and to each other, in the early 1950s. Parts II and III examine the content and the contours of the Boggses' activism and thinking over the next decade. These chapters show how Jimmy and Grace built their marital, political, and intellectual partnership within three important contexts: living in 1950s Detroit and its growing black community, as members of Correspondence, a small Marxist organization, and through their engagement with the black freedom struggle. Part II examines the development of Jimmy and Grace's thinking and the shape of their political practice during the mid- and late 1950s, as they assumed leadership of Correspondence but also began to move away from the group's worker-centered politics. Part III examines the continuing evolution of their ideas and activism from the end of the 1950s to 1963, when the black struggle replaced the Marxist concept of class struggle as the primary focus of their theoretical and political work, and they helped to set the ideological and organizational foundation for the emergence of the Black Power movement. Through this account and analysis of the first decade of the Boggses' partnership, *In Love and Struggle* reveals the organizational, ideological, and political transformations out of which Jimmy and Grace developed their practice of continually evaluating and evolving their concept of revolution.

The book closes with an epilogue that traces the evolution of their thinking about revolutionary change and summarizes their activities over the next three decades, from 1963 to Jimmy's death in 1993. His passing at the age of seventy-four marked the end of their partnership, of course, but not the end of the ideas, politics, or influence that their partnership generated. Grace lived to be 100 years old, outliving Jimmy by twenty-two years and remained politically active throughout all of them save the last, when she was bedridden. She created her own public persona independent of Jimmy, with two decades of experiences and new ideas. Still, their partnership served as a ready foundation for her activism and writing since his death, and her efforts during these years has contributed to or extended the legacy they built together.

Activist, poet, and community leader Aneb Gloria House captured that legacy in her poem written on the occasion of Grace's 100th birthday. House met Jimmy and Grace as a young radical when she moved to Detroit in the late 1960s after organizing in Alabama as a SNCC field secretary. Drawing on these decades of comradeship with the Boggses, House's poetic tribute to Grace expresses a sentiment that could just as easily be about Grace and Jimmy's partnership:

> You gave
> energy, gesture, laughter, you gave flesh and bone
>   to the idea of revolution.
> In your steadfastness we witnessed
> that being a revolutionary
> requires patience and faith
> to walk the evolutionary path
> day by day.[7]

To be sure, Grace and Jimmy gave these and more. They gave much to each other, and together they gave much to the movements they joined, struggles they waged, organizations they built, and the many comrades with which they worked, organized, studied, and struggled.

SOMETIME IN HER eighth decade, Grace began closing her correspondence with the words "in love and struggle." It was a particularly fitting expression, as so much of her life—her thinking and writing, her activism, her personal and political relationships—revolved around or in some way grew from her commitment to social and political struggles. Moreover, she embraced struggle not just in opposing a system or external enemy but also as a difficult but necessary internal process—in a movement, an organization, and even oneself—required to resolve contradictions. She shared that embrace of struggle with Jimmy. Indeed, their partnership shaped and deepened this embrace of struggle for each of them. Her phrase, then, is just as fitting for a book that tells their story. These two things, love and struggle, were central to their lives together. Moreover, combining the two words not only indicates the importance that Jimmy and Grace assigned to each but also signals their view that struggle, like love, is an inevitable and enduring part of life. In their jointly authored book *Revolution and Evolution in the Twentieth Century*, Jimmy and Grace concluded that there is no "final struggle" to be waged or "promised land" to be reached, as "humankind will always be engaged in struggle, because struggle is in fact the highest expression of human creativity."[8]

PART I

CHAPTER ONE

Making a Way Out of No Way

Jimmy's Southern Roots and Urban Groundings

"I grew up in a little town called Marion Junction, Alabama," James Boggs frequently recalled, "where white people were ladies and gentlemen by day and Ku Klux Klanners by night."[1] During his childhood in the 1920s and 1930s, he explained, whites committed acts of violence "nearly every weekend to set an example so you would be a nice fellow the rest of the week."[2] Saturday night the sheriff from nearby Selma would "come in shooting and raising Cain to see the Colored folks run." The refrain of the sheriff and those with him was "see the Niggers run." Meanwhile, local white youth who had been drinking at the service station Saturday night might "go up the road to have a little fun. They would perhaps meet some Negro and beat him up and leave him laying on the side of the road."[3] The victims of these beatings usually did not die, but in some cases the violence of whites against their black neighbors did result in murder. "Every once and a while," Boggs remembered, "you see somebody kill somebody." The murderers would leave the deceased in plain view, while other white citizens would "sit around and play checkers with the body laying out there."[4]

Racial terror and white supremacy permeated the state of Alabama and shaped the environment in which James Boggs was raised. The Ku Klux Klan grew to be an ominous and at times powerful force in the world young Jimmy encountered. The "second" Ku Klux Klan (KKK) was founded in 1915, four years before he was born, and flourished during the 1920s, sweeping the state's elections in 1926. Its members assumed the positions of governor, attorney general, and U.S. senator, while numerous local officials such as judges, solicitors, sheriffs, and county clerks also considered themselves Klansmen. A decade later, when Jimmy was in high school, several counties in central Alabama had become hotbeds of Klan terror.[5] At the same time, white communities increasingly used the practice of lynching to terrorize their black neighbors and enforce racial boundaries. During the 1890s, the decade that produced Jim Crow, Alabama led the nation in lynching. Between the years 1889 and 1921, more black people were lynched in Jimmy's county than in any other in the state.[6] Moreover, his birth coincided with escalating racial violence nationally; he was born during the "Red Summer" of 1919, when white mobs attacked, and then faced resistance and counterattacks from, black citizens and communities in twenty-five cities and towns across the nation between April and October.[7] At multiple and mutually reinforcing levels, then, racial violence and white supremacy shaped the world into which James Boggs was born.

Still, racial terror was not the only, nor even the most powerful, force in his childhood. Jimmy also told stories of his family and community and how they created a nurturing environment that affirmed and encouraged him as a counter to the oppressive social climate of Jim Crow and white supremacy. While the larger white world imposed limits and boundaries, his internal community life fostered a sense of possibility. "The environment which I grew up in said to me very early, 'You have to make a way out of no way,'" he told an audience of friends and comrades late in his life. Rather than accept the intended message to "stay in your place," Jimmy learned to confront societal constraints, even to embrace them "as a challenge to take us to another plateau."[8]

Jimmy's use of the black folk saying "a way out of no way"[9] is a telling expression of his early twentieth-century, rural, southern upbringing. It signifies both a collective cultural consciousness and a credo of individual behavior built upon a shared experience of faith, resilience, and hope in African American communities. The phrase reflects a sensibility forged in the postemancipation and Jim Crow South and a tradition of empowerment passed down through subsequent generations.[10] Jimmy invoked the phrase not only to highlight the importance of this tradition in his early life but also to signal that this consciousness was central to his political identity. Speaking more than half a century after leaving the South (and having spent most of these years engaged in political activism), he recalled the lesson he learned from his mother: "She always told me, 'Baby, you do whatever makes you happy in life.' But she also said you ought to always try to do something that makes the world a little better."[11]

James Boggs would dedicate himself to thinking about and working toward revolutionary change. While his conception of revolution evolved over the course of five decades, Jimmy's reflections on his childhood and hometown offer an instructive starting point for identifying the sources, contours, and trajectory of his thinking. Embedded in his reflections are key signposts—violent repression, family and community resilience, "making a way out of no way," commitment to making change—that map the wellsprings of his subsequent intellectual and political work. These early years taught him enduring lessons. It is to those years we now turn, to discern how Jimmy's early experiences propelled him on his journey from Marion Junction to Detroit and set the foundation for the political vision through which he came to see the world and his role in changing it.

Southern Roots

James Boggs was born on May 28, 1919, the youngest of four children born to Leila and Ernest Boggs.[12] As a child Jimmy filled his days with agricultural work, such as picking blackberries, working in the cotton field, and raising animals. He also kept busy with household chores. "When I was growing up," he recalled near the end of his life, "I had no time to be 'bored.' I had so many things to do around the house: taking out the ashes, emptying the pan under the icebox, running to the store. Every day I looked forward to finally finishing my chores so that I could go out and play with my friends or go walking in the woods." He would later credit his family life and childhood experiences with teaching him the value of family, not just for its individual members but for communities and society. In the world of his youth, children "had a sense of their value," he wrote, "because they knew they were making a contribution." Since every member was tasked with meaningful activities, the family was "a place where children learned that to be a full human being you need to do your share of the work that is necessary to maintain the household. By working around the house children learned early in life what it meant to belong and to be socially responsible."[13]

Young James Boggs also spent time in the home of a white couple, Dr. Donald and his wife, Miss Elvie, who lived outside of Selma.[14] Both of his parents worked for the couple, and their home became an important site for his early lessons about the South. Ernest, who had been a miner and a blacksmith, at one point began working for the couple, using his ability to work machine presses, drive a tractor, and other skills—"my father was very mechanically inclined," Jimmy remembered—to become a valued worker for the couple.[15] Ernest died of typhoid fever when Jimmy was just eight years old. Jimmy recalled that after his father's passing, the couple made it "very clear that because of their former relationship with my father that as long as they ate, we were going to eat."[16] Leila likely started working for the couple after her husband began with them, though perhaps only just before his passing. The couple employed her as a domestic, and she had a cottage behind the couple's house, allowing young Jimmy to spend a lot of time there.

James Boggs later described the couple as "what you called 'good' to colored folks."[17] He remembered Dr. Donald as a well-regarded physician and Miss Elvie as a devout Christian from Texas, where her family owned a large plantation and other economic interests. Miss Elvie took an interest in helping young James to read, working with him and providing reading material such as newspapers that she saved specifically for him. "So I read like hell when I was a kid," he later recalled, an experience he credited with helping to ignite his imagination.[18] The couple's home became something of a safe haven for Jimmy growing up, not only nurturing his imagination and intellectual development, but also affording him a measure of protection. As soon as he made it to the doctor's yard, Jimmy recalled years later, "I was safe from the white community."[19] Because of the doctor's social standing, few whites would think to bother young Jimmy. As he grew older, the couple entrusted him to look after their affairs when they went out of town. He recalled taking care of the bank account, overseeing the food and dairy, and giving out the payments to the people who worked the farm. For the most part Jimmy was able to maneuver among white people, with the exception of a justice of the peace (JP), who tried to give him a hard time. He never overtly harassed Jimmy, but when Jimmy was out running errands for the couple, this JP would stop him and drill him with questions.

The protection that young Jimmy enjoyed was always tenuous. In his community there were two girls, one black and one white, who looked alike and whose families had the same kind of car. Jimmy came across one of the girls one evening when he was on his way to get the couple's mail. He recounted the incident years later: "I walked up to the car and said 'Hello.' I thought it was the colored girl but lo and behold it was the white girl. To top this whole thing off, the doctor and his wife was not in town. So I just retreated. . . . I didn't pick up the mail that day and beat it like hell back home. For three days I lived in a reign of terror thinking that any minute this little girl might say . . . that this colored guy came up and said hello to me, smiling as if he know me. Man that was a nightmare."[20]

Dangers and reminders of dangers dotted the landscape of Jimmy's childhood—moving about under the watchful eye of a hostile JP, suffering the fright of being accused of familiarity with a white girl, witnessing or hearing the stories about the Saturday-night attacks on the black community, and facing the terror of lynching. Growing up in Marion Junction, he said, meant "walking a chalk line all the time."[21]

Marion Junction is in Dallas County, about twelve miles west of Selma, the county seat. The town's population stood at about 1,100 throughout Jimmy's childhood.[22] Most of the residents of Marion Junction and Dallas County were black, as was the case throughout central Alabama, an area known as the Black Belt. This name, Horace Mann Bond explains, "was originally given to the area because of the black waxy soils" but has since been "applied loosely as a demographic descriptive."[23] Indeed, since Alabama's founding as a state in 1819, its geology and demography have been closely related. The fertile soil invited cotton production, and during the antebellum period the institution of slavery and the economics of cotton conspired to entrench the plantation system into the region's economic and social fabric. Cotton and the particular labor regimes used to produce it—slavery, sharecropping, and tenancy—so shaped the Black Belt that the region has also been called the "Cotton Belt" and "Plantation Belt."

When young James Boggs was working and playing in the fields of Marion Junction during the 1920s and 1930s, the largely black world around him had been made over several decades. Slaveholding in Alabama concentrated in the Black Belt, which became the only region in the state where blacks far outnumbered whites. In 1860, almost half of the enslaved population of Alabama lived in the region, which constituted less than one-fifth of the state's area.[24] Dallas County's population in 1860 was 76.9 percent African American; a decade later that number had risen to 79 percent.[25] This pattern continued into the early decades of the twentieth century. In 1910, the total population of the county was 53,401, of which 43,511 (81 percent) were black. In 1930, the year Jimmy turned eleven, the African American population had fallen slightly to 40,867, but still constituted 74 percent of Dallas County's total population.[26] Plantation slavery in the Black Belt, where the returns were the highest and most consistent, made cotton highly profitable and in turn ensured that "the plantation and the plantation way of life dominated."[27] Cotton more than any other crop propelled the plantation to its place as the center of not only economic but also social and political life in the region.[28] On the eve of the Civil War, the Black Belt was producing far more cotton than any other region in the United States. In 1860, the area produced over 350,000 bales; the region coming closest to this, the Upper

Coastal Plain, produced only 100,000. In 1890, 325,000 bales came from the Black Belt, more than double the production of the closest region.[29] Cotton production across the state decreased into the twentieth century, but the Black Belt still led the way, with Dallas County one of the most productive. In 1914, just before a boll weevil infestation, Dallas County produced more cotton than any other county in the Black Belt.[30] By the time Jimmy was born in 1919, cotton production and the crop's significance to the economy of the Black Belt had begun to decline, but the region remained shaped by cotton culture.

At the opening of the twentieth century, the Alabama Black Belt also bore the mark of black disfranchisement. In the last decade of the nineteenth century, with political corruption widespread and whites routinely able to openly steal black votes, a wealthy and powerful planter class dominated electoral politics and actively fostered white supremacy to subordinate the black majority. The *Selma Times* newspaper boldly expressed the sentiment in an 1895 editorial: "The *Times* is one of those papers that does not believe it is any harm to rob or appropriate the vote of an illiterate Negro. We do not believe they ought even to have had the privilege of voting."[31] The full triumph of black disfranchisement came at the beginning of the new century when Alabama convened a constitutional convention in 1901. The president of the convention declared plainly in his address to the gathering that their purpose was "to establish white supremacy in this State,"[32] and they did just that, producing a constitution that stripped black men of the ballot, prohibited interracial marriages, and required separate schools for blacks and whites.[33] A year later, one of the signers of the constitution gleefully listed the "virtual disfranchisement of the negro" as one of its three signal accomplishments.[34] The impact on black voting was immediate and pronounced. In 1900, 181,471 black Alabamans had been eligible to vote. This number was reduced to 3,654 after the new constitution. African American registration in the Black Belt declined from 79,311 to 1,081. In Dallas County, 9,871 African Americans had been registered to vote in 1900, but by the following year, only 52 remained on the rolls. By 1906, more than a decade before Jimmy's birth, no black citizen was registered to vote in Dallas County.[35]

Along with the deterioration of black Alabamans' political status, the new century brought economic changes that profoundly altered how and where they earned their livelihoods. At the turn of the century nearly 90 percent of blacks in the state lived in rural communities and worked in agricultural occupations, principally cotton production.[36] This number fell over the coming decades as the state's agricultural economy declined, both in absolute terms and in importance relative to expanding industrialization.[37] The Black Belt especially suffered, leading some farmers to shift their resources away from cotton and thus displace tenants, mostly African Americans.[38] Dallas County exemplified this transformation. In 1914, its residents had produced more than 60,000 bales of cotton. The next year this number dropped to 17,900, and the following year it fell to a low of 8,298 bales.[39]

Nonetheless, Jimmy remembered the Marion Junction of his childhood as a "cotton town" comprised mostly of black farmers. There were, he told an interviewer, about 500 to 600 black people and between 100 and 150 whites. While his estimate of the town's total population was much lower than that recorded by the census, both reflected a proportion of blacks to whites of roughly five to one. Most of the white residents of Marion Junction came from what he described as "about 20 major white families."[40]

Jimmy was actually related to one of these white families. His paternal grandmother was employed as a domestic in the home of Thomas Boggs, Jimmy's paternal grandfather, a white man who owned land in Marion Junction.[41] The full measure of their relationship is unclear, but they had three children: Ernest (Jimmy's father), his twin brother, and a third brother. Predictably, the white Boggses did not acknowledge the black Boggses as family and shut the three brothers out of family affairs, even denying them the opportunity to see their father when he died. Like other dimensions of the segregated South, this denial on the part of the white Boggses sought to manufacture the image of social distance between black and white where there in fact had been close, if inherently unequal, social interaction. Jimmy described this part of his family tree as an example of the South's "integration by rape," explaining that "the cook or the maid or the field hand won't have no alternative to resist the approach made by the boys. Well the white boy's first sexual relations in the south is generally with a colored girl because the white girls are kind of dainty little things that you don't go around spoiling at that early point, you go and catch a colored girl, you know this is a normal way of life in this town. And most towns, but I'm speaking specifically about what I know."[42] Ultimately the white Boggses could not fully hide the family connection that everyone knew existed. Jimmy and his siblings even played with their white cousins as children, apparently aware of their relation even as it was publicly denied.[43] Jimmy would later describe this situation as common: "Lots of Negroes had this kind of family relation in the South."[44]

JIMMY LEARNED MUCH ABOUT family and the South from his great grand-mother, Big Ma, who had been born into slavery during the early 1850s. She lived into her eighties and shared with young Jimmy and his siblings her recollections of the brutalities of slavery, the coming of emancipation, and the many hardships that followed in its wake. She taught him the spirituals sung by the enslaved, and she described the cruelties of masters toward enslaved children. She told him the origins of the "buck dance," when "white people would come up and say 'N——r, dance', and then start shooting around the feet of blacks so that they would dance like everything."[45] Big Ma was an important presence in Jimmy's childhood and adolescence, and he credited her with giving him a unique and powerful sense of historical change. "When she talked about slavery," he recalled, "she always talked not about how they freed the slaves, but about how [slaveholders] surrendered. There was a big difference. She saw the change as something that had been won by somebody, not something that had been given. She realized that there had been a struggle and that somebody had to lose."[46] It would not take much for young Jimmy to see a historical connection and a continu-ity in struggle between these two moments—the buck dance that Big Ma witnessed in her childhood and the marauding Selma sheriff who came to town "shooting and raising Cain to see the colored folks run" during his childhood.

Big Ma lived until the mid-1930s, when Jimmy was in his teens. By this time he could see new spaces of struggle emerging from shifts in the region's economy and black people's employment patterns. These shifts had im-pacted his family, specifically through his father's work opportunities, and would shape his own prospects. Cotton continued to be an important part of the economy, both in the state and in the Black Belt region, but its signi-ficance declined relative to Alabama's growing industrial economy. African Americans saw expanded employment opportunities, as labor shortages, strikes, and union organizing during the first two decades of the century led companies to open up jobs previously unavailable to black workers. The steel industry, which had previously satisfied its need for cheap labor with immigrant workers, came to rely heavily on black labor after World War 1.[47] At the beginning of the century, black workers in the Birmingham-area steel industry were largely common laborers, but after the United States

Steel Corporation came to the area in 1907, blacks made inroads into various other jobs. Many of these were in the less skilled occupations of the industry such as those in the ore mines, blast furnaces, and steel mills, but within two decades the company was hiring blacks as skilled workers and supervisors.[48] The proportion of black iron molders in Alabama rose from 10 percent to 24 percent between 1910 and 1920.[49] During that same period, the number of black molders in Birmingham foundries went from 78 to 329, representing a jump from 19.8 percent to 55.4 percent. In 1918 black workers constituted approximately 70 percent of the labor force in the ore mines and 40–45 percent of the workers in steel plants in the Birmingham area.[50] Such shifts in employment patterns also occurred in mining. By 1923, black workers accounted for more than half of the miners in the state and were holding positions in the mines that were only recently considered "white men's jobs."[51] Jimmy's father, Ernest, whose work as a miner likely took place during the 1910s or early 1920s, would have been part of this shift. So pervasive was the change that a 1930 study of black workers declared, "Mining as a whole in Alabama is slowly becoming a Negro occupation."[52]

Many of these workers came from rural areas like Marion Junction. They left farms (some temporarily, some permanently) seeking industrial employment in cities like Birmingham and Mobile. They also left for cities outside of the South. Indeed, the state contributed significantly to the World War I–era Great Migration of African Americans out of the South, of which one major stream led from Alabama to Detroit. From the spring of 1916, when the migration began in earnest, to the beginning of 1917, nearly 75,000 blacks left Alabama for the North.[53] By the end of 1917, this number had swelled to over 90,000. This mass migration continued through the close of the war at the end of 1918 and was still in progress in the summer of 1919. Thus, by the time Jimmy was born in May of that year, perhaps as much as 10 percent of the state's black population had traded Jim Crow Alabama for the industrial North. Nearly two decades later, Jimmy would follow their lead, arriving in Detroit just ahead of another, larger wave of black migration during World War II. But just as many other migrants had done, before making the move north he first moved to an urban area of the South. In the mid-1930s, when he was fifteen or sixteen years of age, James Boggs moved to Bessemer, an industrial suburb of Birmingham.

In Bessemer he attended Dunbar High School, which would be a pivotal step in his formal education and intellectual development. The path to Dunbar had been laid by several factors and experiences in his early life.

Perhaps first among these was his mother, who taught him at a young age to value education. "When I was growing up, my mother kept urging me to get an education," he recalled later. For her, the essence of education was "the ability to read and write." She wanted him to have the economic opportunities that literacy could create, and she buttressed her appeals by telling him "time and again how, if only she had been able to read and write," her employment options as a cook would have been greater.[54] Although later Jimmy would regard education as more than the ability to read and write, his mother's insistence on it laid the foundation for his view of education and learning as contested spaces of social life.

His mother had been raised in an era when public education was sparsely available to black children in Dallas County, especially in the rural areas.[55] In a state that had been slow to provide public schools in the nineteenth century, and in a county that in the early twentieth century still relied heavily on the agricultural labor of its black population, African American children in Dallas County faced severely limited educational opportunities. The city of Selma, for example, provided no public high school for blacks until the end of World War II. In the rural areas like Marion Junction, black schooling was especially inadequate. Private institutions operated by religious bodies largely filled the void, and by the time Jimmy was of school age in the 1920s there were four such schools in Dallas County. The oldest of these was Knox Academy. Founded by the Central Board of Missions of the Reformed Presbyterian Church in 1874, Knox was perhaps the largest such institution in the Black Belt, with a central school in Selma and three branch schools in other parts of Dallas County for both elementary and high school levels.[56]

Jimmy attended Knox Academy, thanks in large part to Miss Elvie.[57] After he completed elementary and middle school in Marion Junction, Miss Elvie, who had helped to nurture young Jimmy's education by providing reading material, now aided in his formal education by paying his train fare to Knox. She would "buy me a ticket and send me into Selma to school every day on the train," he recounted. "I'd go catch a train at 8:30 in the morning and come back at 4:00."[58] Knox's curriculum comprised both academic subjects and industrial training, and the school charged for tuition (Jimmy recalled that the fee was $12 per year, but he did not say how he paid it). Perhaps most importantly, as a private school run by a religious institution, the school had a unique racial dynamic. "Knox Academy was one of these strange schools," he recalled years later, "where the missionaries . . . sent down certain whites and so it was a mixed faculty, one of the few rare mixed faculties in the South in a Negro high school."[59]

One of these white faculty members figured prominently in Jimmy's later reflections on his time at Knox. Describing the man as "an old Scots-Irishman," Jimmy remembered how the teacher took notice of his voracious reading: "I used to take home a book every night out the library and I'd read it that night and bring it back the next day finished." The books were "mostly fiction and junk," but his reading nonetheless caught the attention of this faculty member. The man took an interest in Jimmy and tried to provide him with some insight into the thinking of whites. Jimmy recalled in particular the lesson that came in this curious syllogistic form: "John stole a chicken, and he was Negro. Therefore all Negroes steal. Sam told a lie, and he was a Negro. Therefore all Negroes lie." This, the man said, "has been more or less the basis on which the whites in the South have judged the Negro." His intent was not to degrade or insult, but rather to instruct, and Jimmy appreciated it: "He was very good to me, I mean good to me in the sense that he explained this philosophy . . . he told me these things."[60]

Jimmy only stayed at Knox through the tenth grade. Under the weight of the Depression, the Reformed Presbyterian Church announced in 1935 that it could no longer operate the academy. The Dallas County Voters League, a recently revived black civic organization, successfully persuaded the Selma school board to take over the school, but it would only offer classes up to the ninth grade.[61] Jimmy suddenly needed to find a new school, and may have already decided to leave before the announcement.[62] Bypassing the two remaining small and underresourced black high schools in Selma (a fourth school had already relocated to Birmingham in 1932), Jimmy chose to leave the county altogether. He moved to the mining town of Bessemer, where he lived with one of his grandmothers, affording him the opportunity to attend Dunbar High School.

Built in 1923 and initially called Bessemer Colored High School, Dunbar no doubt owed its founding, at least in part, to the brutal logic of segregation, but Bessemer's black citizens nonetheless turned it into an important community institution. In 1928 they renamed the school in honor of the famed black writer Paul Laurence Dunbar. By the time Jimmy arrived in 1935, Dunbar provided black children of Jefferson County a nurturing educational experience. "As I think back, it was quite an institution," recalled Rev. Charles Morton, who graduated from Dunbar in the early 1940s and later settled in Detroit as Jimmy and many others had done before him.[63]

Looking back fondly over several decades, Morton's recollections suggest that Dunbar laid a solid foundation for him and many others. He described a wide and fulfilling curriculum—specifically recalling classes in French, business, and commerce, and that "everybody took typing"—a program that combined liberal arts with vocational training. Extracurricular and social activities, such as a debate team and social dances every Friday, supplemented classroom instruction. The school also boasted an auditorium (Morton recalled he and his classmates raising money for a new floor) and a strong athletic department.[64]

One of Jimmy's classmates at Dunbar was his "high school sweetheart," Annie McKinley, who was also from Marion Junction. They had attended elementary school together, and Jimmy had played with Annie's brothers and cousins as children. She later recalled that Jimmy "was always a little quiet boy" when they were growing up, but added that her "grandfather used to say he was a smart young fellow." Sometime before she began high school, McKinley's family moved to Bessemer—which suited her just fine. "Marion Junction is a little country town," she continued, and "[I] never liked the country, I didn't like the fields." She was already attending Dunbar when Jimmy arrived; indeed, her presence may have influenced his decision to attend.[65]

Jimmy did well at Dunbar. "The teachers were very fond of him," McKinley later recalled, and Jimmy's own reflections on the school many years later suggest that he valued his time there. Dunbar's committed and capable teachers exposed their students to a wider world through their teaching and example. Morton recalled that many of the teachers "were on their way to becoming professional people" and remembered in particular students from Nashville's Fisk University, one of the most prestigious of the black universities, who "taught at Dunbar for a couple of years to get money for graduate school." There were also teachers from Alabama's black colleges, such as Alabama State and Tuskegee Institute, while other teachers came from nearby Birmingham. Whatever their individual origins or trajectories, as a group the teachers apparently set a tone of individual achievement and collective responsibility. "The teachers had pride in themselves," Morton recalled. "They were about self-sufficiency."[66] In transmitting this to the students, they were carrying on the tradition of "making a way out of no way."

The individual perhaps most responsible for setting this tone was Dunbar's principal, Arthur D. Shores. Genteel and accomplished, the well-attired educator stood as a proud symbol of African American achievement both on Dunbar's campus and in the broader African American community in and around Birmingham. After graduating in 1927 from Talladega College, the state's oldest private black college, Shores came to Dunbar, where he taught until 1934 and then served as principal until 1939. Studying law at night, he earned his degree through correspondence courses from the University of Kansas, and in 1937 passed the Alabama bar exam, becoming only the third African American admitted to the Alabama bar in the twentieth century. For about a decade he would be the only practicing black attorney in the state.[67] As Morton described him, Shores was "a very dignified person," "strict on his teachers," and an "aristocrat, like a distant Du Bois."[68]

Shores made a lasting impression on James Boggs. A quarter century after leaving Dunbar, Jimmy still referred to Shores by the honorific "Professor," a term commonly used to confer respect and admiration on black principals in segregated communities.[69] His lessons remained with Jimmy decades later. "I still recall your admonishing us how to conduct ourselves in the school and in the community,"[70] Jimmy wrote to Shores long after both men had left Dunbar.

Shores ended his tenure at Dunbar in 1939, two years after Jimmy graduated, and established himself as a prolific lawyer and civil rights activist. That same year, he represented the National Association for the Advancement of Colored People (NAACP) in the successful prosecution of a white Birmingham police officer for police brutality. A string of civil rights victories followed during the 1940s, many of them while he was serving as NAACP legal representative in Alabama, including a case invalidating the state's white primary and a federal ruling against Birmingham's Jim Crow zoning. This last proved to be especially important, as a shortage of houses, congested neighborhoods, and restrictions on black residential areas made housing segregation a major civil rights battlefront in postwar Birmingham. Shores engaged this struggle on another front as well. His firm, Shores and Hollins Real Estate Company, bought and negotiated the sale of homes formerly owned by whites for resale to black people in the North Smithfield area of Birmingham during the late 1940s, when the area earned the nickname "Dynamite Hill" for the frequent bombings perpetrated by white vigilantes trying to keep out black residents. In the 1950s Shores represented Autherine Lucy, the black woman who attempted to be the first African American to attend the University of Alabama. By the early 1960s, Shores occupied an important social space: a fierce advocate for racial equality who was also a solid representative of Birmingham's black middle class.

This made him a prime target of the Ku Klux Klan, which twice bombed his home on Dynamite Hill, the first time a week before the March on Washington and the second two weeks later.[71]

These bombings prompted Jimmy to write the letter to Shores described above. By this time Jimmy had been away from his home state for more than two decades (he would never return to Alabama), and he had not seen "Professor" since graduating from Dunbar. Jimmy began the letter by reminding Shores that he was a member of the class of 1937, whose class motto had been "The elevator to success is broken; take the stairs." The letter expressed Jimmy's pride and appreciation for Shores's contributions, while also conveying his concern for Shores and his wife, who had been injured in the second bombing. Jimmy closed the letter with a brief summary of his own trajectory and current activities. "Since I left Dunbar, my life can be summed up best as that of being primarily an auto worker in the Chrysler plant, active in the labor movement and also in the Negro revolt. Today I believe that the labor movement has subsided to the degree where it has no potential use and that the Negro revolt is the main instrument for creating a new way of life in America, so that is where I intend to devote my energies."[72] Just weeks before writing the letter, Jimmy had his first book published, *The American Revolution: Pages from a Negro Worker's Notebook*, which reflected and drew upon his experiences in Detroit over the preceding two decades as an industrial worker, a union member, a local civil rights activist, and a Marxist revolutionary.

Both men directly participated in the burgeoning black struggles of the early 1960s, but they did so in distinct ways and settings. The contrast of their specific locations and contributions to the postwar black freedom movement underscores the depth and breadth of the movement yet at the same time highlights the latent and sometimes circuitous connections between its many components. This contrast also captures the distance that Jimmy traveled. His journey from the Alabama Black Belt to the Black Bottom neighborhood of Detroit not only meant moving from a rural, agricultural world to an urbanized and aggressively industrial one. It also meant becoming a part of a city being shaken by the emergence of a powerful labor movement and soon to witness even greater upheavals around labor and industrial relations, economic production, and racial tensions catalyzed by the social and economic transformations of war. In ways that he could not fully anticipate at the time, Jimmy's decision to head for Detroit after completing high school in 1937 set his life on a new path.

"Like Birds on Telephone Lines"

The North had long held an appeal for Jimmy. Annie McKinley recalled that Jimmy "always talked about coming to the North," a desire sparked in part by experiences in Marion Junction and Bessemer that gave him a sense of a wider world outside of Alabama.[73] People who had gone north told stories of faraway places, exciting people, and economic opportunities that captured young Jimmy's imagination. Migrants making visits back home returned with emblems of success and tales of northern life, all giving witness to the North's great promise. "Every time someone went north," he explained years later, "they came back talking, telling a bunch of lies about how good things were there. . . . You didn't come back until you had a big car and other stuff to let people know you were doing well up North. I believed all those lies, too."[74] The accumulation of these lies, he said, gave him an illusion of what it was like up north: "I thought all the houses were brick, all the peoples had beautiful green lawns, colored and white lived side by side, and their kids played together. Oh I had some crazy vision of how the North was."[75]

The prospect of going north became for Jimmy all the more compelling as he faced the slim prospects for work in Depression-era Alabama. Many years later he recalled how a black job seeker could expect to be met with the response, "Hell I ain't got no job for a nigger." There was still agricultural work, but that "wasn't no money."[76] Like many other aspiring migrants, Jimmy had relatives in the North. Considering that he had uncles and two older brothers already in Detroit, the booming city looked especially appealing.[77]

Another important factor in Jimmy's interest in going north was his growing desire to leave behind the racial codes of the South. One incident in particular may have pushed him to leave. Jimmy and three friends, another boy and two girls, were walking to the movies one evening when a firefighter approached and accused them of breaching the well-established racial convention of black people stepping aside when passing by a white woman. "Hey, didn't you see that white woman coming up the street?" the firefighter challenged. Jimmy replied that they had not seen any white woman, but the firefighter insisted they had. "Really, there was no white woman at all," Jimmy explained more than two-and-a-half decades later. "The fact is that he just didn't like seeing these Negroes cleaned up and going to the show. So he followed us for four blocks, pestering us."[78]

The incident had a strong impact on Jimmy. Given the frequency and severity of white violence against blacks in the rural South during the 1930s, this episode could be described as relatively minor harassment. But it stood as yet another indignity signifying the white South's intention to keep black people in their place. Moreover, it illustrated how arbitrary and irrational the racial logic of his native region could be. These were not new lessons: Jimmy had learned them in various ways throughout his childhood. But as a teenager, this experience figured into his calculations about adulthood in this environment. After this incident, he said, "[I] began to make up my mind that I'm gonna leave this place. Because you have two alternatives there. You can keep your big mouth shut, or you can leave."[79]

James Boggs graduated from Dunbar High School on May 19, 1937, nine days shy of his eighteenth birthday, and within days he was on his way to Detroit.[80] He and his Dunbar classmate and close childhood friend Joe Perry climbed aboard a freight train. With no change of clothes and $1 between them (they ran out of money on the second day), they quickly learned how to "bum" for food and utilize other measures of survival. "You'd go up to the nearest house and knock on the back door," he recalled. "I went over to a farmer's house, and a lady gave us some cabbage and hamhocks."[81] It was a difficult way to travel, but it was the Depression, and the two friends did not want for company. As Jimmy explained to an interviewer years later, "Bums were hoboing all over the country. Guys would be sitting on top of freight trains like birds on telephone lines." With so many people out of work, "it was expected that people would drift."[82] He recalled places like Cincinnati, "a bum town" where "people built a shanty town there on the river," and Saint Louis, where people built houses along the Mississippi River made of railroad cross ties. As for actually riding the trains, this could be an almost communal experience. He remembered, "There'd be fifty people on the freight train scattered all over, some sitting on top, some inside, some in gondolas, just riding where you could ride. The thing you had to worry about was, when you come into a town and the freight train slowed down, everybody jumped off and walked around the town to catch the train when it would leave out the other end of town."[83]

Of course, hoboing entailed risks. Black men riding the rails in the 1930s traveled under the shadow of the Scottsboro Boys case, the infamous 1931 arrest and conviction on specious rape charges of nine African American boys riding a train in northern Alabama. Jimmy recalled that the passions and violence occasioned by the case were still very present six years later.

And the charge of rape was not the only reason to be on guard for the police: "Down south in Tennessee if they caught you, they put you on the peanut farm to pick peanuts. If they caught you in another place, they didn't want you at all. They'd want you to get the hell out of town." In some towns such as Dayton, Ohio, police came to the train station "to make sure that you didn't get off the train." There the biggest fear was being caught by the "dirty bulls," or railroad yard detectives, as this would lead to forced work on penal farms without pay.[84]

The trains themselves could be the source of harm as well. Jimmy's oldest son, James Boggs Jr., remembered his father telling him a story about when he temporarily lost his vision while riding a freight train. "The cinders from the coal engines flew back and got in my dad's eyes and blinded him," as James Jr. retold the story. "He and Joe Perry wandered around the country-side, I don't know how long, going from stream to stream, and Joe would wash his eyes out until he got his vision back. But it impaired his vision so that when he went to the draft board they declared him 4F because of his sight. It really did impair his vision."[85]

Jimmy successfully navigated the dangers of riding the rails, and early one June morning he finally arrived in the Detroit area. The train he was riding from Toledo, Ohio, stopped at the Ford Motor Company's River Rouge factory in the city of Dearborn, a suburb on the southwestern edge of Detroit. He hopped off the train and made his way into the city he would call home for the rest of his life.[86]

The Big City

Jimmy came to Detroit in search of work in the auto industry, and the Rouge plant stood as perhaps the industry's greatest icon. An enormous industrial complex, the Rouge covered more than two square miles with dozens of machine shops, steel and rubber plants, foundries, and assembly plants spread over nineteen separate buildings. The plant also boasted a man-made harbor for coal and iron barges and ninety-two miles of railroad tracking. Built between 1917 and 1925, the Rouge plant offered testament to the city's industrial might and, more broadly, represented what many saw as the promise of mass production.[87] At the time of Jimmy's arrival, the plant had a full-time workforce of 87,000, visitors marveled at its enormity, and artists memorialized it.[88] Diego Rivera's *Detroit Industry Murals*, created in 1932–33 and housed in the Detroit Institute of the Arts, captured the intricate and multilayered processes constituting the Rouge's triumphant auto production; at the same time, they expressed what Rivera and others came to believe were the perilous implications of this industrialization for society at large. Thus, amid the frescoes' busy scenes depicting life in and around the plant, there are machines and workers and raw materials and scientific breakthroughs, all meant to illuminate the relationship between the natural world and technology, comment on the wider chain of production (reaching as far as South American rubber plantations), and of course highlight the rising conflict between workers and their industrial overlords.

Even as the Rouge plant epitomized the ascendancy of industrial production, it also came to symbolize Detroit's labor movement. Just days before Jimmy's arrival, the plant had been the site of a bloody conflict between members of the United Auto Workers (UAW) and the Ford Motor Company called the "Battle of the Overpass." The Rouge proved the central front in the UAW's battle to win recognition at the Ford Motor Company, which the union finally achieved in 1941. From that point the Rouge's local union, UAW Local 600, grew to be one of the largest, most powerful, and most progressive forces in the labor movement.

Black workers at the Rouge and in Local 600, in concert with the larger black community of Detroit, very much shaped the world of work, labor activism, and black politics that Jimmy entered. The Rouge was by far the area's largest employer of African American workers, both in absolute numbers and as a proportion of total workers. The UAW needed the allegiance of these black workers to organize Ford Motor Company, and they proved pivotal in the union's victory over Ford in 1941. Importantly, black workers at Ford came to the UAW largely through the efforts of black activists forging a labor-oriented civil rights agenda and social unionism that extended citywide.[89] Jimmy was initiated into, and soon fully participated in, these labor movement and black community politics when he began working in the auto industry. But before that, when he first arrived in the city, his task was simply to find his uncle's home.

After many days riding freight trains, Jimmy made the final part of his journey to Detroit on foot. From the Rouge he walked east down Michigan Avenue toward downtown, stopping along the way to ask for directions to his uncle's east-side home. The sights and sounds that he took in along Michigan Avenue told the story of a city transforming. At the beginning of his trek Jimmy would have passed through outlying areas on the western edge of Detroit just recently annexed by the city. One or two of these neighborhoods along Michigan were among the few African American districts outside of the lower east side.[90] Farther along Michigan Avenue he would have passed Most Holy Trinity, the first Irish church in Detroit, which had anchored the Irish community of Corktown around the turn of the century. Some of these neighborhoods had also been areas of German settlement. By the 1920s and 1930s, however, the neighborhoods along Michigan Avenue were no longer ethnic enclaves, but had become working-class communities made up of various white ethnic groups.[91] Crossing Livernois Avenue, Jimmy would have seen a number of factories dotted along Michigan Avenue, some of them covering entire city blocks. These factories ranged widely in their output—from automobiles, brick works, and steel to chemicals, fuels, and consumer goods—collectively attesting to the city's massive industrial activity.

Nearing downtown, another symbol of the city's recent expansion would have come into his view. Spreading over the Detroit River and connecting Detroit to Windsor, Ontario, the Ambassador Bridge was the longest suspension bridge in the world when it was completed in November 1929. Situated well south of Michigan Avenue, it was not directly on Jimmy's route, but with two steel towers 363 feet high, a main span 1,850 feet long and 55 feet wide, and a total length of 9,602 feet with approaches, it could not have escaped Jimmy's view.[92] Reaching downtown, Jimmy would have encountered more of Detroit's awe-inspiring structures. For example, his path took him in the shadow of the city's tallest building, the forty-seven-story Penobscot Building at the corner of Fort and Griswold. Nearby stood the Guardian Building, a Detroit landmark marveled at for its colorfully patterned Pewabic pottery tiles and intricate brickwork. Viewing these and other towering skyscrapers, the most impressive of them having been built within the preceding decade, would have given Jimmy yet another window onto Detroit's recent and rather rapid emergence as a vital urban center.

Jimmy saw a very different face of the urban landscape when he crossed into the lower east side, the area of the city that housed the largest concentration of African Americans. Significantly expanded through the World War I–era Great Migration, these black neighborhoods once known as the "East Side Colored District" were increasingly known by the monikers "Black Bottom" and "Paradise Valley."[93] While these two names have come to be used interchangeably, they initially referred to distinct areas. Black Bottom—which, like Jimmy's native Black Belt region of Alabama, earned its name in the nineteenth century for its rich black soil and agricultural origins—was the residential district just east of downtown.[94] Generally understood to be bounded by Gratiot to the north and the Detroit River to the south, Black Bottom's eastern boundary, depending on whom you asked and when, was Hastings Street or one of the streets farther east. "Paradise Valley" referred to an entertainment and commercial district extending north from Gratiot. Its boundaries, too, were not completely settled. As African American migrants continued to arrive in the city and settle in the lower east side during the 1930s and 1940s, housing pressures extended the residential district northward into Paradise Valley, thus blurring the boundaries between the original residential district and the commercial district.

Walking along the streets of the black east side, Jimmy would have found something of a city within a city, where successive waves of black migrants, many of them from his native Alabama, had filled neighborhoods and built institutions and forged communities. One of those Alabama transplants who preceded Jimmy in the Motor City was Coleman Young, who grew up in Black Bottom and went on to become the city's first black mayor. "We never locked our doors," Young wrote in his memoir, reflecting on his childhood days in Black Bottom. "By face, family, name or nickname, everybody knew everybody else and embraced the responsibility of looking after one another in a neighborly way, notwithstanding some flagrant differences in lifestyle and agenda."[95] In addition to this sense of community cohesiveness he experienced, Young nicely captured the complexity of this segregated but vibrant world of Black Bottom, describing it as "a thrilling convergence of people, a wonderfully versatile and self-contained society. It was degenerate, but not without a lofty level of compassion. It was isolated, but sustained by its own passion. It was uneducated, but teeming with ideas. It was crowded, but clean. It was poor, for the most part, but it was fine."[96]

The most vivid expression of this was Hastings Street. As the major thoroughfare of the area, Hastings served as the cultural and economic epicenter of black Detroit. Along Hastings could be found bars and nightclubs, churches and grocery stores, apartment buildings and hotels, funeral homes and illegal gambling houses—nearly all aspects of business, entertainment, and social life.[97] Celebrated and memorialized in the artistry of blues musicians and poets, Hastings became black Detroit's most famous street.[98] It both resulted from and symbolized a rapidly growing urban black community, women and men building institutions and cultural life in the context of—and against—the adversity of racial discrimination and economic privation.

Evidence of this would have surrounded Jimmy as he made his way to his uncle's home at the corner of Theodore and Hastings Streets. If he walked up Gratiot to Hastings Street, Jimmy would have passed a cluster of clubs, restaurants, and other establishments centered on Adams and Saint Antoine Streets—what was then "the heart of Paradise Valley," according to Sunnie Wilson, one of the area's most energetic boosters and entrepreneurs. Along this route Jimmy might have smelled the fish being fried at B&B Fish Dock or spotted the upstairs office of John Roxborough, numbers man and manager of boxer Joe Louis, Black Bottom's favorite son (and also an Alabama transplant), who was just days away from winning the heavyweight championship.[99]

Walking north along Hastings, Jimmy would have come to the future site of the Brewster Homes, one of the first two federally funded—and segregated—housing projects in the city. The project's opening was a year away, but it had already been two years since the city began clearing the project site—designated by the Detroit City Plan Commission as the "East Side Blighted Area"—displacing hundreds of families (the vast majority of them African American) and several businesses. The project was part of the city's racially coded slum clearance plan, which reinforced residential segregation and did little to ameliorate the city's housing crisis.[100] The cleared site was in effect an expression of one of black Detroit's major struggles—access to housing—anticipating the extreme wartime tensions around race and housing that exploded five years later with the controversy and mini-riot at the Sojourner Truth Homes.

Farther along Hastings, Jimmy would have passed landmarks of black business and entrepreneurship. Among them was the Cozy Corner, at that time the only black-owned bar on Hastings.[101] At Hastings and Alexandrine he would have passed the very successful Supreme Linen and Laundry, and three blocks later he would have encountered the McFall Bros. Funeral Home on Canfield. Located at the corner of Hastings and Forest, just three blocks south of his uncle's home, was the renowned Forest Club. This sprawling entertainment complex included a banquet hall, dance floor, two-level roller-skating rink, and twenty-six lanes for bowling.[102] The Forest Club was not yet, in the summer of 1937, black owned, but that changed in 1941 when Sunnie Wilson bought the club and quickly built it into such a popular spot that the intersection became known as "Sunnie's Corner."[103]

Jimmy's long trek from the Rouge plant to Hastings Street made an impression on him. The sights and sounds of the Motor City revealed a new world to the eighteen-year-old from Marion Junction. "This is the first time I had ever been to a big city," he told an interviewer years later.[104] Indeed, Detroit was the "big city." In 1940 Detroit ranked as the fourth-largest city in the nation, with a population of 1,623,452 people—only New York, Chicago, and Philadelphia had more. Both black and white migrants from the South fueled the city's population boom, and while the influx of whites was larger, African Americans' migration significantly increased their proportion of the city's total population. Between 1910 and 1920, which includes the World War I–era Great Migration, the black population increased nearly eightfold, from 5,741 to 40,838. During the 1920s the number of blacks in the city tripled to 120,066, and during the Depression years it climbed to 149,119. In 1910 African Americans made up 1.2 percent of Detroit's population; by 1940 they constituted 9.2 percent.[105]

The factory job that Jimmy sought initially proved elusive, though Detroit certainly offered him a myriad of new things to do and see. During his first weeks in the city he secured occasional employment doing day work, painting houses, and washing cars before eventually landing a Works Progress Administration (WPA) job digging curbstones in the northwestern area of the city.[106] Meanwhile, Jimmy had several social and entertainment outlets available to him. Within days of his arrival, black Detroit erupted in celebration of Joe Louis's June 22 heavyweight boxing championship victory. As for music, Jimmy could spend a Monday night, the only night of the week open to blacks, listening and dancing to the sounds of some of the country's greatest black artists when they visited the Graystone Ballroom on Woodward Avenue. During July and August alone, the Graystone hosted Cab Calloway and his Cotton Club Orchestra, Louis Armstrong (advertised in the Detroit Tribune as the "Trumpet King of Swing"), and a "battle of music" between the orchestras of Fletcher Henderson and Earl Hines.[107] On other nights Jimmy could take in local talent at places such as the Melody Club in the heart of Paradise Valley or attend a midnight showing of Oscar Micheaux's new film Temptation at the Downtown Theatre.[108]

In addition to this rich entertainment and cultural life, during the summer of 1937 black Detroit vibrated with political activity. For example, the Tribune actively solicited black Detroiters' participation in the coming fall mayoral election. Jimmy may well have read the front-page banner in late August exhorting readers to "Go and Register." The accompanying article extolled the dual power of the franchise: "When we register and go to the polls in large numbers . . . we not only perform thereby a duty which is obligatory upon good citizens, but our votes make public officials more obligated to give us the recognition and consideration to which we are entitled."[109] This paper and others sought to whip up excitement about the recent passage of a civil rights bill championed by Democratic state senator Charles C. Diggs. Declaring with some hyperbole that the bill would be the "New Emancipation," the black Democratic organization Michigan Federated Democratic Clubs sought to use the bill to both galvanize the community and shore up support for Diggs with the "First Annual Emancipation Picnic and Dance" in his honor on August 1, 1937. Attendees received "a small pocket-size souvenir-copy of Senator Diggs Civil Rights Bill" along with "a statement of what to do if the Bill is violated."[110] More than a decade later, Jimmy would be among a group of activists associated with the Detroit NAACP and the United Auto Workers (UAW) who mounted an effort to enforce this law by "breaking down" restaurants that discriminated against African Americans. By that time, black Detroiters had made important inroads into the UAW, and a strong coalition emerged between labor and civil rights organizations.

In 1937, however, this coalition did not yet exist. Jimmy had arrived in the city as black Detroiters intensified a debate several years in the making over if and how they should relate to the UAW and the rising movement of industrial unionism. This debate over unionization would ultimately help decide the place of black workers in the house of labor and directly condition Jimmy's opportunities for political activism.

Much of the debate took place in the local black press. The *Detroit Tribune*, founded in 1933, was by 1937 the city's most prominent black weekly.[111] It espoused an economic self-help philosophy, tended to be Republican and proindustry in its politics, and like most black papers represented segments of the black middle class. But the paper also devoted space to advocates of various black nationalist positions, reported on all types of struggles against racial discrimination, and provided favorable coverage of the Communist Party's efforts to recruit in the black community of Detroit while highlighting the party's national involvement in defending the Scottsboro boys. The *Tribune* also developed an increasingly open position on labor. As the question of unionization came to the fore in the spring of 1937, the paper facilitated debate by running news stories, letters from readers, and editorials on both sides of the issue. On June 12, the front page declared the *Tribune*'s commitment to airing the "sharp cleavage in opinions among colored citizens in and around Detroit" regarding "whether or not Negro automobile workers should affiliate with labor unions." The paper aimed to provide a forum for discussion without taking sides: "In keeping with its broad policy the *Detroit Tribune* has published from time to time the opinions of workers on both sides of the controversy in order that the reading public might have the opportunity to become more fully informed on the issue."[112] The rest of that edition did indeed seem to demonstrate the paper's declared neutrality. Under a large front-page banner headline stating, "Negro Worker Defends Ford," the paper presented the letter of a Ford worker responding to and countering the charges leveled against Ford in a previous letter by a minister who supported the UAW. On page four was the "Negro Labor Forum," a column appearing regularly in the spring and summer by black unionist Paul Kirk, who in April had been appointed as the UAW's first black paid organizer.[113]

The city's other black weekly, the *Michigan Chronicle*, was openly pro-labor. Over the next four years it would play a prominent role in the black community's shift toward labor and its alliance with the UAW. In June 1937 the paper, which had just been founded the year before, was not yet a major organ of black political debate, but its young editor, Louis Martin, had already emerged as a vocal and influential advocate for unionization. A recent graduate of the University of Michigan, Martin worked briefly for the *Chicago Defender* before being sent by its publisher, John Sengstacke, to Detroit in June 1936 as the editor and publisher of the new *Michigan Chronicle*.[114] Only twenty-three years old when he arrived in Detroit, Martin was a vigorous supporter of the New Deal and urged black people to embrace the Democratic Party as the best political course for black advancement. During the fall of 1936, in the *Chronicle*'s early months when Martin ran the paper on a tight budget and virtually no staff, he wrote editorials calling for blacks to vote for Franklin Roosevelt, and he strongly supported Diggs's successful run for state senate (Martin recalled giving Diggs "all the publicity he needed").[115] Martin and Diggs, whose election made him the first black Democrat elected to the Michigan legislature, shared an enthusiasm for the labor movement both as a vehicle for black advancement and as a catalyst for social change more broadly. Martin used the *Chronicle* and other venues—he also wrote in national publications such as *Life* magazine and the NAACP's magazine, the *Crisis*—to argue that industrial unionism afforded an opportunity to forge multiracial democratic practices. On the hopeful occasion of the successful Ford strike he wrote, "Within the democratic processes of the union the Negro worker can fashion a new place for himself in American labor and develop a new relationship between the races."[116]

As this debate unfolded during the summer of 1937, Jimmy was unable to break into Detroit's industrial economy. In the fall the national economy relapsed into depression, with Detroit hit harder than any other city. By January 1938, the city's unemployment rate had reached 41 percent, with 80 percent of the UAW's 250,000 members out of work.[117] Sometime in the late summer or fall of 1937 Jimmy again hit the road. "I caught a freight train and I hoboed out west," he told an interviewer, recalling how the experience showed him how the Depression was impacting a wide range of people. "I bummed around with peoples from all different categories, there was guys from Harvard and Yale was bumming around in those years because it wasn't any jobs." This experience also gave him his first exposure to the labor movement, as he "saw some of the great railroad strikes out there bumming around."[118] He passed through Chicago, spent some time in Minnesota cutting ice, and worked in the hop fields of Washington. His journey continued through the winter, and for several months on the road Jimmy faced trying times, including a case of frostbite.[119]

Though perilous, this proved to be an important early point in Jimmy's political development. "Hoboing my way by train across the county," he said, was "one of the greatest influences" on his early thinking. Not only did he see, in the many people riding the rails with him, the impact of economic calamity, he also gained a sense of the great expanse and variegated landscape of the country. "Hoboing enabled me to get a complete picture," he reported. "That's important, especially if you're going to be talking about making a revolution in this country."[120] In 1938 he had not yet committed himself to the goal of making an American revolution, but his experiences and developing perspectives in that period would lay the foundation for political commitments soon to emerge.

In the spring of that year, he returned to Alabama for what would be the last time. While there, in May 1938, one year after graduating from high school and just days before turning nineteen, James Boggs married his high school girlfriend Annie McKinley. Soon thereafter, he left his new bride and headed back to Detroit, this time making the city his permanent home. He returned to the WPA, painting city buildings such as Denby High School and Kiefer Hospital and digging ditches and curbstones for newly laid streets. He also found a job at a service station on Hastings Street. Annie joined him in Detroit in 1939, and later that year they celebrated the birth of a son, James Boggs Jr., the first of the couple's seven children.[121]

Like Jimmy, Annie had always heard that things were better in the North, and upon arrival she noticed that white people in Detroit were different from those in Alabama. For example, "you didn't have to say yes sir and no sir, and you could get on the bus and sit wherever you want to sit."[122] Jimmy noticed another difference when he arrived in Detroit: "That's the first time I ever saw white people who were hungry." Surprised to see so many soup kitchens and soup lines in the city, he found an interesting contrast with Alabama: "Down South nobody was hungry, not even black folks. We always had chickens, hogs, and cows down South. Down South people were ragged. We didn't have no shoes, no clothes much; but you had food. When I came to Detroit people didn't have no food." He was shocked to find both blacks and whites "in line at the soup kitchens and the soup lines. They weren't segregated."[123]

Jimmy, Annie, and James Jr. lived in black neighborhoods on the east side. The young family first rented a room in a house on Medbury, between Hastings and Rivard, just north of Paradise Valley. They lived there with another couple and their daughter along with the landlady.[124] As Jimmy recalled, such rooming houses were quite common then. "Anybody who had a six-room house could rent out two rooms or more to help pay the rent. Those days people were still having rent parties. . . . This was the depression."[125] Jimmy and Annie eventually bought a house in Black Bottom, near Joseph Campau and McDougal Streets. As part of the WPA work program, Jimmy completed an eighteen-month machine tool course at the George Washington Trade School on Russell near Mack Avenue. He was among the lucky few African Americans to garner such a spot in a vocational training program, and completion of the course earned him entry into an apprentice program at Aeronautic Tool Company, an aircraft plant on Ryan Road. But he turned down this coveted apprenticeship in favor of an even more desirable and higher-paying job opportunity: he took a job as a material handler at the Chrysler Jefferson Avenue plant located on Detroit's east side.[126] In the early 1940s, as the Depression slowly gave way to a war economy, James Boggs finally found the job he had left Alabama in search of: he became an autoworker.

CHAPTER TWO

Black Radical Detroit
Jimmy, the Labor Movement, and the Left

Jimmy explained his entry into the auto industry by saying, "Hitler and Tojo put me to work in the plant." This was not to say "that I was for Hitler and Tojo," he clarified, "but it was they who gave blacks the opportunity to work in the factories en masse."[1] This statement, versions of which he repeated on several occasions, reflected his understanding of the shifting place of African Americans in Detroit's industrial economy during World War II. Notwithstanding his political interpretation of the causes and meaning of this shift, Jimmy's identification of World War II as a turning point for black employment in the auto industry echoed an observation made by commentators at the time and since.[2] "The general pattern in the industry at the outbreak of the second World War," wrote Robert C. Weaver in his 1946 book *Negro Labor: A National Problem*, "was to restrict Negroes to foundry, general laboring and janitorial assignments."[3] The war disrupted this pattern, forcing open previously closed avenues of industrial employment. Weaver found that by March 1945 black autoworkers in Detroit numbered 75,000, constituting approximately 15 percent of all the workers in the city's principal plants. "A necessary condition of this expanded employment," Weaver wrote, was "significant occupational advancement."[4] Indeed, the gains that black workers made during the war were a matter of both scale and type, as black Detroiters won increases in their volume of employment and job upgrades that provided new opportunities for semiskilled and skilled production jobs.

The Chrysler Corporation, where Jimmy worked, exemplified this. In the spring of 1941 Chrysler employed just over 1,850 black workers, all of them male, and approximately 1,400 of them worked in the foundry or as janitors in the Dodge Motor Division. This constituted about 2.5 percent of the company's total labor supply.[5] By April 1945, Chrysler employed approximately 10,500 black workers—nearly half of them women. Black workers now made up 15 percent of the corporation's Detroit workforce, and they had pushed beyond the confines of janitorial and foundry work. "By V-E Day," Weaver reported, "Negro men and women were working in each of the Detroit Chrysler plants in nearly every production capacity and in every unskilled capacity. Some colored men were in skilled positions. Colored women were engaged principally in aircraft manufacturing as riveters and kindred assembly operators, in maintenance as sweepers and cleaners, in truck assembly, and as coremakers in foundry. Negro men, including some who in prewar days were janitors, yard laborers, and foundry workers, were working in many types of machine production, assembly, inspection, and maintenance jobs."[6]

Jimmy was one of the workers captured in Weaver's tabulations. Shut out of the auto industry when he first came to Detroit in 1937, the war brought him the opportunity he sought. His first factory job was in the foundry at Dodge, but he soon landed a production job at Chrysler, where he became one of the first black material handlers at his plant. Jimmy credited the coming of World War II with creating the opportunity for black people to protest job discrimination. As the nation prepared for a war against fascism, black Americans threatened to march on Washington, forcing President Roosevelt to issue an executive order that mandated non-discrimination in war industries. Jimmy noted that, once employed, black workers "carried on an offensive battle against both management and the white workers."[7] In his early twenties when he entered the plant, Jimmy began his political life not just as an autoworker but as a participant in this massive shift in black Detroiters' position in the city's industrial economy and the particularly strong political culture it produced.[8]

The Labor Movement and Black Detroit

Within this political culture, triangulated by community struggles for racial justice, the labor movement, and the political left, the auto plant emerged for Jimmy as the earliest and, at least initially, the most intense space of politicization. He spent his nearly thirty-year career as an autoworker with the Chrysler Corporation. Jimmy's first job was in the foundry, "the onliest place they hired Negroes." The job did not last, but it exposed him to the labor movement. "At that point," he recalled, "they had a seniority system where you had to have six months before you could get on the seniority list, and Dodge would always lay you off. They would even lay guys off at five months and 29 days to make sure that he didn't acquire seniority. In fact at that time some guys worked at Dodge for seven years and didn't have seniority."[9] After being let go by Dodge, Jimmy went back to work for the Works Progress Administration (WPA) until the wartime employment boom led to his being hired at Chrysler's Jefferson Avenue assembly plant, where he would work until 1968.[10] The plant employed 7,000 people at the beginning of World War II, and it shifted to war production in the months following Pearl Harbor, manufacturing guns, tank parts, fire trucks, marine motors, and airplane wings, expanding its workforce to a wartime peak of 9,500, doubling the number of black workers and tripling the number of women workers.[11]

In 1940, the year Jimmy became an autoworker, not only were wartime changes in motion, but the shifting contours of black protest—organizing and agitation that would profoundly shape the period—were also coming into view. As automakers converted to war production, African Americans still faced systematic exclusion. In 1940 black workers constituted only 4 percent of Detroit autoworkers, a percentage that had remained constant throughout the 1930s, and they were concentrated in unskilled jobs, such as janitorial and production assistant positions, and in the most dangerous and least desirable departments, such as the foundry.[12] Conversion raised the question of opening up higher-paid and more skilled jobs for black workers, setting the stage for a concerted agitation for black participation in the war economy. Some expressions of this militancy emerged as early as 1940, when a coalition of black civic and labor groups formed the Temporary Negro Coordinating Committee for National Defense to publicly protest discrimination in vocational training and defense employment by government, industry, and the union.[13] By the spring of 1941 a full-scale apparatus of protest was in place.

The goal of unionizing Ford became a major focus of this new mobilization. The United Auto Workers (UAW) renewed its Ford organizational drive in September 1940, this time with an aggressive push to earn the support of the black community and bring black workers into the union. A seventy-member staff for the drive included seven salaried black organizers. Among them were veteran Ford foundry workers Joseph Billups, Veal Clough, and Bill McKie, and Chrysler Jefferson employee John Conyers Sr., one of the earliest black members of UAW Local 7. Black unionists filled other roles as well. Walter Hardin served as director of Negro organizational activities at Ford, Chris Alston edited the special Negro edition of the union newspaper, *Ford Facts*, and Paul Kirk headed a joint Negro organizing committee established by members of four locals to recruit black workers at Ford's River Rouge plant. Through the end of 1940 and into the spring of 1941 the UAW continued to slowly win favor in the black community. It enjoyed the sustained support of community leaders Louis Martin, Horace White, Charles C. Diggs, Malcolm Dade, and Charles Hill, the last of whom in early 1941 was elected president of the local division of the National Negro Congress. UAW officials received an audience in both of the black newspapers, where they reaffirmed the union's commitment to challenging the racism of white workers and pledged to establish job equality between black and white workers. The board of the National Association for the Advancement of Colored People (NAACP) remained divided over unionism, though it now leaned toward support while antiunion sentiment among black professionals began to soften as loyalty to Ford waned.[14]

The Ford drive came suddenly to a head when a spontaneous strike broke out at the River Rouge plant on April 1, 1941. Ford's use of black strikebreakers, among other things, fanned racial tensions and led to violence on the picket line, and over the next week and a half the union and black community leaders worked together to rally community support and convince black workers to leave the plant. On April 3, Louis Martin held a luncheon with a cross-section of 100 community leaders to hear the appeal of the UAW. The night before, the NAACP youth council held a midnight meeting during which the group voted to support the strike, and the next day—while the luncheon was in progress—Horace Sheffield, a Ford foundry worker and west side NAACP youth council president, drove a UAW-CIO sound car around the Rouge plant urging black strikebreakers to leave. Over the coming days both a federal labor conciliator and NAACP national secretary Walter White tried to convince strikebreaking black workers to leave the plant. All of this galvanized the local NAACP and Urban League to support the strike and the union.[15]

The strike finally came to an end on April 11, when the company agreed to a National Labor Relations Board (NLRB) election to be held six weeks later. The UAW-CIO overwhelmingly won, defeating the Ford-backed UAW-AFL and becoming the sole representative and bargaining agent for all Ford workers. With this victory the trade union movement achieved its central goal of consolidating one industrial union for all autoworkers. Moreover, the UAW-CIO victory at Ford established Local 600. Representing the Rouge plant's more than 60,000 workers, Local 600 immediately became one of the nation's largest and most militant locals, and it provided a powerful base of black political activity well into the postwar period.[16] Just as important for black Detroiters, the Ford victory signaled an alliance between the UAW and black Detroit. Black workers had forged this alliance on their terms, after pushing civil rights unionism during the decade preceding the strike. The Ford victory dramatized the importance of black workers and the black community to the triumph of industrial unionism in Detroit.[17]

The Ford strike coincided with the emergence of the March on Washington Movement (MOWM) as a major mobilization of African American protest. They shared a noteworthy complementarity in focus and reciprocity in impact. The MOWM originated in early 1941 when A. Philip Randolph began organizing around his proposal for a nationwide mass demonstration of African Americans for greater participation in defense efforts. His call for 10,000 African Americans to "march on Washington" on July 1 gained momentum during the spring, with both grassroots support and the endorsement of the black press. On June 25, when it appeared that as many as 100,000 people would participate, President Roosevelt relented, issuing Executive Order 8802 banning discrimination in defense industries and establishing the Fair Employment Practices Committee (FEPC). In response, Randolph called off the march (officially it was "postponed"). But he and the MOWM planning committee resolved to carry their efforts forward, turning their energy into an organization that would continue to apply pressure on the president and the nation.[18]

By 1942, the spirit of the MOWM merged with another national protest, the "Double V for Victory" campaign calling for victory over fascism abroad and Jim Crow at home. Initiated by the *Pittsburgh Courier* in February and soon picked up by the rest of the black press, the campaign fused patriotic support for the war effort with a commitment to the fight for full equality. The *Courier* and other black newspapers pushed the campaign with news coverage of Double V events, editorials, columns, letters from readers, editorial cartoons, and pictures.[19] Meanwhile, during the summer of 1942 the MOWM held a series of mass rallies across the country in places such as New York's Madison Square Garden, the Chicago Coliseum, and the Saint Louis Auditorium. These dramatic demonstrations of black solidarity and militancy fueled Randolph's strategy of building a mass movement that could continue to apply political pressure. In September 1942 the MOWM held a national policy conference in Detroit, an example of national African American political mobilization's feeding into and helping to frame wartime black protest in the city. To be sure, the idea of double victory had an immediacy and direct application for black Detroiters: their struggle for jobs in defense plants was simultaneously an effort to participate in the war effort and a fight against racial discrimination.[20]

This link between national and local black activism emerged in concrete form in Victory Committees, which were essentially caucuses within union locals formed by black workers to put pressure on UAW leadership. Bringing the spirit of Double V into the plant, they advocated for the rights of black workers to participate in defense work, specifically by safeguarding seniority rights and securing promotions, both on the job and within the union staff. Additionally, Victory Committees served as a base for advocating for black women workers, both in hiring and, once they began to enter the plant in small numbers in 1943, for equal treatment of black and white women workers in the plant. These committees also formed the basis for the Metropolitan Labor Council, established in 1943 by black unionists from several locals to better coordinate their attacks on discrimination. In creating the Victory Committees and the Metropolitan Labor Council, black unionists were building structures inside but somewhat independent of the union, giving them sites for broad-based activism. They used these semiformal groups to address shop-floor issues, to challenge the union, and even to fight discrimination beyond the plant.[21] The foundation for these efforts had been set in the 1930s by the power of large numbers of black workers at the Rouge plant whose activism shaped a tradition of relatively autonomous and community-based black union activism in Detroit that would extend at least through the 1960s.[22] During the war this activism drove an expanding apparatus of black protest that was central to the world Jimmy encountered when he began working at Chrysler and that he both learned from and participated in as a labor organizer and civil rights activist.

By 1943 black Detroit had developed various bases of political action allowing for multiple levels of protest. The Detroit NAACP, for instance, had established a labor committee in April that organized a mass rally against continuing discrimination in defense work. Two months later the branch held an "Emergency Conference" on the "Status of the Negro in the War for Freedom."[23] These and other efforts pushed for federal action, either through the FEPC or through the wartime bureaucracies created to oversee war production. Meanwhile, much of the contestation over black employment took place in the plants, as black workers staged wildcat strikes to secure job upgrades while white workers, seeking to protect the color line, mounted hate strikes to maintain their exclusive rights to higher-paying defense jobs.[24]

Jimmy had immediate connections to this protest activity and close knowledge of these developments. As a Chrysler Jefferson worker and member of Local 7, he witnessed the overlapping dramas of the labor movement and black protests during the war. UAW president R. J. Thomas, who frequently and very publicly articulated the union's policy of antidiscrimination and its commitment to racial equality, was a member of Local 7. One of Jimmy's earliest influences in the labor movement, fellow Chrysler Jefferson worker Nick DiGaetano, was among the 1,000 volunteers during the Ford strike.[25] Another member of Local 7, John Conyers Sr. (father of John Conyers Jr., eventual U.S. congressperson from Detroit), was one of the most prominent black unionists during the crucial struggles of the late 1930s and early 1940s. After the citywide Chrysler strike the year before Jimmy entered the plant, Conyers headed one of the UAW offices in preparation for the NLRB vote at Ford.[26] In 1942, Conyers and other black Chrysler Jefferson workers organized one of the city's first Victory Committees.[27] In the spring of 1943 Chrysler plants across the city experienced a series of work stoppages, including a citywide wildcat strike in May. The previous month 600 black male workers at Chrysler's Highland Park plant had walked out to protest the working conditions faced by black women in the plant. Jefferson Avenue soon followed suit, with black male workers there staging multiple walkouts to protest the treatment of recently hired black women.[28] Thus, a flurry of activity took place in and around Jimmy's plant during his first three years there, exposing him to the ongoing struggle of black workers.

He also experienced the city's dire housing shortage, another pressing problem for African Americans in wartime Detroit. The city was unprepared for its rapid population growth as thousands of people migrated to the Detroit area in search of defense jobs. The influx taxed an already insufficient housing stock, pushing the city to a state of crisis. In "Detroit Is Dynamite," an August 1942 *Life* magazine article, Louis Martin and Ted Poston reported that 98.7 percent of all dwelling units in Detroit had been occupied as of April, a figure well past the 85 percent "danger mark."[29] Making matters worse, many of these residences were of poor quality. In 1938 over

58,000 dwellings were categorized as substandard, and two years later this number was nearly 70,000.[30] "Detroit's incredible housing mess," Martin and Poston warned, was the city's "sorest problem."[31]

The situation was much more severe for African Americans. Discrimination in the housing market, coupled with the continued growth of the black population, led to chronic overcrowding on the black east side. With suitable housing exceedingly difficult to find, families lived "doubled up" or took up residence in dilapidated dwellings. With better options in short supply, landlords drove a hard bargain. Jimmy recalled the difficulty his young family encountered in 1939. "When my first kid was born, I was still rooming," he told an interviewer, recalling the widespread practice of renting rooms. "I paid three dollars, and the landlady made me pay an extra fifty cents a week for the lights," he continued. "They say you burn more light when you have a baby." Jimmy would "sit up half the night" singing to his child, he recalled, "cause if the baby cried the landlord was going to tell you, 'Move!'" Throughout the war the housing difficulties persisted. "Practically all folks was rooming and rent was high—three dollars. You could get a fancy room for four dollars" that would provide you with "kitchen privileges," but "there would be all kind of notes up on the wall over the sink: 'Don't do this . . . Wash the dishes when you get through . . .'" As the situation worsened during the war, it was often easier to find a job than a place to live. Near Jimmy's plant, people rented "them old houses" by the shift. "You slept in the bed during the morning shift," he recalled, "and somebody else slept in it that night while you were at work."[32]

The housing crisis produced its own set of conflicts and confrontations between black and white Detroiters, dramatically illustrated by the controversy around the Sojourner Truth Homes. By 1941, an already acute housing shortage and the continued influx of war workers compelled federal intervention in the form of temporary housing projects. A seven-month controversy over plans to build a housing project for African Americans named after the black abolitionist Sojourner Truth erupted into a mini-riot at the end of February 1942 when white mobs, seeking to prevent the first black families from taking occupancy, confronted a militant and unified black community in the form of the Sojourner Truth Citizens Committee, a broad-based coalition led by Rev. Charles Hill. This crisis unfolded alongside a rash of hate strikes from the fall of 1941 through mid-1942, as white workers conducted sit-down strikes or walked off the job to protest the transfer or upgrading of blacks to wartime production jobs in factories across the city. A new wave of hate strikes occurred during the first half of 1943, punctuated by a massive strike at Packard Motor Car Company that began on May 24 when the upgrading of three black workers prompted more than 20,000 white unionists to walk out in protest. In response, the company's black workers, numbering 5,000, also walked out.[33]

Less than three weeks later, on Sunday, June 20, fights between blacks and whites erupted on Belle Isle, the city's island park. This popular recreation destination drew black and white residents from across the city, particularly during the summer months, making it a cauldron for the racial tensions that had been growing in the city. Minor skirmishes between blacks and whites occurred on the island during the day, and by night full-blown fighting erupted on the bridge connecting Belle Isle to Jefferson Avenue. Rioting spread citywide and grew particularly intense along Woodward Avenue and in nearby neighborhoods, where rumors of gender-inflected atrocities enflamed tensions on both sides of the color line.[34] In the black communities to the east of Woodward, a rumor circulated that whites had thrown a black woman and her baby over the Belle Isle bridge. In the white neighborhoods to the west of Woodward, rumors spread of a black man raping a white woman on Belle Isle. Through three days of rioting, which ended only after the mayor and governor called in federal troops, black Detroiters looted stores, clashed with police, stoned white motorists, and attacked whites riding on streetcars in black neighborhoods. Whites similarly attacked blacks, though often with police complicity or even direct involvement. Along Woodward Avenue, whites stopped traffic, pulled blacks from trolley cars or automobiles, beat them, and overturned and set fire to their cars. Thirty-four people died during the riot, twenty-five of them African American (seventeen of whom were killed by police).[35]

Jimmy and his family were on Belle Isle the day that the riot began. Jimmy and Annie had taken their two small children to the island (their second child had been born in 1942), joining the approximately 100,000 Detroiters who visited Belle Isle that hot summer day.[36] Jimmy remembered seeing some skirmishes on the island that day, but the Boggs family left before the major fighting began. They learned about the race riot when a neighbor told them about "shooting and people getting killed" and warned Jimmy "don't you go to work." Following her advice, he and Annie sat on the porch, each holding one of their children, when "the police or someone shot a gun," Annie remembered. "The bullet went right up over [Jimmy's] head. I bet you we went in after that."[37]

This proximity to the violence of the 1943 riot that Jimmy's family experienced—on Belle Isle and in their neighborhood—reinscribed the racial tension and potential for racial conflict that he was already seeing and experiencing in the factory. "Three weeks before the riot," he would later recall, "because of all the tension in the plant, one of my friends said what we need *is* to have a riot." Of course, when it actually happened, "none of us was ready for it." But the fact that it happened was no surprise because this racial tension "was in the air" and Belle Isle was a predictable location for it to erupt. As Jimmy recalled, the island was a place "where anything that had already been kind of on the slow burner could explode." As an autoworker, Jimmy saw firsthand how Detroit's factories during World War II generated these tensions. Indeed, in his estimation, the riot that began on Belle Isle could just as easily "have happened in the factory."[38]

The Education of a Black Radical

Working at the Chrysler Jefferson plant gave Jimmy an invaluable education in racial politics. He saw firsthand the impact that increased numbers of black workers coming into the plant pushing for better-paying jobs after 1942 had on black-white relations. Decades later, Jimmy recalled details of the racial conflicts that emerged during World War II and informed his understanding of the black struggle:

> Black workers began to create a new social milieu and an arena of struggle inside the plant. For the first time, whites were confronted directly with many of the contradictions which they had been evading because of their position of privilege and isolation from blacks. White men and women were forced to confront questions which they had never dreamed of—and which at the time seemed monumental. Would they or would they not sit on the same toilet stool as blacks? Would they or would they not eat in the same restaurant or cafeteria? Would they work side by side with blacks? Many times, the line would grind to a halt because a white worker would answer these questions in the negative, believing confidently that the whole future of civilization depended on his refusing to sit on the same toilet stool as a black man.[39]

Predictably, the matter of interracial sex contributed its own layer of conflict. "Leading to even more vicious controversy," Jimmy recalled, was "the question of whether black men had a right to talk to white women—even when the conversation might be related only to the job. If a white man saw a black man talking to a white woman, he would walk over to check on the conversation and see whether he could intimidate the black man enough so that he would split."[40]

Membership in the UAW provided a vital space for political activity and organizing experience. In the union, black workers like Jimmy developed organizing skills, gained exposure to many currents in radical thought, and built a political base from which to mount critiques of racial discrimination both inside and outside the plant. African American lawyer George Crocket, a prominent figure among black and labor activists, noted, "It was in the framework of the trade union movement that Detroit's Black leadership got its start in politics. They learned their political ropes in being elected or influencing the election of trade union leaders, and from that they went on to organize the community."[41] Jimmy recalled of his early years in the UAW that "being in the union meant something in those days." Though eventually he would become a strident critic of the UAW and the labor movement, Jimmy consistently acknowledged the significance of his union days. "My early experience was in the union, and that's where I got my real organizing skills—in strikes, wildcats, picketing, goon squads, stuff like that."[42]

"Goon squads" were the UAW's "flying squadrons," groups of union members devoted to providing protection and support for striking workers throughout the industry. They functioned as the UAW's "paramilitary arm," and could be described as "youthful militants, ready to hop in their cars and drive anywhere in southeastern Michigan for a fight, either against the union's corporate antagonists or, with equal frequency, to protect the meetings and strengthen the picket lines of the union faction to which they offered their loyalty."[43] B. J. "Jack" Widick, who worked at Chrysler, was a member of the Socialist Workers Party (SWP), and wrote widely on the UAW and the labor movement, identified members of the UAW flying squadrons as "colorfully garbed union militants chosen for their aggressiveness in defending picket lines."[44] Joe Maddox, another one of Jimmy's Chrysler coworkers, similarly recalled that the goon squads would "go out and crack heads," with the primary target being "people crossing the picket line."[45]

Jimmy had joined Local 7's flying squadron by 1943. Formally named the Organization Committee, Local 7's squadron stated its twofold purpose: "to promote and safeguard the general welfare of the members of Local 7," and "to coordinate all problems pertinent to the policing of the Local Union and its membership, especially during strikes or labor disputes."[46] However, in Jimmy's description the squadron had a more violent purpose: "Our job was to force folks into the union."[47] During strikes, Jimmy explained, the squadron would ostensibly recruit people into the union, "but really we just used to beat them up until they joined. It was tough. A lot of people were afraid to join the union, but we needed them. Most people who joined were beaten into the union."[48] He described a scenario that would occur during union dues drives: "We'd line up out at the gate and wouldn't let them in unless they belonged to the union. They'd go around the back and jump over the fence and go to work anyway. The next day or so, we'd go out to their house and throw bricks through there or beat the hell out of them and they'd join. That was a part of organizing. Then we used go out and help other locals organize."[49] These clashes on the picket line and at the factory gate, like his participation in the flying squadron more generally, gave him a critical education in labor politics.

Jimmy received further tutelage in the history and politics of the labor movement from fellow Chrysler Jefferson worker Nick DiGaetano. A veteran trade unionist, DiGaetano had come to Detroit from southern Italy at the age of fifteen in 1909 and soon began working as a helper in a nickel-plating plant on West Jefferson Avenue near the Michigan Central Railroad Station. In 1912 he joined the Italian Socialist Federation and three years later, when the federation joined the Industrial Workers of the World (IWW), he became a member of the "Wobblies." He credited the IWW with giving him a good understanding of the labor movement and the principles of industrial unionism. He deepened this knowledge through his experiences working in Detroit's expanding industrial economy during the 1910s and 1920s at such plants as Michigan Stove Works, U.S. Rubber, and Ferro Stamping. In 1928 he came to Chrysler Jefferson as a metal polisher and was an active trade unionist from the beginnings of the movement in the 1930s. When the sit-down strike wave hit Detroit in 1937 he was the first person in the metal polisher department to switch from the AFL to the UAW (the metal polishers had a union but it was not recognized by the company). Over the next two decades he played many leadership roles in Local 7. In 1939 he became chief steward and remained in the role for seventeen years until he retired. He also served as editor of Local 7's newspaper, the *Citadel*, and as a member of the local executive board, the shop committee, and the education committee. Twenty-five years Jimmy's senior, DiGaetano taught the younger man how to process union grievances and shared his wealth of information and experience in the city's trade union movement and the Left.[50]

DiGaetano's tutelage and mentorship extended to the intellectual realm and helped shape Jimmy's development as a thinker. "Nick was an old Wobbly so he had read all this Italian" radical literature, Jimmy recalled. DiGaetano gave him a taste for radical European political thought, such as that of Italian Marxist Antonio Gramsci.[51] Other influences included *Dynamite: The Story of Class Violence in America, 1830–1930* by Louis Adamic, and Ferdinand Lundberg's *America's Sixty Families*.[52] Lundberg's book in particular, and Jimmy's reading of it with DiGaetano, defined an important moment in Jimmy's development. The book argues that "the United States is owned and dominated today by a hierarchy of its sixty richest families, buttressed by no more than ninety families of lesser wealth." Writing during the Depression, Lundberg noted with disdain that "instead of decreasing in wealth and power during the crisis of 1929–1933 America's sixty richest families were actually strengthened in relation to the hordes of citizens reduced to beggary."[53] After reading the book, the two of them made a presentation at the union hall. Recalling the event years later, Jimmy excitedly recounted how he and his mentor "went down to UAW and did an education," giving a "book review" for union members. "Ain't that something," he mused, "now here me, little ol' country ass Alabama cat, was educating these white cats on America's leading families."[54] Jimmy regarded this experience as both formative and revelatory, for it helped him recognize his capacity for intellectual engagement and marked an early step in his self-concept as an intellectual.

Jimmy also began to write during this period. Toward the end of the war, perhaps during DiGaetano's editorship, Jimmy started contributing to the *Citadel*. As he described it, "I was just writing trade union stuff" focused on labor organizing and exposing the corruption of the ruling class.[55] While the focus of the early writings had little in common with that of his later writings, these first writings for the union paper nonetheless initiated a writing career—not as an occupation but as vocation and political activity—that would extend through the rest of his life. The particular context of the union paper as the place in which he began writing also helped to solidify his identity as a writer who was also a worker, an identity that he would proclaim with particular force in later years. For example, the point is made in the subtitle of his first book, *The American Revolution: Pages from a Negro Worker's Notebook*. The book's introduction declares, "I am a factory worker, but I know more than just factory work."[56] *The American Revolution* was published in 1963, by which time Jimmy had spent more than two decades as an autoworker. The book contains a strident critique of the labor movement, tracing its degeneration from its heyday of the 1930s to its very different composition and orientation in the early 1960s. Thus, it reflects the distance he had traveled—and his analysis of the distance that the UAW and American society had traveled—since the early 1940s. Pondering the evolution of his writing, Jimmy said a shift occurred around 1951, when "I kind of changed my writing" based on "my exposure to Marxism."[57]

The multiple conduits of radical politics in the worlds Jimmy inhabited in World War II–era Detroit put Marxism, and radical ideas more generally, in wide circulation. "Whether specific policies and attitudes were acceptable to workers or not," writes Martin Glaberman in his study of wartime strikes, "radical ideas, socialist ideas, anti-capitalist ideas, and anti-war ideas were common currency among Detroit auto workers during World War II."[58] Glaberman, himself an autoworker in the 1940s, knew very well the intellectual and political atmosphere in which Jimmy was radicalized. During the 1950s Jimmy and Glaberman were in the same Marxist organization. By 1980, when Glaberman published his study, they had long since parted ways politically, but Glaberman nonetheless illuminates their common roots. "Generally speaking, all sorts of left-wing papers circulated freely in the plants during the war," he wrote, adding that the "parties of the left participated actively in the affairs of the UAW during World War II."[59] The three groups that exerted the most influence were the Communist Party (CP) and two Trotskyist organizations, the Socialist Workers Party (SWP) and the Workers Party (WP), but others such as the IWW contributed to this mixture as well.

Jimmy's first interaction with the organized Left likely came by way of the CP.[60] Despite its wartime shifts in policy and program, the party enjoyed significant influence with black workers and was able to recruit many black autoworkers during the war years.[61] The party's support of the war effort after June 1941 did compromise its support for black rights, but this was not so much an abandonment of black rights as a narrowing of focus, as the CP limited its efforts on black rights to those areas linked to the war effort.[62] Glaberman pointed out the importance of interactions at the local level between black workers and the CP: "Although on a national scale they attempted to restrain the militancy of the black movement, on a personal level and on the shop floor, CP members were the most consistent and principled element in the labor movement in fighting for the rights of black workers."[63] Jimmy had coworkers, friends, and neighbors who were members of the Communist Party, and he belonged to the UAW's "left-wing caucus," a factional bloc whose base of support included the union's Communist Party members and most of the union's African American activists.[64]

Jimmy also joined a CP organization called American Youth for Democracy (AYD).[65] Founded in the fall of 1943 as the successor to the Young Communist League, the AYD committed itself to working, as expressed in the preamble to its constitution, "for full equality in every phase of American life for the Negro people," while pledging to "champion the special needs and interests of Negro youth and work for unity of Negro and white in realizing our common goals."[66] Jimmy was likely among the AYD's short-term members who did not fully adhere to the CP's ideology or consider themselves communists.[67] He ultimately found the experience less than satisfying, and his membership was short lived. He later said he came to the CP looking for ideas, but all the group could offer him was "Jimmy Higgins work," a reference to a fictional character who came to represent the anonymous rank-and-file comrade who dutifully performed the humble tasks needed to keep the organization going and who did so with neither the opportunity nor the desire for promotion to higher posts in the party.[68]

Despite this, Jimmy identified his association with the Communist Party as a small but still noteworthy moment in his political trajectory, and he consistently maintained a measured view of the party's historical significance in relationship to black people.[69] In a lengthy interview conducted in 1976 by fellow activist Xavier Nicholas and published by the Institute of the Black World as a pamphlet titled "Questions of the American Revolution: Conversations with James Boggs," Jimmy discussed the Scottsboro Boys case, the role of the Communist Party in their defense, and the NAACP's criticism of that role. When asked whether he felt the Communist Party used blacks for their own ideological interests, Jimmy said yes, in many instances they did, before adding, "On the other hand, many blacks got their first radical politics from the Communist Party. So *who* used *whom* is questionable."[70]

Drawing from his association with the CP as well the experiences of other black people he knew and worked with in Detroit during the 1940s, Jimmy sought to dislodge the view that the Communist Party's history with black people had been in the main an unbroken line of deception and manipulation. This view had grown on the authority of figures such as Richard Wright and Ralph Ellison, whose celebrated books and personal histories with Communism, especially Wright's very public and acrimonious departure from the CP, announced Communist paternalism and self-interest as driving themes in the CP's relationship to black artists, communities, and struggles.[71] These themes gained a renewed voice a generation later with the publication in 1967 of Harold Cruse's *Crisis of the Negro Intellectual*, which assailed an astonishingly broad collection of black thinkers for being dupes of the Communists. In Cruse's telling, nearly an entire generation of black intellectuals had their analyses blunted or creative capacities ruinously stifled by the Communist Left.[72] Jimmy rejected this view, instead approaching the relationship between black people and Communism as a question of what black communities and black activists got from Communism.

Published in 1976, Jimmy's "Questions of the American Revolution" appeared just as scholars of African American protest were beginning to take up questions similar to that which he raised about the history of blacks and the CP.[73] These new analyses set the stage for a reinterpretation of the relationship between black protest and the CP, moving beyond the familiar but incomplete picture of CP manipulation and black subservience. Subsequent scholarship has shown us that there is much to know and examine about the ideas, actions, and personal experiences of black activists in or affiliated with the CP, and that the complex relationship between the CP and the black freedom struggle is an important dimension of the larger history of black social movements in the twentieth century.[74] For his part, Jimmy had arrived at his understanding of this relationship through his evaluation of his own political trajectory. This included his brief relationship with the CP, but it also included the broader context of black political development in 1940s Detroit, of which the CP was one of many actors and in which black Communists operated and interacted with a range of activists.[75]

If the CP helped to initiate Jimmy into the world of radical politics, his full immersion into that world came through a rival group, the Socialist Workers Party (SWP). He became aware of the SWP during World War II, and he likely had joined the organization by 1946.[76] Thus, it is possible that his membership in the AYD overlapped with his early association with the SWP, which, as a Trotskyist organization, was a staunch ideological and political opponent of the CP.[77] As a young autoworker testing the waters of radical politics, Jimmy did not much concern himself with the rivalries between Trotskyists and Communists. He and his friends would "leave one meeting and go to the other," he recalled. Describing himself and his friends as "young bucks who were looking around for ideas," Jimmy explained that the "CP put you in a situation where you acted out your politics," but it did not provide "much of an education." This search for ideas and intellectual engagement led them to attend SWP public meetings, where they found a more appealing intellectual and political environment. Members of the SWP were, in Jimmy's estimation, more "the intellectual types," and he was drawn to them because "they had a nice little politics." By the early postwar years, Jimmy had, in his words, "more or less shifted from the CP to the SWP."[78]

Still, the UAW had been Jimmy's entry point to political activism, and the labor movement functioned as his political foundation. His involvement with the SWP coincided with, and to a significant degree can be understood as, a response to the UAW's retreat from labor militancy and the possibilities for political radicalism. These possibilities had brought Jimmy into the labor movement during the war, but his relationship to the UAW and the labor movement began to shift with the ascendancy of Walter Reuther and his anti-Communist caucus in the leadership of the UAW during the immediate postwar years. Reflecting the Congress of Industrial Organization's embrace of a growing national Cold War consensus, the UAW under Reuther purged Communists and began implementing policies that stifled shop-floor activism and muted the role of rank-and-file workers in the union. The union began to abandon its claims for a role in production decision making in favor of the more limited goal of securing wage concessions. Moreover, the postwar UAW solidified for itself a place in the Democratic Party, taking it further from its roots as an insurgent labor organization and toward something resembling a political interest group.[79] Jimmy critiqued this devolution throughout the 1950s, and by the early 1960s he wrote and spoke about "the rise and fall of the union" and "the end of an epoch in the UAW."[80]

Even as he critiqued the UAW, Jimmy remained a member throughout his nearly thirty-year career as an autoworker. But the intensity and focus of his activity in the union evolved in accordance with his assessment of the union's politics and his involvement with other political projects. In the early years, he threw himself into union organizing through the flying squadron, strikes, and picketing. But after the war, his union activity increasingly focused on antidiscrimination efforts and the concerns of black workers.

In 1944 the UAW, in response to pressure from black unionists, created a fair practices department, establishing fair practices committees in local unions. Jimmy became active in Local 7's committee, serving for many years as its secretary. The focus of the committee, as he told an interviewer, was "to break up discrimination in and around the plant."[81] In the factory, this involved challenging company hiring policies, such as placing all black workers in one classification or section of the plant, as well as ensuring fair application of seniority and upgrading into skill trades. Outside the factory gates, Local 7's fair practices committee challenged racial discrimination at eateries and other establishments near the Chrysler Jefferson plant. Jimmy recalled that the committee was extremely active from 1946 through the end of the decade, which meant that its efforts overlapped with civil rights protest activity in Detroit at the end of the 1940s and into the 1950s.

By the beginning of the 1950s, Jimmy was fully immersed in a network of black Detroit workers simultaneously engaged in union activities, civil rights struggles, and radical politics. One such protest was the Detroit NAACP's Discrimination Action Committee (DAC), an effort to fight racial discrimination in restaurants and other public places.

"Breaking Down Discrimination"

Formed by the Detroit branch of the NAACP, the DAC was initially called the Committee on Restaurant Discrimination. It was created in October 1949 in response to numerous complaints of discrimination at restaurants in the downtown area and along Woodward Avenue, the city's main north–south thoroughfare. Since the late nineteenth century, African Americans had routinely faced racist treatment in Detroit restaurants. Many establishments flatly refused to serve black would-be patrons, ignored them, treated them rudely to get them to leave voluntarily, or allowed them only takeout orders.[82] While attempts by whites to contain the growing black population and maintain the racial status quo took place in nearly all public spaces, "some of the worst discrimination" faced by black Detroiters "occurred in white restaurants," and these establishments "proved to be the most resistant to equal accommodation laws and social pressure."[83] In 1948, estimates suggested that more than half of Detroit's 2,250 restaurants practiced racial segregation.[84]

Black Detroiters had already mounted several challenges to these practices. For example, the National Alliance of Postal Employees, a black union, fought the issue in the courts in April 1934.[85] During the 1937 NAACP national convention, the youth council of the Detroit branch organized demonstrations against discriminating restaurants.[86] Throughout the 1940s various African American women confronted segregated restaurants, often enlisting the UAW, the Detroit Commission for Community Relations, or the NAACP to mount legal challenges.[87] In 1948, Jimmy's union local, UAW Local 7, was one of three locals that initiated campaigns to end restaurant discrimination near their plants.[88]

The Michigan Civil Rights Law became a major weapon in this fight. Originally passed in 1885, it declared racial discrimination in public accommodations illegal. In 1937 the state legislature amended the law to widen its coverage and increase the minimum penalty for violation. Since then it has been known as the "Diggs Act," after state senator Charles Diggs, the first black Democrat to be elected to the Michigan legislature, who led the effort to amend and strengthen the law. The new law withstood a legal challenge in the Michigan Supreme Court in 1948, encouraging the black protest community and its labor allies to begin a campaign to expose the open and persistent violations of the law.[89]

Toward this end, the Detroit NAACP created the DAC. The thirty-nine-member committee held weekly meetings at the Saint Antoine YMCA from October 1949 to September 1951 and made regular visits to bars, restaurants, cafés, and other eateries to identify offending establishments. On Friday evenings they sent interracial teams of volunteers to these establishments to test compliance with the Diggs Act. If refused service, or forced to wait for an extended period of time, the team called the police. They carried a report sheet with them to record information about the incident, documenting the name and location of the establishment, the number of patrons and their reactions to the DAC members, the actions of wait staff and managers, specific discriminatory acts, and the police response. All of this would be used to file a complaint against the establishment.[90] Legal action, however, was the DAC's last resort. When cases did go to trial, the juries rarely if ever convicted the restaurant owners. Nevertheless, once the trial was set, violators invariably began serving blacks, and after the trials DAC members followed up with visits and found that none of the restaurants returned to their discriminatory policies. Thus, despite the legal outcomes, the DAC chair could report that "our committee has had one hundred per cent success" in fighting restaurant discrimination.[91] The committee initially focused on establishments along Woodward Avenue from the Detroit River north to Highland Park. It then targeted restaurants in other areas of the city, including around the factory where Jimmy worked, the Chrysler Jefferson plant, and even expanded its focus to include other public places such as roller rinks, bowling alleys, bars, and hotels. During its two-year campaign, the DAC involved approximately 200 volunteers and challenged segregation at dozens of establishments throughout the city.[92]

Jimmy became one of the most active of those volunteers. He saw his participation in the Discrimination Action Committee as an extension of his activism with the UAW Fair Practices Committee. He noted, lightheartedly, that he and the other UAW members "called ourselves infiltrating the NAACP in order to make them carry out a more aggressive campaign."[93] "Infiltration" was perhaps too strong a word, as the borders between the NAACP, black workers in the UAW, and other black political spaces were often fluid and permeable, but Jimmy and his fellow unionists no doubt brought to the DAC the type of militancy they had learned from the labor movement. "We would go in, and we would be refused service," he recounted. "So we'd call the police, and we'd tell them we'd want to file a complaint." The police, however, tried to discourage the protest by asking, "What are you complaining about? If they don't want you over here, why don't you go over on Hastings Street and get yourself something?" This led to the following exchange:

> DAC members: We don't want to eat on Hastings.
>   We want to eat here.
> Police officer: Well, the man said he don't want to serve you.
> DAC members: Yes, but the law says he has to serve us.

This could lead to "an argument with the police officer, but he eventually would write up the case." After securing an agreement from the restaurant that it would now welcome black patrons, and then sending a DAC team to ensure that African Americans did indeed receive service, Jimmy and his fellow activists still might face resistance and hostility. "We'd have lots of people that didn't want us in there," he recalled. "Even the customers in there would say, 'we're going home, get our guns, and run these niggers out of here." Indeed, Jimmy recalled confronting hostile responses at various locations and in multiple forms. At the Hotel Detroiter, for example, the DAC team received service, but the food "was full of salt," while other establishments would "deliberately break the glasses up in front of us to let us know they wasn't going to eat out of something some nigger ate out of."[94]

Black workers and trade unionists played a decisive role in the DAC. This is illustrated, for example, by the activities of Ernest Dillard and Simon Owens, with whom Jimmy worked closely in the DAC and whose broader activist profiles help to further illuminate and contextualize Jimmy's activism during the late 1940s and early 1950s. The three men followed remarkably similar trajectories. Each was born and raised in Alabama, migrated to Detroit as a young man, and found work in the auto industry. All three men joined the UAW during World War II, became involved with the Socialist Workers Party (SWP) in the years leading up to the formation of the DAC, and continued to be active in some combination of labor, civil rights, and radical politics well beyond their work in the DAC. In 1950, in the midst of the DAC campaign, Jimmy, Dillard, and Owens each served as a captain in an NAACP membership drive operated through its labor division.[95]

Dillard organized and chaired the DAC. Working at the General Motors Fisher Body Fleetwood plant, he had already become an active member of UAW Local 15, holding union positions that made him, in his words, "the first black everything: chairman of Fair Employment Practices Committee, member of the Executive Board, committeeman of the paint shop, editor of the local union paper, *Fleetwood Organizer*, chairman of the Shop Committee, and recording secretary."[96] In 1949 the Detroit branch of the NAACP appointed him as a member of its board of directors, and that same year he led the effort to establish the Discrimination Action Committee. His interest in fighting restaurant discrimination took root when he learned of the Diggs Act from a white member of "this little left wing group" to which he belonged (likely a reference to the SWP or a small grouping within it). First, Dillard set out on a solitary mission to challenge the discriminatory practices of restaurants. "I went out and caught the streetcar and rode all the way up to beyond [Grand] Boulevard," he recalled of that initial step. "I got off and went into every place on the way back to downtown. Didn't a single one serve me."[97] He quickly realized that he needed a group to do this, so he "told the guys in the plant." Next he called a meeting during which an attorney advised the assembled group—which included Dillard's wife, Jessie, who became an active member of the DAC, and the couple's two children—how best to use the Diggs Act.[98]

Owens found the DAC to be a timely outlet for his own political convictions. By the end of the 1940s, his politics were increasingly in conflict with the UAW, which he had joined in 1943, and with the SWP, which he joined at the end of World War II. In his memoir, *Indignant Heart*, published under a pen name in 1952, Owens scored each organization for its failure on "the race question."[99] He argued that the UAW and the SWP each presented itself as a supporter of the Negro struggle, publicly projecting a policy of racial equality, yet each remained inattentive to its own internal racial problems and discriminatory practices. The memoir was likely written while Owens was participating in the DAC, and it was published shortly after the committee completed its work. The book only mentions the DAC in passing, but it gives a picture of the ways that restaurant discrimination impacted black workers and pushed them to action. "All the restaurants around the plant are jim crowed, there are only three places where Negroes can eat, and there are about three thousand Negroes on my shift," he wrote. "I went into the NAACP," he added, "to fight restaurant discrimination, not because I wanted to sit side of some white person. I did these things because I see them as a struggle for the rights of Negroes in this country."[100]

Jimmy and Owens were both members of a political grouping that broke from the SWP in 1951 to form a new organization called Correspondence. *Indignant Heart* was essentially a collaborative project of the organization, conceived by the group's leadership, C. L. R. James and Raya Dunayevskaya, written via amanuensis by Correspondence member Constance Webb (later James), and published by the organization.[101] *Indignant Heart* chronicles Owens's trajectory growing up in the segregated South, migrating to Detroit in search of factory work, working in an auto plant, joining the UAW and participating in the labor movement, facing and fighting against racial discrimination in Detroit, and finally joining the radical movement. Jimmy's life, of course, mirrored this, and both men had been recruited into the organization precisely because they represented the type of rank-and-file worker that the group envisioned as the embodiment and arbiter of revolutionary struggle.

Jimmy particularly took to Correspondence. At the time of the organization's founding in 1951, he was simultaneously involved with it, the DAC (and by extension the NAACP), and the UAW, but Correspondence quickly moved to the center of his political life and became his political base for the next decade. Most members of Correspondence had been members of the group's forerunner, the Johnson-Forest Tendency, a grouping within the SWP and before that the Workers Party. Thus, some members shared a previous association going back as much as a decade. Jimmy did not share such long-standing ties with fellow members of the group, but he quickly gained the recognition and respect of his new comrades.

Grace Lee was one of these new comrades. Jimmy's entry into the organization set the stage for the personal, political, and intellectual partnership that he and Grace were soon to build, but in 1951 that partnership would have seemed most unlikely. She was one of the leaders of the organization and had traveled a path to the group that was very different from Jimmy's. In 1940, the year that he began working in the auto industry, she earned a Ph.D. in philosophy. But rather than an academic career, Grace's studies propelled her toward the study of Marxism and radical political activism. By 1942 she had joined the newly formed Johnson-Forest Tendency, and over the next decade she became one of the group's key theoreticians. Thus, Grace's relationship to and place in the organization as a longtime theoretician and leader was the inverse of Jimmy's, a worker who was new to the organization. Divergent social backgrounds and experiences also separated Grace and Jimmy. The American-born daughter of Chinese immigrants, she was raised in New York City, where her personality and worldview were shaped by the comforts, constraints, and challenges of a second-generation immigrant in a middle-class family. The sharp contrast between her and Jimmy's personal histories mirrors their equally different processes of politicization. His embrace of revolutionary politics grew from his social identity, namely his experiences as an African American born and raised in the South and then as migrant to the industrial North, where he was radicalized in the labor movement. Grace, by contrast, negotiated a less certain set of identities, and she forged a less predictable path to radical politics.

CHAPTER THREE

Embracing Contradictions
Grace's Philosophic Journey and Political Emergence

Grace Lee Boggs was both product and producer of an improbable history. "I grew up in New York as a first generation Chinese American in an all-Caucasian community with no role models," she once told an audience. "So I realized early on that I had to blaze my own trail." It was this background, she continued, that likely "predisposed me to make so many unconventional decisions when I became an adult, for example, to become an activist in the African American community and to marry an African American worker."[1] On other occasions, she attributed the origins of her "revolutionary activism to a combination of my mother's rebelliousness and my father's commitment to country and community."[2] By mapping what can be known of her childhood, early intellectual development, and formal education, we can identify central experiences and influences during the first quarter century of her life that called forth and shaped her subsequent political commitments and intellectual work.

If Grace's background was the source of qualities that would later provide a foundation for her activism—independence, resolve, and commitment to change—it also generated a contradictory set of experiences around her ethnic identity. As a Chinese American growing up in a largely white world during the 1920s and 1930s, a sense of social marginalization marked her formative years. "Asian Americans were so few and far between," she recalled, "that from an early age we were raised to make ourselves as inconspicuous as possible, in part because so many of us had relatives or knew people who were illegal immigrants."[3] Indeed, she came of age during the era of exclusion, as the Chinese Exclusion Act of 1882 (extended in 1904) remained in force well into her adulthood. It was repealed during World War II as she approached the age of thirty, marking her as a member of the last generation whose childhood and young adulthood unfolded before the Chinese in America saw significant opportunities "to move out from the shadows of exclusion and become fuller participants in American life."[4] She did not have available during her formative years the concept of "Asian Americans" or of a pan-Asian ethnic identity, which did not emerge until the 1960s. Furthermore, her parents transmitted conflicting attitudes toward Chinese identity. While her father proudly embraced his Chinese heritage and sought to instill an appreciation of it in his children, her mother increasingly identified with the United States and derived fulfillment from seeing herself as more American than Chinese.

As a teenager and young adult during the 1930s, Grace grappled with these conflicts surrounding identity in the midst of the Depression. Initially, she responded by turning inward, pondering questions about the meaning of life and her place in the world. This led her to the study of philosophy in college and graduate school, and it was there that she discovered Hegel and the dialectic method. Dialectics gave her a way to connect her inward struggles around social identity and her place in the world with outward struggles revolving around social conflicts and political contestation. More broadly, dialectics offered her a framework—one that was intellectual but also profoundly personal—with which to understand and resolve the contradictory realities she observed around her. Rather than avoid contradictions, she learned to accept them as productive and necessary. This set an enduring foundation: she would make the practice of embracing contradictions and dialectical thinking hallmarks of her intellectual and political activities for the rest of her life.

Born with Two Names

Grace Chin Lee was born on June 27, 1915, to Yin Lan and Chin Dong Goon, immigrants to the United States from China four years earlier. The year of her birth marked profound developments in two distinct patterns of American racialization. That year saw the release of the film *The Birth of a Nation*, based on the 1905 novel *The Clansman*, and the formation of the second Ku Klux Klan.[5] The widely hailed film—which romanticized the old South, lambasted black political empowerment, reinscribed racial stereotypes such as the black rapist and the faithful servant, and celebrated the Klan— reinvigorated and gave cultural authority to national articulations of black inferiority. The film also sparked protest, most notably the National Association for the Advancement of Colored People's national campaign against the film that would help to build the young organization, then in its sixth year, and establish the parameters of twentieth-century black protest.[6] The year 1915 also saw the emergence of what one scholar describes as "a distinctive Chinese American identity."[7] The formation, for example, of the China Mail Steamship Company as a purely Chinese American venture (as opposed to a joint venture with the Chinese government) and the founding of the Chinese American Citizen Alliance, both in 1915, reflected this emergent consciousness of Chinese in America as a cohesive ethnic minority.[8]

For Grace, however, this consciousness and identity as a Chinese American would not be straightforward. She was the fifth of seven children. Her parents gave each of their children a Chinese and an American first name, foretelling Grace's somewhat bifurcated and conflicted relationship to these two facets of her identity. Her father chose to name Grace after the American missionary who taught him English when he first arrived in the United States. Grace's Chinese name was Yuk Ping (Jade Peace). She was called Ping at home and at her father's restaurant, where all of the workers were Chinese. She was called Grace everywhere else, in an overwhelmingly white world. These two names thus corresponded with the two racially and culturally distinct worlds of her childhood. Even Grace's last name evolved. Her father's last name was Chin, but after he took a new first name, Lee, he became known as Mr. Chin Lee or Mr. Lee. Eventually, Chin Lee and then Lee became the family's surname.

Grace's parents came from Toishan County in Guangdong Province, which produced the majority of Chinese immigrants to the United States during the late nineteenth and early twentieth centuries.[9] Born in 1870 in the village of Zhouzhong, her father followed the path of many young Chinese men during the second half of the nineteenth century who went abroad in search of work. In his teens he went to Singapore for work, and by the early years of the new century he had saved enough money to secure passage to the United States. The details of this initial trip, including the year he arrived, are not known. He never revealed to Grace and her siblings how he circumvented the Chinese exclusion laws, which restricted entry to a small number of strictly defined and heavily policed categories.[10] He may have been a "paper son," a term used to describe a Chinese man who purchased papers from another immigrant who had already gained entry and agreed to claim him as a son.[11] Like nearly all Chinese men coming to the United States, he made the trip alone, despite being married before he left home. After arriving in California he began working as a laborer while taking English-language classes in Chinatown. As his English skills grew, he found work in hotels, restaurants, and especially as a cook. He eventually started a small business, which earned him enough money to go back to China where he married his second wife. In 1911 he returned to the United States with his new wife, twenty-one-year-old Yin Lan.[12]

Theirs was an arranged marriage. Yin effectively had no say in the matter, but apparently accepted the union because it opened up the possibility of a new life. Yin's mother, a widow who taught sewing to girls in their village, was illiterate and struggled to provide for her two children. The village had no schools for girls, and Grace's mother similarly did not learn to read and write. The stories of village life that she would later recount to Grace and her siblings told of desperate circumstances. "My mother and her brother used to have to scavenge for food," Grace recalled. "They would go to the graves of the ancestors and steal the food, and she would talk about that sort of proudly."[13] Grace also recalled her mother's stories of an "evil" uncle who sold Yin Lan to "the people in the big house" to make money. She managed to escape, but later this same uncle arranged her marriage to Grace's father. This presented a new type of bondage, but one that offered an escape from the poverty and helplessness she experienced in China. By the time the new couple arrived in the United States, Yin's mother and brother had died, and any ties that might have connected her to China were essentially gone.[14]

Yin Lan's immigration to the United States was improbable. Until well into the twentieth century, the vast majority of Chinese immigrants were men. U.S. law prevented wives of Chinese laborers from entering the country, and Chinese tradition discouraged women from traveling great distances.[15] Between 1882 and 1924 the only Chinese women allowed entry were wives of import-export merchants, one of the groups allowed under the Chinese exclusion laws.[16] In 1910, the total number of Chinese females in America (including married women and minor girls) was 4,675, which was just 6.5 percent of the total Chinese population of 71,531.[17] In 1911, the year that Grace's parents arrived, nearly 5,000 Chinese were admitted to the United States. Only 329 of those were women, and of this number, 80 were wives of U.S. citizens and 136 were wives of merchants.[18] It seems likely that Yin Lan was admitted in one of these two categories.[19] The business that Chin Dong Goon had established during his earlier sojourn in the country may have qualified him as a merchant, allowing him to bring his wife. Or perhaps he successfully passed himself off as a merchant, as some did, by bribing a merchant to list him as a partner or by buying shares in a business.[20] Alternatively, he may have claimed U.S. citizenship, as many Chinese immigrants would do, by taking advantage of the opportunity created by the 1906 San Francisco earthquake, which destroyed almost all of the city's municipal records, allowing Chinese men to claim they had been born in San Francisco without evidence to contradict them. As citizens they could bring their wives to the United States. Yet even with this newly created opportunity, the number of Chinese women immigrating to the United States remained small until the 1920s.[21]

Yin Lan and Chin Dong Goon's arrival was even more unlikely because they arrived with a newborn baby. Toward the end of their journey in steerage, Yin Lan gave birth to her first child, Grace's oldest sister, Katharine. This made the couple a rarity in a largely bachelor society where children were an unusual sight. Most Chinese men in the United States had left behind families, hoping to return with their earnings. Grace's father, by contrast, planned to build his fortune and family in the United States.

They were surely an oddity when they disembarked at Seattle in 1911. However, in other ways they fit squarely within the demographic and economic patterns of early twentieth-century ethnic Chinese. Beginning in the 1890s, the Chinese population increasingly shifted eastward and to urban areas. These trends were driven by growing anti-Chinese racial hostility in the West and by the economic opportunity that densely populated eastern cities offered.[22] A combination of discriminatory federal and state laws along with exclusionary union policies prohibited Chinese from many fields of employment such as mining, civil service, teaching, medicine, dentistry, and various types of manufacturing. This economic isolation compelled many to make use of the few work opportunities available to them, such as running laundries, operating restaurants, working in garment factories, and providing menial services. Located primarily in large cities, these constricted opportunities led to growing concentrations of Chinese in urban areas.[23] In keeping with such trends, Grace's family did not stay in Seattle long, but headed east, where her father began his career as a restaurant entrepreneur.

Grace's family made stops in several eastern cities during the 1910s, and along the way the size of the family and the scope of the family business grew. In 1913 Grace's father opened a restaurant in Lawrence, Massachusetts, where the couple's first son, Philip, was born. Just over a year later he sold that restaurant and opened one in Boston, where another son, Robert, was born. The family moved next to Providence, Rhode Island, where Grace's father opened yet another restaurant, called Chin Lee's, downtown. The family lived above the restaurant on Westminster Street, which is where Grace was born in the summer of 1915. They soon moved to a house on Somerset Street, where Grace's two younger brothers were born, Harry in 1918 and Edward in 1920. The house was a short walk from the restaurant, around the corner from the school Grace attended, Friendship Street Elementary, and a block away from Trinity Methodist Episcopal Church, where she attended Sunday school. Meanwhile, Grace's father frequently traveled to Buffalo, New York, where he opened another restaurant (which he apparently operated simultaneously with the Providence restaurant), and also to New York City, where he hoped to open a much larger restaurant.[24]

He realized this goal in 1924. At the age of eight, Grace and her family moved to New York City and her father opened up a Chin Lee's at 1604 Broadway in Times Square. The sprawling establishment seated nearly 1,000 people, featured two marquee-framed entrances, and garnered mayoral endorsement upon opening. In addition to food, Chin Lee's offered floor shows, live bands, and dancing. The restaurant was very successful, and Grace's father, always setting his ambitions high, opened another, larger restaurant in 1928, this one called Chin's, at Forty-Fourth and Broadway.[25] With the success of his New York establishments, Grace's father was on his way to becoming, in the words of one commentator, the "king of restaurant businessmen among the Chinese."[26] This brought him, and by extension his family, no small measure of status because of the economic and cultural prominence that restaurants held among Chinese Americans.

By 1920, approximately one-quarter of all Chinese workers in the United States worked in restaurants. Most of these were small establishments with few employees beyond family members. Grace's father was among the few with the capital necessary to open a bigger enterprise with a large staff.[27] The initial capital required to open a large restaurant in 1928 was likely more than $75,000. His two establishments were part of a growing number of Chinese restaurants opening after World War I. Some enjoyed success, but the failure rate was high. During the ten-year period from January 1928 to September 1938, 447 restaurants opened. One hundred forty of them lasted no more than 1 year, while 5 percent lasted 10 years or longer, and the average time in business was 2.39 years.[28] Chin Lee's and Chin's fared much better, providing food and entertainment for tourists and New Yorkers alike until business slowed after the war and forced both restaurants to close in 1949.

Chin Lee's shaped Grace's childhood. Initially, this was out of convenience and necessity. For their first several months in New York, the family lived in the Hotel Bristol as they waited for the completion of their new home in the Jackson Heights neighborhood of Queens, but they ate their meals in the restaurant, which was nearby. As she got older, Grace continued to spend many hours at Chin Lee's, sometimes helping out as a cashier or making reservations, other times talking with the entertainers and musicians (which, she said, "made me feel worldly").[29] Years later she explained that the restaurant was "like a family"—some of the workers were in fact relatives from China. "For twenty-five years," she recalled, "the restaurant had been like my second home. Every time I walked up the twenty or more broad marble steps from the street level and entered the dining room, I was greeted by waiters and headwaiters who had known me since I was a child."[30] She also took comfort in the atmosphere of the restaurant: "It was heartwarming to see so many people enjoying themselves at lunch or dinner." Especially pleasing was watching her father preside over the whole scene: "I loved watching my father as he sat behind the rolltop desk from which he could see everything going on or as he welcomed people and urged them to 'Eat, drink, and be merry!'"[31]

While Grace delighted in the memory of her father as the congenial host at Chin Lee's, she remembered him as "an old-fashioned tyrant" at home. As the family patriarch, he insisted on a rather strict code of behavior. He was often away from home, working seventeen- or eighteen-hour days at the restaurants, but when "he was in the house everyone tiptoed around."[32] His worldview was shaped by Confucianism and traditional Chinese cultural values, which mandated precise standards of moral and social conduct as well as clearly defined roles for each member of the family.[33] "He drew up rules of conduct," Grace recalled, "spelling out in detail the role that each of us should play in relationship to my mother and to our siblings and how we should take care of our rooms."[34] Chin Dong Goon's rules included a clearly defined if circumscribed role for himself as husband. "He assumed," Grace explained, "that providing for [Yin Lan] in her role as mother of his children and insisting that her children respect her in this role were all that was required of him." The predictable corollary to this view was that he related to Yin Lan through a fixed notion of womanhood completely defined by motherhood and marital subordination. "My father never saw my mother as an individual," Grace wrote. "I don't remember ever hearing him address her by her given name. He never spoke to her directly unless he was shouting back at her. Usually he spoke of her in the third person as 'Mother.'" He related this relentlessly patriarchal framework to his children in direct ways as well. Grace recalls him explaining, "Your mother is a good woman who tends you, feeds you, loves you, and cares for you when you are sick. But she is a woman. When you need advice and guidance for the outside world, come to me. She only knows what is inside the boundaries of the house, while I meet all kinds."[35]

Grace's mother was unhappy in the marriage and eventually left her husband. Grace described her mother as an attractive and vivacious woman with abundant charm, qualities that apparently conflicted with or were suppressed by the domestic arrangements imposed—or at least expected—by her husband. Twenty years younger than her husband and unable to read and write, she clearly found herself in some ways at his mercy. Yet, while Chin Dong Goon sought to replicate the family structure that he had known in late nineteenth- and early twentieth-century China, Yin Lan wanted something closer to what she saw all around her in 1910s and 1920s American culture. Indeed, she had, in Grace's words, "relentlessly turned her back on China," and increasingly saw herself through the lens of her adopted country. "Comparing her life with that of American women, especially as portrayed in the movies, she saw herself as a victim and her loveless marriage and domesticity as a continuation of her oppression in China."[36]

Yin Lan's identification with the United States began early and was intimately linked to the shaping of her identity as a woman. Grace believed that her mother "really loved America" primarily because it offered significantly more freedom for women than did China.[37] This feeling began with her gratitude to the American doctor who delivered her first child on the steerage floor. During Grace's childhood her mother's identification with the United States intensified. She aspired to learn how to read and write English as a path to citizenship, and Grace noticed that her mother "began dressing and conducting herself as if she had been born in the United States." Grace's mother joined a local church, and soon Christian hymns such as "Jesus Loves Me, This I Know" and "What a Friend We Have in Jesus" replaced the Chinese folk songs that she once sang to Grace and her siblings. All of the children would line up, Grace recalled, and her mother "would wash our hair in the basin in the bathroom. And she would sing to us while washing our hair. . . . She started off singing it in Chinese and then eventually started singing it in English."[38] She began to prepare typically American dishes such as pot roast for family meals (though rice, which Grace's father brought home in 100-pound bags, was always on the table), and at one point she renamed herself Esther, after a character in the Old Testament.[39]

Grace's father, unlike her mother, maintained a fierce pride in his Chinese background and very much identified with the homeland. He read a Chinese-language newspaper every day and actively corresponded with family in China. His arrival in the United States in 1911 coincided with a rising nationalist sentiment among Chinese in the United States sparked by the Chinese Revolution, which in October 1911 overthrew the Qing dynasty and its imperial government.[40] Under the leadership of Sun Yat-sen, the revolution established a new democratic government, the Republic of China. Like most Chinese émigrés, Grace's father supported the revolution and its leader, with whom he shared a similar background. Like Grace's father, Sun was from Guangdong Province and grew up in a rural coastal village near Canton. Both men came from peasant families and in their early backgrounds demonstrated the type of ambition and desire for upward mobility that led many other nineteenth- and early twentieth-century Chinese to immigrate to the United States.[41] A picture of Sun Yat-sen, who became the first president of the Republic of China, hung proudly on the wall in Chin Lee's, next to a certificate of appreciation from the ruling Kuomintang, also known as the Chinese Nationalist Party.[42]

Grace noted that her father's "social and political consciousness was reserved for China,"[43] and it seems clear that his relationship to the United States was mediated through his identity as a Chinese in America. For him as for many others, this nationalist mood and search for a modern China led to support for modernization programs in China. Grace recalls that her father dreamed of ways to modernize his village, even commissioning a commercial artist in the 1930s to make a sketch of his village with schools, a railroad station, and an airport. His social and political consciousness grew out of his identity as an overseas Chinese, and he encouraged his children to keep a skeptical distance from American society. "Even though he obviously enjoyed being a businessman," Grace explains, "he was Confucian in his respect for intellectuals and peasants and in his distrust of merchants. So he was always emphasizing the importance of education and hard work and warning against the commercialization of American culture, especially in a big city like New York."[44]

Thus, like many second-generation immigrants, Grace and her siblings inherited from their parents a complicated relationship to China and Chinese identity. Her father certainly tried to impart an appreciation of—if not strong familiarity with—Chinese culture to his children. For example, he regularly recited homilies he attributed to Confucius, and he hired a tutor to give the children weekly Chinese-language instruction.[45] But he met with limited success, largely because, on the whole, their exposure to other Chinese people was limited. Resilient patterns of residential segregation resulted in most Chinese living near other Chinese, usually in the "gilded ghettos" of Chinatowns.[46] In 1924, the year that Grace and her family moved to New York, restrictive covenants barred Chinese from purchasing homes in areas reserved for whites. Grace's family, however, lived in a white neighborhood; her father maneuvered around restrictions by putting the deed for the land for their home in the name of his Irish contractor. Thus, Grace's family had the rather unique experience of living in an area with no other Chinese families.

Grace's upbringing was also unique in another way that reinforced her isolation from other Chinese. Most Chinese families in New York, as in other large cities, spent time in Chinatown; those who did not live or work there made it a point to visit when they could. Grace's family, however, never went to Chinatown. In the nineteenth century, Chinatowns functioned as way stations for single male workers on their way to the gold fields, farms, and railroads. By the early twentieth century, they had become "segregated ethnic islands in American cities," serving simultaneously as residential communities for families, Chinese economic enclaves, and tourist centers.[47] New York's Chinatown, the second largest in the country after San Francisco, certainly had plenty to offer, making it appealing to Chinese and non-Chinese, New Yorkers and visitors. But Grace's family—more specifically, her father—chose to stay away. Grace explained the decision this way: "On Sundays, New York's Chinatown was alive with Chinese laundry and restaurant men who, after spending six days surrounded by 'foreign devils,' looked forward to one day of conviviality with people from their village. In contrast, my father didn't need to go to Chinatown to associate with Chinese because he spent the week with a couple of dozen Chinese waiters and cooks (among whom were many relatives) in his restaurants."[48]

Instead, Grace's family had a different Sunday ritual. "Sunday was a very special day," she recalled, "the only day that my father was home because the restaurants did not open until 4 P.M." After breakfast Grace and her siblings went with their mother to church and Sunday school at Community Church, about a mile from their home. When they returned home, her father would be cooking the large dinner that the family ate together each Sunday. This was the only time during the week when the entire family was together, and Grace could not recall "a single Sunday when any one of us was excused from this ritual." On some Sundays dinner was followed by a drive in the family's chauffeur-driven, seven-passenger La Salle.[49]

Grace's family home and these Sunday drives frame for us the middle-class life that she enjoyed growing up. She described their house in Jackson Heights as the largest on the block, spacious enough for the family to live comfortably on the second and third floors while renting out the seven-room downstairs flat. The fenced-in area adjacent to the house doubled, depending on the season, as a short tennis court and a personal hockey rink, which suited Grace's tomboy persona and interest in sports. They enjoyed recreation outside the city as well, spending summers in a small village named Island Park on the south shore of Long Island where they passed the days swimming, diving for clams, and rowing across the bay. After two years of renting a home, Grace's father had a house built right on the beach in 1929. Sometime during the next decade, as the children grew older and the ravages of the Depression grew deeper, the family stopped spending summers together, leaving the house vacant until it was confiscated due to unpaid taxes. Nonetheless, the family survived the Depression relatively unscathed. Grace's father managed to keep both restaurants open while Grace and most of her siblings attended college during the 1930s.[50]

Another significant aspect of Grace's childhood was the fact that it unfolded in a largely white world. Even if she never developed a strong racial or ethnic identity, racial difference was a keen part of her social consciousness. "We were the only Chinese in our neighborhood," Grace recounted in her memoir, "and everyone we met or had anything to do with—our neighbors, classmates, and teachers—was Caucasian." As a child in New York she encountered ideas of racial and ethnic difference, or, as she put it, she "began to face racial discrimination and the necessity of creating defenses against it."[51] For example, while riding the subway to school every day, she and her siblings confronted the disquieting gaze reserved for society's outsiders. "It was only an eight-minute ride," she remembered, "but it was an ordeal because people would stare at us as if they had never seen anyone like us before, making us feel that there was something wrong with us." This was one of Grace's earliest lessons in the ways of American othering, and it helped her develop defenses against such treatment: "To make them feel that there was something wrong with *them*, we would stare back at their feet."[52]

Reminders of her difference followed Grace throughout her childhood and young adulthood. She recalled that "it bothered me that my almond-shaped eyes and straight black hair struck people as 'cute' when I was a toddler." Even worse, "I hated being viewed as 'exotic.'" As a child she bristled at "being identified with Fu Manchu," the fictional villain who came to symbolize the "yellow peril" supposedly threatening the West. In college, she "wanted to scream" when people said she reminded them of Madame Chiang Kai-shek, the wife of the leader of China's Kuomintang nationalist government. "Even though I was too ignorant and politically unaware to take sides in the Civil War in China," Grace recalled, "I knew enough to recognize that I was being stereotyped."[53]

Of these experiences, the one that perhaps most shaped Grace's young consciousness was the annoying and frequently asked question, "What is your nationality?" The query came from her peers as well as adults (including teachers), and even decades later she recalled how it "used to infuriate me."[54] She nonetheless developed a measured response. "I would reply patiently, as if giving a civics lesson, that my nationality was American because I was born in the United States but that my parents were Chinese. But no matter how often or how carefully I explained, I would be asked the question again and again, as if to say that I could not be Chinese and American at the same time."[55] These exchanges often included a statement of praise for how well Grace spoke English. It did not matter that Grace, a precocious and academically gifted child, may well have had a better grasp of the English language or the dynamics of American cultural identity than the white person issuing the intended compliment. These interactions made a clear statement: "Being Chinese and speaking English well were just as incompatible as being Chinese and American."[56]

However alienating such experiences were, Grace's encounters with such racialized notions of citizenship and nationality were not unique. Helen Zia, a Chinese American journalist and activist born nearly four decades after Grace, has called the type of questions Grace faced part of "a drill that nearly all Asians in America have experienced more times than they can count." Zia describes strangers asking the "absurdly existential question 'What are you?' Or the equally common inquiry 'Where are you from?,'" to which she generally replied "American" and "New Jersey," respectively. The rest of the dialogue, which paints a strikingly similar experience to that which Grace endured, included the following: "Eyebrows arch as the questioner tries again. 'No, where are you really from?' I patiently explain that really, I am from New Jersey. Inevitably this will lead to something like 'Well then, what country are your people from?' Sooner or later I relent and tell them that my 'people' are from China. But when I turn the tables and ask, 'And what country are your people from?' the reply is invariably an indignant 'I'm from America, of course.'" While these queries were "generally well intentioned," Zia explains that she was aware that when she was growing up during the 1950s and 1960s "Asians were referred to most often as Orientals, Mongrels, Asiatics, heathens, the yellow hordes, and an assortment of even less endearing terms. Whatever the terminology, the message was clear: we were definitely not Americans."[57] Zia experienced what Grace had decades earlier: a fixed vision of Asian alienness in the white American mind.[58]

Grace experienced a distinct form of American racialization as a second-generation immigrant growing up in the 1920s and 1930s.[59] The treatment of Chinese Americans as aliens became a central dynamic in the identity formation of early twentieth-century Chinese Americans, and for Grace, this process of identity formation was further complicated by her relative isolation from other Chinese.[60] "As first-generation Chinese Americans," she recalled of her childhood, "we had to create our own identities. We had no role models."[61] She sought Chinese characters with which she could identify in literature and film, but the 1930s offered a limited range. She tells us, for instance, that "for years I especially looked for novels on Chinese people."[62] Her search introduced her to the works of Pearl Buck, the American writer who had been raised in China and whose 1931 novel *The Good Earth* established her reputation as an expert on China. "At the movies," Grace recalled, "I used to keep my eyes peeled for" the "fleeting appearances" of Chinese American actress Anna May Wong.[63] During the 1930s, Buck and Wong, along with Mayling Soong (Madame Chiang Kai-shek), were the most prominent women associated with China.[64] Wong, in particular, was the rare public figure with whom Grace could rightly identify. Just ten years younger than the actress, Grace found in Wong someone whose experiences in some ways mirrored her own.

Ultimately, Grace noted, she and her siblings "were Chinese Americans who were more American than Chinese in our behavior." Like the children of many immigrants, knowledge of their parents' language diminished over time. They did not take very seriously the Chinese-language tutoring that their father arranged for them. "We had no great desire to learn Chinese," she recalled. "When we were very young, we spoke it at home because my mother did not know any English. But as soon as she knew enough English to understand us, we stopped speaking Chinese. It was also easy to forget what we learned because we had little or no contact with Chinese people and no opportunities to speak, read, or write Chinese."[65] The one place where she encountered other Chinese was at her father's restaurant. While this did provide her with a sense of comfort and belonging, such encounters did not foster a particularly strong sense of cultural or ethnic identity.[66]

Grace's ambivalent ethnic consciousness during her formative years helped to lay the foundation of her political consciousness. As an introspective and intellectually curious teenager, she grappled with questions about her place in the world. As a young adult, she came to resolve the contradictions of her social identity by forging a political identity as an activist and a revolutionary. The foundation of this political identity emerged from her effort to make sense of her ethnic identity. With time, her political identity expanded through her love of reading.

An Intellectual in the Making

Books held a central place in young Grace's world, providing both enjoyment and solace. "At home I was always reading," she recalled, explaining that this was part of her strategy for "staying as far away as possible from the kitchen and housework." The first book she ever owned was *The Secret Garden* by Frances Hodgson Burnett, given to her by her Sunday school teacher as a going-away present when the family left Providence. Soon after their arrival in New York the family acquired a ten-volume set of *Wonder World* from a friend. Grace read and reread these volumes. She also made good use of the New York Public Library. "As soon as I was old enough to use the library," she wrote, "I would bring home an armful of books, devour them, and go back for more," a practice she continued throughout her life.[67] Specific books read at specific moments significantly influenced her political thinking as well as her personal self-understanding.[68] At fifteen she read Charlotte Perkins Gilman's book *Women and Economics*. Grace credited this pioneering feminist analysis of women's economic dependence with shaping her early awareness of gender roles, even citing *Women and Economics* as the main reason she "never thought of getting married."[69]

Grace achieved success throughout her schooling. Graduating from the eighth grade when she was just shy of twelve years old and from Newtown High School at fifteen, she won a Regents Scholarship for college. She performed well enough in high school to have completed all the requirements save one class by her last term. To fill the remaining time she took typing and shorthand at Merchants and Bankers Business School. This gave Grace skills she would use both to secure employment at various times through the 1950s and 1960s and in her political work, particularly in the many editorial and organizational roles she played during most of her activist career.[70]

In the fall of 1931, at the age of sixteen, Grace enrolled at Barnard College, the women's college affiliated with Columbia University in New York City. Her scholarship provided $100, which helped to defray the $700 tuition, with the rest of the money coming from her father, supplemented by the money she earned typing papers for other students. The support from her father reflected his strong belief in education. He wanted all of his children to attend college, and Grace was the most academically inclined of them all.[71] By her own admission, Grace was an impressionable and "very immature" college student at sixteen. The experience opened up to her a larger social and intellectual world. "My first two years at college were exciting," she recalled. "I wanted to try everything."[72] She did not have clear plans for study or a career path to take, though she had already decided that she did not want to become a teacher. She briefly considered international affairs, perhaps prompted by a political science class she took in her first year. The paper that she wrote for that class, the first of her college career, examined the Japanese invasion of Chinese Manchuria in September 1931. Having studied Spanish and French in high school, Grace took German in college. During her first year Grace also participated in a weeklong conference at Silver Bay near Lake George, where Ira D. Reid, then of the National Urban League, was one of the speakers. His presentation exposed her to the practice of racial segregation and discrimination, a topic of which she knew little. Nearly eighty years later, she still recalled the impact that Reid's speech made on her in 1932.[73]

The professor who had the greatest impact on her that year was Professor Crampton, who taught her most exciting class, zoology. "I shall never forget our laboratory experiments," she recalled decades later, "where we dissected earthworms and dogfish to internalize evolutionary progress, and I can still feel the excitement of writing an exam paper on the meaning of the concept 'Ontogeny Recapitulates Phylogeny.'"[74] Grace considered becoming a scientist, but this desire faded as she became dissatisfied with Darwinism. In addition, the lab classes conflicted with extracurricular activities, which included swimming, tennis, and participation in the Women's Athletic Association, a campus-wide organization for which she served as treasurer and then vice president.

The social ferment of the Depression led Grace toward a major in philosophy. At the start of her junior year she suddenly lost interest in school. With signs of the crises created by the Depression and the rise of Hitler in Europe cropping up all around her, Grace's classes and extracurricular activities became "boring and empty." Unlike some of her classmates, she "did not feel moved to social action," but she nonetheless took note of their activities and the various ways people responded to the crises.[75] From one classmate she learned of the demands for emergency relief and the mass demonstrations to stop evictions. Another classmate proudly reported her membership to the Communist Party. Two of her friends attended meetings of the Young Communist League. Apart from the one peace march in which she participated, Grace stayed away from the protests and demonstrations of the day, even as she dwelt deeply on the meaning of the times. As she explained it, she "responded to the deepening crisis by turning inward."[76] Eventually, her personal quest began to intersect with a new interest in philosophy. "I began asking myself and my friends questions about the meaning of life and engaging in endless discussions," she recalled of this period. "Not satisfied with these discussions, I suddenly decided to drop all or most of my classes and began auditing philosophy classes."[77] She ultimately chose to major in philosophy, which became a vehicle to aid her search for meaning and a locus for her intellectual development.

Grace was still finding her place in the world, and her college years offered no easy answers. Not only was she younger than her peers, but she was one of only four women of color in the entire school.[78] Moreover, she was painfully shy. "In the dorm," she recalled, "my friends used to tease me because gossip and dirty jokes made me so uncomfortable that I would leave the room when the conversation took this turn."[79] In other ways, too, Grace did not quite fit in at Barnard. Her family's income and residence gave her a middle-class lifestyle, but she could never fit the full profile of the upper-middle-class and elite white students with whom she found herself interacting. Grace was the first girl in her family to attend college (her brother Phil attended Columbia at the same time she attended Barnard). Though she had lived in a largely white world, Barnard's culture differed from her immigrant New York City neighborhood. "I had never been around so many WASPs and middle-class Jews before," she recalled. "Most of the WASPs were from out of town. The Jews came from the Central Park West and West End Avenue neighborhood."[80] Even more than most college students, Grace's process of self-discovery and identity formation remained complicated.

She recalled that her friends "thought I was crazy to major in a subject which offered so little prospects for gainful employment."[81] This, of course, was not an idle concern during the Depression, but Grace had not gone to college with upward mobility in mind; indeed, throughout her life, employment and economic security would never be foremost in her decision making. "When people asked me why I had become so interested in philosophy or what I was going to do with a major in philosophy," she recalled, "I was unable to explain." What mattered most was the opportunity to grapple with ideas. "I could not even tell them what philosophy was about. All I knew was that I was feeling the need to think for myself. What other people had discovered, what other people thought was no longer enough for me."[82] To a significant extent, this marked the beginning of a life journey characterized by Grace's practice of intimately grappling with ideas.

Philosophic Journey

Grace's attraction to philosophy was intensely personal. Though the discipline attracted her in part because of the social crises of the 1930s, probably the most powerful pull came out of her desire to answer questions about the meaning of her own life. If at times her studies did not fully or directly provide the answers she sought—some of her professors approached philosophy as a professional activity and were uncomfortable with the notion of using it as a route to personal examination or self-discovery—philosophy nonetheless pushed her to a deeper and broader intellectual engagement, including encounters with books beyond her classes that would prove very important to her.

For example, reading *The Modern Temper* during this period was sufficiently significant for Grace that she enthusiastically recalled the experience decades later. "I don't know how it came to my attention," she wrote of Joseph Wood Krutch's 1929 book, "but I vividly remember how it captured my unease."[83] She likely identified with Krutch's quest to describe and account for widely held convictions in a changing society. Perhaps, too, the book appealed to her because it sought a synthesis of introspection and social explanation, as suggested by its subtitle, *A Study and a Confession*. In his examination of contemporary American thought, Krutch found both religion and science to be inadequate to the task of organizing a new sense of order in the modern world. "Weak and uninstructed intelligences take refuge in the monotonous repetition of once living creeds," he wrote. But the "the formulae of the flabby pseudo-religions in which the modern world is so prolific" were of no "aid to the robust but serious mind which is searching for some terms upon which it may live."[84] We can imagine Grace, having left behind the Christianity of her childhood and recently become disillusioned with the image if not practice of detached science, easily identifying with such passages. Perhaps she even counted herself among those "robust but serious mind[s]" engaged in this grand if solemn search.

Grace's undergraduate college experience set her on a course of intellectual exploration and eventual political engagement that proved to be central to her life's work. After graduating from Barnard she spent some weeks at Harvard Summer School and then won a Chinese graduate scholarship that covered tuition, room, and board and paid a stipend of $400 a year. In the fall of 1935, at the age of twenty, Grace left New York to study for a Ph.D. in philosophy at Bryn Mawr College, the first of the nation's women's colleges to offer a Ph.D.

She remembered life on the Bryn Mawr campus as "close to idyllic."[85] Situated in rolling hill country outside of Philadelphia, the college boasted majestic stone buildings spread out over several acres. It struck a noticeable contrast in size and beauty with Barnard's dense urban campus. In other ways, of course, the two schools were more alike than different, serving roughly the same number of students and sharing the status of elite institutions. As a graduate fellow Grace enjoyed the "plush" accommodations of Radnor Hall, where she recalled that "Black maids, dressed in gray uniforms with white collars, made our beds, cleaned our rooms, and served our meals three times a day at tables with fine china, cutlery, and cloth napkins."[86] Bryn Mawr also offered a much-improved social atmosphere compared to what she experienced at Barnard. "After each meal we would rush upstairs to smoke, drink coffee, and play bridge for an hour before going to class or to our rooms to study."[87] For recreation, Grace and the other students walked to the local main street and movie theater on Friday nights, and they took trips to nearby Philadelphia or New York, about 100 miles north of campus. Grace supplemented her scholarship money by working in the graduate school office for $1 an hour under the National Youth Administration program.

She found Bryn Mawr academically stimulating and intellectually rewarding. The primary reason for this was a young assistant professor of philosophy named Paul Weiss. The first Jewish member of Bryn Mawr's faculty, Weiss had grown up in a working-class community of immigrant Jewish families on the Lower East Side of New York and studied at Harvard under the British philosopher and mathematician Alfred North Whitehead.[88] "Weiss philosophized as if his life depended on it," Grace recalled. He "not only got an almost palpable pleasure from grappling with ideas but was passionately engaged in creating a new philosophy that would meet both his own needs and those of a society for whom science was no longer sacrosanct."[89] In his classroom, the study of philosophy came alive. Describing him as "small of stature, feisty, and quick-witted," Grace recalled how Weiss "jumped around the room as he asked hard questions about the meaning of the world around us, not only of his students but of himself. As the words tumbled from his mouth in a New York Jewish accent, you got the feeling that he did not know in advance what he was going to say and that what he said had never been said or thought before by him or anybody else."[90]

Under Weiss's direction, Grace began to delve deeply into writings and ideas that would shape the rest of her life. To begin with, Weiss introduced her to the works of German philosophers Immanuel Kant and Georg Wilhelm Friedrich Hegel. "Kant made a lot of sense to me," she recalled, because his *Critique of Pure Reason* (1781) and *Critique of Practical Reason* (1788) resonated with and affirmed her skepticism of traditional philosophy. She was especially drawn to Kant's dismissal of the idea of a final, eternal, static truth and to his concept of knowledge. Knowledge, Kant argued, was not simply the correspondence between ideas and objective reality but rather resulted from the dynamic interaction between our selves and reality. In his view, human minds impose forms on experience, giving us our reality. Grace found Kant "tremendously empowering," even describing his philosophy as a "watershed" in her life. Not only was her intellectual trajectory taking shape, Grace could also see opening up a path to the answers she had sought back at Barnard. "Slowly but surely I was being prepared to take my place in the world. For if we shape reality by how we think, we can also change reality by what we do."[91]

Studying Hegel had an even greater impact. Grace reported reading and rereading his *Phenomenology of Mind* (1807) and *Science of Logic* (1812–16), finding them "excruciatingly difficult" but well worth the effort. "I kept studying them," she wrote decades later, "because at a gut level I sensed that understanding them was the key to the rest of my life."[92] This is an especially strong statement, and it may be that her subsequent engagements with Marxism and radical politics colored this description of her early response to Hegel. But this sentiment nonetheless captures the depth of personal meaning and growth that the study of philosophy triggered for Grace. There is no doubt that Hegel became a major intellectual force in her life. For example, his understanding of freedom, a cornerstone of his philosophical system,[93] profoundly influenced Grace. She was drawn to Hegel's articulation of the human spirit as constantly evolving and engaged in a progressive realization of freedom. "From Hegel," she wrote, "I had gained an appreciation of how human beings have evolved over many thousands of years as they struggled for Freedom (or what we today call 'self-determination'), constantly striving to overcome the contradictions or negatives which inevitably arise in the course of struggle, constantly challenged to break free from ideas which were at one time liberating but had become fetters on our minds because reality had changed."[94] Grace was also drawn to Hegel's philosophy of history and his formulation of the dialectic method. Her later engagement with Marxism, her theoretical writings, and her autobiographical reflections all confirm the influence on her thinking of Hegel's ideas regarding the movement of history.

Given her sustained application of these ideas to the struggles of African Americans through the second half of the twentieth century, it is worth noting that there is no evidence that Grace was especially disturbed by—or for that matter aware of—the racism and Eurocentrism that marred Hegel's understanding of history. Such thinking is revealed in his now infamous passage from *The Philosophy of History* (1837): "At this point we leave Africa, not to mention it again. For it is no historical part of the World; it has no movement or development to exhibit. Historical movements in it—that is in its northern part—belong to the Asiatic or European World."[95] Hegel's racial worldview presumably did not become a topic of discussion in Weiss's courses—there is no evidence to judge otherwise.

Grace drew four sets of ideas from her study of Hegel that in large measure formed a foundation for her own intellectual work and political vision: a recognition of the duality of the positive and negative in everything, the idea of contradiction as a historical and political force, the need to create new ideas as reality changes, and a sense of history as a continuing struggle to determine what it means to be free. All of these ideas would enjoy pride of place in her emerging revolutionary ideology. Reading Hegel in her early years of graduate school also helped her to further resolve the questions that had brought her to philosophy. "Hegel helped me to see my own struggle for meaning as part of the continuing struggle of the individual to become part of the universal struggle for Freedom," she recalled in her autobiography. "Empowered by these ideas, I began to view my unease and restlessness as not a weakness but a strength, a sign that I was ready to move to a new and higher state of being."[96]

The work of the American pragmatist George Herbert Mead became the next catalyst in Grace's personal philosophic journey. Unlike her introduction to Kant and Hegel, Grace did not encounter Mead through Weiss; rather she happened upon Mead's posthumously published works in Bryn Mawr's philosophy library in 1939. Before finding these four volumes, published between 1932 and 1938, Grace had never heard of Mead, and had already begun writing her dissertation on Aristotle. She was so taken by Mead's work, however, that she abruptly changed her topic. The result was her dissertation, "George Herbert Mead: Philosopher of the Social Individual," completed in 1940.[97] Pragmatism appealed to Grace in part because it cast thinking as a practical activity, as opposed to the exercise of "pure reason." This helped Grace to deepen her emerging sense of the power of ideas to change society. She was drawn to Mead as someone who, in her words, "pioneered tirelessly for [pragmatism's] acceptance as the system most germane to modern American ways of living." The following passage from the dissertation's opening paragraph further reveals Mead's appeal to her: "A genuinely original and independent thinker, Mead nevertheless had little consciousness of his own genius. Rather, with his characteristic effort to introduce the scientific method into philosophy, he regarded himself as a co-worker of all other investigators. Thus, as an associate of John Dewey during the formative years of the Chicago school of Pragmatism, he contributed much to the development of the ideas of his better-known colleague."[98] This statement also suggests that it was not only Mead's penetrating insights but also his diffidence and commitment to a common intellectual project that made him an attractive subject for study: perhaps Grace saw a bit of herself in Mead, as well as a model of intellectual practice worthy of admiration and emulation.

Grace deeply identified with Mead's view that ideas evolve historically. "Unlike the average American teacher of philosophy of his day," she wrote,

Mead "urged his students to relate the ideas of the great philosophers to the periods in which they lived and the social problems which they faced."[99] For example, in his book *Movements of Thought in the Nineteenth Century* (1936), a collection of lectures Mead delivered in his history of philosophy classes, Mead explained how the French Revolution conditioned or served as the context for the ideas of Kant, whose *Critique of Pure Reason* appeared on the eve of the revolution, and Hegel, whose *Phenomenology of Mind* was published shortly after its conclusion. More generally, Grace described what appealed to her most about Mead's intellectual project: "A fundamental problem of all men and therefore of all philosophy is the relation of the individual to the whole of things," she wrote. "It is to the solution of this problem that Mead devotes his earnest attention."[100]

Grace's analysis of Mead's ideas—building on her study of Kant and Hegel—helped to solidify two valuable components of her philosophical vision. The first was to conceptualize a view of ideas in their connection with great advances or leaps forward in history. The second was to develop an analysis of how the individual self and the society develop in relation to each other. Grace's dissertation thus marked a signal moment in her philosophical journey. Studying Mead propelled her to new stages of philosophic exploration and, more importantly, a newfound political activism. "In retrospect," she wrote, "it seems clear that what attracted me to Mead was that he gave me what I needed in that period—a body of ideas that challenged and empowered me to move from a life of contemplation to a life of action."[101] She would begin to construct this life of action in Chicago.

Chicago

After the completion of her dissertation in 1940 Grace found herself without plans for the future. She was not interested in academia, and furthermore she anticipated that racial and gender barriers would significantly restrict her employment prospects. It "would have been a waste of time for me, a Chinese woman with a Ph.D. in philosophy, to apply to a university for a teaching job," she reasoned.[102] To be sure, Grace's education made her a rarity—by virtue both of level of attainment (Ph.D.) and specific field (philosophy)—and there is plenty of evidence that she would indeed have faced limited opportunities. In 1940, the year that she earned her Ph.D., American-born Chinese women had on average only 8.6 years of education, and the number for women in general was 8.5 years. The numbers for American-born Chinese men (6.2 years) and men in general (8.3 years) further make the point that her educational attainment made her unique.[103] Those few Chinese Americans who did graduate from college faced overt discrimination, and were sometimes told to "go back to Chinatown where you belong."[104] World War II brought social and economic changes that improved work prospects for Chinese Americans, as it did for most groups, but at the start of the 1940s, when Grace left Bryn Mawr, second- and third-generation Chinese Americans still found limited employment opportunities, irrespective of education or training.[105] The situation proved especially bad for Chinese American women.[106] In 1938 a government employment service report found that most firms discriminated against Chinese, including well-educated U.S. citizens.[107] When Grace left Bryn Mawr, there were fewer than 200 Chinese and Chinese American professors teaching in American colleges and universities.[108]

After graduation, Grace returned to New York, energized by her studies and her newly acquired desire to become politically active. Living in her mother's house (her parents separated in the late 1930s), she spent the summer recuperating from back pain resulting from an injury she sustained playing basketball years earlier. When she felt up to it, she sought outlets for her burgeoning activism.[109] She found her way first to the Socialist Party and then to the Communists. "It didn't take long for me for me to conclude that I didn't want to join them," she wrote of her visit to the Socialist Party headquarters. "After learning that I had a Ph.D. from Byrn Mawr, the young man I spoke to suggested that I speak at one of their upcoming meetings. Groucho Marx said he didn't need to be a member of any club that would have him as a member. In the same spirit I couldn't see myself joining a group that could overlook my obvious ignorance because of my academic credentials. Because of that experience, I have steadfastly refused over the years to identify myself as a Ph.D."[110]

Unsatisfied in New York, Grace boarded a train to Chicago in the fall of 1940. The city appealed to her in part because Mead had been at the University of Chicago and she could look at his papers there. She was also in search of something much larger. "I came to Chicago quite consciously seeking a new civilization," she recalled later.[111] The completion of her studies coincided with the rise of Nazi aggression in Europe, and with Germany's invasion of France in June, the same month that she earned the Ph.D. "I received my doctorate just at the time that France was falling. And it was quite a blow to me because all of my studies really had been in European philosophy, and now with the fall of France it seemed like this was the end of Europe."[112] She hoped that Chicago might offer a path apart from European traditions. She saw in Mead's intellectual trajectory a guide and model for her own. Like her, Mead and his more celebrated colleague John Dewey were both born in New England, but it was at the University of Chicago that they developed their distinctly American philosophic tradition of pragmatism. Grace hoped that she too would find Chicago invigorating, both intellectually and politically. But leaving New York for Chicago was an abrupt and daring move. She had no friends or relatives there, no job prospects, and no place to live. The only person in Chicago she had contact with was Charles Morris, the University of Chicago professor who had edited Mead's works. Beyond this, she had no connection to the city.[113]

Grace left for Chicago with a buoyant excitement but little else. She arrived "with only a few dollars in my pocket and a suitcase containing a change of clothing and some books."[114] She recalled going door to door seeking a room to rent but repeatedly being told "that they didn't rent to Orientals or that the room was already rented, which amounted to the same thing."[115] She eventually found a place when "a little Jewish woman . . . took pity on me." The woman allowed her to live rent-free in her basement on South Ellis Avenue in Hyde Park, at that time a white neighborhood, near the University of Chicago. The basement was damp and uncomfortably close to the large coal furnace, which a black handyman checked every morning. Like him, Grace "had to face down a lineup of rats each time" she entered the basement. But it was free, so she "leapt at the opportunity." As for employment, Professor Morris helped Grace get a job in the University of Chicago's philosophy library paying $10 per week. "That is what I lived on for the next year and a half," she recalled nearly six decades later. "It meant going without what we today consider necessities, like a refrigerator or a car. I wore the same blue corduroy jumper and saddle oxfords until it became a kind of uniform (worn under my leopard coat during the blustery winters). But you could ride the street car for a nickel or dime, and a glass of beer cost a nickel."[116]

Suddenly, Grace found herself far removed from her middle-class roots. Just a few months earlier she had earned a Ph.D. in an esoteric discipline from an elite institution; following commencement she spent the summer in the familiarity and relative comfort of New York and her childhood home. Now she was in a new city, living in a stranger's basement, and making do on earnings much below what her educational attainment could presumably command. But she found a measure of satisfaction in the future that she believed this modest lifestyle offered. "I do not mean to romanticize poverty," she explained later, "but living simply gives you a freedom to make life choices that is lost when you begin to think you need everything that is for sale."[117] At the age of twenty-five, Grace set herself squarely on a life course in which employment, economic security, and professional reward would never be her central concerns.

The introspection, intellectual curiosity, and process of self-discovery that had marked her first quarter century of life were now the ingredients with which Grace would forge a political identity centered on the theory and practice of revolution. Indeed, making a revolution in the United States would prove to be the central passion of the rest of her long and fruitful life.

CHAPTER FOUR

Revolutionary Marxism

Grace, Black Protest, and the Johnson-Forest Tendency

Walking across the University of Chicago campus one day in 1941, Grace saw a notice for a meeting of a group called the South Side Tenants Organization that was fighting rat-infested housing in the black neighborhoods near the university. She attended the meeting and soon joined the group, immersing herself in organizing activities. This brought her into contact with the Workers Party (WP), one of the many radical groupings that vied for space and influence on the Left during World War II. The WP had set up the South Side Tenants Organization to help deepen its connection to and influence among African Americans. Involvement with the South Side Tenants Organization and the WP introduced Grace to radical politics, Chicago's black community, and the dynamics of black protest.[1]

The experience proved timely. The year 1941 was momentous both for the internal development of the WP—especially for the branch of revolutionary socialism that Grace would join—and for African American protest, in Chicago and nationally. Grace found herself emerging as an activist and thinker, engaging these parallel and at times intersecting political worlds of revolutionary socialism and black protest. World War II Chicago was the context that shaped the primary axes of her politics over the next two decades: Marxism and the black struggle.

The Workers Party provided Grace with a specific point of entry into radical politics. As a member of the party, she became a Trotskyist. Founded in the 1920s by Leon Trotsky, a leader of the Russian Revolution, Trotskyism emerged as an influential branch of revolutionary socialism encompassing groups and political parties across the globe. Trotskyists forged an international political movement based on Trotsky's leadership and ideas, including his theory of permanent revolution and opposition to Soviet communism under Joseph Stalin. American Trotskyism emerged in 1928 with the expulsion of James Cannon, Max Shachtman, Martin Abern, and others from the Communist Party (CP) who were opposed to official Communism, or "Stalinism." This led, a decade later, to the founding of the Socialist Workers Party (SWP), the premier Trotskyist organization in the United States, consisting of roughly 1,200 members. They were central to the emergence of an anti-Stalinist left in the mid-1930s, and they competed with the Communist Party. While the latter mounted its popular front strategy in the mid- to late 1930s, Trotskyists called for the political independence of the working class, insisted on the primacy of class struggle, and argued that socialist revolution was the only effective counter to fascism and war.[2]

During World War II, American Trotskyists were split over what they called the "Russian Question," a vigorous if insular debate over the nature of the Soviet Union and how Marxists should relate to it. This in fact encompassed a series of questions: How and why had the workers' councils of the Russian Revolution devolved into Stalin's despotic bureaucratic state? If the Soviet Union under Stalin was not socialist, what was it? Did it represent a transitional stage between capitalism and communism, along the lines predicted by Marx, or did it embody a new type of class society that Marxist theory had not anticipated? How should Marxist ideas about property forms, social relations, and the revolutionary process be applied to the Soviet Union? Should Marxists revolutionaries defend the Soviet Union or renounce it?[3]

These questions, and especially the matter of defending the Soviet Union, assumed an immediacy in 1939–40 with the outbreak of war, the Hitler-Stalin pact, and the Soviet Union's invasion of Poland and Finland. The majority in the SWP, led by James Cannon, held to Trotsky's analysis that the Soviet Union was a "degenerated workers' state." According to this view, Stalin's ruthless bureaucratic regime had corrupted the Russian Revolution and impeded its progress toward socialism, but because nationalized property had supplanted private ownership the Soviet Union was still a postcapitalist society. Thus, while advocating a political revolution to overthrow the reactionary Stalinist bureaucracy, this position called for the defense of the Soviet Union against external imperialist threats. Against this view, a minority faction in the SWP argued that the Soviet Union was "bureaucratic collectivism," a new form of oppressive class society that socialists should not defend. Led by Max Shachtman, this group (about 40 percent of the SWP membership) split off to form the Workers Party in April 1940, just a year before Grace joined.

Grace was not particularly interested in the WP's position on the Russian Question or its role in Trotskyite factional divisions—she was drawn to its work in Chicago's black community and its strong antiwar stance—but this history nonetheless shaped the WP's organizational identity and framed her early political experiences.

Ria Stone

Grace would learn most of this history from Martin Abern, a founding leader of both the SWP and the WP who had experienced much of recent American radical history firsthand. He had joined the Industrial Workers of the World (IWW) and the Young People's Socialist League as a teenager, and he spent six months in prison for refusing, on political grounds, to serve in World War I. In 1920 he was elected as the youngest member of the central committee of the underground convention held to unite the Communist Labor Party and the Communist Party. As the national secretary of the Young Workers League, he was sent to Chicago, where he brought Max Shachtman in to help him publish a newspaper, the *Young Worker*. He also worked with Shachtman and James Cannon in 1927 as a leader of the International Labor Defense. The following year the three of them helped to organize the Communist League of America, which eventually grew into the SWP. During the 1930s he played a leading role in the Trotskyists' political maneuvering and organizational growth as they competed with the CP for the mantle of leadership among workers and radicals. When Grace joined the WP, Abern was a member of the national committee of the party, and he came to Chicago to help reconcile differences between the Chicago local's two branches, one on the South Side, which Grace joined, and the other on the Northwest Side. Abern spent a great deal of time with Grace, sharing with the new recruit recollections of his experiences in the radical movement, stories about the exploits of party leaders like Cannon and Shachtman, and an insider perspective on the movement's many factional splits. "I found Marty's stories fascinating," she recalled. "I recognized that it was an extraordinary privilege for a young person like me to be receiving an account of such a critical period in the history of the radical movement in the United States from one of its leading participants."[4]

Abern's mentorship helped Grace settle into the world of radical politics.[5] He suggested the party name that she adopted, Ria Stone, and he likely helped facilitate her participation in the intellectual life of the Workers Party. In 1942, they jointly authored a series of articles in the WP's theoretical journal the *New International* titled "World War I in Retrospect: An Historical Examination."[6] Later, he encouraged her to write a piece on China for the journal, resulting in a series of four articles in which she examined China's recent political history and contemporary class dynamics.[7]

While Grace received from Abern a rich sense of the historical evolution of the radical movement, this was only part of the political development she sought. "Marty had always been an organizer rather than a theoretician," she recalled. "He was a storehouse of information, but his stories were mainly about schemes and maneuvers and personalities, not the development of ideas."[8] As an eager political neophyte, and as a budding intellectual recently energized by her study of evolving philosophical concepts, Grace sought political activism that was engaged with and driven by ideas. She hoped that the WP would provide her with a rigorous political development, but this was largely unrealized.[9] Years later, as a seasoned activist, she reflected that when she was a new member, no one in the organization "talked to me about Trotsky, Lenin, or Marx." Indeed, "no one made any effort to educate me politically beyond recommending that I read Trotsky's *History of the Russian Revolution* and some pamphlets by Marx."[10] She recalled further that there had been no program or ongoing forum for the type of political education and theoretical development that she desired. Branch meetings included political discussions, but these only covered current events or political debates going on in the national organization, such as the Russian Question and the fault lines of Trotskyite factional divisions, most of which Grace did not find particularly interesting.

Two dimensions of the party's work did interest her. One was its antiwar position. Trotskyists in general and the WP in particular opposed the war (though increasingly strong differences arose among Trotskyists during and after the split in the SWP). When Grace left Bryn Mawr and began her search for political activism, the one concrete position she held and for which she sought an organizational space was opposition to World War II. She was therefore drawn to the WP's forceful argument that the war was a conflict between imperialists, just as the first had been, a position she had heard and found convincing while at Barnard. The other component of the

Workers Party that captured Grace was its organizing in Chicago's black community.

Like most radical groupings during World War II, the WP sought influence and recruits among African Americans. In Chicago, this meant spending time in Washington Park, adjacent to the increasingly crowded community south of downtown known variously as the Black Belt, the South Side, and Bronzeville. Two astute observers of black Chicago, St. Clair Drake and Horace Cayton, noted in their classic study *Black Metropolis* that the park served simultaneously as the "playground of the South Side" and a "public, open-air 'forum'" for political debate.[11] This was especially true in the summer, when Washington Park was "Bronzeville's equivalent of Hyde Park," drawing a range of speakers competing for attention and adherents among the black masses. It was a place, Drake and Cayton wrote, where "'jack-leg' preachers joust with curbstone atheists, and Black Zionists break a lance with sundry varieties of Reds."[12]

The Workers Party was among these "Reds." Grace ventured to Washington Park with her WP comrades and observed the free flow of ideas there. She even eventually rose as a speaker herself. No record remains of what she said or how many times she spoke. Her recollections of the experience have focused only on the reception she received and on the lesson she took. "When I got up to speak some people would come around, mainly because as a Chinese woman I was a novelty and they were curious about where I had come from and what I thought. . . . Their willingness to listen made me very conscious of how little I had to say."[13] Such reticence notwithstanding, Grace found herself emerging as an activist, and occasionally as a speaker, within this matrix of antiwar, noncommunist Left, and black protest politics.

In one instance, a rally in 1941 or 1942 to protest the recent killing of black soldiers in the South, circumstances threw Grace into the role of public speaker. During the planning of the rally, someone gave her the task of securing Horace Cayton, who was then conducting research for *Black Metropolis*, as the main speaker.[14] Cayton enjoyed prominent community standing on the South Side as the executive director of the Parkway Community House, a major community gathering place, social work center, and art house for black Chicagoans, reported to be the largest and most comprehensive such black-run institution in the country.[15] Cayton told Grace that a prior engagement would prevent him from attending the rally, but he would allow Grace to read a speech he prepared. "It was a huge meeting, about a thousand people," she recalled. "Because I was moved by the speech, I presented it in a very moving way. As a result, at the end of the speech it seemed as if people were ready to follow me in a mass march downtown. It scared the living daylights out of me. Just out of university and getting my toes wet in radical politics, what did I know about leading masses of people? . . . I resolved to avoid speaking at mass meetings until I was a lot better informed."[16]

Whatever her lack of knowledge, Grace had the benefit of an invaluable learning environment. Talking and interacting with people in a black community for the first time, she was gaining insight into the dynamics of racial oppression, hearing about the lived experience of segregation and discrimination, and learning how to organize meetings and protests. Grace's exposure to African American protest politics in Chicago during World War II was foundational to her emergence and growth as an activist.

The March on Washington Movement

Grace regarded her participation in the March on Washington Movement (MOWM) in Chicago as "the turning point in my life" because, as she told Horace Cayton years later, she had come to Chicago searching for the basis of a "new civilization" and found it "in the Negroes mobilizing themselves for the March on Washington. I shall never forget the transformation that took place in them with the call for the march."[17] As a young, emerging radical, the sense of political possibility embodied in the MOWM made a considerable impression on her thinking. Specifically, it gave her a workable model and clear vision of a mass movement. Furthermore, it gave her an appreciation for the potential of grassroots politics not only to confront social injustice but also to effect individual and community transformation. Finally, the MOWM cemented Grace's commitment to black political struggle. "The March on Washington changed my life," she wrote more than half a century later. It "taught me lessons that have shaped my activities ever since." One of these lessons was "that a movement begins when large numbers of people, having reached the point where they feel they can't take the way things are any longer, find hope for improving their daily lives in an action that they can take together." Even more important for her own political trajectory, she "also discovered the power that the black community has within itself to change this country when it begins to move. As a result, I decided that what I wanted to do with the rest of my life was to become a movement activist in the black community."[18]

The idea of a march originated in December 1940, as war production was gearing up and black protest against racial discrimination began to mount. Black labor leader A. Philip Randolph had determined that previous wartime modes of protest—public statements condemning segregation, sharply worded telegrams to Washington, and meetings with White House officials—were demonstrably ineffectual. New and more dramatic measures were in order. Mass action, Randolph reasoned, would be required, and he proposed a protest of 10,000 black people marching down Pennsylvania Avenue to demand an end to segregation in the armed forces and exclusion from jobs in the defense industry. Drawing on community organizing and protest networks developed during the 1920s and 1930s, this would be a broad, national mobilization of African Americans. The substance of their demand would be full and equal participation in the national defense effort, and the form of the demand would be a mass mobilization designed to compel the federal government to action. The MOWM, in effect, pioneered the type of protest politics that was used to considerable effect during the civil rights movement to push the federal government to enforce or enact African American citizenship rights.

Randolph announced the March on Washington proposal in a January 1941 statement to the press. He declared that "power and pressure do not reside in the few, and intelligentsia, they lie in and flow from the masses. . . . Power is the active principle of only the organized masses, the masses united for a definitive purpose."[19] Two months later Randolph issued the official call for the march, set for July 1, 1941. Drawing on his standing as a prominent black leader, and especially as the head of the Brotherhood of Sleeping Car Porters (BSCP), Randolph made his case that the time was right. "In this period of power politics, nothing counts but pressure, more pressure, and still more pressure," he wrote in the call to march. "To this end we propose that 10,000 Negroes MARCH ON WASHINGTON FOR JOBS IN NATIONAL DEFENSE AND EQUAL INTEGRATION IN THE FIGHTING FORCES."[20] To coordinate this massive effort, organizers established a March on Washington Committee, headed by Randolph, along with a sponsoring committee and regional committees in cities across the country. Galvanized by a rising desire for action within black communities, the idea found enthusiastic approval in the black press and eventually won the endorsement of the National Association for the Advancement of Colored People (NAACP), the National Urban League, and other elements of black leadership.[21] By the end of May, Randolph estimated that 100,000 black Americans would march. A national grassroots movement was afoot, and Randolph grew even more confident in his vision for the demonstration. "Let the Negro masses march!" he declared. "Let the Negro masses speak!"[22]

This threat pushed President Roosevelt to action. The all-black character of the MOWM and the prospect of 100,000 marchers made this an explosive and potentially disruptive spectacle as the president ramped up wartime production. On June 25, just days before the scheduled July 1 demonstration, he issue Executive Order 8802, banning racial discrimination in defense industries and agencies of the federal government and establishing the Fair Employment Practices Committee (FEPC) to carry out the order. The order did not meet both of the March on Washington Committee's demands—Roosevelt did nothing to stop racial segregation in the military—but it was nonetheless greeted as a great victory. Having realized the main goal of the demonstration, Randolph and the March on Washington Committee called off—or "postponed"—the march. This drew criticism from some quarters, but in the main Randolph and the committee earned praise for their leadership, and the executive order was roundly described as a major event in African American history. Some even hailed it as a "Second Emancipation Proclamation."[23]

Of course, implementation of the order still remained. Industry compliance was in no way assured, especially given that the FEPC lacked enforcement power. Randolph therefore sought to transform the energy galvanized by the march into a protest organization that would serve as a "watchdog" over implementation of the executive order. The committee that had organized the march was thus turned into the March on Washington *Movement* (MOWM). From September of 1941 until the attack on Pearl Harbor in December, Randolph went across the country helping to build local MOWM chapters. The entry of the United States into the war focused the MOWM toward dramatic protest activity. Under the slogan "Winning Democracy for the Negro Is Winning the War for Democracy" (inspired by the Double V campaign), the MOWM organized a series of three large, widely successful rallies during the summer of 1942 in New York, Chicago, and Saint Louis. Individual MOWM chapters also staged various local protests against discriminatory employers. This effort to turn the March on Washington idea into a permanent entity ultimately failed, but during 1941–42 the MOWM was a leading vehicle for black militancy and political mobilization.[24]

Grassroots organizing drove the MOWM's growth and success, and Chicago activists made their city one of the largest and most effective organizing centers. BSCP chapters and their social and political networks enabled much of the MOWM's organizational work across the country. This was very much the case in Chicago, where the BSCP office served as the major site for organizing, and brotherhood dues provided the majority of funding. Current and former BSCP officials Milton Webster, Charles Burton, and Irene McCoy Gaines were key March on Washington organizers, and they worked with established protest networks such as the Chicago Congress of Negro Organizations. Indeed, the March on Washington idea merged with and galvanized an existing framework of protest politics in black Chicago, making the city one of the earliest and most active sites of March on Washington organizing.[25]

For example, on Sunday, February 9, 1941, black Chicagoans launched Negro History Week and celebrated "Race Relations Sunday" with a huge parade to protest discrimination in defense industries and training programs and segregation in the armed services. Over 1,000 people braved snow and harsh temperatures to participate in this "Demonstration for Democracy," which was organized or endorsed by a cross section of black leadership—including Irene McCoy Gaines, St. Clair Drake (who was secretary of the demonstration committee), the Chicago branches of the NAACP and the National Urban League, Ishmael Flory of the National Negro Congress, two Chicago aldermen, and various pastors—representing 120 organizations. The parade ended with a meeting during which participants discussed and endorsed the March on Washington idea.[26]

News and commentary about this new idea spread through the pages of the ubiquitous and widely influential black weekly newspaper, the *Chicago Defender*.[27] It devoted considerable space to reporting on and debating the March on Washington. Between February and the planned march date of July 1, the *Defender* carried pieces by and about Randolph, editorials supporting the march (though an early one doubted that 10,000 people could be mobilized), and reports on march organizing activities. On the eve of the march, the newspaper ran an editorial expressing in sharp terms the grievances and the hopes embodied in the march: "Goaded by unabated Jim Crowism and relentless insults, the Negro people of America are no longer content to mumble prayers of hope at a wailing wall. . . . Many thousands of black men and women, from all walks of life and from all sections of the United States, will march, July 1, on Washington in the greatest crusade for democracy ever staged by America's black minority. . . . If the 'March on Washington' does nothing else, it will convince white America that the American black man has decided henceforth and forever to abandon the timid role of Uncle-Tomism in the struggle for social justice, no matter what the sacrifice. On to Washington!"[28]

The Chicago MOWM chapter worked with twenty South Side ministers to promote the mass rally in the summer of 1942. They encouraged rally attendance in their sermons, set aside the Sunday before the rally as "MOWM Sunday," and donated their offerings from that day to the rally.[29] Literature advertising the rally carried the banner "Fight or Be Slaves!"[30] and organizers distributed flyers throughout black Chicago encouraging people to "STORM THE COLISEUM" for "THE GREATEST, BIGGEST AND MOST STUPENDOUS GATHERING OF NEGRO PEOPLE FOR JUSTICE—DEMOCRACY—FREEDOM AND MANHOOD RIGHTS IN THE HISTORY OF THE WORLD!"[31] As was the case with the other rallies, mobilization for the rally involved nearly the whole of black Chicago. On the eve of the demonstration, the *New York Amsterdam News* reported that the "entire colored section" of Chicago "is bedecked with flags, placards and street signs reinforced with sound trucks cruising all over announcing tomorrow night's March on Washington Movement's meeting."[32] A "Black Out," during which businesses and residents turned out their lights from 9:00 to 10:00 P.M., elicited enthusiasm among black Chicagoans during the rally preparation and was successful that night.[33]

The rally took place on June 26, 1942, one year, almost to the day, after Roosevelt's issuing of Executive Order 8802. A dramatic display of racial militancy and solidarity, the rally vividly portrayed the "fighting spirit" that the MOWM had galvanized in Chicago.[34] Upward of 12,000 people packed the Chicago Coliseum, with several thousand more overflowing into the street.[35] The *Defender* reported that the crowd was "made up of an overwhelming number of working men and women,"[36] a fact that not only illustrated the MOWM's working-class character but also fulfilled the rally's goal of projecting a mood of mass protest. The clearest expression of this mood, and the emotional highpoint of the night, came during a short stage performance titled "The Watchword Is Forward," taking its title from a slogan Randolph used to close his letters.[37] Written especially for the summer rallies by Dick Campbell, director of the Rose McClendon Players from New York, the play drew "thunder-like applause" for its portrayal of wartime militancy. The most popular scene included a line delivered by Canada Lee, who portrayed a young black draftee speaking to a draft board official:

"Yes sir, I am against them Japs. I'm against them Germans, them Italians—and I'm also against them Negro-hating crackers down south." According to the *Defender*, the "pandemonium which greeted this declaration is indescribable."[38] The rally concluded with an address by Randolph that came to be known as his "We Don't Give a Damn" speech.[39] He issued sharp denunciations of discriminatory practices in industry and government along with uncompromising and crowd-pleasing calls for mass action to oppose black Americans' second-class citizenship. In the midst of these appeals, he resurrected the threat of a march on Washington: "If the President does not issue a war proclamation to abolish jim crow in Washington, the District of Columbia and all government departments and the armed forces, Negroes are going to march and we don't give a damn what happens."[40] This threat never materialized, but the movement behind it helped to forge a monumental shift in black protest and World War II–era American racial politics.

Grace wrote several articles in the Trotskyite press about the MOWM and the intersection of black rights and the labor movement. Published during the summer and fall of 1942, these articles in part document Grace's emergence as an intellectual in the radical movement as well as the beginning of her commitment to analyzing the contours and prospects of black political struggle. In particular, they show that the MOWM served two important roles in Grace's early political development. First, it filled important gaps in the political education that she sought, giving her concrete, local, and immediate examples of political struggle, whereas the WP had generally provided only theoretical abstractions and far-removed events. Secondly, these articles were among the very first of her many writings. The March on Washington Movement served as the object of her first sustained intellectual engagement as a Marxist radical.

The Workers Party saw the MOWM as a potentially progressive movement, but only partially embraced its politics. The WP supported the march idea and gave the movement frequent and favorable coverage in its newspaper, *Labor Action*. However, this support was conditioned—and in some ways circumscribed—by the WP's own political priorities. For example, while the WP nominally accepted the MOWM's policy of remaining an all-black organization, calls for support of the MOWM in *Labor Action* were consistently accompanied by calls for black and white worker solidarity and qualified by an insistence that the MOWM recognize the labor movement as its natural ally. What appealed to the WP most about the MOWM was its mass character, and the party drew a sharp distinction between the leadership, which they stridently criticized, and the black masses, which the party fully and rather uncritically celebrated. According to the WP, the masses were duly militant and thus ahead of their leaders, who were reformist in outlook and too closely tied to the president and the war effort. The WP believed that Randolph and the other leaders had sought to curb mass pressure, that this was the reason they called off the march, and that the black masses felt betrayed by this decision. As we have seen, there were certainly some black people and leaders who disagreed with the decision to call off the march, but the WP overstated this dissension. They also understated Randolph's appeal and standing in the black community. Thus, the WP's position was a reflection of its own politics much more than it was an accurate reading of black movement politics.[41]

This shortcoming marred Grace's first article on the MOWM. Chastising the Double V campaign and the MOWM's related slogan, "Winning Democracy for the Negro Is Winning the War for Democracy," she argued that these slogans amounted to "pretending to fight for democracy at home while at the same time sponsoring the imperialist war abroad." She further asserted that such "campaigners for 'Double Victory' actually straddle the issue and subordinate the struggle against domestic oppression to 'national unity.'"[42] These statements reflected the WP's staunch antiwar position and its interpretation of such slogans as little more than cover for Roosevelt and the war. But this view lacked appreciation for the nuances and valences of contemporary black political thought. The WP's position and Grace's analysis misread an important strand of World War II black politics. Double V represented an elevation of black Americans' struggle for democratic rights. Far from subordinating that struggle to the war effort (though it is true that some black leaders took pains not to disturb national unity), Double V and similar efforts strategically used the war as an opportunity and a wedge. Looking through the prism of the WP's Marxist internationalism, Grace saw no politically justifiable position that did not directly oppose the war. She therefore could not recognize Double V as deriving from a political logic independent of Roosevelt and legitimate on its own terms.

In other ways, however, Grace's MOWM articles showed an astute understanding of black politics. Indeed, while her reporting on MOWM activities and interpretation of its policies rehearsed some of the WP's ideologically driven line, her analysis of the MOWM's significance for black politics and communities showed impressive insight and a measure of independent thought. For example, she perceptively assessed the meaning and significance of the March on Washington Movement by viewing it in a relatively broad context of black political development, both historically and contemporarily. Like many observers, she compared the MOWM to the powerful mass movement led by Marcus Garvey and his organization, the Universal Negro Improvement Association, two decades earlier. However, she drew different conclusions from the comparison. Most analysts noted that both Randolph and Garvey built mass and largely working-class organizations with all-black memberships, and many of these commentators pondered the extent to which Randolph's decision to keep the MOWM an all-black organization reflected a Garvey-style black nationalism.[43] By contrast, Grace placed the two movements in a historical relationship that highlighted their similar sociopolitical origins, namely world war and domestic crisis. She also identified their divergence in political philosophy and program. Writing in the *New International* under the name Ria Stone, she explained that the MOWM, "like the Garveyite movement of the First World War, arises at a time when Negroes are conscious of the discrepancy between the professed aims of the ruling class to spread democracy abroad and the actual denial of democracy at home. But unlike the Garveyite movement, with its emphasis on black solidarity over the world, the MOW is an authentic native American movement, stemming from the American Negro masses and directed toward the goal of democratic rights for Negroes in America."[44]

Grace's articles also compared the MOWM to its two main contemporary national organizations, the NAACP and the National Urban League. By virtue of its mass character, elements of working-class leadership, and connection to organized labor, she favorably evaluated the MOWM's leadership structure and class orientation relative to the two older national organizations. Yet, she was aware that with the movement's success, "dozens of so-called Negro leaders have also climbed onto the bandwagon of the MOW."[45] She critiqued this rising faction of MOWM leadership, composed of middle-class and professional people, citing it and an undemocratic streak in its organizational culture as major forces gutting the movement's militancy and threatening its viability. Indeed, scholars of the movement would later confirm that these two characteristics contributed to the organization's decline.[46] Writing about the movement during the summer of 1942, as it reached its zenith, Grace managed to capture it not just as a dramatic expression of black discontent, but also as a dynamic political event, the exact character and specific impact of which were as yet unclear.

Her ideological commitments notwithstanding, Grace's reporting on and analysis of the MOWM thoughtfully presented its contours and political potentiality, which oscillated, as she saw it, between a genuine mass movement capable of confronting the seat of power and a "propaganda pressure group" that set its sights on low-lying goals and was content with futile executive orders.

Grace's *Labor Action* and *New International* articles demonstrated that she had acquired an impressive knowledge and understanding of black protest politics in her short time in Chicago. She began with no reservoir of experience or information on the black struggle for racial justice from which to draw and little understanding of the dynamics of antiblack racism. But she began to construct her identity as an activist living, working, and engaging in political organizing in proximity to black Chicago, and by the summer of 1942, her articles thoughtfully rendered historical and contemporary contours of racial oppression, African American protest, and emergent struggles against Jim Crow. This passage, for example, describes a black perspective on the meaning of World War II:

> Thirteen million Negroes in America have never known three of the "Four Freedoms" which America is supposedly spreading to the rest of the world. "Freedom from want" is a mockery to Negroes when they are last to be hired and first to be fired; when so many usually obtain only domestic work of short duration: when their wages are the lowest and their rents and food prices the highest. "Freedom from fear" is a myth to Negroes when they have no recourse against the "righteous" Southern citizenry who periodically find excuses to hold lynching parties; against the Northern citizenry who magnify every petty theft into a crime wave; or against those military police whose trigger fingers itch to soil a Negro soldier's uniform with blood.
>
> "Freedom of speech" is meaningless to millions of Negroes who are kept in enforced ignorance and illiteracy by the most meager educational facilities in the South and who are sent to the most crowded schools in the North, so that throughout the country, 2,700,000 Negroes (or more than twenty per cent of the total Negro population) have had no schooling beyond the fourth grade. "Freedom of religion" is the only one of the "four freedoms" for the Negro which the ruling class has encouraged. The latter has hoped to keep

Negroes satisfied by sky-pilots, saturated with spirituals, shouting for peace and security in another world and therefore content with their misery in this world.[47]

Grace's understanding of the black struggle largely derived from what she saw and experienced in Chicago. Her words anticipated those of St. Clair Drake, who wrote in 1944 that "Negro leaders in Chicago, of all social classes and levels of 'culture,' have been united under one platform—that the touchstone of America's sincerity about the Four Freedoms is her treatment of Negroes."[48] Her commentary likewise echoed A. Philip Randolph's speech at the Chicago MOWM rally in June 1942 (just two months before her article): "How can we carry the Four Freedoms to Manila in the Pacific," he asked the crowd, "when we don't have the Four Freedoms in Mississippi, in the Atlantic?"[49]

As Grace was writing these analyses of the MOWM she was also beginning to realign herself politically. Within the WP she began associating with a small grouping known as the "State Capitalist Tendency" (or "State Capitalist Minority"[50]) that earned its moniker from its position on the Russian Question, arguing that "state capitalism" best described contemporary Russia. The group also distinguished itself from the rest of the WP by its unique position on the "Negro Question." Early in 1942, just months before her *Labor Action* and *New International* articles appeared, Grace had met C. L. R. James, the central figure of the State Capitalist Tendency. When they met, she was a political neophyte newly inaugurated into the anti-Stalinist left, whereas he occupied a prominent place in that world. Though he took her under his tutelage, the instruction flowed both ways. Her familiarity with Hegel and knowledge of German complemented and supplemented C. L. R.'s own talents. The collaboration between the two of them over the next two decades had a tremendous impact on Grace's development.

C. L. R. James

Born in 1901 in Trinidad, Cyril Lionel Robert James's middle-class colonial upbringing fostered an early and lasting love of reading and an equally abiding affection for the game of cricket. He received a solid education at Trinidad's premier school, Queens Royal College, which gave him, among other things, an intimate knowledge of European history and culture. He returned to the school as a teacher during the 1920s. At the same time, he pursued a range of literary activities, including cricket journalism, writing for and editing magazines, and writing fiction. In 1932, he left Trinidad for England, where he hoped to more fully pursue his ambitions as a writer. C. L. R. spent the next six years there, making a name for himself as a cricket reporter, creative writer, and Marxist theoretician.[51]

In England, C. L. R. focused on socialism and Pan-Africanism.[52] He studied Marxism, joined the British section of the international Trotskyist movement, and could be described as British Trotskyism's "deepest thinker and most popular public figure."[53] C. L. R. simultaneously threw himself into Pan-African politics. Some of his early writings contained sharply critical commentary on British imperialism, and during the 1920s he took an interest in debates around West Indian independence.[54] When he sailed to England he carried with him the manuscript of his book *The Case for West-Indian Self Government*. At the age of nineteen or twenty, C. L. R. read Marcus Garvey's newspaper *Negro World* with his childhood friend Malcolm Nurse, who later took the name George Padmore. C. L. R. joined with other black ex-patriots in anticolonial agitation and advocacy for African and West Indian independence. Their work included journalism and institution building such as the International African Service Bureau, which C. L. R. created with Padmore, Amy Ashwood Garvey, Jomo Kenyatta, and T. Ras Makonnen.[55]

In 1938, C. L. R. went to the United States as a speaker for the Socialist Workers Party and ended up staying for fifteen years. He arrived as a prominent Trotskyist and also a committed Pan-Africanist who was well versed in the history and culture of European civilization. He quickly reframed his interests in international Trotskyism and global black liberation struggles for an American political context. His engagement in the international Trotskyist movement turned into intense theoretical work on Marxist theory, its articulation within American Trotskyism, and its application to the mid-twentieth-century United States, while his Pan-Africanist work now shifted to the so-called Negro Question. These remained parallel concerns, at times overlapping and even merging to some extent.

C. L. R. traveled to Mexico in April 1939 to have discussions on the Negro Question with Leon Trotsky. Upon his return to the United States in early May he drafted two resolutions—"The SWP and Negro Work" and "The Rights of Self-Determination and the Negro in the United States of North America"—for the SWP convention in early July, both of which were accepted at the convention and in effect outlined the SWP's position on the Negro Question. He continued to push for the SWP to work with black Americans and helped to shape this work, which led to the establishment of the SWP's National Negro Department, with C. L. R. as its director. In the coming months he conducted a popular class on black history and had a hand in the party's recruitment of approximately thirty-nine new black members. He also used the Trotskyist press to advance his ideas, starting a column on "The Negro Question" in *Socialist Appeal* and writing a longer, theoretical piece on the topic in the December 1939 issue of *The New International*.[56]

It was during this period that the SWP erupted in factional struggle. At the SWP convention in the spring of 1940, C. L. R. voted with the minority, whose split founded the WP in April 1940. "In this now much smaller pond," C. L. R. "became a still bigger fish," making his largest impact through his theoretical intervention on the Russian Question.[57] Early in 1941 he undertook a renewed and closer study of Marx's *Capital*, leading to his conceptualization of the Soviet Union as essentially a capitalist society along the lines that Marx had identified. As a result, C. L. R. rejected the WP's position that Russia was a bureaucratic collectivist society, arguing instead that it had reverted to a form of capitalism characterized by state control of production. A small portion of the membership agreed with this analysis. He presented his document as a resolution on the Russian Question at the first WP national convention in September 1941, and those who shared this view, particularly a Russian-born member with a deep theoretical grounding named Raya Dunayevskaya, joined with C. L. R. and constituted themselves as the State Capitalist Tendency within the Workers Party.[58] This was the beginning of what would become known as the Johnson-Forest Tendency (JFT), which took its name from its pseudonymous leaders, J. R. Johnson (C. L. R. James) and Freddie Forest (Raya Dunayevskaya).

C. L. R. soon met the person who would become the third leader of the group. Shortly after the WP convention he traveled to Missouri, spending five months in strike support work with a group of black sharecroppers and union activists. He wrote a pamphlet to articulate the demands and basic issues of the strike and covered the story for *Labor Action*. This experience deepened his engagement with and understanding of black American social dynamics and politics. On his way back to New York in early 1942, C. L. R. made a stop to visit the Chicago branch of the SWP, where he met Grace Lee. When she and another comrade went to meet him at the train station, "he was carrying two thick books, volume 1 of Marx's *Capital* and Hegel's *Science of Logic*, both heavily underlined. When he discovered that I had studied Hegel and knew German, we withdrew to my basement room where we spent hours sitting on my old red couch comparing passages in Marx and Hegel, checking the English against the original German."[59] C. L. R. also maintained a clear memory of their meeting, years later recalling "going to Chicago and meeting Grace . . . a woman of immense qualifications, great abilities and great energy."[60]

Grace's meeting of C. L. R. marked another transition in her life. She left Chicago for New York, where the JFT was centered, so she could fully participate in the activities and life of the tendency. Not yet thirty years old, she was a committed revolutionary, a member of a formidable if insular and recondite group of radicals. They were committed and creative Marxists exploring the possibilities and directions of revolutionary politics in the United States of the 1940s, a country and a moment they believed to be alive with great potential for popular insurgency. Grace would find being a member (and eventually a leader) of the JFT to be intellectually exhilarating, well beyond what she had experienced studying philosophy at Bryn Mawr. She immersed herself in the life of the organization, thereby reinforcing and deepening her political identity.

"A Collective Way to Know Reality"

The Johnson-Forest Tendency (JFT) functioned as a political collective organized around a decidedly cooperative and collaborative practice of intellectual work. This fact is essential for understanding the JFT's history, for properly interpreting C. L. R. James and his relationship to Grace and other members of the group, and for grasping the influences that acted on her thinking and shaped her political practice.[61] A 1945 letter by C. L. R. described the process by which he, Grace, and two other comrades discussed a political matter and then produced a written document: "As we talked I felt very pleased. One person writes but in the world in which we live all serious contributions have to be collective; the unification of all phases of life make[s] it impossible for a single mind to grasp it in all its aspects. Although one mind may unify, the contributory material and ideas must come from all sources and types of mind. . . . The best mind is the one so basically sound in analytical approach and capacity to absorb, imagination to fuse, that he makes a totality of all these diverse streams."[62]

Members of the group drew upon each other's specific skills, interests, and experiences, and through this they created a shared space to work out an understanding of a given issue and collectively arrive at a position. This resulted in a wide array of written texts published by the JFT, some with no author, some attributed to the entire collective, others published under the names (often pseudonyms) of multiple members, and still others carrying a sole author.

Grace described the Johnson-Forest Tendency and its collaborative practice as "a collective way to know reality."[63] JFT members not only learned from each other, they grew to rely on each other as cotheorists and cocreators of knowledge. Composed of approximately sixty to seventy members (out of the larger SWP membership of several hundred), the JFT was a relatively small political grouping. But its members' shared a commitment to a set of ideas, and a sense of revolutionary purpose buoyed them. "Our energy was fantastic," Grace recalled of the early JFT days. "We would spend a morning or afternoon writing, talking, and eating and then go home and write voluminous letters to one another extending or enlarging on what we had discussed, sending these around to other members of our tendency in barely legible carbon copies."[64] These letters performed considerable work for the organization. In them, JFT members discussed and dissected Marxists texts, analyzed contemporary events, and plotted the group's writing projects, which would articulate the JFT line and constitute its interventions into Trotskyist debates. Grace became one of the most active and consistent participants in this correspondence. As such, she came to occupy an essential place in the group's leadership, not just as a theorist, but also as something of a repository for the group's ideological and political evolution. She not only wrote many letters, but she typed some penned by C. L. R. and others. Moreover, she regularly took on the task of distributing these letters and related documents, both to JFT members and to political allies outside the group, and through this she facilitated and fostered the intellectual exchanges that proved vital to the organization. Through her combined intellectual and practical labors, she assumed the functions of chronicling, coordinating, and planning the group's work.

Grace was of course familiar with New York, but living in the city as a member of the JFT offered new experiences. After briefly living with her mother in the Jackson Heights home of her childhood, Grace rented an apartment on 114th Street near Broadway and then moved to a fifth-floor walk-up apartment on the Lower East Side. Next she rented a basement apartment on East Seventeenth Street in Gramercy Park, and finally a place on West Nineteenth Street near Ninth Avenue. She supported herself through an assortment of jobs, including working part time in her father's restaurant and doing temporary secretarial work. Toward the end of World War II she briefly worked in a defense plant in Brooklyn, wiring and soldering electrical parts. Because of the changes brought by the war, this was "a marvelous time for going into the plant,"[65] as she recalled it, where radicals like her hoped to make contact with production workers. Most of her coworkers were young black women whose previous employment had primarily been domestic work. A highlight of this job for Grace was being part of a group that held Negro history study groups during coffee breaks. Later, through the League for Mutual Aid, she secured a job as secretary to James McDonald, the first U.S. secretary to Israel. It paid an initial salary of $60 per week, later raised to $100.[66]

These jobs foretold Grace's employment pattern for the rest of her working life. Since the purpose of her education was personal growth and self-realization, not economic gain or career opportunities, her work life would never be driven by earning potential or prestige. She sought employment opportunities that she could bend to her political commitments. Throughout her life she chose jobs, often undemanding secretarial positions, that offered her flexibility and afforded her the space, both literal and figurative, to engage in her political work. She remembered that the McDonald secretarial position "was more money than I have ever made," which allowed her to move, but the more satisfying aspect of the job was that "all I had to do was arrange McDonald's speaking schedule. He was out of town most of the time, and I could read, write, and hold meetings with comrades during working hours in the office."[67]

Being a member of the Johnson-Forest Tendency in 1940s New York opened up "a whole new world of people, ideas, and activity."[68] Grace traveled across the city, conducting JFT work in the homes of members in the Bronx, Harlem, and Manhattan. Beyond that, she spent time in Harlem visiting the renowned Schomburg Collection to study the writings of black nationalist leader Marcus Garvey; attending forums of the Workers Party's Interracial Club, chaired by her close JFT comrade Lyman Paine (under the party name Tom Brown), at its office on 125th Street; and enjoying Harlem's nightlife and entertainment. Visiting Harlem landmarks such as the Apollo Theater, the Savoy Ballroom, and Small's Paradise, she moved in social circles that included Katherine Dunham, Richard Wright, James Baldwin, and Pearl Primus.[69]

The Johnson-Forest Tendency and the experience that it fostered for Grace in the 1940s provided her with precisely what she sought at that moment: a space to develop not just political ideas, but political relationships and a social context through which the development of ideas could have deeper meaning. In the JFT she was able to work with fellow activists who were at once of like mind and sufficiently varied in background, social experience, and worldview as to open up for her new avenues of social awareness and engagement. The particular combination of people with whom she worked in the JFT helped to make it a stimulating and invigorating environment and one in which she could continue to grow as a thinker and an activist.

629 Hudson Street

Grace enjoyed a special and enduring bond with JFT charter members Freddy and Lyman Paine. A married couple with vastly divergent social backgrounds, the Paines met in the Trotskyist movement during the mid-1930s and witnessed all of the internal party dynamics that led to the formation of the WP and the emergence of the JFT. Freddy (Frances) Paine grew up as an orphan with a formal education that stopped at the third grade. Her young adulthood included stints as a waitress, dancer, and artist's model in New York, but her most formative and enduring activity was as a labor organizer. She started organizing in the garment district of New York in 1928 at the age of sixteen. Two years later she joined A. J. Muste's Conference for Progressive Labor Action, which became the American Workers Party (AWP). Her labor activity also included organizing in anthracite coal mines in West Virginia and Pennsylvania and the famous Auto-Lite sit-down strike in Toledo, Ohio, during the 1930s. During the early 1930s she attended the Bryn Mawr Summer School for Women Workers (just two or three years before Grace arrived at Bryn Mawr for graduate school). In 1936 Freddy became part of the Trotskyist movement when the American Workers Party merged with the Trotskyist Communist League of America. Despite being socialized politically through labor struggles and having the background of a street-smart organizer, she approached politics with an appreciation for ethical considerations and made political judgments based on moral-philosophical leadership.[70] Grace regarded her close relationship with Freddy as a combination of comradeship, friendship, and mentorship. "Freddy knew everybody who was anybody in the radical movement," she recalled. "She was only three years my senior, but when I came around in the early 1940s, Freddy viewed me as a pipsqueak intellectual (which I was), giving me instructions on how to dress and behave, as she did everyone else."[71]

Lyman brought a very different background and set of abilities to the organization. A descendant of Robert Treat Paine, one of the signers of the Declaration of Independence, Lyman was born in New York in 1901. His childhood playmates included Rockefeller children, with whom he sailed in Maine. After earning an architecture degree at Harvard in 1922 he married his first wife, and the couple spent eighteen months in Europe, living and working in Italy, Spain, and France. Upon returning to New York he continued working as an architect in his own office, designing private houses while developing concern for the varying housing conditions across the country. He began to pursue larger intellectual and political questions, though in no systematic or formal way, through the rest of the 1920s. The Depression pushed him to more serious contemplation. It also brought him work with the New York City Housing Authority, through the New Deal's Civil Works Administration, after his office closed. He joined the Federation of Architects, Engineers, Chemists, and Technicians, which brought him in contact with radical organizations and introduced him to Marxism. Finding illumination and a deeper understanding of the current crisis from his reading of Marx, Engels, Lenin, and Trotsky, he embraced the theory of historical materialism. By 1935 he had joined the Trotskyist movement.[72] As Grace described him, Lyman "looked like the WASP that he was . . . tall, lean, blue-eyed, with small features and thin lips." But once he joined the radical movement, he "committed not only his physical and intellectual energies but his financial resources to the movement."[73] As her relationship with him grew, Grace came to appreciate "the persistence with which Lyman would raise tough questions," how he challenged "each of us to realize that freedom involves the exercise of our distinctively human capacity to make responsible choices," and simply "for always giving a damn."[74]

Freddy and Lyman's New York home, 629 Hudson Street, served as a center of JFT intellectual and social life. Through much of the 1940s it served as a meeting place and an unofficial headquarters for the organization. In Grace's estimation, the Paines "had a genius for hosting small gatherings where people from many different walks of life could eat, drink, hold far-reaching conversations, and listen to the music of Beethoven and Louis

Armstrong. So their house at 629 Hudson Street became the kind of center that every political group needs—where revolutionary politics and culture flowed naturally into one another."[75] Accordingly, 629 Hudson Street "was also the place where most of the work of the Johnson-Forest Tendency was done."[76] C. L. R. similarly marked the significance of 629 Hudson Street for the organization, recalling that during "decisive periods of our organization about a dozen of us" met there "week after week. All I have to say about it is that I do not remember a single instance when I was late for the meeting. Few of us were late."[77] On another occasion, C. L. R. reiterated the significance of 629 Hudson Street by declaring it and its hosts as "the solid rock and foundation on which the Johnson-Forest was built." Well after he had severed ties with the Paines, and more than two decades after they last gathered at 629 Hudson Street, C. L. R. made a point to say to his former comrades how much they had meant to him and to the organization. "You were the environment," he wrote to Freddy and Lyman, "and your unfailing support of our successes and failures were the force which kept us together. There is no small organization or never has been in the world one in which it was able to begin, gather strength, and meet its difficulties and continue along its theoretical lines without the kind of support that you gave us at 629."[78]

One of the most important collaborators at 629 Hudson Street was Raya Dunayevskaya. She served with C. L. R. as the coleader of the JFT. Born in Russia, Dunayevskaya came to the United States in 1922 at the age of twelve and quickly entered radical politics. Despite the fact that her orthodox Jewish parents had come to the country fleeing the Bolsheviks, she joined the youth section of the Communist Party. She also found her political sympathies lying with the African Americans she encountered in her Chicago neighborhood. Her early activism included leading a strike at school over anti-Semitism and the practice of corporal punishment, and protesting racial discrimination faced by a black schoolmate. During the 1920s and 1930s she was very active in labor struggles and black struggles, participating in numerous strikes and even serving as a founder of the Communist-supported labor organization, the American Negro Labor Congress, founded in Chicago in 1925. She wrote for its organ the *Negro Champion* as well as the Associated Negro Press. By the start of the Depression she had been expelled from the CP but continued her involvement in labor and black struggles in Chicago and then New York. She eventually joined the Trotskyist movement, serving for nearly a year as translator and secretary to Leon Trotsky during his exile in Mexico, and becoming a member of the newly formed

Workers Party upon her return to New York. Within the WP, Dunayevskaya (who was also known as Rae, Weaver, and Spiegel) analyzed the economic development of Russia, which led her, independently of C. L. R., to the state capitalism analysis. Her specific intellectual contributions to the JFT were her theoretical formulations of state capitalism, studies of Marxism and Hegel, and interpretation and translation of significant texts in the development of Russian theory such as Lenin's *Philosophical Notebooks*.[79]

Grace found it exciting to be in an organization where a woman exerted such leadership. Still, this did not mean that the group fully escaped the gendered roles and interpersonal dynamics found in other groups. "Rae and I would do things that women do in the radical movement in order to make it possible for men to write and speak," Grace recalled. This included typing as well as "shit work" such as cooking and washing the floors. "But we also did other things," she added. "We did a lot of research and study and carried on an enormous intellectual endeavor. It was very, very exciting, very stimulating."[80]

One of the most active and important JFT members outside of New York during the 1940s was Martin Glaberman. Raised in a socialist family, Glaberman once told an interviewer that he did not undergo a process of radicalization but rather was "born that way."[81] In 1933, at the age of thirteen, he joined the Young People's Socialist League and became politically active in his East Flatbush, Brooklyn, neighborhood. Around 1938 he left the Socialist Party to join the Socialist Workers Party (SWP), drawn to it in part because he felt it offered a more serious understanding of Marxism and Leninism as well as the ideas of Trotsky. In 1939 he moved to Washington, D.C., where he took a job as a messenger and clerk and joined a small SWP branch. He met C. L. R. and became one of the first "Johnsonites" (as members of the tendency were called), attending the first WP national conference as a delegate for the tendency from Washington, D.C. In 1942 he was recruited to help set up a WP branch in Detroit, where he became an autoworker and a devoted Johnsonite, helping to lay the foundation for the JFT's relocation of its base to Detroit in 1951.[82] Through the many splits, organizational alignments, and shifts in political climate that they would experience, Glaberman remained one of C. L. R.'s closest and longest comrades, fully committed to the political ideas and perspective often called "Johnsonism."

The sensibilities and excitement of Johnsonism also captured the political imagination of Selma Deitch, who joined the JFT in Los Angeles in 1945 at the age of fifteen. She would become an important contributor to the life of the JFT and its successor groups over the next two decades, much of that time working closely with C. L. R., whom she married in the mid-1950s.[83] Reflecting back on that period, she judged the JFT to be one of C. L. R.'s two "masterworks" (the other being his book *The Black Jacobins*). "Political organizations that aim to overthrow capitalism," she explained, "are not usually taken seriously enough to be considered as creations, let alone masterworks." The JFT, however, "was based on a root-and-branch critique of the Left and its role within the working class movement, and offered an organizational reorientation. . . . Johnson-Forest aimed to express in political perspective and in organizational structure the revolutionary impulse and self-activity of working-class people." She went on to cite the JFT's composition, offering it both as a reflection of the group's ideological and political orientation and as further evidence of its uniqueness among the Left: "The leader was a Black man, an immigrant from the West Indies and a historian; his two closest colleagues were women, one a Russian immigrant, the other a first generation Chinese-American. Much of the membership worked in industry including those who had begun life in the middle class. We were multicultural. We were confident. We felt we were 'going somewhere,' individually and collectively; with history rather than against it; building not a vanguard party so we could one day be the State, but a movement; antiracist and also antisexist; respectful of the people we worked and lived with, rather than imagining ourselves an elite amongst the backward. . . . We saw ourselves as uncovering and helping to articulate the infinite variety of ways grassroots people expressed [their] rebellion."[84]

The Marxism of the Johnson-Forest Tendency

The JFT's approach to radical politics not only solidified a shared commitment to its work during the 1940s; it also laid a foundation for the ongoing political development of members like Grace who would build activist careers extending well beyond the life of the group. Grace's experience in the JFT significantly shaped her thinking and political practice during her subsequent decades of activism. She did not remain committed to all of the political convictions she once held in the JFT—by the 1960s she would come to rethink, rework, or reject many of the ideas she and her JFT comrades developed during the 1940s—but she fully embraced and consistently employed the methods of thought and practice that she had learned in the tendency. Specifically, she internalized the practice of "thinking and acting dialectically."[85] Indeed, dialectical reasoning constituted a core aspect of the group's thinking. The JFT's desire to apprehend the philosophical moorings of Marxism led the group to study Hegel and the dialectic, to examine its influence and application in the thought of Marx and Lenin, and then to apply the dialectical method in their own work on the history of the international labor movement, the Soviet Union, the question of building a socialist organization, and other historical and political problems.

Much of this intellectual effort is on display in C. L. R.'s *Notes on Dialectics*, which received scholarly recognition for its philosophical insights, such as its use of Hegel's thought to analyze the history of the European labor movement, identify Stalinism as a part of that historical process, and critique Trotskyism's failure to transcend old categories.[86] Originating as a series of letters written in 1948, the work was compiled into a confidential document privately circulated among JFT members, who called it "The Nevada Document" because C. L. R. wrote it in Reno, Nevada, where he was living at the time.[87] The document bore the influence and insights of Grace and Dunayevskaya[88] and reflected the type of theoretical development in which the group had been engaged throughout its existence. If *Notes on Dialectics* is now taken as C. L. R.'s singular examination and application of Hegel's method,[89] in 1948 JFT members viewed "The Nevada Document" as an expression of ideas held collectively. For them, it was one step among many in their shared project of using the dialectical method to grasp historical processes and interpret contemporary political dynamics.

Grace thrived in this rich intellectual environment. Ideological differences would eventually lead her and C. L. R. to part company, nonetheless Grace continued to acknowledge, well after their split, the role that their collaboration played in her development: "I shall always be grateful for what I learned during the years we worked together. What has remained in my heart and mind are not the political positions we took which were in response to the realities of the time ... but a method of thinking and acting." This method gave her a way to see the movement of history, to think about the interactions among history, political movements, and social change, and to recognize the need to transcend once-powerful categories of thought. As such, studying and using the dialectical method in the JFT gave her a way to combine theory and practice, or more specifically, she gained a theory by which to guide her political practice: "What I internalized during those years was the importance of always keeping one's ear to the ground to hear the new questions that are being asked at the grassroots; always combining real struggles with philosophical exploration." The essence and importance of thinking dialectically for a revolutionary was "always being on the alert for the changes taking place in reality that force us to break loose from the fixed concepts that have come out of earlier struggles; always recognizing that everything and everyone contains contradictions so that what was progressive at one stage can become reactionary at another."[90] Grace carried this commitment into her subsequent political work, making it the most enduring part of her JFT experience.

An unshakable faith in the revolutionary potential of the working class constituted another defining characteristic of the Johnson-Forest Tendency. Just as Hegelian and Marxist dialectics gave the JFT its methodological foundation, the group's political framework could be encapsulated in the dictum, attributed to Marx and often repeated by C. L. R., that "the proletariat is revolutionary or it is nothing."[91] From its reading of Marx, the Johnson-Forest Tendency theorized that the working class, through its own actions conceived and carried out by the workers themselves, without direction or leadership from labor organizations (unions) or radical parties, could create methods for transforming society. This led them to place a thoroughgoing emphasis on working-class self-activity. In its study of history, current economic and political developments, and contemporary popular culture, the JFT sought out and analyzed examples of the creative expression of the masses, seeing these as motive forces in the struggle for socialism.

Accordingly, the JFT argued that the role of the Marxist party was not to teach the workers or to develop a plan for them, but rather to identify, document, and celebrate efforts that the workers made of their own accord, through which they would fulfill their role as the agents of revolution. From this, the JFT drew two corollary conclusions about the revolutionary process. First, they rejected the so-called backwardness of the workers idea, by which they meant the view in the WP and among other radicals that workers were insufficiently class conscious, leading them to act against their own interests. Second, the group came to reject the idea of a "vanguard party," a political organization composed of professional revolutionaries whose tasks are to conceive of a program for the workers and to guide and direct them in their struggle. The JFT produced a wide range of writings, varying in approach and content, but binding them all was an emphasis on the self-activity of the working class. In all of its work, the group held firm in the conviction that this idea—the revolutionary potential of the working class—constituted the core of Marxism.

The Johnson-Forest Tendency quite consciously fashioned its Marxism in opposition to and distinct from what they termed *official* Marxism, by which they meant that Marxism articulated by the Soviet Union or by the main groups and parties of the Left. Though the JFT was a tendency within the WP, and much of the group's written work aimed specifically to intervene in Trotskyist debates or to influence the direction of the WP, the group saw itself first and above all else as Marxists rather than Trotskyists. JFT members certainly were Trotskyists, and proudly so—including an enthusiastic identification with anti-Stalinism—but the group's driving identity was as a Marxist organization devoted to uncovering and advancing Marxism as a framework for understanding the modern world and showing the way toward a socialist future. That is to say, the JFT's identity as members of the Workers Party, as Trotskyists, and as anti-Stalinists came to be based upon—indeed, was an expression of—the group's particular study and understanding of Marxism that celebrated and centered working-class self-activity as the fount of revolution.

Another critical feature of the JFT's Marxism, and one that significantly shaped Grace's political outlook, was the organization's intention to make Marxism relevant to the mid-twentieth-century United States. While a shared position on the Russian Question was the basis of the group's formation in 1941, the JFT also developed a concern with American history and culture. From its founding, the tendency devoted much of its energies to thinking about the prospects for revolutionary change in the country and about the specific requirements and characteristics necessary for an American Marxist organization. C. L. R. demonstrated this commitment in much of his writing. This includes pieces on U.S. history, the American working class, and the place of the United States in world politics published in *The New International* in 1943 and 1944; his writings on African American history and politics throughout the 1940s; and his "Notes on American Civilization," a prospectus he wrote in 1949–50 for a planned book on American culture.[92]

Perhaps most reflective of the JFT's goal of applying Marxism to American society was "Education, Propaganda, and Agitation: Post-War America and Bolshevism," written by C. L. R. in 1944 and submitted for discussion in the WP. As an internal document, this was a major statement from the tendency regarding the party's organizational priorities and practices. The document called for "the Americanization of Bolshevism," by which C. L. R. meant the grounding of Marxist analysis in American history and culture.[93]

"The classics of Marxism are European in origin and content," he declared.[94] Thus, Marxist texts such as *The Communist Manifesto*, *The Eighteenth Brumaire*, and *Peasant War in Germany* have "solid associations" for the English, French, or German worker, who "finds the history of his own country made significant for him as never before." By contrast, "for the average American worker these books as a beginning are alien. . . . What they cannot give him in sufficient measure is that sense of reality of the development of his own country, that feeling that in addition to the daily class struggle, he is part of something beyond himself that is the beginning of theoretical Bolshevism and the rejection of bourgeois ideology." The first task, then, was to "build up the American counterparts" to these texts.[95] But the WP also had work to be done internally. "Not only raw workers need this Americanization. The party members from the highest to the lowest need it also. No one has any serious grasp of Marxism, can handle the doctrine or teach it unless he is, in accordance with his capabilities and opportunities, an exponent of it in relation to the social life and development around him."[96] Finally, the document argued that the United States' standing as the leading capitalist country demanded critical examination. "America is the center of world attention," C. L. R. wrote. "It is the last hope for imperialism and the old democracy." As such, a special responsibility fell to the U.S.-based WP. "The theoretical interpretation of the United States, its past, present, and future becomes . . . a part of the international struggle for socialism and the national independence of oppressed peoples. And in this, the central issue of our times, we have an exhaustive role to play," C. L. R. wrote. Ever confident in the historical significance of his and his comrades' efforts, he reminded them, "Our revolution is after all the American Revolution."[97]

Grace fully embraced this goal of building a distinctly American revolution. Her conception of the revolutionary process—who would lead the revolution, the theoretical frameworks that would guide them, even the meaning or purpose of a revolution—would change over the course of her life and growth as an activist. But the goal of making an American revolution remained central to her politics and to her political identity as a revolutionist who has assumed the responsibility of theorizing, projecting, and organizing for the transformation of the country, using methods and goals derived specifically from the historical development and contemporary social dynamics of the United States.

The JFT's commitment to an American revolution and its intention to ground Marxism in American soil found expression in the group's attention to and analysis of the Negro Question. As debated in radical circles, this was essentially the question of how radical movements should interpret and relate to African Americans and their struggle against racial oppression. This involved "a very specific set of theoretical and practical problems. Did black people in the United States constitute a national minority? Did black workers share the same interests as the white proletariat? How should the (white) labor movement respond to African-American demands for equality? Was meaningful equality even *possible* under capitalism? And how should socialists relate to existing African-American organizations and institutions?"[98] The JFT made this a major theoretical focus. Throughout the 1940s they developed a Marxist analysis of African American life and staked out a clear position on the Negro Question. C. L. R. had articulated elements of this position even before the tendency formed. In his conversation with Trotsky in 1939, C. L. R. had declared that "the Negro represents potentially the most revolutionary section of the population," and he chastised the Trotskyist movement for failing to give the Negro Question the attention it deserved. "The Negro question as an integral part of the American revolution can no longer be neglected," he insisted.[99] C. L. R. proposed several steps for addressing the practical problem of determining and carrying out the party's "Negro work"—that is, the form and content of Trotskyists' organizing and propaganda efforts in and toward black communities.[100] Most notably C. L. R. called for the party to encourage and assist a mass black organization and movement based on the everyday struggles and demands of black people. He said that the party should "frankly and openly endorse such a movement," but it must not try to direct or lead it.[101]

These ideas appealed to Grace and helped draw her to the JFT. C. L. R.'s identification of black militancy as a potentially revolutionary force and his advocacy of independent black political action confirmed what she had witnessed in the March on Washington Movement and black activist politics in Chicago. Moreover, his analysis put her observations and experiences with black protest politics into a theoretical framework. When she became a member of the JFT in 1942, she joined the group's efforts to further this theoretical work and put forward its position on the Negro Question.

Within two years of Grace's joining the group, the JFT produced a major statement on the Negro Question. Initially circulated as a memorandum within the WP in December 1943, then submitted to the 1944 national convention of the party, and finally published in the *New International* in January 1945 as "Negroes and the Revolution: Resolution of the Minority," the document seemed to break with socialist orthodoxy by rejecting the idea that (white) labor unions must provide leadership to the black freedom struggle.[102] The lengthy resolution repeated and extended ideas C. L. R. had articulated in 1939, incorporating insights and perspectives drawn from the JFT's analysis of the tremendous changes taking place in black politics and the labor movement during World War II. "Negroes and the Revolution" emphasized the role played by black people in the political development of the country, and it assessed the historical and contemporary relationship of black people to organized labor. From this it concluded that the black struggle and the proletarian struggle necessarily depended on each other, and most importantly, that the black struggle actually had the historical role of stimulating the proletariat. Thus, the resolution argued, even though the black struggle developed independently of the labor movement and was reformist in nature, it must be seen theoretically and practically as an essential component of the struggle for socialism in the United States. The following two statements from "Negroes and the Revolution" encapsulate how the JFT tried to convince its comrades of this position:

> The whole history of the United States and the role of the Negro in American economy and society are a constant proof and reminder of the fact that it is absolutely impossible for the Negroes to gain equality under American capitalism. . . . The Negroes' struggle for democratic rights brings the Negroes almost immediately face to face with capital and the state. The Marxist support of the Negro struggle for democratic rights is not a concession that Marxists make to the Negroes. . . . [The Negro] struggle is a direct part of the struggle for socialism.[103]

> In the United States social revolution is impossible without the independent mass struggles of the Negroes. . . . Such is the historical role of the Negroes in the United States; such today is their proletarian composition and such is the interrelation with the American proletariat itself that their independent struggles form perhaps the most powerful stimulus in American society to the recognition by the organized proletariat of its real responsibilities to the national development as a whole and of its power against American imperialism.[104]

JFT members continued to discuss, debate, and develop their position on the Negro Question through the rest of the decade. C. L. R.'s 1948 convention speech "The Revolutionary Answer to the Negro Problem in the United States," which has subsequently become one of his most reproduced writings, represented a culmination of the JFT's thinking and writing on African American politics in relation to the labor movement and the struggle for socialism.[105] C. L. R. delivered the speech in conjunction with a JFT resolution on the Negro Question (based largely on the 1944 resolution), both of which were designed to shape party thinking and policy on the black struggle.[106] "The proletariat, as we know, must lead the struggles of all the oppressed and all those who are persecuted by capitalism," he said, affirming the common ground that the JFT shared with their Marxist comrades in the party. But he then challenged socialists—"some very good socialists too"—for interpreting this to mean that the struggles of African Americans are of little more than episodic value and may even "constitute a great danger" if they weaken or distract from the struggle of the proletariat. According to this position, "the real leadership of the Negro struggle must rest in the hands of organized labor and of the Marxist party." Flatly rejecting this conclusion, C. L. R. explained that the JFT had something very different to say:

> We say, number one, that the Negro struggle, independent Negro struggle, has a vitality and validity of its own; that it has deep historic roots in the past of America and in present struggles; it has an organic political perspective. . . . We say, number two, that this independent Negro movement is able to intervene with terrific force upon the general social and political life of the nation, despite the fact that it is waged under the banner of democratic rights. . . . We say, number three, and this is the most important, that it is able to exercise a powerful influence upon the revolutionary proletariat, that it has got a great contribution to make to the development of the proletariat in the United States, and that it is in itself a constituent part of the struggle for socialism. In this way we challenge directly any attempt to subordinate or to push to the rear the social and political significance of the independent Negro for democratic rights.[107]

In its position on the Negro Question, as in all of the group's positions and theoretical projections, the JFT grounded its analysis in the writings and ideas of the founding Marxist thinkers. Here they called on the authority of Lenin. "The whole historical development of the Negro struggle in the United States and its relations to the social struggles of the revolutionary classes," the 1944 resolution declared, "shows that the Leninist analysis of the Negro question as part of the national question is the correct method with which to approach this problem."[108] To demonstrate this method, the document cited four separate paragraphs from Lenin's "The Discussion on Self-Determination Summed Up," which presents his positions on the question of self-determination for small nations in Europe and for the colonies and the blow delivered to British imperialism by the Irish Rebellion of 1916. Each of the cited paragraphs is followed by a paragraph in which the JFT applies Lenin's ideas to the United States. In this way the document interprets Lenin for the American context, building a case that the Leninist analysis of the American scene must recognize the political significance of the black struggle as a stimulating factor in the struggle against American capital.[109] This use of Lenin's writing in the JFT resolution illustrated the group's practice of intensive study—and then attempted application—of Marxists texts.

Indeed, such had been the JFT's approach from its beginnings. C. L. R., Dunayevskaya, and the JFT delved deep into Marx's *Capital* to make their signature theoretical intervention, the state capitalism position on the Russian Question. Martin Glaberman recalled that the JFT "became notorious in the WP as the people who were always holding classes on Marx's *Capital*."[110] Dunayevskaya often led the group's efforts in studying and teaching *Capital*, with Grace making a significant contribution as a theorist. Occasionally, she also played a role in the public presentation of the group's ideas. For example, in January 1949 the Trotskyist press announced that Grace (under her party name, Ria Stone) would teach a weekly course on "Wage Labor and Capital," one of "Two Courses in Marxist Economics" at the Progressive Workers School in Newark, New Jersey.[111]

"Natural and Acquired Powers": Grace as Marxist Theoretician and Political Leader

Grace's choice of subject matter reflected not only her critical engagement with *Capital* but also the JFT's recent discovery of another of Marx's texts. Grace recounted the discovery this way: "Raya [Dunayevskaya] spent hours in the New York Public Library reading the collected works of Marx and Engels in Russian, while I bought and pored over the fourteen-volume set in German. We made exciting discoveries, which we immediately shared with other Johnsonites around the country. For example, I will never forget the day that Raya came back from the library with the news that she had found a Russian translation of the *Economic and Philosophic Manuscripts*."[112] For

Marxists, this was indeed a remarkable find. But Dunayevskaya's discovery is only half of the story.

Grace played the pivotal role in the recovery of this work. She found the essays in the original German and then took the extraordinary step of translating three of the essays, "Alienated Labor," "Private Property and Communism," and "Critique of the Hegelian Dialectic." Her translations marked the first time that part of Marx's *Economic and Philosophic Manuscripts of 1844* appeared in English. Decades later this text would garner considerable attention and has now risen to a prominent place in the Marxist canon, but in the 1940s, few adherents to Marxism and even fewer in the English-speaking world knew of the *Economic and Philosophic Manuscripts*. Written when Marx was twenty-six years old, these manuscripts preceded *The Communist Manifesto* by four years and the publication of *Capital* by more than two decades.

In the summer of 1947 the JFT mimeographed and published Grace's translations under the title *Essays by Karl Marx, Selected from the Economic and Philosophic Manuscripts*. It included an introduction written by Grace, C. L. R., and Dunayevskaya brimming with their excitement over the discovery of Marx's text and their belief in its timeliness: "We do not publish these translations as archives. Far from it. They are far more alive today than when they were written."[113] The introduction summarized the analytical and theoretical focus of each essay, explained the place of each in Marx's theoretical system, and suggested that the insights found in them could describe with forceful precision "the current crisis" in capitalist production. They argued that the foundation of Marx's essays—methodologically, analytically, and philosophically—was his analysis of the labor process and of the activity of workers within that process. Upon this foundation, Marx developed his concept of alienated labor, the most important theoretical contribution of these essays. This focus, they said, distinguished Marx from the classical economists and allowed him to conceptualize labor as having a twofold nature, abstract labor and concrete labor, which is the central concept (along with the related analysis of use value and exchange value) in the opening chapter of *Capital*. "Here," they said of the 1844 manuscripts, "we see the first fruits of his studies of political economy."[114] Thus, for Grace and her comrades, these translated essays helped to clarify and illuminate Marx's thinking and analysis in *Capital*. Indeed, they believed that "the analysis of alienated labor" was "the precursor to *Capital*."[115] In these essays and in *Capital*, they argued in the introduction, Marx captured the contradiction of labor under capitalism. "The worker was dominated by the objective results of his labor," they wrote. "It became the private property of someone other than the laborer."[116] Thus, labor in the capitalist mode of production made this appropriation inevitable, and this was the essence of alienation. In contrast to some subsequent interpreters of Marx who would draw a distinction between the early or young Marx of the *Economic and Philosophic Manuscripts* and the later Marx of *Capital*, Grace and her comrades found a theoretical unity between the two texts.

The primary reason they expressed such enthusiasm for Marx's text and devoted so much attention to it was that they found in his essays authoritative affirmation of their own conceptualization of Marxism. "This is Marxism," declared the introduction. "These essays will, we hope, remind us of what Marx stood for."[117] The introduction was explicit in declaring the JFT's identification with the essays: "Every political line that we have written has been fertilized by the concept contained in these translations and the others we are unable to reprint. . . . The political tendency which we represent has therefore a great pride and satisfaction in making available for the first time to American readers these precious antecedents to revolutionary Marxism."[118]

Indeed, the JFT's fundamental ideas—its theory of state capitalism, its attention to and celebration of the independent activity of the masses, its emphasis on the revolutionary capacity of the working class, and its prioritization of working-class self-activity above the leadership of a radical party or labor organization—all seemed to be confirmed in Marx's analysis of alienation and private property. They found, for example, that the essay on alienated labor demonstrated that "Marxism is concerned first and foremost with the creative powers of the masses." They wrote that Marx placed "the solution of all economic and political problems upon the powers of the workers. . . . It is the creative power of millions of men which alone can solve the problems of modern society."[119] Similarly, in the essay "Private Property and Communism," they said, Marx denounced "the *mere* transcendence of private property" as "vulgar Communism" and proposed that the essence of a new society was not found in the abolition of private property but in the abolition of alienation.[120] The third essay, "Critique of the Hegelian Dialectic," they argued, shows Marx picking up and extending Hegel's theory. Marx "is saying over and over again" that Hegel identified the problem of alienation and found its roots in the labor process, but "could not see in the labor process itself the positive, creative elements which would overcome the alienation." That is, Marx was saying that Hegel could not see the positive that would complete the dialectical process, the resolution to the problem of alienation. Grace and her comrades wrote that Hegel solved the problem of alienation "by making thinking man, the philosopher, overcome it in thought," to which Marx offered a revision. "Man was striving for full self-consciousness and for Marx full self-consciousness was not the insight of a few philosophers, but the active participation of all men in social life, beginning with production, and expressing and developing their natural and acquired powers."[121]

Marx's phrase "natural and acquired powers" appears frequently in JFT writings.[122] Its usage highlights Grace's role in developing the group's ideas and the impact that the JFT experience had on her thinking.[123] The phrase comes from the chapter titled "Machinery and Modern Industry" in *Capital*. It became for the JFT a favored expression, a shorthand for Marx's—and their—ultimate emphasis on the self-realization of workers as the central dynamic in the struggle against capitalism and the transformation of society. Grace, C. L. R., and Dunayevskaya presented the phrase three times in their seven-page introduction to *Essays by Karl Marx*. In two of these (including the one cited above), the phrase appears without attribution to Marx, revealing the extent to which they took the phrase as their own. They invoked the phrase to argue that "the complete flowering of all the capabilities of the individual"—that is, the need to unleash the social power of workers who were deskilled and dehumanized by capitalism—had been essential to Marx's thinking and must be held as a central tenet of Marxism.[124] The third appearance is directly quoted from Marx's original usage in *Capital*: "Modern Industry indeed, compels society, under penalty of death, to replace the detail-power of today, crippled by life-long repetition of one and the same trivial operation, and thus reduced to the mere fragment of a man, by the fully developed individual, fit for a variety of labours, ready to face any change of production, and to whom the different social functions he performs, are but so many modes of giving free scope to his own natural and acquired powers."[125]

The JFT read this passage as a prescient description of "modern industry" as it appeared in 1947, and they presented it as social analysis of immediate and urgent relevance. Of course, the publication of *Essays by Karl Marx* was primarily (or at least most immediately) directed toward debates within the world of American Trotskyism and intended to make the case for the JFT articulation of Marxism. Indeed, the significance that Grace and her comrades assigned to *Essays by Karl Marx* derived largely from the explicit theoretical linking they made to *Capital*, identifying Marx's analysis of alienation in the 1844 essays as a foundational concept and a cornerstone of the theoretical system he laid out a quarter of a century later in *Capital*. But the theory of alienation held a wider intellectual and political importance for them. At stake was not just an understanding of Marxism but its application as the theory of capitalist development, workers' insurgency, and the reconstruction of society in the postwar world. That is, they saw the analysis of alienation as crucial to understanding the contemporary process of industrial production and the workers' place and experiences within the production process. Only with this understanding, they argued, could revolutionaries truly grasp (and then help to activate) the basis of workers' revolt against this system of production. When workers assumed control over the production process, they could transform it from a system of exploitation to both an expression and a means of human liberation.

Grace played the pivotal role in theorizing and articulating alienation as part of the JFT position on the revolutionary capacity of the working class. Her translation of Marx's 1844 essays was the first major step. This allowed the group to present, in *Essays by Karl Marx*, what was for them a pure and direct distillation of Marx's theory of alienation under capitalism. The next step was a pamphlet that she cowrote, also published in the summer of 1947, titled *The American Worker*, in which she set out to apply Marx's theory to the contemporary American working class.

The American Worker

The JFT reached a new plateau with the publication of *The American Worker*. Giving the fullest exposition yet of the group's analysis of the industrial worker and the political potentiality of the contemporary U.S. working class, *The American Worker* consolidated the group's thinking over the preceding five years about workers in American industry. The pamphlet was a major statement of JFT ideas. It comprises two narratively distinct but complementary essays, the first written by autoworker Phil Singer (under the name Paul Romano) and the second by Grace (under the name Ria Stone). Part 1, "Life in the Factory," is based on Singer's experiences as an industrial worker, and part 2, "The Reconstruction of Society," is Grace's philosophical analysis of workers in American industry. The dual authorship and organization of the pamphlet reflected the JFT's goal of combining practice with theory.[126] A third JFT member, Detroit union committeeman Johnny Zupan, wrote the preface, announcing a seemingly modest ambition: "This little pamphlet concerns itself with the life of the working class in the process of production. Its purpose is to understand what the workers are thinking and doing while actually at work on the bench or on the line." Indeed, *The American Worker* helped to solidify the group's emphasis on the self-activity of rank-and-file workers as a hallmark of its politics. The pamphlet also represented the JFT's particular contribution to a growing concern during the immediate postwar years among intellectuals such as C. Wright Mills and Elton May with industrial workers, their unions, and the labor relations of mass production.[127]

Singer's "Life in the Factory" describes the thoughts and actions of rank-and-file mass production workers. Identifying himself as "a young worker in my late twenties," Singer draws on his experiences and observations working in a General Motors plant. His stories of factory life address such topics as workers' attitudes toward their work, their interactions with management, and their feelings about the company. The essay also exposed the layers and operations of the union, described the social divisions among workers in the shop, and considered the impact of all this on workers' lives outside of the factory. Singer's first-person account and analysis perfectly embodied the JFT's commitment to privileging what rank-and-file workers were doing, thinking, and saying. Identifying the workers themselves— and not "the intellectuals who are detached from the working class"—as his audience, Singer sought to reflect back to his fellow workers their own reality, and in the process he hoped to "uncover the reasons for the worker's deep dissatisfaction which has reached its peak in recent years." This was precisely the method and mode of analysis called for by JFT theory: the pamphlet took as its starting point the workers' own understanding of their life, a distillation of "the daily experiences of the laboring masses," as Singer wrote, and upon this foundation it aimed to build an analysis of the American worker. Moreover, the JFT's emphasis on the self-activity and revolutionary potential of the working class undergirded Singer's intention "to illustrate to the workers themselves that sometimes when their conditions seem everlasting and hopeless, they are in actuality revealing by their every-day reactions and expressions that they are the road to a far-reaching change."[128]

Grace's essay, "The Reconstruction of Society," brings an epistemological and narrative shift in the pamphlet, pivoting from the voice of a worker offering an internal view of working-class life to that of a Marxist theo-retician making a philosophical examination of workers within the world of production. Her analysis is unmistakably that of a Marxist intellectual. After five years in the JFT, she was fully immersed in and committed to Marx's theoretical system, and *The American Worker* shows her facility with Marx's texts and ideas. The essay cites from a range of Marx's writings, in-cluding *Capital*, *The German Ideology*, and *Essays by Karl Marx*, Grace's recent translations of his 1844 manuscripts. Despite its heavily theoretical content, and though missing the first-person and experiential basis of the first essay, Grace's essay nonetheless conveys personal conviction and a deep sense of purpose. "Today, in all strata of society, a search is going on for the way to create a world," she wrote, "one world, in which men can live as social and creative individuals, where they can live as all-around men and not just as average men. Out of this search a new philosophy of life is being created."[129] Drawing on both the authority and the example of Marx, she was writing to apprehend and forestall "the barbarism and chaos which govern the daily existence and immediate perspectives of men from one end of the earth to the other."[130] Grace punctuated her analysis with impassioned language and expressions of righteous indignation, stamping her intellectual person-ality on the pamphlet while articulating the JFT's analysis of capitalism at midcentury. She gave the group's strongest statement yet of its theorization of a contemporary striving toward a liberated humanity.

The pamphlet's title plainly announced the JFT's theorized architects and agents of this striving. "We make our analysis of the American work-ing class, not only because it is the working class which we know best but also because it is the most powerful, the most advanced in the world in social perspective," Grace wrote in the opening pages of her essay. "In the nineteenth century, Marx made British capitalism the foundation for his economic analysis of capitalism. Today, it is the American working class which provides the foundation for an analysis of the economic transition from capitalism to socialism, or the concrete demonstration of the new society developing within the old."[131] To make this case, the essay traces the historical development and evolution of American industrial organization during the first half of the twentieth century, highlighting changes in the means of production and the incorporation of new workers, particularly women and African American men. Some of these workers, Grace wrote, were brought into this "newly developed productive apparatus" during the first three decades of the century, while others were "torn from their traditional moorings" during the Depression and then joined the "stampede into the shipyards, aircraft factories, and radio shops" during World War II. Combining the millions of war workers with the 17 million unemployed, she deemed this "the largest and most powerful industrial working class that the world has ever known."[132]

The American Worker embodied the merging of Grace's philosophic journey with her political identify. Her concern with the social individual and the analysis that she conducted in her dissertation of how the individual self and society develop in relation to each other now found a specific, richly theorized, and distinctly political expression in the new social individual she saw emerging in the postwar factory. Grace's explication of this new social individual also forcefully presented the JFT's political worldview. Her essay drew heavily upon her recently completed translation of Marx's 1844 manuscripts, with Marx's concept of alienated labor providing much of the theoretical framework. She argued that the new American working class of the immediate postwar years was the realization or fruition of what Marx predicted in both *Capital* and the *Economic and Philosophic Manuscripts*. Grace's analysis passionately displays the JFT's emphasis on rank-and-file self-activity and its deep distrust of the union bureaucracy. The essay also provides a clear example of the group's use of the dialectical method, through which the pamphlet concluded that industrial workers were by historical circumstance and social experience coming to the realization that they must fight against the capitalist forces so circumscribing their lives and aspirations. In so doing, the workers would set in motion the transition from capitalism to socialism. "Never has society so needed the direct intervention of the workers," Grace concluded in the pamphlet's final paragraph. "Never have the workers been so ready to come to grips with the fundamental problems of society. The destinies of the two are indissolubly united. When workers take their fate into their own hands, when they seize the power and begin their reconstruction of society, all of mankind will leap from the realm of necessity into the realm of freedom."[133]

In and Out of Trotskyism

The American Worker appeared during a three-month interval in 1947 that the JFT called its "interim period." Earlier in the year the WP and SWP had seemingly reached an agreement to reunite. The JFT supported this reunification, in part because by 1947 they had begun to question their presence as a minority tendency within the WP.[134] By the end of World War II, the JFT's growing emphasis on the self-activity and revolutionary potential of the American working class put them at odds with the majority in the WP. "The differences between us were brought home to me the week of V-J Day when the war with Japan came to an end," Grace recalled decades later. She was then employed at a Brooklyn defense plant, along with another Johnsonite and several other WP members. Some of these majority WP members were also leaders of the union local. "When we came into work after V-J Day," Grace continued, "the Johnsonite comrade and I decided to organize a sit-in to demand that we be kept on the payroll to help reconvert the plant to peacetime production. While we were agitating the workers, who were very responsive, and running from department to department organizing discussions of how to reorganize production, our comrades as union leaders were meeting with management to work out how to get us to leave the plant peacefully!"[135] Grace and the JFT believed that as Marxist revolutionaries they should encourage the mobilization of workers, not stifle it. Martin Glaberman summarized the differences by saying simply that the WP "had lost all confidence in the American working class." The JFT felt that, by contrast, the SWP still had ties to the union movement and the working class and "had maintained at least lip service to an American revolutionary perspective."[136] Thus, when the reunification discussions stalled in April, the JFT sought to rejoin the SWP itself. The tendency left the WP in July 1947 and arranged to enter the SWP that fall. The three months in between constituted the aforementioned interim period, when they held no organizational affiliation and devoted themselves to an intense publishing program.[137]

The JFT made the most of these "three months of independence."[138] Free to publish their works unencumbered by party discipline or restrictions, the group rented an office in Midtown Manhattan from which they published an impressive array of works conveying their body of ideas developed over the preceding five years. In addition to *The American Worker* and *Essays by Karl Marx*, this included *Dialectical Materialism and the Fate of Humanity*, an exposition of Hegelian and Marxist dialectics placing mass revolt as the key engine of human history; *The Invading Socialist Society* (an Engels-inspired title), a statement of the JFT's opposition to orthodox Trotskyism's positions on the Russian Question, Communist parties around the world, and the nationalization of private property as the hallmark of socialism; and a weekly journal written collaboratively by JFT members and workers in various industries. The interim period publishing program also produced *Balance Sheet: The Workers Party and the Johnson-Forest Tendency*, a thirty-two-page document summarizing the group's experience in the WP. The document gave the JFT's accounting of Trotskyism in the United States since the WP split from the SWP in 1940, the group's critique of the policies and practices of the WP, and its justification for joining the SWP.[139] By codifying the JFT's differences with and exit from the WP, *Balance Sheet* served as a "split document," the first of several that Grace would be involved in over the course of her political life.

Balance Sheet also articulated a framework for understanding and developing a revolutionary organization that the JFT would soon employ when it became an independent organization. The framework was inspired by Lenin's characterization of the Bolshevik party as made up of three groups, or layers: party leadership and intellectuals, trade union officials, and rank-and-file workers. The JFT assigned a special significance to the third layer. They were "the least vocal, the least educated in Marxism, the most diffident in expressing themselves among the fast-talking layers above." Yet, the third layer constituted "the social vanguard of the party" because they were decidedly "revolutionary, sensitive to the movement of the proletariat and potentially great recruiters, once they clarify themselves. These represent the mass outside." Yet, the JFT complained, the WP failed to recognize this: the party "has never understood the third layer, never listened to them, never learnt anything from them."[140] By contrast, the JFT vowed, in this document and in its subsequent efforts, to place a particular emphasis on the third layer.

The JFT entered the SWP and this new phase of its existence with Grace as the acknowledged third leader of the group. Her leadership both rested on and manifested itself through her abilities as a theoretician, as exemplified by her contribution to *The American Worker* and her role in the discovery, translation, and interpretation of *Essays by Karl Marx*. These publications were crucial to the development and articulation of the JFT's theoretical projections and helped to solidify her place in the JFT leadership. As another measure of her leadership, Grace increasingly represented the group and its ideas through her writings for the Trotskyist press, talks she delivered at party meetings, and participation in other activities.

In the spring of 1948, Grace traveled to Paris as a JFT delegate to the Second World Congress of the Fourth International, the organization launched by Trotsky a decade earlier to lead the Trotskyist movement. Dunayevskaya had gone to Europe several months before Grace's visit to present the JFT's state capitalist position to members of the Fourth International as they prepared for the world congress, and now Grace represented the JFT at the gathering. Trotskyists from various parts of the world debated and passed resolutions on several issues that they deemed crucial to the building of an international socialist movement, the most important and hotly contested of these issues being the Russian Question.[141] However, Grace did not throw herself into the official proceedings; rather, she found herself much more interested in engaging a group of French Trotskyists with whom she and the JFT shared an ideological bond. Dunayevskaya had made contact with this group during her trip, and the two groups discovered that they had parallel interests in working-class self-activity and were developing similar critiques of official Trotskyism. Dunayevskaya had been particularly impressed with the group's central figure, Cornelius Castoriadis (also known by the pseudonyms Pierre Chaulieu and Paul Cardan), a young Greek socialist who had recently moved to Paris and joined the French section of the Fourth International.[142] When Grace met Castoriadis, the two quickly found their interests especially aligned. "We soon discovered that we had the same interest in the daily lives of workers in the capitalist process of production and similar views about revolution as the liberation of human creativity," Grace recalled.[143] They also shared an engagement with Hegel, each of them having spent time translating, studying, and applying Hegel's thought to their analyses of the modern proletariat. As Castoriadis explained, this helped to crystallize "a sort of intellectual love affair between Grace and me." This included Castoriadis's appreciation for *The American Worker*, which he and his group would translate and publish just months after the world congress, and which Castoriadis later acknowledged for its contribution to his thinking.[144]

This recognition of common ideas and political perspectives gave Grace and Castoriadis fruitful space to interact with and learn from each other during Grace's stay in Paris, which extended well beyond the dates of the congress. "I spent a wonderful four months in Paris, mostly socializing with Chaulieu and the members of his group," she recalled. "I spoke French poorly but I could read and understand it fairly well, and it was a pleasure to hear discussions about political and philosophical ideas in French."[145] For his part, Castoriadis later described his discussions with Grace as playing "a decisive role at a stage when my thoughts were taking form."[146] Early in 1949, Castoriadis and his group left the Fourth International and Trotskyism, formed a new group called Socialisme ou Barbarie (Socialism or Barbarism), and began publishing a journal under the same name. The link that Grace helped establish between the JFT and Castoriadis in 1948 led to a mutually enriching collaboration involving lively cross-Atlantic exchanges, sharing and publishing of each other's writings, joint writing projects, and occasional meetings between the two groups over the next decade.[147]

Grace's trip to Paris and her place in the JFT leadership brought her under the watchful eye of the FBI. In April and May of 1948, the U.S. Department of State, the American embassy in Paris, and the FBI shared communication about Grace's presence at the world congress. The FBI immediately placed her under surveillance upon her return to New York by passenger ship on June 18, and two agents secretly searched her baggage. Over the next two weeks agents tracked her attendance at SWP meetings, including the party's Thirteenth National Convention, where she gave a short report on the world congress.[148] In addition to this surveillance, the FBI investigated her background. By the end of 1948 it had constructed a rather thorough file on her, compiling details about her family, education, Workers Party activities during the years 1940–47, and her party activities since the JFT entered the Socialist Workers Party. FBI agents accessed her educational records— from Newtown High School in Queens, undergraduate studies at Barnard College, and graduate studies at Bryn Mawr—and even spoke to an educator at her high school. The FBI also drew information from Grace's voter registration, customs agents, and the owner of the residence where Grace lived in Chicago. Perhaps most importantly, the FBI received information from people identified as "confidential informants," no doubt some of them having some affiliation with the WP, SWP, and even the JFT.[149] Twenty such informants provided information to the FBI as it kept Grace under surveillance for the next two decades.

When Grace returned from Paris in June 1948, the JFT was entering another period of transition. The group had been in the SWP less than a year, but political differences were already emerging between the tendency and the SWP majority. Over the next three years, the JFT's gathering critique of key elements of Trotskyism led to the group's leaving the SWP and the Trotskyist movement altogether.[150] The JFT's path out of Trotskyism can be traced through three documents written by the tendency between the summer of 1948 to the summer of 1951: the aforementioned "The Nevada Document," *State Capitalism and World Revolution*, and *The Balance Sheet*

Completed: Ten Years of American Trotskyism. Written as an effort to apply Hegelian concepts and logic to the study of the historical development of the working class, "The Nevada Document" concluded that the Leninist concept of a vanguard party had outlived its usefulness, thereby developing the philosophical, theoretical, and historical rationale for what would become one of the central elements in the group's break with Trotskyism and one of its key ideological commitments after leaving the SWP. *State Capitalism and World Revolution*, submitted to the 1950 SWP convention and published in the September 1950 SWP *Bulletin*, articulated the JFT's rejection of the vanguard party idea within a larger critique of the policies of the Fourth International and sought to differentiate the JFT's analysis and politics from those in the international Trotskyist movement who genuinely claimed to be "interpreting and bringing up to date the basic ideas of Trotsky." The JFT stated, "We are not doing that. Our position is that the chaos in the International is due to the fact that Trotsky's method of analysis and system of ideas are wrong."[151] Finally, the JFT wrote *The Balance Sheet Completed* to announce its break with the Trotskyists. Released in August of 1951 as they resigned from the SWP, this was the group's split document (the second in four years), and as such it presented charged polemics in defense of JFT positions relative to the SWP majority and orthodox Trotskyism. At once defensive and accusatory, *The Balance Sheet Completed* issued a caustic appraisal of the JFT's decade in the WP and SWP.

The Balance Sheet Completed was surely a settling of scores, but it also served as a declaration of independence and purpose. "'Johnson-Forest' has now made its final and complete break with what the Fourth International of today stands for. We are leaving behind forever the ideas of those who today represent Trotskyism, their unsocialist, anti-proletarian practice and organizational life," the document declared. "'Johnson-Forest' now sets out as an independent force preparing itself for the revolutionary tasks ahead of us. It will not be easy but the revolution is not easy either. . . . We know where we are going and we will now be able to give all our energies to the tasks for which we joined the movement."[152] Building on the third-layer concept, *The Balance Sheet Completed* identified four sectors of society that, the JFT argued, had been neglected, demoralized, or driven away by the SWP but would receive pride of place in the politics and organizational structure of the newly independent JFT: rank-and-file workers, Negroes, women, and youth.

In the fall of 1951, Grace and her JFT comrades formed a new, independent Marxist organization. They initially called it Committees of Correspondence, named after the committees formed in the thirteen colonies during the years leading up to the American Revolution, but soon came to call it Correspondence Publishing Committee or simply Correspondence. As they envisioned it, the new group would reflect their identity as revolutionary Marxists, embodying the theories and politics they had developed over the preceding decade. The theoretical work and political program of Correspondence would center on—and amplify their belief in—the self-activity, creative expression, and revolutionary capacity of the American working class.

Correspondence would have a tremendous impact on Grace's evolution. She gained strength as a leader and a thinker through the new group, and it grounded her focus on the making of a revolution in the United States. Whereas Trotskyism, World War II (and the immediate postwar years), and the Russian Question had significantly structured the JFT's identity, Correspondence would define itself through its singular focus on identifying the potential revolutionary forces in 1950s America. Grace's initial experiences with the March on Washington Movement and the JFT's analysis of the Negro Question had generated this commitment. Through the activities of Correspondence and a network of people connected to it, she would become a closer observer of and then participant in grassroots black political struggles. Moreover, Correspondence brought Grace to the city of Detroit. Two years after its founding, the group made the city its base. Grace followed, making Detroit her home and her political base for the rest of her life. Above all, the most profound way that Correspondence impacted Grace's evolution was by bringing her into contact with James Boggs. They met in Correspondence, and it was as comrades that they began their personal, intellectual, and political partnership.

Postcard advertisements for Chin Lee and Chin's, the two restaurants owned by Grace's father located in New York City's Times Square. The top postcard describes the two restaurants as situated "at the crossroads of the world." The other postcard reads: "Welcome World friends to Chin Lee and Chin's, Eat, Drink, and be Merry." The back of the card provides instructions for locating New York City street addresses and gives the phone numbers for Chin Lee and Chin's restaurants. Grace described her father's restaurant as her second home, recalling the many hours she spent there during her childhood. From the collection of Sharon Howell and Freddy Paine.

Grace in graduation robe, either at her undergraduate graduation from
Barnard College in 1935 or her PhD graduation from Bryn Mawr College in 1940.
From the collection of Sharon Howell and Freddy Paine.

Grace and Jimmy relaxing at a park in the early stages of their courtship, 1954. From the collection of Sharon Howell and Freddy Paine.

Grace and Jimmy on vacation in California, 1956.
From the collection of Sharon Howell and Freddy Paine.

Jimmy in his backyard in Detroit, 1957. From the collection of
Sharon Howell and Freddy Paine.

Jimmy in 1960.
From the collection
of Sharon Howell
and Freddy Paine.

Grace and Jimmy in 1961. From the collection of
Sharon Howell and Freddy Paine.

Jimmy and Grace celebrating the holidays at the end of 1962. Earlier in the year they had moved into their new home, 3061 Field Street, making this the first of many celebrations to happen there. In the coming months and over the remaining years of their partnership, Jimmy and Grace made their eastside Detroit home a gathering place for movement people and a central site for their intellectual and political activities. Since 1995 the house has been the home of the James and Grace Lee Boggs Center to Nurture Community Leadership, and in 2010 it became a City of Detroit historic site. From the collection of Sharon Howell and Freddy Paine.

"Grace clowning, Jimmy frowning. It happens all the time." Grace inscribed
these words on the back of this photo of her and Jimmy taken in the 1970s. Photo by
Kenneth Snodgrass. From the collection of Sharon Howell and Freddy Paine.

Jimmy (standing) speaks during one of the sessions of the Northern Negro Grass Roots Leadership Conference, held in Detroit in November 1963. A picture of Grace is among the photos on the wall behind Jimmy. Grace was one of the primary organizers of the conference, and Jimmy served as its chairperson. Photo by Milton Henry from the collection of Sharon Howell and Freddy Paine.

PART II

CHAPTER FIVE

Marxism and Marriage in Detroit

Having self-consciously declared itself a new and unique political entity and proudly proclaimed itself to be freed from the strictures and modes not just of Trotskyism but of the whole of the organized Left, Correspondence faced the task of establishing its organizational structure and practice. The organization was centered in New York, with branches, or "locals," in Detroit, Los Angeles, Flint, and West Virginia, their national membership totaling approximately seventy-five people.[1] They shared a commitment to a set of ideas and a common politics, and were convinced of their capacity to contribute something unique to the revolutionary movement. This imbued the group from its beginnings with a strong sense of purpose—they were fully confident in the ideas and politics upon which their new organization was based. But strong as their identity as revolutionary Marxists may have been, the group lacked a clear organizational identity. Thus, the challenge before them was to determine the organizational framework that would most effectively carry out and advance these ideas and politics. If successful, they reasoned, Correspondence would pioneer something new in the radical movement: it would show the power and potential of the small Marxist organization to help forge a revolution in mid-twentieth-century America. To launch this ambitious project, the group produced a mimeographed biweekly newsletter from the fall of 1951 to the fall of 1953 called *Correspondence*, which served as a vehicle for articulating the group's politics. The two years of mimeographed issues functioned as a trial run for the full-fledged printed newspaper they would start in October of 1953. During these two years, Correspondence also held three major gatherings through which the group determined the shape and direction of its day-to-day activities, its theoretical work, and its organizational life.

Grace Lee and James Boggs both contributed significantly to these efforts, though they had very different relationships to the organization. She was a political leader and a key theorist of the group; he was new to the organization, but as an autoworker, a labor movement activist who was critical of the union, and an African American, he was a direct representative of the revolutionary masses that Correspondence intended to place at the center of their theoretical and political work. Thus, Grace and Jimmy played distinct, though complementary, roles in the early development of the organization. Having come to Correspondence through differing personal and political histories, they brought very different things to the group—and eventually to each other.

The organizational dynamics and leadership structure of Correspondence were to some extent in flux from the group's inception due to C. L. R. James's immigration status. At the end of 1947 immigration authorities issued a warrant for his arrest for overstaying his visitor's visa. He surrendered and was released on bond, and then over the next four and a half years he filed multiple, ultimately unsuccessful appeals. In June 1952, he was arrested and incarcerated on Ellis Island. The next year, facing imminent deportation, he chose to leave for England. Thus, while C. L. R.'s political personality and ideas had been the crucial driving force in the formation of Correspondence, his immigration status complicated and circumscribed his role in its early development. His battles against deportation kept him from attending any of the three gatherings that the group held in the years 1951–53, and he was forced to leave the country just as the group embarked on its major venture of publishing the *Correspondence* newspaper.[2] He would maintain an active role in the group from abroad, first in London and later Trinidad, but his separation from the American comrades significantly impacted the development of the organization. Among other things, it led to the deepening of Grace's leadership role in the group and opened space for Jimmy's emergence as a leader.

We Are for the Other America

Jimmy attended the first major gathering of the newly constituted Correspondence, but he did not immediately commit himself to the organization. In September 1951, one month after leaving the Socialist Workers Party (SWP), the group held a founding convention in Detroit. It likely met there, rather than in New York, where most members lived, for two reasons. First, gathering outside of New York might help the group extract itself from the insular world previously inhabited by the Johnson-Forest Tendency (JFT).

Second, the group had already established a small presence in Detroit and hoped to attract new members there, particularly industrial workers like Jimmy. He was there at the invitation of a member of Correspondence, to whom Jimmy must have seemed the ideal recruit.[3] For his part, Jimmy came to the convention in search of a viable political space beyond what he had known the previous decade. "I just wanted to be around something. I had been around the old political organizations. The union was gone for me," he later recalled. Thus, he joined Correspondence. However, over the next year he did not immerse himself in its activities, as he sensed a lack of clarity regarding the group's purpose and problems in its leadership dynamics. "So I just sat on the sidelines," he remembered. "Then I went to the school."[4]

He was referring to the group's Third Layer School. Held in New York during two weeks in September 1952, this was the second major Correspondence gathering, and it was here that Jimmy emerged as an active and committed member of Correspondence. Like the convention held the previous year, this gathering was meant to help establish the group's organizational identity and practice, but unlike the convention, the Third Layer School was not for the full organization, but rather brought together approximately two dozen members, most of them from the "third layer." The school was conceived as a way to put into practice the third-layer concept that the JFT had started to develop theoretically in *Balance Sheet* and *The Balance Sheet Completed*. In the latter they had identified four groups—rank-and-file workers, Negroes, women, and youth—as the new revolutionary social forces in contemporary America, and Correspondence now recognized members of these groups as the organization's third layer. To actualize its vision of having the ideas, perspectives, and voices of the third layer at the forefront of the group's thinking and work, Correspondence held what it called the Third Layer School, comprising a series of structured political discussions led by rank-and-file members like Jimmy who served as the teachers, while the intellectuals and leaders like Grace listened and learned from them.[5] The ultimate goal was to "elicit the sentiments and attitudes of the rank and file and make that the fundamental basis of the organization," Martin Glaberman recalled. "The point was to get the intellectuals discussing what workers had put forward, rather than workers discussing what intellectuals had put forward."[6] One of those workers, Selma Weinstein (later Selma James), who participated as a third-layer comrade alongside Jimmy, recalled the format of the school: "The leaders were to sit down and learn from us. If I remember rightly, for two or three hours a day for two weeks, two groups of six or eight of us, mixed by race, gender, age, etc., met to discuss with the leadership . . . and tell them what we thought."[7]

Jimmy made a strong impression at the Third Layer School. He took an active role in the discussions throughout the two weeks, and spoke on topics that might have been taboo or controversial. For example, during one session he addressed the relationship between white women and black men; in another he spoke about conflicts that he saw within the Detroit branch of Correspondence. He also talked about his own political trajectory. This included relating his concerns about his continued participation in the United Auto Workers (UAW) given his aversion to the union bureaucracy, his decision years ago to leave the SWP (they "did not understand the workers"), and his recent decision to join Correspondence (they "did not try to put words in the workers' mouths but would ask them what they think").[8] Weinstein remembered well his energetic presence at the Third Layer School. "We working class people were to write a report of the two weeks of sessions, the thought of which daunted me," she explained, but Jimmy "saved us all: he wrote the whole damn thing, accurately reporting, among other discussions, the one on 'the woman question.'" She also remembered the impressive personal and political characteristics that he displayed during the Third Layer School. "Jimmy's wealth of information about how society actually functioned, his warm and sweet temperament and his enormous social gifts were all already prominent then," she recalled. "He was in training to be the community teacher others knew later."[9]

Indeed, Jimmy served as one of the "teachers" at the Third Layer School, and Grace, as part of Correspondence's leadership—the organization's first layer—was one of the "students." She did not, however, directly learn from or observe Jimmy's contributions to the school. As Grace recalled, the school was held in two sessions, with Jimmy in the first and Grace in the second. "So I didn't meet him until we held a social one night, although I had already heard that he had practically taken over leadership of the school, for example, volunteering to write the reports of the discussions and actually doing so from day to day." At the social, she asked him to dance, but "he declined because, as he said, he had already made clear to the comrades in Detroit that he 'didn't come around the radical movement to get himself a woman.'"[10] Both parts of Grace's recollection of Jimmy at the Third Layer School—the broad recognition of his active role, and his statement about his motivations—may be taken as indication of the seriousness or commitment that he surely conveyed to his new comrades. Jimmy was new to the organization, but he was not new to radical politics, and he came to this gathering and to Correspondence with a clear sense of identity and purpose. With his participation in the Third Layer School, Jimmy forecasted his eventual leadership role in the group.

The Third Layer School propelled the group to its third major gathering, a convention held in 1953 to launch *Correspondence* as a printed newspaper. Publishing *Correspondence* would be the group's main activity, and they expended considerable time, thought, and resources on its planning and execution. The Third Layer School prepared the way by helping the group solidify its membership and organizational culture while staking out the philosophical approach to be expressed in the paper. The group also published several works in 1952–53 that highlighted the types of analyses to be found in *Correspondence*: a pamphlet by Selma Weinstein (James) titled *A Woman's Place*, detailing the experiences, perspectives, and self-actualization of housewives and working-class women; *Punching Out*, a pamphlet by Glaberman describing rank-and-file workers acting against the trade union leadership and labor bureaucracy; Simon Owens's memoir *Indignant Heart*; and C. L. R.'s book *Mariners, Renegades, and Castaways*, written while he was on Ellis Island.[11] These writing projects, along with the mimeographed issues of *Correspondence*, helped to carry the momentum generated by the Third Layer School into the next gathering.

The convention to launch the *Correspondence* newspaper, which the group called the Convention of Correspondence Committees, began on July 3, 1953. The same day, C. L. R. made his forced departure from the country. This coincidence in timing dramatically marked the moment as one of transition for the organization. As the group gathered in Detroit to finalize plans for publishing the newspaper, which would become the group's central focus, C. L. R. left New York for London, where he would settle into a new role as, in effect, leader-in-exile of Correspondence. His departure not only required the group to work out new organizational dynamics, but forced them to do so just as they embarked upon the publication of *Correspondence*. This brought an elevation in the leadership roles of Grace and Raya Dunayevskaya, the latter becoming the new "chairman" of the organization. Their elevated roles were evident at the convention, with Dunayevskaya presiding over the five-day affair and Grace delivering the opening speech to the gathering.

Grace's speech set an enthusiastic, self-assured tone. In bold strokes, she issued a passionate projection of the role *Correspondence* could play in chronicling and helping to advance the coming mass revolt in the United States. She opened her speech by insisting that the gathering must begin "with a Marxist analysis of the objective national and international situation, in other words, of the world in which we live. Without a sure footing in that, what we talk about and will be running riot with in our paper will just be socialist gossip."[12] To do this she presented an analysis of four political developments of the preceding two weeks: American troops shooting down escaping anticommunist prisoners of war in Korea; the June 17 workers uprising in East Germany; British executions of Mau Mau fighters in Kenya; and the American government's execution of Ethel and Julius Rosenberg on June 19. These developments, she concluded, revealed that "today the whole world is breaking up."[13] Each of these was a display of power in which the state used deadly force to crush dissent, but Grace also saw in these acts of suppression evidence that those in power were in fact, in country after country, losing their hold. Thus, these events revealed that the balance of power was globally shifting to the masses. "The ruling class," she said, "has never shown such lack of confidence in itself. . . . There has never been such wailing and moaning, such hesitation and panic. On the other hand, the workers have never been so close to seeing not only that on both sides those who rule prepare only ruin and disaster, but that the strength and unity is all on the side of the workers."[14]

She made this argument most forcefully in her analysis of the East German uprising. The uprising began when workers took to the streets to protest a substantial increase in government-mandated production quotas and the trade unions' support of this increase. This initial action sparked further protests by workers across the country. Though the uprising was quickly and brutally suppressed by Soviet troops and East German police, Grace and Correspondence took it as an indication that, as Grace said in her speech, "the new stage of the European revolution has begun." Indeed, they took the uprising as confirmation of three key aspects of their theory of revolutionary action. First, Correspondence interpreted the actions of the East German workers—spontaneously erupting in revolt against the state and doing so in defiance of the union—as a decisive display of their willingness and ability to challenge the most powerful forms of capitalist (in this case, state capitalist) bureaucracy. Second, Correspondence identified the increased production quotas that sparked the uprising as another example of the "speed-up" that workers in the West and elsewhere faced. Thus, the East German workers' opposition to the new quotas spoke for all workers. "The question of speed-up," Grace said in her speech, "is so simple, so concrete and universal that every worker, no matter what language he speaks, can understand it—Russians, Americans, Chinese, Mexican, Japanese, Italian. You can't name a worker anywhere who doesn't know that his fight is against speed-up." Third, Correspondence believed that the East German uprising exemplified the socialization of labor that Marx theorized would result from what he called "the historical tendency of capitalist accumulation."

In her speech, Grace read a long passage from Capital in which Marx outlines the steps in his theory of capitalist centralization: competition among firms brings the consolidation of many firms into fewer, larger firms; this generates a continuously expanding workforce; these workers are thrown together in an increasingly cooperative labor process; and out of this production process workers organize themselves into a disciplined, unified class. The passage ends with Marx's prediction that along with the exploitation and misery produced by capitalism there also "grows the revolt of the working class, a class always increasing in numbers, and disciplined, united, organized by the very mechanism of the process of capitalist production itself."[15] This passage was often cited by the JFT and Correspondence, particularly by C. L. R.[16] They took Marx's statement about the growth and unification of the working class under capitalism as an article of faith, supporting their unshakable vision of working-class agency and capacity for revolutionary action. By the end of the decade, Grace and Jimmy began to move away from this view as applied to the American working class, and this would be central to the conflict that emerged between them and C. L. R. But in 1953, Grace held dear this passage and its articulation of working-class revolt, citing it at the convention to punctuate her analysis of the East German uprising and the politics to be expressed in Correspondence.

From East Germany Grace turned to Kenya and the importance of Africa in the current global political scene. Her reference point was the uprising of the Kenya Land and Freedom Army, known as the Mau Mau, which she offered as evidence that a will to revolt "is not only in Europe, it is happening everywhere." She made a plea for the organization "to make Africa our field" and for Correspondence to project a revolutionary analysis of Africa "from every point of view, historically, economically, theoretically." This analysis would be in the context of, and in opposition to, that presented by "the Stalinists and the American ruling class," who, she said, "are now readying for the fight over Africa as over Germany and over Korea." In contradistinction to this Cold War logic, Correspondence would approach Africa with an appreciation for its contributions to the emergent moment of global mass revolt. "We are interested because African people are fighting for self-independence and developing a new form of self-activity." She called on the organization to do "serious theoretical work" on Africa so as to properly situate the continent historically and in the contemporary political economy. "We have to show that if Africans are backward today it is because the capitalists and their slave-trade ruined them. If they are backward and often degraded, the responsibility is entirely that of imperialism." This theoretical work, she continued, should encompass past African civilizations and the contemporary "fight of the *peasants* there to escape the degradation of capitalism and yet achieve a modern civilization. The peasants are in the lead there, not the workers."[17]

Grace's emphasis on the African peasantry—and the role she assigned to it, relative to the working class, in creating a new society—would certainly have been noticed, and perhaps questioned, by most of her audience. While Correspondence had identified four groups as the revolutionary social forces in the United States—rank-and-file workers, Negroes, women, and youth—the group consistently foregrounded workers. Thus, Grace's analysis of the African situation, clearly removing workers from that primary role, might have given some pause. She insisted, however, that this was not contrary to Marxism or to the group's theoretical framework. Indeed, she argued that her analysis grew out of the group's history and theoretical development. "We have been freed," she said, "of the theory of the old organizations that only the proletariat can lead the struggle for national independence in the colonial countries." Furthermore, she asserted that the group's own history called for a careful analysis of African anticolonial struggles, an analysis that would identify new theoretical constructions needed to capture the specific circumstances of African societies and their struggles. To bring home her point, she drew a parallel to the early days of the JFT and the group's initial and foundational theory: "We have to work *as hard* to see the antagonisms and the new social forces in Africa as we worked to see them in Russia *and until we feel as secure about them* as we feel about state-capitalism and its contradictions. Without that, all we will actually be talking about is the heroism of the Mau Mau."[18]

This statement reflected Grace's fidelity to the group's history and to her use of the dialectical method. It also served her larger aim of articulating a vision and a program for *Correspondence*. The challenge she sought to issue to her comrades was not to conceive of an "African Question" and elevate it to the place occupied by the Russian Question in their work, but rather to conceptualize the newspaper as a means to constantly seek out, theorize, and give voice to the new revolutionary social forces wherever they may be found. As she shifted her speech's focus from the international to the national, Grace reaffirmed the organization's primary political coordinates and its focus on the American masses as represented by the four social forces to be at the center of *Correspondence*. "The decisive problem of our day," she declared, "is the reorganization of society without bureaucracy, without officials, without administrators. That is the opposition—between the cooperative labor of the workers and the bureaucracy which plans their speed-up. That opposition is everywhere in the world but nowhere is it clearer than in the United States. It is everywhere in American society among the rank and file workers, the Negroes, the women and the youth, who are working towards this reorganization in their everyday life and relations. That is the job of our paper, to present this."[19]

Grace brought her speech to a close with a passage from Marx and Engel's 1848 tract *The Communist Manifesto*. She offered it as a companion to the one she had read earlier from Marx's *Capital*, intending for the words from these two foundational Marxist texts to serve as bookends to the speech: "Between these two [passages] we can have a balanced judgment of the world in which we live." Drawing on the words of Marx and Engels in this way, she sought to punctuate her analysis of the contemporary political situation. She was also enlisting the authority of Marx and Engels to bolster her argument that the contemporary moment was one of revolutionary possibility, not unlike that which led the pair, more than a century earlier, to pen the words she cited from *The Communist Manifesto*: "Constant revolutionizing of production, uninterrupted disturbance of all social conditions, everlasting uncertainty and agitation distinguished the bourgeois epoch from all earlier ones. All fixed, fast frozen relations, with their train of ancient and venerable prejudices and opinions, are swept away, all new-formed ones become antiquated before they can ossify. All that is solid melts into air, all that is holy is profaned, and man is at last compelled to face *with sober senses* his real conditions of life and his relations with his kind."[20]

Fully aware that *The Communist Manifesto* was the product of another time and place—Western Europe in the era of the 1848 revolutions—Grace encouraged her comrades to find in these words not just inspiration but confirmation of their own revolutionary moment and the historic task before them as they launched *Correspondence* in the America of 1953. "Today, in every sphere, the vast majority of the American people are facing with *sober senses* their conditions of life and their relations with their kind," she declared. "To the large masses of the population, more important than anything else is their relations with their co-workers, their families, their neighbors. That is the America, the other America, that will appear in our paper."[21]

Grace's confident articulation of Correspondence's politics and possibilities made her speech a fitting opening to the five-day gathering. According to one observer, her speech generated considerable interest and discussion among the group. "It seemed that a whole new world had been opened up to these workers and young people by the analysis," the observer wrote in a detailed report on the convention. The report noted several appreciative comments by Correspondence members in response to her speech, including a "Southern white production worker" who "urged that the speech be printed so that he could study it."[22] The speech and the discussion it occasioned helped to reinforce the strong sense of purpose that had brought them together. Despite the glaring and potentially disorienting absence of C. L. R., the gathering generated a mood of excitement and enthusiasm. Dunayevskaya ably presided over the gathering as chair of the organization. "It was clear that the chairman had a wealth of experience in the political movement as well as theoretical background and that this entitled her to leadership," the observer wrote.[23] On the third day, she delivered a "profound and all-embracing" speech, described as "the most intensive and impressive report of the whole conference."[24] Several other people also gave speeches throughout the five days. The specific topics varied but they all shared the goal of establishing the group's collective work in publishing *Correspondence*, and the proceedings were structured to elicit the widest input of the approximately seventy-five-person membership.

The convention built upon Correspondence's preceding two gatherings, with particular emphasis on putting into practice the third-layer concept. "They are always talking about layers," wrote the observer, describing how the concept permeated the gathering not only as a method of generating ideas but also in developing relations among members in the group.[25] "What struck me as most remarkable," the observer declared, "was the readiness with which workers, both white and Negro, of obviously very little formal education spoke up—often they were among the first to speak—and the impact their speeches made on the course of the proceedings." Jimmy could have been one of these workers, though there is no direct mention of him in the report. Nonetheless, it is likely that he played an active role in the convention, and there are several places in the report where the person referenced could be Jimmy. For example, the observer took note of the respect accorded a white worker and a black worker at the convention, "both of whom have obviously had great experience in the organized American labor movement . . . and were recognized by everybody there as men of authority in their own right in terms of the world of production from which they had come."[26] This certainly applied to Jimmy and the role he was assuming in the organization.

The convention produced the desired result of establishing the structures and practices through which *Correspondence* would be published. Reports from the locals on the work they had done in publishing the mimeographed paper and carrying out other writing projects in preparation for the printed paper demonstrated that group editing in the locals had made the mimeographed paper "move ahead by leaps and bounds." They decided that this should carry forward in the form of local editorial boards, and settled on a structure for the printed paper organized around a Resident Editorial Board (REB) in Detroit, the body that would be most directly responsible for publishing the paper. Grace and Jimmy were named as members of the REB, which also included Dunayevskaya, Johnny Zupan, and Martin Glaberman. The organization also created a National Editorial Board to oversee a network of local committees across the country, particularly New York, Los Angeles, and West Virginia, but also in Flint, Philadelphia, San Francisco, and Boston. Each location functioned as an editorial collective and distribution center. From London, C. L. R. would participate in the planning and ongoing functioning of the paper by writing frequent and often lengthy letters to the organization, submitting material to be published in the paper, and building links between *Correspondence* and British workers and radicals. Zupan left his job at the Ford Rouge plant to become the paper's full-time editor, and Glaberman came to Detroit from Flint to serve as managing editor.

The convention also established goals for the paper's readership. They set a target of 5,000 readers, to be achieved first through the solicitation of advance subscriptions and then through a process of Correspondence members' interacting with their coworkers, neighbors, and others as potential readers of the paper. These potential readers were also potential writers.

The convention solidified Correspondence's vision of the paper as being written and edited not just by members but in conjunction and collaboration with people for whom the paper was published, namely the four groups that Correspondence identified as the revolutionary social forces in midcentury America. In this way, as Grace declared in her speech, the paper would embody and project Correspondence's vision "of a new society, the total reorganization of society by the rank and file workers, the Negroes, the women, and the youth, what we call the 'invading socialist society.'"[27] The group had used the phrase "invading socialist society," which they borrowed from Engels, as the title of their 1947 pamphlet explaining the JFT's widening ideological rift with the Workers Party and forecasting their break with Trotskyism altogether. Now Grace deployed the phrase to describe Correspondence's theory of the revolutionary masses and "the other America" she proudly declared would be featured in the paper.

The other America that Correspondence conceptualized was nowhere more present or possible than in Detroit. During the months leading up to the convention, Correspondence had decided to move the center of the organization from New York to that city, a decision that had been in the making since the JFT left the SWP and held the first Correspondence convention in Detroit in 1951. It was in the Motor City, where the eruption of autoworkers and others had been so central to the creation of the Congress of Industrial Organizations during the 1930s, where workers' autonomy surged in the form of wildcat strikes during World War II, and where all of the contradictions of modern mass production so clearly manifested themselves in the postwar years, that Correspondence intended to situate itself firmly among the masses. Coming into the convention, they made the Detroit local the base of the organization and thus the place where *Correspondence* would be published. In Detroit, Correspondence found the conditions for the fulfillment of its theory of workers' self-emancipation and its vision of social transformation.

Grace arrived in Detroit in the summer of 1953, just ahead of the convention. As one of the group's primary leaders and a member of the *Correspondence* editorial board, relocating there was a natural decision. It is also easy to see how moving to Detroit, at that time the fourth-largest city in the country, would have brought her a measure of comfort. For one thing, she had grown accustomed to big cities. She had lived most of her life and undergone all of her political and intellectual experiences in or around the three largest cities in the country: New York, Chicago, and Philadelphia.[28]

Moreover, Grace arrived in Detroit with a clear purpose and plan. Unlike her move to Chicago, where she went in search of a space for personal and political growth, she was coming to Detroit with the express purpose of building an organization to which she already belonged—indeed, she functioned in a leadership role—and to which she was wholly committed. And the organization was coming to Detroit, the place they deemed ideal for their ambitious goal of publishing a novel and transformative newspaper. Finally, she came to the Motor City not only with a solid organizational and ideological foundation, but also with a clear sense of herself as a radical activist. With more than a decade of experience in radical politics behind her, Detroit represented for Grace, as it did for the organization, the next stage in her political development—a continuation but also an exciting extension of the political world she had forged in Chicago and New York. In time, Detroit would far surpass those cities as a generative force in her political and intellectual life.

Detroit, 1953

Detroit appeared especially durable when Grace arrived in 1953, but this was deceptive. In fact, the city was entering a period of transition whereby it would be substantially transformed. The well-known markers of Detroit's apparent vitality—a robust industrial base, well-organized and politically connected labor unions, and a steadily increasing population—concealed what in actuality were massive fault lines. In 1953 Detroit rested firmly on its reputation as an economic powerhouse, and, as the home of the auto industry and the epicenter of organized labor, the city was a seemingly stable generator of the American middle class. Yet, it was precisely that year that industry and people began leaving Detroit in such numbers as to set in motion economic and demographic trends that would reshape the city. Between 1953 and 1957, for example, three major auto manufacturers closed down, while Dodge Main—the city's second-largest auto factory, at one time employing over 35,000 workers—cut its workforce by several thousand during the late 1950s.[29] The economic changes of the 1950s constituted a massive process of deindustrialization—plant closings, the introduction of automation, downsizing and layoffs, plant relocations outside of the city—that resulted in more than temporary job losses and spikes in unemployment; it essentially amounted to the shrinking and virtual unmaking of the industrial economy upon which the city had been built.[30] In

1953, when the nation and the world still looked to Detroit as an industrial leviathan, the city was in fact starting down the road to the postindustrial economy that so dramatically manifested itself in the final decades of the twentieth century.

The year 1953 saw Detroit reach the summit of its population growth. After decades of in-migration and a steadily increasing population, Detroit's population peaked at approximately 2 million in 1953. The year thus marks an inflection point in a history of great population growth during the first half of the century and an equally dramatic—and consequential—decline during the second half. From the mid-1950s onward, the city's population steadily declined, as a flight of residents, particularly white residents moving to the suburbs, accompanied the flight of industry.[31] This helped fuel a dramatic shift in Detroit's racial composition. During the 1950s the city's white population fell by more than 350,000, representing a 23.4 percent change, while continued African American migration from the South grew Detroit's black population by more than 180,000 during this period. As the city's total population dropped by nearly 200,000 during the decade, the percentage of black Detroiters almost doubled, rising from 16.4 in 1950 to 29.4 in 1960.[32] Thus, Grace arrived in Detroit in time to witness the beginning of a demographic pattern that would prevail for the rest of the twentieth century and into the twenty-first: Detroit's total population steadily declined, while the proportion of African Americans continuously rose. Jimmy, of course, had an even closer connection to this history. By 1953 he had been in Detroit for nearly fifteen years, all of them lived in African American neighborhoods on the city's east side in or near Black Bottom. The city's changing racial demographics would prove to be, like the other fundamental changes of this period, an important backdrop against which Grace and Jimmy built their intellectual, political, and marital partnership.

A contributing factor to these racial dynamics, and a significant force in reshaping the physical and social landscape of the city, was Detroit's ambitious postwar redevelopment agenda, which, by 1953, centered on urban renewal. Detroit took its first steps toward an urban renewal program in the 1930s, when city officials and planners instituted slum clearance and public housing programs to replace dilapidated housing and clear "blighted" areas. But the actual program that took the name "urban renewal"—a federally funded program by which the city acquired and cleared land for private development—had its origins in the grand designs of city officials and planners (with the prompting of private builders and real estate interests) for rebuilding the city that emerged during World War II and the immediate postwar years. In 1947 the city crafted its "Detroit Plan: A Program for Blight Elimination," a statement of the city's plans for redevelopment, including slum clearance, central business district revitalization, and the construction of low-cost housing. The plan originally included construction of public housing and was to be financed by the city, but two developments in 1949, one national and one local, significantly altered the shape of the plan: the enactment of the 1949 Housing Act in July, and the election of city treasurer and fiscal conservative Albert Cobo as Detroit's mayor in November. The Housing Act established the federal urban renewal program, supplying federal funds for urban redevelopment under the direction of local authorities. Meanwhile, Cobo promptly dismantled the city's public housing program and stacked the Detroit Housing Commission with people from the real estate and construction industries, both of which helped to ensure that Detroit's urban renewal favored private developers at the expense of the city's poorest residents.[33]

Between 1950 and 1953 the city aggressively proceeded with the first redevelopment site of the Detroit Plan, the clearing of deteriorated housing on 129 acres of land in Black Bottom to make way for new housing. This came to be known as the Gratiot redevelopment area, and the Gratiot project initiated more than two decades of redevelopment activities that reconfigured the city's physical and social landscape. Bolstered by the city's 1951 master plan (an update of the Detroit Plan) and the federal government's extension of urban renewal with the 1954 Housing Act, these activities included the construction of expressways, the Gratiot–Lafayette Park residential area, and industrial Corktown; the rehabilitation or building of municipal services such as schools and recreational resources; and the expansion of Wayne State University, the Cultural Center, and the Medical Center complex.[34]

Detroit's leaders earned high praise from some quarters for their redevelopment efforts, but such praise ignored the devastating impact on black and poor Detroiters.[35] The construction of expressways provides a case in point. As was happening in cities across the country, Detroit's freeway system sliced through poor, usually black neighborhoods and displaced thousands of people. The Oakland-Hastings (now Chrysler) Freeway, for example, overran Paradise Valley and uprooted the famed Hastings Street. This not only wiped out the Hastings Street business district—and along with it vital black institutions—but also forced several thousand people to seek residences in other parts of the city amid an already acute shortage of housing. Thus Jimmy watched the destruction of a place that had been the focal point of the community he entered when he came to Detroit. Hastings was the first location he sought upon his arrival in 1937, and it was the center of black community life on the Detroit's east side, the community in which he lived upon settling in the city that he made his home for all of his adult life. The John C. Lodge and Edsel Ford Freeways similarly disrupted neighborhoods on the city's west side, including a part of the city's Chinatown.[36] Grace's arrival in 1953 allowed her to see the bulldozing of these neighborhoods to make way for the highways, thus giving her a vantage point from which to assess the city's transformation and the struggles attendant to it.

Freeway construction exacerbated the devastating problems generated by urban renewal projects. This was particularly so with the problem of displacement and relocation, which continued well into the 1960s.[37] By 1953, the Gratiot project had already revealed the extreme hardship that urban renewal could produce. Residents forced to move from the area received little or no relocation assistance from the city (despite federal requirements mandating such assistance), and they confronted a shortage in the private housing market, racial segregation in public housing, and the weighty indifference of the Cobo administration.

The Detroit Urban League (DUL) documented the unfolding drama of urban renewal and what DUL official William Price called "the staggering magnitude of the relocation problem."[38] The numbers revealed a bleak picture. At the end of 1950, the Detroit Housing Commission claimed to have relocated only 1,418 families out of 2,593 in need of relocation. Worse still, the DUL found that of the 1,418 families, only 364 were in permanent housing. Of the rest, 226 were placed in "dilapidated temporary housing," while the remaining 828 actually had no housing offered to them.[39] This temporary housing was actually dwellings in the Gratiot redevelopment area used as on-site locations to which people were temporarily transferred. This practice pushed displaced residents into living conditions equally as bad as and in some cases worse than their original dwellings. "Our findings show," concluded a DUL report, "that much of this [temporary] housing is unfit for human habitation." Many of these housing units were "hard to heat because of their dilapidated condition," and they suffered from faulty plumbing resulting in "over-flowing toilets, transferring of water from bath to kitchen for cooking purposes, and the lack of proper bathing facilities." Other conditions included the "absence of doors to insure [sic] privacy, broken window panes stuffed with rags and paper, leaking roofs, and falling plaster."[40] For the many families left to fend for themselves, the only option often proved to be "doubling up"—that is, two families sharing one single-family home. The city's practice of placing evicted families in temporary on-site housing and failing to provide any assistance to others not only violated federal requirements and posed hardships for individual families; it also reproduced the slum conditions that the project was ostensibly meant to reduce. The DUL found "that families 'relocating' themselves into other areas" were in effect "transplanting the same over-crowding and sharing pattern that existed in the Gratiot Redevelopment Area."[41]

By 1953, with upward of 6,000 people already or soon to be evicted from the Gratiot redevelopment area, and several more thousands displaced for expressway construction, urban renewal claimed a prominent place among the major problems confronting black Detroiters. The most affected were the poorest residents of Black Bottom and Paradise Valley, but the nature of the problem animated concern and action among African Americans broadly. Urban renewal not only involved a housing crisis; it also highlighted the city's treatment of black citizens. In addition to the city's failure to address relocation needs, the DUL reported that city officials violated the rights of project area residents in multiple ways, including aggressive and "questionable administrative practices . . . to place undue pressure on the residents to force them to move. In many instances these pressures result in the breaking up of families and other forms of social disorganization."[42] Indeed, that some families had no other option but to split up and take residence in dispersed locations is perhaps one of the hidden but no less disastrous consequences of Detroit's urban renewal. Harold Norris, a civil rights activist and attorney who represented many of the evicted families in proceedings before the Wayne County Circuit Court commissioners, witnessed people testifying in court that eviction forced their families to split up. Norris quotes one mother: "I've had to send my son to live with my sister in Alabama, and my daughter to my mother in Chicago. . . . I don't have any place to move now."[43] Speaking to the Greater Detroit Public Housing Tenants Council in 1952, Norris lambasted Mayor Cobo and his "inhuman policy" of urban renewal, which Norris labeled "dislocation without relocation." He described the situation as "illegal, immoral, and dangerous," explaining that "what is really happening is that poor people, mostly Negro people, are being removed from what little housing they have." Norris also articulated what came to be a truism among a generation of African

Americans nationally: "This really amounts to Negro removal, not urban renewal."[44]

Black Detroit's experience with "Negro removal" constituted one component of the larger contestation over the place of African Americans in the city during the early 1950s, a contestation that expressed itself in multiple ways in 1953. That year marked a decade since the Detroit race riot of 1943, a defining moment in the city's racial history. This milestone occasioned a series of articles in the *Michigan Chronicle*, Detroit's major black weekly newspaper, published under the title "Detroit—Ten Years After!"[45] Written by the paper's executive editor, Charles J. Wartman, the series included seven pieces exploring the progress made in race relations over the decade in five key areas: population growth, housing, employment, discrimination in public accommodations and civic life, and police-community relations. Wartman identified areas of continuing discrimination and stubborn racial barriers, but he also found clear indicators of racial progress. "Racial myths and community stereotypes have collapsed under the impact of recent changes,"[46] he wrote. Among the changes he cited were increased home ownership, expanding ranks of African American professionals, and a robust network of black-owned and -operated businesses. "Hundreds of blocks of well-kept, substantial houses attest to the economic progress which has been made . . . in the Negro community,"[47] he proclaimed. Wartman also proudly reported that "Detroit has been hailed across the country as the home of more Negro-owned and operated businesses than any other city."[48] These businesses were not only meeting the needs of the community, he wrote, but also affording its young people the requisite training and career building "for integration in the total life of the city."[49]

The series ultimately tilted toward and reflected a middle-class perspective. "Detroit—Ten Years After!" gave voice to an important set of experiences, aspirations, and markers of progress, and in the process produced an informed picture of the social challenges facing African Americans in Detroit between 1943 and 1953. But it did so to the relative exclusion of other strategies and terrains of racial struggle, in particular minimizing or leaving unexamined issues most directly related to poor African Americans. There is no mention, for example, of urban renewal or the Gratiot redevelopment project. The result was a cheery optimism about the current status of black Detroiters and the prospects for improved race relations. "In general the Negro population has prospered"[50] over the last ten years, Wartman concluded at the end of the series. "The year 1953," he added, "finds Detroit moving forward in many fields of race relations."[51]

Wartman's racial liberalism also excluded from consideration the relationship among African Americans, labor, and the Left, a relationship that was at times uneasy and certainly shifting but nonetheless figured prominently in African American politics in 1953. This relationship had famously been on display exactly one year prior to the *Michigan Chronicle* series when, at the end of February 1952, the House Un-American Activities Committee held hearings in Detroit. Among those called to testify were prominent African American leftists such as Rev. Charles Hill, C. LeBron Simmons, Arthur McPhaul, and Coleman Young, with attorney George Crocket representing Hill, Young, and McPhaul (among other witnesses). The ostensible purpose of the hearings was to investigate Communist influence in the auto industry, and the primary target was UAW Local 600, the largest local union in the world.[52] Local 600 served as a solid base of black radicalism, including the recently formed National Negro Labor Council, of which Young was an officer. Young's hour-and-a-half-long testimony—during which he forcefully condemned racist violence and denial of rights as "un-American activities" and chastised two southern congressmen for their pronunciation of the word "Negro"—produced perhaps the most dramatic and well-remembered moments of the hearings.[53] Detroiters heard Young's triumphant testimony over the radio and on a phonograph record that circulated in black communities, earning him high praise among African Americans. Nonetheless, the hearings shook the Left in Detroit, whipping up an anticommunist hysteria that imperiled a range of individuals and organizations. The hearings cast a Cold War shadow—including work stoppages and physical attacks against witnesses—over labor and its allies in the Left and civil rights communities.

This, then, was the mix of circumstances and forces at play in Detroit in 1953 when Grace moved to the city where she, Jimmy, and the rest of the organization began publishing *Correspondence*. In the midst of economic shifts, demographic transformation, racial conflict and struggle, and a heightened repression of leftists, they embarked upon the publication of a newspaper designed as a vehicle for working-class expression and a means to invigorate working-class self-activity. The newspaper was the expression of the group's politics—its attempt to bring something new to the Left, to the working-class movement, and to American Marxism. Detroit was the group's new home—and the city quickly became not only a base of operations but also a source of political experience and theorizing.

"Grace Got *Me*"

Both political and personal considerations had driven Grace's decision to move to Detroit. Indeed, this move reflected how much the two had become intertwined in her life. "I liked Detroit," she recalled years later, describing her impressions of the city upon arriving there. "It was much smaller than New York, people seemed to know one another, and it was a city of neighborhoods and beautiful trees. It also felt like a 'Movement' city where radical history had been made and could be made again."[54] Moreover, Grace arrived in Detroit with a clear purpose. Unlike her move to Chicago, where she went in search of a space for personal and political growth, she was coming to Detroit with the express purpose of building an organization to which she already belonged. And the organization was coming to Detroit with a specific and ambitious goal: to publish in the Motor City, the center of the labor movement, a "workers' paper" that they hoped would be a completely novel and transformative newspaper. Finally, she came to the Motor City not only with a solid organizational and ideological foundation, but also with a clear sense of herself as a radical activist. With more than a decade of experience in radical politics behind her, Detroit represented for Grace (as it did for the organization) the next stage in her political development—a continuation but also an exciting extension of the political life she had forged in Chicago and New York.

During the preceding thirteen years, since leaving Bryn Mawr in 1940, Grace "had been involved in nearly a half dozen relationships and lived in more than a half dozen places," she recalled. "The contradictions in this nomadic existence had been growing, and even though I had not said it to myself or anyone else, I needed to settle down in a place and in a relationship that would be both nurturing and challenging." Whether she made this realization immediately or came to it over time, there is no question that she indeed found both in Detroit: Grace settled in there in June 1953 and never left, making the city her home and political base, and within a year of her arrival Grace and Jimmy were married. The city became not only the place in which they built their lives together but a central referent for the intellectual and political partnership they shared for the next four decades. Grace's arrival in Detroit and the start of her and Jimmy's relationship in

1953, just as the city began to be reshaped by the deep, decades-long changes described above, meant that Grace and Jimmy would experience and participate in the city's evolution together, with the city and its transformation becoming a crucial component to their politics and their thinking.

Grace and Jimmy began their courtship almost immediately after her arrival in Detroit during the summer of 1953. They had both attended the Correspondence convention in 1951, but apparently did not meet until the Third Layer School the following year. Now, with Grace living in Detroit and both of them actively engaged in the group's effort to launch *Correspondence*, they spent a lot of time together. The relationship developed quickly, though its progression was apparently not altogether clear or predictable, Nor did it follow conventional patterns. "I always say, Grace got *me*," Jimmy told friends years later as he and Grace recounted the circumstances of their courtship and marriage. Speaking with a smile on his face and pausing between words for emphasis, Jimmy put stress on the word *me* to indicate that Grace had pursued him. "So Grace invited me up for dinner," Jimmy recounted, describing an important early moment in their courtship. As he narrated the events of the night, Grace joined in, recalling with laughter the multiple ways in which the dinner did not go as planned. He arrived late, scoffed at the food she had prepared, and disparaged her selection of music. Still, the night catalyzed their mutual affections and romantic interest. Whether these had been latent or were already developing before this night, they grew rather intensely following the dinner. Jimmy began spending considerable time at Grace's apartment on Blaine and Fourteenth Streets on the west side, and then they moved in together, taking an apartment on the east side, at Chene and Lafayette, closer to Jimmy's job at Chrysler Jefferson and near many of his friends and coworkers.[55]

This was a period of transition in both of their lives. Jimmy was thirty-four years old and had just finalized his divorce from Annie, his first wife. Grace was thirty-eight and living in a new city, where she excitedly faced a new set of personal and social circumstances. They built their relationship against the backdrop of Correspondence's own transition, as the group moved its center to Detroit and launched *Correspondence*. This set of personal and political circumstances formed the context in which Grace and Jimmy built what would be an enduring bond that in those initial months of summer and fall 1953 likely blurred the lines between friendship, comradeship, and romance. This blurring may help to explain the seemingly incongruent train of events Grace described leading up to and during the night of the proposal, and would surely characterize their personal and political companionship over the course of forty years of marriage and activism.

Jimmy and Grace's relationship rather quickly found its way into the files of the FBI. The FBI's monitoring of Grace that began in New York in 1948 continued unabated, with the bureau tracking her arrival in Detroit and soon after moving the "office of origin" for her file from New York to Detroit.[56] In 1952, the bureau began collecting information on Jimmy, and by the spring of 1953, the Detroit office had assembled an extensive and growing file on him and his activities. Their file included Jimmy's employment records, his marriage and divorce records, and various records from the Bureau of Vital Statistics in Montgomery, Alabama (for his birth and other family information); the Merchants Credit Bureau (which reflected "no derogatory information"); the Detroit Police Department and the Wayne County Sheriff's Office (which found "no record identifiable with the subject"); and the Selective Service ("During World War II the subject was registered under the Selective Service Act but was deferred due to occupational reasons and a chronic inaptitude for military service"). The FBI's main source of information was its network of informants, who gave frequent and at times detailed reports on the meetings he attended, the things he said and wrote, his political affiliations, and his personal information. Some even furnished tape recordings and Correspondence's printed material.[57] Thus, by the summer of 1953, when Grace and Jimmy began their courtship, the FBI had each of them under surveillance, and by the fall, agents had noted their relationship. For example, they noted that Grace and Jimmy were "probably living in a common-law status." At least two informants told FBI agents that by November 1953 the couple was living together and Grace was using the name Mrs. James Boggs. One of these informants reported that Grace and Jimmy initially "were planning to be married about Thanksgiving Day, 1953," but the terms of Jimmy's recent divorce decree required them to wait "approximately one year."[58]

In fact, Grace Lee and James Boggs were married on July 17, 1954. The marriage solidified a partnership that was at once personal, political, and intellectual, and that would in coming years productively draw from their divergent backgrounds. Grace and Jimmy's racial/ethnic identities surely marked their marriage as unique in mid-twentieth-century America. But their other differences—urban and rural upbringings, divergent social classes, distinct educational backgrounds and intellectual styles—proved more important for the union, as these significantly shaped and enhanced the partnership that Jimmy and Grace were able to build.

So too was their relationship shaped by the city of Detroit, the place in which they built their partnership, and Correspondence, the organization that brought them together. Each played a vital role in the Boggses' intellectual and political partnership. Detroit did not simply serve as the backdrop to their activities; it furnished specific spaces of political engagement and sources of theoretical development, including the labor movement, black community struggles against segregation, and black nationalist politics. Likewise, their marriage and partnership directly grew from their shared commitment to and participation in Correspondence. The organization—and particularly its main activity, publishing *Correspondence*—occupied a central place in the life that the couple was building together. Jimmy and Grace each became a driving force in its publication throughout the paper's nearly eleven-year existence, making *Correspondence* both a vehicle for the expression of their politics and a source of their continuing political development.

CHAPTER SIX

Building *Correspondence*

The first issue of *Correspondence* appeared on October 3, 1953, exactly three months after Grace's opening speech at the Convention of Correspondence Committees, where the group formally committed itself to launching the paper. In those three months the group secured the equipment required to produce the paper, opened its headquarters in a basement office at 5050 Joy Road on Detroit's west side, and established the Correspondence Publishing Company as the legal entity responsible for the paper. By the release of the inaugural issue, the organization and newspaper had essentially become indistinguishable. The group in effect became the Correspondence Publishing Company. The group's "chairman," Raya Dunayevskaya, said as much in a speech to the Detroit membership just two weeks after the convention when she described the paper not just as a project of the organization or a stage in its life, "but as the organization itself. We breathe the paper all over the place now as *our way of life*, and all else follows."[1] *Correspondence* was to be the center of their activity and the full expression of their politics.

Dunayevskaya made the speech during the first meeting of the Detroit membership since the convention, but this was also the last meeting that she would attend for several months, as she would soon be leaving on an extended trip. She used the occasion to "deputize" Grace as the group's "chairman" in her absence. Dunayevskaya said this would ensure "that the continuity of theoretical and practical work can go on."[2] This was an affirmation of Grace's leadership role in the organization over the preceding decade, and it was also a projection and forecasting of her coming role in *Correspondence*. Likewise, Dunayevskaya highlighted Jimmy's role in building the paper. While she did not identify him by name, she easily could have been speaking of him when she described the group's early efforts—in the two key spaces of the factory and the neighborhood—to garner readers and generate interest in the new publication. "Concretely, we do not go knocking on strange doors for two bucks as hucksters and the old radicals did. We go, first and foremost, to our own shopmates, and we go not as salesmen but as *builders*," she said. "When we do knock on doors, [we go] not to strange neighborhoods where no one saw us before or will after we have collected the buck, but to our *own neighbors*, friends, housewives."[3]

Jimmy, as much as anyone in the organization, embodied this *builder* persona. Throughout the life of the paper, he actively undertook all four of the main tasks involved with its publication: securing subscriptions, which the group called "subgetting"; soliciting submissions, articles of all lengths and types, for the paper from coworkers, neighbors, and others; writing articles himself; and editing. His earnest and consistent interactions with his coworkers and neighbors, engaging them with and through *Correspondence*, contributed both in spirit and in practice to the life of the paper and proved essential to its existence. And in throwing himself fully into building the publication, Jimmy received as he gave. "Jimmy loved *Correspondence*," Grace recalled many years later, because "it gave him the opportunity to write, which he loved to do[, and] it gave him the opportunity to get stories from workers, which he loved to do."[4] Grace and Jimmy also regularly went door to door in their neighborhood, visiting people "to get subscriptions and sit around and talk to them," which she described as "a way of linking up with the community."[5] This fusion of politics and community, where the work of building the paper drew upon, merged with, and even helped to reinforce neighborhood connections, epitomized Jimmy's political identity.

Correspondence, then, played a formative role in Jimmy's intellectual and political development. Writing for the paper gave him an early outlet for his ideas and a venue to develop himself as a writer and political thinker while he simultaneously made the paper a vehicle for connecting with people in ways that engaged political and social questions on a personal basis. Additionally, he deepened his organizational and political skills as a member of the paper's editorial board as it took on repeated crises surrounding readership, finances, and organizational capacity.

The experience of working on *Correspondence* also shaped Grace's intellectual and political identity, though the roles she assumed in publishing the paper were different from Jimmy's. She initially took responsibility for two parts of the newspaper's layout: the lead news story on the cover of each issue, which the group called the "front-pager"; and the "Readers' Views" section, essentially a reworking and expansion of the traditional letters-to-the-editor section. She also served as a silent (unnamed) assistant editor for much of the first few years before becoming the editor in 1957. At the same time, she carried on a heavy correspondence with C. L. R. James about the paper and the group. They discussed the paper's day-to-day operations, with C. L. R. at times giving instructions but also receiving from Grace her assessments of the paper's problems and prospects. The letters between Grace and C. L. R. also contain ongoing theoretical and political discussions that reveal Grace's active role in shaping the group's politics. In an organization that conducted much of its business through voluminous letters between members, this constituted a significant conduit for C. L. R.'s involvement in the paper. Through these activities Grace developed the habits of mind and patterns of practice that she would carry with her in subsequent organizations and movements for the rest of her life.

Correspondence also played a formative role in the development of Grace and Jimmy's relationship and partnership. Their courtship unfolded during the second half of 1953 and the opening months of 1954, that is, at the same time as they were working together in publishing *Correspondence*. Thus, they were building their relationship and building *Correspondence* simultaneously, and their shared commitment to the paper occupied a prominent place in their relationship. The paper served as their primary political activity throughout their first decade together.

"The Search for New Human Relations"

Three closely linked ideas formed the ideological foundation of *Correspondence*: affirming the role of the working class as the agent of revolutionary change; rejecting the concept of the vanguard party and instead celebrating the self-activity and spontaneous mobilization of the working class; and standing in full opposition to all forms of bureaucratic control. Like other Marxists, the group held that workers—particularly those in the mass production industries—were the one social force in society who, in confronting their exploitation in the capitalist system and in taking action to force the system to meet their needs, could effect a revolutionary transformation of society. But the group self-consciously and proudly distinguished itself from other Marxists in emphasizing and encouraging the creativity, spontaneity, and self-activity of the working class. It argued that the working class had the capacity to act on its own behalf without the leadership of labor unions or radical parties, and that such spontaneous self-organization was in fact crucial to the creation of a new society. As a corollary to this, it stridently spoke against all forms of bureaucratic control and management—a position derived over the preceding decade from the leaders' reading of Marxists texts, their analysis of the labor movement, and their experiences in, and sharp critiques of, Trotskyism—whether that management came from capitalists and institutions of civil society or from labor unions and leftist political parties.

Accordingly, *Correspondence* set out to record and amplify the interior worlds of "ordinary people." The group believed that ordinary people wanted and needed a space to share their experiences, express their thoughts, and voice their opinions about society. As they had decided at the launching convention, the paper focused in particular on four groups or segments of society they identified as most marginalized: rank-and-file workers, Negroes, women, and youth.

Of the four groups, rank-and-file workers enjoyed pride of place in the group's conceptualization of *Correspondence*. The layout afforded nominally equal coverage, and the organization expressly sought to include members of all four groups in the work of the paper. However, labor-related articles tended to find a more prominent place in the pages of *Correspondence* than other articles, and the experiences and contributions of members like Jimmy who were factory workers often garnered greater weight or attention. The group quickly came to describe *Correspondence* as a "workers' paper," by which they meant a publication that workers would genuinely and uniquely recognize as their own. It was to be a novel publication in that it did not just speak to or for workers, but rather allowed them to speak for themselves and see their full selves reflected. It was to be distinct from traditional labor papers that revolved around unions or the activities of workers in the plant and in relation to the company. So too did they seek to differentiate *Correspondence* from rival publications that sought to educate workers, instruct them in the correct political line, or organize them into a union or radical party. By contrast, *Correspondence* would consider the totality of workers' lives, giving them the space to share their experiences beyond the plant or union hall and to explore their social and intellectual worlds.

Curiously, *Correspondence* did not explicitly disclose its Marxist orientation. While the paper announced in multiple ways its fealty to workers, consistently championed the working class as the agent of change, and openly stated the need for "a new society," the words "Marxism" and "socialism" almost never appeared in the paper. Only in cryptic passages found in editorial statements did the Correspondence Publishing Company vaguely hint at its roots in the organized Left. The group's motivation was likely not so much to hide or deny its Marxism as to keep the pages of *Correspondence* free from strong ideological language or positions. It could thereby welcome into its pages the voices and thoughts of "ordinary people" for whom Marxism had no resonance but whose ideas in fact expressed the same political convictions that motivated *Correspondence*.

To be sure, the group may have been making a strategic decision to downplay its roots in the organized Left. Launching a radical newspaper at the height of McCarthyism not only courted persecution for the individuals involved, but virtually ensured that the fledging paper would confront the charge of communism. The organization's own vocal anticommunism—they staunchly opposed the Soviet Union, the Communist Party of the United States, and nearly all things associated with official Communism—plainly and regularly appeared in *Correspondence*, but this could not shield it from the harsh winds of Cold War politics.[6] Indeed, suspicion first came from some of the paper's early potential readers who perceived *Correspondence* as a communist paper and therefore inherently anti-American and dangerous. Then, after little more than a year of publication, the Office of the Attorney General placed *Correspondence* on its subversive list. Still, the paper positioned itself as a counterweight to this repressive environment in which dissent was silenced and open expression curtailed.

The form and content of the paper proudly announced its politics. A twelve-page newspaper published every two weeks,[7] *Correspondence* took no advertisements, instead financing itself through subscriptions and contributions from members of the organization (particularly Lyman and Freddy Paine). The paper devoted a separate section to each of the four social groups that the organization hoped to attract to the paper—workers, youth, women, and African Americans, whose section was called "Special Negro News" (SNN). This format was intended to afford each group its own unique and independent significance within the paper's larger focus on "ordinary people." As mentioned previously, the labor section was the largest of the four and clearly received the greatest emphasis in the organization. Nonetheless, each section treated readers to a lively and varied array of content relevant to that particular group, including news stories, first-person accounts of events, columns, and the ruminations of readers on all manner of subjects (from topical matters to personal experiences). The front page prominently featured the "Worker's Journal," a column written by Simon Owens under the pen name Charles Denby. Three other members of the organization also wrote regular columns: Jimmy in the "Special Negro News" section, Selma Weinstein in the women's section, and Dunayevskaya on the editorial page. Appearing opposite the "Worker's Journal" was the front-pager, which usually dealt with a national or international event.

Three other regular components of the paper rounded out the format. The aforementioned "Readers' Views" section on the editorial page very much reflected the spirit and purpose of the paper. This section appeared prominently in the middle of the newspaper and carried the comments, suggestions, and exhortations of various readers, some as short as one sentence, others as long as several paragraphs.[8] These statements presented a wide spectrum of opinions about and responses to the paper, including praise and approval, dissenting views, and sharp critique. Items ranged in subject matter from commentary on specific articles in past issues, to reflections on an individual's experiences helping to publish the paper, to ideas for improving the paper as a whole. The political cartoons, many of them with recurring characters and themes such as the corruption of unions, the problem of unemployment, and the day-to-day challenges of child rearing, proved an effective way not only to foreground the experiences of ordinary people but also to signal the power of their perspectives on the social worlds they inhabited. Finally, a section called "Viewing and Reviewing" provided another dimension to the paper's engagement with the lives of ordinary people with short pieces discussing television, movies, music, sports, and other elements of American popular culture.

The appearance of *Correspondence*'s inaugural issue marked a milestone for the group, but journalistically it did not much impress. Much of the writing was flat, the design was unimaginative, and the crowded layout gave the paper an amateurish feel. Still, this first issue made a bold declaration of the paper's intervention into radical politics. A "Statement of the Editor" on the front page unambiguously located the paper's commitments: "*Correspondence* is a paper in which ordinary people can say what they want to say and are so eager to say. Workers, Negroes, women, youth will tell in this paper their own story of their lives, in the plant, at home, in school, in their neighborhoods, what they are doing, what they are thinking about. All that they have to say, about everything that interests them, will fill our pages." The statement also made clear that *Correspondence* would hold "a total hostility to all forms of bureaucratic domination, anti-Communist as well as Communist," while helping to advance "the search for new human relations" in every corner of society, "between a worker and his work, between races and nations, between men and women, between youth and adults."[9]

Expressions of these two strivings—to be free of bureaucratic domination and to craft new social relations—could be found throughout the first issue. For example, several pieces by Detroit factory workers described their experiences with machines in the assembly line, their interactions with foremen and with other workers, and a recent fire in a General Motors plant. Other labor articles presented the reflections of a West Virginia coal miner and a report on German workers. The front-pager, "The Beria Purge," issued a lengthy critique of Soviet Communism, while another front-page article reported on Lucille Ball's recent appearance before the House Un-American Activities Committee. Two workers wrote about racial dynamics—particularly between white women and black men—in their respective plants, while a cartoon titled "Up from Under" on the front page added a comic commentary on race relations. It depicted two women, one African American and one white, awaiting the arrival of their coal miner husbands. As the men approach, both covered in black soot, one woman remarks to the other, "Do you think that we'll get them mixed up again?" The recently released Kinsey Report garnered brief statements in "Viewing and Reviewing" and an analysis on the women's page.

Jimmy's contribution to the inaugural issue anchored the "Special Negro News" page. He wrote the lead article, "I Talk about What I Please—To Whom I Please," about an incident in his factory, the Chrysler Jefferson Avenue assembly plant, involving a conversation between a white woman and a black man. The woman, an assembly line worker, went outside during her break and asked the man, a jitney truck driver, for the time. The man and woman learned that they were both from Tennessee and struck up a lively conversation. Her foreman, however, took exception to this transgression of racial and gender conventions, rounding up other white men in the department, who rushed outside with him to intervene. "You can't talk to this woman," they told the black man. "You got no business talking to her. You just go on with your truck." The black man, "being very mild," simply replied, "OK," and returned to work. But the matter did not end there, as the foreman spoke to the black man's foreman, seeking to get him fired. Word spread through the plant, and many black workers became upset, saying, "This foreman's trying to start trouble here, and we got to do something about him. He's the guy that needs to be punished." The black worker did nothing wrong, they insisted, so the company "better not say anything to him."[10] He was called into the office, but no action was taken against him because the black workers, demanding that the union get involved, forced the chief steward to talk with the foreman, leading ultimately to the matter being dropped.

The main point of the article was to highlight in this series of events the assertion of black male workers (and secondarily the muted response of the union), but Jimmy also pointed to some of the gender implications of the story. He closed the article by explaining how the white workers who had gone with the foreman to stop the conversation also came "under pressure" from the black workers in their department who "were giving them hell" for the stance they had taken. This led one of the white workers, who "wanted to get in right with" his black shopmates, to say, "Look, I didn't know this girl was going to start all this trouble. I'll take her back down to Tennessee." This, of course, was an unsatisfactory and unsettling response to the situation. It placed the blame for the incident on the woman, not on the foreman and white male workers in her department, and thereby reinforced the racist and sexist precepts that led to the altercation in the first place. The article does not say how the black workers responded to the man's statement, but it does report the woman's response: "You ain't taking me no place." Jimmy closed the piece with a brief comment on the depth of the man's patriarchal presumption: "The peculiar thing about it, this girl was no relation to him, no wife or nothing, he was just going to take her back to Tennessee."[11] With this, Jimmy hinted at the type of analysis that readers found in abundance in the women's section.

The lead article in that section in the first issue, "A New Relationship," presented an especially forward-looking approach to gender dynamics.[12] It also articulated, perhaps better than any other piece in the issue, the paper's vision of a new society coming into being. The article begins with the author relating a story told to her by a friend about a "time that her husband took off his belt and was going to beat her." The friend sat down on the bed and told him, "O.K., go ahead, beat the hell out of me. But sometime you're going to have to go to sleep. And when you do, I'll butcher you." In the face of this threat, the man "put his belt back on." The article cites this as an example of changing patterns that were "breaking up old thoughts, attitudes and feelings of women toward men and men toward women." The article discusses the meaning of marriage, which the writer distills down to consideration and sharing, and presents an egalitarian ethos for marital life not frequently articulated in the early 1950s: "When a woman says . . . she wants to share things with her husband, she doesn't mean she has half and he has half. She means much more than that. She means that they must share their lives and their experiences together; that they must work together for the things that they want; that they must share the decisions of the family and nobody is to be boss."[13] This, the article explains, reflects that women are increasingly coming to clarify their ideas about what a marriage should be, their determination to work toward realizing this, and their willingness to leave unsatisfactory marriages.

This article illustrated the key function of *Correspondence*'s women's page, namely, to expose the tensions and antagonisms that arise as new ideas clash with old ones and as new social relations replace old ones. The writer asserted, "Divorce rates will not be statistics but the struggles of men and women to live together in a new way." Indeed, the article concludes with a statement reaffirming the vision of social transformation upon which *Correspondence* was founded and the paper's intended role in realizing that vision: "Over a cup of coffee, in the factory, during the daily workday of a housewife, and her husband's eight hour day—here is where new attitudes, a whole new way of life is emerging. Our newspaper is part of this. And this is where these new ideas, attitudes, and a whole new way of life will appear."[14]

Correspondence solicited responses from readers to the paper's debut and published them in the second issue under the banner "Readers Say What They Think of the First Issue." Reflecting the importance that the paper assigned to the thoughts of its readers, these comments appeared on the front page and continued in the middle of the editorial page (the space that "Readers' Views" would occupy in coming issues). Signed with descriptions such as "Woman Reader," "Negro Housewife," "A Young Guy," "Ford Worker," or simply "Reader," many were short, some just a sentence or two. They offered a mixture of criticism and praise, with some finding fault with specific features or aspects of the paper—a few of them offering concrete suggestions for future issues—but on balance the response was positive. For example, "Woman Reader" from Morgantown, West Virginia, offered praise that surely gave the organization confidence that they were realizing their objective: "What struck me about the paper," she wrote, "is that there was hardly a section that you could not turn to with any person and say, 'Here is your life.'"[15]

The organization placed a high value on this commentary. The significance of these responses rested not so much in what readers said *about* the paper as in what the comments revealed about readers' level of engagement *with* the paper. Members of the organization solicited comments, and some responses likely came from people who were friends of the organization or in some way loosely affiliated with it. Therefore, these were not, in the main, the spontaneous and random reactions of anonymous readers, as in more traditional letters to the editor. Rather, the comments in "Readers Say What They Think of the First Issue" resulted from and reflected a more direct interaction between the paper (through members of the organization) and its readers. This was a direct effort to build precisely the type of dialogic process—in a word, correspondence—hoped for by the organization. As one of the group's internal documents asserted, "The form of the paper is correspondence, that is to say: *dialogue*."[16]

To deepen readers' participation in the paper, the organization created a section called "Building Correspondence," designed to convey the process by which the paper was published, highlight the role of readers within that process, and engage the widest possible segment of the readership in solving the problems of maintaining and strengthening the paper. The first installment of "Building Correspondence" appeared in the third issue of the paper. It declared, "*Correspondence* is a paper written, edited, and circulated by its readers."[17] This statement—which by the beginning of 1954 graced the masthead of every issue—subtly misrepresented the actual dynamics behind the paper, downplaying the fact that an organization conceived of the paper and remained primarily responsible for its publication. It nonetheless highlighted a crucial fact of *Correspondence*'s existence: readers participated in the production of the paper by writing for it, participating in local editorial committees, distributing it among their neighbors and coworkers, supporting it through subscriptions, and soliciting new subscribers. In the coming issues, "Building Correspondence" carried reports on many of these activities—particularly efforts to increase the circulation and distribution of the paper, but also things such as fund-raising parties—thereby ensuring that some discussion of the week-to-week functioning of the paper appeared in every issue. "Building Correspondence" also addressed problems such as securing subscriptions, increasing circulation, and financing the paper, problems that a paper predicated, as *Correspondence* was, on the active and increasing participation of the readership, would predictably encounter. Indeed, the paper's relationship to its readers proved to be at once it most unique feature and the source of enduring debate and difficulties.

These difficulties contained both practical and philosophical dimensions. As to the former, the organization consistently struggled to attract people in large numbers to write for the paper and participate in the editorial committees. "The fact is," they had to admit after ten months of publishing, "that despite its intentions *Correspondence* is not really being written and edited by its readers."[18] The editor reported 3,000 to 4,000 regular readers, but "no more than 100" of them "are seriously writing for the paper." Thus, approximately 3 percent of readers actively wrote for the paper—a much smaller yield than the organization envisioned, to be sure. Among those who did write for the paper, some voiced reservations about or objections to the paper's political projections and journalistic choices, thereby heightening the philosophical dimensions of the paper's difficulties. From the organization's belief in the self-activity and self-organization of the working class followed the paper's determination not to put forward any particular program or plan but instead to be an organ for the unencumbered expression of workers and ordinary people. "We are not out 'to lead,'"[19] the editor, Johnny Zupan, explained in one issue. Yet, many readers found the absence of a clear program or political line in the paper to be problematic. This was true as early as the fourth issue. Its front page carried a "Statement of the Editor" responding to readers who complained that *Correspondence* was filled with grievances or griping and questioned the paper's utility. "What good does it do to just write?" asked one reader. "It's just a beef if you are not ready to do something about it."[20] Drawing on the history and authority of the early Congress of Industrial Organizations (CIO), Zupan reasserted the value of workers' articulating their grievances and the political ends to which the paper was committed:

> Workers in the modern mass production industries went for years living under abuses before they finally were able to do something about it. But the organization that they established to do something about it didn't spring from nowhere. A large part of that struggle was workers letting each other know how they felt about their conditions and what they thought should be done about it.
>
> The function of *Correspondence* is to provide a framework in which these dissatisfactions can be expressed *freely*. Out of this *freedom* to express dissatisfactions will crystallize ideas. When enough are agreed on what ought to be done, then there will develop the organization that will correspond to the needs and necessities of the day. That was the way of the CIO; that will be the way of any serious workers' organization that is determined "to do something about it."[21]

Zupan's response by no means settled the matter. He addressed these criticisms again in the very next issue, and they continued to arise over the ensuing months. In April, with six months of publishing the paper behind them, the editor reported that "in almost every issue" readers had issued "repeated complaints" about *Correspondence*: "What is the purpose of the paper? What good does it do to write for the paper? Or, what is all the griping about?" Zupan responded to these challenges in "Our Aim and Our Program," an editorial that defended the paper's vision and in the process articulated its politics. "Yes, it is true we propose no program," he wrote. "It's also true that we don't tell workers, Negroes, and others, how or for what to struggle. On the other hand, we do have ideas. What are the ideas that we have? The main and most important one is that no one, absolutely no one, except the workers and the millions of others who go along with the workers, can settle the questions of war, depression and totalitarianism." Emphasizing the point, Zupan added, "The paper considers that what the workers have to say is what is decisive."[22]

This full devotion to workers produced a wide-ranging and often engaging look at the American working class. Pieces by and about workers appeared throughout every issue, including the "Worker's Journal" on the front page, the labor section (which usually covered two and a half pages, nearly a quarter of each issue), and "Readers' Views." In addition, labor-related articles or pieces by workers regularly appeared as the front-pager and on the editorial, "Special Negro News," and women's pages. This material showcased the experiences and perspectives of people working in a wide range of industries and geographic locations. Not surprisingly, Detroit autoworkers figured frequently and prominently among them, as nearly every issue related firsthand accounts of life in auto factories (particularly Chrysler and Ford) and ruminations on speed-up and other work conditions, the threat of layoffs and the pall of unemployment, the foibles of foremen, or the weaknesses of the union. This gave the paper grounding in the rich cultural experience of working-class Detroit. At the same time, the experiences and observations of workers in other places and industries also filled the pages of *Correspondence*, giving the paper something of a multiregional and multi-industry, if not fully national, scope. For example, the Correspondence committee in West Virginia produced a regular feature appearing in the labor section on miners called "Coal and Its People." More broadly, any given issue might contain articles from a New York waterfront worker, railway workers in various cities, an oil worker in Los Angeles, or a Pittsburgh steel mill worker.

While industrial workers such as autoworkers and coal miners—the type of workers who had formed the foundation of the CIO in the 1930s and who in the 1950s constituted the center of the working class, both ideologically and practically—enjoyed pride of place in the pages of *Correspondence*, the paper's commitment to "ordinary people" and its fierce opposition to bureaucracy ensured that it also gave voice to a much wider spectrum of workers and people from various walks of life. This included articles from people employed in such diverse occupations as cab driver, waitress, dishwasher, bus driver, New York City transit worker, office worker, and private secretary. Women identifying themselves as housewives frequently wrote for the paper. Occasionally even small business owners (such as an "Owner of a Barbecue Shop") contributed articles to the paper. Some people wrote first-person narratives relating personal experiences on the job or at home, in the process sharing aspects of their lives. Some wrote about their experiences (and struggles) with layoffs and unemployment. Others contributed to one of the paper's features, such as the "Family Budget," a series appearing in the labor section in which families of different types reported their weekly income and expenditures. Examples included the budgets of "An Average Worker's Family," a "Miner with Five Dependents," a "Working Couple," and a "Skilled Worker."

Correspondence also attempted to incorporate the experiences and voices of people of color. A "Special Mexican-American Feature" on the youth page of an early issue included several articles by and about Chicano youth in Los Angeles.[23] Another issue carried a feature on "Puerto Ricans in America" that addressed the Puerto Rican nationalist movement and related the experiences and perspective of a Puerto Rican migrant to New York.[24] In the spring and summer of 1954, the paper ran a five-part series by a Japanese American on "Life in an American Concentration Camp."[25] The author, a Nisei (second-generation Japanese American) who was a school child in San Francisco at the time of the Pearl Harbor attack, gives an engaging and informative account of internment, taking readers through the many steps in the process and recounting the experience as endured by him and his family.

The women's page of another issue carried a compelling if disturbing article titled "They Wanted Only Boys," about a woman with striking similarities to Grace's mother. An unidentified narrator tells the story of a Chinese woman who came to the United States around 1910:

Her husband, who had made some money in America, came to
China and bought her. She didn't want to leave her sick mother,

but with the money there was a chance her mother could recover. On the American ship her first daughter was born, but her husband wanted to sell it, or give it away. She refused and started to yell. Her husband allowed her to keep it as he was afraid of what the other passengers, some Chinese but mostly Americans, would think, say, or do.

She said that in China, at that time, the women would have their babies while helping their husbands in the fields, plowing, digging, and so on. If it were a girl, they would sometimes bury it rather than see it given away or sold into slavery. The men wanted only boys so they could help in the fields or get out to work to bring money in.[26]

The husband retained these "old fashioned Chinese ideas" as the couple made their lives in the United States. Yet, the woman increasingly identified with her new country and came to see herself as an American. After their children were grown, she left her husband. This article shows how *Correspondence* sought to draw out political meaning from personal experiences and narratives. Most of the short piece detailed the alienation and dehumanization that the woman felt as an immigrant bride, but it ended with an affirmation of her determination to go beyond these confines. For *Correspondence*, the woman's embrace of an American identity and decision to leave her husband made hers a story of self-actualization.

This story paralleled that of Grace's own family, as discussed in chapter 3. Like the husband in the story, Grace's father came to United States, earned money, then returned to China for a wife, bringing Grace's mother back to the United States with him at the beginning of the second decade of the twentieth century. In the story, the husband bought his wife; in the case of Grace's parents, the marriage was arranged by her mother's "evil" uncle, who had previously "sold her as a slave" to wealthy people in their village.[27] Grace's mother and the woman in the story each gave birth to their first child, a girl, on the ship bringing them to the United States. While Grace did not report that her father wanted to give this child away, as the husband in the story does, Grace did later recount an anecdote from her own experience that reflected this disregard and dismissal of girls: "I was born above my father's Chinese American restaurant. . . . When I cried, the waiters used to say, 'Leave her on the hillside to die. She's only a girl.'"[28] Grace's mother also developed a relationship to America and American identity mirroring that of the protagonist of the story. "She fell in love with America," Grace said of her mother, who started "dreaming of the day when her children would be grown so that she could go to school to learn how to read and write enough English to become an American citizen in her own right."[29] Finally, Grace's mother left her husband after Grace and her siblings grew to adulthood, just as the woman in the story did.

It is not clear what, if any, role Grace played in producing the article or if she had any connection to the woman whose life it chronicles, but she surely would have recognized the struggles and decisions described in the piece. As a child of Chinese immigrants, Grace watched and later analyzed the dynamics of her parents' relationship to their new country and to each other. Of course she faced a parallel but unique set of questions, those that confront the second-generation immigrant regarding nationality and ethnic identity. When this article appeared in 1954, Grace was thirty-eight years old and practiced in, if still not fully comfortable with, negotiating her presumed Chinese and American identities. In the Johnson-Forest Tendency (JFT) she had forged a political identity that downplayed and in some respects superseded her ethnic and racial identity. Over the coming decade, through working on *Correspondence* and through her relationship with Jimmy, she would solidify this transmutation of her identity, where her Chinese American ethnicity was secondary to and overshadowed by her identity as an American revolutionary.

By contrast, Jimmy's racial identity directly motivated his political engagement and shaped his emerging identity as an American revolutionary. His background and early life experiences had laid the groundwork for his racial consciousness, which in turn served as a foundation upon which he forged his political identity during the 1940s. While *Correspondence* helped Grace construct a political identity that was largely independent of her ethnicity, for Jimmy the paper facilitated the inverse, providing him with a space where his racial and political identities not only reinforced each other but merged seamlessly together. In the pages of *Correspondence* as well as in editorial meetings, he sharply articulated his interpretation of black politics and in the process shaped the paper's approach to the black struggle and its position on race in American life. Jimmy was the strongest and most active force directing the paper's attention to black history and politics, though his contributions to the paper went well beyond this; as important as he was for the SNN page and the paper's approach to black history and politics, he was instrumental in nearly every aspect of the paper.

Living and Breathing the Paper

Everyone involved with *Correspondence* took notice of Jimmy's deep commitment to the paper and his immense contributions to it. In May 1954, Jimmy's comrades elected him to the paper's Resident Editorial Board (REB), bringing him into the leadership of the organization.[30] In the eight months of the paper's existence to that point, he had been fully engaged in all dimensions of the paper, embodying the dynamic interaction with readers that the group called "going out and writing in."[31] As described in an editorial board meeting, "going out means going back to our subscribers and asking them to renew their subscriptions and ask *their* friends to subscribe, establishing a relationship with them, living our lives with them and having them live their lives with us, encouraging them to involve *their social groups* in the activity around the paper."[32] Jimmy emerged as one of the most active and successful members of the group in soliciting subscriptions, developing a consistent string of coworkers and neighbors with whom he discussed the paper and who submitted material. According to one of the informants who tracked Jimmy's activities for the FBI, Jimmy "was doing the bulk of the work in passing out the *Correspondence*, obtaining subscriptions and making contacts."[33] Other informants reported specific numbers illustrating this: during one week in January, Jimmy sold 38 issues and secured two subscriptions to the paper; between January 10 and March 28, he sold 285 single copies and brought in twenty-six subscriptions.[34]

He was also an energetic contributor. In addition to his column on the "Special Negro News" (SNN) page, Jimmy wrote several other pieces, particularly on the labor page. He also brought in submissions from his coworkers, neighbors, and other readers. These appeared throughout the paper, such as in the SNN section, the labor section, and the "Readers' Views" section. Johnny Zupan called the "Readers' Views" installments that Jimmy assembled the best because they presented "just what the workers say," and he identified them as the kind of material "that will make the paper."[35] Jimmy was responsible for multiple submissions for each issue of the paper. For example, he had twenty-three items and articles in the issue published at the time he joined the REB. This number and the heavy responsibility it represented came up for discussion at the next REB meeting, during which Dunayevskaya pressed for some relief for Jimmy, "whom we have so overburdened with work."[36] Whatever the burden he felt, Jimmy continued to devote himself to the paper. "I can't put my finger on any one particular thing," he said, talking about the reason for this devotion during another REB meeting. "I just know I feel proud as hell of the paper."[37]

Dunayevskaya singled Jimmy out for praise in May 1954. In a report assessing the paper, she said that Jimmy "has lived and breathed the paper" from the moment they began publishing it. She called him the group's "professional subgetter," not only because he "chalked up the most" subscriptions, but because he did so in an integrated and holistic way that made "no distinction whatever between subgetting, eliciting articles for the paper, writing himself, and being on the local editorial board for labor and Negro sections." She held him up as an exemplar for his efforts in every sphere of the paper, "from the column he writes for the Negro page of which he is also an editor, to the Reader's Views he gathers in the shop and in the neighborhood . . . from the labor articles he writes to the dozens of people he brings to socials."[38] The socials to which she referred were informal gatherings and parties that the organization held to broaden its social interactions and deepen the paper's community ties.

Jimmy articulated his politics and those of the organization in his regular column on the "Special Negro News" page written under the pen name Al Whitney. The most strident and consistent themes of his column were his critical assessment of established black leadership, the changing relationship between these leaders and the black masses, and the relative roles of leaders and masses in the rising black struggle. He also frequently wrote about organized labor, particularly in relation to black workers and the black struggle. He combined all of these in the first installment of his column, which appeared in the January 23, 1954, issue of the paper. Titled "Talent for Sale," it chastised Walter White, head of the National Association for the Advancement of Colored People (NAACP), and labor leader Walter Reuther, for typifying the status-conscious and prestige-seeking leader. He said such leaders "are actually individualists" more focused on maintaining their lofty positions than on leading the Negro or class struggle. "They would sell anybody out just to stay in that atmosphere."[39] His next column, "Wasted Energy," took aim at the Detroit branch of the NAACP for its plans to hold a march to city hall to save the job of a member of the local black elite who served as a representative of the city's Negroes on the mayor's interracial commission. The NAACP, Jimmy said, so valued this type of position that it would mount a protest march "to fight for the job of this one person" but not for jobs for the larger black community. "That's the way these Talented Tenth act," he scolded, drawing on his own experience in the organization to make his point. "I remember the time we were having elections in the NAACP and they said they needed more lawyers and doctors and others who could speak with more authority rather than so many workers who always wanted to do something. I am quite sure they really want Negroes to get their rights," Jimmy wrote, but it was clear that the branch's leaders "want their rights too, and that is the right to speak with authority." The lesson for the masses was clear: "They not only have to fight white society; they have to fight this Talented Tenth bunch of Negroes who are also part of official society."[40]

Such criticism of the black elite and established black leadership appeared in nearly all of Jimmy's columns in the paper's first year of publication. For example, in "Negroes and Negro Organizations," he said that Negroes across the country were leaving organizations such as the NAACP, the National Urban League, and the CIO's Fair Employment Practices Committee because "they recognize that these organizations no longer satisfy their needs." These groups were actually "the first ones who [tried] to head off any Negro mass action," instead pushing more gradual approaches. However, "the Negro masses are aware of all the conditions in society and want no part of passive action. Mere words will not satisfy them, even when uttered by Negroes. . . . The era of 'Uncle Tom' is gone. A search for human needs and relations is the struggle of Negroes today."[41] In another column, Jimmy addressed what he saw as the futility of Negro leadership in the union: "Every year, just before election time, the white union leader comes around and gets some Negro to put on his slate." The mass of black workers will support him and vote for him because this represents an advancement, but when they go to him after he is elected, it becomes clear that he can or will do little. "After the election they will go to him and ask him to see what he can do about certain things concerning Negroes in the shop and he will say I'll talk it over with the other union leaders in the local. When they (the workers) ask him again (and they always have to ask him again for he doesn't come back himself) he always answers by saying that they're going to do something about it." This goes on for two or three months but then, after he has been in office for five or six months, "this same leader will begin to talk down to the Negroes and defend the union. This Negro leader may have been ever so sincere when he was running for election for this position, but he has to yield to the other union leaders and thus becomes corrupted in the process." Jimmy explained that he was not opposed to black leaders; rather, "what I am opposed to is the corruption that takes place when these leaders capitulate to this society. . . . When can a Negro leader take a position for Negro equality and remain a leader? From past experience, I can think of only a few. All I know is a new method has got to be worked out in regard to these leaders. This we are trying to do in *Correspondence*."[42]

Jimmy also used historical figures or the broader topic of Negro history to expose and examine the development of black leadership and the assertion of the black masses. He began a column titled "Negro Challenge" with a reference to Margaret Garner, who in 1856 escaped from slavery in Kentucky with her family. Facing imminent capture and a return to enslavement, Garner chose to kill her two-year-old daughter, "giving [her] back to [her] Maker," Jimmy wrote, "rather than give [her] to slavery." Jimmy found in Garner's act of infanticide a dramatic antecedent to the current resolve among black people to finally end the subordination that lingered on from Garner's day. Today, among black people everywhere, he wrote, there was a common refrain: "I'm fighting and working that my son will not have to go through what I had to endure." He described this simple statement as "the expression of a fighting race, not to be subdued under the footsteps of slavery and servitude."[43] Thus, Jimmy sought to link the historical resistance to slavery to an emergent sensibility and determination among black people one century later to challenge and uproot the contemporary mechanisms of black subordination.

Months before this column, Jimmy used the occasion of Negro History Week to engage his readers in a consideration of the political uses of black people's historical experiences. The pioneering black historian Carter G. Woodson and his organization, the Association for the Study of Negro Life and History, launched Negro History Week (the forerunner to Black History Month) in February 1926, three months before Jimmy reached his seventh birthday. Designed to counter the elision and denigration of African Americans in the standard narratives of the nation's past by celebrating the group's exceptional individuals, group achievements, and collective contributions to the country, this annual celebration concentrated the dynamics and contradictions of race in Jimmy's early years. "I'll always remember my school days, when on this week there would be much preparation, just as there is for Christmas," he wrote. "This was the only time I had an opportunity to really find out about Negro people, their accomplishments, and their struggles for recognition of their human dignity. But somehow, after this week I never noticed any change in Negro and white relations." Instead, Negro History Week seemed to reinforce the way things were. The celebrations at his school followed a familiar format: "There would be two or more speakers who were invited to speak on Negro history that week, generally one was a Negro and one was white. Each speaker would go back into history and pick out some Negro figure and praise him to us. Most of the time it was Booker T. Washington or George Washington Carver." Jimmy felt pride hearing about the accomplishments of these historical figures, but he was also "much upset over" the way that the speakers emphasized the personal behavior of these figures. "I would be very confused when it was all over," Jimmy explained.[44]

The column goes on to describe how later, as a young man, Jimmy experienced this same frustration in relation to boxing champion and hero Joe Louis. "I had a swelling pride in him as a fighter, especially when he was in the ring fighting a white. I would be so nervous, I would be trembling until the fight was over. I felt proud of him for he was a Negro and he was disproving everything that was said about Negroes' inability to do things and proving Negroes were equal to all in every way." But white people sought to uphold a different image of Joe Louis. "Whenever he was talked about by white society for what he meant to Negroes," Jimmy complained, whites praised Louis as a model of "Negro behavior" who "advanced his race from his personal conduct." White people sought to define and restrict Louis's meaning for black people, just as was done with the historical figures presented during the Negro History Week celebrations of Jimmy's youth. By focusing on Louis's behavior and personal conduct—and not his powerful refutation of black inferiority or the racial pride he generated—white people were essentially praising the boxer for staying in his "place," Jimmy said. "Negroes detest the idea that they have a 'place,'" Jimmy demanded, but "capitalist society has a standard policy to never mention any Negroes who do not accept its idea that they have a 'place.' To me a Negro's 'place' is any 'place.'" The lesson to be gleaned from "Viewing Negro History Week," as Jimmy titled his column, was the duality of black history. It could be used to instill racial pride, or to reinforce racial subjugation; it could challenge the idea of black inferiority or justify it. Jimmy closed the column by saying: "I am proud of Negro History Week and what it is supposed to represent. It is the corrupt way of white society that I detest, which uses certain Negroes to portray what they would like Negroes to be."[45]

Jimmy's identification of the duality and conflicting uses of Negro history reflected a dialectical understanding of the Negro struggle. He presented this understanding in his December 11, 1954 column, "Tension and

Social Change." It does not use the word "dialectic" (or the related terms "thesis," "antithesis," and "synthesis"), but it clearly articulates a concept of change driven by the resolution of internal conflicts. "What has seemed to be progress for the Negro in America, better housing and job opportunity, has been just the opposite," he wrote, "for the better job and housing has been the basis for the ever-increasing demand by Negroes for a better life. Pressure from Negroes which once came only sporadically, is constant now and the tension is constant also." Here, as in the title and throughout the piece, Jimmy's use of "tension" might be read as capturing the Marxist "contradiction" at the heart of the dialectical process. "What do I see in this tension?" Jimmy asked. "Somebody has to yield in any tense situation. And that is what makes change take place in any society, whether people like it or don't like it. It breaks down the old ideas and opinions and leads to the new."[46]

Jimmy's column helped set the tone for the "Special Negro News" (SNN) page, which ensured a constant presence of African American voices in the paper.[47] The page also encouraged readers to grapple with the problems of race relations and segregation. While the SNN drew material from across the country, printing articles on such topics as police brutality in Pittsburgh, housing and "the Negro's living conditions" in Chicago, and segregation in Los Angeles, it carried many pieces on Detroit. They spoke to a range of experiences and topics, with common themes being social and political issues of the day. For example, in one issue readers found commentary on the recent congressional primary victory of Detroit businessman and politician Charles C. Diggs Jr., soon to be Michigan's first black congressperson. The same issue ran a first-person account of police brutality. "I was lying in bed in my own home. It was about 11 P.M.," the article began. "The police woke me up by slapping me in the face. They asked me where the gun was at. I said 'What are you talking about? What are you doing in my house?'"[48] Another issue carried an article titled "Housing Shortage—They Move You with Bulldozers," giving the author's personal experience with the displacement caused by urban renewal and highway construction that was then impacting thousands of families. "I was living in a house where the new highway was supposed to come through. They gave me three months to move. But we couldn't find a place and we had to go to court to see how much longer they would let us stay in the house. The judge told us that he would give us one more month to stay there, and if we would not be out by the end of that time, he would send bulldozers out to each house and let them be mowed down." The family was forced to "get a place that we didn't want" that charged an exorbitant rent. This expense, combined with "high priced food" and other expenses, posed an acute but sadly familiar hardship. "The cost of living is now so high," the author lamented, that it "takes up each week's pay and leaves not one cent to reach from one pay to the other. We just can't see no way out."[49]

Contributors to the SNN regularly ridiculed or chastised the racial attitudes and racially coded practices of white Americans, including the mechanics of segregation in both the North and the South. This was sometimes expressed with humor, such as in a cartoon depicting a black man in a boat fishing while a white man on the nearby dock, standing next to a sign that reads "Boats Reserved for Whites Only," angrily shakes his fist. The caption to the cartoon says, "Reserved? But I don't see a sign on the water."[50] In more direct ways, too, the SNN expressed African Americans' determination to expose and thwart segregation, such as an editorial on segregation that asserted freedom was the heart of the matter: "The freedom to do what [the Negro] wants to do, when he wants to do it. It's not that he wants to be with whites, it's not that he thinks he's white and not that he wants to marry whites."[51] Particularly strong language occasionally punctuated such sentiments, as in a short piece titled "Americanism" that told of one person's anger with the interconnected and contradictory logic of the Cold War, racial antagonism, and urban transformation in 1950s American political culture. He had watched televised images of "the first Negro family moving into a new housing project in Chicago" where "a crowd of whites [was] throwing stones and other things. They were standing there booing and shouting. Then they have the nerve to tell me about Communism. The Communists aren't doing this to me. They are. When things like that happen, I feel like killing all whites I see."[52]

The "Special Negro News" page occasioned debate among readers in the pages of *Correspondence*. This is perhaps not surprising given the paper's interracial audience. Nonetheless, it posed a conundrum. While the organization saw the SNN as a vital component to its political project and journalistic mission, readers raised sharp questions about its content and usefulness. Criticism came quickly. In just the fourth issue, *Correspondence* printed a full page of readers' comments under the banner "Say Negro News Dominates Paper."[53] Many of those writing in complained that the paper devoted too much space and attention to African Americans. "I noticed that about two-thirds of the paper had something about the Negroes," wrote one reader, with some exaggeration. "I wouldn't like to see the Negro question dominate the paper." Others challenged the utility or purpose of the page itself, as this sympathetic but no less skeptical reader did: "I can understand why some of the colored people from the South write letters that express hatred for the whites. It is something that has embedded itself deep in the minds of the writers. I don't doubt in the least that all this is true, but what does living in the past profit us? We should all strive to understand each other and unite in the cause for freedom." There were also outright detractors who voiced clear opposition to the very idea of a Negro page and the promotion of racial harmony. "Colored people don't need any pillows to rest on," railed one letter. "They are doing all right on their own. We needn't make it our business to promote this Negro-white relations." This reader exhibited a white racial defensiveness that others shared: "It's not my fault that I'm white. Whatever color people are, they are the same. I thought that's what we were trying to say all along, but these articles just try to divide people." Predictably perhaps, the racial anxieties of the times led at least one reader to detect in the paper's racial politics a more sinister motive: "All the paper wants to do is promote sex relations between Negro men and white women."[54] Such rhetoric soon yielded to more reasoned debate, as discussions of the merits of the SNN page continued in subsequent issues.

A month later *Correspondence* ran on the front page an editorial statement, "On the Negro Discussion," to address the "considerable criticism from our readers protesting the dominance of the Negro question in the paper and the reduction of the question to a non-political level."[55] The editor acknowledged the validity of the criticism, yet at the same time assured readers that the paper recognized the importance and complexity of the Negro Question. "We believe that the Negroes have an independent role to play in their own emancipation, and a double role, both as workers and as Negroes, in the emancipation of the American workers and the great body of American people." He also defended the paper against some of the criticism: "It is not a question of 'sympathetic treatment' of the Negro question. The Negro is not out for sympathy. He is engaged, every day, in the factory and out of it, in a struggle for equality, from upgrading to housing to politics. . . . The point is that his continuous struggles bring into question the whole capitalist system. The question therefore is: what is your attitude to these independent struggles.[56]

The SNN carried letters from readers in subsequent issues that continued to discuss and debate the page's merits. These letters, which primarily were from black readers, appeared under a banner labeled "What Do You Think?" that functioned as a smaller, SNN-focused version of "Readers' Views." While some said that having a separate Negro page was akin to segregation, many more expressed support for the page. "I like to see a Special Negro Page," wrote one, "because Negroes are in a special category in American society." Another reader wrote, "Everybody must know that Negroes say things to each other that they don't say to whites. I see the Special Negro Page as a place where Negroes can say what they don't ordinarily say to whites, and where they can talk to each other, straight." Some black readers supported the existence of the page, but thought the word "special" should be removed. As a reader identified as a "Young Negro Woman" put it, "What goes on every day in Negro life is not special. It would be special if it were a race riot or something." She drew a distinction between *Correspondence* and the mainstream daily press, in which the only articles on Negroes "slander them or show in some form that they are inhuman."[57] The strongest rebuttal to this line of thinking came from a member of Correspondence, Simon Owens, writing under his pseudonym Charles Denby. In the June 12, 1954, edition of "What Do You Think?" he took exception to those who "say there is nothing special about Negro life, Negroes do not have special problems," and who therefore wanted to change the name of the page. This was a slight misrepresentation of a previous reader's position, but it served as a useful point of departure for Owens's spirited defense of the page and its name. "I would like to ask those who say this, is there one Negro in the U.S. that has all the freedom privileges, without any form of segregation that the least white has? That makes it special; and the Negroes did not create it, they do not want it, but it is forced upon them. And in many instances they alone, or leading the way, have carried out tremendous struggles combating it down through history and at present. When they are fully integrated into American white society, then you can change the name of this page."[58]

The strongest criticism of the SNN came from a "Firm Supporter" in New York who wrote a letter challenging the page to capture "the Negro struggle and its social implications for the country as a whole."[59] The SNN carried the letter with an accompanying editor's note explaining that they took very seriously this "fundamental criticism of the Negro page." They decided to print the letter in its entirety "because of its importance . . . and ask our readers to study it and write us their opinions on the points raised."[60] "Your Negro page is in a serious mess," the letter began. "All you are showing is the Negroes suffering from prejudice and oppression. But the fact that Negroes suffer from prejudice and oppression compels them to organize themselves and live in a way which is a positive contribution to the struggle of the American people as a whole. These struggles frequently show others how to meet their own problems. That is what your page has not got." According to the writer, this unique character of the black struggle—that African Americans experienced a unique form of racial oppression, but their response to it had a universal quality—held the key to the debate over the usefulness of the paper. "If your separate section emphasizes ways and means Negroes have developed in the struggle against the common oppressor, everybody would read it, and feel himself vitally involved." The writer affirmed the "undoubted need for a separate Negro section," but urged the paper not to fall in the pattern of highlighting oppression and then citing historical examples "of how Negroes struggle." "You have not got to go back to history," he continued. "The Negro is carrying on historical struggles today. But the whole point of his struggles is that today they have a deep social significance. It is these struggles and their significance that you have to put forward and your Negro page will be a great success."[61]

"Firm Supporter" offered the issue of housing in Detroit as an example of where the "Special Negro News" page fell short of its potential. Citing the article "Housing Shortage—They Move You with Bulldozers" (described above), the writer says the SNN had amply shown "the fact that Negroes are being pushed around," but the page showed nothing of their response. The result was a story of discrimination, which was "sad indeed," but "that is only half the story." The missing half was how African American communities, forced to buy houses at elevated prices, regularly held "note parties" to help each other meet their monthly house payments. "In this way they have organized their social life not just for recreation but as a means of coping with prejudice cooperatively. Without any fuss or leadership Negroes have simply organized themselves to meet a concrete political situation."[62] While ostensibly a critique of the SNN, this letter actually articulated quite well the paper's emphasis on spontaneity and self-activity. Moreover, the analysis was consistent with the paper's approach to the Negro Question.

The paper's commitment to the black struggle also found expression in occasional references to historical figures. A short piece on Crispus Attucks, "the first well known Negro in American history," chronicled his contributions to revolutionary-era Boston and labeled him the very embodiment of the idea of freedom that the new American nation gave "to the 18th century world."[63] Dunayevskaya drew on the historical authority of David Walker and his famous "Appeal" in a column asserting the paper's revolutionary potential. Linking Walker's widely distributed antislavery tract with *Correspondence*'s own political project, she wrote that the "pamphlet gave the reader back his own feelings and experiences in a form that he could recognize as changing history in a fundamental way. . . . Walker's pamphlet is part of our history and *Correspondence* is part of that proven method, which enables all the insignificant and obscure people in the world to clear their own minds from the hypnotism of the plans and programs put out by the elite, and trust only themselves to change their conditions of life in a fundamental way."[64]

Commentary in the pages of *Correspondence* tended to champion the Negro struggle for democratic rights as an especially powerful force in American life, touting in particular the potential of grassroots perspectives and initiatives of this struggle to transform not only the American racial landscape but also its political and social structures as well. The front page of the March 6, 1954, issue—the same issue in which the letter from "Firm Supporter" appeared—illustrated this perspective. The front-page lead article, "American Politics and the Negro," argued that the black struggle was helping to change "the whole face of American politics" by forging a crisis in—and even threatening to break up—the Democratic Party. "The politics of the continuous and always growing protests of Negroes against discrimination," the article declared, was "the most conspicuous example of that type of politics in the United States today" that can clear "away the old rubbish and [change] the fate of nations."[65] Accompanying the article was a cartoon titled "Always a Bridesmaid, Never a Bride," depicting the two political parties as male suitors, each with flowers in hand, courting a smiling woman in a dress bearing the word "Dixiecrat." Falling off to the side of the "liberal Dem" is a tearful woman identified as "Civil Liberty" who is being rejected in favor of the more desirable companion. The cartoon caption reads, "She was just a harmless flirtation. You are the one we cannot do without."[66]

Two months later, the U.S. Supreme Court decision in the *Brown v. Board of Education* case, handed down on May 17, 1954, refocused and intensified national attention on the place of black people in American life and politics. Coming just eight months into *Correspondence*'s publication history, the case elicited considerable commentary, analysis, and discussion in the paper. The *Correspondence* Resident Editorial Board (REB) had a "lively and broad" discussion of the political significance of the decision during its

May 25 meeting, out of which they agreed to immediately send out letters to friends in the South to solicit their reactions and opinions on the case as well as prepare other material on *Brown* for the June 12 issue.[67] This included Owens's "Worker's Journal" discussing the implications of the case (and thus departing from its usual first-person and labor-focused format), a letter from Kentucky describing how black communities in that state had already begun mobilizing to make the court's decision real in practice, and an editorial on the SNN page asserting that the decision—and "the determination of the Negro people" that animated it—had "shaken this old America from end to end."[68]

In addition, the "Readers' Views" section of that issue included fourteen comments on *Brown*. They presented an eclectic mix of opinion, though nearly all of them expressed support of, praise for, or gratification at the decision. "The struggle of the Negro people is solely responsible for the decision of the Supreme Court," wrote a Detroit autoworker. "I never did want to volunteer for any army or any fighting, but if anything starts in Georgia I will . . . go defend the rights of my people." A very different but complementary enthusiasm came from a "University President" in Washington, D.C. (an interesting identity given that the legal strategy behind *Brown* owed so much to Washington's Howard University), who proclaimed the case "the greatest intellectual gain made by the Negro in the past fifty years." Some readers saw clearly the Cold War context and international implications of the decision. A West Virginia miner, for example, called *Brown* "the best thing that could have happened. We go telling other people to clean their linens and we got our own homes dirty." A reader identified as an "African Student" from Washington, D.C., similarly opined, "I was amazed that in this 20th century when people talk of equality and liberty, discrimination still exists in the United States despite the fact that the U.S. shouts loudest in the United Nations against Communist tyranny." And a few predicted the hostility and resistance to come. "I'm not prejudiced," wrote an "Old-Timer" in Detroit, "but I'm from the deep South and I know the white people won't stand for it. There will be Civil War first." Even the very young, who would in time be cast as central characters in a violent and angry drama, received the message. "My principal was against [the *Brown* decision]," wrote a "Nine-Year-Old" from West Virginia. "He said when they come, if they give any trouble to grab a ball bat and hit them over the head."[69]

Jimmy devoted his SNN column to the *Brown* decision in each of the three issues immediately following its announcement. He addressed what he saw as the larger politics of the decision: its impact on the broad struggle against segregation, its relationship to grassroots mobilization, its implications for African Americans' evolving position relative to the national polity, and its meaning for black internal class dynamics. His columns dissented from the widely held view that *Brown* was a landmark decision, that it was a great victory with a clear and immediate impact, and that it alone signaled a major change. "The average Negro isn't excited about this decision," he wrote. "They figure it had to come. They figure passing the law won't be the last word anyhow."[70] Jimmy also argued in his columns that popular protest—"the power of the Negroes . . . in their day to day struggles demanding their rights"[71]—remained the most powerful force in the black struggle, in the wake of *Brown* no less than leading up to it. In the title of his June 12 column he labeled the verdict the "Supreme Court Indecision" because of the unspecified method of enforcement and still-uncertain impact, and in the column's title in the next issue he called it "A Decision of Necessity" in the face of domestic and international pressures. "They can 'if' and 'but' in the most backward part of the South," he wrote, "but the rolling tide of the Negroes in pursuit of their civil rights will not falter."[72] This "rolling tide," plus the rising pressure created by the independence struggles taking place throughout the colonial world, had compelled the unanimous Supreme Court ruling. Thus, *Brown* was properly understood as "another concession by the United States," designed "not to rectify the injustice of the past, but to justify their claim that they are a democracy. The average Negro knows this wasn't a decision of sympathetic feeling, but a decision of necessity. Just as Abraham Lincoln said, if he could save the Union and still keep slavery he would do that, but if to save the Union, slavery would have to be abolished, he would do that—so is the Supreme Court decision."[73]

Jimmy also wrote an editorial that boldly declared that *Brown* "was no gift to the Negro people."[74] Rather, the decision was simply "the rulers of America" yielding "in the face of the mounting rejection by millions of Negroes in the South of the old white supremacy doctrine." Titled "Talented Tenth Are Retreating," it took aim at "the so-called Negro leaders" with a critique in particular of Thurgood Marshall and the NAACP for their willingness to wait until September 1955 for the ruling to take effect, thus accommodating the nation's stalling in enforcement of the decision. By contrast, Jimmy said, actions and sentiments at the grassroots revealed a readiness to move faster and further than established leaders. "Since the decision, the southern Negroes have shown that they are preparing for non-segregated schools as soon as possible. At the same time the north-ern Negroes are watching what their southern brothers are doing. Should the southern Negroes start enforcing the Supreme Court decision, the northern Negroes will pour into the South to help their brothers." The editorial ends with a quip that, coming just two months after the ruling, would have surely been read by many as an irreverent if not completely unfair analysis of *Brown*'s driving force: "It looks as if Thurgood Marshall and the rest of the Negro pro-fessional people are more afraid of the Negro people making a law more than a piece of paper than of continued segregation and second class citizenship."[75]

The *Brown* decision continued to receive attention in *Correspondence* through much of the summer. The major theme of these pieces was that the case in and of itself did not mean much, that despite the initial (and con-tinuing) enthusiasm and sense of victory surrounding the ruling, its actual impact and thus its true meaning for African Americans depended in the first instance on enforcement (which was very much an open question in the months following the ruling) and, more broadly, on the continuing mo-bilization of black communities. An article in the July 10 issue titled "Labor Struggles and Negro Struggles" argued that *Brown* (like legal victories more generally) was the beginning, not the end, of the struggle. It drew parallels between the labor movement during the 1930s and the civil rights move-ment of the 1950s, highlighting the relationship between legal victories and popular struggles in each movement. The writer analogized *Brown* to the Norris-LaGuardia Act of 1932, which ended injunctions against strikes and boycotts. This law served as an early victory for workers' right to organize, but "it didn't follow automatically that the unions became a reality," the article explained. "It took much more than a law to establish unions. It was only by long serious and violent struggles that workers were able to estab-lish the CIO and make a reality of legal rights." Similarly, "the struggle to end segregation in schooling will not end with the Supreme Court ruling. The struggle of the Negroes against segregation, like that of workers to es-tablish unions, only begins."[76] The next issue carried a letter from a "Negro Housewife" that expressed little faith that the decision would be enforced.[77]

Grace in London

During the spring and summer of 1954, while Jimmy anchored *Correspon-dence*'s coverage of the *Brown* decision and domestic racial politics, Grace engaged the transnational political space of anticolonial agitation, nationalism, and African independence. Since leaving the United States and reset-tling in England in the summer of 1953, C. L. R. had maintained constant contact with his American comrades through frequent letters while also reconnecting with individuals, networks, and movements with which he had been associated during his first stay in England during the 1930s. It was during that initial six-year stay, when he worked with George Padmore and others in the International African Service Bureau, that C. L. R. first agitated for African independence and started developing his extensive Pan-African networks. Two decades later, he was again operating within this London-based network, but this time the agitation had grown to full-blown independence movements in several African countries. C. L. R. had direct contact with key African independence figures and leaders, particularly in the Gold Coast (soon to be Ghana) and Kenya, such as Mbiyu Koinange, a Kenyan nationalist leader living in London. Early in 1954, C. L. R. and his Correspondence comrades began planning a writing project with Koin-ange that would support the Kenyan struggle and serve as an intervention into an international debate created by the Mau Mau Uprising in Kenya. They decided that Grace and another Correspondence member, Filomena Daddario, would go to London to work with C. L. R. and Koinange on this project.[78] In March 1954, Grace left Detroit for New York and from there sailed to London.

Grace's four-month stay in London was an extension of her Correspon-dence work, much like her 1948 trip to Paris had been for the Johnson-Forest Tendency. In this case, she was deploying her writing and editing skills in collaboration with Koinange to produce an account of the Kenyan independence struggle to be published by Correspondence. Her presence in London also gave her and C. L. R. the chance to approximate the type of political collaboration they had shared in the United States before his forced departure the previous year. C. L. R. "subscribed to all of the news-papers," including the *London Times*, the *Daily Telegraph*, and the *Manchester Guardian*, "and we read them religiously," Grace recalled. They also went to cricket matches, met with some of the new activists with whom C. L. R. had recently made contact, and made two or three trips to Manchester to see the Pan-Africanist T. Ras Makonnen, his old comrade who, along with George Padmore and Kwame Nkrumah, had organized the famed Fifth Pan-African Congress in 1945.[79]

The FBI took notice of Grace's trip to London, just as it had with her trip to Paris six years earlier. The Detroit office learned of her plans to travel in

February and alerted the FBI director, J. Edgar Hoover, as well as the New York and Washington, D.C., offices.[80] The FBI agents tracking Grace knew that she had been in touch with C. L. R., and they correctly suspected that she would be connecting with him in London, but they apparently were unable to learn details about Grace's trip or track her activities while there. Indeed, the FBI seemed to be unaware that the purpose of Grace's trip was to collaborate with Koinange in producing an account of the Kenyan independence movement.

Koinange was, however, well known to U.S. (and British) officials.[81] The son of a chief who helped spark the Kenyan nationalist movement, Koinange traveled a path that was similar to that of other African independence leaders—his fellow Kenyan Jomo Kenyatta, Nigeria's Nnamdi Azikiwe, and Ghana's Nkrumah—who studied, agitated, and organized in the United States and Britain before returning home to lead nationalist movements. Koinange came to the United States in 1927 and attended Hampton Institute (now Hampton University) and then Ohio Wesleyan University, where he earned a bachelor's degree in political science in 1934. He continued his education at Columbia University Teachers College, earning a master's degree in 1936 (his first year there overlapped with Grace's final year as an undergraduate at Columbia's Barnard College). Koinange spent the next two years studying at Cambridge University in England, where he met Kenyatta and other African nationalists. In 1938, he returned home and helped to found Kenya Teachers' College, for which he served as president. This pivotal institution helped stimulate intellectual debates and political consciousness and attracted nationalists such as Kenyatta, who served as a teacher and administrator after he returned to the colony in 1946. Koinange also helped to found what became the Kenya African Union (KAU), a political organization that put forward a program of African self-government and eventually became the ruling party under the leadership of independent Kenya's first president, Kenyatta. In the fall of 1951, the KAU selected Koinange to lead a two-person delegation to London to petition the British government and the United Nations and to put the case of the Kenyan Africans before the British public. The next year, the colonial government issued a state of emergency in Kenya in response to an offensive of the Kenya Land and Freedom Army, labeled by some as the "Mau Mau." Colonial authorities used this as an opportunity to round up and detain many opponents of the white settlers and the colonial regime, including Koinange's father and other family members. Authorities also declared Koinange subject to arrest if he returned to the colony. He thus remained in London as the KAU representative.[82]

When Grace arrived to work with Koinange, he had earned the reputation for being "an uncompromising nationalist," in the words of the author of a book on Kenya just published in London. "Next to Kenyatta," the author explained, Koinange "is the most influential of the Kikuyu leaders."[83] Like much of the mainstream reporting on Kenya, this book sought to explain to a British audience the meaning of the Mau Mau Uprising, its "campaign of terrorism to drive the Europeans off the land that had once been African," and the resulting state of emergency declared by colonial authorities. Grace and Koinange's collaboration, by contrast, aimed to spread among American readers an awareness of the Kenyan people's long-simmering and now irrepressible struggle against a brutal colonial regime and its white settlers. Grace helped Koinange tell a story that proceeded not from his standing as a leader but rather from his relationship to the Kenyan masses and his knowledge of their actions. "What I want to tell here is how before the Emergency the Africans were trying to help themselves and make themselves part of the best that is in civilization," he wrote in the preface to the document they produced. "I want to tell people what my people were doing, of their own energies, how they were doing for themselves what the Government should have been doing for them. It is when you suppress these energies, which are the driving force of any civilization, that you have barbarism." Moreover, the story of Kenya's anticolonial revolt, he insisted, "concerns the whole of Africa."[84] Indeed, Grace, C. L. R., and their Correspondence comrades sought with this project to elevate and inspire support for the cause of African independence. The anticolonial uprisings and nationalist movements across the continent were for them further examples of the masses in motion and proof of global revolutionary activity.

When Grace left London in July, C. L. R. gave her a book as a parting gift. Inside, he wrote the inscription, "We know, we hope our friends know, the world outside will know." Many years later Grace would recall C. L. R.'s words as "typically enigmatic."[85] Cryptic as it was, it also reflected his confidence in the group's political vision. It captured the shared sense of political purpose that had animated Grace's trip to work with Koinange. When C. L. R. penned those words in the summer of 1954, Grace likely understood and agreed with the sentiment.

Kenya Sundays

Grace returned to Detroit in July 1954, bringing with her not only the manu-script that she and Koinange had completed over the preceding months, but also the determination to resume building the new life she had started making for herself in Detroit. The four months she spent in London amounted to roughly half the time she had lived in Detroit, and Grace was anxious to pick up where she had left off. This included her relationship with Jimmy.

As mentioned in the previous chapter, Jimmy and Grace had likely dis-cussed marriage before her departure for London. It is not clear what if any plans were set, but Jimmy and Grace were married very soon after her return to Detroit. They traveled to nearby Toledo, Ohio, where they were married by a justice of the peace on July 17, 1954. Their courtship had emerged out of their shared political work, and their continued political engagement would have the effect of deepening their relationship. Now, as a married couple, their personal partnership would come to be inseparable from their intellectual and political partnership.

Correspondence remained their primary political activity, but for the next several months, Grace and Jimmy took on the additional task of publishing, distributing, and promoting Koinange's manuscript, which they released in January 1955 as a booklet titled *The People of Kenya Speak for Themselves*. Grace was the driving force behind this effort, though Jimmy, who contin-ued to work full time at Chrysler on top of his political activity, joined her at crucial points. Her first task was to raise money for publication, and to do this they formed the Kenya Publication Fund. While separate, this fund was of a piece with the Correspondence organization. The group had been chronicling the Kenyan struggle throughout the year by running pieces in *Correspondence*, most of them appearing in the paper's "News and Views of the World" section. The first of these ran in the January 9, 1954, issue, before Grace left for London. Titled "Murder Inc.," it told of British soldiers killing Kenyan Africans for sport. "The units compete with one another and keep scorecards of 'kills,'" the piece reported. "There is the barbarism of the Mau Mau and there is the barbarism of the settlers and the Government," it continued. "But one barbarism is for freedom and the other for the per-petuation of oppression, race prejudice, and slavery."[86] This set the tone for the subsequent stories that described the treachery of the colonial regime, exposed the British empire's attempt to use the "white man's burden" argument to justify its "violent tenacity in Kenya," and extolled the mounting push for self-government among Africans in Kenya and elsewhere on the continent.[87] In September, *Correspondence* devoted the entire "News and Views of the World" section to printing a letter from Koinange to British prime minister Winston Churchill.

An article titled "The People Are a Mighty Fortress in East Africa" in the November 27, 1954, issue gave perhaps the strongest statement on the Kenyan struggle of all those appearing in *Correspondence*. "It has become the fashion, in the powerful English language newspapers of the Western world," the article began, "to call the Kikuyu people barbarians because they now fight for what is rightfully theirs in Kenya. They are called backward and uneducated, heathen and ungodly." The writer took exception to this misrepresentation of the Kenyan situation, and thus set out the purpose of the article: "It is necessary to brand the lie and tell the truth." This truth, the writer said, was to be found in the story of African education in colonial Kenya. The story begins with the government's failure to provide for compulsory education for Africans, prompting them to create African independent schools. When the government closed these schools, citing a lack of trained teachers, the Africans responded by founding Kenya Teachers' College, which was sustained and made to flourish through the many material sacrifices and collective efforts of the people. The writer stressed that this story of how the Africans of Kenya thwarted the ruling whites' efforts to deny their children education reflected a determined people pushing toward their liberation. "In such fashion did the children of Israel build their Temple when they fled from bondage in Egypt. For this is the way people build who have the mark of civilization upon them." Building upon this dramatic language, the piece closed with these strong words: "In the face of such a remarkable outpouring of cooperative human endeavor, the white settlers of Kenya took fright. Far from welcoming this advance of civilization, they accused the Africans of anti-European activity. *They* declared the Emergency in 1952 which precipitated the bloodshed in Kenya. *They* are the ungodly ones."[88]

By the time that this piece appeared in *Correspondence*, Grace had devoted several months to raising funds for the Koinange booklet, and she was very close to having it published. The article did not mention the booklet or identify Koinange by name, but it clearly augmented the organizing work that Grace was doing around the booklet. Indeed, the story of Kenya Teachers' College and its place in the people's anticolonial struggle that readers found in "The People Are a Mighty Fortress in East Africa" would be told in greater detail in *The People of Kenya Speak for Themselves.*

Grace's efforts included meetings with black church and social groups to tell them about the soon-to-be-published booklet. She also met with Charles Wartman, the executive editor of the city's influential black weekly the *Michigan Chronicle*, who agreed to help promote the book in his newspaper.[89] She spread the word through another local weekly publication as well, which in December published a letter she wrote to one of its columnists. In it she stated, "Today in Kenya, nearly a thousand people are being killed every month" under the state of emergency imposed by the white settlers. She said that while many people think "these Africans are backward," Koinange shows in the booklet "how advanced his people are" as they work to build the society they need and deserve. "I believe that you and many of your readers will want to read and spread this story of the progress that Africans have made and can make if allowed to speak for themselves," she wrote. The article told readers that "contributions, requests for speaking engagements and advance orders (25¢ each) can be sent to Dr. Grace C. Lee, Executive Treasurer, Kenya Publication Fund, 14832 Parkside, Detroit, Michigan."[90] The next week this same publication ran an article titled "Works for Freedom for All Africans—Introducing Dr. Grace C. Lee Humanitarian" that reported, "Dr. Lee, since her return from England last spring, has made it one of her projects to raise funds for the publication of a book about Kenya in Africa. This book is to be called 'The People of Kenya Speak for Themselves' by Mbiyu Koinange, whose father and brothers are today in concentration camps in Africa."[91]

The author of this article also thought it important to note that "in private life Dr. Lee is Mrs. James Boggs, the wife of a Chrysler employee, but in her writings and lecturing she continues to use her maiden name." The reason, he explained, was that it was as "Dr. Grace C. Lee" that she wrote her Ph.D. dissertation and as such that she "has pursued her scholarly and professional activities for more than a decade."[92] In fact, Grace had rarely used "Dr." in her name during the nearly fifteen years since earning the Ph.D. However, her strategic usage of the title in this case established a practice of using it on rare occasions in which it would lend legitimacy or garner attention, such as one decade later, when she would help to organize the all-black Freedom Now Party.

Grace's organizing for the Kenya booklet also brought attention to her ethnicity, another facet of her identity that she usually downplayed. When she spoke about the booklet, she noticed "the tremendous interest which audiences showed" in the fact that she, a Chinese American living in Detroit, "was so concerned with Africa." This curiosity made Grace uncomfortable. "I try to ignore it but the pressure put upon me to talk personally about myself was enormous," she recalled.[93] Over the next decade, as she immersed herself in black political networks and communities of Detroit, this curiosity would subside. She left no record of what precisely she said while she was still new to Detroit and felt compelled to explain how and why she came to be engaged in this activism, but it is clear that as she solidified her identity as an activist in the black movement, she no longer faced this curiosity about her presence or the expectation to explain it.

Though Grace appeared to some an unlikely agitator for African independence, her work around the booklet contributed an important strand of activity to the larger effort to support, defend, and raise awareness about the Kenyan anticolonial struggle. The efforts mounted by Grace and Correspondence coincided with the activity and writing of a network of black radicals—among them George Padmore, W. E. B. Du Bois, and Paul Robeson—concerning Kenya and the larger project of African liberation.[94] As a primary task, they faced the need to counter the standard reporting on Kenya and the official Western interpretation of the struggle, which tended to reduce the anticolonial movement to a distorted picture of the Mau Mau. White and black liberals, including the black press, repeated the charge that the Mau Mau were terrorists and that the Kikuyu people were primitive, with much of this reporting and analysis coming through a Cold War, anticommunist frame.[95] As we saw above, Grace's statements in local publications and the Correspondence articles on Kenya refuted this picture and offered an alternative. Padmore similarly issued a corrective in his essay "Behind the Mau Mau," published in the African American journal Phylon at the end of 1953. The influential Pan-Africanist activist and theorist (and longtime comrade of C. L. R.) implored readers to recognize the historical significance of the Kenyan struggle for its people and all across Africa, where "the indigenous races are struggling to throw off the yoke of colonialism and achieve their rightful place as free nations of a free world. This agitation for self-government is nowhere more dramatically manifested than in Kenya, where the violence of the struggle of the African peoples against alien domination has captured the attention of the entire world."[96] Padmore ended his essay by insisting that as the Kenyan struggle "goes on, all the races of Africa and Asia are watching and making their own conclusions," which he offered as dramatic confirmation that Du Bois (who founded *Phylon* in 1940 to be a vehicle for politically engaged intellectual work) was correct in his famous declaration that the problem of the century would be the color line.[97]

Du Bois also directly engaged in African independence as a driving force in the Council on African Affairs (CAA), a major organization involved in anticolonial politics.[98] With Paul Robeson (also a comrade of C. L. R. from the 1930s) as its chairperson, and Mary McLeod Bethune, Eslanda Robeson, W. Alphaeus Hunton, Max Yergan, and Charlotta Bass among its active members, the CAA undertook a range of activities in support of the Kenyan struggle, most of them centered in New York. In April 1954, while Grace was in London working with Koinange, the CAA held a conference in Harlem titled "A Working Conference in Support of African Liberation" and created the Kenya Aid Committee with the goal of raising $5,000 by August. The money would be used to deliver dried milk, vitamin pills, and first aid supplies, with Koinange serving as the contact person. The CAA also moved to form local aid committees, held monthly educational forums, and presented a series of summer street-corner rallies in New York during which activists distributed news from Kenya to pedestrians and motorists while speakers detailed the connections between colonialism and Jim Crow and the necessity of linking the two struggles.[99]

In Detroit, parallel efforts by Grace and Correspondence resulted in the publication of *The People of Kenya Speak for Themselves*. The 115-page booklet presented perhaps the fullest account available to an American audience of the unfolding Kenyan struggle told from the vantage point of the KAU, the nationalist movement, and Koinange's direct knowledge of the people of Kenya. The booklet also reflected Correspondence's core political belief in the revolutionary potential of the masses and their capacity for self-mobilization. This belief is signaled in the booklet's title as well as in the first words the reader encounters, the acknowledgments, which report that the publication "was made possible by the help of thousands of Americans, white and colored, of all walks of life, who feel a kinship to the Kenya people in their strivings to build a new Africa and who believe that the Africans should be free to speak for themselves, go to school, work, trade, build their own organizations, and take their place in the modern world."[100] Throughout the booklet, readers could learn of the ways in which the Kenyan people arose in rebellion against the colonial order, mobilized to meet their needs, and brought forth leaders of their own, such as Njeri, the leader of the African Women's League imprisoned by colonial authorities, to whom the booklet it dedicated.

Correspondence's orientation toward the power of mass action is also present in "A Letter from American Clergymen," the last document in the booklet's appendix. Grace wrote the letter and sent to various religious leaders in Detroit seeking their signature as part of the effort to promote the booklet. The letter said of the booklet, "chapter after chapter is testimony to the tremendous creative powers that rest within people who are trying to develop themselves and which once released, would be of such great value to people everywhere."[101] Dated January 10, 1955, the letter announced the publication of *The People of Kenya Speak for Themselves* five days later and signaled the intention of all the undersigned to bring the booklet to the attention of their congregations during their service on the last weekend of the month. Moreover, these Detroit clergy members were urging others all over the country to do the same: "Will you join us in this demonstration of the brotherhood of man . . . and share in this welcome of the African people to their place in the modern world?"[102]

This invitation was to participate in what Grace and Jimmy called "Kenya Sundays." Building upon their meetings with church groups over the preceding months, they now enlisted several preachers to select a designated service—a Kenya Sunday—on which they might talk to their congregations about the Kenyan struggle and encourage them to purchase the booklet. Among those participating were prominent Detroit black ministers such as Rev. A. A. Banks of Second Baptist Church, Rev. Robert L. Bradby of Greater King Solomon Baptist Church, Rev. Horace A. White of Plymouth Congregational Church, and Rev. Jos. Lawrence Roberts of Bethel African Methodist Episcopal Church, all signatories of the letter, and Rev. C. L. Franklin of New Bethel Baptist Church, who did not sign but was an enthusiastic supporter and participant in the Kenya Sundays project. As Grace recalled, she and Jimmy sold more than 400 copies of the booklet to members of Franklin's church during New Bethel's Kenya Sunday.[103]

Organizing the Kenya Sundays project was the first political activity outside of working on *Correspondence* that Jimmy and Grace undertook as a married couple. As such it served as an early opportunity for them to begin working out the effective and mutually supportive political style that they developed in the coming years. Their work around *The People of Kenya Speak for Themselves* also proved to be an important model and experience upon which they would draw seven years later when planning and organizing around a pamphlet by Robert Williams detailing his battles with white supremacists in Monroe, North Carolina.[104]

Correspondence in Crisis

At the same time as the group successfully organized around *The People of Kenya Speak for Themselves* and Kenya Sundays, the group experienced a multilayered crisis that would ultimately result in a split in the organization. Government interference generated one dimension of the crisis. First, the U.S. Postal Service labeled the July 24, 1954, issue of *Correspondence* "nonmailable" based on a section of the *Postal Manual* "prohibiting the mailing of matter tending to incite murder and assassination."[105] Nothing in this issue, the first to be published after Grace's return from London, advocated murder or assassination, and the Postal Service did not identify specific articles or passages. Then in December 1954 the U.S. attorney general placed the "Johnson-Forest Group" on its subversive list. While no such group existed, and Correspondence was not put on the list, it was clear that Correspondence was the intended target.[106] Suddenly made acutely aware of their vulnerability, the group discussed what they should do in response to the possibility of being swept up in a still potent McCarthyism. A major fault line emerged when Dunayevskaya proposed that the organization go underground, which Jimmy, Lyman Paine, and other members firmly opposed.[107]

These differences compounded existing disagreements surrounding the viability of *Correspondence*. The problem of "subgetting" continued to plague the group, contributing to its difficulty in financing the paper, and their inability to consistently acquire new subscriptions from industrial workers in particular reflected the larger difficulty they had in attracting more workers to participate in the life of *Correspondence*. While various workers did read the paper, submit submissions for it, or talk to members such as Jimmy who wrote up their thoughts, these engagements with the paper were often uneven and generally fell short of what the group envisioned and believed necessary. Workers' level of involvement in the paper posed a significant problem, as it threatened the very purpose of the paper and called into question its aspiration of being a "workers' paper." By the spring of 1954, this problem had become a frequent topic of discussion in the paper itself. For example, an installment of "Building Correspondence" written by

Correspondence member William Page posed the question "Can we build a workers' paper?" to which he answered, "Frankly, we do not know. We are making an effort. We are putting every ounce of energy that we have, every dollar that we can find, every waking moment into making *Correspondence* into the first newspaper that can be truly called a workers' paper." If they were successful, *Correspondence* would "become the true expression of the thought embodied in the minds of the mass workers," but this could only happen if a wide range of workers joined in the work of putting out the paper, with each of them "freely expressing himself in the pages of *Correspondence*."[108]

Jimmy had been successful in getting workers to subscribe and either write or relate something to him that he then wrote up, and he saw such efforts as an important aspect of the paper's current stage. Now, in the pages of *Correspondence* he stressed that the next step was to get workers to participate in the weekly editing meetings. "Take the Polish worker I saw the other night," he wrote. "He was ready to buy the sub when we got there. He made up his own mind—just found the paper on his porch, nobody sold him nothing. He read that copy, and when I got there, he just reached in his hip pocket." The man told Jimmy the he liked the things he read in the paper, and Jimmy invited him to attend a meeting. The man declined, replying, "I think the paper is good. If it gets wrong, then I'll write something." This demonstrated the challenge before them: workers must want to assume the responsibility of being part of the group putting out the paper. He offered as the means to this end "a new form or association" that would be created "with the people that you know to let them know that what they have to say is so important that you feel they have to be there or the paper won't continue to exist."[109]

In October, Jimmy addressed these lingering challenges and made a stronger plea for readers' participation in the life of the paper, this time in a front-pager titled "The Paper and a New Society." Whereas previous discussions emphasized workers in particular, here Jimmy addressed readers and subscribers generally. By now the mounting conflict in the organization meant that not just *Correspondence*'s identity as a workers' paper but its very survival was at stake. He first touted what they had achieved and hoped to preserve, boasting that in *Correspondence* "people who never thought that what they said meant anything are saying it. It's being read by thousands of others. We who put out the paper have gained strength. Those we have met have gained strength. They found out that what they felt and thought mattered." The paper only had about 1,000 subscribers, but Jimmy encouraged them to see themselves and their shared connection to the paper as remakers of society. "If what *Correspondence* has published could be put into action, it would be the basis of establishing a new society, a society based on what the majority feels." He then made his appeal directly to the subscribers to become involved, take responsibility for growing the paper, and help it realize this potential. "The only way it can be done is if you, one of our thousand subscribers, yourself begin to take the steps of coming to meet us at our editing meetings and at our parties, sending *Correspondence* to your friends, shopmates and neighbors in your community, sending in your own dimes, quarters, and subscriptions and asking your friends to send in theirs. . . . You are in 1,000 neighborhoods and have thousands of friends and shopmates which we 75 will never be able to reach."[110]

The "we 75" referred to the number of members of Correspondence—a number that would soon be halved. On top of the problems with the paper, the group was experiencing internal turmoil that raised questions about Dunayevskaya's leadership. These involved the debate over whether the organization should go underground in the face of McCarthyist repression, the state and handling of the group's finances, and philosophical divergences among the group. Another factor was the relationship between Dunayevskaya and C. L. R., who maintained a heavy involvement with the group from London. While they had shared leadership, albeit unevenly, throughout the life of the JFT and Correspondence, and she had held the title of "chairman" since his departure, C. L. R. had always been the group's strongest figure, and he continued to see himself as such while in London. Early in 1955 open conflict erupted, pushing the existing organizational crisis to a breaking point. In March, Dunayevskaya, Zupan, Owens, and about half of the organization's members left the group. They formed their own organization, the News and Letters Committee, and published a periodical, *News and Letters*. C. L. R. took this as an act of "shameful apostasy"; Dunayevskaya, on the other hand, said she had freed herself from "the rottenness" of Johnsonism built upon C. L. R.'s sense of himself as "the measure of all things."[111]

The split forced the remaining members of the organization to regroup and to reevaluate the form and function of *Correspondence*, as well as its future. They ceased publication during April and May of 1955, and when the paper resumed in June it appeared in a drastically different format. For the next two years, *Correspondence* was in effect a journal of commentary and political theory rather than a newspaper. Carrying the designation "Discussion Bulletin" in the masthead, these issues appeared only every other month, were four or eight pages in length, and consisted of theoretical or historical pieces (most written by C. L. R.), examinations of factory life in various industries, and articles by or about European workers, radical organizations, and political developments. This interim phase in *Correspondence*'s publishing history lasted from the summer of 1955 through the summer of 1957.

Jimmy and Grace emerged during the interim period as the group's new leadership. The membership elected Jimmy to be Dunayevskaya's replacement as the organization's chairperson, and Grace became the editor of *Correspondence*, which returned to its regular publication as a newspaper in October 1957. The return of the paper marked a new phase of the group's organizational history, which they entered with optimism and a sense of renewal, having finally regrouped following the split with Dunayevskaya. They were also energized by significant world political events of the past year that they believed validated their vision of revolutionary transformation. The three words appearing on the masthead of the October 1957 issue of *Correspondence* captured the excitement the group felt about its ability to contribute to this world revolutionary moment: "The Future—Today."[112]

Yet this moment of renewed political activity contained within it the makings of new organizational fissures. The group's engagement with the world political situation in 1957, which they all believed was a moment of great revolutionary potential, revealed subtle political divergences between the Boggses and C. L. R. Seemingly small differences in emphasis and interpretation eventually grew into competing conceptions of the current political situation and, ultimately, of what should be the political direction of the group. This became apparent at the end of the 1950s as Jimmy and Grace began to push *Correspondence* beyond its origins as a workers' paper, forging a shift away from workers' struggles and toward a greater focus on the black struggle. This shift reflected ideological divisions in the organization and generated tensions that would result in a split between the Boggses and C. L. R. in 1961. These tensions and divisions developed through the organization's response to three major political events in 1956 and 1957: the Hungarian Revolution, the independence of Ghana, and the Montgomery Bus Boycott.

CHAPTER SEVEN

Facing Multiple Realities

"The revolutionary crisis is here," C. L. R. declared in a letter to his comrades in the United States in the fall of 1956. The dramatic confrontation with "totalitarian power" embodied in the recent eruptions of popular protest and challenges to Communist Party rule in Poland and Hungary, he said, unmistakably announced its arrival. "From now on the whole world knows that the European proletariat as well as the colonial peoples [are] ready to settle the problems *arms in hand.*" C. L. R. urged the group to turn its attention to Europe and the Third World. Correspondence, he insisted, because of its history and its theoretical orientation, had a unique and specific contribution to make to what he saw as world-historic developments. His letter asked everyone in the group to respond to each of the points he raised—"I must ask you to reply, numbered paragraph by numbered paragraph"—and to make this the focus of their work, turning their powers of interpretation and analysis to these global developments. Above all else, he insisted that they look to Hungary as the most important of all.[1]

"The Hungarian Revolution Is the Ultimate"

On October 23, 1956, a spontaneous antigovernment protest broke out in Budapest and spread across Hungary. It quickly grew into a mass movement, creating a revolutionary challenge to the established order of the Communist Bloc. News of this uprising immediately excited and energized C. L. R., and it generated a new mood of possibility and intellectual activity in Correspondence. The group championed the Hungarian Revolution as a historic experiment in direct democracy and a great leap in the world working-class movement. Most of all, the group was excited by Hungary's workers' councils, which industrial workers formed during the revolution as their own rank-and-file organizations. Correspondence, and C. L. R. in particular, took the Hungarian Revolution as historical validation of the group's most central ideas: a belief in the spontaneous organization of the working class, an unequivocal opposition to bureaucratic state management, and an unshakable faith in the capacity of working-class self-activity and workers' self-governance not only to expose the bankruptcy of the bureaucratic elite but to ultimately replace it.

C. L. R. penned his letter about the current revolutionary situation on November 3. The next day, 6,000 Russian tanks entered Hungary and put down the revolt. Yet, the event did little to temper his enthusiasm, and C. L. R.'s directives to the group multiplied in the days and weeks that followed. The day after Soviet troops crushed the rebellion (and only two days after his initial letter), C. L. R. wrote to the group again, emphasizing the importance of Hungary and elevating it above other developments. "I don't think you all recognize what the Hungarian Rev'n means," he insisted. "*Since 1917 nothing has so shaken the world.*"[2] Allusions to the Russian Revolution of 1917 appeared frequently in C. L. R.'s assessments of Hungary, and he did not use them lightly. Since his earliest days in the Trotskyist movement in the 1930s, and especially during the intense ideological and organization battles around the Russian Question in the 1940s, the Russian Revolution loomed in his consciousness as a singular event in modern world history and an undisputed flashpoint for Marxist theory. He used the Russian Revolution both as a reference point to mark time in the history of revolutionary struggle and as a barometer of Hungary's historical significance. He repeatedly asserted that Hungary represented something new in the theory and practice of revolution. Just ten days later, he wrote the group again: "I hope you realise that the present crisis is one of the greatest turning points of history. The Hungarian Revolution is the ultimate. There cannot be a future revolution that can surpass it. I doubt if there will be many to equal it."[3]

This unequivocal elevation of Hungary above anticolonial movements might have given pause, as C. L. R. was writing in the shadow of the Bandung Conference, in the midst of the Suez Crisis, and less than four weeks after colonial authorities had arrested Kenya Land and Freedom Army ("Mau Mau") leader Dedan Kimathi. Indeed, in the past two years C. L. R. and Correspondence had arranged for Grace's work with Mbiyu Koinange and published *The People of Kenya Speak for Themselves* to tell the story of Kenya's independence struggle and advocate for the liberation of Africa. Broadly speaking, Hungary occurred contemporaneously with the civil rights movement in the United States and rising nationalist movements across Africa that threatened to overthrow the global racial order and re-make societies on both sides of the Atlantic. Yet Hungary rose to the fore of C. L. R.'s thinking and claimed his attention in the fall of 1956. He believed that Correspondence had a unique role to play in interpreting Hungary as part of a world revolutionary advance. Thus, his bold statements about the Hungarian Revolution can be read as a charge to his comrades in the United States to celebrate the group's unique theoretical perspective and to seize this opportunity to show, through the ideas of the Johnson-Forest Tendency (JFT) and Correspondence, that Hungary represents the most advanced embodiment of revolutionary theory and practice for the con-temporary world. "This endurance of the Hungarian workers is a social thing," he declared. "We have to analyse it and draw the theoretical conclu-sions. I don't know anybody else who can."[4]

With the notable exception of Jimmy, and to a lesser extent Grace, most of the organization agreed with C. L. R.'s assessment of the Hungarian Revolution, sharing in his excitement about the future it seemed to sug-gest. The group rather quickly decided to write a pamphlet articulating this future, a collective project that eventually turned into the book *Facing Real-ity*. In addition to the impact they expected the Hungarian Revolution to have in Eastern Europe, Correspondence believed (without much basis, it turned out) that the events in Hungary would impact workers in the United States, perhaps even inspiring them to political action. To hasten this, the group resolved to advance public consciousness and discussion about the Hungarian Revolution through public forums. They held their first forum in early November in Detroit, and then the New York office of Corre-spondence held one over Thanksgiving weekend.[5] Titled "Hungarian and Polish Workers Show the Way to a New World," the New York event was billed as a "discussion meeting on the recent exciting events in Eastern Europe"[6] featuring an introductory talk by Martin Glaberman followed by questions from the floor and general discussion. A press release from the Detroit office announcing the New York event suggested that Hungary was important to American workers because it showed "the people's ability to take politics out of the offices of government and the halls of Parliament and transfer it directly to the factory floor, college campuses and neigh-borhood communities."[7] In its promotion for the forum, the New York office explained that this discussion of events in Hungary and Poland was a direct expression of the mission of the group and its paper: "The purpose of *Correspondence* is to report, interpret and encourage the independent activity of ordinary people everywhere in their struggle for freedom and self-government and against domination by leaders, *beginning at their place of work.*"[8]

Indeed, the Hungarian Revolution became a featured topic in the pages of *Correspondence*, which was still being published as a "Discussion Bulletin" in the fall of 1956. The December 1956 bulletin, the first to appear since the outbreak of the Hungarian Revolution, featured a front-page article on the uprising. Carrying no byline but likely written by C. L. R., the article repeats his contention that the revolution was a decisive political and historical moment. "The Hungarian Revolution is the turning point in modern history," the article began. "From now on, in every country (and sometimes in the country where it is least expected), the open struggle may erupt at any time between the factory councils of the workers and the centralized governments of Party and Plan or of Parliament and Executive." The article strikes a forward-looking tone, advocating a solid break with past ideas and the embrace of new possibilities for revolutionary action, yet beneath this are echoes of old arguments. Indeed, this article, like the group's analysis of Hungary more generally, seemed to use the revolution as evidence of the correctness of their theoretical projections. For example, in its list of the Hungarian Revolution's accomplishments, the article rehearses ideas that animated the Johnson-Forest Tendency's theory of state capitalism in the 1940s: "The Hungarian Revolution demolished for all time the idea that bureaucrats can plan the national economy. It has destroyed the idea that nationalization of property or government ownership means the end of the exploitation of labor in production." Similarly, the article reaffirms the wisdom of the JFT's abandonment of the vanguard party idea (which, as we have seen, was central to its desertion of Trotskyism and regrouping of itself as Correspondence in the early 1950s): "The Hungarian Revolution has struck a death blow at the concept of the Vanguard Party, the party to govern, the part to control the workers and administer the plan. . . . The new form of political organization is the total mobilization of the working class."[9]

"I Can't Get Half as Excited over the Hungarian Revolt as I Can over the Colonial Revolts"

Jimmy in particular, and to a lesser extent Grace, did not share this unbridled enthusiasm for the Hungarian Revolution. Grace essentially agreed with C. L. R. that a period of revolutionary activity was emerging, but she did not see Hungary as singular. She anticipated that the type of clashes between workers and centralized forms of power (governmental, labor organizations, or political parties) that occurred in Hungary would soon appear in various forms "in country after country," and she further predicted that "forms of dual power" like the Hungarian workers' councils "are going to appear suddenly" and often "with arms in hand." But Hungary was only one aspect of this global picture. Of equal importance, she said, was the rising opposition to colonialism, which she believed carried as much weight in the postwar world. "One thing we have to get clear in our own minds," she insisted in a letter to C. L. R., "is that the colonial people have been living since the end of WW II by a series of milestones—the freeing of India in 1947, the victory of the Chinese Communists in 1949, the formation of an Asia-African bloc in the UN, the Bandung Conference."[10] Of course, C. L. R. recognized these milestones as well, and he agreed that they were, in the sense of a global picture of political upheaval, complementary to Hungary. The difference was that he saw the revolt of colonial people as secondary and subordinate to the Hungarian Revolution. Grace urged a different ordering, arguing that Hungary and the colonial revolt deserved equal weight and analysis.

Jimmy went much further. Writing to C. L. R. at the end of November, he took issue with Correspondence's nearly singular focus on Hungary over the preceding month, and he sharply called into question the group's excitement over Hungary relative to popular insurgency in Africa and Asia. "The whole organization is reading and talking about the Hungarian revolution night and day as if this is all that is happening in the world," he wrote. "Now, with me, I am excited over any revolt. I don't care if it is only a sporadic one in the shop that lasts only half a day. But I can't get half as excited over the Hungarian revolt as I can over the colonial revolts." Jimmy urged a fuller appreciation among his comrades of the revolutionary potential in the Afro-Asian states and liberation movements. He saw in this rising Third World, with its nationalist ferment and Bandung-style spirit of nonalignment, a political creativity with the potential to reconfigure global politics and fashion revolutionary change the world over. Moreover, Jimmy judged Hungary's impact to be limited, in terms of both its historical significance and its potential to shape the contemporary political situation. "So far as I am concerned the Russians only had the Hungarians for about 12 years, but the British have had the Egyptians and all these countries for over a hundred years. I feel that the colonial question is going to go far beyond the

Hungarian question," he wrote. "The Hungarian revolt is small and isn't going to have the world-wide repercussions that the colonial revolts have. It just isn't," he insisted. "That colonial question is going to shake up the whole world."[11]

Three lines of argument undergirded Jimmy's elevation of the colonial revolts over Hungary. First, he said that Hungary was having very little impact on the Western world, whereas the Western bourgeoisie, particularly in the United States and Britain, "are worried about the Middle East affair and the colonial question in Africa and also the Asian question." Unlike Hungary, these movements in the Third World were "being thought about, worried about, felt here" because they were "threatening the whole lifeline" of Western nations and thus "threatening the whole country just as the Negroes in this country shut down the buses in the South." Second, Jimmy challenged C. L. R.'s belief that Hungary could impact Western workers. He reported that American workers did not relate to the Hungarian Revolution as workers. They saw Hungary as a social or humanitarian crisis but not as a meaningful political event, and it remained far removed from their own lives. These workers did not draw from Hungary an inspiration to protest, political lessons to study, or methods of protest to emulate. "The same people who are sympathetic with the Hungarian revolution from the standpoint of cruelty are the same ones who will lynch a colored guy tonight and the same one who will be a company stooge in the plant too." In short, the Hungarian Revolution had no impact on workers' politics or their consciousness, either from "a revolutionary standpoint" or "from the point of view of production. I haven't heard anyone talk about it from the view of production."[12]

Finally, Jimmy insisted that because of the colonial peoples' historically constituted subordinate position in the world political economy, the nationalist uprisings offered something that the other uprisings could not. "All I can see that Russia and the West can give to the world is technological advancement." On the other hand, the anticolonial revolts were fighting for "a new form of organization of life," a struggle that included but went beyond economic arrangements or relations of production. "Western civilization has been geared to production and all I see coming out of it is some psychological attempt to reorganize production. We have been so tied up in materialism in Western civilization." The colonial nations, by contrast, had the potential to break from this. Admittedly, they have "a few corrupt puppets," he said, who have "been paid off by both the U.S. and Russia" and who remain committed to the patterns and values of the existing order. "But the public in these countries have not been raised up in materialism and they have a much better chance to find a better civilization that isn't directly wrapped up in production." To amplify his point, Jimmy offered a comparison "between Nkrumah's country" and its fellow West African nation of Liberia. "Liberia has its puppets from America and they are Negroes and they are profiting off the country. Nkrumah isn't doing that."[13]

Jimmy knew that his reference to "Nkrumah's country" would be meaningful to C. L. R. Kwame Nkrumah was the leader of the anticolonial movement in the Gold Coast, the West African nation that was, at the time of Jimmy's writing, less than four months away from achieving independence from Britain. C. L. R. and other members of Correspondence including Grace had met Nkrumah during World War II when the latter was a student in the United States and an aspiring anticolonial leader. C. L. R.'s work during the 1930s with George Padmore and others in the International African Service Bureau, including his editorship of its journal *International African Opinion*, had made him a prominent figure in the world of Pan-African politics, and he served as a political mentor to the soon-to-be leader of Ghana's independence movement. When Nkrumah left the United States in 1945, C. L. R. helped to put the young freedom fighter in touch with Padmore and a network of anticolonial activists in London, which led to Nkrumah's assuming a prominent role alongside Padmore in organizing the Fifth Pan-African Congress later that year. Nkrumah returned to his native Gold Coast in 1947 to join and eventually lead the anticolonial struggle. That struggle culminated a decade later in the transfer of power and the founding of the new nation of Ghana, with Nkrumah as its leader.

Grace and Jimmy took a particular interest in the nationalist movement in Ghana. Throughout 1956 they anticipated the coming of independence and plotted ways to contribute to the development of the new nation. "For over a year now, Jim and Willis and I have been talking about emigration to Ghana," Grace wrote in a letter to C. L. R. in late March of 1957, just after Ghana achieved its independence. "We have discussed schemes for exchanging Chrysler workers with African workers and I have even discussed with an airline agency the idea of a raffle in the plant each week to choose workers to go abroad." These conversations that Grace and Jimmy had with their friend Willis, who worked with Jimmy at Chrysler but was not a member of Correspondence, reflected a specific approach and attempt to contribute to the building of independent Ghana. "In our discussions, it has not only been a personal matter of wanting to go. We have seen it in terms of the building of the African economy, the need for investment, the types of technicians etc. the U.S. govt. would send, the types of help the Africans need from American workers, not in CARE packages and not only in technical skills alone but from that sense of building an economy." She said this sensibility "exist[s] particularly in the American Negro workers."[14] Grace and Jimmy had raised the importance of African independence movements with black Detroiters in 1954–55 when they created Kenya Sundays and promoted *The People of Kenya Speak for Themselves*. Now they were exploring the relationship between black Americans and new African nations in another way. Jimmy and Grace would revisit the links between Africa and black Americans again in the late 1960s, including a visit to West Africa to meet with Nkrumah to discuss a new set of political issues arising in the context of Nkrumah's removal from power and the emergence of the Black Power movement in the United States. But now, in 1956–57, they were exploring questions and opportunities relating to building a newly independent African nation.

"The Greatest Political Achievement in Africa for a Hundred Years"

On September 18, 1956—a month before the beginning of the Hungarian Revolution—Nkrumah announced that a date had been set for the transfer of power in the Gold Coast: on March 6, 1957, the Gold Coast colony would become the independent nation of Ghana.[15] C. L. R. apparently took little notice of this announcement. Despite his connections to Nkrumah and his long-standing interest in the Gold Coast's anticolonial struggle, it seems that C. L. R. paid little if any attention to the movement during the months leading up to independence. There was no discussion within the group about the Gold Coast Revolution or its impending independence during the final months of 1956, nor are there references to it in the *Correspondence* discussion bulletins. That this would be the case is somewhat surprising, not only because of C. L. R.'s relationship to Nkrumah and the revolution in the Gold Coast but also because he had theorized and labored for African independence since the 1930s. As he would proudly recall in the preface to the 1963 edition of his book *The Black Jacobins*, originally published in 1938, the closing pages of the study "envisage[d] and were intended to stimulate the coming emancipation of Africa." The new preface further boasts that when the book originally appeared, "only the writer and a handful of close associates thought, wrote, and spoke as if the African events of the last quarter century were imminent."[16] The "African events" to which he referred, of course, was the post–World War II upsurge of nationalist politics and mass protest in colonial Africa resulting in dozens of newly independent states. Ghana was the first of these south of the Sahara, and under Nkrumah's leadership the new republic self-consciously became a touchstone for a renewed Pan-Africanist project and a vision of African liberation that owed no small debt to C. L. R. and his labors.

The Ghanaian and Hungarian Revolutions were essentially contemporaneous events, competing for the group's attention and exposing its ideological fault lines. As noted above, the September 1956 announcement of the date for Ghana's independence preceded by a month the start of the uprising in Hungary. Thus, the final preparations for Ghana's independence coincided with the outbreak and aftermath of the Hungarian Revolution. C. L. R. and the group did come to focus on Ghana for a brief period during the spring of 1957, even affording it some priority over Hungary, but this was short lived.

Most of the group's activity at the end of 1956, including discussions carried out in their voluminous transatlantic correspondence, centered on the significance of Hungary and the need to project the group's analysis of it. "Towering above all," C. L. R. wrote to Glaberman on December 13, "is the urgent necessity of a pamphlet on Hungary."[17] C. L. R. initially hoped that the pamphlet, written mostly by him but with editorial and production work done by members of the group in the United States, would be published by January. However, work on it continued well into the new year, as C. L. R. continued to devote considerable energy to the theoretical and political implications of the Hungarian Revolution. For example, after reading a mass of material on Hungary, he wrote a long letter to the group dated February 10, 1957, critically assessing the analyses of French intellectual Jean-Paul Sartre and others. Engaging leftist interpretations of Hungary in this way expanded the scope of the pamphlet and pushed C. L. R. (and most of the group) to see the pamphlet as a major statement of contemporary Marxism and a defining statement of the group. "Sartre and the rest of them do not know, cannot recognize the significance of what has taken place [in Hungary]," he wrote. "I have said before that we and we alone are in a position to do so." C. L. R.'s letter also seems to be an indirect response to the points Jimmy raised about Hungary and his detraction of the group's view. For example, C. L. R. asserted, "There is a danger that these analyses may seem to the less experienced of you somewhat remote from conditions in the United States. You would be wrong. Completely wrong." He insisted that the group make the Hungary pamphlet its priority, both theoretically and practically—that is, publishing and distributing it as widely as possible. "Let us get the Hungarian Revolution right and all will follow."[18]

At the end of January, in the midst of the group's many letters about the Hungary pamphlet, C. L. R. received an invitation from Nkrumah to attend Ghana's independence ceremonies. C. L. R. initially greeted the invitation with only mild interest. He sent a copy of Nkrumah's letter to his comrades in the United States, but he struck a rather neutral tone. "I have received the following letter from Nkrumah, the Prime Minister of the Gold Coast," he wrote in his accompanying note. "Some of you will remember him in the U.S. and the time he spent with us."[19] C. L. R. surmised that his invitation reflected the new government's desire "to get as many people of color with some reputation to the celebrations." Moreover, he knew that his Pan-African organizing and advocacy during the 1930s "has always been remembered by the Gold Coast nationalists." C. L. R. seemed to feel some obligation to attend Ghana's independence celebration, but he did not demonstrate much intrinsic interest or enthusiasm. Indeed, his initial response showed him to be hesitant, even conflicted, about attending. "It makes a tremendous mess in many respects," he wrote about the prospect of traveling to Ghana, likely referring to a combination of the interruption of his work, the financial strain it could pose, and the potential impact on his health.[20] "But I am sure I ought to go," he added. "I shall try to go and I certainly will enjoy it, learn a great deal, do my best to pass on certain ideas to all whom I meet and, when I return, pass on what I have seen." Whatever his reservations, C. L. R. of course recognized the significance of Ghana's independence. "How big the occasion is in the minds of the political world is shown by the fact that Nixon is going."[21]

Its importance in C. L. R.'s own mind grew in the coming days. "As it is now," he reported ten days later, "I think there is every possibility of me going." He began planning a two-week trip, and he also began to conceive of a writing project to come out of the trip. "I hope to see something of the country and I intend to get hold of a typist and dictate what I hope will become a small volume, letters from Accra," he told the group. "If everything is well with me I shall have it ready for publication within two or three days of my return."[22] Predictably, he did not meet this time frame, in part because it was overly optimistic, but also because his appreciation for

Ghana's independence movement and the scope of his planned book both expanded based on what he saw and experienced during the two-week visit.

C. L. R. left for the Gold Coast on February 24, allowing him to witness and participate in many of the independence activities culminating in the historic ceremony on March 6 formally marking Ghana's birth. "I am getting around, twice as much as most folks here and seeing and hearing plenty," he wrote in one of his many letters to his American comrades. He said this was giving him rich material for the book, starting with his observations and impressions from the many Ghanaians he met, from the university student who served as his guide and the man who served as his driver (and both of their families, whom he also met) to the hotel attendants, civil servants, and ministers. He spoke to people in the city of Takoradi, which he described as a "modern" part of the country "with a proletariat of 10,000. You could have picked up any one of them and dropped him in Detroit." He also traveled to the interior, where he saw "the peasants," and he took note of the market women, the segment of society that Nkrumah told him had "made the party." C. L. R. similarly told his comrades about conversations and interactions he had with an impressively wide array of people who came for the celebration: Africans and West Indians "who hang on my words"; black Americans "who are here by the dozens"; two Poles with whom he had ongoing conversations; a Sudanese newspaper man who invited him to the Sudan; two Romanians, whom he met "by accident" (they were among the Stalinists there who "look at me with a strange look" and "wish me elsewhere, but they listen and keep silent, thinking"); and others from various places such as Laos, Cambodia, and Siam (Thailand). C. L. R. attended a ceremony to launch *Ghana: The Autobiography of Kwame Nkrumah*, the prime minister's memoir of the movement published to coincide with the independence ceremony. And of course C. L. R. went to the dramatic midnight rally where the British flag came down and the flag of Ghana was raised for the first time.[23]

One of C. L. R.'s most impactful experiences was "a social evening" he spent with Nkrumah, his cabinet, and the Central Committee of the Convention People's Party (CPP). His conversations with Nkrumah and others there deepened his laudatory assessment of the CPP, the mass-based political party that Nkrumah cofounded and led through the successful drive to independence. C. L. R. wrote to his comrades the next day telling them about this gathering, relating some of his conversations there, and sharing the analytical conclusions he was drawing about the Ghanaian Revolution. "I said quite in the course of things that the great achievement was the *building of the party*," referring to the CPP, which C. L. R. saw as the embodiment of popular insurgency and mass political organization. He even described it as "the greatest political achievement in Africa for a hundred years." Nkrumah apparently responded favorably to this, telling C. L. R. that he had simply narrated the story of CPP and the anticolonial movement in his just-released memoir, but his hope was for others to follow with the necessary political analysis of Ghana's revolution. "N[krumah] says that he wants his story 'philosophized' and 'put into principles,'" C. L. R. told his American comrades, self-assuredly accepting the task. "He practically asked me to do it and I told him I would. . . . Who else can do it but we?"[24]

The planned book, then, was taking on a slightly different shape. C. L. R. told the group that it would still be a small book, for a "bourgeois publisher," and it would be easy to write, but it would also speak to and for the Ghanaian masses who built the party and the independence movement, holding up for serious analysis and praise their contributions to the theory and practice of revolution. "We shall give them everything," he said, excitedly projecting an analysis of their actions and achievements as a model for the whole of Africa and possibly Asia and Latin America as well. "The last chapter will be as serious an analysis as I can make of their experience, the party above all."[25]

This was, like most of their intellectual work, to be a collective effort— "We are in a beautiful position to do it," C. L. R. wrote excitedly—with Grace taking a lead role alongside C. L. R. "Now this is for *Grace*," he declared in a letter addressed to the whole group, "though everyone is invited." He said this to preface his thoughts on the CPP and Nkrumah's autobiography, and he concluded with specific instructions: "Now G[race] must get his book, read it and do a job on it and send me letters. . . . Everyone can help, of course, but G[race] must do it at once."[26] Though he had been in London for more than four years, C. L. R. still operated as the leader of the group, as indicated by his brash directive, telling Grace what she *must* do. At the same time, his words affirmed Grace's unique abilities, as well as his reliance on them. It was no surprise that C. L. R. relied on Grace in this way. She had the philosophical grounding and political experience C. L. R. valued and needed for this project. She was, as well, the member of the group most familiar with and perhaps most adept at this mode of theoretical and intellectual collaboration—for instance, the letters exchanged in 1948 that became C. L. R.'s book *Notes on Dialectics*—which he desperately tried to maintain despite his distance from the group. Moreover, among the Correspondence members who dated back to the early JFT days, Grace would likely be the one who most remembered Nkrumah. In this same letter, C. L. R. reported that Nkrumah asked how he might arrange for Grace to come to Ghana. C. L. R. responded that she should be invited to give a series of lectures on philosophy at a Ghanaian university, to which Nkrumah agreed. C. L. R. seemed excited about this prospect, and included Jimmy in the plans. "She and J[immy] will create a sensation here. Everything in time," he wrote.[27]

This plan did not materialize, but Grace and Jimmy did eventually visit Nkrumah. It was, though, under very different circumstances. In 1968, eleven years after independence, they spent a week with him, not in Ghana but in Conakry, Guinea, where Nkrumah was living in exile after a coup deposed him in 1966. As conveyed by C. L. R.'s letters, this turn of events—the coup, Nkrumah's exile, and Ghana's retreat from its position of Pan-African leadership—could hardly be imagined in 1957. "There is such a collection of people here as have never been assembled in Africa," C. L. R. wrote of those gathered for the independence celebration, all sharing in the triumphant and euphoric sense of possibility generated by the birth of Ghana. "It is not only the future of Africa," he explained, "but the future of the world, that is in all minds."[28] C. L. R.'s presence certainly put Ghana, momentarily but prominently, on his mind and the collective mind of Correspondence.

Upon his return to London, C. L. R. gave his strongest statement yet about the importance of Ghana, his plans for the book, and its priority in his and the group's work: "I propose to postpone the Hungarian pamphlet for 4–6 weeks and do instead a 70,000 word book on Ghana." This reprioritization, which surely surprised the membership of the group, reflected the lofty expectations he had for the book. For one thing, he anticipated that it would be an immediate commercial success. He also believed it would serve as an articulation of "our *whole program* in a most concrete context, for Ghana and for everybody else." As such, the book would be "a flying start for the general publicizing" of the group's ideas in Europe, the United States, and Africa.[29]

C. L. R. laid out the structure and content of the proposed book, emphasizing in particular the three dimensions that he believed would give the book its unique and powerful quality. First was the rich set of insights gained from his observations during his visit to Ghana. "I saw and understood more in 14 days," he wrote in his characteristically self-confident fashion, "than people who have been studying the subject for 14 years." It was this, he surmised, that explained why Nkrumah and his government "spent so many hours with me in that busy time." The new government was "looking forward to the book as the first satisfactory exposition of what has happened there," C. L. R. assured his American comrades, adding that the Ghanaians "will give all possible assistance." Second, he proposed to build on his past work, particularly *The Black Jacobins*, his study of Toussaint L'Ouverture and the Haitian Revolution published in 1938, the year that C. L. R. came to the United States. Here he would show how he had in that book anticipated the African revolution that Ghana represented, but he would break from the theory of colonial revolution articulated in *The Black Jacobins* in which the success of the colonial revolution was linked to European proletarian mass movements. This new book would reject that, presenting his revised view that "the African Revolution (as a process) is no longer to be seen as supplementary to or subordinate to the revolution in Western Europe." This conclusion closely aligned with the position Jimmy had articulated back in the fall of 1956 when the organization began to analyze the Hungarian Revolution, a fact C. L. R. quietly acknowledged with this parenthetical statement identifying Jimmy by his old JFT alias: "I want Heinz to note this particularly." C. L. R. also singled Jimmy out on a related point: "I shall expect from you all and from Heinz in particular a statement as to what is the attitude of the American Negroes in particular to Ghana."[30] The surviving letters show no response from Jimmy on either of these points; whatever ideological convergence may have been suggested here faded in the coming years. The third distinguishing feature of the proposed book, C. L. R. said, would be its close analysis of the CPP, including detailed assessments of both the success of the revolution and the challenges the CPP faced as it made the transition from a revolutionary party to a ruling party.

Grace had already given the subject serious thought. As she wrote in reply to C. L. R.'s letter instructing her to assess Nkrumah's book and his political party, "I have not yet read Nkrumah's autobiography. It is not obtainable here, so I have sent to NY for it. However, I am going to venture some analysis of what is involved in the Convention People's Party movement on the basis of what I have read about it." Her reading included three of the earliest books on Ghana's independence movement—Richard Wright's *Black Power*, George Padmore's *The Gold Coast Revolution*, and David Apter's *Ghana in Transition*—and the text of Nkrumah's "Motion of Destiny" speech, which pushed the British government to set constitutional and administrative arrangements for independence. Delivered before the Gold Coast Legislative Assembly in July 1953, the speech marked a decisive step in the movement to end colonial rule and has subsequently been identified by Nkrumah's biographers as "one of the most important speeches in his life" and "possibly the finest expression of his vision for Ghana and Africa."[31] Grace's evaluation of Nkrumah's speech reached even higher: "In my opinion it will go down in history as one of the great speeches of all time." It was, she believed, comparable in significance to Pericles's Funeral Oration and the speeches of Wendell Phillips. By identifying Athenian democracy and American abolitionism as historical reference points for what was taking place in Ghana, Grace was making a claim for the Ghanaian struggle as a political expression of "the age to which we are now entering." She said that Ghana's CPP, along with the workers' councils in Hungary and Poland, most clearly evidenced this new age. "The essence of these movements is that they demonstrate the inseparability for our day between the struggle for total political freedom and the struggle for economic emancipation in the specific form of the liberation of the natural and acquired powers of mankind for cooperative labor."[32]

The appearance of the phrase "natural and acquired powers," which Grace had used in *The American Worker* and *Essays by Karl Marx*, and would appear in her later writings as well, highlights how her analysis of Ghana and the CPP extended from her philosophical thinking begun in graduate school and her Marxism from the JFT period. Her argument about the CPP as part of "the fundamental revolutionary character of the age into which we have now entered" began with showing how the party represented a leap beyond "the political ideologies that were created by the great philosophers for the political revolutions that ushered in rising capitalism," summed up in the concepts of natural rights and social contract as seen in the philosophies of Hobbes, Hume, Locke, and Rousseau and culminating in that of Kant. She then moved to Hegel and Marx, who had identified a fundamental duality of capitalist society. "Hegel, and after him Marx, said that the key to the understanding of modern society is its duality," she wrote, "that on the one hand, in political life every man is a citizen, equal to every other man, an end in himself; while on the other hand, in his actual empirical social and economic existence, he is unequal, a means to an end. In his political life his mission is to be social; in his actual social and economic life, his economic ties are constantly being broken up and destroyed." Reminiscent of the JFT days, Grace then cited a long passage from Marx to illustrate this point. She followed this with further discussion of how Hegel and Marx developed ideas about the duality between the state and society and the alienation of the modern capitalist order characterized by the separation of the wage earners from their land and social ties, the intellectual from the masses, the mind from the body, and science from ethical values, ritual, and religion. "In the city-state in Ancient Greece there was no such separation. The polis was not just a means of maintaining order. It was a religious confession, an economic concern, a cultural association and an ethical society," she wrote. "That is what is being created under our very eyes in Hungary, Poland, and Ghana."[33]

This brought Grace to the concluding point of her analysis: the theoretical and historical significance of the Convention People's Party. "For 400 years we have lived through this duality" of the state and society, she said, and the political party as an institution in the democratic states of the West, England and the United States in particular, emerged to mediate this duality. The emergence of state capitalism began to break down the separation of the state and society, with the Communist and Nazi movements, she said, trying to remove this separation from above by incorporating society into the state. This, in turn, created the movement from below to assume the functions of the state. "An understanding of this general world movement enables us to understand what is taking place in the CPP of Ghana," Grace insisted, "and the CPP of Ghana in turn enables us to understand what is taking place in Hungary and Poland. . . . The essence of the CPP, as I understand it, is that it unites the struggle for political freedom with the tasks of education, economic activity and political activity."[34]

One week later, Grace again wrote to C. L. R., this time responding to his letter describing his plans to review and update the premise of *The Black Jacobins*. "As soon as I got your letter," she began, "I went to the library and got out two copies" of the book, "one for myself and the other to make available. I have since re-read it. It is the greatest book that you have ever written, comparable in range and sureness of judgment only with the 18th Brumaire. . . . I say that not in praise but because of what I think it means for the forthcoming book."[35] Intended or not, this was the highest of praise. Karl Marx's book *The Eighteenth Brumaire of Louis Bonaparte*, which chronicles the revolution in France during 1848–51 leading to the coup d'état of Louis Bonaparte, articulates fundamental Marxist theories of historical materialism, class struggle, proletarian revolution, and the dictatorship of the proletariat. With this comparison, Grace was placing C. L. R.'s book on par with "one of the masterpieces of Marxism," as the editors of the 1963 edition of *The Eighteenth Brumaire* labeled it.[36] Though written in the months immediately following the events it describes, *The Eighteenth Brumaire* has come to be regarded as a powerful work of history. It stands, one scholar noted, as "one of Marx's most important and glittering historical writings."[37] Grace gave *The Black Jacobins* parallel praise, saying that it was at once "human, social, [and] individual," containing "a dramatic tension and suspense that I know of in no other history." Most importantly, she felt that the analysis achieved in the book gave C. L. R. standing to write the book on Ghana. "It is because of the vision of African freedom reached in [*The Black Jacobins*] 20 years ago that today you have the right, freedom, and responsibility to project your criticism of the newly independent state on such a profound level."[38]

By this time Grace had secured a copy of Nkrumah's autobiography, and she included her analysis of it in the same letter. "I got the Nkrumah autobiography the other day and read it through at practically one sitting," she wrote. "Although I found my eyes warm with tears at the climax and the certainty of Independence, I was on the whole disappointed in the book." Her disappointment derived from the theoretical and analytical limitations she saw in the book and its author, basing her analysis not only on the book but also on the JFT's interaction with Nkrumah during World War II when he was in New York and her rereading of C. L. R.'s *The Black Jacobins*. "What the book lacks and what Nkrumah lacks still," she wrote sharply, "is a sense of the economy and of economic interrelations as they become embodied in human beings and human sensitivities. . . . I emphasize 'still' because I have some idea of what he lacked in the way of knowledge of organization when he left here in 1945 and what he acquired in a few short years with Padmore." She concluded that if Nkrumah "does not acquire this, consciously cultivating it . . . he will find himself left behind as Toussaint was by Dessalines." In addition to her reference to the leadership rivalry of these two figures of the Haitian Revolution, Grace's analysis of Nkrumah's autobiography included comparisons to Marx and his *Economic and Philosophic Manuscripts of 1844*, the relationship of Chinese workers to the Chinese Communist Party, and "the new social-economic ties" being forged by Ghanaian rowers, uranium miners in the Congo, and Rhodesian copper workers.[39]

This intense though brief transatlantic exchange about Ghana showcased Grace's intellectual practice. By this time she was a committed radical, a fifteen-year veteran of Marxist organizations secure in her identity as a revolutionary. She forged this identity through a pattern of impressive intellectual work anchored in her prodigious reading. As these letters show, the probing and purposeful way in which she had read Hegel, the dedication with which she read Marx, and the focused intensity with which studied Marxist theory all informed her engagement with contemporary political questions and the books she read to understand them. Throughout her political life, specific books made meaningful and lasting imprints on Grace's thinking, with a small number of them, such as Hegel's *Phenomenology of Mind*, becoming foundational and lifelong reference points and many others serving as guideposts in particular moments or for certain political questions.[40] These letters reflect this, showing the importance she assigned to her reading, the excitement she derived from books, and the ways her reading informed her political analyses and shaped her political work.

Of course, the letters also revealed dimensions of C. L. R.'s intellectual practice. Just as he had used this correspondence to quickly shift the group's attention to Ghana, one of his letters written shortly after his return to London introduced another shift in the group's focus. "Tomorrow night I am going to meet the Rev. Luther King," he informed his comrades. Martin Luther King Jr., newly famous for his leadership of the Montgomery Bus Boycott concluded just three months earlier, had also been in Ghana for the independence celebration. He and C. L. R. did not meet there, but King and his wife were traveling through Europe on their way back to the United States, and a mutual friend arranged for them to all attend a dinner in London. C. L. R. was excited about exploring the parallels he saw between Montgomery and Ghana. "Nkrumah has worked on much the same ideas as Luther King," he offered, saying that both had accomplished something "profoundly" revolutionary. The Ghana book would include a section on the Montgomery Bus Boycott that "should make both sides of the Atlantic aware of what is involved."[41] This letter clearly showed that C. L. R. had an appreciation for the Montgomery struggle before he met King; this appreciation would grow even stronger after he had a conversation with him.

"One of the Most Astonishing Events in the History of Human Struggle"

On the afternoon of March 24, 1957, C. L. R. and Selma James welcomed to their London home Martin and Coretta King for lunch and conversation. Joining them for what turned out to be a full afternoon of discussion were two prominent members of black Britain, Barbadian writer George Lamming, author of *In the Castle of My Skin*, and political aspirant Dr. David Pitt. Ghana's independence served as impetus for this gathering. All but Lamming had attended the independence ceremonies two and a half weeks earlier, and Lamming planned to travel to Ghana in the near future through a literary prize he had recently won for *In the Castle of My Skin*. The group shared a wide-ranging conversation that inevitably turned to the Montgomery Bus Boycott. The Kings related the remarkable story of the boycott, giving a firsthand account of the mood occasioned by Rosa Parks's act of defiance, the response of local leaders, the rallying of the black community, and the building of a mass movement.[42] The opportunity to hear about the boycott from its celebrated leader deepened C. L. R.'s enthusiasm for the Montgomery movement and reinforced his conviction that a new, world revolutionary situation was afoot.

The next day C. L. R. penned a letter to his comrades back in the United States eagerly recounting the meeting. "I have stopped everything to do this," he began, "because in my opinion it is extremely urgent that you study it and penetrate as deeply as possible into what I have been trying to say over the last week or two."[43] He related in some detail the events of the boycott's initial days, focusing especially on the process by which King emerged as the leader. C. L. R. then offered commentary on the movement's political and theoretical implications. Throughout the six-page letter James issued unreserved praise for the boycott. Ranking it "one of the most astonishing events in the history of human struggle," he implored his comrades not to miss the profound historical statement registered by the Montgomery movement. "I hope no-one underestimates the tremendous inner power of a movement which results in 99% of a population refusing to ride in the buses for over a whole year. . . . It is one of the most astonishing events of endurance by a whole population that I have ever heard of."[44]

While these statements might seem to suggest that C. L. R. saw Montgomery as singular, in fact it was the connections he drew between Montgomery and Ghana—and between both of them and Hungary—that most interested and excited him. "The more I look at this," he wrote, referring to the parallels between Montgomery and Ghana, "the more I see that we are in the phase of a new experience which demands the most serious analysis."[45] He had initially identified this "new experience" with the outbreak of the Hungarian Revolution. Now, his experience in Ghana, followed almost immediately by the conversation with King, led C. L. R. to the belief that these were not only world-historical events important in their own right, but, even more significantly, they dramatically and irrefutably revealed a new stage in the history of popular struggle. Hungary, Ghana, and Montgomery were, as he saw it, constitutive of something entirely new in the history of mass protest and revolutionary change.

C. L. R. took the commonalities and parallels that he identified in all three movements as empirical support for his theoretical formulations regarding the revolutionary potential of mass action. "The most astonishing thing about the Gold Coast Revolution," he wrote, "is the fact that the masses of the people in a few months recognised Nkrumah as their leader and were prepared to go to the end with him. In Montgomery, Alabama they recognised King as their leader in a few hours and were prepared to go to the end with him. In Hungary I doubt if they recognised any particular person as the leader at all. Yet they went to the end, organising and recognising the leadership as they went along." These parallels in political development, along with their parallel timing—the Hungarian Revolution, the successful conclusion of the Montgomery Bus Boycott, and Ghana's independence all occurred between late October 1956 and early March 1957— led C. L. R. firmly to this conclusion: "The general level of the mass movement in both advanced and backward countries, particularly since the end of World War II, is such that they recognise immediately any leadership which is saying that thing that they want to hear." He urged his American comrades to see Hungary, Ghana, and Montgomery as parts of an interconnected whole that served as a "warning to all revolutionaries not to under estimate the readiness of modern people everywhere to overthrow the old regime."[46]

On the face of it, the attention that C. L. R. devoted to Ghana and Montgomery during the spring of 1957 seemed to suggest a narrowing of the distance between his and Jimmy's positions as articulated in the fall of 1956. The historical and theoretical significance that C. L. R. assigned to the Ghanaian Revolution—declaring it a milestone in world revolutionary activity; linking it with Montgomery, a major event in the black American struggle; and placing it on par with (rather than subordinate to) Hungary—might be read as C. L. R.'s answering Jimmy's plea, issued in his letter strongly dissenting from C. L. R.'s analysis of Hungary, for the group to give more attention and weight to the anticolonial revolts. In fact, differences in their positions remained in the spring of 1957. The core of these differences was this: Jimmy highlighted the *racial assertion* at the heart of these two movements, while C. L. R. highlighted *popular insurgency* as the most salient feature. For example, Jimmy took Montgomery as evidence that the black masses were ready to confront Jim Crow. He therefore championed the boycott as a forward leap in black protest and as an advance in the challenge to the southern system of racial oppression. C. L. R., by contrast, found a different meaning: for him the most meaningful and most revolutionary characteristic of the boycott was the relationship between the masses and their leaders.[47] Thus, while the more familiar analysis of Montgomery emphasized the significance of this local black population rising up in confrontation of the larger white society and its system of racial oppression, C. L. R.'s lens on Montgomery emphasized the boycott as a mass movement and looked for its greatest lessons in its leadership dynamics.

Theoretical questions about the relationship between masses and leaders in popular struggles had interested C. L. R. since at least the 1930s, when he published *The Black Jacobins*, and such questions drove his analysis of Ghana and Montgomery. He emphasized how both movements grew out of rapidly developing popular protests, which he believed ultimately demonstrated to the world "the always unsuspected power of the mass movement." In both cases, the masses called for and continuously supported the leadership that they desired and needed. Indeed, C. L. R. believed the great gift that these two leaders shared was the ability to recognize the determination of the masses, identify the directions in which they wanted to move, and then "put forward decisive programmes"—King's nonviolence and Nkrumah's Positive Action campaign—that fit the political circumstances, provided what the people themselves wanted, and therefore mobilized the masses. He judged Nkrumah and King to be remarkable political figures, but he insisted that the masses were instrumental in propelling each leader and his program. In the case of Nkrumah and the formation of the CPP, he identified "critical moments when the leadership seemed to waiver," at which point "it was always the demonstration by the mass of its force and determination and its confidence in them that enabled them to take the forward step." He drew a parallel to a "precisely similar situation" during the earliest stages of the Montgomery Bus Boycott, when its future was uncertain but the leadership was "impelled to go on by the thousands who were lining up since afternoon for the meeting that they had called that night."[48]

C. L. R. surely recognized these two movements as marking major advances in black and Pan-African political struggle, but unlike Jimmy, this was not the framework within which he analyzed or approached them. Jimmy had urged the group to see Ghana and other anticolonial revolts as revolutionary breakthroughs precisely because they wrote the newest and most transformative chapter in the struggle against colonialism and the domination of Western Europe over racialized people in the Third World. He similarly judged Montgomery to be full of revolutionary possibility because it represented an irreparable rupture in the system of Jim Crow and the practice of racial subordination in the United States. By contrast, C. L. R. celebrated Ghana and Montgomery not primarily as great moments in African liberation or black struggle, but for what they contributed to a more general theory of popular protest and a history of revolutionary change. When he traveled to Ghana for the independence ceremonies, and when he hosted Martin Luther King in his home, he was doing so as a black man and a colonial whose earliest political influences and experiences included Caribbean nationalism and African independence, but he was also a revolutionary socialist whose deepest political commitments grew from a quarter-century-long engagement with Marxism and radical politics. Specifically, his engagement with Marxism provided the worldview and intellectual framework through which he evaluated the Montgomery Bus Boycott, interpreted the protest, and analyzed its leadership following his meeting with King in March 1957.

The next *Correspondence* "Discussion Bulletin" following the meeting with King reflected C. L. R.'s newfound interest in Montgomery and his analysis of it alongside Ghana and Hungary. Nothing about the boycott had appeared in *Correspondence* during the nearly thirteen-month protest (from December 5, 1955, to December 21, 1956), during which time the group produced seven bulletins. Now the April 1957 bulletin contained two references to Montgomery, one of them an announcement about *Correspondence*'s future publishing plans saying that recent "world events" underscored the need for the paper to move to a weekly format. The announcement lists the Montgomery Bus Boycott as one of these events, along with the Suez Crisis, the uprisings in Hungary and Poland, and Ghana's independence. The other reference to Montgomery came in the peculiarly titled "Montgomery and Melville," a short piece about an upcoming civil rights demonstration in Washington, D.C., called the "Prayer Pilgrimage for Freedom." King and the newly formed Southern Christian Leadership Conference (SCLC), which was created to carry forward the momentum of the boycott, conceived the Prayer Pilgrimage as a response to President Eisenhower's refusal to speak in support of desegregation.⁴⁹ The significance of the upcoming pilgrimage, according to the *Correspondence* article, was a firm demonstration that southern blacks—"this supposedly most backward section of the Negroes in the United States"—were determined to challenge Jim Crow.⁵⁰ The article also referenced C. L. R.'s 1953 book, *Mariners, Renegades, and Castaways: The Story of Herman Melville and the World We Live In*, to suggest a link between Herman Melville's allegorical novel *Moby-Dick* and African Americans' rising protest mood embodied in the Prayer Pilgrimage.

"Montgomery and Melville" typified the group's mode of political engagement as well as its optimistic mood in the spring of 1957. The political ferment created by these "world events" of 1956–57 generated within the organization a heightened confidence in their ideas and in their ability to interpret these events for an international audience. The rather odd act of connecting Melville and *Moby-Dick* to the Montgomery movement reflected the excitement that the organization felt about their writing projects and the opportunities, as they saw them, to apply Correspondence's specific brand of Marxism. They saw these writing projects as a means of projecting Correspondence's interpretation of popular protest and socialist revolution in the modern world; these books and pamphlets were so many opportunities to intervene in the contemporary political situation.

A Return to London and the Return of *Correspondence*

Correspondence was also to be a vehicle for this intervention. However, the paper was to be a different type of intervention, and it brought its own set of challenges and potentially competing imperatives. While the group exchanged transatlantic letters analyzing Ghana and Montgomery during the spring of 1957, the American comrades, and especially those in Detroit, also worked on relaunching *Correspondence* as a biweekly newspaper. Indeed, the planning of the paper became a consistent topic in these letters alongside discussion of the Ghana book and the Hungary pamphlet, and the relationship between the two endeavors—moving *Correspondence* from "Discussion Bulletins" to a weekly paper, on one hand, and carrying out a writing program of books and pamphlets on the other—proved to be a source of contention. At issue was the group's capacity to simultaneously publish the paper and carry out its other writing projects, and how best to relate them to each other. The paper's function was to cover current affairs and global political developments, document popular protest, and give voice to the experiences and perspectives of ordinary people. The books and pamphlets, by contrast, were theoretical works designed to project in the most direct sense the organization's politics. As C. L. R. wrote of the proposed Ghana book, "We shall put forward our *whole program* in a most concrete context."[51]

Jimmy and C. L. R. again found themselves articulating competing visions of the group's work. For C. L. R., the paper and the theoretical work were in fact two parts of a whole; the organization could and should pursue the two simultaneously. However, he gave the books and pamphlets priority over *Correspondence*, believing that new global political realities had created the opportunity for projects like the Ghana book to find a receptive readership and earn wide distribution. This, in turn, would generate a broad-based international audience for the group's ideas. "Once we get the larger books out," he explained, "they will read the paper."[52] By "they" C. L. R. meant colonial peoples as well as European and American workers, all of whom "have to be prepared for the next great upheaval along the lines of Hungary and to know what side to take immediately."[53] They would be searching for the type of theoretical insights that the Ghana book and the Hungary pamphlet would deliver, C. L. R. insisted. Therefore, these works would help the group "meet the reception that is waiting for us." This was yet another expression of his unbounded confidence in the group's analysis of the contemporary world political situation. "You never can tell when the break will come," he wrote in a letter to the membership. "The thing is to see it and seize it, in fact sometimes to push out into the darkness confident that events are shaping and will come to meet you."[54]

Jimmy made a less favorable assessment of the group's ability to navigate these events. During a discussion of C. L. R.'s letters, Jimmy gave his view that "the organization goes to pieces every time something new is proposed. We can't go from pillar to post. Every time a new event takes place, we get lost." He also questioned whether the Hungary and Ghana projects had any meaningful relationship to the goal of putting out the paper. "To me the [Hungary] pamphlet is now obsolete. Maybe in 20 years it will have the same effect as [*The Black Jacobins*]" but now it served to detract from the group's efforts to relaunch the paper. "We have to have a fixed program," he urged, one based on a sober assessment of resources and that could be reasonably sustained when new political developments and opportunities arose, as they surely would, whether they be created by events like those in Hungary and Ghana, or experiences such as C. L. R.'s trip to Ghana and meeting with Martin Luther King.[55]

Grace's view fell between these two positions. She firmly believed that the group needed a fixed program for the paper, and she agreed with Jimmy that there was a tendency in the organization to let world events justify further delays in relaunching the paper. "Until this is cleared up," she wrote to C. L. R., "every new opportunity, every new revolutionary development, is going to plunge the organization into a crisis, as the Hungarian revolution has already done."[56] But she was less skeptical than Jimmy of the viability and significance of the books and pamphlets. Indeed, while Jimmy wanted the paper to take primacy over the theoretical works, and C. L. R. leaned in the other direction, Grace believed each one served a unique and vital purpose and therefore the two should claim equal attention. "We have to realize," she continued, that "revolutions and revolutionary crises are going to break out" in various places, "demanding from us continuously analytical pamphlets of a fundamental character which demonstrate our theory and drive it forward. But the only form total enough, big enough, to embrace the new ferment, is the paper. The two must go side by side, each enriching the other. . . . I believe that it has to be posed as pamphlets *and* the weekly paper, not pamphlets *or* the weekly paper."[57]

Grace's efforts proved to be pivotal in advancing both. In Detroit she was one of the members of the organization working most directly in the effort to relaunch the paper, including in her role as editor when *Correspondence* resumed regular publication. At the same time, C. L. R. relied heavily on her input and help on the Hungary and Ghana projects. As we have seen, much of C. L. R.'s correspondence with the group was letters between him and Grace in which she provided much in the way of helping him clarify his ideas for the Hungary pamphlet and then the Ghana book. As early as December 1956, she and other members of the organization began considering the possibility of her going to London to more directly assist C. L. R. with the Hungary pamphlet as she had done in 1954 to work with him and Mbiyu Koinange on *The People of Kenya Speak for Themselves*. By March 1957, with the expansion of C. L. R.'s proposed writing program following the trip to Ghana and his meeting with Martin Luther King, Grace gave the idea of her going to London serious consideration.

C. L. R. was adamant that he needed Grace's assistance to do all that he planned. In mid-March he lamented, "God help us how I wish Grace was around" as he discussed his writing plans upon returning to London.[58] A week later, at the end of a long letter laying out his emerging plans for the Ghana book, he urged the group to "free Thompson as much as you can," referring to Grace by one of her aliases. "I want to, *I have to*, lean heavily on Thompson," he confessed, "or I couldn't do it at all."[59] Nine days later he wrote to Glaberman with an even stronger plea: "After weeks and weeks of looking at it from every possible angle, I am certain that you should send Thompson here by April 15th if you can."[60]

It was not, of course, for Glaberman or C. L. R. to decide if and when Grace would go to London. The manner in which the two men discussed the matter suggests a measure of male presumption and prerogative. C. L. R.'s words also betrayed a gendered, male-centered leadership style. At the same time, his directive reflects how thoroughly he and all members of the group, including Grace herself, viewed such matters in organizational rather than personal terms. Still, the decision would not be without personal implications. Jimmy had reservations about Grace going to London. As she surveyed the possible strain on their marriage of her absence for several months, Grace explained to C. L. R. that "the separation this time [would be] a lot different from before," referring to the four months she spent in London working with C. L. R. in 1954. That trip occurred at an earlier point in Grace and Jimmy's relationship, just before they were married. Since then they had grown closer, personally and politically. "Over the past years," Grace continued, she and Jimmy "have become very close and dependent on one another."[61]

Indeed, through three years of marriage, Grace and Jimmy were growing together, learning from each other, and benefiting from each other's intellectual and political strengths. Grace provided a glimpse of this in one of her letters to C. L. R. discussing Kwame Nkrumah and Ghana: "As I write, I have in my mind a picture of the rowers in Accra who take the cocoa bags out in canoes to the ships in deep water . . . and in my ear is the music they sing as they work which I heard over the TV last week on the Report of Nixon's Tour. In this work, in these rowers, are not only the limitations, but [also] the perspectives of the African economy as part of the work economy. In one sense they remind me of rowers at Pirseus in Ancient Greece. In another more important sense, they make me think of what I learned from [Jimmy] on our cross-country trips—that sense of the continent as having been created by human labor, a sense of the inter-relations of labor which is now in the personality of each worker."[62]

By highlighting what she learned from Jimmy on these cross-country trips, Grace was affirming the political wisdom that he derived from his background and experiences that differed from hers—namely, his rural upbringing, experiences riding freight trains, and many years as an autoworker. She was also asserting the significance of their divergent backgrounds for their relationship.[63] Decades later, after they had made many more such trips over many years, she reinforced this point with a telling description of their trips: "Traveling along the highway, I would have my head in a book, while he was pointing out the cows and sheep, counting the freight cars and trying to figure out what they were carrying based on his knowledge of industry and agriculture in the region." And this, she said, reflected not just their divergent personal styles but also their differing political styles: "My approach to political questions came more from books, his from experience."[64]

This duality of books and experience may have been exaggerated—theoretical concepts informed Jimmy's political practice more than the statement would suggest—but it captures the complementary and cumulative nature of their collaboration. Combining their respective approaches to the politics that they engaged together, Grace and Jimmy could learn from each other, influence each other's thinking, and grow together. This mutual growth came to be a crucial dynamic of their intellectual and political partnership, and this is what Grace was coming to see, and reporting to C. L. R. in their 1957 correspondence, as she weighed the decision to join him in London for several months.

Grace did decide to make the trip, and by early April she was arranging her plans. She and Jimmy apparently agreed that this was best, despite his clearly registered reservations. Nonetheless, Grace assured C. L. R. that Jimmy "will do everything he can to make it possible, whatever his doubts. That is the sort of person he is."[65] In addition to the personal toll, one of his doubts was that Grace's absence would further distract the group from the goal of reestablishing *Correspondence* as a biweekly newspaper.

Publishing their discussion bulletins was part of this effort, and the one released just as Grace prepared to leave for London carried a front-page story by Jimmy (using his pseudonym Al Whitney) that captured his thinking and political focus. "A Report on the March on Washington" gave a first-hand account of the Prayer Pilgrimage to Washington, D.C. the preceding May, a major civil rights demonstration. Thousands of people from across the country congregated at the Lincoln Memorial to register their support for civil rights and to call for federal legislation. They listened to a series of speeches by civil rights luminaries, capped off by a rousing, crowd-pleasing address by Martin Luther King. While the SCLC named their protest "Prayer Pilgrimage for Freedom," its stated goals of expressing black unity and urging federal action on civil rights made the moniker that Jimmy gave it, "the March on Washington," equally appropriate. That name, of course, was subsequently claimed by the much larger and more famous civil rights demonstration six years later. The huge crowds and celebrated oratory of the 1963 "March on Washington for Jobs and Justice" completely superseded the Prayer Pilgrimage in both size and importance, but the thousands who attended the 1957 affair made it the largest civil rights demonstration to date and a significant moment in the rising civil rights movement of the mid-1950s. Jimmy concluded his article with this assessment of the impact of the Prayer Pilgrimage: "The southern people went home determined beyond the expectations of even King. No one in the South is big enough to stop this march of people and no one can call it off."[66]

C. L. R. felt an equal conviction about the movements in Ghana and Hungary, and his next letter to the group laid out specific and ambitious plans for the writing projects on them that he and Grace would carry out upon her arrival. In close collaboration with Selma James, who had moved to London in 1956, Grace would provide intellectual, editorial, and secretarial contributions to these projects that were in various states of planning or preparation. The most important of these were three books. The first was to be the Ghana book, then the book on the Hungarian Revolution, and finally a book on cricket that would make an analysis of the sport alongside analyses of British society and political history. This partially autobiographical work aimed to tackle "the question of what constitutes an education" in "human terms" and through a writing style "uniting the profoundest universals with the concrete, the individual."[67] These books would be "written in a style that can be understood at once by thousands of people," C. L. R. explained shortly before Grace's arrival. He wanted them all to "appear quickly" and to contain "from the first the basis for wide circulation among all strata, [in] many countries, forming the *bulwark* of mass support."[68]

Grace set sail toward the end of April, arriving in London at the end of the month. She would spend four months there, working closely with C. L. R. and Selma. The trio quickly fell into "a fixed program" of work, as Grace explained in a letter to her comrades back in the United States shortly after her arrival. Their schedule called for "so many hours each day, so many words to be written each day, a total of 200,000 in four months." She was also glad to report that "the daily program includes time for a walk on the heath every morning before breakfast and time to listen to the radio after dinner for an hour before doing more work."[69] There were other diversions from the hectic pace of work as well, such as the cricket season. They mostly took in the matches on a television set rented for that purpose to save on the time and expense of attending matches while facilitating C. L. R.'s cricket journalism.[70]

The most important diversion for Grace was Jimmy, who spent about one month with her in London.[71] The previous two or three summers, Grace and Jimmy had driven to Los Angeles to spend his vacation from Chrysler with Freddy and Lyman Paine. This year they decided Jimmy would travel to London for his vacation. This provided a nice interruption of the long separation that Grace's trip was causing. It seems that there was also a therapeutic goal behind Jimmy's going to London. He had recently recovered from an illness, and members of the group, including C. L. R., believed that this vacation would be a much needed and deserved respite,[72] which it turned out to be. This was Jimmy's first trip abroad, "and he was intrigued by what was happening all around him," Grace recalled many years later. For example, "Jimmy was fascinated by the fact that plumbing pipes were still outside and therefore much more accessible than the enclosed ones in the United States." Among their many activities, Grace and Jimmy attended African independence rallies, visited Windsor Castle in England and Cardiff Castle in Wales, and even took an excursion to Paris.[73]

Grace still managed to be especially productive during her four-month stay in London. This time gave her and C. L. R. their first opportunity since his departure from the United States in 1953 for daily collaboration, where they could develop a rhythm and a productive pace while working simultaneously on multiple writing projects.[74] Indeed, part of C. L. R.'s insistence that Grace join him and Selma in London may have been his attempt to recreate the exciting intellectual partnership they had built in the JFT in New York during the 1940s.[75] They made progress on all three writing projects during the spring and summer of 1957. However, the books did not all "appear quickly," as C. L. R. had hoped they would, nor were they completed in the order he had projected. C. L. R.'s initial plan called for the Ghana book to be completed first. He had already developed much of the book before Grace got to London, and it was that book on which they focused upon her arrival. She indicated in a letter written to the group shortly after that they expected the book to be done by the end of May. However, the Hungary book quickly took primacy, and they devoted much of their time and effort to that project. This rather suddenly adjusted the group's writing and publishing priorities—as recently as April 13, C. L. R. had restated his plan that the Ghana book would precede that on Hungary. In the months to follow, the organization made the publication and promotion of the Hungary book a central focus; the Ghana and cricket books, though both had been mostly completed in 1957, were published years later.[76]

Jimmy and Grace returned to Detroit in late August, in time to participate in the final work to relaunch *Correspondence*. On September 21–22 the organization held a national convention in Detroit attended by the full membership across the country, just as they had done with the initial founding of the paper. During the convention Jimmy and Lyman were elected as the cochairmen of the organization.[77] This reflected a solidification of Jimmy's leadership of the organization. In title Jimmy and Lyman shared responsibility, but in practice, with Jimmy there in Detroit and Lyman in Los Angeles, "90% of the burden of national leadership rest[ed] with" Jimmy, as Glaberman described the situation. In a letter to C. L. R., Glaberman reported that Jimmy had been "the key figure in the convention" and "he remains that today. He consciously and vigorously took over the direction of the organization and his leadership was accepted by everyone." Given the many activities and spaces in which Jimmy had taken responsibility for building the organization—leading editorial committees and reaching out to workers in his neighborhood and at Chrysler—Glaberman expressed concern that Jimmy not overextend himself: "The organization looks to him to give direction on all these things and he is not very cooperative when any attempt is made to slow him down."[78]

The convention also confirmed the decision that Grace would be the new editor of *Correspondence*. They published the first issue under her editorship, and the first in this new phase of the paper as a monthly, in October 1957. It appeared just days after the nation witnessed the dramatic scenes of the Little Rock school desegregation crisis. In early September, nine black students attempted to enroll in the previously all-white Central High School in Little Rock, Arkansas, in accordance with a plan adopted by the local school board. The students faced the opposition of white mobs and Arkansas governor Orval Faubus, who ordered the National Guard to prevent the students from enrolling. Following three weeks of court proceedings, Faubus's refusal to fully comply with the federal court, and ultimately mob violence, the escalating crisis compelled President Eisenhower to send federal troops to Little Rock, opening the way for the students' admission to Central. As the first full-blown confrontation between the federal government and southern resistance to school desegregation (and the first use of federal power to enforce equal treatment of African Americans in the South since Reconstruction), the nearly month-long crisis became a flashpoint in the civil rights movement as well as one of the earliest major news stories of the still-young television era. Little Rock claimed the nation's (and the world's) attention during the latter part of September 1957 as Correspondence prepared the October issue of the paper. This is reflected in the three editorials on Little Rock in that issue appearing under the banner "Events in Little Rock Mark the End of an Era."[79]

Jimmy likely wrote all three editorials, and one, titled "Who Is for Law and Order?" carried his byline. He argued that the spectacle, seen in other recent conflicts and then repeated most dramatically in the Little Rock crisis, of white people defying police as well as state and federal troops raised the question, "If white people defy the Constitution, who then are the law-abiding citizens of the U.S. and who is for democracy?" Inherent in his answer was a reshaping of the relations between blacks and whites. On one hand this meant the loss of white people's claim to civic and moral authority. "The Little Rock crisis has put an end to the era of the white man's burden to preserve democracy," he asserted. "The white man's burden now is to prove that he believes in democracy and that he can follow the example of the colored people in upholding law and order." As for black Americans, their newfound racial assertion struck a blow to the edifice upon which their subordination had long rested. "For years untold colored people have been forced to maneuver in all directions trying to avoid a head-on collision," Jimmy wrote. "They have allowed white people to name them 'Negroes' by which the whites mean a thing and not a person. They have stayed out of the public parks, restaurants, hotels and golf courses, walked on the cinder path when meeting whites on the sidewalk, gone to separate schools, worked on the worst jobs under the worst conditions, smiled and acted unhurt when abused in public places." But the recent tide of black protest revealed that African Americans were making "an about face." Black people, he wrote, were not only pressing for their rights but were also beginning to "denounce" the people and practices that had denied them those rights.[80]

Jimmy's analysis of Little Rock differed from other commentaries, which tended to emphasize it as an advance in the struggle for integration, highlight the moral questions it raised, or discuss it as a crisis of authority played out through conflict among the local, state, and national governments. Instead, Jimmy said Little Rock represented a rather sudden transformation now taking place among black people. The importance of Little Rock for him was in revealing how black people were seeing themselves differently and thus making this "about face," no longer accepting the southern way of life and even rejecting the standards by which white people had organized society and elevated themselves. This analysis, and all of the editorials on Little Rock more generally, continued the focus and tone of Jimmy's previous writings in the paper, but they also reflected the greater attention that *Correspondence* was soon to give to the escalating civil rights movement. The paper no longer had the "Special Negro News" page. Instead, material on civil rights protests, what the group still called the Negro Question or the Negro Struggle, appeared with increasing frequency and more widely throughout the paper under Grace's editorship and Jimmy's leadership of the organization.

Different Worlds of Work

The FBI took note of these developments within the organization and newspaper through its continued surveillance of Grace and Jimmy. The bureau maintained its contingent of informants, who provided often detailed and usually accurate information on the Boggses' activities. FBI agents kept in regular contact with these informants, who reported on such things as the meetings Jimmy and Grace attended, their writings and speaking engagements, the publication plans for the paper, their financial contributions to the organization, and their travel. As with her 1948 trip to Paris, the FBI took particular note of Grace's London trip, and informants gave it information regarding her travel dates, the purpose of her trip, and Jimmy's visit. Informants served as just one of many means of surveillance. FBI agents also conducted "physical surveillance" of Jimmy and Grace at their home, checked a credit bureau and the files of local law enforcement agencies for damning information on them (of which there was none), and conducted "pretext interviews" by calling the Boggses' home under assumed identities, in one case posing as an insurance salesperson. The FBI even obtained a sample of Grace's handwriting by securing a copy of *The People of Kenya Speak for Themselves* that Grace had signed and given to the owner of the mail service that she used to distribute the book.[81] Agents also extended their surveillance into Jimmy's and Grace's places of employment. In what became a yearly practice, agents spoke with Chrysler's Employment and Employee Services office to confirm Jimmy's employment.[82] Grace's employment was intermittent and more difficult to confirm, leading the FBI to use the even more surreptitious tactic of monitoring her at work. According to Grace's FBI file, "the Subject was observed by a Special Agent of the FBI at her employment as a receptionist" on multiple occasions and at different employers over several years.[83]

While the FBI was able to learn Grace's work history and employment patterns, its agents did not discern the relationship between her employment and her politics. On the surface it would seem that the two were not related, as politics were central to Grace's life, whereas employment seemed to occupy only a small corner of her time and attention. However, her choices of and approach to employment reflected an important dimension of her political identity and practice. Remarkably, Grace never considered pursuing a career and very rarely sought consistent employment. At no time in her long life was Grace driven by the question of how to make a living. Accordingly, political considerations frequently guided her choices about employment, including where to work, for how long, and even whether to take a job. This set of choices, of course, was available to her because of the relative material security she enjoyed at most stages of her life: her comfortable middle-class upbringing and the family support she continued to enjoy when she returned to New York during the 1940s; her marital union with Jimmy; and the support of her political community, as she sometimes worked as a member of the organization's (minimally) paid staff and later received financial support from Freddy and Lyman. But that alone does not explain her employment decisions. Grace's indifference to career and upward mobility reflected her decidedly nonacquisitive personality and a complete disinterest in status or the trappings of any sort of professional life.

This was evident in 1940 when Grace earned her Ph.D. Securing an academic job "was never on my mind," she said decades later, thinking back to her mind-set and priorities while completing the degree. With no aspiration of becoming a professor—"I had not studied philosophy in order to teach it"—Grace had allowed herself to sink into her studies without regard for where they would lead, intellectually or materially. The need to eventually find employment beyond what she had already been doing "was never in my consciousness. It just never bothered me," she recalled. "What I knew was that by and large I had been able to make a living because I was a very good typist and I figured, if I needed money I can type."[84] And that is what she did over the next two decades, taking various secretarial and clerical jobs, most of them short term or temporary and some of them part time.

Grace held a string of such office jobs in Detroit during the second half of the 1950s.[85] She thought about her employment through the prism of her politics and the needs of Correspondence, making decisions about the type of jobs to seek, which offers to accept, and when or how often to work with the organization foremost in mind. "I got a job today and started this afternoon," she wrote to C. L. R. in April 1955, describing what may have been her first office job in Detroit. It was as a receptionist in the office of an auto parts supplier located on West Grand Boulevard. "It's temporary and it doesn't pay much by Detroit standards, but it's just the sort of thing I want, and when this one ends (at the end of the week) I'm quite sure there will be others." The job fit well into her plan for the type of work she sought. "What I have in mind is this," she explained. "I don't want an executive secretary job which demands thinking about your job all day long and outside of working hours as well. I could probably get one of those if I tried hard enough, and it would probably pay quite well. But then I would have to be responsible on the job." Instead, she wanted jobs where she would use her strong typing and shorthand skills but that required little commitment from her; she wanted jobs that would not impede, and would possibly even facilitate, her political work. She found an agency that would match her with such jobs, and it brought immediate results. "I went down there this morning, the fellow there was impressed with my qualifications and sent me out immediately." A hidden benefit to this arrangement was that the companies who utilized the agency were, as Grace noted, "usually in a tight fix so they can't be particular about race." Her statement suggests that she had previous personal experience with workplace racial discrimination, or that she simply recognized the possibility of facing it. She made no further reference to race, other than to say that her boss at the new job was a white southerner. The two of them "got along remarkably well," and the man repeatedly told Grace that she was doing a good job. If he reported the same to the agency, they would call Grace for other jobs.[86]

Perhaps the greatest benefit was flexibility. The agency gave her the option of refusing any job without jeopardizing future opportunities. This meant that at those times when political or organizational matters demanded her attention, "I can be free to do whatever is needed." Her paid work would not interfere with her political work. "So all in all, I am quite satisfied ... for the time being," Grace concluded. She acknowledged "an element of uncertainty" regarding pay. "This week I may make $25. Next week perhaps nothing. The following week $60 or the like."[87] She earned the $25 working only two and a half days that week, during which time she received a permanent full-time offer: "While I was working there, a man from an office on the same floor came in and asked if I would like to work full time for him. I told him that I was working part-time because I was a writer and needed free time for myself and I didn't want to tie myself down to any particular job." The man responded by saying the job only required her to answer the phone and write letters, leaving her with a great deal of time to herself. "It is very tempting," Grace admitted, but still declined.[88]

Grace's and Jimmy's respective employment patterns and relationships to the world of paid labor marked another significant contrast between them. While she worked intermittently and often part time at various jobs, he worked full time at Chrysler continuously. Grace's jobs gave her the flexibility and time to engage in her political work, sometimes working two or three days per week and devoting the other days to organizational or political activities. Jimmy's job afforded no such opportunity. Grace's office jobs also allowed her to use time and other resources. "I am making these notes while at work, on my lunch hour," she wrote at the beginning of a letter to C. L. R. "One good thing about an office job is that you are never too far away from a typewriter."[89] Working at Chrysler afforded Jimmy something very different: the factory and the union were primary sites of his political development and political activity. From his participation in strikes, the flying squadron, and political education work during his early years as an autoworker to his activism in the Discrimination Action Committee and his ongoing work with Chrysler Local 7's Fair Employment Practices Committee, Jimmy's employment at Chrysler significantly configured his politics.

By the mid-1950s, Jimmy's political engagement at work and in the union was largely distilled through his daily interactions and relationships with his coworkers. In 1957 Grace described an ongoing conversation that she and Jimmy had about his experiences at work: "Every day in the shop he is under pressure from hundreds and indirectly thousands of guys expecting from him answers on everything—from the history of Egypt to the climate in Africa. Being able to answer these questions is almost a question of survival for him."[90] Jimmy's coworkers learned to rely on him in this way through years of his demonstrated knowledgeability and active engagement with the wider world, and this dynamic was just one dimension of the relationships Jimmy built with people in the plant. He shared close friendships with all types of people at Chrysler Jefferson, such as Nick DiGaetano, who mentored him; Willis, who joined with Jimmy in several political activities; and coworkers like Joe Maddox who were not political. Maddox and Jimmy worked together in the material control department, and they got to know each other very well starting in the late 1940s. "Jimmy was one of the best persons that I ever met, one of my best friends," Maddox recalled. He said everyone in the shop knew that Jimmy was very active and committed to his political views, but Jimmy never forced them on anyone. Maddox recalled the "sick club" as an example of Jimmy's organizing and his relations with his shopmates: "Jimmy said we should form a group to help each other when we get sick." Club members paid dues and held monthly meetings in each other's homes. When a member fell sick, the club paid $25 to help them until they returned to work.[91]

The union continued to be an important space for Jimmy's activism, though the character of that activism and the weight it carried relative to his other political concerns had shifted by the mid-1950s. He remained active in his home local, United Auto Workers (UAW) Local 7, but was a staunch opponent of the union leadership. Jimmy was especially critical of Walter Reuther, who had been elected president of the UAW in 1946 and then president of the Congress of Industrial Organizations (CIO) in 1952, and the union machine over which he had presided during the preceding decade. Writing to radical pacifist, preacher, and labor organizer A. J. Muste in 1956, Jimmy said Reuther "has red-baited more than any statesmen with the exception of McCarthy, and particularly against his opponents in the union" and he derided the head of the CIO for his racial politics: "Reuther will go to India or Europe and out-do the State Department in lauding the democratic virtues of America by explaining how Negroes and whites work side by side in the shop. But he says nothing about the fact that the moment the whistle blows, each race goes to its separate neighborhood."[92] Jimmy challenged the union leadership at various turns, including through Local 7's Fair Employment Practices Committee, of which he was a founding member and the secretary for ten years. At the time of his exchange with Muste, Jimmy was also challenging the leadership through union politics surrounding the recent election at Local 7. An antiadministration slate narrowly lost the election in a runoff vote, which Jimmy and Willis believed reflected a weakness in the Reuther administration and a new willingness among Chrysler workers to challenge it, and the two men began developing a strategy to stimulate and grow this "revolt against Reuther."[93]

The plan was to create a year-round program of education and agitation among their coworkers that would galvanize anti-Reuther sentiment and lead to future election victories. To do this, Jimmy and Willis would distribute leaflets in the plant monthly designed to show the prospects for a new path beyond the Reuther machine. Covering topics such as the powers and limits of a chief steward, the duties of a shop committeeman, and the working of machine politics, the leaflets would expose two competing views, contrasting "what the rank and filers are thinking" with "the union set-up." Parallel to this, the anti-Reuther forces would need to be building a slate for the next election. Some of the leaflets would lay out the views of the people on the slate and show how they were against the machine and supported the rank and file. The goal was "not just opposing" the administration but also "giving the workers something. Explaining to them . . . facts."[94] Jimmy and Willis would write and run off the leaflets, and they hoped to enlist others who opposed the Reuther administration to help with distribution. All of the leaflets would be anonymous, signed with a fictional name such as "Eagle Eye" or "Watch Dog."[95]

Jimmy's strategy for union elections showed another emergent point of ideological divergence in Correspondence. Jimmy and Willis met with Martin Glaberman to share this plan, which Glaberman received "with a great deal of reserve." The next day he wrote to C. L. R. expressing his fears that Jimmy was reverting back to two things the group had left behind when they left Trotskyism: "small mass partyism," and the idea of the "backwardness of the workers." The former related to Jimmy's role in the plant. "It is not the same," Glaberman acknowledged, but Jimmy and Willis's plan "strikes me as being mighty close to the old Trotskyist trade union policy of writing revolutionary leaflets which left-wing bureaucrats could use to their advantage." Jimmy and Willis, he explained, were known throughout the plant as radicals and thus would not be distributing the leaflets as rank-and-file workers. Rather, they would be acting as "politicos, impatient politicos," meaning they were driven by a desire to "shake up the local." In his view, the leaflets would not be what Correspondence valued most: a spontaneous articulation of rank-and-file workers' thoughts. This related to Glaberman's second concern, which spoke to Jimmy's role in the organization. He felt that Jimmy and Willis's plan lacked "an attempt to find out what workers were thinking and doing, or are willing to do" in relation to the organization Correspondence or *Correspondence* newspaper. In this sense, he believed that Jimmy, if only temporarily, had given up on a core principle of the organization and purpose of the paper. "To me," he concluded, Jimmy new activism in the plant "reflects a turning away from" Correspondence and toward "the milieu where he is most at home and at ease."[96]

The Age of Automation

In fact, during the second half of the 1950s, Jimmy began turning from both the milieu of the union and the worker-centered politics of Correspondence. A central reason was his analysis of automation. Since the beginning of the decade he had made a serious examination of this technological innovation that was bringing rapid changes to the factory, increasingly impacting workers, and exercising the minds of a wide range of social commentators and policy makers.

By the early 1960s he had concluded that automation represented a new stage in capitalist production. This formed the basis of his analysis of the nation's economic and technological development—and along with it his analyses of the meaning and potential of the black struggle and of the prospects for an American revolution—in his 1963 book *The American Revolution: Pages from a Negro Worker's Notebook*, which threw Jimmy into a decade-long national conversation about the impacts of automation.

That conversation had its origins in the immediate postwar years, when this new technology began to generate great interest, even fascination. The term "automation" could apply to a range of new production technologies, at times being used as an all-encompassing term to describe widespread, rapid technological change, but the generally accepted use of the term was to describe specific, new production processes involving three components: automatic machines to perform the production, specific devices to pass material from one automatic machine to another, and a control mechanism with feedback capacities to regulate the entire series of operations.[97] The potential for drastic economic and social implications sparked wide interest.

The fascination with automation in part reflected the country's mood in the immediate postwar period, including a solid ideological commitment to technological progress. Representatives of industry (along with their counterparts in science and engineering) captured this mood by championing automation as the next step in the development of new production machinery and American industrial prowess. These boosters quickly built up automation into "a new gospel of postwar economics," lauding it as "a universal ideal" that would "revolutionize every area of industry."[98] For example, the November 1946 issue of *Fortune* magazine focused on the prospects for "The Automatic Factory." The issue included an article titled "Machines without Men" that envisioned a completely automated factory where virtually no human labor would be needed.[99] With visions of "transforming the entire manufacturing sector into a virtually labor-free enterprise," factory owners in a range of industries began to introduce automation in the postwar period.[100]

The auto industry moved with particular haste. After the massive wave of strikes in 1945–46, automakers seized on automation as a way to replace workers with machines.[101] As they converted back to civilian auto production after World War II, they took the opportunity to install new labor-saving automatic production equipment. The two largest automakers, Ford and General Motors, set the pace. General Motors introduced the first successful automated transfer line at its Buick engine plant in Flint in 1946 (shortly after a 113-day strike, the longest in the industry's history). The next year Ford established an automation department (a Ford executive, Del S. Harder, is credited with coining the word "automation"). By October 1948 the department had approved $3 million in spending on 500 automated devices, with early company estimates predicting that these devices would result in a 20 percent productivity increase and the elimination of 1,000 jobs. Through the late 1940s and 1950s Ford led the way in what became known as "Detroit automation," undertaking an expensive automation program, which it carried out in concert with the company's plans to decentralize operations away from the city. A major component of this effort was the Ford plant in the Cleveland suburb of Brook Park, a $2 billion engine-making complex that attracted visitors from government, industry, and labor and became a national symbol of automation in the 1950s.[102]

Jimmy's writings about automation coincided with a national debate about its meaning and impact. Initially, the debate leaned more toward celebration as automation's enthusiasts successfully generated great interest in and positive press for the new technology during the early 1950s. Periodicals such as *Business Week*, *Time*, and *U.S. News and World Report* extolled the virtues and coming advances of automation, giving readers excited forecasts of fully automated factories in articles titled "Automation: A Factory Runs Itself," "Coming Industrial Era: The Wholly Automatic Factory," and "Push Button Plant: It's Here—Machines Do the Work and a Man Looks On."[103] Corporate interests raised a nearly unified voice heralding automation as a certain and universal beneficial advancement. However, some observers saw the new technology as a cause for concern and cautioned that the final word on automation would depend on the choices that industry and the nation made in the face of difficult questions regarding the pace of automation's implementation, the uses of the new productivity, and the fate of displaced workers as well as depleted or eliminated job classifications, communities, and even industries. Norbert Wiener, for example, a prominent MIT mathematician and pioneer in the science of cybernetics, emphasized the potentially calamitous economic and social consequences of the new production technology. Wiener had begun to express concerns about the impacts of automation on labor and the entire society during World War II, and he authored two books in the immediate Cold War years warning that potentially disastrous unemployment and related social problems may come from industry's drive toward automation. He characterized automation and computer controls in the production process as the "modern" or "second" industrial revolution, which even more than the first held "unbounded possibilities for good and evil."[104] In particular, Wiener feared that the larger impact of the changes caused by automation would be a massive displacement of workers, compounded by the profit-driven indifference of industry. "The automatic machine . . . will produce an unemployment situation, in comparison with which the present recession and even the depression of the thirties will seem a pleasant joke."[105]

If not quite to the level of the Depression, automation did exact a considerable toll on Detroit's economy. It has been identified as the single most important force in restructuring Detroit's economy after the war, with black workers hardest hit.[106] Automation-related job loss in Detroit-area Ford plants rose above 4,000 between 1951 and 1953.[107] Chrysler's flagship plant, Dodge Main, reduced employment in its paint shop by almost 2,500 and by more than 3,000 on two of its assembly lines. At his own plant, Chrysler Jefferson, Jimmy saw how the company, which pushed an aggressive program of automation during the 1950s in an effort to catch up with Ford and General Motors, eliminated an entire shop by sending the work to the newly automated plant in Trenton, Michigan, where it took only 596 workers to do what 1,800 had done at Chrysler Jefferson.[108] He also witnessed the impact on suppliers and independent auto manufacturers who were forced to close, such as the Packard plant located near his east side neighborhood. After reducing its workforce from 16,000 to 4,000 during the preceding four years, Packard closed the plant in 1956. With several other plants in the area also closing around the same time, Detroit's east side lost over 70,000 jobs between 1954 and 1960.[109] These numbers bespeak Detroit's protracted and painful process of deindustrialization, with automation at the center of enormous job loss, economic decay, and social disaster.[110]

Jimmy was among the earliest to give serious consideration to the impact of automation on workers and their world in the plant. Writing to C. L. R. in 1955, Grace reported that early on Jimmy had gone to the central Marxist text as a guide. With the first sign of implementation of automation in his plant, Jimmy "took down *Capital* from the shelf, began reading it and drawing up charts of the workers in his shop, the number of skilled, the number of unskilled, the assembly, the shipping workers etc."[111] A decade later his analysis of automation would in part lead him to challenge and eventually reject key tenets of Marxism. Along the way, he grappled with questions that went beyond the immediate problems of worker displacement and unemployment to larger questions of production. What did automation mean for the next generation of would-be autoworkers? Rather than simply taking a defensive posture of protecting jobs, how should autoworkers respond to automation? What new social possibilities could this new productive capacity open up? Did automation signal a new era of production? If so, what new roles should workers and unions assume in production?

These questions grew from Jimmy's identity and experiences as a worker, but they reflected as well his growing disengagement with the worker-centered politics of Correspondence. Meanwhile, the organization celebrated a publication that further projected those politics.

Facing Reality

The June 1958 issue of *Correspondence* included a "Correspondence Special Book Supplement," marking a significant step in the group's publishing program. Under the headline "Facing Reality—1958," the supplement presented an excerpt from *Facing Reality*, a book being published that month by Correspondence Publishing Company. The book carried no subtitle, but explanatory words on the cover declared its focus:

The New Society . . .
Where to look for it
How to bring it closer
A statement for our time

The organization touted the book's arrival as a milestone in socialist thought, and they also celebrated the book as a major achievement for the group itself. Written largely in the fall of 1956 and the spring and summer of 1957 when Grace was in London, the project grew in scope from a pamphlet on Hungary to a book analyzing the Hungarian Revolution in relation to other world events. Members of the organization began referring to it as "the manifesto," reflecting their determination to present the book as a major statement of the group's ideas. During the end of 1957 and the first half of 1958 the group expended considerable energy in the arduous task of self-publishing the work. Jimmy, as we have seen, held strong reservations about the project, but as chair of the organization, he continued to support the group's work in its publication. In fact, it was Jimmy who suggested the book's title.[112] The group organized a book release party, and subsequent issues of *Correspondence* carried announcements for the book as well as material from it. This sentence from the book appeared on the top of the second page of several issues: "Our Purpose: 'To recognize that the new society exists and to record the facts of its existence'" (from *Facing Reality*).

The focal point of *Facing Reality* is the Hungarian Revolution and C. L. R.'s contention that it marked a decisive moment in the history of ordinary people's struggle against the bureaucratic state and its control over their lives. The book's analytical and narrative starting point is the workers' councils that sprang from the revolution. They were, for C. L. R. and most members of Correspondence, the antidote to official society and "the shadow of state power" that it cast all over the world. "By the total uprising of a people," the book asserts, "the Hungarian Revolution has disclosed the political form which not only destroys the bureaucratic state power, but substitutes in its place a socialist democracy, based not on the control of people but on the mastery of things. This political form is the Workers Councils, embracing the whole of the working population from bottom to top, organized at the source of all power, the place of work, making all decisions in the shop or in the office."[113] The book travels well beyond Hungary for examples of popular insurgency—the reader learns of struggles in the United States and Britain, Russia and France, and Ghana and the other "new nations" of the Third World. Likewise, *Facing Reality* examines multiple sites and sources of struggle, including wildcat strikes, shop-floor organizations, African Americans' fight for full citizenship, and the roles to be played by artists, intellectuals, and the middle classes. Another concern of the book is the appropriate form and function of a Marxist organization in the revolutionary upheavals to come, reflecting Correspondence's own history. But *Facing Reality* drives inexorably toward the conclusion that workers' councils are the purest and most sure form of contemporary socialism.[114]

The book's discussion of automation provides one example of how it arrives at this conclusion and also reveals how C. L. R.'s analysis of automation differed from Jimmy's. A section titled "Automation and the Total Crisis" argued that the new technology went to the heart of workers' struggle with management because automation had begun to "dominate American industry and all forms of economic organization." In some ways the analysis of automation in *Facing Reality* closely paralleled Jimmy's analysis. Both said that automation constituted a new stage of production. The stage of mass production—and with it the assembly-line worker—was coming to an end. Thus, unlike the introduction of previous stages, automation represented a change in production technology that would reduce rather than grow the workforce. Similarly, both believed that the trade union movement—itself an outgrowth of mass production—had no answer for automation because it had conceded to management all control over production. Thus, Jimmy and C. L. R. agreed that the advent of automation was pushing society toward crisis. However, *Facing Reality* came to a conclusion that was very different from Jimmy's regarding the ultimate meaning of automation for workers and social transformation. "It is from the growing realization that society faces total collapse," C. L. R. wrote in *Facing Reality*, "that has arisen the determination of American workers to take the control of total production away from the capitalists and into their own hands. Up to now American workers have only organized to defend themselves from the machine inside the individual factories. Now, in defense of all society, they are being driven to organize themselves to regulate total production. . . . Far more than in any country, the automation of industry in the United States is creating the actual conditions for a Government of Workers Councils."[115]

Jimmy's experiences as an autoworker inspired no such confidence in the acumen or political vision of American industrial workers. He saw no indication that workers would seize the control of production and respond to automation in the way *Facing Reality* predicted. To the contrary, based on what he saw happening in his plant and in Detroit generally, Jimmy argued that automation was further weakening workers' power. Moreover, he feared that it would deepen their participation in and ideological commitment to the consumption-driven progress that he lamented in his early *Correspondence* articles on the impact of automation.

Jimmy and C. L. R. were increasingly in disagreement regarding the role of the American working class. For C. L. R., automation would propel the working class to assume its historic role: by taking control of production and then creating structures of self-government in the plant, workers would lead the way in transforming society and thus fulfill the role assigned to them in Marxist theory as the agents of revolutionary change. By contrast, Jimmy argued that automation, as a new stage of production, forced a rethinking of Marx's scenario of revolution. By the early 1960s, Jimmy believed that black Americans, not the industrial working class, constituted the social force best suited to lead a revolution in the United States. In 1961–62, this theoretical difference would contribute to larger political differences and an organizational crisis culminating in the collapse of Correspondence.

The roots of these contending theoretical perspectives and their attendant political trajectories were evident in 1958, the year that *Facing Reality* appeared. The book reinforced the worker-centrism that had been at the heart of the organization since the founding of the Johnson-Forest Tendency. This emphasis on worker-centered self-organization served as the original guiding principle of *Correspondence*, and it now animated *Facing Reality*'s celebration of workers' councils. However, as Grace and Jimmy busied themselves within an ever-wider network of black radicals, *Correspondence* began to shift away from its previous identity as a workers' paper. Under Grace's editorial direction, material on the civil rights movement and black protest politics supplemented and eventually supplanted the paper's coverage of workers' and workplace struggles. For example, the July 1958 issue of *Correspondence*, the issue immediately following the one with the *Facing Reality* book supplement, ran a front-page story on the continuing efforts to secure compliance in the Little Rock school desegregation case. Subsequent issues carried a political cartoon comparing the Little Rock case to the U.S. involvement in Lebanon, more coverage of Little Rock as well as other actions to force school desegregation across the South, and articles on a large youth march for integration in Washington, D.C. These pieces shared a common theme of emphasizing grassroots initiatives in the civil rights movement and reflected the paper's editorial tenor of highlighting the potential of grassroots political mobilization to both bypass established black leadership and confront the fulcrums of power in official society.

The November 1958 issue of *Correspondence* carried an article by attorney Conrad Lynn titled "Accommodating Negro Leadership" that epitomizes this editorial focus. It also points to Jimmy and Grace's presence within a national network of black radical activists and thinkers in the late 1950s. Lynn was a civil rights attorney with a long record of activism and leftist political activity. As a student at Syracuse University in the late 1920s he joined the Young Communist League. By 1934 he was a lawyer and Communist Party activist in New York City, where he worked with the Works Progress Administration (WPA), participated in various popular front activities, and interacted with various black intellectuals in Harlem and tendencies of the Left. Expelled from the Communist Party in 1937 after sharply dissenting from the party's position on a Trinidadian oil workers' strike during which British forces killed several strikers, Lynn continued his law practice and participation in left-wing activities, including serving as legal counsel for the Socialist Workers Party in 1939. Through this he met C. L. R. and became close friends with him in the early 1940s. During World War II he waged an extraordinary fight against discrimination in the armed services, including mounting a legal challenge (with famed lawyer Arthur Garfield Hayes) of his brother's arrest for refusing induction into the segregated army and then submitting to the draft himself and challenging his discriminatory treatment. After the war, he went on to participate in the Journey of Reconciliation, the 1947 direct action protest sponsored by the Congress of Racial Equality that served as the model for the Freedom Rides in 1961. During the 1950s Lynn mounted several impactful cases against civil rights violations and McCarthy-style repression, including the defense of Carl and Anne Braden, who were arrested in 1954 for selling their home to a black couple in an all-white neighborhood in Louisville, Kentucky.[116]

Lynn's article in *Correspondence* presented his considered perspective on the current state of the African American struggle. "In contemporary America," he wrote, "the Negro has a unique opportunity [to] strike out boldly for first class citizenship." The major impediment, however, was "timid, inept leadership." The article called upon historical and contemporary examples of black leaders to demarcate two persistent currents of black thought and to illustrate the conflict and tension between them. "After the Civil War we witnessed the rise to esteem of the Negro 'Uncle Tom,' Booker T. Washington being the prime example." In the contemporary moment, with the potential upsurge of the masses, the problem lay with the likes of Martin Luther King, Roy Wilkins of the National Association for the Advancement of Colored People, Lester Granger of the National Urban League, and A. Philip Randolph—"the present moderates who make up the hierarchy of Negro leadership." Citing machinations involving recent protest efforts, Lynn derided these leaders for their cozy relationship to the White House or other levers of power and their demonstrated willingness to "pour oil on the waves of Negro discontent." Lynn approvingly referenced a "second echelon" of black leaders, including stalwarts Ella Baker and Bayard Rustin, who were "uncorrupted in the main." But he lamented that they "have been slow to give voice to their dissatisfaction," thus clearing the way for the "supine leadership" of the current civil rights orthodoxy. Ultimately, Lynn called for a militant, principled, and more effective leadership, one that would be fully committed and responsive to the black masses. "Until the current leadership is exposed," he concluded, "the Negro will continue to be betrayed."[117]

Lynn would receive a phone call in early November that seemed to be a direct response to his plea for new leadership.[118] The caller was Robert Williams of Monroe, North Carolina, who in the coming months would emerge as perhaps the most fitting candidate for precisely the type of leader called for in Lynn's article. The purpose of his call was to enlist Lynn and his legal skills in what became known as the Kissing Case.

PART III

PART III

CHAPTER EIGHT

Only One Side Is Right

On October 28, 1958, in the town of Monroe in Union County, North Carolina, two young African American boys, David Ezell "Fuzzy" Simpson (age
eight) and James Hanover Thompson (age ten) were involved in a game with
white playmates. During the game, Thompson exchanged a kiss with Sissy
Sutton, an eight-year-old white girl. Word of the kiss got back to Sutton's
parents and then the police, activating white sexual fears and the South's
virulent and violent politics of rape. As a mob gathered, the police arrested
and beat the two young boys, holding them in the basement of the Monroe
jail. For six days they were held without a hearing and barred from contact
with their parents or attorneys, and then on November 4 a judge sentenced
Thompson and Simpson to indeterminate terms, perhaps for the rest of
their childhoods, in a reform school. The mothers of the two boys came to
Robert Williams for help, and he immediately became their adviser and advocate. He was, in October 1958, already a well-recognized local leader, and
the Kissing Case would be the first in a series of developments between 1958
and 1961 that propelled Williams to national and international standing.

Williams's background conditioned his emergence as a militant black
leader during the 1950s.[1] Born in 1925 in Monroe, his early trajectory also
holds some parallels to that of Jimmy. Raised during the 1920s and 1930s in
different parts of the South, Williams and Jimmy each enjoyed a nurturing
childhood that would serve as the foundation for their later activism. Williams inherited from his family a proud heritage of independence, political
activism, and racial assertion. At the same time, young Robert's life, like
Jimmy's, was punctuated with ready and repeated expressions of white
supremacist violence and racial terror. For blacks of Union County this
was symbolized, for example, by Jesse Alexander Helms, nicknamed "Big
Jesse," Monroe's infamously brutal police officer and the father of U.S. senator Jesse Helms. Jimmy and Williams both left the South as teenagers and

headed for Detroit. They each had male relatives working in the auto indus-try, and when seventeen-year old Williams arrived by bus in 1942 (five years after Jimmy's initial trek by freight train), his older brother, who worked at Ford's famous River Rouge plant, was able to secure him a job. He also joined UAW Local 600, putting himself at the center of interracial trade unionism, labor militancy, and black worker agency in World War II Detroit. His work in the Rouge and his membership in Local 600 also exposed him to a range of leftist ideas, tendencies, and groups (including the Social-ist Workers Party [SWP], which later would provide considerable support to Williams and the black community of Monroe in the 1950s). Thus, Wil-liams was exposed to the same currents and influences (and experiences) that helped to shape Jimmy during the early 1940s. Moreover, both men witnessed the overt racial hostility that World War II Detroit produced. Indeed, they even shared the experience of being on Belle Isle, the city's massive recreation and amusement park on an island in the Detroit River, the day the 1943 Detroit race riot began there. Jimmy; his wife, Annie; and their young child left the island shortly before the fighting began. Williams went to the island with his brother and wife and another couple, and they found themselves forced to fight through white mobs as they tried to leave on the Belle Isle Bridge that evening.[2]

Williams's subsequent trajectory differed from Jimmy's in two key re-spects. For one, Williams returned to the South. Monroe served as his po-litical base, and the struggles he led in his hometown anchored his rise to national prominence, whereas Jimmy never went back to the South, and his activist career centered on northern struggles. Second, Williams entered the military, where he gained training, access to a network of black veter-ans, and further resolve to steadfastly confront southern white violence. In 1944 Williams left Detroit and, after a short time working in a shipyard in California, returned to Monroe. He observed the multiple ways that the war was transforming his hometown, and in the summer of 1945 (just weeks before Hiroshima) he was drafted into the U.S. Army, where he stayed for eighteen months. Williams returned to Monroe in November 1946 at the age of twenty-one, and within months he joined other black veterans in Monroe who took up arms to face down the local klavern of the Ku Klux Klan. This proved to be a precursor to the self-defense efforts that Williams would lead during the 1950s, but before that he would spend several years away from his hometown. He briefly returned to Detroit, this time working at a Cadillac plant. Then he used his GI benefits to attend college, studying psychology and writing poetry at three different southern black colleges. In 1953, after a lack of money stalled his college career, Williams returned to military service, this time joining the marines.

Williams returned to Monroe in 1955 with a growing commitment to confronting racial injustice. He joined the local branch of the National Association for the Advancement of Colored People (NAACP), but in the face of rising intimidation—Klan rallies with crowds as large as 15,000, dynamite blasts at the homes of black activists, and other acts of terror—the branch was in decline. The few remaining members elected Williams as president, and he promptly rebuilt the organization by bringing in other veterans and women who worked as domestics. He recruited in pool halls and on street corners, giving the Monroe branch a uniquely working-class character. Among the efforts of the rejuvenated branch was a struggle in 1957 to desegregate Monroe's lone swimming pool after several black children, barred from the tax-supported public pool, drowned in isolated farm ponds. In response to this resurgence of black activism, the Klan mounted an armed motorcade to the home of Dr. Albert Perry, a veteran and the vice president of the Monroe NAACP. Williams and other black veterans organized self-defense networks and successfully repelled the Klan. The Kissing Case arrived in the wake of these developments and escalated Monroe's inflamed racial tension. Williams's emerging leadership made him the likely candidate to lead the effort to free the two boys and defend the black community.

Conrad Lynn, too, was a likely ally. Though a New Yorker and seemingly far removed from the racial vagaries of Union County, North Carolina, Lynn had in fact worked with Williams and the black community of Monroe the preceding year when he provided legal aid during the campaign to desegregate the town swimming pool. Now Williams was asking Lynn to represent the Thompson and Simpson families in this most disturbing case. "I would not have believed the case that Robert Williams described," Lynn recalled years later, "had I not already been to Monroe. Two children were in jail without a reason that could make sense to civilized people."[3] In addition to his relationship to Williams, Lynn was a probable choice because he was a committed civil rights attorney known for taking on such cases. "My office has been called 'the house of last resort,'" Lynn later wrote about his decision to take the case, "because I have been willing to handle cases that were unpopular or dangerous."[4] The Kissing Case was both. Williams first tried to get the NAACP involved, at both the state and the national levels, but was declined. It was then that he sought Lynn, who immediately went to Monroe and began working on the case. Lynn's primary role was to handle legal matters, but he also helped Williams in his effort to generate publicity and bring international attention to the case. To this end, Lynn brought with him George Weissman of the SWP to write a story on the case for the *Nation*.[5] This also marked the beginning of *Correspondence*'s support of the Monroe struggle.

Behind the Iron Curtain: Robert Williams and the Monroe Struggle in *Correspondence*

The February 1959 issue of *Correspondence* ran a front-page story about "the now world-famous" case. Indeed, by this time the case had generated what *Time* magazine called a "rolling snowball" of publicity. While the local press avoided the case, it garnered widespread coverage outside the South and internationally. By the end of 1958 the case made its way into newspaper headlines in various languages, spurred the creation of protest committees throughout Europe, and sparked demonstrations at U.S. embassies across the world. This international attention began with a front-page story in the *London News-Chronicle*, accompanied by a photo of the boys in the reformatory and a stinging editorial on the case. The reporter, Joyce Egginton, traveled to Monroe in late November and was able to report the story with the help of her hosts, Dr. Perry and his wife, Bertha. Egginton also managed to secure an interview with the town's unwitting mayor, who was not pleased when he subsequently discovered the writer's obvious sympathies with the incarcerated boys and the campaign to free them. The offending story appeared on December 15, 1958. Within days of Egginton's story, *Correspondence* sent its own reporter, Constance Webb, to Monroe. Webb was a member of the New York section of the organization and former wife of C. L. R. James. She had likely known Conrad Lynn since the 1940s, and it was Lynn, along with Robert Williams and Albert Perry, who arranged Webb's trip—including discussions of how best to ensure her safety. They planned her trip carefully so that she would interview white officials first, then spend time in the black community to allow her to get material she could use to further expose the struggles of Monroe's black citizens.

This of course followed closely the reportorial path Egginton had recently forged. As such, Webb was aware that she would be subject to the skepticism and ire of local officials, a fact she found ominously enough confirmed in the details of her passage. "The plane was the 'Golden Hawk,' an apt name, for I was swooping down on Monroe, N.C.," she explained in her *Correspondence* article. "The press has not been welcome in Monroe" since Webb's British predecessor had "won southern officials' confidence, then printed the truth."[6] Egginton had portrayed herself as a social worker to gain access to the boys in reform school. Now Webb would similarly seek to mask her identity and purpose, concealing her political orientation and her connections to Lynn, Williams, and black Monroe. If Webb and Egginton shared methods of reporting, there were similarities between the two reporters' backgrounds as well. Both were white women, coming from places that made them obvious outsiders in the South, and both sought interviews with Monroe officials for stories sympathetic to the incarcerated boys. This surely made Webb's task more difficult, given the recent deception achieved by Egginton. But Webb played on the fact that she did not fit the idea or image of a Yankee radical that was lodged in the imagination of Monroe officialdom. As a former actress and model with southern roots—"I intended to cash in, for the first time, on the birth of my parents in Atlanta, Ga.,"[7] she wrote—it seems that Webb found ways to at least partially offset the suspicions that greeted her.

Webb garnered very little in the way of interviews with white city leaders. Predictably, the mayor evaded her requests. Her attempts to speak with the editor of the local paper and the mother of Sissy Sutton, the girl involved in the infamous kiss, also produced nothing. The judge who sentenced James Thompson and David Simpson to the reformatory "broke down enough" to show Webb a report from the reform school, but she got nothing more from him. The one interview Webb managed to secure was with the man she identified as "the real boss of the city," the chair of the local Democratic Party. "He talked at random while wondering how much to trust me," Webb recounted in *Correspondence*, until "my southern ancestry won out and he spilled his guts." The contents thereof included a predictable range of derogation—from the ubiquitous (and, in this context, relatively more polite) "Nigras" to the more forceful but still familiar "niggers," "mongrels," and "pickaninnies." This powerful local figure also made the seemingly obligatory declaration that "there will never be integration in Monroe."[8]

Webb then moved on to Monroe's black community for the second and much more fruitful part of her journey. Interviewing members of the community was an entirely different experience, netting her a wealth of material. Leaving the white part of town also gave Webb a measure of relief from the tension she had experienced from the moment she arrived in Monroe.

She described it as going "home to the colored community."[9] She spent much of her time at the Perrys' home, which sat on a hill and "had sandbags all around it and a heavy metal chain guarded the drive,"[10] she recalled years later. These were fortifications against Klan attacks, a testament to the rifle squad's successful stand against the Klan before the Kissing Case. Since the resurgence of the Monroe branch of the NAACP, the Perrys' home had remained constantly under threat, but they and the whole community had resolved to defend it. Inside Webb found more evidence of this resolve. "Dr. Perry opened the door and invited me in, where I was surrounded by what appeared to be the whole community, all holding guns," she recounted. "The room was almost packed. Perry introduced me to his wife, who greeted me warmly, and Williams introduced me to Mrs. Thompson and Mrs. Simpson, the mothers of the children. He explained that walking through the neighborhood might not be safe for me, so everyone decided to meet at the Perrys'. They would take turns so everyone would have a chance to speak." With her recorder at the ready, Webb listened as several black Monroe residents, in contrast to the tight-lipped white Monroe officials, related the details of recent events, welcoming the opportunity to have their voices heard and stories told. This is how Webb recalled the scene: "My first recording was with the mothers of the children, who were, of course, upset and worried. They had not been allowed in the jail to see the boys and were able to visit only once at the reform school. Both women cried a little, not for themselves but imagining the fear and terror their children were experiencing. When the mothers finished talking, others in the room were eager to have their stories recorded."[11]

As they spoke in the Perry home, potential danger mounted outside. The interviews went well into the night, and the self-defense networks that Williams and others had organized in recent months kept armed guard. As Webb recounted in her *Correspondence* story, "Members of the guard, both men and women, began to come to the house. For my benefit, each was asked, 'Did you bring something?' and the coat was flicked back exposing the guns." The guard noticed at least one police car drive up to the house, and they also got word that three Klan members were nearby "discussing Mr. Williams." Williams and two other men went to investigate. Meanwhile Webb continued to conduct her interviews in an atmosphere that was relatively relaxed, though all remained on guard. "There was laughter," she recalled, "but with each car light we were ready." The experience duly impressed Webb, and she sought to convey to her readers why: "There was no fear, only determination and the tension of people under fire. These are freedom fighters in our own land. The Klan didn't show—it is intimidated by this community which goes forth to meet war with war. We went to bed late, guns in each room."[12]

Webb's account of her trip carried the title "I Went Behind the Iron Curtain—in U.S.A." The "iron curtain" metaphor may have been designed to conjure the Cold War context that invariably amplified stories such as the Kissing Case, where an instance of American racial strife reached an international audience. But the metaphor also signaled *Correspondence's* particular framing of the case, presenting it not as a dramatic moment of senseless injustice, but rather as a logical, even predictable occurrence in the twisted setting of white supremacy in Monroe. In fact, Webb's reporting focused less on the Kissing Case itself than on the struggles of Monroe's black community. This distinguished *Correspondence's* coverage from most others'.

While Egginton's reporting exposed to an international audience the senseless injustice of the Kissing Case, Webb sought to show a domestic audience the fortitude and political resolve of Monroe's black community by reporting on its struggles against Monroe's system of white supremacy, not just in response to the Kissing Case but leading up to it as well. Moreover, Webb continued to report on Monroe's black community beyond the case, resulting in a series of articles in *Correspondence* over several months. The material she gathered and the extended coverage of Monroe in *Correspondence* not only documented the community's armed self-defense efforts but revealed Williams's arrival as a local leader onto the national stage.

Webb's reporting on Monroe coincided with an important moment in the paper's evolution. In March 1959, Grace assumed full-time duties as editor of *Correspondence* (during the preceding month, the organization raised funds to allow her to quit her job and devote her full attention to the paper), and the paper moved from a monthly to being published every two weeks. Grace now had more opportunities to develop and implement her editorial vision for the paper, and throughout 1959 Monroe figured prominently in that vision. Grace counted Conrad Lynn as a longtime ally (their friendship likely went back to the early 1940s), and she quickly perceived what was happening in Monroe to be of great importance. Excited about the material that Webb had gathered from Monroe, Grace resolved to feature it prominently in the pages of *Correspondence*. In a letter to the group in mid-January, she enthusiastically wrote that the first story to come from Webb's reporting, "I Went Behind the Iron Curtain," would run on the front page of the next issue. "The only word for this article is 'sensational,'"[13] Grace wrote. She was also eager to determine "how best to utilize the magnificent material which Constance had recorded from her trip." She proposed rather ambitious options (which were not mutually exclusive) including a book, a pamphlet, public meetings, and a supplement in *Correspondence* (similar to the excerpt of *Facing Reality* in 1957). While the organization explored these options, Grace wanted to ensure that readers knew more was on the way: an announcement appearing next to Webb's initial article in the February 1959 issue read: "COMING! The Inside Story from Monroe, N.C., as recorded on tapes. EXCLUSIVE!"[14]

Webb arranged for a portion of the tapes to be broadcast over a New York radio station. The forty-minute broadcast gave listeners the opportunity, as a *Correspondence* article described it, "to hear the ordinary citizens of the Monroe Negro community tell how they had armed themselves in July 1957 to turn back an assault of the KKK and how they are still ready to lay down their lives in the defense of liberty and justice."[15] Timed to coincide with a hearing in New York held by a subcommittee of the NAACP national board to discuss Williams's suspension, this broadcast helped to further carry the Monroe story to African Americans in New York, which would become William's strongest base of support outside of Monroe.

Meanwhile, articles on Monroe appeared in nearly every issue of *Correspondence* between March and August and in several other issues beyond that. These included Webb's "Behind the Iron Curtain" series, which continued her reporting on her trip to Monroe. The articles went well beyond the Kissing Case, relating the larger story of Monroe's black community, its extraordinary efforts against Klan terror, and the meaning, as Webb saw it, of the Monroe struggle for the black struggle nationally. For example, one article related the instance in 1957 when an armed black guard repelled a Klan motorcade (this incident led city officials to pass an ordinance against motorcades, which amounted to an anti-Klan measure). An article on the methods devised by Monroe's black community to organize itself and quickly respond to threats celebrated the community's clever resourcefulness as they rallied together and built an effective grassroots struggle. "The entire Negro community (with exception of the professional class) was on alert for months," Webb wrote of this system. "Individuals formerly considered 'Uncle Toms' began to prove their loyalty to the community, reporting information that white people unwittingly revealed." Another article profiled

Dr. Albert Perry, giving details of his remarkable personal story, reporting the reservoir of admiration and appreciation for him among the black community as well as some poor whites, and also outlining the persecution to which Perry was subjected by Monroe officials.

Grace supplemented this material with prominently placed editorial cartoons castigating the vile practices and official hypocrisy involved in the Monroe struggle. For example, a cartoon accompanying one front-page article on Monroe derided the FBI's lackluster response to racial violence. It pictures a smiling FBI agent in friendly conversation with a group of armed Klansmen dressed in full robes and hoods. The agent says: "An' while you're mushroom hunting, if you do see a lynching mob crossing the state line, we'd be much obliged if you called us."[16] Another cartoon mocked the FBI again, this time for its liberal use of the charge (or ruse) of communism against civil rights efforts.[17]

Correspondence also carried articles specifically documenting Robert Williams's activism and leadership. Written by Webb and usually appearing on the front page, these stories gave further insight into the Monroe struggle while chronicling Williams's rise as a national figure in the African American freedom struggle. Williams began to achieve some notoriety nationally in late 1958 and early 1959 through his activism around the Kissing Case, which included a speaking tour outside the South and meetings with activists and supports in places like Harlem, where he established particularly close ties to a community of black nationalists and radicals. In the spring of 1959 he again threw himself onto the national civil rights stage with a much-publicized advocacy of armed self-defense.

The time had come for African Americans in the South to "meet violence with violence," Williams told reporters on the steps of the Monroe courthouse on May 5, 1959. "We must be willing to kill if necessary," he said. Williams spoke out of the anger and intensity of the moment, but he nonetheless provided a compelling rationale born of both recent and long-standing experiences and grievances. "I feel this is the only way of survival. Since the federal government will not bring a halt to lynching in the South and since the so-called courts lynch our people legally, if it's necessary to stop lynching with lynching, then we must be willing to resort to that method."[18]

Reporters immediately broadcast these words far and wide, making Williams and his sentiments big news. But the context and impetus were absent from these reports. Left out was the fact that he had made his statements on the day that the Monroe courts heard two cases of assault of black women by white men. Before the trials, members of the Monroe NAACP, particularly several women, had called for the community to retaliate against one of the perpetrators, but Williams discouraged this in favor of a legal remedy. The two cases came to trial on May 5, 1959, and all-white male juries acquitted both men. Williams attended the trials along with several African Americans, most of them women who witnessed the proceedings with intense interest and concern. When the verdicts came down, the women made known their consternation. The pain of watching the perpetrators go free seemed to confirm the soundness of the black community's initial inclination to inflict the punishment due the attackers. Williams suddenly faced the shame of having counseled the community to seek resolution in the courts, where, these verdicts confirmed, nothing resembling justice could be expected. As Williams's biographer Tim Tyson writes, "The black women castigated the courts for betraying them and Williams for begin naïve enough to let it happen."[19] This castigation, coupled with the jarring injustice of the verdict itself, no doubt inspired Williams's remarks to reporters on the courthouse steps.

The national office of the NAACP and its executive secretary Roy Wilkins cared little about the context or impetus for Williams's statements, but they took great concern with the resulting uproar and the damage it was causing to the association. Indeed, to newspapers in the North and South the story simply became "Negro Calls for Lynch of Whites" and "N.A.A.C.P. Leader Urges Violence." For them, Williams's "bloodthirsty remark" was sure confirmation that "hatred is the stock in trade of the NAACP."[20] Wilkins quickly suspended Williams from his post as president of the Monroe NAACP. With the aid of Conrad Lynn as counsel, Williams fought his suspension, and *Correspondence* aided in this effort. In three successive front-page stories, Webb reported on the fight between Williams and the national NAACP, presenting Williams's side of the controversy and his effort to both clear his name and state his position on what he called "armed self-reliance." Lynn insisted that Williams's suspension was unconstitutional and demanded a hearing for Williams at the NAACP national convention in July. Williams knew his chances of winning were slight, but airing the matter at the annual convention would allow him the opportunity to advance his position on self-defense. "Negroes are not taught generally, and particularly in the South, that they have a right to resist violence and a duty to subdue the criminal," Lynn wrote in his petition for the hearing. "This is the major reason that the respondent requests a hearing open to any member of the

NAACP. If this hearing serves no other purpose, it, at least, may cause an awareness on the part of Negroes deprived of the elementary safeguards of law, as in Union County, North Carolina, that they can themselves help to restore civilized order."[21]

The hostile reception Williams received from the national office did not diminish the support he enjoyed from a substantial segment of the rank-and-file membership. Local branches passed resolutions in support of Williams and sent messages to the national board indicating their agreement with Williams's statements and calling for his reinstatement.[22] Individuals, too, wrote in support of the Union County branch president, "and from all over the country," Webb reported, "letters containing $1 and $2 bills are pouring into Mr. Lynn's office to aid Williams' legal expenses." The strongest support came from Williams's own branch. Webb reported their "open defiance" of his suspension, including branch vice president Ethel Azalea Johnson's saying the group would not accept the decision of the national office. "We do not intend to have any president but Williams," Johnson declared. "If it means losing our charter and going it alone, we are prepared to do this." A deep resentment toward the national office reinforced this strong support for Williams. "Despite continued reprisals against the colored community" of Monroe, she explained, "the national office has given us no help." She castigated the leaders in the national office who "don't know what it is to live in the South" and who "expect us to lie down and cry before the race supremacists."[23]

Williams did receive his hearing during the annual convention, which met in New York during mid-July, but predictably lost his bid for reinstatement. "The matter of Robert Williams" came before the convention during the fifth session of the resolutions committee, after which the attendees voted to uphold Williams's suspension as president of the Monroe NAACP. But it took much more than the words and prestige of Roy Wilkins to persuade the committee. The convention heard an amazing forty speakers come out against Williams, including Martin Luther King Jr., baseball hero and respected civil rights spokesman Jackie Robinson, and finally Daisy Bates, at that time one of the most celebrated figures in the NAACP for her leadership in the 1957 Little Rock school desegregation effort. Nonetheless, Williams made the most of his opportunity to take the podium, speaking passionately and persuasively in his defense and for the position that African Americans should enact what he called "armed self-reliance." In the face of "the social jungle called Dixie," Williams declared, "there is no Fourteenth Amendment" and "no equal protection under the law."[24]

His powerful address to the convention demonstrated that, though Williams received the censure of the national NAACP, he would not be silenced. Quite the opposite, as it turned out. He continued to serve as a leader of the Monroe struggle, and in the coming months he would rise both in national recognition and in standing among the more militant dimensions of the black freedom struggle.[25]

Just before the NAACP convention, Williams; his wife, Mabel; and fellow Monroe activist Azalea Johnson had established the *Crusader Weekly Newsletter*. The trio first began discussing the idea of publishing a newsletter in the summer of 1958. By the next summer their confrontation with Roy Wilkins and the national office had underscored the need for an outlet through which they could project their ideas and analysis of the freedom movement. As Mabel Williams explained, the newsletter was a response to both "how the white press slanted and distorted facts of incidents regarding Negroes, and our great need for a news media that would be able to tell the whole story."[26] The *Crusader* combined political commentary on both local and international developments with features on black history and culture, all punctuated with an unflinching critique of segregation and black passivity. The consistent themes of the newsletter were black pride, armed self-defense, international solidarity, and economic autonomy. Though the *Crusader* was a decidedly local effort, they were able to quickly reach a broader audience through Robert Williams's national contacts and notoriety, achieving approximately 2,000 subscribers nationally.[27]

The *Crusader* and *Correspondence* enjoyed close ties, including shared material. The first issue of the *Crusader*, released on June 26, 1959, reprinted an editorial cartoon from *Correspondence*. The drawing by Correspondence member Frank Monico depicts a black man, attired in a suit, returning home to Africa, apparently after having studied in the United States. In his jacket pocket is a newspaper with the headline "U.S.A. Negroes Lynched and Raped." He is facing his father, who is dressed in African clothing and holding a spear, with similarly dressed men looking on in the background. Draping his arms around his father, the younger man announces, "My father, you don't know how happy I am to be home away from those savages."[28] In *Correspondence*, the cartoon accompanied Constance Webb's article about Williams's "meet violence with violence" comments. The *Crusader* paired the cartoon with an article by Williams in which he declared, "We like to think of Africa as the land of savages and jungles, but there are not many jungles more savage than this section of America called Dixie."[29] *Correspon-*

dence likewise printed material from the *Crusader*, including an article by Mabel Williams and two by Robert Williams, all appearing between September 1959 and February 1960.[30]

Webb's last article on Williams appeared on the front page of the August 1, 1959, issue of *Correspondence*, shortly after the founding of the *Crusader*. Published in the immediate aftermath of the NAACP convention, Webb's article carried the title "R. F. Williams: New Type of Leader" and it presented a comparison of Williams and Roy Wilkins. Webb began by quoting Williams: "I would rather walk on my feet for one minute as a man than crawl on my knees for a hundred years." Webb offered this statement as a "brilliant" example of the militant and uncompromising rhetoric that so clearly differentiated Williams from Wilkins. But she hastened to add that "it is not just words which distinguish" the one from the other. "Williams is superior to Wilkins in leadership," she concluded, "not because he is a nicer, finer, or more intelligent man but because he lives with and in his community." This simple but all-important fact, she insisted, set the two men worlds apart: "Mr. Wilkins lives the life of all leaders the world over, whether governmental, big business, big union, or big church. Williams lives the life of his community. Whereas Wilkins must weigh his words and actions in order not to offend this or that politician, Williams is responsible only to his community. Williams has no office and no stacks of paperwork. Instead of luncheons or meetings with politicians, Williams goes three times a week with members of his community to the Welfare office in Monroe and fights and harasses them until the people are given the money due them. Several times each week he meets with the women of the community and they plan how to raise money."[31] For Webb (and Correspondence), this organic form of leadership placed Williams at the fore of the black struggle, far ahead of his well-heeled adversary.

Webb's article spoke directly to the analysis presented in Conrad Lynn's article in *Correspondence* eight months earlier. Lynn had decried the "timid leadership" of the contemporary moderates directing black protest politics, naming Wilkins as one of them, and he called for a new leadership to supplant this anemic and tame "civil rights hierarchy." Webb and *Correspondence* championed the type of leadership that Williams represented, both by presenting him as an extraordinary figure, particularly relative to Wilkins and his ilk, and also by finding in the story of Williams and the Monroe struggle the suggestion of a broader of grassroots insurgency. "R. F. Williams: New Type of Leader" ends with the assertion, made by Williams himself, that neither the Monroe struggle nor his leadership of it was wholly exceptional or unique: "Williams claims that there are communities like Monroe all over the South," Webb wrote, "and that there are leaders like himself and people who will stand and die fighting rather than continue to live without their civil rights."[32] In identifying Williams as a "new type of leader," Webb and *Correspondence* were among those who saw early the potential of Williams (and others like him) to shape the character and future directions of the black struggle.

Assessments of Williams's significance, of course, varied across the political spectrum, and most did not champion him as *Correspondence* did. Still, few failed to acknowledge his sudden rise as a protest figure or to note his appeal to the militant sections of the black movement. Indeed, by the summer of 1959—with his leadership in the Kissing Case, his pledge to meet violence with violence, and his resulting confrontation with the NAACP—Williams had become one of the biggest civil rights stories of the year.[33] In the fall and winter of 1959 and in early 1960, he would enter a series of very public debates with Martin Luther King Jr. and others over the use of nonviolent direct action, solidifying his position as arguably the most visible and articulate critic of nonviolence.[34]

But Only One Side Is Right

Correspondence's coverage of Williams and the Monroe struggle in 1959 anchored the paper's increasing attention to racial matters and its growing focus on the black freedom struggle. This included articles by Constance Webb on developments in Harlem such as recent community responses to the persistent problem of police brutality and other expressions of "the growing political consciousness of the Negro people."[35] Jimmy addressed contemporary racial developments in columns and editorials that frequently challenged readers to question received ways of framing racial matters and urged them to rethink their understanding of the black struggle. For example, an editorial titled "Two Sides—But Only One Is Right" used the recent lynching of Mack Parker in Mississippi and the failure to charge anyone for his murder to issue a strong critique of the Cold War framing of this case and of civil rights more generally. "As the situation develops," he wrote at the end of 1959, "we can expect thousands of words to be said and written in all of the organs of American official society, warning that America itself is on trial and that unless the lynchers are punished, the

Russians will win in the world struggle for allegiance of the Asians, Africans, Arabs, and Latin-Americans." For many, of course, consideration of civil rights cases in the light of international diplomacy and American standing was a perfectly legitimate practice if not a pressing national imperative. But Jimmy flatly dismissed such thinking: "This opportunistic approach is at the heart of the moral bankruptcy of the United States."[36]

This opportunism and moral bankruptcy, Jimmy insisted, did not originate with the Cold War but rather had only found in that conflict their most recent breeding grounds. Indeed, these were well-worn characteristics permeating the nation's historical treatment of African Americans. "Only the Negroes," he wrote, "first brought here as instruments of production, continue to be exploited both for the original purpose and as instruments of domestic and foreign policy. Never are they looked at first and foremost as human beings with rights as human beings." This, in fact, was the central contention of the editorial: not only was the long-practiced refusal to recognize black humanity the foundation of America's racial history; it also brought with it a corresponding deterioration of the nation's moral capacity. "Abraham Lincoln took the position that if he could save the Union without destroying slavery, he would do that, but that if the emancipation of the slaves was necessary to save the Union, that was his position," Jimmy wrote. "That opportunism has distinguished American society ever since." The editorial goes on to list subsequent episodes in which this Lincoln-style evasion of black humanity has repeated itself precisely at those moments when it seemed that the nation was making advancements in the treatment of its black citizens and the management of the race problem:

When the unions were organized in the 1930s, the colored workers were admitted not because they were first and foremost workers, but because the unions were afraid that the corporations would use them as strikebreakers. The unions were only trying to save the union. When World War II broke out, Roosevelt, afraid of a Negro march on Washington and that Hitler would use this to split the nation, issued the Executive Order that admitted Negroes to defense factories. He was only trying to save the country. When the massive strike movement broke out after World War II, Harry S. Truman seized upon the Civil Rights issue as the only one big enough to overshadow the class struggle and win the Presidency again for the Democratic Party. He too was trying to save capitalism and the party.

The same thing is happening today. Bit by bit, begrudgingly, America is yielding various civil rights to the Negro people only because of the pressure of the Negro people themselves and the awareness that the colored people make up three-fifths of the world's population. At no point has an organization of American official society raised its voice and launched a campaign on behalf of the Negroes themselves, as human beings, with rights and aspirations equal and indistinguishable from those of every other human being.

This is the shame of American society, which manifests itself in every sphere but above all on the question of the Negro people. Not until the Negro is granted rights as a human being, because he is a human being, not until then will America be on the right side. Rights granted for the sake of the "union," "the nation," "international politics," "the party," etc. are not rights but base bribes. Whites may be fooled by such grants; the Negroes are not.[37]

The coverage of racial dynamics and expressions of African American protest in *Correspondence* at the end of the 1950s directly reflected the paper's continued shift away from its worker-centered roots. This shift manifested both in the amount of space devoted to African Americans relative to workers and in the character of the coverage of each. The paper had always placed an emphasis on black Americans, such as with the "Special Negro News" page, but its focus had been on giving voice to black experiences, perspectives, and aspirations primarily through individual testimonials and local commentary examining dimensions of black life and exposing the hypocrisy or irrationality of racial prejudice as experienced in the workplace, local communities, or various social settings. By contrast, the coverage of African Americans in the late 1950s emphasized the rising civil rights movement (including distinctions and divisions within it) and the range of black protest as well as its challenge to "official society." Initially the paper's coverage of African Americans had sought to demonstrate the compatibility of black struggles with a larger working-class movement. However, by the end of the decade, coverage of African Americans projected the rising black struggle as a legitimate and mounting challenge to the foundations of society, independent of workers or a working-class movement.

A related change occurred in the paper's coverage of workers. Two central goals of the early *Correspondence*—to emphasize worker self-organization, and to facilitate workers' expression of their own ideas by enabling them to speak for and to themselves through the paper—had declined in importance. The paper had been founded, first, on the theoretical proposition that the spontaneous eruption and self-organization of the American working class was the key to fundamental social transformation and, second, a belief that the paper could play a role in galvanizing this revolutionary potential. This belief was not fully gone by 1959, but it was fading. The evolution of *Correspondence* from a self-identified workers' paper to an organ increasingly drawn to black insurgency began to subtly downplay or mute some of the ideas and political perspectives that had sustained the organization for nearly two decades.

Jimmy's writings for the paper during this period illustrate this evolution. In 1959 he contributed at least one article to every issue, and in several issues he wrote multiple pieces, some under his name, others as Al Whitney, and still others unsigned. Much of his writing addressed workplace issues and analyzed American industry, with particular focus on the auto industry. These were for the most part animated or inspired by what he experienced, witnessed, and discussed with fellow workers at the Chrysler Jefferson plant. He continued to deal with the inhumanity of the companies, the resistance of rank-and-file workers, the bankruptcy of the union bureaucracy, and the impacts of automation. But at the end of the 1950s Jimmy's writing began to challenge and even chide workers.

For example, "The High Cost of Production"[38] relates two incidents in Jimmy's plant in which a worker passed out on the job and fellow workers, intimidated by their superiors and scared of losing their jobs, hesitated to stop their work to come to their coworker's aid. In one case, the other workers "were stepping over and around their sick brother, busily catching their job operations. Twenty minutes later the line was stopped and they lifted him out and carried him over to first aid." In the other incident, the passed-out man actually had a heart attack, though "the company said it was only a stomach ache." Jimmy cited this as emblematic of the oppressive environment under which the workers of the Chrysler Jefferson plant toiled. "So great has been the increase in heart attacks, cuts and bruises due to the speed-up in production that the company does not want the truth circulating among employees." But his critique was directed at the workers as well, not only for their timidity in accepting these conditions and the resulting inhumanity experienced on the shop floor, but also for their seeming hypocrisy in readily decrying the same elsewhere. "These are the same workers who are amazed at what the Russian and Chinese workers take from their bosses,"[39] Jimmy chided.

These changes in *Correspondence*'s focus took place under Grace's editorial direction, and they reflected the shape and direction of her and Jimmy's thinking at the end of the 1950s. Subtly at first, and then with more focused intention, Grace oversaw and guided the paper's evolution during the late 1950s and early 1960s into a very different publication, one that placed greater emphasis on the civil rights movement and other expressions of the black struggle relative to workers and labor struggles. This shift in the paper's political perspective mirrored Grace's and especially Jimmy's growing conviction that the black struggle had the potential to bypass the working class as the agent of revolutionary change in the United States. This theoretical position, as articulated in various pieces appearing in the paper in 1961, would activate yet another conflict within the organization. That conflict had been seeded during the second half of the 1950s; it began to sprout during the first year of the new decade, when developments both internal and external to the group sharpened the antagonisms within the organization.

"To All Student Strikers"

In February of 1960, black political assertion in North Carolina once again claimed national attention. Black college students brought a new expression of protest, very different from Robert Williams but equally dramatic, to further challenge the ways of Dixie. If Williams's advocacy of armed self-defense and the Monroe movement was the biggest civil rights story of 1959, the southern sit-in movement, initiated in the nearby city of Greensboro, easily claimed that title the following year. While the number of stories in *Correspondence* on the sit-ins did not quite reach the number on Williams and Monroe, the tone and underlying intent of the coverage were essentially the same. *Correspondence* presented the students, as it had the black community of Monroe, as authentic agents of political action, an autonomous grassroots mobilization forcing irreversible changes in American social relations.

The paper's analysis of the sit-ins, much of it appearing in front-page articles written by Constance Webb, emphasized the far-reaching implications of this rapidly spreading youth movement. The "sitdowners" were not simply protesting for the rights of one group, but more fundamentally were challenging the basis upon which southern life was organized, galvanizing youth of all colors in both the North and the South, and exposing the bankruptcy of national politicians. Webb's analysis hinged to some extent on the Johnson-Forest Tendency (JFT) themes of self-organization and spontaneity: "This unorganized, totally spontaneous move by the students was without leadership, as we commonly know it, and without the aid of any organizations. It moved so quickly no organization could have kept pace."[40] She juxtaposed the bankruptcy and futility of an inactive federal government with the sit-ins, positioning them as the newest form in a line of mass insurgency and popular democracy. "While these honorable men have deliberated and discussed and maneuvered year after year," Webb opined, "every gain in civil rights in this country has come from the actions of the people themselves, using the powers they have at hand. The crowning futility of the present situation is that while these petty politicians pose as men of heroic stamina, whatever decision comes out of their long-windedness and short-sleepiness can mean absolutely nothing. By the time the decision is reached, the people themselves will have gone far beyond that stage in their actions and demands."[41]

Webb's liberal use of the phrase "the people themselves" reflects the tendency in some of her writing to cast the sit-ins and other expressions of black protest in a broader, almost nonracial frame of mass action. Within this frame, which was consistent with the Johnson-Forest Tendency and Correspondence's emphasis on "ordinary people" acting in opposition to "official society," Webb's articles at times discussed the sit-ins with remarkably little reference to them as racial struggles. But this is not to say that she absolved the forces of white reaction. In one story she ridiculed the police, politicians, "and other leading citizens" for being no better than "white hoodlums who parade with miniature baseball bats and Confederate flags. These, together, constitute a mob, and their acts, whether official or unofficial, are, purely and simply, mob violence."[42] Still, it was the federal government's inaction that came in for the sharpest rebuke: "The most striking feature of the national government in Washington is its uselessness," Webb concluded. "The President speaks only for himself, exposing his own hollowness with every word he utters. The Senators and Congressmen speak only to each other. If the whole pack of them were to be shipped to outer space and an equal number of chattering see-nothing, hear-nothing monkeys put in their place, it is difficult to see what difference it would make to the monumental struggle now going on."[43]

The paper's coverage of the sit-ins placed the greater stress not on the roots or basis of the sit-in leadership or on the failures of official society but on the impact of the protests. Indeed, *Correspondence*'s strongest message about the sit-ins was that the students, by taking action in this manner, were forcing the country to face social divisions and making a path for a genuine reconstruction of society. "The face of our country is changing," Webb wrote. "Through the sitdown movement of Southern Negro students, Americans in all sections of the country and in all situations of life are rediscovering who's who and what's what. Every day, with increasing sharpness, the line is being drawn between those who would reconstruct American society on foundations of which we can all be proud, and those who would maintain it in its present state of barbarism."[44]

A front-page cartoon struck another chord of praise for the student protesters. It shows two white police officers watching a long line of black college students file into the Orangeburg, South Carolina, police department. One of them is reading a book, with several others tucked under his arm. Other students include a couple holding hands, she with books in her free hand, he wearing a college sweatshirt. On the ground are picket signs, one of which reads, "We're through with 5 & 10c prejudice." As the students make their procession, one officer remarks to the other, "Are we arresting them for *dis*orderly conduct—or for *orderly* conduct?"[45]

Appearing below this cartoon was a timeline of the sit-in movement through late March. "The First 50 Days—Chronicle of a Revolution" gave a detailed, sometimes day-by-day account of the movement's progression, listing locations, participants, and outcomes of protests across the South. It also highlighted moments of violence enacted by white counterprotesters as well as relevant events in the North, such as southern senators beginning their filibuster, "Northern liberals giv[ing] up in U.S. Senate," and a march by the Detroit NAACP in the state's capital. Grace placed a prefatory note at the head of the timeline. It revealed the importance that she and *Correspondence* assigned to the sit-ins: "In years to come historians will tell and re-tell the story of the upheaval we are now living through in the U.S. We urge everyone with friends and relatives in the South to send *Correspondence* to them and ask for their stories to publish in the paper. We also want to hear from our Northern readers. No one, of whatever race, age, or class, in any section of the country, is untouched by the revolution now taking place."[46]

In the next issue Grace spoke directly to the student protesters themselves. "To All Student Strikers," a message appearing prominently on the front page, pledged the paper's full support to the young activists and their movement. "The pages of *Correspondence* are at your disposal," the message began. "We know that the wire services and local papers are not printing the full story of your actions. . . . We know that your student papers are being confiscated." Therefore, *Correspondence* was offering itself as a vehicle to counter this conspiracy of silence and to help spread word broadly to those who desired and needed to know the full measure of the movement. "We in the North have not heard the full story." Moreover, "others in the South engaged in the same fight want to hear what is happening in other areas."[47]

Of course, plenty of writing about the sit-ins had appeared in the mainstream press, but *Correspondence* asserted that this coverage was incomplete so long as it failed to project the voices of the students themselves. And this was a task to which *Correspondence* was both committed and well suited. "Since its inception," the message boasted, *Correspondence* had "placed its columns at the disposal of various communities." It cited several examples, the most recent being the black community of Monroe. The message also touted the paper's unique position relative to other outlets: "We are an independent paper, unattached to any political organization or pressure group, supported by 20 reporters and the subscriptions and contributions made by our readers. Therefore there is no restriction on the news we will print."[48]

If it was somewhat disingenuous to assert that *Correspondence* held no organizational affiliation, "To All Student Strikers" nonetheless demonstrated the paper's commitment to supporting the students and their movement without any intention of interfering with its future course. Despite this earnest appeal, nothing from the "sitdowners" appeared in the paper. The sit-in movement generated considerable momentum during the spring of 1960, and this created multiple other outlets for the student activists to tell their story. In fact, only days before *Correspondence* published "To All Student Strikers," hundreds of student activists had gathered at a major conference to coordinate and further plan their efforts. It was convened by longtime activist Ella Baker, whose deep-seated commitment to nurturing grassroots leadership ensured that the students maintained their independence and a measure of autonomy from existing organizations. As such, the meeting allowed the students to purposely begin carving out their space within the larger struggle, resulting in the founding of the Student Nonviolent Coordinating Committee and with it a new dimension in the civil rights movement. In this context, the platforms available to the new organization, either those provided by its allies or those it could create for itself, exceeded anything the pages of *Correspondence* could offer.

While attempting to publicly support and connect with the student sit-in movement during the spring of 1960, Correspondence also turned inward. To help bolster the internal dynamics of the organization, they developed plans for Jimmy and Grace to visit C. L. R. that summer and for the group to hold a convention in the fall. In June, Jimmy, Grace, and their friend Kathleen Gough, an anthropologist and activist then teaching at Wayne State University in Detroit, flew to C. L. R.'s native Trinidad, where he and Selma had moved in 1958. C. L. R. had returned at the invitation of Trinidad's new government, headed by his old friend Eric Williams, who asked C. L. R. to serve as managing editor of his party's newspaper, the *Nation*. Jimmy and Grace's three-week stay was much shorter than Grace's trips to London in 1954 and 1957, and it was also less productive. C. L. R. had been corresponding with Grace about his planned revision of *Facing Reality* and a series of lectures on "Modern Politics" that he was preparing. However, it seems that little was accomplished during the visit. When Grace and Jimmy returned to Detroit at the beginning of August, their relationship with C. L. R. was no better than before the trip, and it may have worsened.[49]

One month after their return, Jimmy and Grace presided over Correspondence's next convention, held at the organization's office on Mack Avenue near the Boggses's home. Grace had been central in the planning group, which issued this call to the convention: "Among the tasks of the convention will be to analyze the rapidly moving revolutionary developments in the world during the last three years and our place in these developments. It will be necessary for us to face the organizational problems that have been growing recently and take whatever steps we feel necessary to remedy them."[50]

Jimmy addressed what he saw as a prime source of such problems in his report to the convention, "The Politics of Publishing *Correspondence.*"[51] The report likely rehearsed ideas he conveyed to his comrades in multiple venues or formats, as he had been pushing the organization to rethink the role of *Correspondence*. He wanted the paper to expand beyond simply reporting or recording the actions of workers. "We have accumulated facts and episodes to justify our position that the workers are today creating *the new society,*" he said. However, he felt that the paper fell short because it had not provided "analysis to help the workers in the constant struggle to uncover, make more specific the nature of the new society, which, except as a phrase

among us, does not yet exist. . . . We've abandoned role[s] of educators, il-
luminators, leaders, advocates, to become mere reporters."[52]

The Coming Year of 1961

Jimmy's vision for *Correspondence* found expression in a quartet of Detroit
activists. By 1960, Reginald and Dolores Wilson and Conrad and Gwen
Mallett were important contributors to the paper, bringing to it a new set
of political sensibilities and histories. These two married couples joined
Grace and Jimmy not only in publishing the paper but also in analyzing the
ideological development of the black movement and simultaneously insti-
gating a range of protest activities during the opening years of the 1960s.
This quartet also deepened *Correspondence*'s material connection to black
Detroit and its capacity to contribute to local struggles. At the same time,
the paper gave the four of them a base for their activism and a space to grow
as thinkers.

The Wilsons and Malletts were drawn to *Correspondence* by the group's
public meetings held at the newspaper's office. Through these meetings and
other events, the office became an important political and social space, facilitating interactions among people with varying connections to the paper
and levels of interest in radical politics. The meetings helped to raise the
organization's profile and to more deeply immerse Jimmy and Grace—as
leaders of the group and as the two members (perhaps along with Martin
Glaberman) most responsible for writing, promoting, and publishing the
paper—in the activist networks to emerge in early 1960s Detroit.

Such meetings were not new for Correspondence. But whereas in the
past they had been somewhat spontaneous or situational (for example, the
meetings held on the Hungarian Revolution), during the late 1950s the group
began to hold public meetings regularly and to more systematically emphasize them as an extension of the work of the paper. All of the meetings,
normally held on the third Friday of each month, received announcement
in the paper, and frequently the text of presentations at these meetings subsequently appeared in *Correspondence*. The topics, while varied, reflected
the paper's evolution. One example is a March 1959 meeting on "The Meaning of Negro History" (at this time *Correspondence* also announced it had
for sale at a discounted price *Black Reconstruction* by W. E. B. Du Bois, "A
Famous Book That Tells What the History Books Leave Out"). Most meetings featured a member of Correspondence delivering a talk, such as Grace

speaking on "The New Nations" at a meeting on Third World independence movements in April 1959. In June, Filomena Daddario addressed
"The American Woman and the New Society." That fall, Jimmy spoke on a
topic to which he had given considerable thought: "Negroes and the Trade
Unions."[53]

Jimmy in particular played a pivotal role in drawing the Wilsons and
Malletts into the organization. As one of its leaders, his unassuming political style, easy manner of engaging people, and generosity of spirit made
for a welcoming, even nurturing political environment. The Wilsons
and Malletts also found appealing the seriousness with which Jimmy approached politics, as exhibited through his long-standing commitment to
radical social change and his obvious enthusiasm for the development of
ideas. It was also the case that Jimmy's wealth of activist experience made
him an ideal mentor. "Jimmy was a down to earth humanist," Gwen Mallett
recalled. "He was a very intelligent man, but he was also a very down to earth
man, a human man. He loved human beings individually as human beings
and not as some political entity."[54] Dolores Wilson similarly described
Jimmy as "earthy," "warm," and "just a wonderful man." She added that he
was "a very clear thinking person" and explained that she learned a great
deal from him: "He was the kind of person that could just clear away all of
the garbage and stuff and zero right in with very plain language. . . . He was
able to clarify a lot for me."[55] Reginald Wilson expressed the same appreciation for what he got from *Correspondence* and particularly from Jimmy: "I
grew politically and intellectually about a thousand fold, and most of that
is due to Jim Boggs. He was a wonderful person, and he was a wonderful
intellect."[56]

Of course, Jimmy did not have the credentials or the polish usually
associated with intellectuals. For this reason, his intellectual abilities were
not, for some, instantly recognizable, particularly for university-trained
activists like the Wilsons and Malletts. For one thing, though he never returned to Marion Junction, he maintained his "Alabamese," the accent and
speech patterns of his native land. Jimmy "was a country boy, who talked
like he was down home," Reginald Wilson recalled. "When he opened his
mouth, [it] sounded like he had just gotten off of the train." But if Jimmy's
style departed from that of an eloquent radical, erudite professor, or a member of the cultured literati, he nonetheless offered those listening to him a
compelling alternative model of an intellectual. "You had to put aside his
accent and all his country ways and start listening to what he was saying,"

Wilson remembered. "Then we realized that the way he spoke and what he articulated was strictly from the dynamism" of his life experiences and his concrete engagement in grassroots struggles. Eventually, "most people who heard him speak pretty much gave a great deal of deference to him."[57]

As the year 1960 came to an end, the participation of the Wilsons and Malletts in the publication of *Correspondence* proved a key element in the changing dynamics of the paper and the organization. As Jimmy and Grace extended their networks of activists and thinkers, nationally and in Detroit, they became fully engaged with an emerging black nationalist and black radical politics. This political focus increasingly appeared in the paper along with a corresponding disavowal of the worker-centered politics that had been at the heart of the JFT and Correspondence projects. As a result, their relationship to C. L. R. continued to fray, and the group lurched toward a final organizational crisis in 1961.

The year began with Jimmy's sending a New Year's message to the membership. "This year marks 20 years of the excitement of this group," he began, opening with a celebratory tone that acknowledged the group's history, "20 years in which we have been held together by our ideas, deeply steeped in our Marxist viewpoint." He then turned to the current moment. The year 1960 had seen "the greatest revolutionary upsurge since 1848," he said. "Today old Africa is dead" and the continents of Asia and South America "are in constant upheaval." The masses of the Third World, "by trying to decide their own destinies," had forced "a colossal change in the map. . . . Even more spectacular is the consternation their awakening has created in the old powers like France, England, U.S., Belgium, Portugal, Spain, etc." This assessment duly reflected Correspondence's celebration of the masses in motion, but it also restated Jimmy's position that the anticolonial movements, and not the European proletariat or American workers, stood at the fore of the world's current revolutionary forces. Jimmy's main point, however, was about the American revolution: "It is here where the test for us will become sharper and sharper. This coming year 1961 will call for us to take [a] position in relation to the American situation, not the Russian or something like that."[58] His insistence that the organization recognize its unique opportunity but also its responsibility to build an American revolution would be a consistent theme in the debates and divisions experienced in Correspondence over the coming year.

CHAPTER NINE

An Ending and a Beginning

In the spring of 1961, James Boggs and Malcolm X offered Detroit-area audiences parallel analyses of black protest politics. Each of them employed the familiar "house Negro versus field Negro" trope as a rhetorical and analytical device to describe the social divisions of enslavement. Speaking to students at the University of Michigan (and later printed in *Correspondence*), Jimmy said, "From the very beginning the Negro masses (or 'field hands') and not the educated Negroes (or 'house Negroes') have been the ones to drive the struggle forward. . . . This began with the slave revolts, continued with the runaway slaves and those who fled to join the union armies in the Civil War, causing a virtual general strike." Drawing on this historical evidence and on the authority of W. E. B. Du Bois, who made the "general strike" argument in his book *Black Reconstruction*, Jimmy drew a line from the nineteenth century to the present, identifying the Nation of Islam (NOI), commonly known as the Black Muslims, as a contemporary version of the field hands while casting the mainstream civil rights leaders and their middle-class backers as house Negroes. "The Black Muslims today have the support of masses of Negroes" because they offer an alternative to the "the legalistic limitations of Negro middle classes."[1] Jimmy was describing an important division in the current configuration of the black freedom struggle, in which the NOI, easily the most visible and influential black nationalist organization in 1961, reflected the aspirations and worldview of the black masses in ways that the more moderate groups and integration-focused segment of the movement did not.

Malcolm X, the NOI's most articulate spokesperson, spoke in Detroit at the Nation of Islam mosque less than a month after Jimmy's appearance at the nearby University of Michigan. Among those in the audience was Reginald Wilson, who wrote about Malcolm's talk in *Correspondence*. Malcolm spoke for nearly four hours to "an attentive capacity audience," explaining the group's theology and program "in minute detail with brilliant lucidity and irresistible logic." Key elements of this program, Wilson told *Correspondence* readers, included the NOI's "total rejection of integration, non-violence (as an active technique), and accommodation within American society." Amplifying Jimmy's assessment of the NOI, Wilson said that these elements made the Black Muslim program "more dynamic and radical than any proposed by leadership of the NAACP variety, and in this lies its dramatic appeal to the masses." He further advised that the NOI, "growing in influence and membership, should be closely watched as a significant force among American Negroes." Malcolm's compelling delivery of the NOI's message was the main draw. "With a blackboard next to a podium," Wilson wrote, "Minister Malcolm X proceeded by word and illustration to depict the degraded position of the 'so-called Negro' in America, the intransigence of the white man, and thus, the necessity of 'Separation or Death!'" Wilson further described how Malcolm put the "field Negro versus house Negro" construct in service of his explanation of the NOI's program: "In a striking illustration, he used the familiar terms, 'house Negroes' and 'field Negroes' to show that when the white man's house (civilization) burns down, the 'house Negroes' will perish with him and the 'field Negroes' will survive."[2]

The emphasis on the black masses—field Negroes—that Malcolm and Jimmy shared led each to a different conclusion. They both elevated the black masses as the key to black struggles historically and contemporarily. Jimmy linked this point to other theoretical propositions: that there is a historical and political link between capitalism and racial oppression; that black people were currently on the offensive in a way that was "dealing powerful blows to U.S. capitalism"; and that the black struggle had the potential to transform society. "When the Negroes gain their equality," he said, "it won't be a capitalist society any more. It can't be."[3]

The invitation for Jimmy to address students at the University of Michigan, where he made these remarks, followed recent speaking engagements there by other members of Correspondence. In January, Martin Glaberman spoke on the Hungarian Revolution and gave lectures on Marxism. Grace spoke to the Democratic Socialist Club, addressing a crowd of 75 to 100 people on the topic "Winds of Change: Before Lumumba and After," on March 1, two weeks after the announcement of Lumumba's death.[4] Questions and a discussion followed, at the conclusion of which Jimmy addressed the crowd for about three minutes. The next day Grace reported that Jimmy "spoke magnificently . . . and drew a burst of applause."[5] In January several students attended a Correspondence public meeting at which Jimmy spoke, and afterward they made plans to have him deliver the speech on campus.[6] Now, in May, he was back on campus for a forum titled "The Negro Mass Movement: Which Way Is It Going?"[7]

"If in the morning paper you read that a revolt has erupted in Mississippi, don't be surprised," Jimmy told the audience.[8] As his forecast suggested, this was a particularly explosive moment to entertain the chosen topic. The date of the forum, May 17, marked the seventh anniversary of the historic *Brown v. Board of Education* Supreme Court decision. While the full legal impact of the decision still remained to be seen, *Brown* no doubt had opened up new spaces for civil rights protest. The anniversary provided an ideal opportunity to both assess the nation's progress and raise questions about the shape and direction of the struggle for black equality. More immediately, the forum occurred in the midst of the Freedom Rides, which in the spring of 1961 were the most dramatic and visible expression of that struggle. As a direct attack on segregation, the Freedom Rides occasioned violent counterprotests that, in turn, garnered intense media attention. This gave an urgency and immediacy to questions regarding the direction of the civil rights movement, whether debated in the halls of government, discussed at kitchen tables, or addressed on college campuses.

Jimmy's prediction of unrest in Mississippi referred to the Freedom Rides. The Congress of Racial Equality (CORE) initiated the Freedom Ride as non-violent direct action modeled on the group's 1947 Journey of Reconciliation. It began on May 4 when an interracial group of thirteen "Riders" boarded two southbound buses in Washington, D.C., in an effort to test the federal ban on racial segregation in interstate travel, which had been strengthened in December 1960 by the *Boyton v. Virginia* Supreme Court decision that extended the prohibition against segregation in interstate travel to terminal accommodations as well as buses and trains. They would travel across the South seated anywhere they wished on buses and insisting on their rights to use waiting rooms and lunch counters without regard to race. The two-week pilgrimage would conclude with the Freedom Riders' arrival in New Orleans on May 17 to participate in a celebration of the *Brown* anniversary. As it turned out, the violent response of counterdemonstrators and local Ku Klux Klan mobs altered—and ultimately extended—the trajectory of the Freedom Rides, helping to make this the biggest civil rights story of the year.

The first incidence of violence occurred on May 9 in Rock Hill, South Carolina, when a mob beat two Riders at the entrance to a white waiting room. A week later, massive violence broke out. In Alabama, white supremacists firebombed one of the buses near Anniston, and a mob brutally attacked Riders in Birmingham. These repressive forces and the threat of escalating violence compelled the Riders to fly to New Orleans, where they attended the *Brown* anniversary rally as intended. Their arrival by plane had effectively ended the original CORE Freedom Ride, but their effort sparked wider action. A group of black college student activists from Nashville resolved to continue the protest, and on very day of the *Brown* celebration, they arrived in Alabama to resume the Freedom Rides through Mississippi.[9]

Thus, Jimmy was speaking to a group of northern university students just as CORE and others celebrated the *Brown* anniversary and a group of college students in the South initiated the second stage of the Freedom Rides. The CORE Freedom Ride had captured the nation's attention, but Jimmy's reading of the situation differed from the standard interpretation. He encouraged his youthful audience to see past the dramatic images of peaceful protesters (black and white) assaulted by white mobs. Instead, he focused on what to him was the underlying dynamic and driving force at play: an emergent black political resolve. His prediction of violence was not only a statement about recalcitrant white supremacists. He was also calling attention to "how belligerent and indignant the colored people in the United States are today over the race issue."[10]

Sure enough, white supremacist violence did ensue. Three days after Jimmy's talk, a white mob led by Klansmen struck in Montgomery, Alabama, attacking Freedom Riders in the bus terminal and black citizens on nearby streets. "News of the riot," Jimmy wrote in *Correspondence*, "came as no shock to me." He argued that this dynamic of protest, violence against it, and further protest exposed the hypocrisy and political decline of the American labor movement, embodied in the person of UAW president Walter Reuther. "Busloads of Freedom Riders are now rolling across Alabama and Mississippi," Jimmy wrote, "and Negroes are determined to keep them rolling, despite Kennedy's appeal for a 'cooling-off period,' an appeal in the same spirit and for the same purpose as Walter Reuther's constant appeals to workers to 'cool off' strikers against the company." Jimmy charged that "the labor movement is standing by, doing nothing" in response to the racist violence in the South, while its leader prominently involved himself in the other major news story of the day.[11] Reuther joined Eleanor Roosevelt and others to lead the Tractors for Freedom Committee, formed to negotiate the release of anti-Castro commandos taken prisoner in Cuba the previous month during the failed Bay of Pigs invasion.[12] Jimmy found that this combination of American race relations, Cold War geopolitics, and union politics—all taking place in the context of a new economics of industrial production—made for a "very strange" situation: "This great American labor movement can't organize the South because of the race prejudice there and can't put up a decent fight against the companies in the North because they can run South with their plants. Yet, 'in the name of common humanity,' it can rush off at a moment's notice to the rescue of counterrevolutionary prisoners in Cuba." The word coming from the UAW headquarters, Solidarity House, on the night of May 25 gave further evidence of Reuther's priorities: "The 11:00 news bulletin reports that Reuther is keeping Solidarity House open all night for a reply from Castro."[13]

When Jimmy saw this news report, he quickly sent a telegram to Reuther at Solidarity House expressing his frustration with the politics of the UAW and the direction of the labor movement. It read, "In the name of common humanity and as an expression of labor's support of the cause of Freedom and equality at home, urgently request that the UAW-AFL-CIO immediately organize and send a fleet of integrated buses of Freedom Riders to Alabama."[14]

Jimmy's appeal implicitly and somewhat mockingly criticized Reuther's prioritizing of the prisoners in Cuba over the Freedom Riders. More importantly, it explicitly challenged the UAW to demonstrate a deeper commitment to the cause of racial justice.[15] Jimmy had, of course, been pushing the UAW in this regard for years, most recently in a letter he wrote to the executive board of his union local that January requesting support for the members of the local's fair practices committee to attend the upcoming conference of the newly formed Negro-American Labor Council. He justified the request by saying, "The Negro question is the No. 1 question in the country today and is particularly acute in the City of Detroit because of the present tension between the races, and our organization, the UAW-CIO, can no longer afford to measure its concern with the question in dollars and cents as has been its past practice in this field."[16] This last point was Jimmy's primary concern. By calling for black *and white* workers to go to Alabama, Jimmy was pushing the union, and white workers in particular, to render a type of support to the civil rights movement. "I was, of course, not only interested in testing the Alabama Klan," Jimmy later explained. "I was also testing the readiness of the organized labor movement and of Northern white workers to clash with other whites on the issue of integration—which they allegedly supported, particularly because all the action was taking place down south."[17]

Jimmy was not surprised to find out that "the UAW took the easy way out. Instead of confronting the rank and file with this proposal, the leadership made a financial contribution" to the Congress of Racial Equality (CORE), the organization that launched the Freedom Rides.[18] Though he did not expect the union to accept his invitation to throw itself into the fight, he still lambasted its leaders for failing to take the step of active participation and thereby demonstrate that labor genuinely stood with the black struggle. "The UAW international will send $10,000 to the Negro movement," he said, "but they won't tell one white worker in the plant, or in the organization, that he has to do something concretely in relation to it, like getting out in a picket line and struggling side by side with the Negro the same way he wanted the Negro to struggle side by side with him when he was organizing the union."[19] Jimmy's call for the UAW to send its members, not just its money, reflected his vision of social transformation. In addition to changing the laws and social structures of the South, the struggle must also compel change among white workers of the North. By going to Alabama, they would see and experience the racism, and they would be forced to better understand the struggle being waged. Moreover, they themselves would be transformed in the process.[20]

Jimmy's *Correspondence* article on the UAW and the Freedom Rides carried the title "The First Giant Step," a reference to the momentum of the civil rights movement and especially the still-in-progress Freedom Rides. "As of now, the buses are still rolling," he said in the closing paragraph, "and it is up to the labor leaders whether common decency is enough to bring them to act. The Negroes themselves have no other choice but to act, and they are not waiting on the labor movement. They have taken the first giant step."[21] This juxtaposition of labor and the black struggle showed how Jimmy judged the relative strength of each movement and its potential for changing society. In effect, this "first giant step" showed that the black masses were bypassing workers as the force most prepared or able to disrupt society. Jimmy's assessment further fueled the growing ideological division within Correspondence.

Recognition and celebration of both workers and black struggles had of course been central to the Johnson-Forest Tendency (JFT) and Correspondence for the past two decades. Likewise, Jimmy had engaged and held dear both struggles, having been an autoworker, active union member, and civil rights activist during this same period. But through most of the 1950s, and even more so in the opening years of the new decade, Jimmy's evaluation of the balance between the two shifted as he saw a deterioration in the capacity or willingness of worker-led struggles alongside the intensification of black political assertion. Thus, Jimmy (and Grace) increasingly offered critical assessments of workers while shifting his political activities and focus, in the paper and otherwise, to the black struggle. However, C. L. R. James and others in the organization saw this as a wrongheaded shift away from the group's established focus on the rank-and-file worker—a shift they would come to take as political apostasy.

Jimmy further exposed this ideological conflict in the organization with his article "The Second Civil War Has Begun in the United States of America," which appeared next to "The First Giant Step" on the front page of the June 3, 1961, issue of *Correspondence*. It also took the Freedom Rides as its point of departure, but whereas "The First Giant Step" critiqued the labor movement, this one said nothing about it. Instead, "The Second Civil War" offered a fuller analysis of the civil rights movement and Jimmy's contention that "the issues of freedom and equality which the American people refused to resolve 100 years ago are now going to be settled, and not settled by constitutional means but once again by bodies of armed men." The Freedom Rides placed this conflict "squarely and irrevocably before the nation," Jimmy wrote, noting that "this war has been on its way for a long time." He said battle lines were set with the acquittal of Emmett Till's murderers in 1955 and intensified through the Montgomery Bus Boycott of 1955–56; the armed defense of the black community of Monroe, North Carolina, led by Robert Williams in 1958–59; and the sit-ins of 1960. Now, the Freedom Rides helped to expose the fundamental contradictions of American society and force the nation to confront these contradictions. "The most important thing about these young Freedom Fighters . . . is the fire burning inside them, their determination to exercise their own rights to freedom of association and of movement, and to establish thereby these rights for everyone else. Their determination has brought into the political arena all the conflicting passions and forces which have been gathering momentum inside American society."[22] This article generated debate in the organization because some members disagreed with Jimmy's use of the term "civil war" to characterize the present situation, an argument that he would later concede had merit.[23] Another cause for debate was his seeming vision of a social transformation driven by the black struggle and not the mass actions of workers: "Now the battle has been joined, and it will end only when the present state power in the South has been completely deposed or has bowed to the superior might and right of the Negro people and their allies. Of this outcome there is no doubt. It is equally certain that in the course of this war and before it is finally resolved, there will be a total reconstruction of all social, political, and economic relations in the nation."[24]

Jimmy's discussion of the Freedom Rides and the meaning he ascribed to them in these two articles distinguished his analysis from the standard interpretation. The Freedom Rides were a self-consciously interracial action, designed to force compliance with new federal laws outlawing segregation in interstate travel and, by extension, in all public places. They were part of a broader movement aimed at achieving racial integration. That is, the Freedom Rides reflected *racial liberalism*, the primary protest trajectory of the civil rights movement, characterized by interracial activism, nonviolent direct action, and appeals to constitutional authority. By contrast, Jimmy emphasized *racial assertion* as the underlying dynamic and most important feature of the Freedom Rides. "In the merciless light thrown by the fire of" the Freedom Riders' determination, he believed the nation was forced to see both "the hate-ridden, savage mobs of white men, women, and children" and "the Negro community, calm, confident, and conscious that the hour has come for it to strike the final blow for freedom and that there is no more room for retreat or compromise."[25]

At the same time, Jimmy was focusing on a rising militancy among black activists that was, to his mind, as much a part of "the race issue" as the Freedom Rides and which was equally explosive. The Freedom Rides certainly took center stage in the national civil rights struggle during the spring of 1961, but other forms of protest also shaped this moment, and these forms represented a competing protest agenda and political project that operated largely outside of—and at times in direct conflict with—the mainstream civil rights movement. This protest trajectory of *independent black radicalism* challenged the precepts of racial liberalism with a protest agenda built on a combination of black nationalist and leftist ideas and buttressed with ideological influences and historical examples from the Third World. Both of these protest trajectories were present and growing during the spring of 1961; one of them—the civil rights movement—grew in full view by way of news coverage and national debate, while the other—independent black radicalism—operated at lower frequencies. Jimmy and Grace participated in the latter while also using *Correspondence* to amplify it.

Rising Tide of Afro-American Nationalism

Correspondence reported on the black radical politics that congealed during the spring of 1961 in "Tide of Afro-American Nationalism Is Rising in the United States." The front-page story of the April 8, 1961, issue, it told of the "revolutionary tone and temper" expressed in the new "Negro extremist groups" gaining members and influence across the country. In the language of early 1960s political discourse, the label "Negro extremist group" would typically be deployed to dismiss or discredit an organization. To call a group extremist was to mark it as irresponsible, unrepresentative of mainstream Negro opinion, and a potential threat to established and respectable black leadership. However, *Correspondence* used the label to convey the opposite. The article compared these groups favorably with the "moderate organizations like the NAACP and the Urban League" whose membership and appeal among the masses were in decline. Other than a reference to the Black Muslims, the article did not name the groups being discussed, but it cogently presented their general political perspective, the bases of their critiques, and their place relative to the traditional organizations in the larger black freedom struggle. "The new groups," the article explained, "are distinguished by the fierce pride with which they identify themselves with the African struggles for national independence. Unlike the traditional Negro leaders who regard themselves first of all as Americans, these new groups boast of their African origins." While the politics of racial liberalism rested on appeals to national consciousness or national political ideals, the new nationalism explicitly claimed an ideological and emotional distance from the nation state and took a decidedly oppositional stance toward the government. "They flaunt the growing power of the new African nations, take every advantage of the crisis of Western civilization, preach unrelieved hostility to the white community, exclude whites from their organizations, [and] openly defy the government." Further differentiating themselves from the civil rights movement, these groups "do not regard themselves as pressure groups, asking for rights from American society or re-educating whites in democratic values." The article concluded by asserting that "the significance of these new movements . . . lies in the fact that they do not want integration into American society as it is. By the totality of their rejection of existing society and their refusal to compromise with it, they are bringing the American revolution closer."[26]

If one development most clearly represented this emergent nationalism in 1961, it was the response of Harlem activists to the assassination of

Patrice Lumumba. On February 15 a group of approximately fifty activists staged a demonstration in the gallery of the United Nations to protest the murder of the leader of the newly independent Republic of the Congo. That evening, another group of activists staged a parallel protest outside. Both demonstrations sparked confrontations with authorities, arrests, and reports of a supposed communist plot. Such concerns, of course, were unfounded. The protests expressed a deep reservoir of nationalist sentiment, particularly in Harlem, that was just then emerging in organizational form and activist politics.[27] This included the recently formed On Guard for Freedom, led by Calvin Hicks; the Liberation Committee for Africa (LCA), led by Dan Watts; the Harlem Writers Guild (HWG), whose distinguished roster of black literary figures included Rosa Guy, John Oliver Killens, and Maya Angelou; and the Cultural Association for Women of African Heritage, founded by singer Abbey Lincoln and prominent HWG members.[28] These groups shared overlapping membership as well as close personal, artistic, and political ties. Various accounts indicate that activists from these groups (assigning a leading role to Guy and the HWG in particular) conceived of and carried out the UN protests. Their politics included a mixture of racial and cultural pride, a left critique of both America and other Western powers, identification with Africa, and support for African and other Third World struggles against colonialism. The protesters interpreted Lumumba as a hero and champion for all of Africa and his murder as an attack not just on the aspirations of the Congolese people but also on the dignity and freedom of black people worldwide.[29]

The *Correspondence* article credited the UN demonstrations with forcing the American public to pay attention to this rising nationalism. The article opened by recounting a Harlem street-corner meeting shortly after Lumumba's murder during which "a bearded, smartly dressed young man jumps up and down on the platform" denouncing those responsible for the murder. "I blame the United States Government for the death of Lumumba," the article quotes him as saying, "and don't anybody dare call me a Communist. I am just an angry black man."[30]

John Henrik Clarke also identified the UN protest as a clear marker of this emergent nationalism. Clarke, a Harlem-based intellectual and activist and an especially astute observer of black activist politics, began his essay "The New Afro-American Nationalism" by asserting that the "protest against the foul and cowardly murder of Patrice Lumumba introduced the new Afro-American nationalism."[31] Published in the fall of 1961, Clarke's discussion of this new nationalism mirrored and extended the analysis *Correspondence* presented just months earlier in "Tide of Afro-American Nationalism Is Rising in the United States." Surveying the many nationalist groupings in Harlem and their programs, Clarke found that the rise in nationalist activity reflected the fact that "the American dream and the American promise of full citizenship, with dignity, after being so long delayed, is now being discarded as a hope and an objective by large numbers of Afro-Americans."[32] A defining feature of these nationalist groupings was that they were primarily led "by aroused proletarians" in sharp distinction to the "smug middle class leadership of organizations like the NAACP and the National Urban League."[33] The new nationalist groups did not speak in one voice with regard to specific objectives and rhetoric, but they all captured "the new tempo of restlessness among the Afro-American newly alerted masses."[34] That the "moderate Black Bourgeoisie 'leaders'" had either "missed or misjudged" this restlessness further revealed the sizable chasms of class, ideology, and political orientation existing within the black freedom struggle. Indeed, this new wave of nationalist activity registered a repudiation and rejection of the established civil rights leadership. "The Afro-American nationalists," Clarke concluded, "have moved far ahead of the articulate beggars of crumbs, now being called 'leaders.'"[35]

As his sharp and critical language suggests, Clarke wrote not only as an analyst but as a partisan. He was actively engaged in New York black nationalist circles and networks of radical intellectuals and activists. Throughout this period he not only chronicled but helped to fashion critiques of civil rights orthodoxy. He also helped to build vehicles through which these critiques were articulated and projected out to the black freedom struggle. Clarke's essay appeared in *Freedomways*, a newly founded black political and literary journal expressly devoted to the black freedom struggle. It launched in the spring of 1961, the product of an interesting mix of political traditions and influences, including black radicals associated with the Communist Left, the most militant corners of the civil rights movement, and politically oriented black literary figures and artists.[36] Clarke was a member of the collective that initiated the journal.[37] He also served on the editorial board of *Liberator*, a black political magazine founded by Dan Watts and the LCA a few months after the UN protests.[38] These two journals of black radical critique and analysis appeared simultaneously with the Boggses' increasing coverage of black nationalist activity in *Correspondence*. The emergence of these three vehicles for the analysis of the new nationalism reflected the creation of an intellectual infrastructure for not only analyzing but also advancing this trajectory of black radical politics. In other words, these publications served as institutions within the networks of early 1960s independent black radicalism that would critique, challenge, and seek to uproot the racial liberalism of the civil rights movement in the months and years ahead.

Through *Correspondence* and through their growing connections to other activists, Jimmy and Grace became increasingly active in these black radical networks during 1961. These networks formed largely through local struggles, but activists also forged important national links. New York, as the home of *Liberator, Freedomways,* and many of the new nationalist activists and groups, served as a primary center. As we will see, Jimmy and Grace and their comrades in Detroit turned their city, already the site of a proud heritage of multihued radicalism, into another locus of early 1960s black radicalism. And Robert Williams made Monroe yet another focal point. Beginning in 1959, Williams emerged as perhaps the most important individual activist, both ideologically and practically, in the forging of a national network of independent black radicalism. This happened through an ongoing dynamic of interaction whereby his efforts in Monroe drew support from activists in New York, Detroit, and elsewhere who organized in their locales and, in some cases, such as Conrad Lynn, Constance Webb, and Reginald Wilson, traveled to Monroe. Moreover, Williams's continuing efforts took him across the country, creating opportunities for further exchanges and deepening ties that further galvanized these national networks. If the UN demonstrations announced this stream of independent black radicalism in 1961, Williams helped to catalyze and deepen its connections across the country. Indeed, we gain a deeper understanding of how this thread of black radical politics developed by looking at the ways in which Williams's trajectory intersected with the community of New York activists responsible for the UN protests and with the Boggses and their fellow Detroit radicals who forged a distinctive local movement there.[39]

Robert Williams and the Detroit Committee to Aid the Monroe Defendants

The evening before the UN protests, Williams was in New York City discussing politics and movement strategies with some of his Harlem-based comrades and supporters. The conversation included the protest planned for the next day, which Williams was unable to attend because he was in the midst of a national speaking tour and would be leaving for Michigan in the morning.[40] On the evening of February 15, 1961, as the second UN demonstration took place outside the UN headquarters, Williams spoke on "The Negro Revolution: Cuba and the South" at the University of Michigan.[41] The local sponsors of his appearance were the Democratic Socialist Club (the same organization that hosted Grace two weeks later for her speech on Lumumba) and the Committee for Improved Cuban-American Relations, but it was part of a national tour organized by the Fair Play for Cuba Committee (FPCC).[42] Williams had visited Cuba twice in 1960, once as part of the now famous trip of mostly black writers and activists that included John Henrik Clarke, Julian Mayfield, Harold Cruse, and Amiri Baraka.[43] Williams's support for the Cuban Revolution and his linking of it to the black American struggle in the South made his speeches at the University of Michigan and elsewhere powerful and provocative.

His speaking tour next took him to nearby Detroit for the weekend. There he spoke at Debs Hall, the Socialist Workers Party (SWP)'s headquarters, in their Friday Night Socialist Forum, a regular space for discussion and political debate that drew participants from nearly all corners of the city's left and progressive political culture. Dan Georgakas, a regular attendee and keen observer of the forum, described it as "the most significant political institution in the city of Detroit in the late 1950s and early 1960s" and attributed its success to the fact that the initiators "were far less interested in recruiting people than they were interested in just talking and creating a climate, creating a movement."[44] Williams's appearance at the Friday Night Socialist Forum was a generative moment in his relationship to the city's Left, white and black.[45]

While in Detroit, Williams met with the Boggses and other members of Correspondence.[46] Their meeting confirmed for Jimmy that Williams was a new type of leader, and it spurred a strengthening of links between the two men over the coming months.[47] By May, Jimmy had joined an exchange taking place among Conrad Lynn, Julian Mayfield, and Williams about Williams's political views and program. Lynn and Mayfield in particular urged Williams to clarify his position on the black struggle, and Mayfield proposed a conference in Monroe organized by Williams. Jimmy also thought a clarification of Williams's views would advance the larger struggle, in part because of two things that Jimmy believed distinguished Williams. Writing to Lynn, Jimmy explained that Williams, having been born and raised in the South and having returned there to build his political base, "has not been corrupted by the philanthropic attitude" that Jimmy found prevalent among many northern Negroes, "Southern Uncle Toms," and other leaders who "feel they are doing the Negroes a service in speaking for their rights when actually they are only getting the important treatment from white dignitaries because they are supposed to represent the Negroes." Second, Williams "can move with relative flexibility and not be caught in one fixed position." Jimmy contrasted this with Martin Luther King Jr.'s unwavering commitment to nonviolence. "There will be a time and there will have to be times for non-violent resistance as well as times for armed direct action," Jimmy wrote. "There will be times for meeting resistance with resistance, times when white and colored will have to fight each other and other times when Negroes will have to fight Negroes."[48]

Reginald Wilson was especially drawn to Williams and the support efforts around him. By the summer of 1961, Wilson had assumed a significant place in the Detroit and national networks supporting Williams and the Monroe struggle. In late summer he drove to New York to collect a shipment of guns and food that he then secretly delivered to Monroe, a dangerous but needed delivery, as the black community of Monroe was facing the continuing threat of white racist violence as well as repression by local authorities.[49] Like Constance Webb two years earlier, Wilson brought a tape recorder. He stayed one night at the home of Robert and Mabel Williams and taped several people telling what was happening in Monroe.

Shortly after he returned, the situation in Monroe took another dramatic turn. In August 1961, yet another armed confrontation erupted between Monroe's black community and local whites. In the course of the fracas, authorities charged Williams with a plainly false accusation of kidnapping a white couple whom he had actually protected. He and his family quickly made the decision to leave Monroe. With the help of a range of supporters, including Julian Mayfield, the Williams family made their way to New York, Canada, and finally Cuba.

While the FBI searched for Williams, his informal networks of support mobilized to aid him and the Monroe community. They moved to solidify and strengthen their efforts in the form of new organizations, resulting in two parallel groups, the Committee to Aid the Monroe Defendants (CAMD) and the Monroe Defense Committee (MDC). In New York, these two groups developed a bitter rivalry, fought in part along ideological lines. The Socialist Workers Party influenced the CAMD, while some of New York's partisans of the new black nationalism led the MDC. Such competition did not take root in Detroit, where a cross section of black activists joined to form a CAMD chapter that mounted a very effective support campaign without the competition of another group. Reginald Wilson served as a leader of the Detroit CAMD, which also included Rev. Charles Hill and Williams's brothers John and Edward.

For the remainder of 1961 and throughout 1962 Detroit was an important base of support, on par with New York, for Williams and Monroe. One reason for this was that Williams had family members living in Detroit, including John and Edward, who played a unique role in bridging family and activist support. In May 1962 Grace wrote to Conrad Lynn to say that John Williams had "been in very close touch with us" and she remarked that she was impressed with how "he has devoted himself practically full-time to the matters that only a family member can really handle while showing a growing political grasp."[50] The groundwork that *Correspondence* and the Boggses laid proved to be another reason that Detroit formed this important location for galvanizing support activity around Williams and Monroe.

The End of Correspondence

Meanwhile, the ideological conflict in Correspondence was developing into an organizational crisis and rupture. The opening salvo of this yearlong conflict came in January when the group decided to focus an issue of *Correspondence* on Cuba. The Cuban Revolution's emergence in 1959 had not generated the excitement within Correspondence that had followed the Hungarian Revolution three years earlier, but Cuba exposed differences between Jimmy and another leader of the organization just as Hungary had. This time Jimmy clashed not with C. L. R. but with Glaberman, and their debate turned more explicitly to the matter of the American working class. Far more immediate and more consequential for the organization, this conflict went to the core of the group's politics, and played out not only through international correspondence with C. L. R., now living in Trinidad, but also in editorial meetings and in the daily organizational operations.

The conflict arose when Jimmy and Glaberman proposed contrasting formats for the Cuba issue of the paper. Glaberman envisioned an all-Cuba issue with the back page printed in Spanish. Jimmy opposed this idea, arguing that the issue should contain some continuation of the paper's analysis of "the American situation," by which he meant particularly the black struggle, other domestic expressions popular of protest, and ultimately the prospect for revolutionary transformation in the United States. This, he believed, was the paper's primary responsibility. Glaberman countered that the paper had a duty to demonstrate the revolutionary significance of Cuba to the American workers who viewed it through the eyes of the bourgeois. Their debate over this issue of the paper revealed divergent visions for the role of *Correspondence*, and competing articulations of revolutionary politics.

What was at issue, particularly for Glaberman, was the role of workers' control and worker self-organization in the revolutionary process—foundational Johnson-Forest Tendency and Correspondence ideas. As Grace explained to C. L. R., both Glaberman and Jimmy "believe in unqualified support" for the Cuban Revolution, but Jimmy "tends to emphasize that the Cubans have a right to develop their own revolution how they please, while Marty emphasizes what he considers the workers' control developments in Cuba and the creation of new revolutionary non-party forms."[51] As she had done since the mid-1950s, Grace played the role of a mediator as well as a conduit of information, writing to C. L. R. with updates. Glaberman wrote to C. L. R. about the matter as well, making the point even more clearly: "The special Cuba issue has brought out certain substantial differences among us. . . . The real question involved is not Cuba but the American working class."[52]

In the closing months of 1961, Grace and Jimmy each wrote an internal document that captured these competing interpretations of the American working class. Together, these two documents—and the responses they elicited—spelled the end of Correspondence. In October, Grace wrote an "Editor's Report" designed to share with her comrades information and perspective on the current state of *Correspondence* and to offer Grace's plans or vision, as its editor, for the future development of the paper. Going far beyond the specifics about content, circulation, and such, Grace used the report as an opportunity to suggest rethinking some of the group's central theoretical concepts, such as its belief in the revolutionary capacity of the American working class. She also used the document as a space to begin formulating new ideas for possible inclusion in the paper, such as explicit consideration of the roles that conscious moral choice and the struggle for rights might play in a distinctly American revolution. The "Editor's Report" quickly generated intense critique and opposition from Glaberman and others. At the end of the year, Jimmy wrote and submitted to the organization his own document articulating his thinking regarding these now hotly contested ideas. Its focus was to be "the potentialities of the American revolution," by which he meant an examination of the prospects and likely character of a distinctly American revolution. This would involve an analysis of the recent political and economic developments in the United States, a reappraisal of the Marxist scenario of revolution in light of this analysis, and finally the projection of a theory of an American revolution appropriate for the time. "I have felt that there was a great need for such a document," Jimmy wrote to the group at the end of 1961, "because American itself now stands as the citadel of capitalism and it is here more than any place else in the world that the question of whether society will always be governed by capitalism has to be tackled."[53] Jimmy's document, titled "State of a Nation—America, 1962," drew even more fire than Grace's statement for its departure from Marxism.[54]

The opening paragraphs of this nearly ninety-page document directly rebuked the practice and the thinking of Marxists in the United States. "For many years, the American revolutionary groupings have lived and built their hopes on what happens in the European revolutions," he said. "They have taken the conditions of other countries to explain the conditions in America, seldom recognizing in practice that it is the fundamental, organic conditions in any country that make the people of that country revolt." He chided them further for using the Russian Revolution and Marx's *Capital*, "which they have torn apart and analyzed, confusing more than clarifying," as the templates and guiding framework for a revolution in the United States.[55] Jimmy did not go any further in directly identifying any specific targets of his criticism, but with echoes of the group's debates over the Hungarian revolution and more recently Cuba present in Jimmy's comments, and with his rather dismissive reference to *Capital*'s presumed authority, members of the organization could easily interpret this as a subtle, or perhaps not so subtle, denigration of the group's history and politics. In particular, Jimmy's words could be read as a challenge to C. L. R. and others such as Glaberman, who remained consistently loyal to C. L. R. and his positions. Of course, Correspondence (and the JFT before it) defined itself as distinct from, and in some ways in opposition to, orthodox Marxism and radical parties, and more importantly as the generator of an authentic American Marxism. Thus, Jimmy's critique could have been read by C. L. R. and others in the group as a confirmation of their mission and practice.

It was Jimmy's ideas about the U.S. working class that fully exposed his differences within the organization. Based on his analysis of automation and what he was seeing in his plant, Jimmy argued that the country was undergoing such a profound industrial and social transformation that "the question of who is in what class becomes an ever-wider and more complicated question." Neither historical examples nor established theoretical conceptualizations of class formation were sufficient to capture contemporary dynamics. Unlike earlier periods, such as feudal Europe, pre–civil war United States, or the 1930s, he said that the country had reached "the stage where no class is a homogeneous segregated bloc. . . . Today the working class is so dispersed and transformed by the very nature of the changes in production that it is almost impossible to select out any single bloc of workers as working class in the old sense." This was heresy enough, challenging as it did the group's theoretical foundation, but he went further, rejecting the role of the working class at the core of the group's politics: "It is not only the diversification of work that has changed the working class. The working class is growing, as Marx predicted, but it is not the old working class which we persist in believing will create the revolution and establish control over production. That old working class is the vanishing herd."[56]

This document helped raise the ideological and political tensions within the group such that it teetered toward a split. The crisis played out in part through a flurry of letters passed between members of the organization. Glaberman wrote frequent letters, many to C. L. R., discussing with obvious dismay what he saw as the Boggses' betrayal of Marxism and the organization. He called one issue of Correspondence "a complete rejection of everything that Correspondence has ever stood for"[57] and angrily derided Grace's new views as "anti-Marxism" because they rejected three key Marxist ideas: the inevitability of socialism, the concept of the invading socialist society, and the revolutionary capacity of the working class.[58] C. L. R. also took this new turn as an affront to the organization and the Marxist tradition on which it stood. Writing to Glaberman, C. L. R. described Grace's "Editor's Report" and Jimmy's "State of a Nation" as "indefensible," and Jimmy's document in particular as "a vicious concentrated attack on Marxism."[59] His response to the crisis was "once more to make Marxism the centre of our thoughts,"[60] which he proposed to do through two articles he wrote for publication in the Correspondence. When in December Jimmy and Grace passed a resolution, over Glaberman's objections, to have C. L. R.'s articles discussed internally in the organization but not printed in the paper, the final blow to the organization was struck. C. L. R. interpreted this decision as a "settled hostility to the principles of Marxism." In January he responded by saying the resolution was "the final stage in the destruction of our movement" because "those who declare that the very fundamentals of Marxism are matters for discussion are no longer Marxists." He therefore brought a close to his long political relationship with Jimmy and Grace by declaring "henceforth I break all relations, political and personal, with all who subscribe to that resolution."[61]

The year 1962 began with Grace and Jimmy facing a new and to a large extent uncharted political situation. By March they had formally left Correspondence, though they had in effect stopped functioning as members in January. They were no longer part of the organization that had been at the center of their lives, both politically and personally, for their entire seven-year marriage. On the other hand, they had for some time been slowly moving away from the organization's ideological outlook while immersing themselves in a world of black radical politics.

They were able to retain some continuity in spite of the split. Freddy and Lyman Paine left with them, and because Lyman held ownership of *Correspondence*, they continued to publish the paper as a central component of their political work. The Wilsons and Malletts also left the organization; indeed, for them, the break with C. L. R. did not mean much, as their association with the organization was largely through the Boggses and the paper, and this association and collaboration continued as it had before the split. Ultimately, the split freed Grace and Jimmy to move more freely and resolutely in political directions they had already charted. The break with C. L. R. marked the end of one stage in their shared activist career and the beginning of another.

The roster of local activists that Jimmy and Grace met or deepened their association with in 1961–62 marked the beginning of this new stage. Prominent among them was Rev. Albert Cleage, who led the Central Congregational Church on Linwood at Hogarth near Twelfth Street and was fast gaining notice as one of the most militant voices in the city.[62] During the first half of 1961 he and other members of his family launched the *Illustrated News*, a weekly newspaper printed on salmon-colored newsprint in a small print shop owned by the family and used primarily to print grocery circulars. With a circulation of over 35,000 distributed for free through black Detroit churches and other community networks, the *Illustrated News* offered a grassroots and politically oriented alternative to the major black weeklies.[63] During the early 1960s the *Illustrated News* served as a platform for Cleage and played an important role in building a vibrant local movement. Grace and Jimmy would work closely with him during the early and mid-1960s, Grace especially so. In a letter to Conrad Lynn at the end of 1962, she described Cleage as having escaped "being hogtied by the labor movement in this city" and as being "extremely sensitive to the changes that have taken place in the Negro community" there. As a result, he held unique appeal and potential as a local leader. "He is always challenging and defying the union movement," she continued, "and also leading school and neighborhood struggles. In addition, he is a gifted speaker, with a sense of timing much like Will Rogers or Dick Gregory."[64]

Among the Boggses' other new allies in this period were brothers Richard and Milton Henry. In 1962 the Henry brothers, who were also close allies of Cleage, formed the Group on Advanced Leadership (GOAL), a militant group that anchored much of the protest activity in this period. With Cleage and the *Illustrated News*, GOAL and the Henry brothers mounted sustained and often very successful attacks on racism in the city's public schools, urban renewal, and discrimination in the building trades, among other things. During this time Jimmy and Grace also met Wilfred X, leader of the NOI mosque in Detroit and brother of Malcolm X. Grace in particular developed a close relationship with Wilfred, establishing another important link in the diverse black nationalist circles of early 1960s Detroit. As in New York and other places, an impressive network of activists and organizations in early 1960s Detroit forged a somewhat eclectic but sufficiently cohesive protest community. This community, despite the ideological diversity within it, created a vibrant stream of black radical politics. Jimmy and Grace stood at its center. They helped to build and sustain it in many ways, including through their wide connections, their activism, and *Correspondence*. Their activities during one week in June 1962 provide an example. On Sunday they attended a NOI rally, and the next day they spoke with Malcolm X on the phone. Later that evening they spent three hours talking with his brother Wilfred at their home. Then, on Wednesday and Saturday, "we spent many hours with the Williams family," as Grace reported in a letter, "arranging among other things to get material on the U.S. struggle to Rob [Williams] and discussing developments inside the Monroe community."[65] One result of this continued work with the Williams family, the Detroit CAMD, and Conrad Lynn was that Jimmy and Grace published, as a *Correspondence* pamphlet, "Monroe, North Carolina: Turning Point in American History," consisting of two speeches by Lynn and a foreword by Jimmy.

The pace of the Boggses' activities during the spring of 1962 momentarily slowed when they were forced to find a new home. As Grace put it, they were "Urban Removed."[66] The six-room flat they were renting at the corner of Baldwin and Goethe, for which they paid $62 per month, was scheduled to be torn down to make way for Bell Elementary School.[67] They initially planned to "sit out" their ninety-day notice, but Grace happened to drive past a house for rent on nearby Field Street that caught her attention. She went to see it and "couldn't believe it." Thoroughly enamored with the home, she encouraged Jimmy to see it and he too was charmed. "Jimmy loved taking care of things," Grace recalled years later, and this was a place he could take care of. The owner wanted $75 per month, but Grace told her that they could not afford that, so she dropped it to $70.[68] With that, Grace and Jimmy moved into their new home at 3061 Field Street, on the corner of Field and Goethe, one block from East Grand Boulevard. "We have rented a really palatial place," Grace wrote to Freddy Paine in May 1963, "2 baths, 6 ½ rooms, sunporch, recreation room in the cellar, soundproofed recording studio also in the cellar, wall-to-wall carpeting from spacious living room through reception hall to equally spacious dining room, etc."[69] With all of its space, the house served their political activities quite well. Over the coming years they shared in their living room innumerable discussions with a staggering array of activists, artists, intellectuals, and other guests. The spacious basement housed visitors, served as meeting space, and facilitated interactions that are not easily measured but no doubt enhanced the quality of their political engagements. By the time that Black Power emerged in the mid-1960s, the Boggses' home was already becoming a well-known and well-used movement center.[70]

While it could not have been anticipated when they moved in, 3061 Field Street would play a central role in the Boggses' intellectual and political work from that point forward. Thus, their rather sudden move to the house in the spring of 1962, just fourth months after the split with C. L. R., served as a fitting metaphor for new beginnings. It symbolized their move from one stage of their activism and their lives together to another. Having entered this new stage in 1962, they turned fully to its opportunities and challenges in 1963.

CHAPTER TEN

The American Revolution

"Negroes Are the Ones Best-Suited to Govern the United States Today." This declaration appeared on the front page of *Correspondence*'s special Emancipation Proclamation issue published in January 1963.[1] The start of the new year marked the centennial of the proclamation, and the symbolism of "100 years of freedom" sparked numerous and varied responses, including celebrations, commentary, and renewed activism from a wide range of parties with some interest in or opinion on the contemporary black struggle. *Correspondence* used the occasion to present its interpretation of that struggle and to place distance between itself and the Marxist Left. An editorial titled "Why This Issue?" explained that the issue "is unmistakably Nationalist in tone and content. The reason for this is very simple. Anyone who knows the Negro community knows that the greatest emancipation is taking place among those Negroes who are proud of their blackness and separateness. By stressing rejection of the institutions of American society rather than seeking integration into them, these Negroes are achieving an unparalleled freedom and independence of thought."[2] The editorial also articulated the position on the black struggle that Jimmy and Grace had been developing over the preceding two years: "At this time, in this country, revolutionary philosophical and political leadership can only come from the Negroes," and this fact made it clear that "the ideological paternalism which socialists have always maintained in regard to the Negro struggle is only white supremacy in a radical guise."[3]

The special Emancipation Proclamation issue was full of arguments for and expressions of the new nationalism that had emerged since 1961. The lead article argued that the United States needed "a government that is in tune with the world revolution now sweeping Latin-America, Africa, Asia, and the Middle East" and that "the Negroes are the only social force in this country which is part of this world revolution."[4] Also appearing on the front page was a piece by Selma Sparks, a member of the *Liberator* editorial board, describing the growth and depth of Bandung-style internationalism among Harlem nationalists since the UN demonstration following Patrice Lumumba's death, particularly in support of the Cuban Revolution.[5] The fifth installment of Reginald Wilson's "What Are We Fighting for Anyway?" series questioned "the alleged progress of the Negro during the past hundred years" and the notion that the centennial was cause for celebration. The article reported on "the real situation of the Negro in America" by detailing numerous recent cases of racist violence and official malfeasance across the country. "In his revolutionary struggle for freedom," Wilson concluded, "the only thing the Negro in America has to celebrate in 1963 is his awakening."[6] Several pieces in *Correspondence*'s Emancipation Proclamation issue dealt with black history and black pride, such as Gwen Mallett's "I'm Glad I'm a Negro" and Conrad Mallett's "Rediscovering Negro History." A letter in the "Readers' Views" section argued for the rejection of the word "Negro" in favor of "Afro-American," while another letter asserted that nationalism "undoubtedly" brings self-improvement: "Every nationalist becomes a scholar. His scope becomes enlarged to a world scope where before it was just his block. His ego really grows because he truly grows himself. He gets a purpose and becomes a free-thinking person."[7]

Further evidence of the new nationalism appeared under the banner "Introducing Rev. Albert B. Cleage, Jr." in the form of excerpts from a speech Cleage had recently delivered on the future of the black struggle, showcasing his militant rhetoric and bold pronouncements on white duplicity and the need for an assertive black nationalist political program. Grace gave Cleage's remarks the title "The Negro Struggle Is a Struggle for Power" and introduced them with a prefatory statement praising Cleage for his role in the local black movement.[8]

The issue also included a "Black Art" supplement that was in some ways the most telling feature of the issue. It featured works by several Detroit visual artists and poets; a profile of singer, actress, and activist Abbey Lincoln; and two essays on Jazz, one of them by Lincoln's husband, the drummer and activist Max Roach. The supplement aimed to showcase local artists while emphasizing the importance of art and artists in the development of black cultural identity and the larger black struggle. Lincoln and Roach were among the Harlem activists who instigated the UN protests and the anti-imperialist activity that Selma Sparks described on the front page of the issue. The profile of Lincoln, titled "Black Beauty," praised her combination of artistic talent, integrity, and racial pride. It particularly noted that she "refused to press her hair," instead choosing to wear a natural hairstyle as both a statement of personal values and a larger cultural and political statement. "The moment Negro women begin to wear their hair NATURALLY," *Correspondence* asserted, "they will automatically feel different. Then, and only then, will they know that they are beautiful black women—like Abbey Lincoln—based on their own standards."[9]

Correspondence's Emancipation Proclamation issue served as a prescient statement on the arrival and dramatic impact of the Black Power movement during the second half of the decade. Jimmy and Grace were already thinking and writing about a notion of black power in 1963. Writing to Conrad Lynn in January, Grace said that "the past period" of activism and theoretical work had advanced their thinking on two points: the international character of the Negro struggle; and the need for "black power" (her quotation marks), which she specified as being "not in any old eight Southern states but in the cities where Negroes are fast becoming a majority." She also told him he "would be absolutely amazed" if he had seen the enthusiastic response when they raised the idea of Negro self-government in Detroit with people over the past few weeks. "Out of perhaps twenty-five people, most of them Negroes, only one has shown any hesitation—and he is a 'radical'—i.e. someone who says *he* is ready but that the people are not."[10]

Jimmy also began formulating a concept of black power and projecting the significance of the idea in his writings during the early 1960s, when few observers anticipated or took seriously the prospect of the civil rights struggle's transforming into a struggle for black power. In his 1963 "Black Political Power," a review essay of black journalist Louis Lomax's 1962 book *The Negro Revolt*, Jimmy noted that in some quarters of black opinion and politics there was a rising nationalist sentiment, rejection of integration, and desire for black political power, all of which he saw as pointing to the next stage of the black revolt. He chided Lomax for being "a Negro who still thinks in terms of white power as naturally as he thinks of eating when he's hungry. His mind simply has not stretched beyond the idea of whites ruling and giving Negroes a greater share in this rule."[11] The essay ends with a prediction that, within months, would begin to be realized in Detroit by the successful formation of the Freedom Now Party (FNP) and within three years would be dramatically proved accurate with the rise of the Black Power movement. "The struggle of the Negroes in the very near future," he wrote, "will be the struggle for black political power, and by black political power is meant, not the power of Negroes to put white men in office, to whom they can go and ask for things, but rather their own power to dispose of things."[12]

The Black Revolution of 1963

All of this placed Jimmy and Grace in the midst of the currents of black radical politics that were challenging racial liberalism, in Detroit and nationally, and would culminate in the year ahead. The dramatic events of 1963 led participants and observers alike to speak of a racial revolution. During the summer of 1963 *Newsweek* magazine conducted a nationwide survey in an attempt to understand the motivations and meanings of the rising "Negro revolution in America."[13] Martin Luther King Jr. described "the Negro Revolution of 1963" in his book *Why We Can't Wait*, asserting that "no one can doubt that as the Negro left 1963 behind he had taken the longest and fastest leap forward in a century."[14] Journalist and popular historian Lerone Bennett Jr. also used the theme of revolution in his recounting of the year's developments. Drawing on the imagery, emotions, and violence of the year's most dramatic events, Bennett summarized 1963 as "a year of funerals and births, a year of endings and a year of beginnings, a year of hate, a year of love. It was a year of water hoses and high-powered rifles, of struggles in the streets and screams in the night, of homemade bombs and gasoline torches, of snarling dogs and widows in black. It was a year of passion, a year of despair, a year of desperate hope. It was 1963, the 100th year of black emancipation and the first year of the Black Revolution."[15]

Protest activity in the South impacted northern communities and struggles within them. The Birmingham campaign, in particular, provided an impetus for organizing and movement building nationally. The mass movement to desegregate Birmingham dramatically exposed the depths and depravity of white supremacy, but it also showed that the brutal hand of southern reaction could be stayed, at least partially, by mass action. In response, black communities across the country mobilized to demonstrate their solidarity with the struggle in Birmingham. Within a week of the May 10 settlement that brought the campaign to a close, supporters staged large rallies in Cleveland, Los Angeles, and Chicago.[16] Other support rallies occurred in other cities throughout May and into the summer, raising a total of $159,856 for the Southern Christian Leadership Conference (SCLC).[17]

Detroit was one of these cities. In early May, leaders of the Detroit branch of the National Association for the Advancement of Colored People (NAACP) issued a "Call to Action" urging "Freedom loving Detroiters" to "Reinforce the Birmingham Freedom Fighters." The call urged mass participation in a "protest rally and demonstration" on May 10 at the site of Old City Hall in downtown Detroit to "make Detroit and the world more aware of the tragedy in Birmingham Alabama." Cosponsored by the local chapter of the Congress of Racial Equality (CORE), the rally was conceived as an expression of solidarity and also as a demonstration of local political resolve. "We must dramatize our awareness of the Federal Government's responsibility to protect the rights of Negro citizens," the NAACP leaders explained. "We must by our attendance at the rally . . . emphasize the need of immediate and effective action by the Kennedy Administration." The featured speaker at the rally was *Birmingham World* editor and civil rights activist Emory O. Jackson.[18]

The strong language of the call notwithstanding, the rally was hastily organized and poorly attended. The interracial crowd was estimated at 300 people, much less than might be expected in a city that not only boasted strong traditions of political protest and civil rights activism, but was also home to a black population with strong ties to the South, and Alabama in particular. As previously discussed, Detroit's African American population had grown steadily through migration from the South over the preceding half century. Between 1910 and 1940 the city's black population rose from 5,741 to 149,119, reflecting an increase from 1.2 percent of the total population to 9.2 percent. In 1950, the census recorded 300,506 African Americans in the city, reflecting 16.2 percent of the total population. By 1960 there were 482,229 African Americans in Detroit, making up 28.9 percent of the city's nearly 1.7 million residents.[19] Like other cities, the tremendous growth of Detroit's black population during and after World War II was contemporaneous with the rising civil rights movement. Thus, the evolution of political consciousness among black Detroiters in this period was informed both by experiences of southern racism—either directly or through kinship ties and collective memory—and by its urban, northern variant. While the rally did not seem to reflect this consciousness, it did serve as a catalyst for subsequent organizing and political mobilizations.

Cleage delivered an impromptu speech during the rally in which he declared that such a small affair was woefully inadequate, suggesting that a large mass march would be a more appropriate and effective demonstration of the black community's political resolve.[20] By 1963 Cleage had earned a reputation as a powerful speaker and one of the city's most outspoken activists, and his call for a mass march was part of a broader critique he had been making of the city's traditional black leadership. Following the May 10 rally (and perhaps in response to Cleage's exhortation), members of various black community organizations met at the Detroit National Urban League office on Mack Avenue to discuss how they could support the Birmingham struggle.[21] The meeting was planned and organized by Rev. C. L. Franklin, pastor of New Bethel Baptist Church (and father of singer Aretha), and real estate developer James Del Rio. The assembled group agreed to sponsor a march and to raise $100,000 for King and the Birmingham struggle. They selected Franklin to head the organizing effort and scheduled a mass meeting for May 17 to begin planning the march and formally launch the new organization, the Detroit Council for Human Rights (DCHR).

Known for his theatrical preaching and stylish dress, Franklin has been described as "the most popular black, Baptist preacher of his generation" and "the most imitated soul preacher in history."[22] Franklin assumed the leadership of the New Bethel Baptist Church in 1946 and he soon became a local celebrity. His congregation had grown into the thousands during the 1950s, and by 1963 he had achieved national celebrity for his powerful and entertaining sermons, performed on radio broadcasts, on records, and before live audiences during national gospel road shows.[23] By this time he had also assumed a role in the local civil rights struggle, and he had connections to the national civil rights leadership, including King.[24]

Over 800 people attended the May 17 meeting held at Franklin's church, which had moved to its new sanctuary on Linwood Avenue two months earlier. The participants voted to hold a march down Woodward Avenue on June 11 that would conclude with a mass rally at Cobo Arena, where the main speaker would be either Martin Luther King or Ralph Abernathy. Franklin was elected chairman of the organization, and the all-black board of directors included Cleage. Three days later, Franklin wrote to the Detroit City Council requesting permission "to hold a parade on the evening of June 11 which would facilitate an estimated 100,000 marchers on foot." He explained that the purpose of the march was "to demonstrate our sympathy for those American citizens in Birmingham, Alabama who are engaged in a struggle for first class citizenship and to make known to people in Detroit our own displeasure over that segment of our population which is deprived of the full measure of their constitutional rights." He added that the DCHR expected to raise $100,000 at the rally "to be donated to the struggling peoples of Birmingham."[25]

Over the course of the next five weeks, the DCHR finalized the plans for the march and mobilized broad support and enthusiasm. The date was changed to June 23, King's participation was confirmed, and the event was billed as both the "Walk to Freedom" and the "Freedom March." Under the leadership of Franklin, Cleage, Del Rio, and Tony Brown, who had been hired as march coordinator, the DCHR organized all over the city. They held weekly meetings in various churches around the city to build momentum for the march. Many churches held premarch rallies, and other Michigan cities sent delegations.[26]

By all accounts, the march was a tremendous success. Estimates of the number of participants ranged from 125,000 to 250,000, and King told the crowd that "what has been done here today will serve as a source of inspiration for all the freedom-loving people of this nation." He opened his speech by expressing "the deep joy that comes to my heart as I participate with you in what I consider the largest and greatest demonstration for freedom ever held in the United States."[27] Marchers made their way down Woodward Avenue carrying signs that read, "We Shall Be Free," "Evers Did Not Die in Vain!," "Stop Jim Crowism!," "Black Peoples' Revolt," and "White Man Listen, We Will Take Our Rights!"[28] Thousands more lined the streets, cheering the marchers on as they made their way to Cobo Arena, where King delivered "a thunderous, dramatic climax" to the march. During his speech, which included an early version of his famous "I Have a Dream" oration, King brought the crowd to its feet when he asserted, "We want Freedom . . . and we want it now!" The other platform speakers were DCHR board member and longtime activist Snow Grigsby, Detroit mayor Jerome Cavanagh, Representative Charles C. Diggs Jr., United Auto Workers (UAW) president Walter Reuther, and Cleage, with Franklin serving as master of ceremonies.[29]

Correspondence ran a banner at the top of its next issue that read, "250,000 Detroiters Walk for Freedom," along with a front-page report on the march by Gwen Mallett, "Freedom Walkers Pledge 'We Shall Overcome.'" Mallett explained that the sentiment "This is OUR DAY" captured the general feeling among the marchers.[30] She also reported that, despite wide endorsement of the march from white liberal, labor, and religious organizations, the vast majority of the demonstrators were black. Estimating whites as no more than 2 percent of the quarter million demonstrators, she said that the presence of only a mere "sprinkling of whites among the marchers" reinforced the attitude among "more and more Negroes" that "this is our fight."[31] To illustrate the mood of the march, she cited several slogans carried on placards that were more militant than those reported in other news outlets. "White Man Wake Up or Wake Up Dead" read one. A nine-year-old child carried a sign reading "Ready or Not, Here We Come," and another child's placard declared, "100 Years Overdue, Freedom Now." Among the more humorous signs was "Freedom Now, Said Tom, Democratically." Echoing *Correspondence*'s Emancipation Proclamation issue, another placard read, "Negroes Best Suited to Govern Themselves." The political cartoon by Reginald Wilson on the front page of this issue depicted Gus and Greasy, regular characters in his cartoons, talking against the backdrop of two scenes of white police beating African Americans. One scene involves a police dog, suggestive of the televised images of Bull Connor and his police force brutalizing civil rights demonstrators in Birmingham during the preceding weeks. "The question should be," one man says to the other, "when will WHITES be fit for self-government?"[32]

Mallett reported that the "holiday spirit" prevailing along the march route carried over into the rally afterward, but this wore thin when "people began to get disenchanted with the platitudes mouthed by white dignitaries" such as Cavanagh and Reuther. The crowd's discontent vanished when Cleage took the podium to speak. "In the challenging manner for which Cleage is noted," wrote Mallett, who was a friend and political ally of his, Cleage "immediately transformed the holiday spirit of the crowd into a fighting spirit for freedom." He stressed the specific issues faced by blacks in the North around which they must fight. "The crowd let him know they accepted the challenge" as they applauded and cheered, and they responded, "That's right." "When Cleage repeated again and again, 'We must FIGHT and FIGHT, and FIGHT,' the hall shook as they shouted after him, 'FIGHT and FIGHT and FIGHT!'" During his speech Cleage announced a boycott of local supermarkets Kroger and A&P to protest their hiring practices, in response to which "the whole assembly stood and cheered." King followed Cleage at the podium, further exciting the crowd. "As he addressed the audience," Mallett reported, "you could see the faces of some being literally transfigured into the faces of free people." The "fervor" of the crowd especially rose when King repeated the now famous phrase "I have a dream" and then ended the speech with the equally evocative phrase "Free at last," at which point "several women began to shout 'Free at last, my Lord, free at last.'"[33]

Although Detroit's Freedom March was eclipsed by the much more celebrated March on Washington held two months later, the Detroit march was a major event when it happened in the summer of 1963. It made national news and was widely recognized as one of the largest civil rights rallies in the nation's history.[34] With broad participation from Detroit's black community, labor unions, and civic groups, the march raised thousands of dollars for the Southern Christian Leadership Conference (SCLC) and gave an indication of the extent of the support for the efforts of southern freedom fighters in other parts of the country. Furthermore, the energy and activism that the march embodied evidenced the emerging political sensibilities and drive toward political action in Detroit during the early 1960s. As Franklin declared two weeks before the march, the event served as "a warning to the city that what has transpired in the past is no longer acceptable to the Negro community." Punctuating this political resolve, Franklin added, "We want complete amelioration of all injustices."[35]

Franklin's assertive rhetoric reflected the militant mood building among black Detroiters during the spring and summer of 1963. It was, too, a forecast of the increasingly aggressive politics of the coming months and years, though, ironically perhaps, Franklin would soon be positioned (or position himself) at odds with the most militant voices in Detroit's black activist community. The march had helped to foster a sense of unity and collective purpose, and this was an important factor in mobilizing people around previously identified concerns. Indeed, the months that followed the march saw an intensification of black grassroots activism and political organizing, building on and extending the organizational and strategic resources reflected in the march. Yet, this increased political consciousness and activity generated new ideas and organizational forms, and with them came competing articulations of political objectives—as well as different strategic approaches to realizing them. These organizational and leadership rivalries certainly proved counterproductive at times, but they also represented creative tensions that ultimately had a generative impact on the development of black protest politics. Two areas of protest—economic discrimination and police brutality—would be particularly important to the movement that was building.

Detroit activists critiqued and challenged economic discrimination through a series of boycotts and selective-patronage efforts during the spring and summer of 1963. In early June the Detroit chapter of CORE began picketing Kroger's stores in opposition to the chain's discriminatory employment policies, while at the same time, but with no apparent connection, an organization of black clergy leaders named the Negro Preachers of Detroit and Vicinity launched a selective-patronage campaign against the A&P supermarket chain to expand employment opportunities for African Americans. These efforts, which began at least two weeks before the Freedom March, highlight the ways in which, by the summer of 1963, economic activism was reemerging as an important vehicle for black Detroiters to challenge the city's racial status quo. Both Rev. Cleage and Snow Grigsby used the Freedom March as a platform to advocate for aggressive economic activism. Grigsby addressed economic protest strategies during his speech at the Cobo Arena rally, and he distributed an open letter addressed to "All People of Goodwill" that championed the strategy of selective patronage.[36] The letter called for "Negroes [to] set a specific date to cease purchasing anything other than food and medicine for 30 days, to focus attention on the economic contribution of the Negro to the business community, and job discrimination perpetuated by unions. It is high time that job opportunities be more commensurate with purchasing."[37]

Cleage made a similar appeal, calling for Detroit's black community to support the recent campaigns of CORE and the Negro Preachers of Detroit and Vicinity to force the Kroger and A&P food chains to hire black managers and department heads.[38] In the most recent issue of the *Illustrated News*, released just days before the march, Cleage and his coeditors had run a full-page announcement of the selective-patronage campaigns against Kroger and A&P. Urging their readers to support the campaigns with the exhortation "Do Not Buy Where You Cannot Work," Cleage and his collaborators were drawing on the spirit if not the direct historical example of mass protests and boycotts that went under this slogan in the 1930s.[39]

They were also drawing attention to a new mood, as they perceived it, rising in black communities across the country and energizing the civil rights struggle. Both in the South—symbolized most dramatically by the mass protests in Birmingham—and in the growing black urban communities of the North, Cleage and his collaborators found that African Americans showing a marked willingness to engage in militant mass action. Cleage forcefully argued this position in an editorial that appeared in the same issue of the *Illustrated News* as the selective-patronage announcement. Putting a militant intonation to the familiar civil rights movement refrain, Cleage titled his editorial "Not Someday—But Now! We Shall Overcome" and began by asserting that "one hundred years after the Emancipation Proclamation the

Negro has at long last begun his march to freedom." Reflecting in particular on the struggle in Birmingham as well as the mobilization in Detroit for the Freedom March, Cleage proclaimed that "everywhere people are coming to accept the fact that the Negro has completely rejected gradualism and tokenism." Black protest activity was being driven by the militancy and resolve of the masses, with "Negro leadership everywhere," Cleage wrote, "reflecting the fighting temper of the Negro community."[40]

Cleage and his coeditors felt that the economic boycott was one important facet of that fight, and they used the pages of the *Illustrated News* to inform readers about boycotting and selective patronage nationally and to encourage support for such efforts in Detroit. Under the headline "Boycotting May Hit Detroit A&P," the April 29 edition of the paper cited a *Wall Street Journal* report of a boycott of the 150 A&P stores in Philadelphia "until the chain hires additional Negro employees." The *Illustrated News* added that A&P was the twentieth company to be boycotted in Philadelphia during the past three years, and suggested that similar campaigns were beginning to take root in Baltimore and New York, as well as Detroit. The paper explained, "Three Detroit ministers," who had returned to Detroit after "traveling to Philadelphia to study the program there, have organized a boycott for Detroit."[41] Indeed, the Philadelphia selective-patronage campaign was extremely successful. Led by Rev. Leon Sullivan and other members of a group called 400 Ministers, the Philadelphia boycott movement began in 1960 and had won agreements with several employers securing jobs for African Americans—usually supervisory, clerical, and skilled positions.[42]

This wave of activity, he argued, was sweeping up much of the "old guard" black leadership. Indeed, a consistent theme in the paper and in Cleage's analysis and public pronouncements, and one of the things that made him a controversial and often antagonistic or polarizing figure in local black political circles, was a sharp criticism of old-guard leadership, especially in the city. Reflecting on the impact of the Birmingham campaign, he criticized local black leaders who praised John F. Kennedy for his "Civil Rights stand," and he asserted that the president "did nothing until he was forced to act by the increasing pressure of the NEGRO PROTEST. Rev. Martin Luther King dragged Kennedy kicking and screaming into the twentieth century."[43]

Three weeks after the Freedom March, the *Michigan Chronicle* announced that A&P had reached an agreement with the Group on Advanced Leadership (GOAL) to hire five Negro managers within the next year. The agreement also called for the promotion of twenty-one black employees and the hiring of twenty-one to replace those promoted, and included terms about the fair display of "Negro-produced goods." These successful selective-buying campaigns not only represented civil rights activism in Detroit, but were also consistent with the type of activism that was emerging in urban centers across the country. The focus on employment patterns highlighted the economic dimensions of American racism as experienced in the North, and efforts around economic activism and coordinated economic action among black Detroiters were consistent with a broader national effort among black communities—many initiated and led by black clergy.

In the midst of this activity, the murder of Cynthia Scott over the Fourth of July weekend brought the struggle against police brutality to the center of black protest politics in Detroit. Just thirteen days after the Freedom March, black citizens of Detroit launched a major protest against the Detroit Police Department in response to Scott's murder by a white officer. An African American woman known to many in the area as a prostitute, Scott was enjoying after-hours Fourth of July celebrations with an acquaintance, Charles Marshall, when police encountered her. According to police reports, Scott attempted to stab officers who were trying to apprehend her and then ran to escape, at which point patrol officer Theodore Spicher shot her. Marshall, however, disputed the official version of events. He reported that Scott did not attack the officers with a knife, nor did she run to escape. Rather, she told the officers that they had no basis to arrest her and then walked away, at which point the officer began shooting. She was shot twice in the back and then once in the stomach after she had collapsed.[44]

Word of the shooting quickly spread throughout Detroit's black neighborhoods, and within nine hours a crowd of protesters had gathered at police headquarters. Numbering as many as 5,000, the crowd marched around the building chanting "Stop Killer Cops! Stop Killer Cops!" When city prosecutor Samuel H. Olson later declared that the officer's actions were justified, frustration and anger was widespread throughout the black community, and various organizations took action. The NAACP demanded a full and immediate investigation into the shooting. Uhuru, a recently formed radical student organization based at Wayne State University held street rallies and sit-ins, and GOAL organized a picket line at police headquarters. GOAL's Milton Henry served as the attorney for the Scott family.[45]

This was the context and community spirit in which the DCHR made plans for a major civil rights gathering in Detroit and the creation of a formal network of protest organizations to be called the Northern Negro Leadership Conference was conceived. The DCHR had made the call for the conference before the Freedom March. The success of the march and the subsequent activism it helped to inspire further solidified the group's intention to create a formal coalition of northern civil rights groups. Based on the structure and principles of the Southern Christian Leadership Conference (SCLC), this new coalition would link Detroit's civil rights organizations with activists from urban communities throughout the Northeast and Midwest.[46] The DCHR planned a major conference, to be attended by such activists, to launch the new Northern Negro Leadership Conference.

The first mass planning meeting took place at Franklin's New Bethel Baptist Church on September 27, and within a month political and ideological differences manifested themselves. These came to a head on October 21 during a meeting of the organization's executive board. The differences revolved around the organization's relationship to an emerging black nationalist sentiment, the efficacy of integration as an objective, and the strategy of nonviolence for the black freedom movement. In what amounted to a recanting and reversal of the original conference plans, Franklin suddenly imposed restrictions on the event, seeking to limit the range of potential delegates and issues to be discussed at the conference. An article in the *Illustrated News* a week later reported that Franklin, who was the DCHR's chair, had expressed his opposition to "black nationalist and other radical groups" who might infiltrate the conference. Although the board had approved the plans for a conference open to all black organizations in all northern urban centers, Franklin insisted that the participation of such people "must be prevented at all costs," saying that such groups would hold positions counter to his own. One such position was critical of nonviolence. Cleage responded by saying that many black people had begun to question the philosophy of nonviolence and embrace the principle of self-defense.[47]

Franklin's turnabout may have been simply a response to the involvement of the newly created Freedom Now Party (FNP). Earlier in the summer, seasoned activists William Worthy and Conrad Lynn had begun to publicly discuss the idea of an all-black political party. Their vision was to create a vehicle that could move beyond what they—and others—took to be the limiting politics of civil rights protest, as represented most visibly in the summer of 1963 by the March on Washington. Worthy and Lynn used the occasion of the march to announce the formation of the FNP, declaring, "We are the political expression of the mighty black crusade for freedom that nobody can halt or suppress."[48] In the two months to follow, Cleage had become a member of the FNP and had invited Worthy and Lynn to speak at the Northern Negro Leadership Conference, doing so with the approval of the DCHR's board.

Franklin, however, insisted that the conference must not endorse the party. He found himself at odds with the political perspective of the FNP, which "repudiates and breaks with the established party system which serves only to sustain the enslavement of Afro-Americans!" Franklin, unwilling to stray far beyond the integrationist ethic of mainstream civil rights agitation, wanted to avoid association with the FNP's "desire to achieve our own destiny through our own efforts," or its recognition that "our struggle for freedom and equality can issue, meaningfully, only from our own leadership and candidates." As the DCHR's chair, Franklin explained to his fellow board members that he "could not afford to be labeled a black nationalist."[49] In response to Franklin's ideological impositions, Cleage resigned from the DCHR. Explaining his decision, he said, "In renouncing the independent black political action represented by the FREEDOM NOW PARTY and the new Negro image which is called 'black nationalism,' the DCHR has renounced any reason for its existence."[50]

Cleage and GOAL quickly decided to sponsor a competing conference, which they called the Northern Negro *Grass Roots* Leadership Conference, to be held the same weekend. GOAL's Milton Henry was close to Malcolm X and arranged for him to address the conference.[51] Grace and Jimmy assumed prominent roles in the conference, with Grace as one of the central organizers and Jimmy as the conference chairperson.

In Malcolm X, the organizers of the conference found an ideal representative. His presence would draw a sharp contrast to the more moderate DCHR conference taking place downtown. By 1963, Malcolm was perhaps the most able and influential spokesperson for black nationalism. His uncompromising advocacy for black people's humanity; his equally charged railing against white supremacy and white liberal hypocrisy; his unrelenting criticism of mainstream civil rights leaders and their commitment to integration; his powerful rejection of nonviolence and his call for self-defense; all of this made Malcolm the embodiment of the political project that Jimmy, Grace, Cleage, and the other organizers sought with the Northern Negro Grass Roots Conference.

The American Revolution

Against this background, during the summer of 1963 Jimmy's "State of a Nation" found a wider audience. In 1961, Grace and Jimmy met W. H. "Ping" Ferry of the Center for the Study of Democratic Institutions and the Fund for the Republic, whose thinking about the nation's current economic and social challenges paralleled Jimmy's analysis of automation. The next year Grace shared a copy of "State of a Nation" with Ferry. Impressed with the document, Ferry shared it with Leo Huberman for possible publication by Monthly Review Press, which quickly agreed to publish it.[52] Over the next year, Jimmy revised the document into a slightly more broadly conceived manuscript that he initially titled "But Only One Side Is Right: The Industrial and Social Revolution in America."[53] Monthly Review Press published it in July 1963 as *The American Revolution: Pages from a Negro Worker's Notebook*.[54] Thus, the internal document that had helped to solidify the Boggses' split with C. L. R. at the beginning of 1962 now reappeared, in different form, as a statement of Jimmy's thinking about revolutionary change in the midst of the "Black Revolution" of 1963. The appearance of the book at this moment announced its author as both an important interpreter of and contributor to the great escalation of black protest that made 1963 a pivotal year in the black freedom movement.

Published in the summer of 1963, the book arrived at a pivotal moment in the civil rights movement, and its thought-provoking assessment of the movement's meaning and possible trajectory established its author as an original and penetrating analyst of the black freedom struggle.[55] *The American Revolution*, however, is not only or even principally about the civil rights movement or black protest. Its starting point, both narratively and analytically, is the labor movement, tracing its decline and its failure in the face of changes in the industrial economy brought on by automation. It then moves to an analysis of the economic as well as social implications of automation. This proved to be one of the most celebrated features of the book, catapulting Jimmy into a national debate during the early 1960s about the effects of automation on employment and the future of the industrial economy.

Drawing on Jimmy's study of automation during the 1950s, the book argues that automation was making black labor obsolete. This would turn a generation of young people into "outsiders"—a group of people who had no real prospects of entering the system—and this fact, he said, would shape the meaning and future directions of the civil rights movement. Amid an eruption of books on "the Negro revolt" and a similarly exploding body of writing on poverty and economic production, *The American Revolution* was unique in its linking of the technological and economic change of automation to the social and political changes being forged by the black struggle and its exposure of them as related historical processes. The automation debate had already identified increasing job loss among African Americans as a central concern, but Jimmy's singular contribution was to look beyond the relationship between automation and black joblessness to see a deeper connection—both historically and sociologically—between changes in the industrial economy and the unfolding of the black struggle for democratic rights over the preceding two decades. His understanding and particular articulation of the civil rights movement and automation as related social phenomena of the 1960s distinguished the book from others published at the time.

The book also marks a significant point in Jimmy's intellectual and political trajectory. For one thing, it rather suddenly raised his profile as a thinker and activist. Widely read in both black radical and Marxist circles, and published across the world in translations in six languages,[56] the notoriety the book brought to its author opened up new opportunities for intellectual and political engagement. In this sense, *The American Revolution* marked a new stage in his activist career. The book also marked a shift in Jimmy's relationship to the labor movement and to Marxism, both of which had been central coordinates of his political life during the preceding two decades. During most of the 1950s, even as he was an active unionist, Jimmy had been a vocal critic of the UAW and the labor movement in his *Correspondence* columns and elsewhere. By the early 1960s his critiques grew especially strident, culminating in *The American Revolution*, which put forward a devastating indictment of the American labor movement. He argued that it had irreversibly devolved into a special interest group bearing no relation to its origins in the 1930s, when industrial unionism represented a genuine movement for social change.

The American Revolution received an immediate and overwhelmingly positive response. In the issue of *Monthly Review* that directly followed its publication, the editors reported that readers had written them describing *The American Revolution* as "the best thing MR has ever done." Letters commending the book for its clarity and insight into the history and future of the labor movement, the Left, and the black struggle came from across the country and from abroad. "The demand for copies has been so great," wrote editors Huberman and Paul Sweezy, "that we have decided to do a second printing of the issue as a $1 paperback."[57]

Perhaps the most surprising correspondent was Bertrand Russell, the British philosopher and internationally renowned peace activist, who wrote to Jimmy shortly after the book was published saying he was "greatly impressed" with the "power and insight" of his "remarkable book."[58] Russell's letter initiated an improbable but remarkable correspondence between the two men over the next several months in which they discussed such topics as the March on Washington (which occurred eight days after Russell's letter), the efficacy of nonviolence in the civil rights movement, the impact of automation on the consciousness of American workers, and the internal dynamics and divisions of the civil rights struggle.

Actor and activist Ossie Davis was similarly taken by *The American Revolution*. When this "little book came into my life," Davis recalled years later, it left him with the sensation of being "born again": "I read every word of it and it opened my mind, my thoughts. It was immediately apprehended by me in every possible way. When I read it, I said, 'Yes, of course, Amen. Even I could have thought of that.' Immensities of thought reduced to images so simple that coming away from the book I was indeed born again. I could see the struggle in a new light. I was recharged, my batteries were full, and I was able to go back to the struggle carrying this book as my banner. Ruby and I bought up copies and mailed them to all the civil rights leaders, Martin Luther King Jr., Malcolm X, Whitney Young. We thought all of them should have access to this book. It would give them an opportunity to be born again."[59] Davis's comments illuminate the ways in which the book propelled Jimmy into national discussions and activist networks. His remarks also provide a vivid example of how the publication of the book brought Jimmy's analysis and ideas to a broader audience while also opening up new relationships— including the decades-long friendship that Jimmy and Grace shared with Ossie Davis and his wife, Ruby Dee.[60]

The responses from Russell and Davis, situated as they were in distinct spheres and political spaces, suggest the wide reach and impact of the book. *The American Revolution* stretched across conventional realms of political analysis and appealed to a varied readership that included, for example, radical trade unionists, civil rights activists, longtime leftists, young internationalist-minded black radicals, and people watching current trends involving technological and economic change. Indeed, while readers like Russell and Davis found themselves drawn to the book primarily for its analysis of the rising black struggle, its examinations of automation, the meaning of work, and the failure of the labor movement spoke to other readers. For example, Wyndham Mortimer, a major figure in the formation of the UAW and the Congress of Industrial Organizations during the 1930s, wrote to Jimmy after "having just finished reading your very fine and thoughtful book."[61] Mortimer agreed with and appreciated Jimmy's critique of the union. As a participant in the storied Flint sit-down strikes in 1937, the veteran gave the highest praise to his younger comrade: "I think your book is the best thing that has happened to the UAW since the sit-down strikes."[62] Another reader, Minnie Livingston of Technocracy Inc. in the state of Washington, wrote to congratulate Jimmy "on your excellent analysis of America's economy," while a radical labor activist in Chicago appraised the book as "one of the most important, if not the most important, and one of the most lucid books produced by the American left in generations. . . . [This] book surely belongs at the top of the list of works of the 'New Left.'"[63]

Almost immediately after the book's publication, Jimmy began receiving speaking invitations and requests for his writing. In September 1963 alone, letters arrived inviting him to four distinct speaking engagements. One asked him to participate in a conference at Princeton University, and another invited him to give an address on "The Revolution of the Unemployed" at McGill University in Montreal. A community group in Toledo, Ohio, asked Jimmy to address their organization. And Monthly Review, which had published the book and seen firsthand the positive response it elicited, asked Jimmy to be one of the speakers at a forum it was holding at the Town Hall in New York on "Where Is the Negro Liberation Movement Going? How Will It Get There?" In each case, the person extending the invitation had read *The American Revolution* and cited its power and insight as the impetus for the invitation. Thus, when the Northern Negro Grass Roots Leadership Conference convened in early November, Jimmy—already a well-recognized activist in Detroit—was fast becoming known nationally. When GOAL chose Jimmy to chair the conference, they placed before the dozens of activists who came from across the country a veteran activist with strong ties to the local Detroit movement and an increasing visibility in the national movement.

The Northern Negro Grass Roots Leadership Conference

The Northern Negro Grass Roots Leadership Conference opened on the morning of Saturday, November 9, with over 100 activists and leaders of local movements from several cities across the country attending. Among them were Dan Watts, editor of *Liberator* magazine; New York school boycott leader Rev. Milton A. Galamison; journalist and FNP cofounder William Worthy; Don Freeman, director of the Afro-American Institute in Cleveland, Ohio; Selma Sparks, a Brooklyn activist and member of the *Liberator* advisory board; Harlem rent strike leader Jesse Gray; Lawrence Landry, Chicago school boycott organizer; and Sam Jordan of San Francisco. The conference gave them the opportunity to share and discuss ideas with each other and the many Detroit activists who participated, including people that Jimmy and Grace were already working with such as Rev. Cleage, Milton and Richard Henry and other members of GOAL, and Charles Johnson and other members of Uhuru.

The conferees participated in workshops throughout the day at Mr. Kelley's Lounge and Recreation Center on Chene Street that focused on organizing strategies and various political and economic issues arising out of the conditions of urban black communities such as de facto segregation in northern schools and housing discrimination.[64] For example, workshops on self-defense and independent political action fostered spirited discussions probing the precepts of civil rights reform. Conference participants issued sharp critiques of the philosophy of nonviolence and its application by King and others in the mainstream civil rights organizations, arguing in favor of the principle of self-defense. Some people made appeals for retaliatory violence as an appropriate response to continued brutality against African Americans. The idea of independent political action was also a highly charged topic, with several participants declaring the need for black people to organize independently of white influence. A significant portion of the discussion during the workshops was devoted to the Freedom Now Party (FNP), and its cofounder William Worthy responded to a series of questions about the party's platform and program.[65]

A workshop on economics similarly drew conferees into extended discussions of protest tactics and principles. These included consideration of a proposed Christmas boycott initiated by the Association for Artists for Freedom, a new organization formed by John Oliver Killens, James Baldwin, Ruby Dee, Ossie Davis, and others in the wake of the September 1963 bombing of Sixteenth Street Baptist Church in Birmingham. They asked black people to refrain from the season's consumer activity as an act of sacrifice in memory of the six black children murdered (the four girls killed in the bombing and two boys killed in the city later that day), and as a demonstration of unity and economic strength.[66] The workshop also dealt with economic boycotts as a political weapon. During this discussion, activists from Cleveland shared their struggle to force a local General Motors distributor to change their discriminatory hiring practices and asked GOAL and others throughout the country to support a nationwide action against the automaker.[67]

The next morning, the conference participants began plotting the course for a new organization. They drafted and accepted a set of resolutions that emerged from the workshops, elected a nine-person steering committee to work out the procedures for the organization, and selected Chicago as the site of the next national meeting to be held in six months.[68] Among the resolutions were endorsements of the Freedom Now Party and the principle of self-defense.[69] These resolutions indicate how these activists were moving beyond the parameters of established civil rights orthodoxy and were anticipating the ideas and commitments of the Black Power movement. The articulation of these ideas at the conference bears a direct connection to the nationalist organizations and black radical politics that had developed over the preceding two years. The conference created an opportunity for connections and fellowship between activists from various places in a way that fostered a sense of collective purpose and political engagement that also, along with specific political ideas and programs, would soon emerge as a prevailing ethic of Black Power. The foretelling of these ideas and this ethic achieved full expression during the mass rally at the conclusion of the conference on Sunday night. A crowd of approximately 2,000 gathered at King Solomon Baptist Church to hear speeches by Cleage, William Worthy, and Malcolm X. Malcolm's passionate and moving "Message to the Grass Roots" made a fitting climax to the conference.[70]

Malcolm began his speech with a call for black people to unite around a common cause and common struggle. He then addressed the nature of that struggle by describing the difference between what he called a "black revolution" and a "Negro revolution."[71] First, he said, it is necessary to make clear what a revolution is—to apprehend the motives, objectives, methods, and results of a revolution. Malcolm argued that revolutions are fundamentally about land—that is, access to the resources from which a subjugated people obtain an independent existence and build a nation. Furthermore, he asserted that revolution is a necessarily bloody experience, as the dispossessed must fight to gain land and independence. Drawing on the American, Russian, and Chinese Revolutions as historical examples, Malcolm explained, "I cite these revolutions, brothers and sisters, to show you that you don't have a peaceful revolution. You don't have a turn-the-other-cheek revolution. There's no such thing as a nonviolent revolution. The only kind of revolution that is nonviolent is the Negro revolution. The only revolution in which the goal is loving your enemy is the Negro revolution."[72]

Embedded in Malcolm's denunciation of the "Negro revolution" was his critique of civil rights leadership. He brought the point home with satire and rhetorical flair, using the taxonomy of slave society that he referenced in his 1961 appearance in the city. "There were two kinds of slaves," Malcolm asserted, "the house Negro and the field Negro." The house Negro identified with the master, would protect the master's interests as his own, and was reluctant to run away from the plantation. The field Negro, on the other hand, hated the slave master, plotted and prayed for his demise, and would jump at the opportunity to escape.[73] For Malcolm, the slave society approximated contemporary American society, in which class position and proximity to whites conditioned one's response to racial oppression. "This modern house Negro loves his master," Malcolm insisted, chastising African Americans who sought racial integration. "He wants to live near [white people]. He'll pay three times as much as the house is worth just to live near his master." In contrast, blacks who rejected the goal of integration, preferring separation from white society, stood in the tradition of the field Negro. "If someone came to the field Negro and said, 'Let's separate, let's run,' he didn't say 'Where we goin?' He'd say, 'Any place is better than here.'"[74]

Malcolm's analysis of slave society was a parable for the 1960s. The field Negro represented the masses, and his or her rebellious act of running away from the plantation symbolized the nationalists' desire to gain autonomy from white society. On the other hand, the house Negro represented integrationists, and his or her investment in the slave system symbolized civil rights leaders' desire for integration. Through this historical analogy, Malcolm restated the essence of his message to the grass roots: the civil rights movement and its leadership could only offer a "Negro revolution"; it could not bring black liberation. It was up to the black masses—the grass roots—the descendants of field Negroes, to move the struggle ahead and to achieve full and complete liberation.

Malcolm's message met with an enthusiastic reception, in part because it sanctioned the emerging ideas and political sentiments of those gathered for the Northern Negro Grass Roots Leadership Conference. His words gave voice to new forms of oppositional consciousness and endorsed new modes of political engagement, modes that those assembled at the conference had begun to envision or in some cases were already practicing. This was true for the activists and organizations there representing local movements all over the country, and especially those from Detroit. Indeed, herein lies part of Malcolm's power and appeal at the conference. His call for black revolution at King Solomon Baptist Church would reverberate many times during the subsequent months and years in Detroit and beyond.

"Into the Sunshine of a Different Society"

About a week after the Northern Negro Grass Roots Leadership Conference, Jimmy and Grace flew to New York, where Jimmy participated in the aforementioned forum at Town Hall. Organized by Monthly Review Associates, the event engaged a lively crowd in a discussion of the topic "Where Is the Negro Liberation Movement Going? How Will It Get There?" As one of the panelists, Jimmy shared the platform with Bruce Moore from the Student Nonviolent Coordinating Committee (SNCC) and the Boggses' friend Conrad Lynn, veteran civil rights activist and attorney, lawyer to Robert Williams, and most recently the chairperson of the National Committee for a Freedom Now Party.[75] Also appearing on stage was actress and activist Ruby Dee, who "completed the program with exciting dramatic readings from various writers and poets."[76] The Town Hall forum reflected its organizers' belief that there was a growing need to give serious thought to and discussion of the future course of action in the black freedom movement. In its announcement for the meeting, Monthly Review Associates explained the rationale for the event: "Since the Birmingham crisis last May, the Negro liberation movement has experienced an extraordinarily rapid growth. Scores of new towns, cities, and counties in the South have erupted and, no less important, the movement has for the first time taken hold in the great metropolitan centers of the North. Demonstrations of all kinds . . . have shown that this is now a militant mass movement . . . yet it must be admitted that the progress that has been achieved toward the movement's goal of freedom and equality for Negro Americans has been very small."[77]

To examine this "paradox"—the apparent inability of the movement, despite its strength and militancy, to achieve meaningful change in the conditions of African Americans—the forum sought to foster public discussion and debate of critical issues. "Does the difficulty lie in the strategy and tactics of the movement itself?" the organizers asked. "Or is it to be sought in the character of the U.S. power structure? How can more, and more rapid, gains be won in the future?" The forum invited attendees to consider these and other questions concerning the very objective and nature of the struggle by hearing the thoughts of "three men who we know have been thinking deeply about the problems of the liberation movement."[78]

The writer covering the forum for the *Muhammad Speaks* newspaper reported that "knowledgeable observers called" the event "one of the most provocative, analytical, and incisive discussions of the black freedom movement ever to be held in New York." Lynn made the case that massive public investment, along with fundamental economic reorganization, would be required to provide necessary levels of employment as well as tackle major social needs around housing and schools. Moore, whose remarks garnered "a rousing reception," said that "integration is no longer the answer." Forecasting changes in his organization and in the entire movement, Moore told the crowd that "we must shift our emphasis," explaining that the sit-ins—the protest activity that led to SNCC's founding—"are becoming obsolete" in the face of other needs. "The vote is more significant than a hot dog. Economic power is more important than a theatre ticket." Jimmy struck a similarly militant tone, exhorting the audience to recognize and embrace the revolutionary implications of the black revolt and doing so, according to the *Muhammad Speaks* reporter, with a "penetrating and devastating logic" that "brought constant cheers from the audience."[79]

Jimmy's speech at the Town Hall event gave him the opportunity to address a large public gathering with the ideas he had articulated in his book. In a style that he would consistently deploy in speeches and meetings over the coming years, Jimmy sought to challenge and provoke his audience:

> Now I did not come here to comfort you. I came here to disturb you. I did not come here to pacify you. I came here to antagonize you. I did not come here to talk to you about love. I came here to talk to you about conflict.
>
> I say this at the outset because the American people have lived for so long under the illusion that America is an exception to the deep

crises that wreck other countries—that they are totally unprepared to face the brutish realities of the present crisis and the dangers that threaten them. The American people have lived so long with the myth that the United States is a Christian, capitalist, free democratic nation that we can do no wrong, that the question of what is right and wrong completely evades them.[80]

The topic of his speech was "the American Revolution, which as now is primarily a Black Revolution." He told the audience that "sometimes a Revolution starts because the people believed that the country in its present form can do more for them than it is already doing. So they go out and ask for those things which they call their 'Rights' under the system. . . . If they get these 'Rights,' and then don't press any more, then the country has made a social reform. . . . But if they *don't* get what they believe are their 'Rights,' and they continue to fight for them, they begin to make a *Revolution*."[81]

This, he explained, was precisely the pattern that black protest had followed in the years since the 1954 *Brown v. Board of Education* decision, during which time no Supreme Court decision, agency of the government, or social or political institution of American life had been able to guarantee the rights that were granted to black citizens under the Constitution. "The Negroes," he said, "have been left . . . to devise means of struggle for themselves. . . . So the myth that American Democracy protects the rights of Negroes has been exploded." He went on to assert that "under this Democracy of which Americans are so proud, there has been *more systematic exploitation of more people* than there has been under any other political system. This is the truth which the Black Revolution is beginning to expose." He said that as the Black Revolution proceeds, it will show that there is another form of society, an alternative to the status quo of American democracy, which had benefited the few at the expense of the many, for "democracy is a system which has been made possible by the worst kind of class society in the world—the class society that is based upon the systematic exploitation of another *race*."[82]

This public discussion at the Monthly Review forum intersected with the private conversation that Jimmy and Bertrand Russell had been carrying on in their letters during the summer and fall of 1963. Russell had developed a strong interest and concern with the plight of African Americans, leading him to read widely in both the history of African Americans and contemporary material on America's racial conflict.[83] He received newly published works from editors and writers such as James Baldwin, who sent

Russell a copy of his *The Fire Next Time*, published at the beginning of 1963, and Jimmy's *The American Revolution*, which Monthly Review editors Leo Huberman and Paul Sweezy had sent to Russell that summer. Russell believed that the combined effects of America's international policies and its internal social crisis posed the primary threat to world peace. In his initial letter to Jimmy, Russell sought his views on the likely directions that American workers' political consciousness would take in the face of automation and the possibility of a greater reaction in American political culture. "Will [American workers] not embrace a more harsh authoritarianism and delve for new victims . . . ?" he asked. Russell also questioned to what extent "American whites, whose living standards have depended upon the exploitation of American negroes and non-European peoples, will understand the American negro revolt. If they fail to make common cause with it, will not the result be a further impetus towards neo-fascist popular Government?"[84]

Jimmy wrote a reply about two weeks later in which he addressed Russell's questions and further articulated his own ideas about the coming social conflicts. "Your questions are very big questions," he told the philosopher, issuing the caveat that his answers were necessarily speculative, before launching into his analysis. "I believe that it will probably be in the north rather than in the south that the bitterness of the whites will overflow in spontaneous actions of a Fascist character," Jimmy wrote, adding that he foresaw economic issues to be a central catalyst. He felt that confrontations could also come from the threat of blacks gaining political power in many areas of the South where they are the majority of the population. Similar conflicts could come in the North, he said, where in the large cities there had been a "concentration of Negroes in the central districts with the whites in the suburbs commuting daily to the centers of power through (or, by means of expressways, over) the Negro areas."[85]

Russell sent an enthusiastic reply two weeks later, expressing appreciation for Jimmy's comments and seeking to extend the dialogue. "I cannot see how the Negro revolt can stop short of a challenge to capitalism," he offered. He also ascribed to the African American struggle an important role internationally, viewing the black movement as a promising means for opposing the Cold War and its logic of nuclear conflict: "I do think that the Negro revolt could be the means of opposing effectively and for the first time the assumptions of the United States and the race towards nuclear annihilation."[86] Russell also gave his analysis of the March on Washington, which had taken place three weeks earlier. "The March was deeply impressive but disappointing," he wrote, "because the depth of feeling that one imagines negroes in America to experience about their treatment did not gain reflection in the demonstration."[87]

Russell had sent a strong message of support to the march, calling it "the real Emancipation Proclamation," but cautioned that "it must lead to an end to indifference, to suffering and mass murder, in short, to a revolution into thinking and acting as Americans." The text of Russell's message was released to the press in London on August 27 and read during the march the next day. "I am convinced that the march on Washington is a turning point in the history of the United States," he proclaimed. "The Negro in the United States is on the move and he will not stop. The meaning of this is that the values and the practices which have formed the United States over three hundred years are being fundamentally challenged." In a part of the statement that likely resonated with African Americans, but that earned condemnation from the mainstream American press, Russell said "The number of Negroes who have died through torture, lonely murder and systematic maltreatment in this period without doubt is in excess of those killed by the Nazis in the course of their unparalleled barbarism in Europe."[88]

Like he had done with the March on Washington, Bertrand Russell sent a statement to be read during the Town Hall meeting. Unlike the celebrated gathering in Washington, however, where his words seemed to be consistent with the mood of the hour, Russell's message to those assembled in New York was at variance with the general tenor of the event. He expressed his "wholehearted and complete sympathy" with "the movement towards [racial] equality," but declared, "I do not believe that this end will be achieved if the Negro movement adopts methods of violence." He feared that the "rapidly increasing sympathy" with "the Negro cause" among many whites would "very largely cease if the movement abandons persuasion and attempts, instead, to use force."[89] Russell's memorandum was titled "Should the Negro Movement in the U.S. Remain Non-Violent?" and it was timely, as this very question and variants of it were a matter of great discussion and debate at the end of 1963. His counseling against violence was tantamount to an endorsement of nonviolent protest and represented a refusal to consider the possible merits of other forms of protest. This, of course, did not resonate with a meeting devoted to discussing new perspectives on the black struggle. Furthermore, in his reasoning against organized violence, Russell implicitly placed an importance on appeals to white support and sympathy, a strategy that many in the movement had come to question, if not abandon. Russell, in effect, urged a moderation that was out of step with the ideological orientation of the event.[90]

Jimmy challenged and critiqued Russell's analysis. Addressing the audience following the reading of Russell's message, Jimmy refuted the philosopher's position in both tone and substance. For one thing, he asserted that the black freedom movement was for more than just equality, as Russell had indicated. More importantly, Jimmy rejected Russell's advocacy of nonviolence. As he explained to Russell in a letter following the forum, "When I appeared at Town Hall in New York and heard your telegram addressed to that meeting and warning Negroes against violence, I who was speaking next had to say that whereas I too would like to hope that issues of our revolt might be resolved by peaceful means," he believed that "the issues and the grievances were so deeply imbedded in the American system and the American people that the very things you warned against might just have to take place if the Negroes in the U.S.A. to walk are ever to walk the streets as free men."[91]

Jimmy wrote this letter on December 29, three months after Russell's previous letter to him and one month after the Town Hall forum. "It has been a long time since you wrote," the letter began, "and lots of events have transpired, and yet nothing has changed."[92] The most dramatic of these was the assassination of President Kennedy the day after the Town Hall event. This of course had been preceded two months earlier by the Birmingham church bombing, which occurred just four days before Russell's last letter to Jimmy. The year 1963 thus drew to an end shaken by the experience of public violence and threatened by impending confrontations around the status of its black citizens. These were the social dynamics on Jimmy's mind when he sat down to pen his letter to Russell on December 29. "To this date," he wrote, "no one in this country wants to take responsibility for the thousands of Negroes who have been beat up, shot up, jailed up in this country just for asking for some normal rights that are common in most countries." Further challenging Russell's warning African Americans against violence, he cited the experiences of and prevailing mood among many African Americans: "I do not believe that the temper of the Negroes is such that they will take eight more years of the kind of beatings and jailings that they have taken since 1954, just to prove that they are entitled to the things that everyone else has. In fact, I believe that period is over; that the Black masses will either retaliate—or they won't act at all. But the one thing that they will not take any more is beatings."[93]

Jimmy continued to explain the rejection of nonviolence and embrace of self-defense as a political principle. He made statements that were similar in their tone and argument to statements that the many critics of nonviolence would make later in the decade and that some, notably Malcolm X, were already making in 1963. For example, he wrote, "The one thing that always goes unnoticed in all the eulogizing of the nonviolent behavior of the Negro is the open, direct violence of the American whites against the Negroes." Implicit in such eulogizing, he said, was a readiness to accept the violence of the whites. "And if a nation has not felt aroused by the bestialities of whites, it has no right to expect anything different from the Negroes who have been on the receiving end of these bestialities for over 300 years."[94]

Jimmy also responded to Russell's proposal, made in his last letter, that black organizations tax African Americans and their white sympathizers $1 monthly to raise the funds that "would enable much to be done in the struggle." Jimmy responded to this with a comment on the nature and current dynamics of the black movement. "I think that perhaps here you are not aware of what is taking place totally in this country," he said, telling the philosopher that black Americans did not all speak with the same voice, as he seemed to assume. "This is not just a crusade for Negro rights as most Negroes thought it was at the beginning and many still think it is. This is a struggle to change a system, and as it becomes clear that it is not just a struggle for some rights and that each right that the Negroes win will help destroy a system, lots of Negroes are going to fall by the wayside in the struggle." Emphasizing the revolutionary potential of the black struggle, and placing it in historical relation with the Russian Revolution of 1917, he continued: "In fact, already the separation is getting sharper between those who are going to struggle and those who just want to be like other Americans, and splits are developing between Negroes as they developed between the Mensheviks and Bolsheviks in Russia which means that there isn't any organization in this country which all of Negroes can support."[95]

Jimmy recognized and acknowledged that the civil rights movement was to experience divisions and splits, and that a new movement was soon to emerge from this. His statements, in short, anticipated the emergence of the Black Power movement. Though his words predicted trouble ahead, Jimmy closed his letter to Russell on a hopeful note: "Here's hoping . . . that both of us will still be around to weather the storms and emerge into the sunshine of a different society, call it what you may."[96]

Epilogue

In 1963, Jimmy and Grace began describing their philosophy as "dialectical humanism." They crafted this new political theory in response to the four interrelated developments that reshaped their political activity during the early 1960s: their organizational split with C. L. R. James; their ideological break with central Marxist tenets; the conclusions they drew from their analysis of automation and the changes it brought in production; and their immersion in the black freedom movement. Their articulation of dialectical humanism marked a new phase in Grace and Jimmy's partnership, at once a reflection of the dynamic understanding of the revolutionary process they had developed together since 1953 and a projection of the shared intellectual and political work they would continue over the next three decades.

Grace first used the phrase "dialectical humanism" in a June 1963 *Correspondence* editorial explaining the paper's political focus. She insisted that black people stood at the forefront of revolutionary possibility: "We devote a great deal of space to the struggles of the Negroes because they are without question the most revolutionary, the most advanced, and the most human social force in the United States today." Yet "the revolution which has now begun . . . is not just a Negro revolution. . . . What is involved is a totally new and uniquely American revolution, a revolution without historical precedent anywhere in the world, a revolution which essentially will have to bring about a radical change in man's image of himself and of his rights and responsibilities, to correspond with the revolutionary changes that have been achieved in material production. . . . The philosophy of this new revolutionary struggle for new human values and new human relations we call Dialectical Humanism."[1]

Two months later, Grace urged an audience of liberal intellectuals to recognize the philosophical and political-economic significance of "the remarkable historical coincidence of the Negro revolt and the technological revolution." Automation would expand the nation's productive capacity so that it was possible to meet society's material needs, a point that Jimmy made in his new book, *The American Revolution*. Grace said that the civil rights movement was not solely a struggle to change the racial order but "represents the beginning of a new revolutionary epoch, ... which will center around conscious strivings and struggles to achieve and create the dignity of man." The epoch of dialectical materialism was now coming to a close. During that period of revolutionary thinking, which was initiated by the French Revolution, "technological problems of material production were still unsolved," so "revolutionary struggles had to center around goods and goods production." "Now that these technological problems have essentially been solved in America, we are able to enter the epoch of Dialectical Humanism. Of this epoch the Negro revolt is the beginning, but by no means the end."[2]

Jimmy first used the phrase in "The Meaning of the Black Revolt in the U.S.A.," an essay he wrote toward the end of 1963 and published in the journal *Revolution*. He said, "Negro freedom fighters have been confining the struggle within the framework of the system, but each time the struggle reaches an explosive pitch, more Negroes are driven to recognize that the things they are fighting for cannot be achieved within the system"; instead, they are "the ingredients for creating another system." He likened this development to anticolonial struggles around the world, as each newly independent nation "faces the need to create a new economic and political system in order to meet the social needs of the masses of that country." The black struggle, he concluded, was in essence forging this process in the United States: "The Negro revolt exposes the whole American system as it has operated in regard to every sphere of the relations between human beings. Coming in the United States at a time when there is no longer any problem with material scarcity, the Negro revolt is therefore not just a narrow struggle over material necessities. It does not belong to the period of struggle over goods and for the development of productive forces which we can call the era of 'Dialectical Materialism.' Rather, it ushers in the era of 'Dialectical Humanism,' when the burning question is how to create the kind of human responsibility in the distribution of material abundance that will allow everyone to enjoy and create the values of humanity."[3]

THE MARXIST CONCEPTS of dialectical and historical materialism served as Grace and Jimmy's point of departure for conceptualizing dialectical humanism. According to the philosophy of dialectical materialism, everything in nature and society is subject to the fundamental laws of dialectical development, whereby the internal contradictions of any entity or process drive its evolution and transformation over time. Historical materialism, understood by its adherents as empirical social science and Marxist social theory, views human history in terms of economic development. It postulates that historical change is driven by changes in three interrelated forces: a society's prevailing mode of production, the resulting division of society into classes, and the struggle between those classes.[4] Grace and Jimmy's analysis obscured the distinction between the dialectical and historical materialism, implicitly combining the two concepts by subsuming historical materialism under dialectical materialism. They also deviated from standard Marxist language by using "dialectical materialism" to identify an epoch or era. This conceptual shift enabled Grace and Jimmy to make the heretical argument that Marxism's philosophy and theory of society could no longer guide revolutionary thinking. While they did not break completely with the Marxist intellectual tradition, they were clearly turning away from central ideas and ways of thinking that had previously guided their politics.

Specifically, Jimmy and Grace were relinquishing the idea of class struggle as the motive force of history and the Marxist scenario of revolution centered on the working class, replacing this materialist conception of history and revolutionary struggle with one emphasizing broader human relationships. As they wrote years later with their comrades Freddy and Lyman Paine, "We concluded that, whether we liked it or not, the epoch had come to an end when it was progressive to think of the history of humanity as the history of class struggle. . . . Instead of seeing history as class struggle, we must see it as a continuing struggle to create human social relationships." This vigorous dissent from fundamental Marxist precepts did not represent either a form of anti-Marxism or a dampening of Jimmy and Grace's commitment to revolutionary thought; rather, it represented a deepening of that commitment, born of deep theoretical reflection. "The process of questioning our previous thoughts has been painful," they wrote, "but it has also been joyous because we have been searching for another way to view the history of humanity which could inspire as much commitment from ourselves and others as Marx's ideas have done."[5] Indeed, it reflected their commitment to the practice of dialectical thinking: as revolutionaries they must recognize that reality is constantly changing and that ideas that were once progressive may become outmoded; social movements must develop new ideas in response to societal change.

Dialectical humanism, then, was the Boggses' attempt to develop a philosophical framework that could both explain the new social and political realities that they saw emerging in the early 1960s and guide revolutionary struggle. They had spent a decade working with, learning from, and growing with each other. Their conceptualization of dialectical humanism marked a new stage in their shared revolutionary politics, which was characterized by their intensified effort to theorize and advance the revolutionary capacity of the black freedom movement.[6]

Black Power

In the mid-1960s, Grace and Jimmy concentrated their writing and activism on theorizing black political power, launching multiple organizing efforts based on this theoretical work, and intervening in the escalating debates within the movement about the broader concept of black power. They called for a coordinated mobilization of independent black political power, concentrated in cities and focused on exercising municipal control, as a base for an eventual revolutionary reorganization of society.

Jimmy and Grace became recognized as Black Power leaders in Detroit as well as nationally. They continued to work with the impressive community of local black activists that had solidified at the beginning of the 1960s, including Rev. Albert Cleage, with whom Grace developed a strong association. Jimmy emerged as an important and influential theorist of the movement. He published essays in some of the most prominent Black Power–era publications, as well as a range of more mainstream magazines and newspapers.[7] In their writings, as in their activism, Jimmy and Grace sought to develop a theoretical and practical framework that would push Black Power in a revolutionary direction.

Through the late 1960s, Grace and Jimmy critically assessed the growing Black Power movement, its multiple articulations, and its diverse strategies for political action. Jimmy regularly engaged in the ideological debates within the movement. For example, his 1967 essay "Black Power—A Scientific Concept Whose Time Has Come" argues that the concept had "nothing to do with any special moral virtue in being black" but rather grew out of black people's place in American society and the evolution of their struggle beyond civil rights. The essay criticizes "those writing for and against

Black Power" who "would rather keep the concept vague than grapple with the systematic analysis of American capitalism out of which the concept of Black Power has developed."[8] His essay "Culture and Black Power" looks critically at the ways in which segments of the movement deployed notions of culture, African heritage, and black unity. It warns against allowing identification with Africa or celebrations of black cultural heritage to serve as an evasion or mystification of the struggle at hand. "Of what profit is our history and our culture," it asks, "unless it is used in a vision of our future?"[9] Jimmy urged activists to understand the movement in relation to the struggle for civil rights and in the historical development of the country as a whole. In a *New York Times* op-ed written in the early 1970s, he wrote, "Most of those who call themselves black power advocates are trying to find a solution for blacks separate from a solution for the contradictions of the entire United States. Actually, this is impossible. Therefore, many black nationalists are going off into all kinds of fantasies and dreams about what black power means—like heading for Africa, or isolating themselves in a few states, or whites just vanishing into thin air and leaving this country to blacks."[10]

Just as Black Power was coalescing as a national movement, the 1967 Detroit rebellion propelled Grace and Jimmy to a new theoretical consideration. During the last week of July, black residents of Detroit took to the streets, confronting the police and issuing a massive challenge to civil authority that resulted in forty-three deaths (thirty-three black people and ten whites), most at the hands of the police and the National Guard. It was by some measures the largest and most consequential uprising of the period's "long hot summers," the term used to describe successive years when black people in cities across the country burned and looted businesses in the ghetto and fought back against the police. City officials and most commentators labeled them riots, but Jimmy and Grace were among the many activists and well-informed observers who called them rebellions. They recognized that these uprisings were collective and spontaneous eruptions of social protest; more than simple lawlessness, they were acts of rebellion against the symbols and substance of white authority, particularly that wielded by the police, who functioned as an occupying force in black communities. In the urgency, anger, and outrage expressed in the urban rebellions, Jimmy and Grace found an impetus to revise their understanding of the revolutionary process, focusing particularly on the role of urban black youth in spontaneous uprisings. As Grace recalled, the rebellion "forced us to rethink a lot of philosophical questions" and moved them "to draw a clear distinction between rebellion . . . and revolution."[11]

A series of international conversations they had in 1968 helped to crystallize this distinction. In June the Boggses traveled to Paris, where they observed the tail end of the May revolt, and from there they went to Italy, where Jimmy had been invited to undertake a multicity speaking tour. Next they flew to Conakry, Guinea, to meet with Kwame Nkrumah, who had been living there in exile since being deposed as president of Ghana in a 1966 military coup. Nkrumah hosted them for a week, during which the three old friends discussed the political situations both in Africa and in the United States and exchanged ideas about future political projects.[12] Upon their return to the country at the end of the summer, Grace and Jimmy initiated what became an annual practice of vacationing on Sutton Island, Maine, with their longtime comrades Freddy and Lyman Paine. During their stay on Sutton Island, which usually lasted weeks, the two couples engaged in wide-ranging political and philosophical discussions that became known affectionately among the foursome (and the other friends who attended in later years) as the "conversations in Maine" or simply the "conversations."[13] Grace described their powerful impact on her philosophical, political, and personal growth in her autobiography: "As we talked into the night, I felt a liberation comparable to that which I had first experienced back at Bryn Mawr when the study of Hegel had helped me to see my own struggles as an integral part of the evolution of the human race. Inside my heart and mind the materialist concept of revolution as chiefly a redistribution of goods, property, and power was being enriched by a moral and spiritual dimension."[14]

As the Boggses and the Paines reflected on their day-to-day lives and political practice, they decided that Jimmy should immediately resign from his job at Chrysler so that he could devote his full time and energy to political activity. As Grace recounted it, "The more we talked in 1968, the clearer it was that even deciding what questions need to be asked, let alone discovering the answers, would take years, extending far beyond our lifetimes. One of our favorite sayings was 'Things take time!' But in view of the spreading chaos it was also urgent that we get started on finding ways and means to develop these ideas further by putting them into practice. It was ridiculous to think that Jimmy could do this and at the same time work eight hours a day at Chrysler, spending his evenings writing, speaking, and going to meetings and then getting up at 5 A.M. to go to work."[15]

At the age of forty-nine, Jimmy was leaving Chrysler after working there for twenty-eight years, just short of the thirty years required for retirement on pension. To offset the forgone income, Lyman Paine agreed to provide Jimmy and Grace with a modest quarterly stipend from a trust fund that Lyman had recently inherited. Materially and symbolically, this joint decision launched Jimmy and Grace into a new phase of their partnership and deepened their self-identification as revolutionary theorists and activists. When they returned to Detroit that fall, Grace and Jimmy intensified their political activities within and beyond the escalating Black Power movement.

Grace resumed her ubiquitous presence in Detroit's black nationalist circles. During hearings on the Detroit rebellion, a Detroit Police Department lieutenant testified that Grace was one of "our militants in Detroit" and offered his belief that "she is of Chinese and African descent."[16] It is likely that he was not alone in making this mistake. Grace regularly participated in otherwise all-black organizations, was welcomed into explicitly black spaces, and received invitations to speak about the black movement. Her November 1968 speech "The Black Revolution in America" was published two years later in the now-classic book *The Black Woman,* edited by Toni Cade Bambara. Education was an important site of Grace's activism. Throughout the 1960s, she addressed the growing crisis in the school system, the need to redefine education, and struggles over education in black communities and became a central figure in the movement for community control of the public schools in Detroit.

In 1970, Grace cofounded the Asian Political Alliance (APA), a small study group and political organization composed of Asian and Asian American activists in Detroit. Grace remembered this fondly as "the first and only period in my life that I was meeting regularly with political people who shared my background as an Asian American."[17] The APA conducted workshops on Asian identity in the United States, participated in protests against the war in Vietnam, and screened and discussed films from China and Japan.[18]

Jimmy's departure from Chrysler enabled him to participate more actively in the ideological debates and activist spaces of the Black Power movement. His *Racism and the Class Struggle: Further Pages from a Black Worker's Notebook* (1970), a collection of his recent essays and speeches, included "The Myth and Irrationality of Black Capitalism," which he delivered to the National Black Economic Development Conference, a major gathering of Black Power activists held in Detroit in April 1969. At the conference,

Jimmy and Grace distributed copies of their recently published pamphlet, *Manifesto for a Black Revolutionary Party*, which argued "that Black liberation cannot be achieved except through a Black Revolution" that took power "for the purpose of bringing about a fundamental change in the social, economic, and political institutions of the society."[19]

Revolution and Evolution

The manifesto served as an ideological statement and an organizing tool in building a new cadre organization called the Committee for Political Development (CPD). A central idea animating the group's ideology was the view that the United States was the "technologically most advanced and the politically and socially most counter-revolutionary" country in the world.[20] Dan Aldridge, a seasoned activist well known in Detroit's Black Power networks, joined the Boggses in leading the group. It developed a small core membership of young black radicals, exemplified by Kenneth Snodgrass, who joined as a teenager and developed an especially close relationship with Jimmy over two decades. The CPD and the revolutionary study groups it conducted generated a series of successive organizations through which Grace and Jimmy worked with other young Detroit radicals, black and white, and some of them established enduring relationships with the Boggses. Sharon "Shea" Howell, Richard Feldman, and Larry Sparks all met the Boggses in the early 1970s, worked closely with Jimmy and Grace and each other for decades, and continued to apply the ideas about revolutionary change they developed together.

In 1974 the Boggses published a major statement of their political philosophy, *Revolution and Evolution in the Twentieth Century*. This jointly authored book showed how their thinking about revolution had developed since 1963. Based in part on a series of lectures they delivered in 1970 at Wayne State University's Center for Adult Education, the work considers the historical and theoretical lessons to be learned from the Russian, Chinese, and Cuban revolutions, "the African Revolution," the "People's War in Vietnam," and "the Black Revolution in the U.S." Building on their concept of dialectical humanism, their distinction between rebellion and revolution, and their conclusion that the most important contradiction in the contemporary United States was between its economic and technological overdevelopment and its moral, social, and political underdevelopment, Jimmy and Grace articulated their understanding of the revolutionary process and the meaning and purpose of revolutionary change. "A revolution is not just for the purpose of correcting past injustices," they declared. "A revolution involves projecting the notion of a more human human being, i.e. a human being who is more advanced in the specific qualities which only humans have—creativity, consciousness and self-consciousness, a sense of political and social responsibility."[21]

Their desire to put into practice the ideas presented in *Revolution and Evolution in the Twentieth Century*, in combination with the growth of the revolutionary study groups and the collapse of the Black Power movement, led the Boggses and their comrades in Detroit to join with activists they had connected with in other parts of the country to found the National Organization for an American Revolution (NOAR) in 1978. NOAR sought to forge a new organizational form and political practice. It held public forums, organized locals across the country, and published pamphlets and short statements on contemporary national issues and local concerns. *Manifesto for an American Revolutionary Party*, a pamphlet written primarily by Jimmy, articulated NOAR's vision of *a new, self-governing America* and a concept of citizenship in which people accept responsibility for making social, economic, and political decisions. It argued that citizens must not think of themselves as passive victims who can only make demands on the system or on those in power; they must claim agency and make demands on themselves as well. NOAR saw political transformation as tied to personal transformation; the oppressed and their leaders must all reject capitalist values and struggle to confront their own individualism and materialism. This concept was expressed as "two-sided transformation," or working to change oneself and the oppressive structures of society simultaneously.

Grassroots Detroit

As NOAR collapsed under the weight of internal conflicts in the mid-1980s, Jimmy and Grace's political focus returned to the city of Detroit and the challenges of postindustrial cities. In 1990, Jimmy wrote presciently that "most of our life in the 20th century, as Du Bois said, was occupied with the 'problem of the color line.' But, as we approach the 21st century, the issues we face, especially in the United States, are even more complex. The struggle of the 21st century is going to be over what will become of our cities."[22] They identified community building and developing grassroots leadership as crucial elements of the struggle to empower local communities, repair social relationships, and uncover new ways to meet basic economic and human needs. Grace and Jimmy participated in grassroots struggles and helped to found a range of organizations. In the mid-1980s, for example, they helped to organize seniors, most of them women, in Detroiters for Dignity. In 1988 they joined with Dorothy Garner to form We the People Reclaim Our Streets, a citywide network of neighborhood groups that held regular marches against the scourge of crack cocaine. They joined United Detroiters against Gambling, which defeated Mayor Coleman Young's initial proposal to legalize casino gambling and then evolved into Detroiters Uniting, a multiethnic coalition advocating a vision for Detroit based on neighborhood empowerment and opposition to Young's corporation- or developer-driven model of development.

The Boggses became deeply involved with Save Our Sons and Daughters (SOSAD), founded in early 1987 by Clementine Barfield, who had recently lost her sixteen-year-old son in a shooting. Grace and Jimmy worked with SOSAD to reduce violence, foster a culture of healing and hope, and create meaningful pathways for young people's development.[23] In SOSAD the Boggses met activist lawyers Alice Jennings and her husband Carl Edwards, who became valuable allies. In November 1991, this loose coalition of activists held a "People's Festival" to celebrate and advance community-based efforts to meet the challenges facing the city. As explained in the printed program, the festival was conceived as an affirmation of an emergent vision grounded in the principles of social responsibility and self-reliance:

> There is a new spirit rising in Detroit. It is found where people are rehabbing abandoned houses, walking streets against crack and crime, planting gardens, reclaiming our neighborhoods as places of safety and peace for ourselves and our children.
>
> It is a spirit born out of the depths of a city crisis. For too long our neighborhoods have been allowed to deteriorate. For too long our scarce tax dollars have gone to subsidize megaprojects with little return to the people. For too long our streets have been places of violence and danger.
>
> It is the spirit born out of people struggling together. The spirit that builds Community, Compassion, Cooperation, Participation and Enterprise as we strive for harmony with one another and with our Earth. The spirit that says WE THE PEOPLE will education our children. WE will create productive and loving communities. WE will rebuild our city.[24]

One month after the People's Festival, the Boggses started planning Detroit Summer, their most ambitious and enduring project during this period. Jimmy and Grace joined with a small group of activists, including Howell and Barfield, to plan a youth program modeled on Mississippi Freedom Summer that would engage young people in the grassroots revitalization of Detroit. Guided by its mission to "rebuild, redefine, and re-spirit Detroit from the ground up," Detroit Summer brought together young people from the city and around the country who spent four weeks in the summer of 1992 working in small groups on collaborative projects such as planting gardens, rehabilitating homes, and creating murals.[25] Many projects involved intergenerational exchanges, such as planting vegetable and flower gardens with a group of elders called the Gardening Angels. One of the participants, fifteen-year-old Tracy Hollins, said of her experience in Detroit Summer, "It filled your head with answers to questions that you'd had all of your life and questions that no one can answer. It made you feel that you were an important part of the changing and molding of future generations. It made you feel that the hole you dug, the garden you watered or the swing set you painted, made a difference."[26] Another participant, Detroit High School student Julia Pointer (Putnam), recalled that during the Detroit Summer opening ceremony Jimmy "stepped to the mic and challenged every youth in the audience." He told them that "it was up to us to make a difference in our communities," leaving no doubt that the purpose of Detroit Summer was "to empower and inspire youth to reclaim some responsibility in rebuilding our cities. And we wanted to—because Jimmy made it clear that afternoon and every day afterwards that he was proud of us. And that made us proud of ourselves. Because this thin, wiry man, who a moment ago was a stranger, became our friend."[27]

No Final Struggle

The contrast that Putnam identified between the strength of Jimmy's words and the frailty of his body reflected a difficult reality: Jimmy's health was rapidly deteriorating. In 1988 he was diagnosed with bladder cancer, for which he underwent chemotherapy and multiple surgeries. In 1991 doctors found a tumor in Jimmy's lung. Radiation treatments put it into remission, but another tumor was found a year later. In February 1993 Jimmy was put on oxygen, and in the middle of May he entered hospice. He continued writing, attending meetings, and delivering speeches until his condition suddenly worsened on July 20. For two days, as the hospice nurse tended to him, Jimmy's friends, neighbors, and family members filled the house. Jimmy could no longer speak, but Grace and others sat with him playing his favorite music and reading his favorite poems to him. Jimmy passed away on July 22, 1993, at the age of seventy-four.[28]

Grace was acutely aware of what she lost with the death of her partner, collaborator, and closest comrade. "Life is so different without Jimmy to dialogue and share and fuss with," she told Rosemarie and Vincent Harding in a December 1993 letter. "After 40 years you begin taking a lot of things for granted," she confided. "I realize what a unique partnership we enjoyed."[29] Indeed, theirs was very much a partnership of equals, from political work to housework, as Grace referenced in a letter to Xavier Nicholas a month later: "It's strange without Jimmy but he's very present in his absence. Not only when I go to a meeting or prepare a speech or an article, but in and around the house reminding me to keep an eye on the water level in the furnace or rub down the car when I come in from the rain or mop the kitchen floor— all the things that I never thought about because he took care of them."[30]

The memorial services held after Jimmy's passing occasioned multilayered reflections on his life and the life he built with Grace. A memorial service held on October 23 at the First Unitarian-Universalist Church, a vital meeting space for Detroit activists, grassroots organizations, and community-based programs, drew friends and fellow activists from across the country. The tributes and testimonies embodied the sense of community and commitment to change that had been central to Jimmy's life and his partnership with Grace. The program ranged from a moving video by Frances Reid titled "James Boggs: An American Revolutionary" to musical selections from Duke Ellington's "Sacred Concerts." Speakers recited original poems and shared their memories. "The part of the celebration that I suspect [Jimmy] would have liked the best," Grace recalled later, "was when individuals stood up and were introduced according to how many years they had known him, beginning with Faye Brown who had worked with him at the Chrysler-Jefferson plant in the early 1940s and Ping Ferry who had known him since 1962. Those who had known him the shortest time were the young people of Detroit Summer."[31] Characteristically, those who had attended the memorial service were all invited to join a set of roundtable discussions on the theme "The Struggle for the Future" hosted by Detroit Summer youth and adult volunteers.[32]

Ruby Dee and Ossie Davis, the popular artist-activists who had known Grace and Jimmy since the mid-1960s, described their appreciation for Jimmy's plainspoken and clearly written insights, praised his unique ability to challenge and push others in their thinking, and recounted how they had been so convinced of the importance of Jimmy's *The American Revolution* that they sent copies of the book to major civil rights leaders. Davis explained that reading that book was the first in a series of moments when he felt "born again" through encounters with Jimmy's ideas over the course of the two couples' long friendship.[33] Dee paid tribute to Jimmy in her poem "For James, Writer, Activist, and Worker." Written for Jimmy on the eve of his death and now printed in the memorial service program, it expressed gratitude for all that Jimmy and Grace had meant to her and Davis. Representing "the nobleness of life," the Boggses served as "stalwart cheerleaders of the BETTER WAY CONTIGENT," opening new "horizons of thought and theory" and nurturing "the seed bed of exciting and necessary choices."[34]

This recognition of Jimmy's unique gifts and contributions, in combination with an equal appreciation of Jimmy's partnership with Grace, was a consistent theme in the tributes that flowed in, some of them heard that day, others written and collected in a booklet that was distributed at the service. Bill Strickland, an activist and intellectual who was a principal figure in key movement organizations of the 1960s and 1970 such as the Northern Student Movement and the Atlanta-based Institute of the Black World, identified Jimmy as one of four black men by whom he was "politically molded" (along with Malcolm X, Jesse Gray, and Vincent Harding). From each of them he learned something specific and invaluable. "Jimmy Boggs—and when I say 'Jimmy' here I mean, of course, 'Jimmy and Grace'— taught me that it was possible, indeed absolutely necessary, to make sense of the day-to-day reality in which I was immersed. I learned from them that RIGHT NOW was also History, as susceptible to analysis and understanding as anything that happened in decades past." Over the years, Strickland regularly called or visited the Boggses "to hear their thoughts on the real contradictions underlying an unfolding event": "Few memories are as lasting, or as fond, or as important to me intellectually . . . as are my memories of those talks . . . grappling with the latest developments in 'The Struggle.' These discussions enlarged my capacity to know and think and act less blindly. They also gave me a lesson in how a revolutionary intellectual thinks with clarity, reflects with humor, and speaks out in courage. The Boggses University at

3061 Field Street was a great place to learn and be warmed in the fire of a politically exciting intellectual hospitality whose like I have not encountered since. Above all, however, it was a place to get to know Jimmy Boggs, a man worth the knowing, and the loving, and now, the missing."[35] Strickland's witty characterization of 3061 Field Street as "the Boggses University" aptly captured the significance of their home as a site of intergenerational exchange and mentorship of young activists and a gathering place where organizational meetings, movement strategizing, and political discussions constantly took place.

A year later, during an intergenerational gathering to assess Jimmy's legacy, Vincent Harding offered a parallel reflection: "When we first met Grace and Jimmy more than a quarter of a century ago now, it was clear to me that we were meeting people who represented the spirit of continuing struggle." This spirit was exemplified, he said, in Jimmy's recognition "that there is always the need to begin again, that there is no permanent solution of anything, and that every set of solutions creates a new set of challenges. If we are looking for permanent solutions, we are looking for the grave. If we are looking for life, then we are looking for permanent challenges."[36] This was, of course, a recognition that Jimmy and Grace shared. As she wrote just a few years later, "I am often asked what keeps me going after all these years. I think it is the realization that there is no final struggle. Whether you win or lose, each struggle brings forth new contradictions, new and more challenging questions."[37]

The founding of the James and Grace Lee Boggs Center to Nurture Community Leadership (BCNCL) in 1995 provided a organizational and political space through which Grace continued to engage the new contradictions and new questions that she believed were essential to revolutionary change. The idea for the BCNCL, commonly referred to as the Boggs Center, emerged when Jennings and Edwards raised it with Grace shortly after Jimmy's death.[38] In 1995, the three of them founded the Boggs Center as a nonprofit organization to serve as "a Community Think Place and Visioning Center." Its purpose, in Grace's words, was to honor community work and "open up the minds especially of young people and children to rethink fundamental ideas about revolution, politics, and citizenship."[39] Howell and Donald Boggs, Jimmy's youngest son, served as the interim cochairs of its founding board of directors, whose members also included Grace, Jennings, Edwards, and Barfield. By 1998 the Boggs Center had raised the money to purchase 3061 Field Street, the house that Grace and Jimmy had lived in since 1962 and that had "been the site of so many movement-building activities over the years."[40] While Grace continued to live on the first floor, the upper floor became the home of the Boggs Center. The organization soon became an important vehicle for the public presentation and application of Jimmy and Grace's ideas, and it has emerged, through its many activities over several years, as a consistent and generative force within Detroit's vibrant community of grassroots activists. From its founding in 1995 to Grace's passing in 2015, the Boggs Center served as Grace's organizational base as she assumed the overlapping roles of movement elder, community activist, and revolutionary theoretician.[41]

Throughout most of these final two decades of her life, even as she experienced the inevitable physical limitations of advanced age, Grace maintained a consistent and active schedule of writing, attending meetings, organizing programs, speaking, holding discussions, and strategizing. Throughout the 1990s, Grace was an ever-present and influential figure in grassroots struggles to shape Detroit's future. The publication of her autobiography *Living for Change* in 1998 generated new interest in Grace's life and ideas, and by the turn of the twenty-first century she was receiving increasing national recognition as a growing number of people across the country became aware of her long history of activism and found inspiration in her work in Detroit. In 2011 Grace published her last book, *The Next American Revolution: Sustainable Activism for the Twenty-First Century*, presenting a distillation of her thinking during the preceding decade about revolutionary change in the new century. Written in collaboration with historian and Boggs Center board member Scott Kurashige, *The Next American Revolution* provides the historical and theoretical foundation for what Grace and the Boggs Center called "visionary organizing": grassroots political work not focused solely on protesting current injustices, but rather geared toward projecting alternatives and creating new visions for the future. This concept had its roots in Jimmy and Grace's theorizing dialectical humanism, in their distinction between rebellion and revolution, in their belief in two-sided transformation, in their commitment to community building and grassroots leadership, and in Grace's continuing embrace of the "new contradictions" and the "new and more challenging questions" of the twenty-first century that she confronted as a movement elder who not only inspired a new generation of activists but also directly engaged with them.[42]

In 2013, filmmaker Grace Lee (no relation) released the documentary film *American Revolutionary: The Evolution of Grace Lee Boggs*, presenting a compelling portrait of her long life and record of political engagement. "I don't know what the next American revolution is going to be like," Grace says at the end of the film, "but you might be able to imagine it, if your imagination were rich enough."[43] This statement, like the concept of visionary organizing, reflected two central dimensions of the political practice that Grace and Jimmy had fashioned together: an evolutionary conception of revolutionary change, and a commitment to dialectical thinking. She insisted that we question old ideas about the purpose and practice of revolution, allowing our creativity and imagination to envision news ways of relating to each other and the earth, new ways of building our communities, and in the process challenging ourselves to create the world anew.

Grace celebrated her 100th birthday on June 27, 2015. A group of Grace's comrades, friends, and supporters formed a Grace Lee Boggs Birthday Committee to plan a weeklong series of events in Grace's honor taking place at various locations in Detroit.[44] In poor health and bedridden, Grace was unable to attend any of the events, but she received visitors during the week, including friends and former comrades from across the country. The culminating event at the Charles H. Wright Museum of African American History brought together a wonderfully broad collection of people. It included people who admired Grace but never met her and people who had known her for decades, younger people she had inspired and older people who had been in various organizations with her, people who read her writings and people who participated in movements with her. The collection of people gathered to celebrate Grace, and by extension Jimmy, stood as a testament to the legacy Grace and Jimmy left. In this gathering were multiple generations and overlapping networks of the activists, friends, family, and admirers who were a part of Grace and Jimmy's life or shared their commitments.

On October 5, 2015, 100 days after her 100th birthday, Grace passed away peacefully at her home, with her closest friends, longtime comrades, and caregivers by her side. Friends and admirers of Grace held an impromptu memorial that evening outside her home, and then organized a large public memorial service at the end of the month. More than 500 people attended the service, some forced to watch the video feed in an overflow room after the union hall reached its capacity, while others elsewhere watched on live stream. The number of people attending or watching the memorial service, like the outpouring of reflections and tributes in the days and weeks following her passing, reflected Grace's influence and standing among activists, artists, and others in Detroit and beyond. In that moment it was easy, and on some level appropriate, to think of Grace and her legacy in the singular. To be sure, a good number of those in attendance and watching remotely knew of Grace primarily or even exclusively from the public profile she developed and the recognition she garnered during the two decades since Jimmy's death. Still, in important moments, speakers and performers on the memorial service program pointed out that Grace and Jimmy's four decades of activism and theoretical work had been the foundation for her thinking, writing, and activism during this period. Among the various tributes, remembrances, poems, and songs attesting to the depth and meaning of Grace's life, several made it clear that a full assessment of Grace's legacy and impact must recognize the unique and generative partnership that she and Jimmy built together. Activist, poet, and Boggs Center board member Tawana "Honeycomb" Petty, for example, captured the spirit of their relationship in the poem she delivered at the memorial: "Grace was struggle wrapped in love. . . . She was the other half of Jimmy, dynamic duo in the struggle."[45]

Three years before his death, on the occasion of Grace's seventy-fifth birthday, Jimmy made a public tribute that articulated what their partnership meant to him: "To my wife of many years whom I love and respect not only for our good fortune and relationship, but because of my deep appreciation of what I have learned from her. She has enriched my life."[46] The enrichment, of course, flowed both ways, with Grace and Jimmy continually learning from each other as they grew together. With the goal of making the next American revolution as their guiding commitment, James and Grace Lee Boggs crafted a remarkable partnership, forged in love and struggle.

Notes

ABBREVIATIONS

BLMOHC   Blacks in the Labor Movement Oral History Collection, Walter P. Reuther Library, Archives of Labor and Urban Affairs, Wayne State University, Michigan

Boggs Papers   James and Grace Lee Boggs Papers, Walter P. Reuther Library, Archives of Labor and Urban Affairs, Wayne State University, Michigan

Cleage Papers   Albert B. Cleage Jr. Papers, Bentley Historical Library, University of Michigan, Michigan

CRDP   Civil Rights Documentation Project, Ralph J. Bunche Oral History Collection, Moorland-Spingarn Research Center, Howard University, Washington, D.C.

DCCR   Detroit Commission on Community Relations, Human Rights Department Collection, Walter P. Reuther Library, Archives of Labor and Urban Affairs, Wayne State University, Michigan

Dillard Papers   Ernest C. and Jessie M. Dillard Papers, Walter P. Reuther Library, Archives of Labor and Urban Affairs, Wayne State University, Michigan

DULR   Detroit Urban League Records, Bentley Historical Library, University of Michigan, Michigan

Dunayevskaya Papers   Raya Dunayevskaya Papers, Walter P. Reuther Library, Archives of Labor and Urban Affairs, Wayne State University, Michigan

FBI-GLB   Grace Lee Boggs File HQ 100-356160, Federal Bureau of Investigation, Washington, D.C.

FBI-JB   James Boggs File HQ 100-405600, Federal Bureau of Investigation, Washington, D.C.

Franklin Papers   C. L. Franklin Papers, Bentley Historical Library, University of Michigan, Michigan

Glaberman Papers   Martin and Jessie Glaberman Papers, Walter P. Reuther Library, Archives of Labor and Urban Affairs, Wayne State University, Michigan

JALC   Joseph A. Labadie Collection, Special Collections Library, University of Michigan, Michigan

James Papers   C. L. R. James Papers, Rare Book and Manuscript Library, Columbia University, New York

NAACP-DBC	National Association for the Advancement of Colored People Detroit Branch Collection, Walter P. Reuther Library, Archives of Labor and Urban Affairs, Wayne State University, Michigan
OHALC	Oral History of the American Left Collection, Tamiment Library and Robert F. Wagner Labor Archives, New York University, New York
Paine Papers	Frances D. and G. Lyman Paine Papers, Walter P. Reuther Library, Archives of Labor and Urban Affairs, Wayne State University, Michigan
UAWLocal7	United Automobile Workers Local 7 Collection, Walter P. Reuther Library, Archives of Labor and Urban Affairs, Wayne State University, Michigan

INTRODUCTION

1. This is the first full-length treatment of James and Grace Lee Boggs. The following works explore various dimensions of their activism and thinking. Stephen M. Ward, ed., *Pages from a Black Radical's Notebook*, presents a collection of Jimmy's writings over four decades and provides an overview of their careers, focusing in particular on James Boggs's activism and intellectual work. Mullen, *Afro-Orientalism*, includes a chapter on the thought of James and Grace Lee Boggs, calling them "the most significant Afro-Asian collaboration in U.S. radical history" (xliii) and "two of contemporary radicalism's most seminal thinkers" (111), adding that their thinking "awaits a still more complete explication" (162). A special issue of *Souls: A Critical Journal of Black Politics, Culture, and Society* examined James Boggs and his book *The American Revolution*. The issue is titled "Reflections on a Black Worker's Notebook: The Legacy of James Boggs's *The American Revolution*" and is guest edited by Matthew Birkhold (*Souls* 13, no. 3). An examination of James Boggs's thought in relation to Mao Zedong and China is presented in Frazier, "The Assault of the Monkey King on the Hosts of Heaven." Two articles investigating Grace Lee Boggs within Asian American political traditions are Fu, "On Contradiction"; and Choi, "At the Margins of the Asian American Political Experience."

Additional studies identify the Boggses as pivotal figures. Speaking specifically to their place in Detroit's history, Angela Dillard writes, "If cross-generational influence was indeed key to the development of political radicalism in 1960s Detroit, Grace Lee and James Boggs personified that influence" (*Faith in the City*, 226). Literary scholar James Edward Smethurst characterizes James Boggs "as a sort of father figure" (*Black Arts Movement*, 187) to many young radicals, while political scientist Michael Dawson writes that the Boggses' influence "went beyond Detroit's black radicals," noting that their works "were standard fare in black study groups, in worker circles, and among student activist from New York to California" (*Black Visions*, 200–201). Van Gosse cites James Boggs, together with Malcolm X, Harold Cruse, Amiri Baraka, and others, as a key figure who helped to forge the transformation of the civil rights movement into a struggle for black power (*Rethinking the New Left*, 114).

2. Bill Strickland, "Remembering My Man, James Boggs," statement for memorial celebration of James Boggs, October 12, 1993 (in author's possession).

3. James Boggs, "Think Dialectically, Not Biologically," Save Our Sons and Daughters Workshop, March 1993 (videotape in author's possession).

4. James Boggs, "Think Dialectically, Not Biologically," text of speech delivered at Atlanta University, February 17, 1974. This speech is reprinted in Stephen M. Ward, ed., *Pages from a Black Radical's Notebook*. This quotation appears on 273.

5. Stephen M. Ward, *Pages from a Black Radical's Notebook*, 266.

6. Ibid.

7. Aneb Gloria House, "For Grace Lee Boggs' 100th Birthday" (in author's possession). House read this poem at Grace Lee Boggs's 100th birthday celebration at the Charles H. Wright Museum of African American History in Detroit. This event is briefly discussed in the Epilogue.

8. James and Grace Lee Boggs, *Revolution and Evolution in the Twentieth Century*, 128, 226.

CHAPTER I

1. Jimmy made these remarks at the James and Grace Lee Boggs Community Celebration, Detroit, May 1990 (videotape in author's possession; hereafter cited as Community Celebration). His remarks are also cited in Grace Lee Boggs, *Living for Change*, 228. The "About the Author" page at the end of James Boggs, *The American Revolution*, reads in part, "James Boggs, born in Marion Junction, Alabama, forty-four years ago, never dreamed of becoming President or a locomotive engineer. He grew up in a world where the white folks are gentlemen by day and Ku Klux Klanners at night. Marion Junction is in Dallas County where even today, although Negroes make up over 57 percent of the total county population of 57,000, only 130 Negroes are registered voters."

2. Community Celebration.

3. James Boggs, "Walking a Chalk Line," interview by WBAI Pacifica Radio, recorded October 11, 1963; broadcast November 25, 1963.

4. James Boggs interview in OHALC.

5. Glenn Feldman, *Politics, Society, and the Klan*, 20, 261–68; Kelley, *Hammer and Hoe*, 73–76, 101.

6. Flynt, *Alabama in the Twentieth Century*, 318.

7. Krugler, *1919, The Year of Racial Violence*; Tuttle, *Race Riot*, 14, 22.

8. Community Celebration.

9. In *Way Out of No Way*, Swann-Wright cites the following "African American folk saying" on the page facing the table of contents: "Our God can make a way out of no way. . . . He can do anything but fail."

10. For further discussion of this phrase and its meanings, see Ladner, *The Ties That Bind*, chapter 11. Two recent studies of African American culture, focusing particularly on black women, have taken the phrase as their titles: Boehm, *Making a Way Out of No Way: African American Women and the Second Great Migration*, and Coleman, *Making a Way Out of No Way: A Womanist Theology*. Boehm centers resilience—"the capability of a human

being to continue on in the face of great adversity"—as the basis of this shared cultural experience. She writes, "Resilience is an often undervalued attribute; resilience is a form of courage, but it requires a continuity of spirit that is not necessarily a component of all types of bravery. A soldier might gather up his personal fortitude, take a deep breath, and run headlong into danger. Resilience entails not only a momentary conviction of spirit, but a continued devotion to persisting in the face of adversity, a commitment to 'making a way out of no way'" (19). A similar reflection comes in Marian Wright Edelman's discussion of her memory of Martin Luther King Jr. Herself a veteran of the civil rights movement, a child of the South, and a longtime activist, Edelman writes, "I also remember him as someone able to admit how often he was afraid and unsure about his next step. But faith prevailed over fear and uncertainty and fatigue and depression. It was his human vulnerability and his ability to rise above it that I most remember. In this, he was not different from many Black adults whose credo has been to make 'a way out of no way'" (*The Measure of Our Success*, 11).

11. Community Celebration.

12. James Boggs's birth certificate gives May 27 as his date of birth, but May 28 is the date that he and his family celebrated as his birthday. May 28 is the date of birth listed on the program of his memorial service and in the tribute booklet distributed at the service.

The most useful sources of biographical information on James Boggs are the following: James Boggs, "Walking a Chalk Line"; James Boggs's oral history in Moon, *Untold Tales, Unsung Heroes*, 149–56; transcript of the interview with James Boggs conducted by Detroit Urban League (for *Untold Tales, Unsung Heroes*), Boggs Papers, Box 16, Folder 9; the text of James Boggs's statement during the "Pendle Hill Seminar/Search: Martin Luther King, Jr. and the Modern Freedom Movement," led by Vincent Harding and Rosemarie Freeney Harding, July 18, 1979 (in author's possession); Nicholas, *Questions of the American Revolution*; James Boggs interview in OHALC; James Boggs interview in *Detroit Committee for the Liberation of Africa Newsletter* 1, no. 4 (February–March 1974): 1–3; "Biographical Data on James Boggs," Boggs Papers, Box 1, Folder 7; Grace Lee Boggs, *Living for Change*, chapter 4; Phelps, "James Boggs"; Darrell Dawsey, "An American Revolutionary," *Detroit News*, April 21, 1992; and the author's interviews with Grace Lee Boggs.

13. These passages come from James Boggs, "Why Are Our Children So Bored?," which appeared in the *Save Our Sons and Daughters Newsletter* in the summer of 1991. It is reprinted in Stephen M. Ward, ed., *Pages from a Black Radical's Notebook*, 357–58. The quoted passages appear on 357.

14. It seems that "Dr. Donald" and "Miss Elvie" are the names by which James Boggs and other members of the family referred to the couple. I am grateful to Joy Boggs, James Boggs's niece, for sharing this and other family information with me. James Boggs regularly mentioned the couple in interviews, but never by name. He only refers to them as "the doctor and his wife."

15. James Boggs, "Walking a Chalk Line."

16. Ibid.

17. James Boggs interview in OHALC.

18. Ibid.

19. James Boggs, "Walking a Chalk Line."

20. Ibid.

21. Ibid.

22. The state of Alabama reported Marion Junction's population to be 1,114 in 1920, the year after James Boggs was born, and 1,053 in 1930. See State of Alabama Department of Archives and History, *Alabama Official and Statistical Register, 1931*, 440.

23. Bond, *Negro Education in Alabama*, 3.

24. Kolchin, *First Freedom*, 12.

25. Ibid., 16.

26. Fitts, *Selma*, 108

27. Griffith, *Alabama*, 288, 141.

28. Hereford, "A Study of Selma and Dallas County, Alabama," 11.

29. Bond, *Negro Education in Alabama*, 123.

30. Alabama Department of Archives and History, *Alabama Official and Statistical Register, 1919*, 436–37.

31. Flynt, *Alabama in the Twentieth Century*, 6.

32. Ibid., 7.

33. Bond, *Negro Education in Alabama*; Flynt, *Alabama in the Twentieth Century*.

34. Flynt *Alabama in the Twentieth Century*, 3.

35. Ibid., 14; Fitts, *Selma*, 101; Alabama Department of Archives and History, *Alabama Official and Statistical Register, 1915*, 362. One of the most effective disfranchisement measures was the poll tax, which also resulted in a decline of white voters.

36. Bond, *Negro Education in Alabama*, 226.

37. Alabama Department of Archives and History, *Alabama Official and Statistical Register, 1919*, 436. A key reason for the decline in agriculture was the boll weevil, which came to Alabama during the first half of the 1910s and by mid-decade had devastated the state's cotton crops. While Alabama boasted a cotton crop of 1,731,751 bales in 1914, two years later it had plunged nearly 70 percent, to just 552,679 bales.

38. Bosworth, *Black Belt County*, 1–2.

39. Alabama Department of Archives and History, *Alabama Official and Statistical Register, 1919*, 436.

40. James Boggs, "Walking a Chalk Line."

41. I am again grateful to Joy Boggs for confirming the name Thomas Boggs. In James Boggs, "Walking a Chalk Line," Boggs says, "my father's father was white," but does not give his name.

42. Ibid.

43. James Boggs Jr. interview with author. He says that his uncle Bill (his father's older brother) told him that they played with the white cousins as children.

44. James Boggs, "Walking a Chalk Line."

45. James Boggs, "Pendle Hill Seminar/Search," 1. He does not name his great-grandmother in this document, but Grace Lee Boggs identifies her as Big Ma in *Living for Change*. She writes that James Boggs's relationship with Big Ma was an early expression of his lifelong concern for elders and describes another dimension to their relationship: "As a boy

he had taken care of Big Ma, his great-grandmother, feeding and dressing her and emptying her bedpan" (93).

46. James Boggs, "Pendle Hill Seminar/Search," 1.

47. Spero and Harris, *The Black Worker*, 246.

48. Ibid., 248, 168.

49. Ibid., 168–69.

50. Ibid., 248.

51. Ibid., table 19 on 208.

52. Ibid., 169.

53. Phillips, *Alabama North*, 53, citing the Department of Labor study "The Negro at Work."

54. James Boggs made these remarks during a speech titled "The Next Development in Education" delivered in Detroit in 1977. The text of the speech is included in Stephen M. Ward, ed., *Pages from a Black Radical's Notebook*, 284–92. The quoted passage appears on 284.

55. Sisk, "Negro Education in the Alabama Black Belt."

56. Fitts, *Selma*, 118–19. Fitts reports that Knox was one of four private schools for blacks in Selma. The one public school, with 1,300 students, was "highly overcrowded." There were six public schools for whites.

57. Grace Lee Boggs e-mail correspondence with author, August 14, 2009. In this correspondence Grace Lee Boggs relates information related to her by Annie Boggs, James Boggs's first wife, who attended the same elementary school.

58. James Boggs, "Walking a Chalk Line."

59. Ibid.

60. Ibid.

61. Fitts, *Selma*, 119.

62. In "Walking a Chalk Line," James Boggs describes his change of schools but does not say it was because of Knox closing or reducing the grades offered. He says, "I stayed in Selma until I got in the 10th grade, and then I decided I wanted to go to this town called Bessemer, Alabama."

63. After leaving Dunbar, Morton attended Morehouse College and Columbia University before settling in Detroit, where he had an accomplished career as an educator, philosopher, and member of the clergy.

64. Charles Morton interview with author.

65. Annie Boggs interview with author. As she recalls, Jimmy "followed" her to Bessemer.

66. Charles Morton interview with author.

67. Bailey, *They Too Call Alabama Home*, 345–50; Raines, *My Soul Is Rested*, 348–51; Powledge, *Free at Last?*, 45–47, 149–50, 172, 484, 638; and McWhorter, *Carry Me Home*.

68. Charles Morton interview with author.

69. As Vanessa Siddle Walker explains, black communities throughout the South used "professor" to describe "an empowering leader who was the lever elevating racial progress in black schools and communities." Through his leadership of Dunbar, as well as his example of educational and professional attainment, Shores embodied "this community

definition of an educational agent who used his influence to motivate the educational aspirations of black children" (Walker with Byas, *Hello Professor*, xiv).

70. James Boggs to A. D. Shores, September 14, 1963, Boggs Papers, Box 1, Folder 22.

71. Bailey, *They Too Call Alabama Home*; Eskew, *But for Birmingham*, 54–57; McWhorter, *Carry Me Home*, 96–104, 498–501.

72. James Boggs to A. D. Shores, September 14, 1963.

73. Annie Boggs interview with author.

74. Quoted in Dawsey, "An American Revolutionary."

75. James Boggs, "Walking a Chalk Line."

76. James Boggs interview in OHALC.

77. Grace Lee Boggs, *Living for Change*, 84–85; transcript of interview with Jimmy Boggs conducted by Detroit Urban League, 2.

78. James Boggs, "Walking a Chalk Line."

79. Ibid. Boggs offers this story as a prominent reason he decided to leave the South.

80. James Boggs high school diploma (in possession of Grace Lee Boggs); Grace Lee Boggs e-mail correspondence with author, July 13, 2005.

81. Moon, *Untold Tales, Unsung Heroes*, 150

82. Nicholas, *Questions of the American Revolution*, 1.

83. Moon, *Untold Tales, Unsung Heroes*, 150.

84. Transcript of interview with Jimmy Boggs conducted by Detroit Urban League, 4.

85. James Boggs Jr. interview with author.

86. Transcript of interview with Jimmy Boggs conducted by Detroit Urban League, 4.

87. Babson, *Working Detroit*, 42.

88. Ibid., 104.

89. I have drawn this point from Bates, *The Making of Black Detroit in the Age of Henry Ford*. Bates provides an excellent discussion of black workers at Ford and the company's evolving relationship with the city's black community.

90. See map in Richard W. Thomas, *Life for Us Is What We Make It*, 126.

91. Zunz, *The Changing Face of Inequality*, 132, 348–49. Zunz shows how the city's neighborhoods and social dynamics were reshaped by a dissolution of ethnic identification and a strengthening of both a class-based identity and a cross-class white racial identity.

92. Hyde, *Detroit*, unpaginated.

93. For rich discussions of the Great Migration, black settlement patterns, and the intense struggles over housing during the two-and-a-half decades preceding James Boggs's arrival in the city, see Bates, *The Making of Black Detroit in the Age of Henry Ford*, and Miller, *Managing Inequality*.

94. Black Bottom earned its name from the area's dark, fertile soil, on which Detroit's early settlers farmed, but the name took on new meaning as African Americans came to inhabit the area in the first half of the twentieth century. As literary scholar and poet Melba Joyce Boyd explains, "During the Great Migration, that name [Black Bottom] acquired additional symbolic meaning as black southerners crowded into a neighborhood situated on the bottom of the city's social strata" (*Wrestling with the Muse*, 35).

95. Young and Wheeler, *Hard Stuff*, 143.

96. Ibid., 144.

97. For businesses along Hastings, see Wilson with Cohassey, *Toast of the Town*, 104–5; and various selections in Moon, *Untold Tales, Unsung Heroes*.

98. Examples include Detroit Count, "Hastings Street Opera"; John Lee Hooker, "Boogie Chillen"; and Dudley Randall, "Hastings Street Girls."

99. Wilson with Cohassey, *Toast of the Town*, 46. Wilson writes, "Benny Ornsby's B&B Fish Dock served only fried fish. Take-out or sit-down, it had wonderful bass and pickerel sandwiches. You could smell the fish cooking down the street." Roxborough's office was in the Watson Investment Real Estate Company, owned by Everett I. Watson, who was himself a businessman involved in both legal and extralegal affairs. This building may have also housed the recently established black weekly newspaper, the *Michigan Chronicle*. See Poinsett, *Walking with Presidents*.

100. See Miller, *Managing Inequality*, 241, for the "East Side Blighted Area"; Boykin, *A Handbook,* 54, for boundaries of the area; Thomas, *Race and Redevelopment*, 20–22, for the city's plans; and Moon, *Untold Tales, Unsung Heroes*, for multiple former residents describing life in the Brewster Homes.

101. Wilson with Cohassey, *Toast of the Town*, 105–6. Most of the bars as well as many other establishments in the area were Jewish owned, as Jewish immigrants had lived in the area during the decades prior to, and to some extent during, black settlement.

102. Ibid., 104.

103. Ibid., 106, citing the *Detroit Tribune*.

104. This description of James Boggs's arrival in Detroit is drawn from his oral history in Moon, *Untold Tales, Unsung Heroes*. The quotation appears on 150.

105. Detroit population statistics from *United States Census of Population, 1910–1970*, cited in Sugrue, *Origins of the Urban Crisis*, 23.

106. Moon, *Untold Tales, Unsung Heroes*.

107. See *Detroit Tribune*, July 17, 1937, 4, for Calloway advertisement; *Detroit Tribune*, July 31, 1937, 4, for Armstrong advertisement; *Detroit Tribune*, August 21, 1937, for Henderson and Hines advertisement. The Graystone was the largest ballroom in the city and, like others, generally only held dances for blacks on Monday nights. See Bjorn and Gallert, *Before Motown*, 8.

108. "Hot-Cha Sizzles at Melody Club," *Detroit Tribune*, August 28, 1937, 11; advertisement for *Temptation* in *Detroit Tribune*, July 24, 1937, 11.

109. "Go and Register," *Detroit Tribune*, August 28, 1937, 1.

110. Announcement for First Annual Emancipation Picnic and Dance, *Detroit Tribune*, July 24, 1937, 3. On the Michigan Federated Democratic Clubs, see Richard W. Thomas, *Life for Us Is What We Make It*, 267.

111. Richard W. Thomas, *Life for Us Is What We Make It*, 187. Thomas reports that several black papers collapsed during the Depression. The *Tribune* merged with one of these, the *Detroit Independent*.

112. *Detroit Tribune*, June 12, 1937, 1.

113. On Kirk see Meier and Rudwick, *Black Detroit and the Rise of the UAW*, 40.

114. Poinsett, *Walking with Presidents*, 13.

115. Ibid., 17. For more on Diggs, see Richard W. Thomas, *Life for Us Is What We Make It*, 265–70.

116. Louis Martin, "The Ford Contract: An Opportunity," *Crisis*, September 1941, cited in Poinsett, *Walking with Presidents*, 23.

117. Babson, *Working Detroit*, 93.

118. James Boggs, "Walking a Chalk Line."

119. Ibid.; Moon, *Untold Tales, Unsung Heroes*, 150–51.

120. Nicholas, *Questions of the American Revolution*, 1.

121. James Boggs interview in OHALC; Annie Boggs interview with author.

122. Annie Boggs interview with author.

123. Moon, *Untold Tales, Unsung Heroes*, 151.

124. Annie Boggs interview with author.

125. Moon, *Untold Tales, Unsung Heroes*, 151.

126. James Boggs, "Walking a Chalk Line"; "Biographical Data on James Boggs"; Moon, *Untold Tales, Unsung Heroes*, 150–51; Dawsey, "An American Revolutionary." In the apprentice program he would have made 60 cents an hour as a template maker (pattern maker), whereas he would earn 68 cents an hour as a new factory worker. He reported that his earnings at Chrysler had risen to $1.02 an hour by 1945.

CHAPTER 2

1. From the text of James Boggs's statement during the "Pendle Hill Seminar/Search: Martin Luther King, Jr. and the Modern Freedom Movement," led by Vincent Harding and Rosemarie Freeney Harding, July 18, 1979, 2 (in author's possession). He would express this sentiment on multiple occasions during and after his tenure in the plant. See, for example, these interviews: James Boggs, "Walking a Chalk Line" interview by WBAI Pacifica Radio, recorded October 11, 1963; broadcast November 25, 1963; Nicholas, *Questions of the American Revolution*, 6; James Boggs interview in OHALC.

2. Thomas J. Sugrue makes this point in *Origins of the Urban Crisis*. He writes, "World War II represented a turning point in black employment prospects. In 1941 and 1942, firms with predominantly white work forces gradually opened their doors to blacks" (26).

3. Weaver, *Negro Labor*, 63.

4. Ibid., 286.

5. Ibid., 63.

6. Ibid., 289.

7. James Boggs, *The American Revolution*, 80. In this passage, Boggs also restated his interpretation of the war's impact: "Negroes did not give credit for this order to Roosevelt or the American government. Far from it. Recognizing that America and its allies had their backs to the wall in their struggle with Hitler and Tojo, Negroes said that Hitler and Tojo, by creating the war that made the Americans give them jobs in industry, had done more for them in four years than Uncle Sam had done in three hundred years" (*The American Revolution*, 79–80). This book is reproduced in its entirety in Stephen M. Ward, ed., *Pages from a Black Radical's Notebook*. These quotations appear on 133.

8. For wartime black activism see Bates, "'Double V for Victory.'" In *The Making of Black Detroit in the Age of Henry Ford*, Bates provides a provocative and compelling analysis of black community and labor activism during the 1920s and 1930s, making a strong argument for how to understand the transformations during World War II. For other and sometimes competing discussions of the years leading up to World War II, see Meier and Rudwick, *Black Detroit and the Rise of the UAW*; and Miller, *Managing Inequality*. Each of these identifies the significance of the 1937-41 period, though they give contrasting arguments about the specific political dynamics at play. Bates challenges these interpretations, particularly Meier and Rudwick's, and identifies the early 1930s as a crucial moment leading to black workers and the black community acting as a major force in the success of the UAW's victory at Ford in 1941. In *Life for Us Is What We Make It*, Richard W. Thomas says the years 1936-41 were a period of "radical transformation of the social consciousness of black Detroit" (190). Dillard, *Faith in the City*, gives an insightful exposition of the overlapping political spaces leading up to, during, and after World War II, with particular attention to religious expressions of radicalism.

9. James Boggs, "Walking a Chalk Line."

10. Jimmy began working at Chrysler between 1940 and 1942, but his exact starting date is unclear. The year most frequently given is 1940. For example, in his oral history in Moon, *Untold Tales, Unsung Heroes*, he makes a reference to working at Chrysler in 1940 (151). Similarly, in her autobiography Grace says that when they, along with their comrades and friends Freddy and Lyman Paine, collectively made the decision in 1968 that Jimmy should resign from his job at Chrysler to allow him to devote his full energies to political activities, this meant that he would be leaving "two years short of the thirty years required for retirement on pension" (*Living for Change*, 156). This suggests that he began in 1940 and stayed there for twenty-eight years. This time frame is repeated elsewhere, and I followed this usage in the introduction to *Pages from a Black Radical's Notebook* (11). However, other evidence suggests he began at Chrysler in 1941 or 1942. A biographical statement written in 1970 describes him as "an auto worker for 27 years . . . from 1941–1968" ("Biographical Data on James Boggs," Boggs Papers, Box 1, Folder 7). It is not clear if 1941 refers here to his first, and short-lived, job at Dodge, or to his starting date at Chrysler. In an interview decades later, Annie Boggs recalled that James began at Chrysler in 1942, shortly after the birth of their second child in that year (Annie Boggs interview with author). The FBI's file on James Boggs records his starting date at Chrysler as July 21, 1942 (FBI-JB, Summary Report, October 15, 1953, 4).

11. Boyle, "Auto Workers at War," 103, 105; Babson, *Working Detroit*, 80; Jefferys, *Management and Managed*, 84–87.

12. Bailer, "The Negro Automobile Worker"; Korstad and Lichtenstein, "Opportunities Found and Lost"; Sugrue, *Origins of the Urban Crisis*, 95.

13. Weaver, *Negro Labor*, 61–77; Capeci, *Race Relations in Wartime Detroit*, 31.

14. Bates, *The Making of Black Detroit in the Age of Henry Ford*; Meier and Rudwick, *Black Detroit and the Rise of the UAW*; Dillard, *Faith in the City*; Richard W. Thomas, *Life for Us Is What We Make It*.

15. Bates, *The Making of Black Detroit in the Age of Henry Ford*; Meier and Rudwick, *Black Detroit and the Rise of the UAW*, 90, 92.

16. Bates, *The Making of Black Detroit in the Age of Henry Ford*; Meier and Rudwick, *Black Detroit and the Rise of the UAW*; Babson, *Working Detroit*; Sugrue, *Origins of the Urban Crisis*.

17. See Bates, *The Making of Black Detroit in the Age of Henry Ford*, for an analysis of the dynamics involved in this relationship among black workers and the black community of Detroit, the Ford Motor Company, and the city's labor movement.

18. Garfinkel, *When Negroes March*, 38, 54–60. The MOWM is discussed in greater detail in chapter 4.

19. "Publishers at the White House," *Michigan Chronicle*, February 19, 1944, 1, quoted in Washburn, *The African American Newspaper*, 177.

20. Bates, "'Double V for Victory'"; Garfinkel, *When Negroes March*. For the meaning and use of Double V in Detroit, see Shockley, *We, Too, Are Americans*. For more on the MOWM in Detroit, including FEPC-inspired activism, see Dillard, *Faith in the City*, 115–23.

21. Lewis-Colman, *Race against Liberalism*, 25–29; Bates, "'Double V for Victory,'" 27–28.

22. Bates, *The Making of Black Detroit in the Age of Henry Ford*; Lewis-Colman, *Race against Liberalism*. Such organizations include the National Negro Labor Council in the 1950s, the Trade Union Labor Council in the 1950s and 1960s, and the League of Revolutionary Black Workers in the early 1970s.

23. Meier and Rudwick, *Black Detroit and the Rise of the UAW*; Lewis-Colman, *Race against Liberalism*.

24. George Lipsitz gives an especially thoughtful analysis of these wildcats and hate strikes, examining their significance locally and placing them in a national context, in his *Rainbow at Midnight*, chapter 3.

25. For DiGaetano's relationship with James Boggs, see Grace Lee Boggs, *Living for Change*, 93, and discussion below. For DiGaetano's efforts in the Ford strike, see Babson, *Working Detroit*, 105.

26. Meier and Rudwick, *Black Detroit and the Rise of the UAW*, 89, 103.

27. Lewis-Colman, *Race against Liberalism*, 26.

28. Richard W. Thomas, *Life for Us Is What We Make It*, 245. See also Lipsitz, *Rainbow at Midnight*, chapter 3. For a listing of the many walkouts throughout the city during the spring of 1943, see Hill, *FBI's RACON*, 130–35.

29. "Detroit Is Dynamite," *Life*, August 17, 1942. The article was published anonymously, but Meier and Rudwick indicate its authorship. See Meier and Rudwick, *Black Detroit and the Rise of the UAW*, 192, 264n37.

30. June Manning Thomas, *Redevelopment and Race*, 20–21.

31. "Detroit Is Dynamite," 20.

32. Moon, *Untold Tales, Unsung Heroes*, 151–52. For a broader discussion of the wartime housing crisis, see Sugrue, *Origins of the Urban Crisis*.

33. Capeci and Wilkerson, *Layered Violence*, 184; Meier and Rudwick, *Black Detroit and the Rise of the UAW*, 191.

34. For a discussion of the gendered dimensions of these rumors, see Marilynn S. Johnson, "Gender, Race, and Rumours," 264–67.

35. For descriptions and analyses of the riot, see Capeci and Wilkerson, *Layered Violence*; Lee and Humphrey, *Race Riot*; Sitkoff, "The Detroit Riot of 1943"; Marilynn S. Johnson, "Gender, Race, and Rumours."

36. Capeci and Wilkerson report that the number of Belle Isle visitors that day was 100,000 and that on the east side "the temperature broke 90 degrees" that afternoon (*Layered Violence*, 5).

37. Annie Boggs interview with author. James Boggs Jr. also recalled this incident, with slight variation in the details (James Boggs Jr. interview with author).

38. Quoted from the 1995 documentary *Claiming Open Spaces*, which explores the use and significance of public space for black urban communities. It focuses on Franklin Park in Columbus, Ohio, and uses the experiences in four other cities—Detroit, Birmingham, New Orleans, and Oakland—to frame and reevaluate the history and meaning of Franklin Park. James and Grace Lee Boggs appear in the film speaking about Belle Isle and the 1943 Detroit riot.

39. Nicholas, *Questions of the American Revolution*, 4–5.

40. Ibid., 5. These same remarks also appear in James Boggs, "Beyond Militancy." The quotations appear on 38.

41. Mast, *Detroit Lives*.

42. Moon, *Untold Tales, Unsung Heroes*, 153.

43. Lichtenstein, *Walter Reuther*, 100.

44. Widick, *Detroit*, 72.

45. Joe Maddox interview with author.

46. "Local 7 Organization Committee Rules," UAWLocal7, Box 9, Folder 19.

47. Moon, *Untold Tales, Unsung Heroes*, 152.

48. Darrell Dawsey, "An American Revolutionary," *Detroit News*, April 21, 1992.

49. Moon, *Untold Tales, Unsung Heroes*, 152.

50. Nick DiGaetano oral history, BLMOHC; Grace Lee Boggs, *Living for Change*, 93.

51. James Boggs, "Conversations with James Boggs, #2," interview by Kenneth Snodgrass, YouTube video, May 25, 2009, https://www.youtube.com/watch?v=ywjrbGdsrO4 (accessed March 23, 2013). This is one of a series of video segments from a longer interview conducted by Snodgrass, a Detroit activist, writer, and videographer, in 1990. Snodgrass was a longtime comrade of Jimmy, beginning in the late 1960s.

52. Grace Lee Boggs, *Living for Change*, 93.

53. Lundberg, *America's Sixty Families*, 3–4.

54. James Boggs, "Conversations with James Boggs, #2."

55. Ibid.

56. James Boggs, *The American Revolution*, 11; Stephen M. Ward, ed., *Pages from a Black Radical's Notebook*, 84. Similar language appears in the subtitle of James Boggs's second book, *Racism and the Class Struggle: Further Pages from a Black Worker's Notebook*. He stopped working at Chrysler in 1968, thus when this book was published in 1970 he was no longer, at least in terms of current employment and activity, a factory worker. However, his nearly

thirty years as a factory worker remained an important part of his political identity and analysis. Additionally, the title presents this book as something of a sequel to *The American Revolution*, also published by Monthly Review Press. Reflecting the shifting landscape, and political language, of the period, the second volume uses the word "black" in the subtitle rather than "negro," which is used in the first.

57. James Boggs, "Conversations with James Boggs, #2."

58. Glaberman, *Wartime Strikes*, 80.

59. Ibid., 62.

60. While he consistently spoke of an association with the Communist Party, James Boggs would make conflicting statements in interviews given over the course of two decades about his actual membership in the party. In James Boggs, "Walking a Chalk Line," he says, "I always look at it like this: I never been a member of the Communist Party but if Communists have something good, that will make things good for me, well hell give me some of it. I don't care about the labels" (track 8). However, two decades later in an interview for the OHALC he declared, "I belonged to the CP first. I belonged to a group called AYD, American Youth for Democracy." He similarly claimed direct party membership in an interview with Ossie Davis and Ruby Dee for their television program *With Ossie and Ruby*, also in the early 1980s. Discussing his activities during the 1940s, he said, "Some people were around [the Communist Party], I was in it." Whatever his actual membership, the available evidence and the circumstances of his employment and union activities make clear that he had some interaction with the Communist Party and this was a component, however brief, of his early politicization.

61. Glaberman, *Wartime Strikes*, 73; Keeran, *The Communist Party and the Auto Workers Unions*, 234.

62. Isserman, *Which Side Were You On?*, 143.

63. Glaberman, *Wartime Strikes*, 73.

64. Moon, *Untold Tales, Unsung Heroes*, 153; Grace Lee Boggs, *Living for Change*, 95–96.

65. James Boggs interview in OHALC. In this interview Jimmy says he was a member of the AYD. Additionally, FBI-JB identifies him as a member. On March 22, 1946, an informant "furnished a list of 'American Youth for Democracy' members who had signed 1946 membership cards. Included on this list was the name James Boggs" (FBI-JB, Correlation Summary, December 23, 1966, 4).

66. "Preamble and Constitution of American Youth for Democracy" (published January 1947), JALC, Pamphlet A57-5.

67. According to Aileen Kraditor, the AYD "contained the same three types of members who made up the party: the cadre and official leaders, the true believers in the ranks, and the short term members who were never true believers." Jimmy fell into the third group, whom Kraditor says "did not even call themselves Communists." See Kraditor, *Jimmy Higgins*, 10.

68. Ibid., 2.

69. Grace explained that her husband "was always measured in his attitude toward the Soviet Union and the Communist Party, always careful to avoid any association with the anti-Communism of the power structure. . . . Like most of his friends (in Detroit) Jimmy

was aware that the American Communists had provided indispensable leadership in the struggle against Jim Crow and to create the unions" (*Living for Change*, 95–96).

70. Nicholas, *Questions of the American Revolution*, 2 (emphasis in original).

71. Richard Wright engages this in *Native Son*, *The Outsider*, and *Uncle Tom's Children*; Ralph Ellison in *Invisible Man*. Wright discussed his dissatisfaction with the Communist Party and his reasons for leaving it, and particularly his experiences as an aspiring writer in the party's John Reed Club, in his 1944 essay "I Tried to Be a Communist." Wright also took up his experiences with the Communist Party in his posthumously published book *American Hunger*, which was originally conceived as the second half of his autobiographical novel *Black Boy* (1945). The two are combined, thus restoring the full autobiography, in *Black Boy (American Hunger)*, published by the American Library in 1991.

72. Cruse, *The Crisis of the Negro Intellectual*. See also Watts, *Harold Cruse's "The Crisis of the Negro Intellectual" Reconsidered*; and Cobb, *The Essential Harold Cruse*.

73. Also published in 1976 was Charles H. Martin, *The Angelo Herndon Case and Southern Justice*. In the preface Martin writes that "the relationship between Communists and blacks" is a "thorny problem. Traditionally, most historians have treated Communist efforts as nothing more than crude, cynical attempts to exploit blacks for propaganda purposes without actually securing anything tangible for them" (xiii).

74. The view emphasizing CP manipulation and attempts to infiltrate black organizations is represented by two books authored by Wilson Record: *The Negro and the Communist Party* and *Race and Radicalism: The NAACP and the Communist Party in Conflict*. The latter appeared as part of a series of scholarly case studies on "the problem of 'Communism in American Life'" commissioned by the Fund for the Republic (*Race and Radicalism*, v). In that study Wilson asserted, "For over forty years the CP has tried to break what it conceived to be the weakest link in the American social chain, employing first one approach and then another to capture and direct the affairs of indigenous Negro organizations or, failing that, to establish competing groups of its own. The party has viewed racial conflict and unrest in the United States as issues on which a viable Communist movement might be built" (2). Scholarly challenge to and revision of this view emerged in the late 1960s, such as Carter, *Scottsboro*. Building on Carter's work, Martin sought further to demonstrate "that the reality was more complex than previously depicted and that Communists did sometimes produce results." Writing in 1976, he called for "a new synthesis . . . based not merely on rewriting old accounts but also on new research and detailed case studies" (*The Angelo Herndon Case and Southern Justice*, xiii).

Such works did indeed follow, and the study of the relationship between blacks and the Communist Party has achieved considerable analytical sophistication during the past three and a half decades. Three years after Martin's call came Painter's *Narrative of Hosea Hudson*. This was followed by two groundbreaking books: Naison, *Communists in Harlem during the Depression*; and Kelley, *Hammer and Hoe*. These works demonstrated the value of examining the inner lives of black Communists and the work of the party in black communities. The end of the 1990s saw the publication of four works of literary history that brought fresh interpretations of the cultural worlds and products emerging from the early and mid-twentieth-century interactions between blacks and the Communist

Party: Solomon, *Their Cry Was Unity*; Maxwell, *New Negro, Old Left*; Mullen, *Popular Fronts*; and Smethurst, *The New Red Negro*. Subsequent works extended the study of the black-CP relationship into the postwar era, uncovering the connections, influences, and interactions between the Communist Left and younger activists and artists in the postwar black freedom struggle. Two important works in this regard are Biondi, *To Stand and Fight*; and Smethurst, *The Black Arts Movement*. A recent study that considers the relationship between African Americans and the Communist Party within a larger argument about the failure of various socialists and Marxists during the 1920s–1930s and the 1960s–1970s to fully account for race and enjoin black struggle is Dawson, *Blacks In and Out of the Left*.

A range of biographical studies has similarly expanded the scholarship on blacks and the CP by examining the activism and intellectual trajectories of black radicals who were members of or at some point affiliated with the party. Among them are three works by Horne, *Black Liberation/Red Scare*, *Race Woman*, and *Red Seas*; Davies, *Left of Karl Marx*; Lewis, Nash, and Leab, *Red Activists and Black Freedom*; and Ransby, *Eslanda*.

Four books published between 2011 and 2012 signal yet another stage in historical scholarship on the relationship between blacks, and particularly intellectuals, and the CP. Gore's *Radicalism at the Crossroads* and McDuffie's *Sojourning for Freedom* examine the largely neglected experiences and contributions of black women in or associated with the CP and Communist-affiliated organizations. Through their examination of different sets of organizations, activist campaigns, publications, and other political experiences, the two books make separate but complementary arguments about black women's political practices and the place of the CP in the development and genealogy of black feminist politics. Makalani's *In the Cause of Freedom* brings fresh insights to a familiar time period by providing a detailed account of the organizational, ideological, and institutional spaces within which black radicals in the Communist International forged an internationalist politics and movement. Gellman's *Death Blow to Jim Crow* shines light on the CP-black relationship during the Depression and World War II through a case study of the National Negro Congress and its effort to craft a protest model for the emerging postwar movement.

Also noteworthy are recent debates in two journals over black anti-Communism as an aspect of the larger debate over the relationship between blacks and the CP and the role of the party in racial struggles. The Winter 2006 (vol. 3, no. 4) issue of *Labor: Studies in Working-Class History of the Americas* features a forum on Eric Arnesen's article "No 'Graver Danger': Black Anticommunism, the Communist Party, and the Race Question" with responses from Martha Biondi, Carol Anderson, John Earl Haynes, and Kenneth R. Janken. More recently, *American Communist History* devoted its April 2012 issue (vol. 11, no. 1) to a symposium on Arnesen's article "Civil Rights and the Cold War at Home: Postwar Activism, Anticommunism, and the Decline of the Left" with responses from Dayo Gore, Alex Lichtenstein, Judith Stein, and Robert H. Zieger.

75. Beth Bates gives a nice picture of this context through her discussion of the Detroit local of the National Negro Congress in *The Making of Black Detroit in the Age of Henry Ford*, 201–5, and also in her "'Double V for Victory.'" Other important studies providing analysis of Detroit black politics in this period are Dillard, *Faith in the City*; and Miller, "The Color of Citizenship."

76. James Boggs interview in OHALC.

77. According to James Boggs's FBI file, a letter dated April 15, 1946, "indicated that Jim Boggs, accompanied by two men from Chrysler had attended an SWP forum on Sunday." The same report describes "a list of names of individuals who were members of the SWP, East Side Branch, Detroit. This list included the name of Jim Boggs and indicated that he used the Party name of Ross" (FBI-JB, Correlation Summary, December 23, 1966, 4). If these reports of James Boggs's membership in the AYD (cited above) and the SWP are accurate, he would have been a member of both at approximately the same time.

78. James Boggs interview in OHALC.

79. "By the late 1940s," writes historian Kevin Boyle, the UAW and other CIO unions "had become simply another special-interest group." See Boyle, *The UAW and the Heyday of American Liberalism*, 2.

80. "The Rise and Fall of the Union" is the title of chapter 1 of James Boggs, *The American Revolution*, published in 1963. "The End of an Epoch in the UAW" is the title of a talk he delivered in 1961. For both, see Stephen M. Ward, ed., *Pages from a Black Radical's Notebook*, 85, 17, respectively.

81. Moon, *Untold Tales, Unsung Heroes*, 154.

82. Richard W. Thomas, *Life for Us Is What We Make It*, 127–31; Neusom, "The Michigan Civil Rights Law and Its Enforcement."

83. Richard W. Thomas, *Life for Us Is What We Make It*, 127.

84. Neusom, "The Michigan Civil Rights Law and Its Enforcement," 39.

85. Miller, "The Color of Citizenship," 301.

86. "Detroit Conference Largest in History," *Crisis*, August 1937, 250; Richard W. Thomas, *Life for Us Is What We Make It*, 130.

87. Shockley, *We, Too, Are Americans*, 178–81.

88. Howe and Widick, *The UAW and Walter Reuther*, 230.

89. Neusom, "The Michigan Civil Rights Law and Its Enforcement," 7; Moon, *Untold Tales, Unsung Heroes*, 53, 158–59, 258.

90. This description of how the DAC worked is drawn from a document titled "Discrimination Action Committee" in Dillard Papers, Box 1, Folder 44; Neusom, "The Michigan Civil Rights Law and Its Enforcement," 16–17; the oral histories of Dillard and Boggs in Moon, *Untold Tales, Unsung Heroes*; Arthur Johnson's oral history in Mast, *Detroit Lives*; and Arthur L. Johnson, *Race and Remembrance*, 213–14.

91. Quote in Neusom, "The Michigan Civil Rights Law and Its Enforcement," 28.

92. "Jim Crow Broken" and "Discrimination Action Committee" in Dillard Papers, Box 1, Folder 44. See also Fine, *Expanding the Frontiers of Civil Rights*.

93. Nicholas, *Questions of the American Revolution*, 9.

94. Moon, *Untold Tales, Unsung Heroes*, 154–55.

95. Unlabeled document reporting on a meeting held at the YMCA on Saturday, April 1, 1950, Dillard Papers, Box 1, Folder 44. They were among at least a dozen autoworkers representing their local unions.

96. Dillard interview in Moon, *Untold Tales, Unsung Heroes*, 157–58; quote on 158. For more on Dillard, see Dillard, *Faith in the City*, 209–14, 216, 231.

97. Moon, *Untold Tales, Unsung Heroes*, 159.

98. Ibid., 158–60.

99. Owens originally wrote the book under the pen name Matthew Ward, and it appeared as Matthew Ward, *Indignant Heart* (New York: New Books, 1952). Subsequent editions appeared under the pen name Charles Denby, including the edition cited here: Charles Denby, *Indignant Heart: A Black Worker's Journal* (Detroit: Wayne State University Press, 1989).

100. Denby, *Indignant Heart*, 149.

101. Constance Webb and Grace Lee Boggs both report, in their respective memoirs, that Webb wrote *Indignant Heart*: Webb, *Not Without Love*, 247, 249–50, 266; and Grace Lee Boggs, *Living for Change*, 62.

CHAPTER 3

1. Grace Lee Boggs, "Our Country," xvii. This is the text of a speech she delivered on May 15, 1999, at the Asian American Student Center, University of Minnesota.

2. Grace Lee Boggs, *Living for Change*, 16. She made a similar comment in an oral history interview during the early 1990s. At the beginning of the interview, she states, "Insofar as I would say that there are some influences with regard to myself from [my parents], it would be that my mother was a rebel form the very beginning, and my father had . . . some ties with Sun Yat-sen and some consciousness with regard to the need for revolutionary struggle in China." "Transcript of Oral History Interview with Grace Lee Boggs," Boggs Papers, Box 9, Folder "James, C. L. R." This is the transcript of her interview in the Tamiment Library and Robert F. Wagner Labor Archives, New York University.

3. Grace Lee Boggs, "Our Country," xviii.

4. Yung, Chang, and Lai, *Chinese American Voices*, 225.

5. Political scientist Cedric J. Robinson describes the combination of these two developments as leading to the "rewhitening of America." See chapter 2, "In the Year 1915: D. W. Griffith and the Rewhitening of America," in Robinson, *Forgeries of Memory and Meaning*.

6. Sullivan, *Lift Every Voice*, 48–50.

7. Shehong Chen, *Being Chinese, Becoming Chinese American*, 75.

8. For a fuller explication of this argument, see ibid., chapter 3, "Constructing a Chinese American Identity, 1915."

9. For the significance and scale of migration from Toishan (Taishan), see Hsu, *Dreaming of Gold, Dreaming of Home*. See also Erika Lee, *At America's Gates*, 112, 114; Chang, *The Chinese in America*, 170, 216.

10. On Chinese exclusion see Erika Lee, *At America's Gates*; Hsu, *Dreaming of Gold, Dreaming of Home*, chapter 3.

11. On the paper son system see Erika Lee, *At America's Gates*, 4–5, 194–95, 203–7; Hsu, *Dreaming of Gold, Dreaming of Home*, 74–85; Takaki, *Strangers from a Different Shore*, 235; Chang, *The Chinese in America*, 146–47.

12. Grace Lee Boggs, *Living for Change*, 1–4.

13. Grace Lee Boggs interview with author (March 23, 2005).

14. Ibid.; Grace Lee Boggs, *Living for Change*, 4–5.

15. Shehong Chen, *Being Chinese, Becoming Chinese American*, 14.

16. Mark and Chih, *A Place Called Chinese America*, caption on 61.

17. Shehong Chen, *Being Chinese, Becoming Chinese American*, 14; Tung, *The Chinese in America*, 25.

18. Erika Lee, *At America's Gates*, tables on 99 and 101.

19. The chances are remote that she was classified in any of the other categories in which Chinese women immigrants were recorded for that year: student, U.S. citizen, and daughter of merchant.

20. Takaki, *Strangers from a Different Shore*, 234.

21. Erika Lee provides an especially thoughtful discussion of Chinese immigrant women, including a section on exclusions, gender, and sexuality (*At America's Gates*, 92–100).

22. Fessler, *Chinese in America*, 187.

23. Ibid.; Takaki, *Strangers from a Different Shore*, 230–33. Takaki gives these figures: "By 1920, 58 percent of Chinese were in services, mostly restaurants and laundry work, compared to only 5 percent for native whites and 10 percent for foreign whites. Only 9 percent of Chinese were employed in manufacturing, compared to 26 percent for native whites and 47 percent for foreign whites. . . . Chinese workers had been crowded into a Chinese ethnic economy" (240).

24. Grace Lee Boggs, *Living for Change*, 9.

25. Ibid., 8.

26. Lew, *The Chinese in North America*, 42. The statement appears in the caption for a photo of Chin Lee's.

27. Iris Chang writes that most of these restaurants "were tiny mom-and-pop enterprises in which the owner worked as cook and dishwasher and his wife—if he had one—as the waitress and cashier. A few Chinese with sufficient capital rented their own buildings, installed expensive Asian décor, and hired battalions of chefs, waiters, and hostesses" (*The Chinese in America*, 163).

28. Kung, *Chinese in American Life*, 57, 182; Julia I. Hsuan Chen, "The Chinese in New York," 53–54; Takaki, *Strangers from a Different Shore*, 240.

29. Grace Lee Boggs, *Living for Change*, 14–15.

30. Ibid., 14.

31. Grace Lee Boggs interview with author (March 23, 2005).

32. Grace Lee Boggs, *Living for Change*, 15.

33. Shehong Chen, *Becoming Chinese, Becoming Chinese American*, 121.

34. Grace Lee Boggs, *Living for Change*, 10.

35. Ibid., 5.

36. Ibid., 5–6.

37. Grace Lee Boggs interview with author (March 23, 2005).

38. Ibid.

39. Ibid.; Grace Lee Boggs, *Living for Change*, 5, 13.

40. Historian Shehong Chen pinpoints the year 1911 as a key moment in the "transformation of traditional Chinese identity" characterized by an intense nationalist discourse and "the search for modern China" (*Becoming Chinese, Becoming Chinese American*, 10).

41. Chang, *The Chinese in America*, 159.

42. Grace Lee Boggs, *Living for Change*, 16.

43. Ibid.

44. Ibid., 6, 16 (quote appears on 10); Shehong Chen, *Becoming Chinese, Becoming Chinese American*, 10.

45. Grace Lee Boggs interview with author (March 23, 2005); Grace Lee Boggs, *Living for Change*, 10–11.

46. Takaki, *Strangers from a Different Shore*, 245–46.

47. Ibid.

48. Grace Lee Boggs, *Living for Change*, 11. She adds that avoiding Chinatown may have also been a matter of safety because of the violence associated with the tongs, which were secret societies involved with drug distribution, gambling, and prostitution.

49. Grace Lee Boggs interview with author (March 23, 2005); Grace Lee Boggs, *Living for Change*, 13–14.

50. Grace Lee Boggs, *Living for Change*, 12–13.

51. Ibid., 9.

52. Ibid., 10 (emphasis in original).

53. Ibid., 192–93.

54. Ibid., 10. She also discusses the impact of this repeated query on her consciousness at the beginning of her interview in the OHALC.

55. Grace Lee Boggs, *Living for Change*, 10.

56. Ibid.

57. Zia, *Asian American Dreams*, 9.

58. Interestingly, Grace and Zia both received the Legacy Award from the Museum of the Chinese in America in New York in 2002.

59. Comparative literature and Asian American studies scholar Lisa Lowe describe this as "the *contradictions* of Asian immigration." Lowe writes that since the middle of the nineteenth century "the American *citizen* has been defined over against the Asian *immigrant*, legally, economically, and culturally. These definitions have cast Asian immigrants both as persons and populations to be integrated into the national political sphere and as the contradictory, confusing, and unintelligible elements to be marginalized and returned to their alien origins" (*Immigrant Acts*, 8, 4 [emphasis in original]).

60. Reflecting on his childhood in 1930s San Francisco, Victor Wong explained that in the mind of white Americans "we *were* all immigrants in those days, no matter where we were born" (Takaki, *Strangers from a Different Shore*, 268 [emphasis in original]). This view is confirmed by Kit King Louis, a scholar studying the "problems of American-born Chinese" during the early 1930s, who found that "in spite of the fact that they are legally and qualitatively American citizens," Chinese Americans "are treated to all intents and purposes by the Americans as if they were aliens" ("Problems of Second Generation

Chinese," 256). Even in American jurisprudence, where the matter should have been settled by the Fifteenth Amendment to the Constitution, the question of American nationality for a person of Chinese descent born in the United States lingered in the courts until 1898, less than two decades before Grace's birth, when the Supreme Court finally ruled in *United States v. Wong* that a person born in the United States of Chinese parents was indeed of American nationality by birth (Tung, *The Chinese in America*, 21).

61. Grace Lee Boggs, *Living for Change*, 21.

62. Ibid., 25.

63. Ibid. The careers of Buck and Wong, along with analyses of their representations of China, Chinese Americans, and the relations between the two countries during the 1930s and 1940s, are thoughtfully presented in Leong, *The China Mystique*. Leong argues that the lives of Buck, Wong, and Soong (whom most Americans knew as Madame Chiang Kai-shek) illustrate the "romanticized, progressive, and highly gendered image of China" that emerged during the late 1930s, which Leong terms the "China mystique" (1).

64. Leong, *The China Mystique*, 2, 57.

65. Grace Lee Boggs, *Living for Change*, 11.

66. Grace has suggested that part of the reason is that she was the owner's daughter and thus class distinctions prevented her from forming close ties (Grace Lee Boggs interview with author [March 23, 2005]). Though, of course, she also indicated that the restaurant was like family, and some of the workers were in fact relatives.

67. Grace Lee Boggs, *Living for Change*, 25.

68. Grace frequently identified such books. For one example, in 2009 she briefly discussed four books that "have especially sustained my activism over the years": Confucius, *The Analects of Confucius*; Georg W. F. Hegel, *The Phenomenology of Mind*; Immanuel Wallerstein, *The Modern World System I: Capitalist Agriculture and Origins of the European World Economy in the Sixteenth Century*; and Lewis Mumford, *The City in History: Its Origins, Its Transformations, and Its Prospects*. See Grace Lee Boggs, "Movement Reading."

69. Grace Lee Boggs, *Living for Change*, 75. While the book is a landmark in feminist thought, it is also steeped in a turn-of-the-twentieth-century discourse on civilization and its attendant assumptions about white racial superiority and a commitment to racial hierarchy. Gail Bederman provides an insightful discussion of Gilman's use of civilization discourse and racial ideology in *Women and Economics* and in her other writings in Bederman, *Manliness and Civilization*, chapter 4.

70. Grace Lee Boggs, *Living for Change*, 25; Grace Lee Boggs interview with author (March 23, 2005).

71. Ibid.

72. Grace Lee Boggs, *Living for Change*, 25.

73. She describes the experience in ibid, 37. In 2010, seventy-eight years after hearing Reid, she again recalled the event in her weekly column, also titled "Living for Change," published in the *Michigan Citizen*, a Detroit weekly newspaper. There she wrote, "When I was an undergraduate in the early 1930s, I heard Ira D. Reid speak at a weekend college conference and learned truths about the African American experience which I felt had been kept from me. At the time I was in my teens. So Dr. Reid (1901–1968), who was in his 30s

and director of research for the Urban League, seemed much older and wiser than I would ever be. I never met Reid again. But today, 80 years later, when I talk to students, I recall the impact he had on me and wonder whether decades hence they will remember me the way I remember Reid." Grace Lee Boggs, "Living for Change."

74. Grace Lee Boggs, "My Philosophic Journey" (unpublished manuscript in author's possession), 2.

75. Grace Lee Boggs, *Living for Change*, 26.

76. Ibid., 27.

77. Ibid.

78. In her autobiography, Grace writes that there were only two other women of color on campus during her years at Barnard: Louise Chin, a Chinese American also in the graduating class of 1935 whose family owned a small laundry near Grace's house; and Grace Ijima, a Japanese American in the class of 1934 (ibid., 18). In 2000, on a visit to Barnard during which she was named a distinguished alumna, Grace learned that a fourth woman of color, Jean Blackwell Hutson, was also her classmate. Hutson became the second African American (after Zora Neale Hurston) to graduate from Barnard. Hutson's distinguished career as a librarian and intellectual included serving as curator for the Schomburg Center for Research in Black Culture in New York.

79. Ibid., 12.

80. Ibid., 25.

81. Grace Lee Boggs, "My Philosophic Journey," 3.

82. Grace Lee Boggs, *Living for Change*, 27.

83. Ibid.

84. Krutch, *The Modern Temper*, 19.

85. Grace Lee Boggs, *Living for Change*, 28.

86. Ibid., 29.

87. Ibid.

88. On Weiss see Hahn, *The Philosophy of Paul Weiss*.

89. Grace Lee Boggs, *Living for Change*, 29.

90. Ibid., 30.

91. Ibid.; see also Grace Lee Boggs, "My Philosophic Journey," 3.

92. Grace Lee Boggs, *Living for Change*, 31.

93. Blackburn, *Oxford Dictionary of Philosophy*, 16. In his guide to understanding Hegel, David James identifies freedom as a central theme of Hegel's thought (David James, *Hegel*, 1–2).

94. Grace Lee Boggs, "Coming Full Circle" (unpublished manuscript in author's possession), 2.

95. Quoted in Robinson, *Black Marxism*, 73–74. Citing this and other passages, Robinson explains that "Hegel privileged Western Civilization in his historical philosophy, citing the absence of Reason elsewhere. . . . For Hegel, ultimately, the historical development of the species-being was discoverable only in Europe" (Robinson, *An Anthropology of Marxism*, 96).

96. Grace Lee Boggs, *Living for Change*, 31–32.

97. She subsequently had the work published as a book: Grace Chin Lee, *George Herbert Mead*.

98. Ibid., v.

99. Ibid., vi.

100. Ibid., 1.

101. Grace Lee Boggs, *Living for Change*, 33–34.

102. Ibid., 34.

103. Takaki, *Strangers from a Different Shore*, 265.

104. Ibid., 267.

105. Kung, *Chinese in American Life*, 57.

106. Takaki, *Strangers from a Different Shore*, 267.

107. Ibid.

108. Ibid. Kung reports that there were 190 Chinese and Chinese American professors in U.S. colleges and universities between 1935 and 1944 (*Chinese in American Life*, 192).

109. Grace Lee Boggs, *Living for Change*, 34.

110. Ibid.

111. Grace Lee Boggs to Horace Cayton, November 22, 1963, Paine Papers (unprocessed), Box 2, Folder "1962–1963 Grace, Reply."

112. Grace Lee Boggs interview in OHALC.

113. Grace Lee Boggs, "My Philosophic Journey," 3–4; Grace Lee Boggs, *Living for Change*, 34–35.

114. Grace Lee Boggs, *Living for Change*, 35.

115. Ibid.

116. Ibid., 36.

117. Ibid.

CHAPTER 4

1. Grace Lee Boggs interview in OHALC; Grace Lee Boggs, "My Philosophic Journey," 4; Grace Lee Boggs, *Living for Change*, 36.

2. For fuller descriptions and analysis of Trotskyism, see Breitman, Le Blanc, and Wald, *Trotskyism in the United States*; Wald, *The New York Intellectuals*; Callinicos, *Trotskyism*; and Alexander, *International Trotskyism*.

3. Phelps, "C. L. R. James and the Theory of State Capitalism," 158–59.

4. Grace Lee Boggs, *Living for Change*, 42.

5. Ibid. She is somewhat circumspect about the full nature of their relationship in her autobiography, telling us in passing and somewhat cryptically that "what became for me a relatively casual affair became an obsession for him, forcing me to break off all contact" (ibid., 42).

6. They published the series under their party names: Harry Allen and Ria Stone, "World War 1 in Retrospect: An Historical Examination," *New International*, June–July 1942. Grace suggests in her autobiography that Abern wrote the articles alone, despite both names appearing in the byline. See Grace Lee Boggs, *Living for Change*, 274n11.

7. The series appeared under the name Ria Stone in four successive issues of *The New International*: "China: Colossus of the East" (February, 1944), "The China of Chiang Kai-Shek" (March 1944), "China Under the Stalinists" (April 1944), and "China Under Japanese Domination" (May 1944).

8. Grace Lee Boggs, *Living for Change*, 42.

9. Ibid., 39–40.

10. Ibid., 40.

11. Drake and Cayton, *Black Metropolis*, 380; Bates, *Pullman Porters and the Rise of Protest Politics in Black America*, 112.

12. Drake and Cayton, *Black Metropolis*, 380, 603.

13. Grace Lee Boggs, *Living for Change*, 37.

14. She later recalled the circumstances in a letter to Horace Cayton: Grace Lee Boggs to Horace Cayton, November 22, 1963, Paine Papers (unprocessed), Box 2, Folder "1962–1963 Grace, Reply." See also Grace Lee Boggs, *Living for Change*, 37–38.

15. Finding Aid to Horace R. Cayton Papers, Vivian G. Harsh Research Collection of Afro-American History and Literature, Chicago Public Library; Lawrence P. Jackson, *The Indignant Generation*, 96.

16. Grace Lee Boggs, *Living for Change*, 37–38.

17. Grace Lee Boggs to Horace Cayton, November 22, 1963.

18. Grace Lee Boggs, "My Philosophic Journey," 4; Grace Lee Boggs, *Living for Change*, 39.

19. Quoted in Jervis Anderson, *A. Philip Randolph*, 248.

20. Ibid., 250.

21. Garfinkel, *When Negroes March*, 38–66.

22. Anderson, *A. Philip Randolph*, 251.

23. Garfinkel, *When Negroes March*, 6.

24. Garfinkel says the MOWM was "the outstanding mass protest organization in the Negro community in 1941 and 1942" (*When Negroes March*, 112).

25. Bates, *Pullman Porters and the Rise of Protest Politics in Black America*, 155. Bates demonstrates the centrality of grassroots organizing to the MOWM and shows how it was enabled by or drew from BSCP chapters, networks, activists, and experience nationally (*Pullman Porters and the Rise of Protest Politics in Black America*, 148–74). Garfinkel says "a vast amount of organizational work" was required to build the movement (*When Negroes March*, 41).

26. *Chicago Defender*, February 15, 1941, 7; *Amsterdam News*, February 15, 1941, 13.

27. As an important community institution, the *Defender* served as a vital source of information and means of communication for both the local and the national black communities, as well as for activists like Grace. She regularly read the *Defender* and recalled that "everyone in the radical movement read the *Defender*, the *Courier*, and the *Afro-American*" (Grace Lee Boggs interview with author). Her statement refers to the three most widely read black newspapers, each with a national circulation: the *Chicago Defender*, the *Pittsburgh Courier*, and the *Baltimore Afro-American*. During this period Horace Cayton wrote a column for the *Pittsburgh Courier*, including several pieces devoted to Randolph and the MOWM.

28. Editorial, "Crusade for Democracy," *Chicago Defender*, June 28, 1941, 14.

29. Bates, *Pullman Porters and the Rise of Protest Politics in Black America*, 165–66.

30. Ibid., 164–65.

31. Garfinkel, *When Negroes March*, 89.

32. Quoted in ibid., 88. Garfinkel adds that there was "almost total involvement of the Negroes in the MOWM demonstrations" (91).

33. *Pittsburgh Courier*, July 4, 1942, 14; Garfinkel, *When Negroes March*, 90–91.

34. Garfinkel, *When Negroes March*, 93; "fighting spirit" is from George F. McCray, "12,000 in Chicago Voice Demands for Democracy," *Chicago Defender*, July 4, 1942, 3.

35. McCray, "12,000 in Chicago Voice Demands for Democracy," 3; "Chicago Decorated for Monster Rally," *Amsterdam News*, June 27, 1942, 5; George F. McCray, "Chicago March-on-Washington Meeting Cheers, Randolph, White, Webster," *Amsterdam News*, July 4, 1942, 2.

36. McCray, "12,000 in Chicago Voice Demands for Democracy," 3.

37. Bates, *Pullman Porters and the Rise of Protest Politics in Black America*, 165.

38. Quoted in ibid., 165.

39. Garfinkel, *When Negroes March*, 109.

40. McCray, "12,000 in Chicago Voice Demands for Democracy," 3.

41. The WP's analysis of MOWM was shaped and clouded by its rivalry with the CP. The WP overplayed the CP's role in the MOWM, misread the racial politics of the National Negro Congress (which it took to be nothing more than a CP front), and ignored A. Philip Randolph's rocky relationship with—and even hostility to—the CP. Indeed, the WP's criticism of Randolph was particularly problematic. Their charge that he was in tune with the Communists was laughable. In fact, his long record of activism showed an aversion to the CP, and he had recently resigned from the leadership of the National Negro Congress in protest of the Communists' role in that organization. Randolph bitterly opposed Communist participation in the MOWM and took clear steps to exclude them.

42. Ria Stone, "'March on Washington' Movement Stirs Again," *Labor Action*, June 8, 1942, 1.

43. In fact, Randolph's policy of excluding white membership in the MOWM was less an expression of black nationalism than a pragmatic and to some extent ideological decision, designed both to galvanize black political resolve and to help deter Communist involvement. Thus, the two movements did share a commitment to building mass (and largely working-class) movements with all-black memberships, but Randolph's decision to exclude white membership was made for very different reasons from those of Garvey. Contemporaries during the 1920s, Randolph initially worked with Garvey and had praise for the efforts of his Universal Negro Improvement Association, but ultimately the two men diverged significantly in their political programs and economic philosophies. Randolph eventually became one of the black leaders who opposed Garvey—even leading the "Garvey Must Go" campaign in Harlem. Bates provides a thoughtful discussion of Randolph's relationship to Garvey's black nationalism and his insistence on the MOWM remaining all black (*Pullman Porters and the Rise of Protest Politics in Black America*, 167–71). Also see Garfinkel, *When Negroes March*, 128–30.

44. Ria Stone, "A Labor Base for Negro Struggles," *New International*, August 1942, 207–8.

45. Ibid., 208.

46. Ibid. On the decline see Bates, *Pullman Porters and the Rise of Protest Politics in Black America*; Garfinkel, *When Negroes March*.

47. Ria Stone, "A Labor Base for Negro Struggles," *New International*, August 1942. Her comments can easily be read as failing to recognize the vitality and importance of religion in black communities. While she would later develop a more nuanced understanding of black religious experience, in 1942 her view was likely informed by a standard radical view of religion as the opiate of the masses.

48. Drake, "Profiles: Chicago," 268.

49. *Pittsburgh Courier*, July 4, 1942.

50. Anthony Marcus explains that a "tendency" in Trotskyist organizations "refers to a politically defined group, usually within a political party or organization, that does not have factional intent but subscribes to a certain political worldview that may not be shared by the entire organization." This is distinguished from a "faction," which "refers to an internal group within a party or organization that seeks political change in the party and is willing to wage a battle for this change. Factional struggles usually lead to splits" (*Malcolm X and the Third American Revolution*, 19).

51. This biographical information is drawn from Rosengarten, *Urbane Revolutionary*; Paul Buhle, *C. L. R. James: The Artist as Revolutionary*; and Worcester, *C. L. R. James*. See also Bogues, *Caliban's Freedom*; Paul Buhle, *C. L. R. James: His Life and Work*; Cudjoe and Cain, *C. L. R. James*; Glaberman, *Marxism for Our Times*; Grimshaw, *The C. L. R. James Reader*; Grimshaw and Hart, *American Civilization*; McLemee, *C. L. R. James on the "Negro Question"*; McLemee and Le Blanc, *C. L. R. James and Revolutionary Marxism*; Robinson, *Black Marxism*, 241–86.

52. Rosengarten, *Urbane Revolutionary*, very effectively traces the development of these two spaces. Also see Hill, "In England, 1932–1938," for an insightful discussion of the genesis and early formation of this "conjuncture of Pan-African agitation and organized Trotskyism" and the ways it pointed to "the type of organized political activity which would characterize the rest of [C. L. R.'s] entire political career, namely *the small Marxist organization*" (69, emphasis in original).

53. Paul Buhle, *C. L. R. James: The Artist as Revolutionary*, 62.

54. Rosengarten, *Urbane Revolutionary*, 17.

55. See Makalani, *In the Cause of Freedom*, especially 213–18; also see the introduction by Robin D. G. Kelley to C. L. R. James, *A History of Pan-African Revolt*, in addition to the various biographical studies of C. L. R. cited above.

56. See McLemee, *C. L. R. James on the "Negro Question,"* xvii–xxiii, 3–16; Breitman, *Leon Trotsky on Black Nationalism and Self-Determination*.

57. McLemee, *C. L. R. James on the "Negro Question,"* xxiii.

58. Hill, "Literary Executor's Afterword," 304.

59. Grace Lee Boggs, *Living for Change*, 43.

60. This statement is from a letter that C. L. R. wrote to JFT member Martin Glaberman on December 17, 1962, recounting the history of their collaboration after a split in the

organization ended their political relationship. The letter is reprinted in Glaberman, *Marxism for Our Times*, 72–85 (the quotation appears on 81).

61. Scott McLemee reinforces this point when he notes, "The cooperative nature of [the JFT's work] has often been neglected in the rush to celebrate James as a genius" ("Afterword," 217). Paul Buhle makes a similar observation in *C. L. R. James: His Life and Work*. In an essay titled "The Marxism of C. L. R. James," longtime C. L. R. comrade Martin Glaberman identifies three levels on which the organization, by which he means JFT and its successor groups, "was an integral element in the development of [C. L. R.'s] ideas. On one level there was the sharing of work and the production of work that would have been beyond the capacity of any individual. . . . But the significance of organization was far beyond the assistance of individuals. When James said he was not afraid to make mistakes, it was because he knew there was an organization that would sustain its members, would correct mistakes, and he encouraged the members of his group to take risks in the development of their ideas. . . . But an organization meant much more than this. It was the way to participate in class and other struggles. It was the way to see and meet and understand workers who were fighting the class struggle in their daily lives, blacks who were struggling for freedom and equality, women who were trying to transform the social reality of gender in modern society, young people who were battling the oppression and restriction of youth." The essay is cited in Staughton Lynd, *Martin Glaberman*, 187.

62. The letter is cited in Grimshaw, "Introduction," 10.

63. Grace Lee Boggs, *Living for Change*, 61.

64. Ibid., 60–61.

65. Grace Lee Boggs interview in OHALC.

66. Grace Lee Boggs, *Living for Change*, 51–54.

67. Ibid., 52.

68. Ibid.

69. Ibid., 53; Grace Lee Boggs interview with author.

70. Richard Feldman, introduction to *Conversations in Maine*, xv–xvi.

71. Grace Lee Boggs, *Living for Change*, 147.

72. Freddy Paine, "All Living Is Politics—It Embraces Everything," Paine Papers (unprocessed), Box 1, Folder "Correspondence, etc., Lyman." This document includes a biographical statement about Lyman written by Freddy, an interview that Lyman gave in 1941, and an autobiographical sketch that Lyman wrote in 1947 on the occasion of his Harvard School of Architecture twenty-fifth reunion.

73. Grace Lee Boggs, *Living for Change*, 147.

74. Ibid., 148–49, 174.

75. Grace Lee Boggs, "C. L. R. James," 164. A similar passage appears in Grace Lee Boggs, *Living for Change*, 48.

76. Grace Lee Boggs, "When C. L. R. Was a Part of Our Lives—And We of His," Boggs Papers, Box 9, Folder "James, C.L.R.—Correspondence, Speeches, Obituaries." This is the text of a speech Grace delivered on July 7, 1989, in New York City at "An Evening in Memory of C. L. R. James," sponsored by the Coalition for Caribbean and Central American Unity and WBAI Radio.

77. C. L. R. James to Marty Glaberman, January 3, 1963, reproduced in Glaberman, *Marxism for Our Times*, 90. In a footnote to this statement, Glaberman writes that 629 Hudson Street "provided a home for the Johnson-Forest Tendency" (128n16).

78. C. L. R. James to Lyman Paine, December 1, 1976, Paine Papers, Box 1, Folder 21.

79. Raya Dunayevskaya interview in OHALC; Kellner, "Raya Dunayevskaya," 205; Rosengarten, *Urbane Revolutionary*, 67.

80. Grace Lee Boggs interview in OHALC.

81. Martin Glaberman interview in OHALC.

82. Ibid.

83. For some contextualization and a sampling of her work during and after this period, see Selma James, *Sex, Race, and Class*. For a discussion specifically of Selma James's contributions to the JFT and to C. L. R. James, see Rosengarten, *Urbane Revolutionary*, 89–94.

84. Selma James, "Striving for Clarity and Influence: The Political Legacy of C. L. R. James (2001–2012)," in *Sex, Race, and Class*, 285, 288–289.

85. Grace frequently used this phrase, including as the title of a talk she delivered at the "C. L. R. James: The American Years" conference at Brown University in April 1993. The text of the speech was published as Grace Lee Boggs, "Thinking and Acting Dialectically."

86. The most recent scholarly assessment of the book is McClendon, *C. L. R. James's "Notes on Dialectics."* One of the first close readings of *Notes on Dialectics* is found in Robinson, *Black Marxism*, 278–85.

87. The work appeared in mimeographed form as C. L. R. James, *Notes on Dialectics: Hegel and Marxism* (Detroit: Friends of Facing Reality, 1966); and *Notes on Dialectics: Hegel and Marxism*, 2nd ed. (Detroit: Friends of Facing Reality, 1971). In its published book form, the work has appeared as *Notes on Dialectics: Hegel, Marx, Lenin* (Westport, Conn.: Lawrence Hill, 1980); and *Notes on Dialectics: Hegel, Marx, Lenin* (London: Allison and Busby, 1980). For a discussion of the book's origins as "The Nevada Document" and an analysis of its content, see Paul Buhle, *C. L. R. James: The Artist as Revolutionary*, 92–93. Grace Lee Boggs discusses the work in relation to the other studying and writing that the JFT and particularly she, C. L. R., and Dunayevskaya were undertaking at the time (*Living for Change*, 59). For additional (and competing) assessments of the work and its place in C. L. R.'s body of work and in the Johnson-Forest Tendency, see Turner, "Epistemology, Absolutes, and the Party"; Roderick, "Further Adventures of the Dialectic"; and Glaberman, "The Marxism of C. L. R. James." See also McClendon, *C. L. R. James's "Notes on Dialectics."*

88. Rosengarten briefly discusses their influence on C. L. R.'s thinking regarding Hegel and on the text in *Urbane Revolutionary*, 30.

89. For example, the following description of the book reflects the view of the text as singular: "In *Notes on Dialectics*, James set out to teach his followers how to use Hegel's *Science of Logic*. Dialectical reason, he explained, was a way of thinking which reflected the movement of the object of thought, the world in which we live. Analytical thinking and common sense can only identify what is or has been; but the dialectic, in contrast, enables us to imagine a different future by combining speculation with knowledge in the context of action" (Grimshaw and Hart, "*American Civilization*: An Introduction," 12). Grace Lee Boggs acknowledges in *Living for Change* her appreciation for *Notes on Dialectics*, but she

contextualizes and situates that recognition within the shared efforts and contributions within the group. In particular, she first explains that Dunayevskaya made a prior contribution to their collective study of Hegel when she translated Lenin's notes on Hegel and adds that this translation inspired C. L. R.'s *Notes on Dialectics*. Grace Lee Boggs then writes, "I will always be grateful to Raya for making Lenin's notes on Hegel accessible. . . . Together Lenin's notes on Hegel and CLR's *Notes on Dialectics* taught me that, in times of crisis or transition in any organization, movement, or society, it is a matter of life and death for the organization, movement, or society, to recognize that reality is constantly changing, that the contradictions present in everything are bound to develop and become antagonistic, and therefore that ideas or strategies that were progressive and mind-opening at one point have become abstractions and fixations. At such times revolutionary leadership must have the audacity to break free of old ideas or strategies and create a new vision or visions based on concrete actions by the masses that suggest a forward leap in their self-determination or ability to assume greater control and responsibility for their own lives" (*Living for Change*, 60).

90. Grace Lee Boggs, "Thinking and Acting Dialectically," 45–46.

91. Glaberman, "The Marxism of C. L. R. James," 307, 310 (the phrase appears on both pages, in one case with "was" instead of "is").

92. C. L. R. lists the titles of his *New International* pieces in "Education, Propaganda, and Agitation," republished in Glaberman, *Marxism for Our Times*, 26. They were: "Negroes in the Civil War: Their Role in the 2nd American Revolution," "In the American Tradition: The Working Class Movement in Perspective," and "The American People in One World: An Essay in Dialectical Materialism." For a discussion of them and of his and the JFT's engagement with American culture and society, see Grimshaw and Hart, "*American Civilization*: An Introduction," and Robert A. Hill, "Literary Executor's Afterword," especially 13–14, 303–7. On C. L. R.'s thinking and writing about African American history and politics, see McLemee, *C. L. R. James on the "Negro Question."* "Notes on American Civilization" was posthumously published as C. L. R. James, *American Civilization*.

93. In their respective discussions of "Education, Propaganda, and Agitation," Robert Hill and Scott McLemee both make the point that C. L. R. was not the first to call for Americanization of Marxism, and both scholars cite in particular the work of V. F. Calverton. See Hill, "Literary Executor's Afterword," 305–6; and McLemee, "Afterword," 222.

94. C. L. R. James, "Education, Propaganda, and Agitation," 18.

95. Ibid., 19.

96. Ibid., 20.

97. Ibid., 28–29.

98. McLemee, *C. L. R. James on the "Negro Question,"* xvi.

99. C. L. R. James, "Preliminary Notes on the Negro Question," in McLemee, *C. L. R. James on the "Negro Question,"* 4. This document was originally published under the pseudonym J. R. Johnson in the Socialist Workers Party's *Internal Bulletin* 1, no. 9 (June 1939), and then in Breitman, *Leon Trotsky on Black Nationalism and Self-Determination*.

100. The rival Communist Party's work in black communities and recruitment of black members surely helped to motivate C. L. R.'s concern with the Trotskyists' Negro

work and shape his prescriptions. C. L. R. makes several references to the CP throughout "Preliminary Notes on the Negro Question."

101. C. L. R. James, "Preliminary Notes on the Negro Question," 9.

102. This document is reproduced as "The Historical Development of the Negroes in American Society" in McLemee, *C. L. R. James on the "Negro Question,"* 63–89.

103. Ibid., 71.

104. Ibid., 73.

105. The speech was first published under the pseudonym J. Meyer in *Fourth International* 9, no. 8 (December 1948). It has since appeared in these collections of C. L. R.'s writings: a special C. L. R. James issue of *Radical America* 4, no. 4 (May 1970); C. L. R. James, *The Future in the Present*; Grimshaw, *The C. L. R. James Reader*; McLemee and Le Blanc, *C. L. R. James and Revolutionary Marxism*; McLemee, *C. L. R. James on the "Negro Question."*

106. The party referred to here is the Socialist Workers Party (SWP). As described later in the chapter, in 1947 the JFT left the Workers Party and joined the SWP.

107. C. L. R. James, "Revolutionary Answer," in McLemee, *C. L. R. James on the "Negro Question,"* 139.

108. C. L. R. James, "The Historical Development of Negroes in American Society," 72.

109. This analysis appears in ibid., 72–73.

110. Glaberman, "The Marxism of C. L. R. James," 305. Historian and C. L. R. James's literary executor Robert Hill reports the same ("Literary Executor's Afterword," 313).

111. The announcement appears in the *Militant*, January 10, 1949, 2. In her autobiography, Grace Lee Boggs says that Dunayevskaya taught a weekly class on *Capital*, but she does not mention her own teaching. See Grace Lee Boggs, *Living for Change*, 58.

112. Grace Lee Boggs, *Living for Change*, 58.

113. Johnson, Forest, and Stone, *Essays by Karl Marx*, 1. A copy of this publication can be found in the Boggs Papers, Box 28, Folder 4-7.

114. Ibid., 1.

115. Ibid., 5.

116. Ibid., 1.

117. Ibid., 5.

118. Ibid., 7.

119. Ibid., 3.

120. Ibid., 5.

121. Ibid., 6–7.

122. A year before *Essays by Karl Marx*, C. L. R. had cited the phrase in an essay titled "They Showed the Way to Labor Emancipation: On Karl Marx and the 75th Anniversary of the Paris Commune," *Labor Action*, March 18, 1946.

123. In her autobiography, written four decades later, Grace uses the phrase in her recollection of their discovery of Marx's 1844 manuscripts, saying that Marx's essays "were important because they reinforced the Johnson-Forest view that the essence of socialist revolution is the expansion of the natural and acquired powers of human beings, not the nationalization of property" (Grace Lee Boggs, *Living for Change*, 102).

124. Johnson, Forest, and Stone, *Essays by Karl Marx*, 5.

125. Ibid., 6. The quotation appears in the chapter titled "Machinery and Modern Industry" in Marx, *Capital*.

126. Grace recalled this goal in her interview in OHALC.

127. See, for example, Mills, *The New Men of Power*; Mayo, *The Human Problems of an Industrial Civilization*; and Mayo, *The Social Problems of an Industrial Civilization*.

128. Romano and Stone, *The American Worker*, 1.

129. Ibid., 42.

130. Ibid.

131. Ibid., 42–43.

132. Ibid., 43.

133. Ibid., 70. This passage is also quoted in Grace Lee Boggs, *Living for Change*, 65.

134. Johnson-Forest Minority, WP, and Fourth International, "Resolutions Adopted by the Johnson-Forest Minority at Its National Conference," July 5–6, 1947, Glaberman Papers, Box 22, Folder 14.

135. Grace Lee Boggs, *Living for Change*, 63.

136. Glaberman, *Marxism for Our Times*, xv–xvi.

137. Bogues, *Caliban's Freedom*, 97; Glaberman, *Marxism for Our Times*, xv–xvi.

138. Glaberman, *Marxism for Our Times*, xvi.

139. "Report and Discussion on Break with S.W.P.," 3–4, Glaberman Papers, Box 22, Folder 14. This internal JFT document briefly describes the interim period and lists the works published in a 1951 document. For subsequent descriptions of this period from Grace Lee Boggs and Martin Glaberman, see Grace Lee Boggs, *Living for Change*, 64; Glaberman, *Marxism for Our Times*, xvi. Two of the works from the interim period have been published as "Dialectical Materialism and the Fate of Humanity," in Grimshaw, *The C. L. R. James Reader*; and C. L. R. James, Forest, and Stone, *The Invading Socialist Society*.

140. Johnson-Forest Tendency, *Balance Sheet*, 18.

141. Grace Lee Boggs, *Living for Change*, 65; Alexander, *International Trotskyism*, 312.

142. Dunayevskaya excitedly reported meeting Castoriadis in a letter to C. L. R. on September 22, 1947, which is reproduced in "Three Letters," in Cudjoe and Cain, *C. L. R. James*, 298–300. For the biographical information on Castoriadis, see Curtis, *Cornelius Castoriadis*, viii.

143. Grace Lee Boggs, *Living for Change*, 65.

144. Castoriadis, "C. L. R. James and the Fate of Marxism," 283; Curtis, *Cornelius Castoriadis*, 18, 36n5.

145. Grace Lee Boggs, *Living for Change*, 65–66.

146. Curtis, *Cornelius Castoriadis*, xxv.

147. Castoriadis describes his relationship with the Johnson-Forest Tendency and Grace's role in building that relationship in Castoriadis, "C. L. R. James and the Fate of Marxism."

148. FBI-GLB, Section 1, 307, 311–14.

149. Report dated December 20, 1948, in FBI-GLB, Section 1, 300–309.

150. The JFT had of course entered the SWP known as the "state capitalist" minority, with its position on the nature of the Soviet Union deviating from the SWP's position on the Russian Question, but this difference was recognized and accepted, and it was not the source of conflict.

151. Published as C. L. R. James, with Dunayevskaya and Lee, *State Capitalism and World Revolution*. Quotation appears on 3.

152. Johnson-Forest Tendency, *Balance Sheet*, 1, 35.

CHAPTER 5

1. Martin Glaberman interview in OHALC.

2. There is no record of his participation in any of the three gatherings, and the available evidence points to him not attending. In her recollection of the first gathering, held in the fall of 1951, Selma James said "C.L.R. was not at the convention because he was fighting deportation," adding that at the end of the convention she and others were "shepherded to some hall and [C. L. R.] appeared there" (Selma James interview with author). C. L. R. could not have attended the second gathering, which convened in the fall of 1952, because he was then incarcerated on Ellis Island. The third gathering, in July 1953, occurred just as C. L. R. departed for England. Selma James recalled seeing him off in New York just before she left for the convention (ibid.). Robert Hill gives his departure date as July 3, 1953 ("Literary Executor's Afterword," 301), and the convention met July 3–7 in Detroit.

3. FBI-JB, Section 1, 4, 7.

4. Al Whitney, "Why the Split," 1, Glaberman Papers, Box 3, Folder 8.

5. Selma James interview with author; Nettie Kravitz interview with author.

6. Glaberman, *Marxism for Our Times*, xviii, xix.

7. Selma James, *Sex, Race, and Class*, 294. Selma James situated the Third Layer School as an important part of C. L. R.'s legacy. She called the Johnson-Forest Tendency one of the two "masterworks" (285) created by C. L. R. (the other being his book *Black Jacobins*) and identified the Third Layer School as "perhaps the most startling Johnson-Forest innovation" (294). Highlighting the purpose and impact of the Third Layer School, she explained, "It was to train us to stand up to our own leaders. It was to train third layer people who are not used to it to express their point of view to those who are 'educated' or in other ways more socially powerful, whether or not other third layer people joined in. I think a number of us found our voice. I certainly did" (294). By contrast, Glaberman judged the group's effort to implement the third-layer concept "a good faith attempt, but it was probably maintained essentially on the strength of James's support. I cannot say that it was successful" (Glaberman, *Marxism for Our Times*, xxix).

8. These topics and statements were reported by multiple sources and recorded in FBI-JB, 7.

9. These statements are from the memorial booklet produced after James Boggs's death: Zola, Gruchala, and Grace Lee Boggs, *James Boggs*. Her statement begins and ends with these words: "I will remember many things in many places about Jimmy Boggs, but mainly I will remember him in New York in 1952 when we first met. We were at the school which C. L. R. James had devised for working class people like us to educate our intellectual comrades. . . . Jimmy's gifts—acknowledging others' unique needs and therefore making the right help available—are what village life at its best offers. He bestowed these gifts in cities where they rarely re-root and are even more rarely blended with political resistance.

During a better time he would have had a broader arena in which to act. Jimmy was that rare being, a civilizer in politics" (unpaginated).

10. Grace Lee Boggs, *Living for Change*, 77–78.

11. *A Woman's Place* is included in Selma James, *Sex, Race, and Class*, 13–31; *Punching Out* is included in Lynd, *Martin Glaberman*, vi–viii, 2–23; James, *Mariners, Renegades, and Castaways*. Owens published his book under two pseudonyms, Mathew Ward for the first edition and Charles Denby for the second edition. The most frequently cited is the second edition. See Denby, *Indignant Heart*. For a discussion of the book's authorship and evolution, see Jones, *A Dreadful Deceit*, 248, 268–69, 283–84,

12. Grace Lee Boggs, speech to Convention of Correspondence Committees, text in author's possession, 1.

13. Ibid., 8.

14. Ibid.

15. Ibid., 11. The passage appears in Marx, *Capital*, 929.

16. Grace Lee Boggs, *Living for Change*, 48.

17. Grace Lee Boggs, speech to Convention of Correspondence Committees, 25 (emphasis in original).

18. Ibid. (emphasis in original).

19. Ibid., 29–30.

20. Ibid., 39 (emphasis in original). This passage remained one of Grace's favorites in the Marxist canon. In her autobiography, Grace cites this passage to illustrate Marx as a "humanist prophet," "the Marx I love to quote" (51). The original passage is to be found in Marx and Engels, *The Communist Manifesto*, 16–17.

21. Grace Lee Boggs, speech to Convention of Correspondence Committees, 39 (emphasis in original).

22. Anon., report on Convention of Correspondence Committees, 9, Boggs Papers, Box 28, Folder 14. The identity of the author is not indicated. The text of the report suggests that the author was familiar with Correspondence and largely agreed with its politics. The text also suggests that the author may have been a European or was writing for a European audience. The report begins, "I was invited by a group of people to attend a conference they had organized to publish a newspaper which will tell the story of the other America, that is the America little known to the European who gets his picture of America from LIFE, the Voice of America and other such semi-official and official channels. They are a small group, less than 100, of intellectuals and workers, most them quite young, but fairly representative, it seems to me, of the American population, white and Negro workers, women, and young people. The whole conference was centered around launching the paper and all of them are very enthusiastic about it. They feel that America has never had such a paper that tells the story of how the ordinary people live, at work, in their homes, schools, and in their communities, and they feel that you and people like you abroad would be interested not only in the paper but in hearing who they are and how they function" (1).

23. Anon., report on Convention of Correspondence Committees, 2.

24. Ibid., 31.

25. Ibid., 5.

26. Ibid., 2.

27. Grace Lee Boggs, speech to Convention of Correspondence Committees, 4.

28. Grace also had had family in Detroit, as her brothers Harry and Eddie had preceded her in the city, coming in 1949 to work in the auto industry. However, she said that by the time she arrived in Detroit she did not have much contact with them. They "were out of politics" and no longer involved in the organization (Grace Lee Boggs interview with author).

29. Sugrue, *Origins of the Urban Crisis*, 125–26. Sugrue writes that these and other shocks to the city's economy represented "the beginning of a long-term and steady decline in manufacturing employment" that brought "a systematic restructuring of the local economy from which the city never fully recovered" (126).

30. Sugrue provides an exhaustive discussion of Detroit's industrialization (ibid.).

31. The 1950 census recorded the city's population as 1,849,568, and the Census Bureau estimated the population to be 2 million in 1955. Other demographic estimates locate the peak of 2 million residents in 1953. By 1960 the city's population dropped to 1,670,144, and in 1970 it was 1,511,482. See Gavrilovich and McGraw, *The Detroit Almanac*, 289, 294.

32. Aberbach and Walker, *Race in the City*, 9.

33. June Manning Thomas, *Redevelopment and Race*, 45–79; Sugrue, *Origins of the Urban Crisis*, 47–51, 82–86; Dillard, *Faith in the City*, 200–203, 260–62.

34. June Manning Thomas, *Redevelopment and Race*, 56–62, 76–78.

35. June Manning Thomas reports that two of the city's lead planners, as well as the city's comprehensive planning program, were the most widely respected according to a 1961 survey of prominent members of the planning profession. In 1964, Detroit won the American Institute of Planners Honors Award in Comprehensive Planning. See June Manning Thomas, *Redevelopment and Race*, 103–4, 120. For a recent analysis of the impact of urban renewal on black communities nationally, including a strong critique of the notions of progress that undergirded urban renewal programs, see Fullilove, *Root Shock*.

36. Sugrue, *Origins of the Urban Crisis*, 47. One observer noted in 1952 that 17,000 people had already been displaced by the expressways (Norris, "Dislocation without Relocation," 474).

37. June Manning Thomas, *Redevelopment and Race*, 60–61.

38. "The Magnitude of the Relocation Problem," November 21, 1950, 4–5, DULR, Box 38, Folder A2-1.

39. Ibid., 3.

40. "Report of the Housing Situation as It Affects the Community in the Gratiot Redevelopment Area—Survey Findings," 4–5, DULR, Box 38, Folder A2-2.

41. Ibid., 3.

42. "Recommendations to the Executive Board of the Detroit Urban League," March 23, 1951, 1, DULR, Box 38, Folder A2-2.

43. Norris, "Dislocation without Relocation," 475.

44. Ibid.

45. The articles appeared between February 21 and March 28, 1953. The *Michigan Chronicle* subsequently published the series as a pamphlet by Charles J. Wartman under

the same title, "Detroit—Ten Years After!," which can be found at the Bentley Historical Library, University of Michigan (call number EC 2 D4834 W297). All citations below are from the pamphlet.

46. Wartman, "Detroit—Ten Years After!," 14.

47. Ibid., 14–15.

48. Ibid., 15.

49. Ibid.

50. Ibid., 17.

51. Ibid., 14.

52. Halpern, "'I'm Fighting for Freedom.'" See also Dillard, *Faith in the City*, 186–91; and Salvatore, *Singing in a Strange Land*.

53. Halpern, "'I'm Fighting for Freedom,'" 28–30; Salvatore, *Singing in a Strange Land*.

54. Grace Lee Boggs, *Living for Change*, 79.

55. These quotations and this information about the Boggses' courtship are drawn from a video recording of Grace Lee Boggs, James Boggs, and Freddy Paine at Sutton Island, Maine made by France Reid (in author's possession). While the exact date is not known, it was likely during the 1980s. Parts of this recording, including the quotations cited here, appear in a memorial tribute video of James Boggs produced by Reid, titled *James Boggs: An American Revolutionist* (1993). In her autobiography, Grace also describes this night and its place in their courtship. Her account differs in that she says they made the decision to marry that night, whereas he said that decision came months later (*Living for Change*, 78).

56. FBI-GLB, 288–91.

57. FBI-JB, 3, 5, 10, 11. All of the quotations appear on 3.

58. FBI-JB, 16; FBI-GLB, 203, 205. The quotations are from FBI-GLB, in which the two informants are T-1 and T-4.

CHAPTER 6

1. Speech by Weaver, July 17, 1953, 1, Glaberman Papers, Box 10, Folder 2 (emphasis in original).

2. Ibid., 10.

3. Ibid., 2 (emphasis in original).

4. Grace Lee Boggs interview with author.

5. Ibid.

6. See Peterson, "*Correspondence.*" For a broader discussion, see Doody, *Detroit's Cold War*.

7. As we will see later in the chapter, the frequency of publication and number of pages fluctuated over the paper's nearly eleven-year history. It was twelve pages for its first year. The first issue shorter than twelve pages appeared on October 30, 1954 (it was eight pages). Plans to turn it into a weekly never materialized.

8. The initial issues did not yet have "Readers' Views" but instead had sections called "Letters to the Editor" and "Letter Box." By the fourth issue (November 14, 1953) these became "Readers' Views." During the period that *Correspondence* was twelve pages,

"Readers' Views" usually covered three columns of page six and three columns of page seven, thereby constituting the very center of the paper.

9. "Statement of the Editor," *Correspondence*, October 1, 1953, 1.

10. "I Talk about What I Please—To Whom I Please," *Correspondence*, October 3, 1953, 10.

11. Ibid.

12. Selma Weinstein (soon to be Selma James) wrote "A New Relationship." The article's title is drawn from *A Woman's Place*, the pamphlet written by Weinstein that Correspondence published a year earlier, and the article quotes from the pamphlet. Weinstein was the driving force behind the women's page, and *A Woman's Place* provided material for it in several of the initial issues of *Correspondence*. For example, the November 14 ("The Family Divided") and December 12 ("A Feeling of Independence") issues each carried an excerpt from the pamphlet. Beginning with the December 26, 1953, issue, Weinstein wrote a regular column titled "A Woman's Place," with most pieces written under her pseudonym Marie Brandt (sometimes incorrectly spelled Brant). The full text of *A Woman's Place*, along with several other writings by Selma James, is reproduced in her book *Sex, Race, and Class*. For a short discussion of her experiences writing for *Correspondence* see 32–33.

13. "A New Relationship," *Correspondence*, October 3, 1953, 11.

14. Ibid.

15. "Readers Say What They Think of the First Issue," *Correspondence*, October 17, 1953, 1, 6, 7. The front page and particularly its lead article drew most of the criticism. A reader identified as a housewife from Detroit said "the paper on the whole is very good," though she felt that "the articles on the front page are too long and the Beria article is too abstract for the front page." A young Detroit reader said "the front page is dead" with "too many long articles on it," and a Chrysler worker similarly did not think the Beria article belonged on the front page because "political events like that just past, they don't last." Yet another Detroit reader agreed that the Beria article was too long and called the front page "dull," but added that "as you get into the rest of the paper it get pretty interesting." Supporters from West Virginia "felt the front page too crowded and a little too colorless," and also found the first issue "lacked a sense of urgency. The only exception was the Kinsey Report." A more general critique also came from a reader in Los Angeles who said, "The paper has too much content, too much material on how things are loused up in production. There's not enough humor and the give and take of daily life." A secretary in New York similarly found the paper a bit underwhelming, writing, "I don't think it was as terrific as it was built up in advance," though this reader did "like the way it is written not by professional writers." Articulating a dynamic that would play out through much of the paper's early history, a "Ford Woman Worker" in Detroit wrote in to say, "I want to subscribe. . . . At first I thought the paper was Communist, but after reading it, I saw it wasn't."

16. "From January 15 through June," 5, Glaberman Papers, Box 3, Folder 1 (emphasis in original).

17. "Building Correspondence," *Correspondence*, October 31, 1953, 1.

18. *Correspondence*, August 7, 1954, 6.

19. *Correspondence*, December 12, 1953, 6.

20. "Statement of the Editor," *Correspondence*, November 14, 1953, 1.

21. Ibid., 6 (emphasis in original).

22. "Our Aim and Our Program," *Correspondence*, April 17, 1954, 6.

23. "Special Mexican-American Feature," *Correspondence*, January 23, 1954, 10.

24. "Puerto Ricans in America," *Correspondence*, March 20, 1954, 12.

25. The series ran from May 15 to July 10, 1954 (nos. 17–21).

26. "They Wanted Only Boys," *Correspondence*, January 9, 1954, 9.

27. Grace Lee Boggs, *Living for Change*, 4.

28. Ibid., 1.

29. Ibid., 5.

30. Minutes of the REB, May 11, 1954, Glaberman Papers, Box 3, Folder 4.

31. "From January 15 through June," 1, Glaberman Papers, Box 3, Folder 1.

32. "The Transition Point: A Memo to the Membership," 1, Glaberman Papers, Box 10, Folder 3 (emphasis in original).

33. FBI-JB, 29.

34. Ibid., 29–30.

35. "Tour Report, Motions, the Letter," 7, Glaberman Papers, Box 10, Folder 3.

36. Minutes of the REB, May 25, 1954, Glaberman Papers, Box 3, Folder 4.

37. "Tour Report, Motions, the Letter," 8.

38. Ibid., 7, 11.

39. Al Whitney, "Talent for Sale," *Correspondence*, January 23, 1954, 8. This column is reprinted in Stephen M. Ward, ed., *Pages from a Black Radical's Notebook*, 42.

40. Al Whitney, "Wasted Energy," *Correspondence*, February 6, 1954, 8.

41. Al Whitney, "Negroes and Negro Organizations," *Correspondence*, March 20, 1954, 8.

42. Al Whitney, "Negro Leaders and the $64 Question," *Correspondence*, March 6, 1954, 8.

43. Al Whitney, "Negro Challenge," *Correspondence*, August 7, 1954, 8. This column is reprinted in Stephen M. Ward, ed., *Pages from a Black Radical's Notebook*, 45. Margaret Garner's act of infanticide in 1856 dramatically represents gendered experiences of enslavement, the centrality of rape, and the complexity and importance of women's resistance to slavery. Jimmy accurately conveyed the essence of Garner's story, though he inaccurately reported some of the details. He wrote, "It has been over 100 years since Margaret Garner, a Negro mother, tossed her son into the Ohio River, giving him back to his maker rather than give him to slavery." In fact, Garner and her family crossed the Ohio River to escape, but she did not throw her child into the river. Rather, she cut the child's throat with a knife. The child was Garner's two-year-old daughter, not son. I have corrected this last error by replacing the word "his" in the original with "[her]" in my quotation of the text. For a range of thoughtful discussions of Garner's story and its implications, including artistic responses and renderings, see Frederickson and Walters, *Gendered Resistance*.

44. Al Whitney, "Viewing Negro History Week," *Correspondence*, February 20, 1954, 8. This column is also reprinted in Stephen M. Ward, ed., *Pages from a Black Radical's Notebook*, 43–44.

45. Ibid.

46. Al Whitney, "Tension and Social Change," *Correspondence*, December 11, 1954, 6.

47. The name of the page was a deliberate expansion of what constitutes news, as very few actual news reports appeared on the page. Instead, the page mostly carried opinion pieces, personal reflections, letters, and commentary on topical or timely subjects of interest to black communities.

48. J.O., "Police Brutality," *Correspondence*, September 4, 1954, 8.

49. "Housing Shortage—They Move You with Bulldozers," *Correspondence*, December 26, 1953, 8.

50. *Correspondence*, September 4, 1954, 8.

51. "An Editorial: Segregation," *Correspondence*, December 26, 1953, 8.

52. "Americanism," *Correspondence*, January 23, 1954, 8.

53. "Say Negro News Dominates Paper," *Correspondence*, November 14, 1953, 7.

54. Ibid.

55. "On the Negro Discussion," *Correspondence*, December 12, 1953, 1.

56. Ibid.

57. "What Do You Think?," *Correspondence*, January 23, 1954, 8.

58. "What Do You Think?," *Correspondence*, June 12, 1954, 8.

59. "What Is Wrong with Special Negro News," *Correspondence*, March 6, 1954, 8.

60. "Editor's Note," *Correspondence*, March 6, 1954, 8.

61. "What Is Wrong with Special Negro News," *Correspondence*, March 6, 1954, 8.

62. Ibid. A short letter titled "House Parties" from a reader in the "What Do You Think?" section appearing next to the letter from "Firm Supporter" speaks to the significance of note parties: "In most Negro communities, there are all types of house parties. Some are savings clubs, some for poker games where everyone takes turns as the house man, and then there are some to help each other. The latter are the best. Friends rotate to give the parties and attend each other's parties. It may be for a back mortgage payment, for a doctor's bill, or for a new coat, but from my experience, there seems to be a common understanding that we are all in the same boat" (*Correspondence*, March 6, 1954, 8).

63. "Negro History: Crispus Attucks," *Correspondence*, February 20, 1954, 8.

64. "Two Worlds: Notes from a Diary," *Correspondence*, July 24, 1954, 7.

65. "American Politics and the Negro," *Correspondence*, March 6, 1954, 1.

66. *Correspondence*, March 6, 1954, 1.

67. Minutes of the REB, May 25, 1954.

68. "Worker's Journal," *Correspondence*, June 12, 1954, 1; "Letter of the Week: Activity in Kentucky on Supreme Court Decision," *Correspondence*, June 12, 1954, 1; "An Editorial: The Supreme Court," *Correspondence*, June 12, 1954, 8.

69. All comments appeared in "Readers' Views," *Correspondence*, June 12, 1954, 6.

70. Al Whitney, "Supreme Court Indecision," *Correspondence*, June 12, 1954, 8.

71. Al Whitney, "Negroes and the Supreme Court Decision," *Correspondence*, May 29, 1954, 8.

72. Al Whitney, "A Decision of Necessity," *Correspondence*, June 26, 1954, 8.

73. Al Whitney, "Negroes and the Supreme Court Decision"; Al Whitney, "Supreme Court Indecision"; Al Whitney, "A Decision of Necessity."

74. "An Editorial: Talented Tenth Are Retreating," *Correspondence*, July 24, 1954, 8. I have determined that Jimmy wrote this editorial because he was the editor of the SNN page, the editorial is consistent in language and tone with his other writings, and some of the subject matter is similar to that of his other work, such as the critique of the talented tenth and the reference to the Detroit NAACP's acquiescence to a recent ruling on public housing, which is the subject of his column on the same page.

75. Ibid.

76. Stefan, "Labor Struggles and Negro Struggles," *Correspondence*, July 10, 1954, 12.

77. Negro Housewife, "Letter of the Week—Supreme Court Decision," *Correspondence*, July 24, 1954, 1; "An Editorial: Talented Tenth Are Retreating."

78. On the plans for Daddario to make the trip, see FBI-GLB, 221, 250, 256. It seems that the plans initially called for Grace and Daddario to travel together, but this later changed, with them traveling separately and meeting in London. In her autobiography, Grace briefly discusses the trip but does not mention Daddario being there (*Living for Change*, 69).

79. Grace Lee Boggs lists these activities in *Living for Change*, 69.

80. FBI-GLB, 260–63. Having kept Grace under consistent surveillance since that initial trip, the FBI activated its network of informants and government agencies to monitor Grace's activities in London. Shortly after her departure, Hoover wrote a memo about her to the director of the Office of Security in the Department of State sharing the information the bureau had gathered from informants and other sources. Copies of the memo went to the director and deputy director of plans for the Central Intelligence Agency, the Foreign Service Desk, and the legal attaché in London, with a note to the attaché: "Through sources available to you it is requested that subject's contacts and activities be determined while in England" (FBI-GLB, 219–20).

81. Gerald Horne discusses American and British surveillance of Koinange in *Mau Mau in Harlem?*, 97–98, 117.

82. This portrait of Koinange is drawn from these sources: Kithinji, "Koinange, Peter Mbiyu," 408–10; Kithinji, "Koinange wa Mbiyu," 96–98; Koinange, *The People of Kenya Speak for Themselves*, 7–10, 25–28, 56–64, 71.

83. Rawcliffe, *The Struggle for Kenya*, 124.

84. Koinange, *The People of Kenya Speak for Themselves*, 1.

85. She shared this in an interview conducted by Stephen Ferguson and Jennifer Choi (transcript in author's possession). The quotations appear on 1.

86. "Murder Inc.," *Correspondence*, January 9, 1954, 5.

87. "Neither Terror, nor Treachery, nor Bargain," *Correspondence*, May 1, 1954, 5; "Accident and Treachery in Africa," *Correspondence*, May 15, 1954, 5; "White Man's Burden," *Correspondence*, August 7, 1954, 5.

88. "The People Are a Mighty Fortress in East Africa," *Correspondence*, November 27, 1954, 8 (emphasis in original).

89. Grace Boggs to Saul and Bessie, November 5, 1954, Glaberman Papers, Box 3, Folder 3.

90. FBI-GLB, 180–81.

91. Ibid., 180.

92. Ibid., 175.

93. Grace Lee Boggs to Freddy Paine, November 10, 1960, Glaberman Papers, Box 6, Folder 7.

94. For a thoughtful discussion of the relationship between the Kenyan liberation struggle and the United States, including black Americans' response to Kenya and activism in support of the independence movement, see Horne, *Mau Mau in Harlem?*

95. See Plummer, *Rising Wind*, 241–43.

96. Padmore, "Behind the Mau Mau," 355.

97. Ibid., 372.

98. For more on the CAA and an analysis of its place in the history and politics of African American anticolonial activism from the 1930s through the early 1950s, see Von Eschen, *Race against Empire*.

99. Ibid., 141; Horne, *Mau Mau in Harlem?*, 116.

100. Koinange, *The People of Kenya Speak for Themselves*, "Acknowledgment."

101. Ibid., 115.

102. Ibid.

103. Grace Lee Boggs, *Living for Change*, 69; Grace Lee Boggs to Conrad Lynn, May 28, 1962, Paine Papers (unprocessed), Box 2, Folder "1962–1963, Grace Reply."

104. Grace Lee Boggs to Conrad Lynn, May 28, 1962, June 5, 1962, June 18, 1962, all in Paine Papers (unprocessed), Box 2, Folder "1962–1963, Grace Reply."

105. Abe McGregor Goff to Rowland Watts, June 3, 1955, Glaberman Papers, Box 3, Folder 10.

106. Martin Glaberman to friends and supporters of Correspondence, September 30, 1954, Paine Papers, Box 2, Folder 11.

107. Grace Lee Boggs, *Living for Change*, 100.

108. William Page, "Can We Build a Workers' Paper?," *Correspondence*, May 1, 1954, 12.

109. Al Whitney, "A New Form of Association," *Correspondence*, July 24, 1954, 2.

110. Al Whitney, "The Paper and a New Society," *Correspondence*, October 30, 1954, 1. This column is reprinted in Stephen M. Ward, ed., *Pages from a Black Radical's Notebook*, 46–47.

111. Raya Dunayevskaya quoted in Jones, *A Dreadful Deceit*, 269.

112. *Correspondence*, October 1957, 1.

CHAPTER 7

1. C. L. R. James to comrades, November 3, 1956, Glaberman Papers, Box 5, Folder 6 (emphasis in original).

2. Letter dated November 5, 1956, with no signature or addressee, Glaberman Papers, Box 5, Folder 6 (emphasis in original). Read in the context of the other letters, this can be identified as written by C. L. R. The top of the letter says copies have been or are to be sent to "Sh," Th," and "Neff," which are references to Sherman (Glaberman), Thompson (Grace), and Lyman Paine, respectively. C. L. R. struck the same tone in a letter to Glaberman dated December 13, 1956: "I want to repeat, and I say so because it will take you some time to understand; the Hungarian Revolution is the greatest political event since the October Revolution of 1917." C. L. R. James to Martin Glaberman, December 13, 1956, Glaberman Papers, Box 5, Folder 7.

3. J (C. L. R. James) to friends, November 15, 1956, 3, Glaberman Papers, Box 5, Folder 6. This is a letter from C. L. R. to members of the organization in the United States. It includes a copy of a letter from Grace (signed Thompson) to C. L. R. on November 10, 1956. C. L. R.'s statement cited here is from a postscript that he wrote at the end of Grace's letter.

4. J (C. L. R. James) to friends, November 15, 1956.

5. Thompson (Grace Lee Boggs) to friends, November 15, 1956, Glaberman Papers, Box 5, Folder 6.

6. New York Editing Committee of Correspondence to friend, November 17, 1956, Glaberman Papers, Box 5, Folder 6.

7. Press release, November 16, 1956, Glaberman Papers, Box 5, Folder 6.

8. New York Editing Committee of Correspondence to friend, November 17, 1956 (emphasis in original).

9. "The Hungarian Revolution," *Correspondence*, December 1956, 1.

10. Thompson (Grace Lee Boggs) to J (C. L. R. James), November 10, 1956. C. L. R. sent this letter out to the group with his November 15 letter.

11. Jim (James Boggs) to J (C. L. R. James), November 28, 1956, Glaberman Papers, Box 5, Folder 6. All quotations in this paragraph are from this letter.

12. Ibid. All quotations in this paragraph are from this letter.

13. Ibid.

14. Th (Grace Lee Boggs) to J (C. L. R. James), March 24, 1957, Glaberman Papers, Box 5, Folder 10.

15. Nkrumah, *Ghana*, 281–83; Nkrumah, *I Speak of Freedom*, 64–69; Milne, *Kwame Nkrumah*, 73, 75.

16. C. L. R. James, *The Black Jacobins*. The quotations cited here appear in the unpaginated "Preface to the Vintage Edition." The final pages of the study to which C. L. R. refers are 375–77.

17. C. L. R. James to Martin Glaberman, December 13, 1956, Glaberman Papers, Box 5, Folder 7.

18. C. L. R. James to friends, February 10, 1957, Glaberman Papers, Box 5, Folder 9.

19. C. L. R. James to Martin Glaberman, February 8, 1957, Glaberman Papers, Box 5, Folder 9.

20. C. L. R. was still recovering from an illness that had slowed down his writing of the Hungary pamphlet. Nkrumah said that his government would pay for C. L. R.'s passage to and from Ghana and also host him as a guest of the government. Nonetheless, C. L. R. indicated in letters to the American group that there would be other expenses incurred. Lyman Paine subsequently agreed to cover these expenses.

21. C. L. R. James to Martin Glaberman, February 8, 1957.

22. J (C. L. R. James) to friends (February 18, 1957, Glaberman Papers, Box 5, Folder 9.

23. J (C. L. R. James) to friends, March 3, 1957, Glaberman Papers, Box 5, Folder 10; J (C. L. R. James) to [unidentified], March 14, 1957, Glaberman Papers, Box 5, Folder 10; C. L. R. James to everybody, March 20, 1957, Glaberman Papers, Box 5, Folder 10.

24. J (C. L. R. James) to friends, March 3, 1957 (emphasis in original).

25. Ibid.

26. Ibid.

27. Ibid.

28. J (C. L. R. James) to [unidentified], March 14, 1957.

29. C. L. R. James to everybody, March 20, 1957. All quotations in this paragraph are from this letter (emphasis in original).

30. Ibid.

31. For "one of the most important speeches in his life," see Milne, *Forward Ever*, 2. For "possibly the finest expression of his vision for Ghana and Africa," see Rahman, *The Regime Change of Kwame Nkrumah*, 172. In a subsequent biography of Nkrumah, Milne writes that the speech "was one of his finest. Every seat in the Assembly was filled, and large crowds had gathered outside. He spoke at length of events leading up to the demand for an end to colonial rule" and "went on to remind members that independence was not an end itself, but a means to an end." She further explains, "The Motion of Destiny took Britain by surprise. It demanded self-government now, and a clear commitment by Britain to a date for full independence. The colonial planners had not expected such a Motion so soon. At most, they anticipated a Motion on self-government. But Nkrumah, having felt the pulse of the people, wanted to telescope the entire period of preparation to a few years. In doing so, it was Nkrumah who was setting the pace" (Milne, *Kwame Nkrumah*, 65, 66).

32. G (Grace Lee Boggs) to J (C. L. R. James), March 17, 1957, Glaberman Papers, Box 5, Folder 10.

33. Ibid.

34. Ibid.

35. Th (Grace Lee Boggs) to J (C. L. R. James), March 24, 1957.

36. Marx, *The Eighteenth Brumaire of Louis Bonaparte*, 141n1.

37. Miliband, "Bonapartism," 55.

38. Th (Grace Lee Boggs) to J (C. L. R. James), March 24, 1957.

39. Ibid.

40. Grace's first encounter with Hegel and the impact of this book were described in chapter 3. For the book's continuing significance for her, see Grace Lee Boggs, "Movement Reading," and Grace Lee Boggs, *Living for Change*, 31–32.

41. J (C. L. R. James) to friends, March 21, 1957, Glaberman Papers, Box 5, Folder 10.

42. C. L. R. James to friends, March 25, 1957, Glaberman Papers, Box 5, Folder 10. This letter has been published in Grimshaw, *The C. L. R. James Reader*, 271–76; Paul Buhle, *C. L. R. James: His Life and Work*,153–58. These publications provide a valuable contribution in making this letter widely available, however a fuller understanding of the letter can best be gained by reading it in the Glaberman Papers alongside other letters written between C. L. R. and his comrades in the United States during the spring of 1957.

43. C. L. R. James to friends, March 25, 1957.

44. Ibid.

45. Ibid.

46. Ibid. All quotations in this paragraph are from this letter.

47. I am thankful to Matt Birkhold for his insight and editorial work that helped me to arrive at this analysis.

48. C. L. R. James to friends, March 25, 1957. All quotations in this paragraph are from this letter.

49. The organization formed in early 1957, taking the name Southern Leadership Conference. In August the organization added the word "Christian" to its name. Garrow, *Bearing the Cross*, 85, 90, 97.

50. "Montgomery and Melville," *Correspondence*, April 1957, 6.

51. C. L. R. James to everybody, March 20, 1957, 3 (emphasis in original).

52. C. L. R. James to friends [unsigned], April 13, 1957, 2, Glaberman Papers, Box 5, Folder 11.

53. Ibid.

54. C. L. R. James to everybody, March 20, 1957, 4–5.

55. Grace reported this conversation and shared Jimmy's comments in, G (Grace Lee Boggs) to J (C. L. R. James), April 9, 1957, Glaberman Papers, Box 5, Folder 11.

56. Th (Grace Lee Boggs) to J (C. L. R. James), March 24, 1957.

57. Ibid (emphasis in original).

58. J (C. L. R. James) to [unidentified], March 14, 1957.

59. C. L. R. James to everybody, March 20, 1957, 5 (emphasis in original).

60. J (C. L. R. James) to Sherman (Martin Glaberman), March 29, 1957, Glaberman Papers, Box 5, Folder 10.

61. G (Grace Lee Boggs) to J (C. L. R. James), April 9, 1957, Glaberman Papers, Box 5, Folder 11.

62. Th (Grace Lee Boggs) to J (C. L. R. James), March 24, 1957.

63. Within Correspondence it was expected that intellectuals like Grace would learn from workers like Jimmy, who possessed, according to the group's political worldview, unique and invaluable knowledge by virtue of their experiences in the factory and proximity to the world of production. The Third Layer School had formalized and solidified this idea as part of the group's organizational philosophy. However, Grace intended her anecdote to show something slightly different. What she learned from Jimmy resulted not solely from his being a worker but from his broader life experiences and worldview; she attributed his critical insights and influence on her thinking to the type of person he was, the social background that shaped him, and the sharp contrast of his background and personality with hers.

64. Grace Lee Boggs, *Living for Change*, 85.

65. T (Grace Lee Boggs) to J (C. L. R. James), April 9, 1957.

66. Al Whitney, "A Report on the March on Washington," *Correspondence*, April 1, 1957, 1.

67. C. L. R. James to friends, April 13, 1957.

68. Ibid. (emphasis in original).

69. Grace Lee Boggs to friends, May 2, 1957, Glaberman Papers, Box 5, Folder 12.

70. Ibid.

71. Grace Lee Boggs, *Living for Change*, 69; report dated October 7, 1957, FBI-JB, 53.

72. C. L. R. James to Constance, June 15, 1957, Glaberman Papers, Box 5, Folder 13; Marty Glaberman to C. L. R. James, October 13, 1957, Glaberman Papers, Box 5, Folder 15.

73. Grace Lee Boggs, *Living for Change*, 110.

74. During her stay in London in 1954, Grace worked mostly with Mbiyu Koinange on one project.

75. According to Grace's later reports, her time in London was nothing like the Johnson-Forest days. Reflecting decades later on this period, Grace wrote that working with C. L. R in London during both her 1954 and 1957 trips "had been like a tour of duty" and that she felt a distance between them. See Grace Lee Boggs, *Living for Change*, 111.

76. The cricket book appeared five years later as C. L. R. James, *Beyond a Boundary*. The Ghana book was not published until 1977, two decades after C. L. R. attended Ghana's independence celebration and five years after Nkrumah's death, as C. L. R. James, *Nkrumah and the Ghana Revolution*. For discussion of the eventual content of these books as well as the timing of their publication, see Rosengarten, *Urbane Revolutionary*.

77. Report dated March 11, 1958, FBI-JB, 58–59.

78. Marty Glaberman to C. L. R. James, October 13, 1957.

79. *Correspondence*, October 1957, 4. Reprinted in Stephen M. Ward, ed., *Pages from a Black Radical's Notebook*, 52–53.

80. Al Whitney, "Who Is for Law and Order?," *Correspondence*, October 1957, 4. Reprinted in Stephen M. Ward, ed., *Pages from a Black Radical's Notebook*, 54–55.

81. Information from informants and other surveillance is documented throughout both FBI-JB and FBI-GLB. The specific cases cited from Grace's file are from reports dated September 9, 1955, December 12, 1955, February 20, 1956, and April 17, 1958; those from Jimmy's file are dated October 13, 1953, and March 22, 1957.

82. For example, see reports dated March 11, 1958, March 10, 1959, March 14, 1960, and March 27, 1961, FBI-JB.

83. Reports dated April 4, 1957, October 17, 1958, April 4, 1959, April 14, 1959, and June 1, 1960, FBI-GLB.

84. Grace Lee Boggs interview with author.

85. She had worked as a paid functionary for Correspondence during some stretches in the early 1950s, though the work she did for the organization during these periods differed very little if at all from that which she did for the organization at other times.

86. G (Grace Lee Boggs) to J (C. L. R. James), April 13, 1955, Glaberman Papers, Box 3, Folder 8. Also see Grace Lee Boggs, *Living for Change*, 87.

87. G (Grace Lee Boggs) to J (C. L. R. James), April 13, 1955.

88. G (Grace Lee Boggs) to J (C. L. R. James), April 18, 1955, Glaberman Papers, Box 3, Folder 8.

89. G (Grace Lee Boggs) to J (C. L. R. James), April 15, 1955, Glaberman Papers, Box 3, Folder 8.

90. T (Grace Lee Boggs) to J (C. L. R. James), April 9, 1957.

91. Joe Maddox interview with author.

92. Jim Boggs to A. J. Muste, July 24, 1956, Glaberman Papers, Box 5, Folder 2.

93. G (Grace Lee Boggs) to J (C. L. R. James), June 9, 1956, Glaberman Papers, Box 5, Folder 1. With this letter is an untitled document that contains the quotation and describes the Local 7 election and the reasoning that Jimmy and Willis followed in their strategy. The document is also dated June 9, 1956.

94. Untitled document with G (Grace Lee Boggs) to J (C. L. R. James), June 9, 1956.

95. Marty Glaberman to J (C. L. R. James), June 21, 1956, Glaberman Papers, Box 5, Folder 1.

96. Ibid.

97. Pursell, "The Technology of Production." See especially p. 65.

98. Bix, *Inventing Ourselves Out of Jobs?*, 237.

99. "The Automatic Factory," *Fortune*, November 1946, 165–66; Eric W. Leaver and J. J. Brown, "Machines without Men," *Fortune*, November 1946, 92–204. See also Noble, *Forces of Production*, 67–68; and Bix, *Inventing Ourselves Out of Jobs?*, 237–38.

100. Bix, *Inventing Ourselves Out of Jobs?*, 238.

101. For an evocative discussion of the 1945–46 strike wave, see Lipsitz, *Rainbow at Midnight*, part 2.

102. Meyer, "'An Economic Frankenstein'"; Meyer, "The Persistence of Fordism"; Noble, *Forces of Production*, 67; Edsforth, "Why Automation Didn't Shorten the Work Week," 163–67; Sugrue, *Origins of the Urban Crisis*, 130–35; Bix, *Inventing Ourselves Out of Jobs?*, 240.

103. "Automation: A Factory Runs Itself," *Business Week*, March 29, 1952, 146–50; "Coming Industrial Era: The Wholly Automatic Factory," *Business Week*, April 5, 1952, 96–99; and "Push Button Plant: It's Here—Machines Do the Work and a Man Looks On," *U.S. News and World Report*, December 4, 1953, 41–44. For more discussion of this surge in interest in automation, see Bix, *Inventing Ourselves Out of Jobs?*; and Noble, *Forces of Production*.

104. Wiener, *Cybernetics*, 27.

105. Ibid., 220.

106. Sugrue, *Origins of the Urban Crisis*, 130, 144.

107. Ibid., 134 (table 5.1).

108. James Boggs, *The American Revolution*, 23–24; Sugrue, *Origins of the Urban Crisis*, 136.

109. Sugrue, *Origins of the Urban Crisis*, 136–37.

110. "Automation affected virtually every sector of the city's economy," writes Sugrue, "reshaping Detroit's industrial labor market, and unleashing forces whose destructive powers no one—industrialists and workers alike—could fully anticipate" (ibid., 135).

111. G (Grace Lee Boggs) to J (C. L. R. James), February 19, 1955, Glaberman Papers, Box 3, Folder 5.

112. Sherman (Martin Glaberman) to all locals, April 6, 1958, Glaberman Papers, Box 6, Folder 2; Grace Lee Boggs, *Living for Change*, 69.

113. C. L. R. James, Lee, and Chaulieu, *Facing Reality*, 6.

114. Though C. L. R. was the book's primary author, the cover of *Facing Reality* listed three authors: J. R. Johnson, Grace C. Lee, and Pierre Chaulieu. At the initial publishing, the group decided that C. L. R.'s pen name should be used to highlight continuity between *Facing Reality* and the Johnson-Forest Tendency (JFT), identifying the book as a continuation of the ideas developed by J. R. Johnson and the JFT. Subsequent editions use the name C. L. R. James instead of J. R. Johnson.

The third name, Pierre Chaulieu, was the pen name of Cornelius Castoriadis, the founder of the French group Socialisme ou Barbarie (Socialism or Barbarism), whom Grace had made contact with during her 1948 trip to Paris. This attribution of authorship reflected the collaborative spirit in which C. L. R. and the group approached this work. More generally, it reflected the group's practice of collaboration and collective authorship that had been at the heart of the JFT. However, this effort lacked a crucial quality of the group's intellectual production during the 1940s: the unity of purpose and vision—that is, a shared intellectual and political viewpoint—that had bound the members of the JFT was not fully present in 1957. Castoriadis contributed only a small portion of the text, 12 pages of the 174-page book. More importantly, Castoriadis's contribution was, in his words, "edited a bit and perhaps vulgarized in some sense by James," and Castoriadis apparently never granted final approval for his portion to appear in the book. See Castoriadis, "C. L. R. James and the Fate of Marxism," 285.

Grace, too, would distance herself from *Facing Reality*, though much later. "The book is pure C. L. R James," she wrote in her autobiography. "I did not share CLR's excitement about the Hungarian Revolution," she recalled, adding that after living in Detroit for four years she had begun to "have some reservations about [C. L. R.'s] celebration of spontaneity. But I did not challenge him, and although I did little of the actual writing, I went along with including my name with Chaulieu's as a coauthor." See Grace Lee Boggs, *Living for Change*, 69–70. She also says that the book "draws heavily on the experiences of Selma [James]" (70), adding that "Selma's influence on CLR during their long partnership has not been sufficiently recognized" (277n32). Speaking again to her reservations about the book, Grace adds this about C. L. R.: "His idea, while still brilliant, struck me as increasingly abstract because he was not rooted in any place or any ongoing struggle. After living in Detroit and getting a sense of the diversity among workers and blacks and the need for both to struggle to transform themselves, I found his celebrations of spontaneity idealistic and romantic" (111). Of course, this may overstate the reservations she actually felt at the time. The surviving records do not reveal this ambivalence, and this passage was written decades later, by which time the full dimensions of her and Jimmy's differences with C. L. R. had come to light and they had undergone a painful organizational split. Still, subsequent events do suggest that in 1957 she was developing some reservations, if subtle and unarticulated, about some of the ideas in *Facing Reality* and that she was not fully invested in the basic perspective underlying the book.

115. C. L. R. James, Lee, and Chaulieu, *Facing Reality*, 24, 27.

116. This biographical information on Lynn and his career is drawn from his memoir and an oral history interview: Lynn, *There Is a Fountain*; and transcript of tape-recorded interview of Conrad Lynn by Milaika Lumumba, January 27, 1970, CRDP.

117. Conrad Lynn, "Accommodating Negro Leadership," *Correspondence*, November 1958, 3.

118. Lynn reports that the phone call occurred on November 2, 1958, in his autobiography *There Is a Fountain* (143).

CHAPTER 8

1. These biographical details are drawn from Tyson, *Radio Free Dixie*.

2. Ibid., 40–41.

3. Lynn, *There Is a Fountain*, 143.

4. Ibid.

5. Ibid., 144.

6. Constance Webb, "I Went Behind Iron Curtain—in USA," *Correspondence*, February 1959, 1.

7. Ibid.

8. Ibid.

9. Ibid.

10. Webb, *Not Without Love*, 277.

11. Ibid. Caution should be used with Webb's memoir as a source to reconstruct this history. Like the genre as a whole, her memoir relies heavily if not exclusively on memory to recount long-ago events and experiences, in this instance four decades removed. Webb's book seems to be especially burdened by the practice of some memoirists who color their recollections, many times unconsciously, but occasionally with intent, according to subsequent ideas and motivations. The result in this case is a book with clear historical inaccuracies and distortions. To cite one example, she relates at some length the internal organizational discussions centered on Raya Dunayevskaya's response to the book *Facing Reality*, which was published in 1958. However, Dunayevskaya had departed from the group in 1955. More relevant to the present study, Webb provides an especially unflattering portrayal of Grace Lee Boggs. It is difficult if not impossible to refute or verify the events and actions that Webb describes to build her characterization of Grace. However, Webb's portrayal of Grace as constantly seeking power within the organization and as scheming for prestige relative to Dunayevskaya and others stands at odds with considerable evidence to the contrary. This puts Webb's picture of Grace in some question. I have chosen to cite the particular passages from Webb's memoir regarding her trip to Monroe because other evidence, such as that provided by Tyson and Lynn, either corroborates or strongly suggests the accuracy of her account of the Perry home and the larger scene. That is to say, her words are used here to amplify the scene described because they are consistent with other sources.

12. Webb, "I Went Behind Iron Curtain," *Correspondence*, February 1959, 1. In February and March 1959, *Correspondence* only appeared once, rather than bi-weekly.

13. G (Grace Lee Boggs) to friends, January 15, 1959, Glaberman Papers, Box 6, Folder 5.

14. *Correspondence*, February 1959, 1.

15. "Broadcast Correspondence Monroe, N.C. Tapes," *Correspondence*, June 20, 1959, 1.

16. *Correspondence*, July 4, 1959, 1.

17. *Correspondence*, November 21, 1959, 1.

18. Cited in Tyson, *Radio Free Dixie*, 149.

19. Tyson, *Radio Free Dixie*, 149.

20. These quotations are from newspaper headlines and stories cited in Tyson, *Radio Free Dixie*, 149–50.

21. Constance Webb, "Urges Open NAACP Hearing of Negroes' Right to Self-Defense," *Correspondence*, June 20, 1959, 1.

22. Tyson, *Radio Free Dixie*, 156–57.

23. Constance Webb, "Monroe NAACP Defies National Office Suspension of Local President Williams," *Correspondence*, July 4, 1959, 1.

24. Quoted in Tyson, *Radio Free Dixie*, 163.

25. Tim Tyson notes that the proceedings aired on New York radio. Indeed, it was through this broadcast that Mae Mallory, who would become one of Williams's most committed supporters and cofighters, initially heard about and became interested in him. Tyson writes of that moment that Mallory "turned the dial on her radio and heard a voice that changed her life forever" (*Radio Free Dixie*, 189). Mallory is briefly discussed in chapter 9.

26. Quoted in Tyson, *Radio Free Dixie*, 193.

27. Tyson, *Radio Free Dixie*, 195–96. For a fuller discussion of the *Crusader* see chapter 5 of Tyson's excellent book, especially 193–201.

28. *Correspondence*, June 6, 1959, 1; and *Crusader Weekly Newsletter*, June 26, 1959, 1.

29. *Crusader Weekly Newsletter*, June 26, 1959, 1.

30. Mabel Williams, "The Night We Rode in a KKK Motorcade," *Correspondence*, September 26, 1959, 4; Robert. F. Williams, "State Snatches People's Doctor," *Correspondence*, November 21, 1959, 1; Robert F. Williams, "Ghost of Buchenwald," *Correspondence*, February 13, 1960, 4.

31. Constance Webb, "R. F. Williams: New Type of Leader," *Correspondence*, August 1, 1959, 1.

32. Ibid.

33. Tyson cites a North Carolina newspaper as calling Williams "the biggest civil right story of 1959"; Tyson, *Radio Free Dixie*, 149.

34. For a discussion of these debates, see ibid., 213–17.

35. Constance Webb, "Near-Riot Flares in Harlem," *Correspondence*, August 29, 1959, 4.

36. Editorial, "Two Sides—But Only One Is Right," *Correspondence*, December 19, 1959, 2. Jimmy used the phrase "but only one side is right" in other writings as well, including an early title for the manuscript that became *American Revolution* (which is discussed in chapter 9).

37. "Two Sides—But Only One Is Right," 2.

38. Al Whitney, "The High Cost of Production," *Correspondence*, April 11, 1959, 1.

39. Ibid.

40. Constance Webb, "Southern Students Score Victories; Sitdowns for Service Spreading," *Correspondence*, March 12, 1960, 1.

41. Constance Webb, "Bell Tolls for Parliamentary Democracy as Students Act While Politicians Talk," *Correspondence*, March 26, 1960, 1.

42. Constance Webb, "Real Voice of the American People Speaks through Today's Sitdowns," *Correspondence*, April 9, 1960, 1.

43. Ibid.

44. Ibid.

45. Ibid. (emphasis in original).

46. "The First 50 Days—Chronicle of a Revolution," *Correspondence*, April 9, 1960, 1.

47. "To All Student Strikers," *Correspondence*, April 23, 1960, 1.

48. Ibid.

49. G (Grace Lee Boggs) to J (C. L. R. James), June 17, 1960, reprinted in C. L. R. James, *Party Politics in the West Indies*, 81–84; Grace Lee Boggs, *Living for Change*, 112, 280n23; FBI-GLB, 7, 16; FBI-JB, 88, 93.

50. FBI-GLB, 7.

51. FBI-JB, 88.

52. James Boggs notes, 1960, 2, 5, James Papers, Box 14, Folder 3 (emphasis in original).

53. "The Meaning of Negro History" speech was announced in the March 1959 *Correspondence* (a monthly issue), 4, and in the March 28, 1959 (returned to bi-weekly) issue, 4. The announcement for the sale of *Black Reconstruction* appeared in the April 11, 1959, issue. "The New Nations" speech was announced in the April 19, 1959, issue. The "Negroes and the Trade Unions" speech was announced in the November 21, 1959, issue.

54. Claudia Gwendolyn Mallett and Conrad Mallett interview with author.

55. Dolores Wilson interview with author.

56. Reginald Wilson interview with author.

57. Ibid.

58. Jim (James Boggs) to member, January 1, 1961, Glaberman Papers, Box 6, Folder 8.

CHAPTER 9

1. Jimmy's remarks to the class were printed as "Too Little, Too Late—Rights for Negroes in the U.S.A.," *Correspondence*, June 17, 1961, 2.

2. Reginald Wilson, "Black Muslims Meet," *Correspondence*, July 1, 1961.

3. "Too Little, Too Late," 2.

4. Marty Glaberman to Freddy Paine and Frank, March 18, 1961, Glaberman Papers, Box 6, Folder 8; announcement for the speech in *Correspondence*, March 11, 1961, 4. The front-page story in this issue also focused on Lumumba: "After the Death of Lumumba— His Truth Goes Marching On."

5. Grace Lee Boggs to Freddy Paine, March 2, 1961, Glaberman Papers, Box 6, Folder 8.

6. Grace Lee Boggs to Freddy Paine, January 24, 1961, Glaberman Papers, Box 6, Folder 8.

7. Denise Wacker, "Negro Movement: Blame Whites for Racial Problems," *Michigan Daily*, May 18, 1961, 1; "Correspondence on Campus," *Correspondence*, June 3, 1961, 4.

8. James Boggs, "The First Giant Step," *Correspondence*, June 3, 1961, 1. This article is reprinted in Stephen M. Ward, ed., *Pages from a Black Radical's Notebook*, 67–68. The quotation appears on 67.

9. Arsenault, *Freedom Riders*. This "Nashville Movement Freedom Ride" was quickly followed by others, a few conducted by CORE, many others not. Over the next several months, hundreds of people participated in Freedom Rides traversing every state of the South. Arsenault gives a map of the many Freedom Rides between April and December 1961 (319) as well as an appendix listing a roster of Freedom Riders.

10. James Boggs, "The First Giant Step," 1; Stephen M. Ward, ed., *Pages from a Black Radical's Notebook*, 67.

11. Ibid.

12. President Kennedy announced the formation of the coordinating committee led by Roosevelt, Reuther, and Dr. Milton Eisenhower on May 24. See Kennedy, "Statement by the President on the Tractors-for-Freedom Movement."

13. James Boggs, "The First Giant Step," 1; Stephen M. Ward, ed., *Pages from a Black Radical's Notebook*, 67.

14. Ibid.

15. Jimmy's reference in his telegram to the UAW-AFL-CIO reflected the membership of his union, the UAW, in the merged AFL-CIO federation. In 1955, the once rival federations, American Federation of Labor (AFL) and the Congress of Industrial Organizations (CIO), joined together. At its founding in 1935, the CIO was the standard bearer of industrial unionism, offering a more politically progressive, democratic, and militant alternative to the craft unionism of the AFL. The UAW, as a leading member of the new CIO, had briefly been home to radicals and militant trade unionists of the sort that fashioned the labor movement politics Jimmy encountered when he became an autoworker and nurtured his political growth in the early 1940s. His telegram to Reuther, who ascended to the leadership of the UAW and then the CIO during the preceding fifteen years, reflected Jimmy's ongoing challenge to the union and the labor movement during the 1950s and early 1960s in the context of this devolution of the labor movement and the escalating civil rights movement. This comment on the AFL-CIO from historian Steve Babson further contextualizes Jimmy's telegram: "From its founding, the AFL-CIO was riven by this contradiction between its official rhetoric on racial equality and its actual practice, particularly as the latter was carried out by affiliated unions. The national AFL-CIO was generally progressive, supporting implementation of the Supreme Court's desegregation orders, contributing money to voter registration and civil rights groups in the South, and inviting Martin Luther King to speak at its national meetings. But the AFL-CIO made little effort to mobilize its members or align its affiliated unions with the civil rights movement" (Babson, *The Unfinished Struggle*, 142).

16. James Boggs to members of the executive board of Local 7, January 25, 1961 (in author's possession).

17. James Boggs, *Racism and the Class Struggle*, 70.

18. Ibid., 71.

19. James Boggs, "Walking a Chalk Line," interview by WBAI Pacifica Radio, recorded October 11, 1963; broadcast November 25, 1963.

20. I thank Richard Feldman—a longtime friend and comrade of James Boggs and an autoworker for many years—for his critical reading of and conversations about this material, which helped me to arrive at this point.

21. Stephen M. Ward, ed., *Pages from a Black Radical's Notebook*, 68.

22. "The Second Civil War Has Begun in the United States of America," *Correspondence*, June 3, 1961, 1.

23. James Boggs, *Racism and the Class Struggle*, 71–73.

24. "The Second Civil War Has Begun in the United States of America," 1.

25. Ibid.

26. "Tide of Afro-American Nationalism Is Rising in the United States," *Correspondence*, April 8, 1961, 1. As with most front-pagers, no author is given, but it was likely written by either Grace or Jimmy.

27. Smethurst, *The Black Arts Movement*, provides an especially insightful discussion of Harlem's character and significance as a "central topography for African American artists and intellectuals" (111) during this period and an enduring site, symbolically and practically, for black radical politics before and during the early 1960s. As Smethurst points out, some groups located their headquarters in Harlem even when the leaders of the groups did not live there (113).

28. Smethurst gives an illuminating discussion of these figures and organizations, especially with regard to their leftist backgrounds or connections and the intersection (or perhaps inseparability) of artistic and political activity (ibid.).

29. On Lumumba, his meaning for African Americans, and the UN protests, see Baldwin, "A Negro Assays the Negro Mood," reprinted as "East River, Downtown" in Baldwin, *The Price of the Ticket*; De Witte, *The Assassination of Lumumba*; Hansberry, "Congolese Patriot"; Joseph, *Waiting 'til the Midnight Hour*, 38–44; Meriwether, *Proudly We Can Be Africans*, 208–40; Plummer, *Rising Wind*, 300–304; Polsgrove, *Divided Minds*, 138–41; Woodard, *Nation within a Nation*, 54–59.

30. "Tide of Afro-American Nationalism Is Rising in the United States," 1.

31. Clarke, "The New Afro-American Nationalism," 285.

32. Ibid., 292–93.

33. Ibid., 292.

34. Ibid.

35. Ibid., 295.

36. Esther Cooper Jackson, *Freedomways Reader*.

37. Ibid., xxii.

38. On *Liberator*, see Tinson, "The Voice of the Black Protest Movement." The reference to Clarke's being on the editorial board is on 7.

39. For another discussion of Williams's relationship to Detroit radicals, focusing on the period of his exile, see Mullen, *Afro-Orientalism*, chapter 3.

40. Tinson, "The Voice of the Black Protest Movement," 5–6. Richard Gibson recalled giving a small party for Williams at his home on the eve of the UN demonstrations. He even suggests that Williams inspired the protests. Tyson reports that Williams delivered a speech, as part of his Fair Play for Cuba Committee (FPCC) tour, at a Harlem street rally on the night of February 14. Tyson, *Radio Free Dixie*, 237.

41. "Williams Lauds New Cuban Freedom," *Michigan Daily*, February 16, 1961. This story and an accompanying photo of Williams and others at the forum shared the front page with two stories on the UN and a photo of the UN protest.

42. Announcement in *Michigan Daily*, February 15, 1961, 6; Gosse, *Where the Boys Are*, 148.

43. Both trips were facilitated by journalist Richard Gibson, at whose New York home Williams was the night before the University of Michigan talk. Gibson was a leader of the FPCC as well as a prominent figure in New York black radical circles around On Guard for Freedom, *Liberator*, and the others. See Gosse, *Where the Boys Are*, 147; and Tinson, "The Voice of the Black Protest Movement."

44. Georgakas, "Frank Lovell," 43. Also see General Baker's recollections in Mast, *Detroit Lives*; and Dillard, *Faith in the City*, 231.

45. Student Council, February 11, 1961. The next night he spoke at Greater King Solomon Baptist Church on Fourth and Forest, near Wayne State University.

46. Marty Glaberman to Connie, March 5, 1961.

47. James Boggs to Conrad Lynn, June 5, 1961, Paine Papers (unprocessed), Box 2, Folder 8; Grace Lee Boggs to Frank, May 31, 1961, Glaberman Papers, Box 6, Folder 9; Grace Lee Boggs interview with author (May 11, 2005).

48. James Boggs to Conrad Lynn, June 5, 1961.

49. Grace Lee Boggs interview with author (April 6, 2005); Reginald Wilson interview with author. Wilson recalled that he got the guns from Julian Mayfield. Tyson reports that Mayfield and Clarke delivered a truckload of weapons and clothes to Monroe in December 1960. Tyson, *Radio Free Dixie*, 204.

50. Grace Lee Boggs to Conrad Lynn, May 8, 1962, Paine Papers (unprocessed), Box 2, Folder "1962–1963 Grace, Reply."

51. Grace Lee Boggs to C. L. R. James, January 13, 1961 (mistyped as January 31), Glaberman Papers, Box 6, Folder 8.

52. Marty Glaberman to C. L. R. James, January 25, 1961, Glaberman Papers, Box 6, Folder 8.

53. James Boggs to friends, December 30, 1961, Glaberman Papers, Box 6, Folder 12.

54. James Boggs, "State of a Nation—America, 1962," Glaberman Papers, Box 1, Folder 11.

55. Ibid., 1.

56. Ibid., 7, 8, 9.

57. Marty Glaberman to C. L. R. James, September 10, 1961, Glaberman Papers, Box 6, Folder 11.

58. Marty Glaberman to Freddy Paine, November 11, 1961, Glaberman Papers, Box 6, Folder 12.

59. C. L. R. James to Marty Glaberman, February 11, 1961, Glaberman Papers, Box 6, Folder 13.

60. C. L. R. James to Grace Lee Boggs, November 20, 1961, Glaberman Papers, Box 6, Folder 13.

61. C. L. R. James to secretary, Resident Editorial Board, January 15, 1962, Glaberman Papers, Box 6, Folder 13.

62. For an insightful discussion of Cleage's background, including the roots and trajectory of his theological reasoning, as well as an overview of his political activism during the 1960s, see Dillard, *Faith in the City*, especially chapter 6 and conclusion.

63. Grace Lee Boggs to Conrad Lynn, May 28, 1962, Paine Papers (unprocessed), Box 2, Folder "1962–1963 Grace, Reply"; Dillard, *Faith in the City*, 252.

64. Grace Lee Boggs to Conrad Lynn, December 7, 1962, Paine Papers (unprocessed), Box 2, Folder "1962–1963 Grace, Reply."

65. Grace Lee Boggs to Conrad Lynn, June 18, 1962, Paine Papers (unprocessed), Box 2, Folder "1962–1963 Grace, Reply."

66. Grace Lee Boggs to Conrad Lynn, May 28, 1962.

67. Grace Lee Boggs, *Living for Change*, 88.

68. Grace Lee Boggs interview with author (September 15, 2008); Grace Lee Boggs, *Living for Change*, 88. Grace adds that the owner never raised the rent above $150, in part because Jimmy did so much to take care of the house, tending to it as if he owned it.

69. Grace Lee Boggs to Freddy Paine, May 23, 1962, Paine Papers (unprocessed), Box 2, Folder "1962–1963 Grace, Reply."

70. For example, members of the Revolutionary Action Movement (RAM) spent time at the Boggses' home during the early and mid-1960s, including a week in 1964 putting together an issue of their magazine *Black America*. RAM material listed 3061 Field Street as its address, as did RAM leader Max Standford, who was based in Philadelphia. Among the many Detroit activists who spent time at the Boggses' home, General Baker, a central figure in the group Uhuru and later the League of Revolutionary Black Workers, recalled that he and his fellow young activists regularly went to Jimmy and Grace for counsel. At the Boggs home they could discuss revolutionary theory and political strategies, and they could get a wide array of radical literature, including hard-to-find material (General Baker and Marian Kramer interview with author).

CHAPTER 10

1. "Negroes Are the Ones Best-Suited to Govern the United States Today," *Correspondence*, January 1963, 1. In 1963, the paper shifted back to monthly publication.

2. "Why This Issue?," *Correspondence*, January 1963, 2.

3. Ibid.

4. "Negroes Are the Ones Best-Suited to Govern the United States Today," 1.

5. Selma V. Sparks, "Embattled Harlem Makes World Forum of UN," *Correspondence*, January 1963, 1.

6. Reginald Wilson, "Only Our Awakening to Celebrate," part 5 of "What Are We Fighting For Anyway?," *Correspondence*, January 1963, 1.

7. "Why Are We Called Negro?" and "Be Black and Like It," *Correspondence*, January 1963, 2.

8. "Introducing Rev. Albert B. Cleage, Jr.—The Negro Struggle Is a Struggle for Power," *Correspondence*, January 1963, 4.

9. "Black Beauty," *Correspondence*, January 1963, Black Art Special Emancipation Supplement.

10. Grace Lee Boggs to Conrad Lynn, January 31, 1963, Paine Papers (unprocessed), Box 2, Folder "1962–1963, Grace Reply" (emphasis in original).

11. This essay was first published as "Black Political Power" in the March 1963 issue of *Monthly Review* and was subsequently published as "Liberalism, Marxism, and Black Political Power" in James Boggs's second book, *Racism and the Class Struggle*. It has been reprinted in Stephen M. Ward, ed., *Pages from a Black Radical's Notebook*, under that title. The quotation appears on 160–61.

12. James Boggs, *Racism and the Class Struggle*, in Stephen M. Ward, ed., *Pages from a Black Radical's Notebook*, 161.

13. Brink and Harris, *The Negro Revolution in America*.

14. King, *Why We Can't Wait*, 115, 26.

15. Bennett, *Before the Mayflower*, 386.

16. Branch, *Pillar of Fire*, 88.

17. Eskew, *But for Birmingham*, 314–15.

18. "Call to Action!!!," May 8, 1963, NAACP-DBC, Box 21, Community Action Committee, Folder "1963"; Fentin, "The Detroit Council for Human Rights and the Detroit Freedom March of 1963," 20.

19. "A Profile of the Detroit Negro, 1959–1964," prepared by the Research Department of the Detroit Urban League, June 1965, 3; Sugrue, Origins of the Urban Crisis, 23 (chart).

20. Fentin, "The Detroit Council for Human Rights and the Detroit Freedom March of 1963," 20–21; Grace Lee Boggs, *Living for Change*, 124.

21. Both David Thomas Fentin and Grace Lee Boggs report that the meeting took place on the evening of May 10. Fentin writes that the National Urban League meeting occurred "a few hours after the NAACP-sponsored rally" and was attended by "representatives from over 100 organizations" ("The Detroit Council for Human Rights and the Detroit Freedom March of 1963," 22). Grace Lee Boggs does not mention the location of the meeting, but says, "That night [after the rally] we began meeting in small groups to plan the kind of mass march down Woodward Avenue that Cleage had projected" (*Living for Change*, 124).

22. Both statements are from Titon, *Give Me This Mountain*, the first from the preface, the second from the foreword by Jesse L. Jackson.

23. On Franklin, see Salvatore, *Singing in a Strange Land*.

24. Franklin and King had developed a friendship after they met when King was a student at Morehouse College and Franklin served as a board member of the organization that King led, the Southern Christian Leadership Conference. See Robbie L. McCoy, "C. L. Franklin Services Saturday," *Michigan Chronicle*, August 4, 1984, 4A. Also see "Southern Christian Leadership Conference Board Members," n.d., Franklin Papers, Box 1, Folder "Miscellaneous."

25. J. C. Coles to R. V. Marks, "Inter-office Correspondence," subject: Detroit Council for Human Rights, May 22, 1963, DCCR, Box 19, Folder 6.

26. Fentin, "The Detroit Council for Human Rights and the Detroit Freedom March of 1963," 51–58, 70–72; Grace Lee Boggs, *Living for Change*, 124.

27. Carson, *A Call to Conscience*, 60; "125,000 in 'Freedom Walk,'" *Pittsburgh Courier* (national edition), June 29, 1963, 1. This and other newspaper accounts reported police estimates of 125,000 marchers and 125,000 supporters along the streets.

28. Chester Higgins, "$350,000 Spent in Birmingham, King Tells Rally," *Pittsburgh Courier* (national edition), June 29, 1963, 1; *Detroit News*, June 24, 1963, 2A; *Detroit Courier*, June 29, 1963, 8.

29. "125,000 in 'Freedom Walk,'" *Pittsburgh Courier*, 4; Fentin, "The Detroit Council for Human Rights and the Detroit Freedom March of 1963," 86–89. King's speech was recorded as *The Great March to Freedom*, Gordy Records no. 906, distributed by Motown. The text of the speech is available in multiple sources, including Carson, *A Call to Conscience*.

30. Gwendolyn Mallett, "Freedom Walkers Pledge 'We Shall Overcome,'" *Correspondence*, June 1963, 1.

31. Ibid., 32. "Gus and Greasy," *Correspondence*, June 1963, 1.

33. Mallett, "Freedom Walkers Pledge 'We Shall Overcome,'" 1.

34. Fentin, "The Detroit Council for Human Rights and the Detroit Freedom March of 1963," chapter 5.

35. *Detroit News*, June 8, 1963.

36. Fentin, "The Detroit Council for Human Rights and the Detroit Freedom March of 1963," 87. On Grigsby, see Richard W. Thomas, *Life for Us Is What We Make It*; and Miller, *Managing Inequality*.

37. Snow F. Grigsby, "An Open Letter," DCCR, Box 12, Folder 8.

38. Fentin, "The Detroit Council for Human Rights and the Detroit Freedom March of 1963," 87–88. For Cleage's recollection of his statement see Cleage, *Black Christian Nationalism*, 106; Grace Lee Boggs, *Living for Change*, 124.

39. "Don't Buy Where You Can't Work, Support Selective Patronage Campaign" *Illustrated News*, June 24, 1963, 5.

40. Albert B. Cleage, "Not Someday—But Now! We Shall Overcome," *Illustrated News*, June 24, 1963, 3–4.

41. "Boycotting May Hit Detroit A&P," *Illustrated News*, April 29, 1963, 7.

42. Sewell, "The 'Not-Buying Power' of the Black Community," 139–40. For a thorough discussion and analysis of the Philadelphia campaign and its connection to that city's broader black political movements, see Countryman, *Up South*.

43. Albert B. Cleage, "Not Someday—But Now! We Shall Overcome," 3.

44. Smith, *Dancing in the Street*, 52–53.

45. Ibid.; Grace Lee Boggs, *Living for Change*, 126.

46. Smith, *Dancing in the Street*, 56–57.

47. "Differs with Franklin on Policy, Rev. Albert B. Cleage Resigns from DCHR," *Illustrated News*, October 28, 1963, 3–4.

48. "Freedom Now Party Platform," *Illustrated News*, September 28, 1964, 7; Lynn, *There Is a Fountain*, 184.

49. "Differs with Franklin on Policy, Rev. Albert B. Cleage Resigns from DCHR," *Illustrated News*, October 28, 1963, 3.

50. Ibid., 6.

51. Grace Lee Boggs interview with author; Milton Henry oral history transcript in CRDP; Jasmin A. Young, "Detroit's Red," 23. Malcolm's brother Wilfred, of the Detroit NOI mosque, was in conversation with Grace and others, including about the Freedom Now Party. He may also have been involved in arranging Malcolm to speak on what would have been relatively short notice. Malcolm made other speaking engagements in and around Detroit, including at Wayne State University in Detroit on and at the University of Michigan in nearby Ann Arbor, both in late October.

52. Leo Huberman to James Boggs, April 20, 1962, Ping Ferry to friends, April 24, 1962, James Boggs to Leo Huberman and Paul Sweezy, April 30, 1962, all in Boggs Papers, Box 1, Folder 18.

53. Just weeks before publication, the title was still in question. In April 1963 James Boggs confessed to Huberman and Sweezy that he was having "a very hard time trying to arrive

at a title because of the varied nature of the book. If it were just about race, the title would be easier to find; the same if it were just a question of work. But what the book does, in my estimation, is make an analysis of the economic, industrial, social, and political changes that have taken place in the United States and in its relations to world changes, and the effect that these changes are having on the people in molding them into the pattern that they are at present." Explaining his thinking on the title to that point, James Boggs said that with his most recent revisions to the manuscript he felt that "a drive has now been injected into the book that will make it quite a controversial piece and that regardless of which side one is on, it will strike home to a lot of people. It is perhaps for this reason that I am tentatively entitling the book 'But Only One Side is Right'" (James Boggs to Leo Huberman and Paul Sweezy, April 30, 1963, Boggs Papers, Box 1, Folder 18). At one point James Boggs considered as an alternative title "Rights Are What You Take" (table of contents, Boggs Papers, Box 1, Folder 6). Each of these discarded titles made its way as a phrase into the book's introduction, in the opening and closing sentences, respectively. Sweezy suggested *The American Revolution: Pages from a Negro Worker's Notebook* (Paul Sweezy to Jim Boggs, May 27, 1963, Boggs Papers, Box 1, Folder 18).

54. It appeared first as the ninety-six-page special double summer issue (July–August) of *Monthly Review* in 1963 and then in the fall as a Monthly Review Press paperback book.

55. *The American Revolution* remains Jimmy's most well-known and enduring work. After a long period of being out of print, it has been republished twice. It is included in Stephen M. Ward, ed., *Pages from a Black Radical's Notebook*, and was also reissued by Monthly Review Press with short introductory essays by Grace Lee Boggs and six other Detroit-based activists. Each of these essays speaks to how the book contributed to the writer's conceptions and practice of grassroots activism and social change. Together, these introductions give a vivid picture of the book's legacy. Another statement on the book's influence comes from Dan Georgakas's personal reflections on Detroit radical politics from the late 1950s through the 1960s. *The American Revolution* "was widely admired in Detroit radical circles," he writes. "I believe it was read by almost every person who later became a member of the [League of Revolutionary Black Workers] Executive Committee" ("Young Detroit Radicals," 193n2).

56. The languages are French, Italian, Spanish, Japanese, Catalan, and Portuguese.

57. *Monthly Review* 15, no. 5 (September 1963). The statements appear in the "Notes from the Reader" section on the inside cover of the issue.

58. Bertrand Russell to James Boggs, August 20, 1963, Boggs Papers, Box 1, Folder 20. Their correspondence is discussed below.

59. Davis, *Life Lit by Some Large Vision*, 196. This passage comes from Davis's remarks at a memorial service for James Boggs on October 23, 1993, in Detroit. As Davis recounted in his remarks, his reading of *The American Revolution* was the first in a series of times throughout their three-decade association when Davis reported this feeling: "One of the biblical passages I always loved was Christ's response to Nicodemus: 'You must be born again'—not going back to the womb, of course, but undergoing some fundamental change if you are going to save your life. There were several moments when, because of Jimmy, I was indeed born again" (195–96).

60. Grace Lee Boggs, *Living for Change*, 114. See also Ruby Dee's note prefacing Davis's statement in *Life Lit by Some Large Vision*, 195.

61. Wyndham Mortimer to James Boggs, August 12, 1963, Boggs Papers, Box 1, Folder 22.

62. Wyndham Mortimer to Boggs, September 1, 1963, Boggs Papers, Box 1, Folder 22.

63. Minnie Livingston to James Boggs, October 15, 1963, James A. Kennedy to Robert Harris, August 2, 1963, both in Boggs Papers, Box 1, Folder 22.

64. "'Freedom Now' Heads Answer GOAL Call," *Michigan Chronicle*, November 9, 1963, 1; Jim Cleaver, "Malcolm X Blasts 'Big Six,' Grassroots Conference Sets organizational Plans," *Michigan Chronicle*, November 16, 1963, 1; "Black Revolution in North," *Correspondence*, November 1963, 1; Announcement for Northern Negro Grassroots Leadership Conference, *Illustrated News*, November 11, 1963, 2.

65. "Grass Roots Leadership Conference," tape 14, Boggs Papers.

66. "Support the Christmas Boycott: The Proudest Gift," *Illustrated News*, November 25, 1963, 2.

67. "Grass Roots Leadership Conference"; "Black Revolution in North," 1.

68. "Black Revolution in North," 1; Cleaver, "Malcolm X Blasts 'Big Six,' Grassroots Conference Sets organizational Plans," 1.

69. The full list of resolutions passed by the delegates of the Grass Roots Leadership Conference:

1. To organize a national boycott of General Motors
2. To support the Christmas boycott
3. To express and implement solidarity with the oppressed colored peoples of the world
4. To support the International All-Trades Union of the World
5. To organize a national boycott of schools "as necessary" to end biased textbooks and inferior education
6. To support the Freedom Now Party
7. To demand that Governor Rhodes of Ohio grant asylum to Mae Mallory, and that President Kennedy allow Robert Williams to return home

These are listed in "Black Revolution in North," 1.

70. "Black Revolution in North," 1; Cleaver, "Malcolm X Blasts 'Big Six,' Grassroots Conference Sets organizational Plans," 1.

71. Breitman, *Malcolm X Speaks*, 6–10.

72. Ibid., 9.

73. Ibid., 10–11.

74. Ibid.

75. SNCC chairperson John Lewis was originally slated to appear. He had been one of the most militant though somewhat silenced voices at the March on Washington, where he was forced to change his speech by scaling down his criticism and condemnation of the federal government. Though he would maintain a moderate position as SNCC moved to Black Power in 1965 and 1966, in November 1963 Lewis—like SNCC more generally—

represented the emerging militant opposition to accepted forms and assumptions of black protest.

76. Sylvester Leaks, "Definitions of the Negro Revolution," *Muhammad Speaks*, December 20, 1963, 18.

77. Announcement for "Where is the Negro Liberation Movement Going?" included with Sybil May (for Leo Huberman) to James Boggs, November 22, 1963, Boggs Papers, Box 1, Folder 18.

78. Ibid.

79. Leaks, "Definitions of the Negro Revolution," 18. All quotations in the paragraph are from this source.

80. "Final Draft of JB's Speech, Town Hall, Nov. 21, 1963," 2, Boggs Papers, Box 3, Folder 20.

81. Ibid., 7 (emphasis in original).

82. Ibid., 5 (emphasis in original).

83. Feinberg and Kasrils, *Bertrand Russell's America*, 219.

84. Bertrand Russell to James Boggs, August 20, 1963, Boggs Papers, Box 1, Folder 20.

85. James Boggs to Bertrand Russell, September 5, 1963, Boggs Papers, Box 1, Folder 20.

86. Bertrand Russell to James Boggs, September 18, 1963, Boggs Papers, Box 1, Folder 20.

87. Ibid.

88. Feinberg and Kasrils, *Bertrand Russell's America*, 219–21; James Feron, "Russell, Hailing March, Scores 'Atrocity' in Slaves' Treatment," *New York Times*, August 28, 1963, 21.

89. Feinberg and Kasrils, *Bertrand Russell's America*, 227–28; "Negroes Warned by Lord Russell; Briton Says that Violence Would Set Back Cause," *New York Times*, December 8, 1963, 56.

90. Feinberg and Kasrils, *Bertrand Russell's America*, 228. Alice Mary Hilton, who like Russell contacted Jimmy following the publication of *The American Revolution*, had encouraged Russell to send the message and facilitated its arrival. After the forum, she wrote to Russell telling him, "Your reasonable words were not heeded. Jim Boggs expressed his appreciation, but—he said—'unfortunately, Bertrand Russell does not understand revolution'" (Feinberg and Kasrils, 228).

91. James Boggs to Bertrand Russell, December 29, 1963, 1, Boggs Papers, Box 1, Folder 20; Feinberg and Kasrils, *Bertrand Russell's America*, 229.

92. Ibid.

93. Ibid.

94. Ibid.

95. Ibid.

96. Ibid.

EPILOGUE

1. "Neither White Nor Black—But Revolutionary," *Correspondence*, June 1963, 2.

2. Grace Lee Boggs, "Who Will Blow the Trumpet?" Full audio of the speech is available at http://digital.library.ucsb.edu/items/show/5250. The speech was delivered August 20, 1963.

3. James Boggs, *Racism and the Class Struggle*, 418. The essay was written in 1963 and first published in the journal *Revolution—Africa, Latin America, Asia*.

4. On dialectical materialism and historical materialism, see Bottomore, *A Dictionary of Marxist Thought*.

5. James Boggs, Grace Lee Boggs, Freddy Paine, and Lyman Paine, *Conversations in Maine*, 270, 291.

6. In her autobiography, writing three decades later, Grace Lee Boggs modestly credits Lyman Paine with conceptualizing and coining the phrase "dialectical humanism" in 1968 (*Living for Change*, 152). The book's addendum adds that the process by which Lyman Paine came to dialectical humanism began after he visited C. L. R. James in 1956. But the concept was surely a collective one, generated through shared intellectual work and political struggles.

7. James Boggs, "Black Power"; James Boggs, "The Revolutionary Struggle for Black Power"; James Boggs, "The Myth and Irrationality of Black Capitalism."

8. James Boggs, *Racism and the Class Struggle*, 58, 52.

9. Ibid., 68.

10. James Boggs, "Beyond Rebellion," in Ward, ed., *Pages from a Black Radical's Notebook*, 251.

11. Grace Lee Boggs, "My Philosophic Journey" (unpublished manuscript in author's possession), 1998, 7.

12. They continued this dialogue through an exchange of letters and writings that continued until Nkrumah's death in 1972.

13. Grace Lee Boggs, *Living for Change*, 146–50. Portions of conversations from the years 1970–74 were published in *Conversations in Maine*, which has an excellent introduction by Richard Feldman.

14. Grace Lee Boggs, *Living for Change*, 149–50.

15. Ibid., 156.

16. Hearings before the Permanent Subcommittee on Government Operations United States Senate, Ninetieth Congress, Second Session, March 21 and 22, 1968, Part 6. Quotations appear on 1422 and 1440.

17. Grace Lee Boggs, *Living for Change*, 196.

18. For more on the Asian Political Alliance, see Fu, "On Contradiction," which provides a rich analysis of the group's origins, activities, and historical significance.

19. James Boggs, *Manifesto*, 2. This pamphlet carried Jimmy's name as sole author, but it was likely a collaborative effort of Jimmy, Grace, and others, such as their Philadelphia-based comrades James McFadden and Bill Davis.

20. Ibid.

21. James Boggs and Grace Lee Boggs, *Revolution and Evolution*, 15, 19.

22. James Boggs, statement on the inside cover of a pamphlet titled *Grace: Selected Speeches*, which was prepared by James Boggs, Joseph Eggly, Susan Eggly, Richard Feldman, John S. Gruchala, Sharon Howell, Freddy Paine, and Nkenge Zola, for Grace Lee Boggs's seventy-fifth birthday in 1990.

23. For a brief explanation of the founding of Save Our Sons and Daughters, its evolution, and the Boggses' involvement, see Grace Lee Boggs, *Living for Change*, 210–18.

24. People's Festival program, November 16, 1991, in author's possession.

25. Howell, Brock, and Hauser, "A Multicultural, Intergenerational Youth Program; author's electronic correspondence with Sharon Howell, November 25, 2015; Grace Lee Boggs, *Living for Change*, 232–35; Grace Lee Boggs and Kurashige, "Planting the Seeds of Hope."

26. Hollins quoted in Grace Lee Boggs, *Living for Change*, 233.

27. Putnam quoted in Zola, Gruchala, and Grace Lee Boggs, *James Boggs*.

28. Grace Lee Boggs, *Living for Change*, 235–38; Grace Lee Boggs, "Remembering James Boggs."

29. Grace Lee Boggs to Rose and Vincent Harding, December 5, 1993, Boggs Papers, Box 9, Folder 7.

30. Grace Lee Boggs to Nick (Xavier Nicholas), January 11, 1994, in author's possession.

31. Grace Lee Boggs, *Living for Change*, 238.

32. Program for "Celebration a Life," October 23, 1993, First Unitarian-Universalist Church, Detroit, in author's possession.

33. Davis, *Life Lit by Some Large Vision*, 195.

34. "A Celebration of Life." A longer version of Dee's poem appears in the booklet of tributes to Jimmy, *James Boggs: An American Revolutionary*, which was distributed at the memorial service.

35. Zola, Gruchala, and Grace Lee Boggs, *James Boggs* (no pagination); Bill Strickland to author, October 29, 2001; Bill Strickland, "Remembering My Man, James Boggs," October 12, 1993, in author's possession.

36. Transcript of "What Fire Can a Younger Generation Catch from the Work of James Boggs?," November 36, 1994, in author's possession.

37. Grace Lee Boggs, *Living for Change*, xvi.

38. Author's electronic correspondence with Alice Jennings, December 11, 2015.

39. Grace Lee Boggs, *Living for Change*, 260.

40. Ibid. In 2012, the City of Detroit established the house as a historic site, the "Grace Lee and James Boggs House Historic District," based on a petition to the City of Detroit Historic District Commission filed by Alice Jennings and Carl Edwards.

41. For more on the history and continuing activities of the Boggs Center, see http://boggscenter.org/.

42. A full explication of Grace's ideas, activities, and influence during these two decades is not yet available. To begin, see the following: Grace Lee Boggs, *Living for Change*; Grace Lee Boggs with Kurashige, *The Next American Revolution*; Lee, *American Revolutionary*; Grace Lee Boggs, Birkhold, Feldman, and Howell, "A Detroit Story"; and the pamphlet *A New Moment*, published in April 2015 by the James and Grace Lee Boggs Center to Nurture Community Leadership (available at http://boggscenter.org/).

43. Lee, *American Revolutionary*.

44. Information about the celebration can be found here: http://graceleeboggs100.org/

45. Poem delivered at Grace Lee Boggs memorial service, "Celebrating the Life and Legacy of Grace Lee Boggs," October 31, 2015, IBEW Local 58, Detroit, Michigan.

46. James Boggs, statement on the inside cover of James Boggs et al., *Grace: Selected Speeches*.

Bibliography

ARCHIVAL AND MANUSCRIPT COLLECTIONS

Bentley Historical Library, University of Michigan, Michigan
  Albert B. Cleage Jr. Papers
  Detroit Urban League Records
  C. L. Franklin Papers
Moorland-Spingarn Research Center, Howard University, Washington, D.C.
  The Civil Rights Documentation Project, Ralph J. Bunche Oral History Collection
Rare Book and Manuscript Library, Columbia University, New York
  C. L. R. James Papers
Special Collections Library, University of Michigan, Michigan
  Joseph A. Labadie Collection
Tamiment Library and Robert F. Wagner Labor Archives, New York University, New York
  Oral History of the American Left Collection
Walter P. Reuther Library, Archives of Labor and Urban Affairs, Wayne State University,
  Michigan
    Blacks in the Labor Movement Oral History Collection
    Detroit Commission on Community Relations—Human Rights Department Collection
    Ernest C. and Jessie M. Dillard Papers
    Frances D. and G. Lyman Paine Papers
    James and Grace Lee Boggs Papers
    Martin and Jessie Glaberman Papers
    NAACP Detroit Branch Collection
    Raya Dunayevskaya Papers
    United Automobile Workers Local 7 Collection

GOVERNMENT DOCUMENTS

Federal Bureau of Investigation, Washington, D.C.
  Grace Boggs File HQ 100-356160
  James Boggs File HQ 100-405600

INTERVIEWS CONDUCTED BY AUTHOR

Muhammad Ahmad (Maxwell Stanford Jr.), September 21, 2006, Detroit, Michigan
Dan Aldridge, December 13, 2002, Detroit, Michigan

Ernie Allen, September 25, 2004, telephone
General Baker and Marian Kramer, June 29, 2003, Detroit, Michigan
Annie Boggs, January 20, 2004, Detroit, Michigan
Grace Lee Boggs, multiple dates, Detroit, Michigan
James Boggs Jr., October 13, 2007, Fresno, California
John Bracey, August 3, 2010, telephone
James Chaffers, April 13, 2005, Ann Arbor, Michigan
Patricia Colman-Burns, Ann Arbor, Michigan
 July 6, 2005
 July 12, 2005
Richard Feldman, December 16, 2006, Huntington Woods, Michigan
Sharon (Shea) Howell, Detroit, Michigan
 July 18, 2007
 June 10, 2008
Jim Jackson, November 17, 2001, Detroit, Michigan
Selma James, November 23, 2012, telephone
Frank Joyce
 November 11, 2010, Gross Pointe, Michigan
 November 7, 2012, Detroit, Michigan
Nettie Kravitz, July 2, 2008, telephone
Joe Maddox, October 4, 2003, Detroit, Michigan
Claudia Gwendolyn Mallett and Conrad Mallett, February 20, 2006, telephone
James McFadden, April 16, 2008, telephone
Charles Morton, June 21, 2006, Detroit, Michigan
Xavier Nicholas, telephone
 May 20, 2008
 May 22, 2008
Ron Scott, April 11, 2008, Detroit, Michigan
Kenneth Snodgrass, May 9, 2005, Detroit, Michigan
Luke Trip, November 12, 2003, telephone
Dolores Wilson, August 1, 2006, Detroit, Michigan
Reginald Wilson, February 13, 2006, telephone

AUDIO AND VIDEO RECORDINGS

Allen, Austin, dir. *Claiming Open Spaces*. Urban Garden Films, 1995.

Boggs, Grace Lee. "Who Will Blow the Trumpet?" (speech). August 20, 1963. Audio available at http://digital.library.ucsb.edu/items/show/5250.

Boggs, James. "Conversations with James Boggs, #2." Interview by Kenneth Snodgrass. YouTube video. May 25, 2009. https://www.youtube.com/watch?v=ywjrbGdsrO4 (accessed March 23, 2013).

———. "Walking a Chalk Line." Interview by WBAI Pacifica Radio, recorded October 11, 1963; broadcast November 25, 1963. Pacifica Radio Archives BB3071. CD recording.

James and Grace Lee Boggs Community Celebration. Detroit, May 1990. Videotape in
    author's possession.
King, Martin Luther, Jr. *The Great March to Freedom.* Gordy Records no. 906. CD recording.
Lee, Grace, dir. *American Revolutionary: The Evolution of Grace Lee Boggs.* LeeLee Films,
    2013.
Reid, France, dir. *James Boggs: An American Revolutionist.* 1993.

UNPUBLISHED SOURCES

Boggs, Grace Lee. "Coming Full Circle." Manuscript in author's possession.
———. *Grace: Selected Speeches by Grace Lee Boggs.* 1990.
———. Interview by Stephen Ferguson and Jennifer Choi. Transcript in author's possession.
———. "My Philosophic Journey." 1998. Manuscript in author's possession.
———. Speech to Convention of Correspondence Committees. Text in author's possession.
Boggs, James. *Manifesto for a Black Revolutionary Party.* 1969.
———. Statement made during the "Pendle Hill Seminar/Search: Martin Luther King,
    Jr. and the Modern Freedom Movement." Led by Vincent Harding and Rosemarie
    Freeney Harding. July 18, 1979. Text in author's possession.
———. Statement made to Members of the Executive Board of Local 7. January 25, 1961.
    Text in author's possession.
———. "Think Dialectically, Not Biologically." Save Our Sons and Daughters Workshop,
    March 1993. Videotape in author's possession.
"Celebrating a Life." James Boggs memorial service program, First Unitarian-Universalist
    Church, Detroit, Mich., October 23, 1993. In author's possession.
House, Gloria Aneb. "For Grace Lee Boggs' 100th Birthday." In author's possession.
James and Grace Lee Boggs Center to Nurture Community Leadership. *A New Moment.*
    2015. http://boggscenter.org/.
"People's Festival" program, Majestic Theatre, Detroit, Mich., November 16, 1991. In
    author's possession.
Strickland, Bill. "Remembering My Man, James Boggs." Statement for memorial celebration
    of James Boggs, October 12, 1993. In author's possession.
"What Fire Can a Younger Generation Catch from the Work of James Boggs?" Barth Hall,
    The Cathedral Church of St. Paul, Detroit, Mich., November 26, 1994. Transcript in
    author's possession.

PUBLISHED SOURCES

Aberbach, Joel D., and Jack L. Walker. *Race in the City: Political Trust and Public Policy in the
    New Urban System.* Boston: Little, Brown, 1973.
Ahmad, Muhammad. *We Will Return in the Whirlwind: Black Radical Organizations,
    1960–1975.* Chicago: Charles H. Kerr, 2007.
Alabama Department of Archives and History. *Alabama Official and Statistical Register, 1915.*
    Montgomery: Brown Printing, 1915.

———. *Alabama Official and Statistical Register, 1919*. Montgomery: Brown Printing, 1920.

———. *Alabama Official and Statistical Register, 1931*. Montgomery: Wilson Printing, 1931.

Alexander, Robert J. *International Trotskyism, 1929–1985: A Documented Analysis of the Movement*. Durham, N.C.: Duke University Press, 1991.

Alpern, Sara, Joyce Antler, Elisabeth Israels Perry, and Ingrid Winther Scobie, eds. *The Challenge of Feminist Biography: Writing the Lives of Modern American Women*. Urbana: University of Illinois Press, 1992.

Anderson, Jervis. *A. Philip Randolph: A Biographical Portrait*. New York: Harcourt Brace Jovanovich, 1972.

Arnesen, Eric. "Civil Rights and the Cold War at Home: Postwar Activism, Anticommunism, and the Decline of the Left." *American Communist History* 11, no. 1 (April 2012): 5–44.

———. "No 'Graver Danger': Black Anticommunism, the Communist Party, and the Race Question." *Labor: Studies in Working-Class History of the Americas* 3, no. 4 (Winter 2006): 13–52.

Arsenault, Raymond. *Freedom Riders: 1961 and the Struggle for Racial Justice*. New York: Oxford University Press, 2006.

Austin, Algernon. *Achieving Blackness: Race, Black Nationalism, and Afrocentrism in the Twentieth Century*. New York: New York University Press, 2006.

Babson, Steve. *The Unfinished Struggle: Turning Points in American Labor, 1877-Present*. Lanham: Rowman and Littlefield, 1999.

———. *Working Detroit: The Making of a Union Town*. Detroit: Wayne State University Press, 1986.

Bailer, Lloyd H. "The Negro Automobile Worker." *Journal of Political Economy* 51, no. 5 (October 1943): 415–28.

Bailey, Richard. *They Too Call Alabama Home: African American Profiles, 1800–1999*. Montgomery, Ala.: Pyramid, 1999.

Baldwin, James. *The Fire Next Time*. New York: Dial, 1963.

———. "A Negro Assays the Negro Mood." *New York Times Magazine*, March 12, 1961.

———. *The Price of the Ticket: Collected Nonfiction, 1948–1985*. New York: St. Martin's, 1985.

Bambara, Toni Cade. *The Black Woman*. New York: Washington Square, 2005 [1970].

Barbour, Floyd B., ed. *The Black Seventies*. Boston: Porter Sargent, 1970.

Bates, Beth Tomkins. "'Double V for Victory' Mobilizes Black Detroit, 1941–1946." In *Freedom North: Black Freedom Struggles outside the South, 1940–1980*, edited by Jeanne Theoharis and Komozi Woodard, 17–40. New York: Palgrave, 2003.

———. *The Making of Black Detroit in the Age of Henry Ford*. Chapel Hill: University of North Carolina Press, 2012.

———. *Pullman Porters and the Rise of Protest Politics in Black America, 1925–1945*. Chapel Hill: University of North Carolina Press, 2001.

Bederman, Gail. *Manliness and Civilization: A Cultural History of Gender and Race in the United States, 1880–1917*. Chicago: University of Chicago Press, 1995.

Bennett, Lerone, Jr. *Before the Mayflower: A History of Black America*. New York: Penguin, 1988 [1962].

Berger, Dan. *Captive Nation: Black Prison Organizing in the Civil Rights Era*. Chapel Hill: University of North Carolina Press, 2014.

Biondi, Martha. *To Stand and Fight: The Struggle for Civil Rights in Postwar New York City*. Cambridge, Mass.: Harvard University Press, 2003.

Birkhold, Matthew, ed. "Reflections on a Black Worker's Notebook: The Legacy of James Boggs's *The American Revolution*." Special issue, *Souls: A Critical Journal of Black Politics, Culture, and Society* 13, no. 3.

Bix, Amy Sue. *Inventing Ourselves Out of Jobs? America's Debate over Technological Unemployment, 1929–1981*. Baltimore: Johns Hopkins University Press, 2000.

Bjorn, Lars, and Jim Gallert, *Before Motown: A History of Jazz in Detroit, 1920–1960*. Ann Arbor: University of Michigan Press, 2001.

Blackburn, Simon. *Oxford Dictionary of Philosophy*. Oxford: Oxford University Press, 1994.

Boehm, Lisa Krissoff. *Making a Way Out of No Way: African American Women and the Second Great Migration*. Jackson: University Press of Mississippi, 2009.

Boggs, Grace Lee. "C. L. R. James: Organizing in the U.S.A., 1938–1953." In *C. L. R. James: His Intellectual Legacies*, edited by Selwyn R. Cudjoe and William E. Cain, 163–72. Amherst: University of Massachusetts Press, 1995.

———. *Living for Change: An Autobiography*. Minneapolis: University of Minnesota Press, 1998.

———. "Living for Change: Reconnecting Generations." *Michigan Citizen*, May 23, 2010.

———. "Movement Reading." *Hyphen*, Summer 2009.

———. "Our Country—To Change for the Better." *Amerasia Journal* 25, no. 2 (1999): xvii–xxviii.

———. "Remembering James Boggs." *Third World Viewpoint* (Fall 1993): 12.

———. "Thinking and Acting Dialectically: C. L. R. James, the American Years." *Monthly Review*, October 1993, 38–46.

Boggs, Grace Lee, Matthew Birkhold, Rick Feldman, and Shea Howell. "A Detroit Story: Ideas Whose Time Has Come." In *Grabbing Back: Essays against the Global Land Grab*, edited by Alexander Reid Ross, 193–207. Oakland: AK Press, 2014.

Boggs, Grace Lee, with Scott Kurashige. *The Next American Revolution: Sustainable Activism for the Twenty-First Century*. Berkeley: University of California Press, 2011.

———. "Planting the Seeds of Hope." In *A Detroit Anthology*, edited by Anna Clark, 222–24. Cleveland: Rust Belt Chic Press, 2014.

Boggs, James. *The American Revolution: Pages from a Negro Worker's Notebook*. New York: Monthly Review Press, 2009 [1963].

———. "Beyond Militancy." *Monthly Review* 26, no. 4 (September 1974): 34–42.

———. "Black Power—A Scientific Concept Whose Time Has Come." In *Black Fire: An Anthology of Afro-American Writing*, edited by LeRoi Jones and Larry Neal. New York: William Morrow, 1968.

———. Interview in *Detroit Committee for the Liberation of Africa Newsletter* 1, no. 4 (February–March 1974): 1–3.

———. "The Myth and Irrationality of Black Capitalism." *Review of Black Political Economy* 1, no. 1 (Spring–Summer 1970): 27–35.

———. *Racism and the Class Struggle: Further Pages from a Black Worker's Notebook*. New York: Monthly Review Press, 1970.

———. "The Revolutionary Struggle for Black Power." In *The Black Seventies*, edited by Floyd B. Barbour. Boston: Porter Sargent, 1970.

Boggs, James, and Grace Lee Boggs. *Revolution and Evolution in the Twentieth Century*. New York: Monthly Review Press, 1974.

Boggs, James, Grace Lee Boggs, Freddy Paine, and Lyman Paine. *Conversations in Maine: Exploring Our Nation's Future*. Boston: South End, 1978.

Bogues, Anthony. *Caliban's Freedom: The Early Political Thought of C. L. R. James*. London: Pluto, 1997.

Bond, Horace Mann. *Negro Education in Alabama: A Study in Cotton and Steel*. New York: Octagon Books, 1969 [1939].

Bosworth, Karl A. *Black Belt County: Rural Government in the Cotton Country of Alabama*. Birmingham: Birmingham Printing and the University of Alabama, 1941.

Bottomore, Tom, ed. *A Dictionary of Marxist Thought*. Cambridge, Mass.: Blackwell, 1991 [1983].

Boyd, Melba Joyce. *Wrestling with the Muse: Dudley Randall and the Broadside Press*. New York: Columbia University Press, 2003.

———, ed. *Roses and Revolution: The Selected Writings of Dudley Randall*. Detroit: Wayne State University Press, 2009.

Boykin, Ulysses W. *A Handbook on the Detroit Negro (A Preliminary Edition)*. Detroit: Minority Study Associates, 1943.

Boyle, Kevin. "Auto Workers at War: Patriotism and Protest in the American Automobile Industry, 1939–1945." In *Autowork*, edited by Robert Asher and Ronald Edsforth, 99–126. Albany: State University of New York Press, 1995.

———. *The UAW and the Heyday of American Liberalism, 1945–1968*. Ithaca, N.Y.: Cornell University Press, 1995.

Branch, Taylor. *Parting the Waters: America in the King Years, 1954–63*. New York: Simon and Schuster, 1988.

———. *Pillar of Fire: America in the King Years, 1963–1965*. New York: Touchstone, 1998.

Breitman, George, ed. *Leon Trotsky on Black Nationalism and Self-Determination*. New York: Pathfinder, 1978 [1967].

———, ed. *Malcolm X Speaks: Selected Speeches and Statements*. New York: Grove, 1965.

Breitman, George, Paul Le Blanc, and Alan Wald. *Trotskyism in the United States: Historical Essays and Reconsiderations*. Atlantic Highlands, N.J.: Humanities, 1996.

Brink, William, and Louis Harris. *The Negro Revolution in America: What Negroes Want, How and Why They Are Fighting, Whom They Support, and What Whites Think of Them and Their Demands*. New York: Simon and Schuster, 1963.

Brown, Scot. *Fighting for US: Maulana Karenga, the US Organization, and Black Cultural Nationalism*. New York: New York University Press, 2003.

Buhle, Mari Jo, Paul Buhle, and Dan Georgakas, eds. *Encyclopedia of the American Left*. Urbana: University of Illinois Press, 1990.

Buhle, Paul. *C. L. R. James: The Artist as Revolutionary*. New York: Verso, 1997.

———, ed. *C. L. R. James: His Life and Work*. London: Allison and Busby, 1986.

Callinicos, Alex. *Trotskyism*. Buckingham: Open University Press, 1990.

Capeci, Dominic J. *Race Relations in Wartime Detroit: The Sojourner Truth Housing Controversy of 1942*. Philadelphia: Temple University Press, 1984.

Capeci, Dominic J., and Martha Wilkerson. *Layered Violence: The Detroit Rioters of 1943*. Jackson: University Press of Mississippi, 1991.

Carson, Clayborne, ed. *A Call to Conscience: The Landmark Speeches of Martin Luther King, Jr.* New York: Warner Books, 2001.

Carter, Dan T. *Scottsboro: A Tragedy of the American South*. Baton Rouge: Louisiana State University Press, 1969.

Castoriadis, Cornelius. "C. L. R. James and the Fate of Marxism." In *C. L. R. James: His Intellectual Legacies*, edited by Selwyn R. Cudjoe and William E. Cain, 277–97. Amherst: University of Massachusetts Press, 1995.

Chang, Iris. *The Chinese in America: A Narrative History*. New York: Penguin, 2003.

Charron, Katherine Mellen. *Freedom's Teacher: The Life of Septima Clark*. Chapel Hill: University of North Carolina Press, 2009.

Chen, Julia I. Hsuan. "The Chinese in New York: A Study in Their Cultural Adjustment, 1920–1940." Ph.D. diss., American University, 1941. Reprinted by R and E Research Associates, San Francisco, 1974.

Chen, Shehong. *Being Chinese, Becoming Chinese American*. Urbana: University of Illinois Press, 2002.

Choi, Jennifer Jung Hee. "At the Margins of the Asian American Political Experience: The Life of Grace Lee Boggs." *Amerasia Journal* 25, no. 2 (1999): 18–40.

Clarke, John Henrik. "The New Afro-American Nationalism." *Freedomways* 1, no. 3 (Fall 1961): 285–95.

Cleage, Albert B., Jr. *Black Christian Nationalism: New Directions for the Black Church*. Detroit: Luxor, 1987 [1972].

Cobb, William Jelani, ed. *The Essential Harold Cruse: A Reader*. New York: Palgrave, 2002.

Coleman, Monica A. *Making a Way Out of No Way: A Womanist Theology*. Minneapolis: Fortress, 2008.

Conot, Robert. *American Odyssey: A Unique History of America Told through the Life of a Great City*. New York: William Morrow, 1974.

Countryman, Matthew J. *Up South: Civil Rights and Black Power in Philadelphia*. Philadelphia: University of Pennsylvania Press, 2006.

Cruse, Harold. *The Crisis of the Negro Intellectual*. New York: New York Review of Books, 2005 [1967].

Cudjoe, Selwyn R., and William E. Cain, eds. *C. L. R. James: His Intellectual Legacies*. Amherst: University of Massachusetts Press, 1995.

Curtis, David Ames, ed. *Cornelius Castoriadis: Political and Social Writings*. Vol. 1, *1946–1955*. Minneapolis: University of Minnesota Press, 1988.

Darden, Joe. T., Richard Child Hill, June Thomas, and Richard Thomas, eds. *Detroit: Race and Uneven Development*. Philadelphia: Temple University Press, 1987.

Davies, Carole Boyce. *Left of Karl Marx: The Political Life of Black Communist Claudia Jones*. Durham, N.C.: Duke University Press, 2008.

Davis, Ossie. *Life Lit by Some Large Vision: Selected Speeches and Writings.* New York: Atria Books, 2006.

Dawsey, Darrell. "An American Revolutionary." *Detroit News*, April 21, 1992, 4c.

Dawson, Michael. *Blacks In and Out of the Left.* Cambridge, Mass.: Harvard University Press, 2013.

———. *Black Visions: The Roots of Contemporary African-American Political Ideologies.* Chicago: University of Chicago Press, 2001.

Denby, Charles (Simon Owens). *Indignant Heart: A Black Worker's Journal.* Detroit: Wayne State University Press, 1989 [1952].

De Witte, Ludo. *The Assassination of Lumumba.* Translated by Ann Wright and Reneé Fenby. London: Verso, 2001.

Dillard, Angela D. *Faith in the City: Preaching Radical Social Change in Detroit.* Ann Arbor: University of Michigan Press, 2007.

Doody, Colleen. *Detroit's Cold War: The Origins of Postwar Conservatism.* Urbana: University of Illinois Press, 2013.

Drake, St. Clair J. G. "Profiles: Chicago." *Journal of Educational Sociology* 17, no. 5 (January 1944): 261–71.

Drake, St. Clair, and Horace Cayton. *Black Metropolis: A Study of Negro Life in a Northern City.* Chicago: University of Chicago Press, 1993 [1945].

Edelman, Marian Wright. *The Measure of Our Success: A Letter to My Children and Yours.* New York: Harper Perennial, 1992.

Edsforth, Ronald. "Why Automation Didn't Shorten the Work Week: The Politics of Work Time in the Automobile Industry." In *Autowork*, edited by Robert Asher and Ronald Edsforth, 155–79. Albany: State University of New York Press, 1995.

Ellison, Ralph. *Invisible Man.* New York: Random House, 1952.

Eskew, Glenn T. *But for Birmingham: The Local and National Movements in the Civil Rights Struggle.* Chapel Hill: University of North Carolina Press, 1997.

Feinberg, Barry, and Ronald Kasrils, eds. *Bertrand Russell's America.* Volume Two, *His Transatlantic Travels and Writings, 1945–1970.* Boston: South End, 1983.

Feldman, Glenn. *Politics, Society, and the Klan in Alabama, 1915–1949.* Tuscaloosa: University of Alabama Press, 1999.

Feldman, Richard. Introduction to *Conversations in Maine: Exploring Our Nation's Future*, by Grace Lee Boggs, Freddy Paine, and Lyman Paine, xi–xviii. Boston: South End, 1978.

Feldman, Richard, and Michael Betzold, eds. *End of the Line: Autoworkers and the American Dream: An Oral History.* Urbana: University of Illinois Press, 1988.

Fentin, David Thomas. "The Detroit Council for Human Rights and the Detroit Freedom March of 1963." MA thesis, Wayne State University, 1998.

Fergus, Devin. *Liberalism, Black Power, and the Making of American Politics, 1965–1980.* Athens: University of Georgia Press, 2009.

Fessler, Loren, ed. *Chinese in America: Stereotyped Past, Changing Present.* New York: Vantage, 1983.

Fine, Sidney. *Expanding the Frontiers of Civil Rights: Michigan, 1948–1968.* Detroit: Wayne State University Press, 2000.

———. *Violence in the Model City: The Cavanagh Administration, Race Relations, and the Detroit Riot of 1967*. East Lansing: Michigan State University Press, 2007 [1989].

Fitts, Alston. *Selma: Queen City of the Black Belt*. Selma, Ala.: Clairmont, 1989.

Flynt, Wayne. *Alabama in the Twentieth Century*. Tuscaloosa: University of Alabama Press, 2004.

Frazier, Robeson Taj P. "The Assult of the Monkey King on the Hosts of Heaven: The Black Freedom Struggle and China—the New Center of Revolution." In *African Americans in Global Affairs: Contemporary Perspectives*, edited by Michael L. Clemons, 313–44. Boston: Northeastern University Press, 2010.

Frederickson, Mary E., and Delores M. Walters, eds. *Gendered Resistance: Women, Slavery, and the Legacy of Margaret Garner*. Urbana: University of Illinois Press, 2013.

Fu, May C. "On Contradiction: Theory and Transformation in Detroit's Asian Political Alliance." *Amerasia Journal* 35, no. 2 (2009): 1–22.

Fullilove, Mindy Thompson. *Root Shock: How Tearing Up City Neighborhoods Hurts America, and What We Can Do about It*. New York: Ballantine Books, 2004.

Garfinkel, Herbert. *When Negroes March: The March on Washington Movement in the Organizational Politics of the FEPC*. Glencoe, Ill.: Free Press, 1959.

Garrow, David J. *Bearing the Cross: Martin Luther King, Jr., and the Southern Christian Leadership Conference*. New York: Harper Collins, 1986.

Gavrilovich, Peter, and Bill McGraw, eds. *The Detroit Almanac: 300 Years of Life in the Motor City*. Detroit: Detroit Free Press, 2000.

Gellman, Erik S. *Death Blow to Jim Crow: The National Negro Congress and the Rise of Militant Civil Rights*. Chapel Hill: University of North Carolina Press, 2012.

Georgakas, Dan. "Frank Lovell: The Detroit Years." In *Revolutionary Labor Socialist: The Life, Ideas, and Comrades of Frank Lovell*, edited by Paul Le Blanc and Thomas Barrett. Union City, N.J.: Smyrna, 2000.

———. "Young Detroit Radicals, 1955–1965." In *C. L. R. James: His Life and Work*, edited by Paul Buhle, 185–94. London: Allison and Busby, 1986.

Gilman, Charlotte Perkins. *Women and Economics: A Study of the Economic Relation between Women and Men*. New York: Prometheus Books, 1994 [1898].

Glaberman, Martin. "The Marxism of C. L. R. James." In *C. L. R. James: His Intellectual Legacies*, edited by Selwyn R. Cudjoe and William E. Cain, 304–13. Amherst: University of Massachusetts Press, 1995.

———. *Wartime Strikes: The Struggle Against the No-Strike Pledge in the UAW during World War II*. Detroit: Bewick, 1980.

———, ed. *Marxism for Our Times: C. L. R. James on Revolutionary Organization*. Jackson: University of Mississippi Press, 1999.

Glaude, Eddie S., Jr., ed. *Is It Nation Time? Contemporary Essays on Black Power and Black Nationalism*. Chicago: University of Chicago Press, 2002.

Goldberg, David, and Trevor Griffey, eds. *Black Power at Work: Community Control, Affirmative Action, and the Construction Industry*. Ithaca, N.Y.: Cornell University Press, 2010.

Gore, Dayo F. *Radicalism at the Crossroads: African American Woman Activists in the Cold War*. New York: New York University Press, 2011.

Gore, Dayo F., Jeanne Theoharis, and Komozi Woodard, eds. *Want to Start a Revolution? Radical Women in the Black Freedom Struggle*. New York: New York University Press, 2009.

Gosse, Van. *Rethinking the New Left: An Interpretive History*. New York: Palgrave Macmillan, 2005.

———. *Where the Boys Are: Cuba, Cold War, and the Making of a New Left*. London: Verso, 1993.

Grady-Willis, Winston A. *Challenging U.S. Apartheid: Atlanta and Black Struggles for Human Rights, 1960–1977*. Durham, N.C.: Duke University Press, 2006.

Griffith, Lucille. *Alabama: A Documentary History to 1900*. Tuscaloosa: University of Alabama Press, 1972 [1968].

Grimshaw, Anna. "Introduction: C. L. R. James: A Revolutionary Vision." In *The C. L. R. James Reader*, edited by Anna Grimshaw, 1–22. Cambridge, Mass.: Blackwell, 1992.

———, ed. *The C. L. R. James Reader*. Cambridge, Mass.: Blackwell, 1992.

Grimshaw, Anna, and Keith Hart. "*American Civilization*: An Introduction." In C. L. R. James, *American Civilization*, edited by Anna Grimshaw and Keith Hart, 1–25. Cambridge, Mass.: Blackwell, 1993.

Hahn, Lewis Edwin, ed. *The Philosophy of Paul Weiss*. Chicago: Open Court, 1995.

Halpern, Martin. "'I'm Fighting for Freedom': Coleman Young, HUAC, and the Detroit African American Community." *Journal of American Ethnic History* 17, no. 1 (Fall 1997): 19–38.

Hansberry, Lorraine. "Congolese Patriot." *New York Times Magazine*, March 26, 1961, 4.

Hereford, Robert Scott. "A Study of Selma and Dallas County, Alabama, 1930–1970." MA thesis, University of Georgia, 1992.

Hill, Robert A. "In England, 1932–1938." In *C. L. R. James: His Life and Work*, edited by Paul Buhle, 61–80. London: Allison and Busby, 1986.

———. "Literary Executor's Afterword." In *American Civilization*, edited by Anna Grimshaw and Keith Hart, 293–366. Cambridge, Mass.: Blackwell, 1993.

———, ed. *The FBI's RACON: Racial Conditions in the United States during World War II*. Boston: Northeastern University Press, 1995.

Holsaert, Faith S., Martha Prescod Norman Noonan, Judy Richardson, Betty Garman Robinson, Jean Smith Young, and Dorothy M. Zellner, eds. *Hands on the Freedom Plow: Personal Accounts by Women in SNCC*. Urbana: University of Illinois Press, 2010.

Horne, Gerald. *Black Liberation/Red Scare: Ben Davis and the Communist Party*. Newark: University of Delaware Press, 1994.

———. *Black Revolutionary: William Patterson and the Globalization of the African American Freedom Struggle*. Urbana: University of Illinois Press, 2013.

———. *Mau Mau in Harlem? The U.S. and the Liberation of Kenya*. New York: Palgrave Macmillan, 2009.

———. *Race Woman: The Lives of Shirley Graham Du Bois*. New York: New York University Press, 2000.

———. *Red Seas: Ferdinand Smith and Radical Black Sailors in the United States and Jamaica*. New York: New York University Press, 2005.

Howard, Walter T. *We Shall Be Free! Black Communist Protests in Seven Voices*. Philadelphia: Temple University Press, 2013.

Howe, Irving, and B. J. Widick. *The UAW and Walter Reuther*. New York: Da Capo, 1973.

Howell, Sharon, Bernard Brock, and Eric Hauser. "A Multicultural, Intergenerational Youth Program: Creating and Sustaining a Youth Community Group." In *Group Communication in Context: Studies of Bona Fide Groups*, edited by Larry R. Frey. New York: Routledge, 2003.

Hsu, Madeline Yuan-Yin. *Dreaming of Gold, Dreaming of Home: Transnationalism and Migration between the United States and South China, 1882–1943*. Stanford, Calif.: Stanford University Press, 2000.

Hyde, Charles K. *Detroit: An Industrial History Guide*. Detroit: Wayne State University Press, 1982.

Isserman, Maurice. *Which Side Were You On? The American Communist Party during the Second World War*. Urbana: University of Illinois Press, 1993 [1982].

Jackson, Esther Cooper, ed. *Freedomways Reader: Prophets in Their Own Country*. Boulder, Colo.: Westview, 2000.

Jackson, Lawrence P. *The Indignant Generation: A Narrative History of African American Writers and Critics, 1934–1960*. Princeton, N.J.: Princeton University Press, 2011.

James, C. L. R. *American Civilization*. Edited by Anna Grimshaw and Keith Hart. Cambridge, Mass.: Blackwell, 1993.

———. *Beyond a Boundary*. Durham, N.C.: Duke University Press, 1993 [1963].

———. *The Black Jacobins: Toussaint L'Ouverture and the San Domingo Revolution*. New York: Vintage, 1989 [1938].

———. *The Future in the Present: Selected Writings*. London: Allison and Busby, 1977.

———. *A History of Pan-African Revolt*. Chicago: Charles H. Kerr, 1995 [1938].

———. *Mariners, Renegades and Castaways: The Story of Herman Melville and the World We Live In*. Hanover: University Press of New England, 2001 [1953].

———. *Nkrumah and the Ghana Revolution*. London: Allison and Busby, 1982 [1977].

———. *Notes on Dialectics: Hegel, Marx, Lenin*. London: Allison and Busby, 1980.

———. *Party Politics in the West Indies*. San Juan, Trinidad: Vedic Enterprises, 1962.

James, C. L. R., with Raya Dunayevskaya and Grace Lee. *State Capitalism and World Revolution*. Chicago: Charles H. Kerr, 1986.

James, C. L. R., F. Forest, and Ria Stone. *The Invading Socialist Society*. Detroit: Bewick, 1972 [1947].

James, C. L. R., Grace C. Lee, and Pierre Chaulieu. *Facing Reality*. Detroit: Bewick, 1974 [1958].

James, David. *Hegel: A Guide for the Perplexed*. London: Continuum, 2007.

James, Selma. *Sex, Race, and Class: The Perspective of Winning—A Selection of Writings, 1952–2011*. Oakland, Calif.: PM, 2012.

Jefferys, Steve. *Management and Managed: Fifty Years of Crisis at Chrysler*. New York: Cambridge University Press, 1986.

Jeffries, Hasan Kwame. *Bloody Lowndes: Civil Rights and Black Power in Alabama's Black Belt*. New York: New York University Press, 2009.

Jeffries, Judson L., ed. *Black Power in the Belly of the Beast*. Urbana: University of Illinois Press, 2006.

Johnson, Arthur L. *Race and Remembrance: A Memoir*. Detroit: Wayne State University Press, 2008.

Johnson, Cedric. *Revolutionaries to Race Leaders: Black Power and the Making of African American Politics*. Minneapolis: University of Minnesota Press, 2007.

Johnson, J. R., F. Forest, and Ria Stone. *Essays by Karl Marx, Selected from the Economic and Philosophic Manuscripts*. New York: Johnson-Forest Tendency, 1947.

Johnson, Marilynn S. "Gender, Race, and Rumours: Re-examining the 1943 Race Riots." *Gender and History* 10 no. 2 (August 1998): 252–77.

Johnson-Forest Tendency. *Balance Sheet: Trotskyism in the United States, 1940–1947*. New York: Johnson-Forest Tendency, 1947

———. *The Balance Sheet Completed: Ten Years of American Trotskyism*. New York: Johnson-Forest Tendency, 1951.

Jones, Jacqueline. *A Dreadful Deceit: The Myth of Race from the Colonial Era to Obama's America*. New York: Basic Books, 2013.

Jones, LeRoi, and Larry Neal, eds. *Black Fire: An Anthology of Afro-American Writing*. New York: William Morrow, 1968.

Joseph, Peniel E. "The Black Power Movement: A State of the Field." *Journal of American History* 96, no. 3 (December 2009): 751–76.

———. *Waiting 'til the Midnight Hour: A Narrative History of Black Power in America*. New York: Henry Holt, 2006.

———, ed. *The Black Power Movement: Rethinking the Civil Rights-Black Power Era*. New York: Routledge, 2006.

———, ed. *Neighborhood Rebels: Black Power at the Local Level*. New York: Palgrave Macmillan, 2010.

Keeran, Roger. *The Communist Party and the Auto Workers Unions*. Bloomington: Indiana University Press, 1980.

Kelley, Robin D. G. *Freedom Dreams: The Black Radical Imagination*. Boston: Beacon, 2002.

———. *Hammer and Hoe: Alabama Communists during the Great Depression*. Chapel Hill: University of North Carolina Press, 1990.

———. *Race Rebels: Culture, Politics, and the Black Working Class*. New York: Free Press, 1994.

Kellner, Douglas. "Raya Dunayevskaya." In *Encyclopedia of the American Left*, edited by Mari Jo Buhle, Paul Buhle, and Dan Georgakas. Urbana: University of Illinois Press, 1990.

Kennedy, John F. "Statement by the President on the Tractors-for-Freedom Movement." May 24, 1961. *American Presidency Project*. http://www.presidency.ucsb.edu/ws/?pid=8147 (accessed March 7, 2015).

King, Martin Luther, Jr. *Why We Can't Wait*. New York: Harper and Row, 1964.

Kithinji, Michael Mwenda. "Koinange, Peter Mbiyu." In *Dictionary of African Biography*, edited by Emmanuel K. Akyeampong and Henry Louis Gates Jr., 408–10. Oxford: Oxford University Press, 2012.

———. "Koinange wa Mbiyu." In *Dictionary of African Biography*, edited by Emmanuel K. Akyeampong and Henry Louis Gates Jr., 410–11. Oxford: Oxford University Press, 2012.

Koinange, Mbiyu. *The People of Kenya Speak for Themselves.* Detroit: Kenya Publication Fund, 1955.

Kolchin, Peter. *First Freedom: The Responses of Alabama's Blacks to Emancipation and Reconstruction.* Westport, Conn.: Greenwood Press, 1972.

Korstad, Robert, and Nelson Lichtenstein. "Opportunities Found and Lost: Labor, Radicals, and the Early Civil Rights Movement." *Journal of American History* 75, no. 3 (December 1988): 786–811.

Kraditor, Aileen. *Jimmy Higgins: The Mental World of the American Rank-and-File Communist, 1930–1958.* Baton Rouge: Louisiana State University Press, 1981.

Krugler, David F. *1919, The Year of Racial Violence: How African Americans Fought Back.* New York: Cambridge University Press, 2015.

Krutch, Joseph Wood. *The Modern Temper: A Study and a Confession.* New York: Harcourt, Brace, 1929.

Kung, S. W. *Chinese in American Life: Some Aspects of Their History, Status, Problems, and Contributions.* Seattle: University of Washington Press, 1962.

Ladner, Joyce A. *The Ties That Bind: Timeless Values for African American Families.* New York: Wiley, 1998.

Lang, Clarence. *Grassroots at the Gateway: Class Politics and Black Freedom Struggle in St. Louis, 1936–1975.* Ann Arbor: University of Michigan Press, 2009.

Leaver, Eric W., and J. J. Brown. "Machines without Men." *Fortune,* November 1946, 192–204.

Lee, Alfred M., and Norman D. Humphrey. *Race Riot.* New York: Dryden, 1943.

Lee, Erika. *At America's Gates: Chinese Immigration during the Exclusion Era, 1882–1943.* Chapel Hill: University of North Carolina Press, 2003.

Lee, Grace Chin. *George Herbert Mead: The Philosopher of the Social Individual.* New York: King's Crown, 1945.

Lee, Helen Shores, and Barbara S. Shores, with Denise George. *The Gentle Giant of Dynamite Hill: The Untold Story of Arthur Shores and His Family's Fight for Civil Rights.* Grand Rapids, Mich.: Zondervan, 2012.

Leeks, Sylvester. "Definitions of the Negro Revolution." *Muhammad Speaks,* December 20, 1963, 18.

Leong, Karen J. *The China Mystique: Pearl S. Buck, Anna May Wong, Mayling Soong, and the Transformation of American Orientalism.* Berkeley: University of California Press, 2005.

Lewis-Colman, David M. *Race against Liberalism: Black Workers and the UAW in Detroit.* Urbana: University of Illinois Press, 2008.

Lewis, David Levering, Michael H. Nash, and Daniel J. Leab, eds. *Red Activists and Black Freedom: James and Esther Jackson and the Long Civil Rights Revolution.* New York: Routledge, 2010.

Lew, Ling. *The Chinese in North America: A Guide to Their Life and Progress.* Los Angeles: East-West Culture Publishing Association, 1951.

Lichtenstein, Nelson. *Walter Reuther: The Most Dangerous Man in Detroit.* Urbana: University of Illinois Press, 1995.

Lieberman, Robbie, and Clarence Lang, eds. *Anticommunism and the African American Freedom Movement: Another Side of the Story.* New York: Palgrave Macmillan, 2009.

Lipsitz, George. *Rainbow at Midnight: Labor and Culture in the 1940s.* Urbana: University of Illinois Press, 1994.

Louis, Kit King. "Problems of Second Generation Chinese." *Sociology and Social Research* 41, no. 3 (January–February 1932): 250–58.

Lowe, Lisa. *Immigrant Acts: On Asian American Cultural Politics.* Durham, N.C.: Duke University Press, 1996.

Lundberg, Ferdinand. *America's Sixty Families.* New York: Vanguard, 1937.

Lynd, Staughton, ed. *Martin Glaberman: Punching Out and Other Writings.* Chicago: Charles H. Kerr, 2002.

Lynn, Conrad. *There Is a Fountain: The Autobiography of a Civil Rights Lawyer.* Westport, Conn.: Lawrence Hill, 1979.

Makalani, Minkah. *In the Cause of Freedom: Radical Black Internationalism from Harlem to London, 1917–1939.* Chapel Hill: University of North Carolina Press, 2011.

Marcus, Anthony, ed. *Malcolm X and the Third American Revolution: The Writings of George Breitman.* Amherst, N.Y.: Humanity Books, 2005.

Mark, Diane Mei Lin, and Ginger Chih. *A Place Called Chinese America.* Dubuque, Iowa: Kendall Hunt, 1982.

Martin, Charles H. *The Angelo Herndon Case and Southern Justice.* Baton Rouge: Louisiana State University Press, 1976.

Marx, Karl. *Capital: A Critique of Political Economy.* Vol. 1. Translated by Ben Fowkes with an introduction by Ernest Mandel. New York: Vintage Books, 1977.

———. *The Eighteenth Brumaire of Louis Bonaparte.* New York: International Publishers, 1963 [1852].

Marx, Karl, and Frederick Engels. *The Communist Manifesto: 150th Anniversary Edition, 1848–1998.* Introduced by Robin D. G. Kelley. Chicago: Charles H. Kerr, 2003 [1848].

Mast, Robert, ed. *Detroit Lives.* Philadelphia: Temple University Press, 1994.

Maxwell, William J. *New Negro, Old Left: African-American Writing and Communism between the Wars.* New York: Columbia University Press, 1999.

Mayo, Elton. *The Human Problems of an Industrial Civilization.* Boston: Division of Research, Graduate School of Business Administration, Harvard University, 1946.

———. *The Social Problems of an Industrial Civilization.* Boston: Division of Research, Graduate School of Business Administration, Harvard University, 1945.

McClendon, John H. *C. L. R. James's "Notes on Dialectics": Left Hegelianism or Marxism-Leninism?* Lanham, Md.: Lexington Books, 2005.

McDuffie, Erik S. *Sojourning for Freedom: Black Women, American Communism, and the Making of Black Left Feminism.* Durham, N.C.: Duke University Press, 2011.

McLemee, Scott. "Afterword: American Civilization and World Revolution: C. L. R. James in the United States, 1938–1953 and Beyond." In *C. L. R. James and Revolutionary Marxism: Selected Writings of C. L. R. James, 1939–1949,* edited by Scot McLemee and Paul Le Blanc, 209–38. Atlantic Highlands, N.J.: Humanities Press, 1994.

———. *C. L. R. James on the "Negro Question."* Jackson: University Press of Mississippi, 1996.

McLemee, Scott, and Paul Le Blanc, eds. *C. L. R. James and Revolutionary Marxism: Selected Writings of C. L. R. James, 1939–1949*. Atlantic Highlands, N.J.: Humanities Press, 1994.

McWhorter, Diane. *Carry Me Home: Birmingham, Alabama, the Climatic Battle of the Civil Rights Revolution*. New York: Touchstone, 2001.

Meier, August, and Elliot Rudwick. *Black Detroit and the Rise of the UAW*. Ann Arbor: University of Michigan Press, 2007 [1979].

Meriwether, James H. *Proudly We Can Be Africans: Black Americans and Africa, 1935–1961*. Chapel Hill: University of North Carolina Press, 2002.

Meyer, Stephen. "'An Economic Frankenstein': UAW Workers' Responses to Automation at the Ford Brook Park Plant in the 1950s." *Michigan Historical Review* 28, no. 2 (Spring 2002): 63–89.

———. "The Persistence of Fordism: Workers and Technology in the American Automobile Industry, 1900–1960." In *On the Line: Essays in the History of Auto Work*, edited by Nelson Lichtenstein and Stephen Meyer, 86–91. Urbana: University of Illinois Press, 1989.

Miliband, Ralph. "Bonapartism." In *A Dictionary of Marxist Thought*, edited by Tom Bottomore, 55–56. Cambridge, Mass.: Blackwell, 1991 [1983].

Miller, Karen R. *Managing Inequality: Northern Racial Liberalism in Interwar Detroit*. New York: New York University Press, 2015.

Mills, C. Wright. *The New Men of Power: America's Labor Leaders*. New York: Harcourt, Brace, 1948.

Milne, June. *Forward Ever: The Life of Kwame Nkrumah*. London: Panaf Books, 2006 [1977].

———. *Kwame Nkrumah: A Biography*. London: Panaf Books, 2006 [1999].

Moon, Elaine Latzman, ed. *Untold Tales, Unsung Heroes: An Oral History of Detroit's African American Community, 1918–1967*. Detroit: Wayne State University Press, 1994.

Mullen, Bill V. *Afro-Orientalism*. Minneapolis: University of Minnesota Press, 2004.

———. *Popular Fronts: Chicago and African-American Cultural Politics, 1935–46*. Urbana: University of Illinois Press, 1999.

Naison, Mark. *Communists in Harlem during the Depression*. Urbana: University of Illinois Press, 1983.

Neusom, Daniel B. "The Michigan Civil Rights Law and Its Enforcement." MA thesis, Wayne University [now Wayne State University], 1952.

Nicholas, Xavier. *Questions of the American Revolution: Conversations with James Boggs*. Atlanta: Institute of the Black World, 1976.

Nkrumah, Kwame. *Ghana: The Autobiography of Kwame Nkrumah*. New York: International Publishers, 1957.

———. *I Speak of Freedom*. London: Panaf Books, 1973 [1961].

Noar, David. *The Lines of Life: Theories of Biography, 1880–1970*. West Lafayette, Ind.: Purdue University Press, 1986.

Noble, David F. *Forces of Production: A Social History of Industrial Automation*. New York: Alfred A. Knopf, 1984.

Norris, Harold. "Dislocation without Relocation." In *Detroit Perspectives: Crossroads and Turning Points*, edited by Wilma Wood Henrickson, 474–76. Detroit: Wayne State University Press, 1991.

Padmore, George. "Behind the Mau Mau." *Phylon* 14, no. 4 (1953): 355–72.

Painter, Nell Irvin. *The Narrative of Hosea Hudson: His Life as a Negro Communist in the South*. Cambridge, Mass.: Harvard University Press, 1979.

Peterson, Rachael. "*Correspondence*: Journalism, Anticommunism, and Marxism in 1950s Detroit." In *Anticommunism and the African American Freedom Movement*, edited by Robbie Lieberman and Clarence Lang, 115–59. New York: Palgrave Macmillan, 2009.

Petty, Tawana Honeycomb. "100 Years of Bad Ass." Poem delivered at the Grace Lee Boggs memorial service, "Celebrating the Life and Legacy of Grace Lee Boggs," October 31, 2015, IBEW Local 58, Detroit, Michigan.

Phelps, Christopher. "C. L. R. James and the Theory of State Capitalism." In *American Capitalism: Social Thought and Political Economy in the Twentieth Century*, edited by Nelson Lichtenstein, 157–74. Philadelphia: University of Pennsylvania Press, 2006.

———. "James Boggs." In *African American National Biography*, edited by Henry Louis Gates and Evelyn Brooks Higginbotham, 459–60. Oxford: Oxford University Press, 2008.

Phillips, Kimberley L. *Alabama North: African-American Migrants, Community, and Working-Class Activism in Cleveland, 1915–1945*. Urbana: University of Illinois Press, 1999.

Pizzolato, Nicola. *Challenging Global Capitalism: Labor Migration, Radical Struggle, and Urban Change in Detroit and Turin*. New York: Palgrave Macmillan, 2013.

Plummer, Brenda Gayle. *Rising Wind: Black Americans and U.S. Foreign Affairs, 1935–1960*. Chapel Hill: University of North Carolina Press, 1996.

Poinsett, Alex. *Walking with Presidents: Louis Martin and the Rise of Black Political Power*. Lanham, Md.: Rowman and Littlefield, 2000.

Polsgrove, Carol. *Divided Minds: Intellectuals and the Civil Rights Movement*. New York: Norton, 2001.

Powledge, Fred. *Free at Last? The Civil Rights Movement and the People Who Made It*. New York: Harper, 1991.

Pursell, Carroll. "The Technology of Production." In *A Companion to American Technology*, edited by Carroll Pursell, 55–82. Malden, Mass.: Blackwell, 2005.

Rahman, Ahmad A. *The Regime Change of Kwame Nkrumah: Epic Heroism in Africa and the Diaspora*. New York: Palgrave Macmillan, 2007.

Raines, Howell. *My Soul Is Rested: The Story of the Civil Rights Movement in the Deep South*. New York: Penguin, 1977.

Randolph, Sherie M. *Florynce "Flo" Kennedy: The Life of a Feminist Radical*. Chapel Hill: University of North Carolina Press, 2015.

Ransby, Barbara. *Ella Baker and the Black Freedom Movement: A Radical Democratic Vision*. Chapel Hill: University of North Carolina Press, 2003.

———. *Eslanda: The Large and Unconventional Life of Mrs. Paul Robeson*. New Haven, Conn.: Yale University Press, 2013.

Rawcliffe, D. H. *The Struggle for Kenya*. London: Victor Gollancz, 1954.

Record, Wilson. *The Negro and the Communist Party*. Chapel Hill: University of North Carolina Press, 1951.

———. *Race and Radicalism: The NAACP and the Communist Party in Conflict*. Ithaca, N.Y.: Cornell University Press, 1964.

Renton, Dave. *C. L. R. James: Cricket's Philosopher King.* London: Haus Books, 2007.

Robinson, Cedric. *An Anthropology of Marxism.* Burlington, Vt.: Ashgate, 2001.

———. *Black Marxism: The Making of the Black Radical Tradition.* Chapel Hill: University of North Carolina Press, 2000 [1983].

———. *Forgeries of Memory and Meaning: Blacks and the Regimes of Race in American Theater and Film before World War II.* Chapel Hill: University of North Carolina Press, 2007.

Roderick, Rick. "Further Adventures of the Dialectic." In *C. L. R. James: His Intellectual Legacies,* edited by Selwyn R. Cudjoe and William E. Cain, 205–11. Amherst: University of Massachusetts Press, 1995.

Romano, Paul, and Ria Stone. *The American Worker.* Detroit: Bewick, 1972 [1947].

Rosengarten, Frank. *Urbane Revolutionary: C. L. R. James and the Struggle for a New Society.* Jackson: University Press of Mississippi, 2008.

Salvatore, Nick. *Singing in a Strange Land: C. L. Franklin, the Black Church, and the Transformation of America.* New York: Little, Brown, 2005.

Sewell, Stacy Kinlock. "The 'Not-Buying Power' of the Black Community: Urban Boycotts and Equal Employment Opportunity, 1960–1964." *Journal of African American History* 89, no. 2 (Spring 2004): 139–40.

Shockley, Megan Taylor. *We, Too, Are Americans: African American Women in Detroit and Richmond, 1940–1954.* Urbana: University of Illinois Press, 2004.

Sisk, Glenn N. "Negro Education in the Alabama Black Belt, 1875–1900." *Journal of Negro History* 22, no. 2 (Spring 1953): 126–35.

Sitkoff, Harvard. "The Detroit Riot of 1943." *Michigan History* 53 (Fall 1969): 183–206.

Smethurst, James Edward. *The Black Arts Movement: Literary Nationalism in the 1960s and 1970s.* Chapel Hill: University of North Carolina Press, 2005.

———. *The New Red Negro: The Literary Left and African American Poetry, 1930–1946.* New York: Oxford University Press, 1999.

Smith, Suzanne E. *Dancing in the Street: Motown and the Cultural Politics of Detroit.* Cambridge, Mass.: Harvard University Press, 1999.

Solomon, Mark. *Their Cry Was Unity: Communists and African Americans, 1917–1936.* Jackson: University Press of Mississippi, 1998.

Spero, Sterling D., and Abram L. Harris. *The Black Worker: The Negro and the Labor Movement.* New York: Atheneum, 1974 [1931].

Sugrue, Thomas J. *Origins of the Urban Crisis: Race and Inequality in Postwar Detroit.* Princeton, N.J.: Princeton University Press, 1996.

———. *Sweet Land of Liberty: The Forgotten Struggle for Civil Rights in the North.* New York: Random House, 2008.

Sullivan, Patricia. *Lift Every Voice: The NAACP and the Making of the Civil Rights Movement.* New York: New Press, 2009.

Swann-Wright, Dianne. *A Way Out of No Way: Claiming Family and Freedom in the New South.* Charlottesville: University of Virginia Press, 2002.

Takaki, Ronald. *Strangers from a Different Shore: A History of Asian Americans.* Rev. ed. Boston: Little, Brown, 1998 [1989].

Theoharis, Jeanne. *The Rebellious Life of Mrs. Rosa Parks*. Boston: Beacon, 2013.

Thomas, June Manning. *Redevelopment and Race: Planning a Finer City in Postwar Detroit*. Baltimore: Johns Hopkins University Press, 1997.

Thomas, Richard W. *Life for Us Is What We Make It: Building Black Community in Detroit, 1915–1945*. Bloomington: Indiana University Press, 1992.

Thompson, Heather Ann. *Whose Detroit? Politics, Labor, and Race in a Modern American City*. Ithaca, N.Y.: Cornell University Press, 2001.

Tinson, Christopher M. "The Voice of the Black Protest Movement: Notes on the *Liberator* Magazine and Black Radicalism in the Early 1960s." *Black Scholar* 37, no. 4 (Winter 2008): 3–15.

Titon, Jeff Todd, ed. *Give Me This Mountain: Reverend C. L. Franklin, Life History and Selected Sermons*. Urbana-Champaign: University of Illinois Press, 1989.

Tung, William L. *The Chinese in America, 1820–1973: A Chronology and Fact Book*. Dobbs Ferry, N.Y.: Oceana Publications, 1974.

Turner, Lou. "Epistemology, Absolutes, and the Party: A Critical Examination of Philosophical Divergences within the Johnson-Forest Tendency, 1948–1953." In *C. L. R. James: His Intellectual Legacies*, edited by Selwyn R. Cudjoe and William E. Cain, 193–204. Amherst: University of Massachusetts Press, 1995.

Tuttle, William M., Jr. *Race Riot: Chicago in the Red Summer of 1919*. New York: Atheneum, 1970.

Tyson, Timothy B. *Radio Free Dixie: Robert F. Williams and the Roots of Black Power*. Chapel Hill: University of North Carolina Press, 1999.

Von Eschen, Penny M. *Race against Empire: Black Americans and Anticolonialism, 1937–1957*. Ithaca, N.Y.: Cornell University Press, 1997.

Wacker, Denise. "Negro Movement: Blame Whites for Racial Problems." *Michigan Daily*, May 18, 1961.

Wald, Alan. *The New York Intellectuals: The Rise and Decline of the Anti-Stalinist Left from the 1930s to the 1980s*. Chapel Hill: University of North Carolina Press, 1987.

Walker, Vanessa Siddle, with Ulysses Byas. *Hello Professor: A Black Principal and Professional Leadership in the Segregated South*. Chapel Hill: University of North Carolina Press, 2009.

Ward, Matthew. *Indignant Heart*. New York: New Books, 1952.

Ward, Stephen M., ed. *Pages from a Black Radical's Notebook: A James Boggs Reader*. Detroit: Wayne State University Press, 2011.

Washburn, Patrick S. *The African American Newspaper: Voices of Freedom*. Evanston, Ill.: Northwestern University Press, 2006.

Watts, Jerry, ed. *Harold Cruse's "The Crisis of the Negro Intellectual" Reconsidered*. New York: Routledge, 2004.

Weaver, Robert C. *Negro Labor: A National Problem*. Port Washington, N.Y.: Kennikat, 1946.

Webb, Constance. *Not Without Love: Memoirs*. Lebanon, N.H.: University Press of New England, 2003.

Widick, B. J. *Detroit: City of Race and Class Violence*. Detroit: Wayne State University Press, 1989 [1972].

Wieder, Alan. *Ruth First and Joe Slovo in the War against Apartheid*. New York: Monthly Review Press, 2013.

Wiener, Norbert. *Cybernetics; or Control and Communication in the Animal and the Machine*. Cambridge, Mass.: MIT Press, 1961 [1948].

Wilkinson, Sook, and Victor Jew, eds. *Asian Americans in Michigan: Voices from the Midwest*. Detroit: Wayne State University Press, 2015.

Williams, Rhonda Y. *Concrete Demands: The Search for Black Power in the 20th Century*. New York: Routledge, 2015.

Wilson, Sunnie, with John Cohassey. *Toast of the Town: The Life and Times of Sunnie Wilson*. Detroit: Wayne State University Press, 1998.

Woodard, Komozi. *A Nation within a Nation: Amiri Baraka (LeRoi Jones) and Black Power Politics*. Chapel Hill: University of North Carolina Press, 1999.

Worcester, Kent. *C. L. R. James: A Political Biography*. Albany: State University of New York Press, 1996.

Wright, Richard. *Black Boy (American Hunger)*. New York: American Library, 1991 [1945].

———. "I Tried to Be a Communist." *Atlantic Monthly* 174, no. 2 (August 1944).

———. *Native Son*. New York: Harper, 1940.

———. *The Outsider*. New York: Harper, 1953.

———. *Uncle Tom's Children*. New York: Harper, 1938.

Young, Coleman, and Lonnie Wheeler. *Hard Stuff: The Autobiography of Coleman Young*. New York: Viking, 1994.

Young, Jasmin A. "Detroit's Red: Black Radical Detroit and the Political Development of Malcolm X." *Souls* 12, no. 1 (March 2010): 14–31.

Yung, Judy, Gordon H. Chang, and Him Mark Lai, eds. *Chinese American Voices: From the Gold Rush to the Present*. Berkeley: University of California Press, 2006.

Zia, Helen. *Asian American Dreams: The Emergence of an American People*. New York: Farrar, Straus, and Giroux, 2000.

Zola, Nkenge, John S. Gruchala, and Grace Lee Boggs, eds. *James Boggs: An American Revolutionary*. Detroit: New Life, 1993.

Zunz, Olivier. *The Changing Face of Inequality: Urbanization, Industrial Development, and Immigration in Detroit, 1880–1920*. Chicago: University of Chicago Press, 1982.

Index

experience and, 363 (n. 47); *Capital* and, 101, 102, 117–21, 123, 124, 139, 141; CLR and, 110–11, 184–87, 199–200, 224–27, 381 (nn. 74, 75), 382 (n. 114); dialectical thinking, 110, 321–24, 365 (n. 85); duality, 79–80, 212–13; Hegelian concepts and logic, 61, 78–79, 79–81, 99, 102, 108, 109–10, 128, 212–15, 326, 365 (nn. 88, 89); intellectual practice and, 60, 79–81, 102–5, 209–10, 214–15, 396 (n. 6); JFT and, 59, 103–5, 109–14; Kant studies, 78, 81, 212; Kenya project, 229–30; London writing projects, 184–87, 199–200, 224–27, 381 (n. 74; 75); Marxism and, 59, 109–14, 117–21, 122–24, 137–42, 367 (nn. 111, 123); Mead and, 80–81, 83; the Negro Question, 114–17; "Nevada Document" and, 110, 128–29, 365 (n. 87); Nkrumah book project, 208–15; philosophy education, 75–78; pragmatism, 80–81, 83, 362 (n. 43); as reflections on history, 79–80, 96–99; state capitalism and, 99, 108, 117, 119–20, 128–29, 140, 201, 213; theory of alienation, 119–20; Trotskyism and, 87–90, 126–29; truth/knowledge, 78; Weiss and, 78, 79, 80; on working-class agency/capacity, 137–42, 287–88. *See also* partnership, intellectual and political of GLB and JB

Boggs, Grace Lee (writings, speeches, interviews): "Alienated Labor" translation, 118, 119; *The American Worker*, 121–25, 126, 127, 212; "Black Revolution in America," 327; Convention of Correspondence Committees speech, 137–42; *Conversations in Maine* (with JB, F. Paine & L. Paine), 326, 396 (n. 13); *Correspondence* newspaper, 264; "Critique of the Hegelian Dialectic" translation, 118, 119–20; "Editor's Report," 287, 289; *Essays by Karl Marx* translations, 117–21, 123, 125, 126, 212; *Facing Reality* (James, Lee, Chaulieu), 200–201, 241, 382 (n. 114); *Living for Change*, 335; *Manifesto for a Black Revolutionary Party* pamphlet, 327–28; "Monroe: North Carolina," 291; MOWM and, 95–99; *New International* articles, 88, 97, 98–99, 101, 112, 114–15, 360 (n. 6), 366 (n. 92), 367 (n. 7); "New Nations" speech, 386 (n. 53); *Next American Revolution* (with Kurashige), 335–36; "Private Property and Communism" translation, 118, 119; *Revolution and Evolution in the Twenti-*

eth Century (with JB), 7, 328–29; under Ria Stone pseudonym, 88, 97, 117, 121–22, 360 (n. 6), 363 (n.47); *State Capitalism and World Revolution* (with James and Dunayevskaya), 128–29; "When C. L. R. Was a Part of Our Lives" speech, 364 (n. 76); "Winds of Change" remarks, 273; "World War I in Retrospect" (article series with Abern), 88

Boggs, James: activist roots, 11–13, 59; aliases/pseudonyms of, 172, 211, 263, 354 (n. 77); AYD membership, 354 (n. 77); birth/early childhood, 11, 13–19, 270, 341 (n. 1), 343 (nn. 22; 37); courtship and marriage to GLB, 152–55, 188, 223–24, 372 (n. 55); CP and, 351 (n. 69); death/memorial service, 6, 369 (n. 9), 393 (n. 59), 397 (n. 34); Dr. Donald/Miss Elvie and, 13–14, 20, 342 (n. 14); education and schooling, 19–23, 344 (nn. 56, 57, 62); employment patterns, 32, 35–36, 38–39, 232–35, 326–27, 347 (n. 126), 348 (n. 10), 350 (n. 56); family relationships, 13–14, 17–18, 342 (n. 14), 343 (nn. 41, 43, 45); Kenyan independence project (London), 226; marriage/family with Annie (McKinley) Boggs, 22, 25, 35–36, 44, 45–46, 153, 344 (nn. 57, 65), 348 (n. 10); migration north, 25–27, 28–29, 345 (n. 79); politicization process, 20, 22–24, 43, 48–50, 59, 60–61, 344 (n. 69); racial/ethnic identity and, 59, 169–70. *See also* partnership, intellectual and political of GLB and JB

Boggs, James (labor movement activism): antidiscrimination organizing, 53–54, 56–58; *Citadel* contributions, 48–49; employment patterns and, 232–35; with Local 7, 39–40, 43, 47–48, 49–50, 54, 55, 232–34, 381 (n. 93); Marxist analysis and, 238, 288; Organization Committee, 47–48; UAW and, 48–49, 53–54, 136, 276–77, 387 (n. 15); union critiques, 233–35; use of *Capital* theorizations, 238, 288. *See also* partnership, intellectual and political of GLB and JB

Boggs, James (political engagement): AYD membership, 51, 52–53, 351 (nn. 60, 65, 67), 354 (n. 77); black radical education and, 46–54; Correspondence and, 58–59; *Correspondence* and, 156–57, 171–77, 195–96, 197, 220–28; CP and, 50–53, 351 (n. 60), 351 (n. 69); FBI surveillance of, 154, 171, 229–30, 348 (n. 10), 351 (n. 65), 354 (n. 77); grassroots

Boggs, James (political engagement) (*continued*)
activism, 393 (n. 55); on housing, 176, 177, 178, 180; Kenyan independence *Correspondence* project, 188–89, 193–94; Marxism and, 50; NAACP and, 57; Nkrumah and, 210; social identity and, 59, 71–73; SWP and, 52–53, 136, 354 (n. 77). *See also* partnership, intellectual and political of GLB and JB

Boggs, James (theoretical development): anticolonial activities, 211; automation analysis, 145, 235–38, 240–41, 263, 288–89, 307–8, 321–22, 382 (n. 110); on black humanity, 260–61; black masses/black leadership, 172, 174, 218, 272–73, 277, 313, 319; capitalism/racial oppression links, 273–74; critiques of black elite leadership, 172–74, 183–84; dialectical thinking, 175–76, 321–22, 321–24; DiGaetano and, 43, 48–49, 233, 349 (n. 25); duality, 175–76; impact of *Correspondence* on, 170; impact of employment patterns on, 232–35; left intellectual development and, 49–54; Marxist analysis of, 238, 287–90; militancy framework, 278–79; on nonviolent resistance, 284–85, 319–20; political uses of black history, 174–75; racial assertion concept, 217–18, 228–29, 279; racial liberalism, 278–79; use of *Capital* theorizations, 238, 288; vision of social transformation, 240, 262–63, 277, 278–79, 289; Williams collaboration, 284–85; working-class agency/capacity, 287–88, 369 (n. 9). *See also* partnership, intellectual and political of GLB and JB

Boggs, James (writings, speeches, interviews): *The American Revolution: Pages from a Negro Worker's Notebook*, 24, 50, 235, 307, 333, 347 (n. 7), 350 (n. 56), 392 (n. 53), 393 (n. 55); "Beyond Militancy," 350 (n. 4); "Black Political Power," 295, 390 (n. 11); "Black Power—A Scientific Concept Whose Time Has Come," 324–25; Black Power writings, 327–28; *Citadel* contributions, 48, 49–50; Community Celebration remarks, 341 (n. 1); *Conversations in Maine* (JB, Paine, and Paine), 326, 396 (n. 13); *Correspondence* articles and projects, 157, 162, 172–77, 195–96, 228–29, 260–64, 268–69, 277–79, 376 (n. 74); "Culture and Black Power," 325; *Manifesto for a Black Revolutionary Party* pamphlet, 327–28; "Meaning of the Black Revolt in the USA"

(JB), 322; "Monroe: North Carolina," 291; "Myth and Irrationality of Black Capitalism," 32; "Negroes and the Trade Unions" speech, 270, 386 (n. 53); "Next Development in Education," 344 (n. 54); "Questions of the American Revolution" (Nicholas interview), 51, 52; *Racism and Class Struggle*, 327, 350 (n. 56), 390 (n. 11); *Revolution and Evolution in the Twentieth Century* (with GLB), 7, 328–29; "Special Negro News" column, 160–62, 167, 171, 172, 176–78, 180, 229, 262; "State of Nation-America, 1962," 287–89, 307; "Tension and Social Change," 119–20; "The Myth and Irrationality of Black Capitalism" speech, 327; "Too Little Too Late" remarks, 272, 273, 341 (n. 1)

Boggs, James, Jr., 27, 36, 343 (n. 43), 350 (n. 37)

Boggs, Joy, 342 (n. 14), 343 (n. 41)

Boggs, Leila, 13–14, 20

Boggs, Thomas, 17, 343 (n. 41)

Boggs Center to Nurture Community Leadership (BCNCL), 334–35, 397 (n. 41)

Boggses University/3061 Field Street, 3, 292, 333–34, 334–35, 390 (n. 70)

Bond, Horace Mann, 15

Boyd, Melba Joyce, 345 (n. 94)

Boyle, Kevin, 354 (n. 79)

Boyton v. Virginia, 274

Brandt, Marie, 373 (n. 12). *See also* James, Selma

Brotherhood of Sleeping Car Porters (BSCP), 91, 93, 361 (n. 25)

Brown, Faye, 332

Brown, Tony, 299

Brown v. Board of Education, 181–84, 274, 316

Buck, Pearl S., 72, 358 (n. 63)

Buhle, Paul, 364 (n. 61), 365 (n. 87)

Calverton, V. F., 366 (n. 93)

Cannon, James, 86–87

Capital (Marx), 101, 102, 117–21, 123, 124, 139, 141, 238, 288

Case for West-Indian Self-Government (James), 100

Castoriadis, Cornelius (Pierre Chaulieu/Paul Cardan), 127–28, 368 (nn. 142, 147), 382 (n. 114)

Cavanagh, Jerome, 299, 300

Cayton, Horace, 89, 90, 361 (n. 27)

Chang, Iris, 356 (n. 27)

Chaulieu, Pierre (Cornelius Castoriadis), 127–28, 368 (nn. 142, 147), 382 (n. 114)

Chen, Shehong, 357 (n. 40)

Chicago, Illinois, 32, 34, 35, 81–90, 93–95, 98–99, 101–2, 107, 312, 361 (n. 27)

Chicago Congress of Negro Organizations, 93

Chicago Defender, 34, 93, 94–95, 361 (n. 27)

Chin, Louise, 359 (n. 78)

China Mystique (Leong), 358 (n. 63)

Chin Dong Goon, 61, 62–64, 66, 67

Chinese/Chinese Americans: Chinese exclusion, 60–61, 62, 63, 64, 355 (nn. 10, 11), 356 (n. 21); in higher education, 81–82; identity development of, 64, 67–69, 357 (nn. 40, 48); immigrant experiences, 62–64, 68–69, 72, 168–70, 355 (n. 9), 356 (n. 19), 357 (nn. 59, 60); influences on Grace, 68, 355 (n. 2); paper sons, 62, 355 (n. 11); *United States v. Wong*, 357 (n. 60); women, 60–61, 62, 63, 64, 355 (nn. 10, 11), 356 (nn. 19, 21), 358 (n. 63); as workers, 63–66, 356 (nn. 23, 27), 360 (n. 108)

Chinese Exclusion Act of 1882, 60–61, 62, 63, 64, 355 (n. 10), 356 (n. 21)

Chinese in America (Chang), 356 (n. 27)

Chrysler Corporation: apprentice program, 347 (n. 126); Dodge Main, 145, 237–38; Dodge Motor Division, 37–38, 39, 348 (n. 9); Highland Park plant, 43; JB employment at, 347 (n. 126), 348 (n. 10); Jefferson Avenue plant, 36, 39, 43, 45–46, 48, 54, 56, 162, 233, 237–38, 263; SWP and, 354 (n. 77); walkouts, 43, 349 (n. 28); worker demographics, 37–38

Citadel, 48, 49–50

Civil rights movement: Black Power movement and, 4, 311–14, 320, 340 (n. 1); *Brown v. Board of Education* and, 181–84, 274, 316; critiques of, 172–73, 183–84, 259–60, 282–83; Freedom Rides, 242, 274–75, 277, 278, 279, 386 (n. 9); interracial activism, 55–57, 248, 274–75, 278–79; labor movement and, 387 (n. 15); Little Rock school desegregation case, 227–29, 241, 257; Monroe Struggle/Kissing case, 247–55, 283–86; Montgomery Bus Boycott, 215–20; 1963 events, 296–311; nonviolent direct action and, 218, 259, 285, 305, 306, 309, 311, 319–20; racial assertion and, 217–18, 228–29, 279; racial liberalism, 278–79; student strikes/sit-ins, 264–69

Clarke, John Henrik, 281–82, 284, 388 (n. 38), 389 (n. 49)

Cleage, Albert B., Jr., 290–91, 293, 297–306, 311, 312, 314, 389 (n. 62), 391 (n. 21)

Clough, Veal, 39

Cobo, Albert, 147, 148, 149–50

Cold War geopolitics, 53, 139–40, 151, 160, 177, 182, 191, 237, 260–61, 317 –318, 352 (n. 74)

Committee for Improved Cuban-American Relations, 284

Committee for Political Development (CPD), 327

Committee to Aid the Monroe Defendants (CAMD), 285–86, 291

Communism, 37 –318, 53, 139–40, 151, 160, 177, 182, 191, 237, 260–61, 352 (n. 74)

Communist League of America, 87, 105–6. *See also* Socialist Workers Party (SWP)

Communist Manifesto (Marx), 113, 141–42

Communist Party (CP): American Trotskyism and, 85–86; auto industry and, 151; AYD, 51, 52–53, 351 (nn. 60, 65, 67), 354 (n. 77); black anti-Communism, 352 (n. 74); black protest and, 51–52; black recruitment/members, 352 (n. 74), 366 (n. 99); criticisms of, 51–52; internationalism and, 352 (n. 74); John Reed Club, 352 (n. 71); MOWM and, 362 (n. 43); Negro Question and, 366 (n. 100); postwar black freedom struggle and, 352 (n. 74); racial politics and, 362 (n. 43); Trotskyism and, 52–53; UAW and, 50–51; women and, 352 (n. 74)

Communists in Harlem during the Depression (Naison), 352 (n. 74)

Congo, Republic of the, 214, 280–81

Congress of International Organizations (CIO), 40–41, 166, 167–68, 173, 184, 233, 354 (n. 79), 387 (n. 15). *See also* AFL-CIO

Congress of Racial Equality (CORE), 242, 274–75, 277, 297, 301–2, 386 (n. 9)

Convention People's Party (CPP), 208–9, 211–13, 218

Conyers, John, Sr., 39, 43

Correspondence (newspaper): "Behind the Iron Curtain" series, 253, 254–55; Black Art supplement, 294–95; black freedom struggles and, 260–64, 280–83, 293–96; *Brown v. Board of Education* coverage, 181–84, 274, 316; bureaucratic control and, 158–59; civil

labor movement and, 38–46, 144, 345 (n. 91), 348 (n. 8); leftist movements, 33, 54–59, 151, 393 (n. 55); Monroe struggle and, 283–86; political activity, 32–35, 353 (n. 75); racial/ethnic struggles, 345 (n. 91), 346 (n. 101), 348 (n. 8); religious activism and, 219–20, 224–25, 297–306, 302; unionization and, 33–34, 144–45; urban renewal, 146–51, 176, 371 (nn. 35, 36); Woodward Avenue march, 391 (n. 21); youth organizing and, 325–26.

Detroit Committee to Aid the Monroe Defendants, 283–86

Detroit Council for Human Rights (DHCR), 298–99, 304–6

Detroiters for Dignity, 330

Detroiters Uniting, 330

Detroit Freedom March, 299–306

Detroit Rebellion (1967), 325–26, 327

Detroit Summer, 331, 332

"Detroit–Ten Years After!" (Wartman), 150–51, 371 (n. 45)

Detroit Tribune, 32, 33–34, 346 (n. 111)

Dialectical thinking: CLR and, 110, 209–20, 365 (n. 89); critiques of, 119–20; dialectical humanism, 321–24, 328–29, 335–36, 396 (n. 6); dialectical materialism, 125–26, 322–23, 396 (n. 4); GLB and, 61, 79, 109–11, 118, 140–42, 365 (n. 89); Hegel and, 61, 79, 118, 119; JB and, 4, 175–76, 322, 323; JB/GLB partnership and, 3–5, 321–24, 328–29, 335–36, 396 (n. 6); JFT use of, 109–11, 118–21, 124, 125

DiGaetano, Nick, 43, 48–49, 233, 349 (n. 25)

Diggs, Charles C., 33, 34, 40, 55, 176, 299

Diggs Act (Michigan Civil Rights Law), 55–56, 57–58

Dillard, Angela D., 340 (n. 1), 348 (n. 8), 353 (n. 75)

Dillard, Ernest, 57–58

Dillard, Jessie, 57–58

Discrimination: Brewster Homes project, 31; *Brown v. Board of Education*, 181–84, 274, 316; defense industries and, 41, 42–43; Diggs Act, 55–56, 57–58; Discrimination Action Committee (Detroit NAACP), 33, 54–59; Fair Employment Practices Committee, 41, 42–43, 92, 349 (n. 20); housing and urban redevelopment, 43–45; Little Rock school desegregation case, 227–29, 241, 257; Metropolitan Labor Council, 42; MOWM and, 41–42, 90–99, 130, 141, 361 (nn. 24, 25,

27), 362 (nn. 32, 41, 43); NAACP Discrimination Action Committee, 54–59; Philadelphia boycott, 303, 392 (n. 42); supermarket boycotts, 301–3

Discussion Bulletin, 196–97, 201, 205, 219–20, 221, 224–25

Dodge Motor Division, 37–38, 39, 348 (n. 10)

"Double V for Victory" campaign, 41–42, 92, 96, 348 (n. 8), 353 (n. 75). *See also* March on Washington Movement (MOWM)

Drake, St. Clair, 89, 93, 99

Du Bois, W. E. B., 191–92, 269, 272, 329, 386 (n. 53)

Dunayevskaya, Raya: bio and background, 107–8; Castoriadis and, 368 (n. 142); *Correspondence* and, 156, 172, 180–81, 196–97; Freddie Forest pseudonym, 101; Hegel and, 108, 365 (n. 89); *Indignant Heart* collaboration, 58; interpretations/translations of Russian theory, 108; Marx and, 108, 117–18; "Nevada Document" and, 110, 128–29, 365 (n. 87); Russian Question and, 101; 629 Hudson Street collaborators, 106–9, 107, 365 (n. 77); on state capitalism, 108, 128–29; Trotskyism and, 107–8; Webb and, 384 (n. 11); WP and, 107–8. *See also* James, C. L. R.; Johnson-Forest Tendency

Dunbar High School, 19–20, 21–23, 24, 26, 344 (nn. 63, 69)

Economic and Philosophic Manuscripts of 1844 (Marx), 117–19, 124, 214

Edelman, Marian Wright, 341 (n. 10)

"Editor's Report" (GLB), 287, 289

"Education, Propaganda, and Agitation" (James), 112–13

Edwards, Carl, 330, 334–35

Egginton, Joyce, 250–51, 253

Eighteenth Brumaire (Marx), 113, 213–14

Eisenhower, Dwight D., 219, 228

Eisenhower, Milton, 386 (n. 12)

Ellison, Ralph, 52, 352 (n. 71)

Engels, Frederick, 117, 125, 141, 144

Essays by Karl Marx (Johnson, Forest, and Stone translation), 117–21, 123, 125, 126, 212

Facing Reality (Correspondence Publishing Company), 200–201, 237–42 384 (n. 11), 241, 382 (n. 114)

Phenomenology of the Mind (Hegel), 78–79, 81, 215

Pitt, David, 216

Pointer (Putnam), Julia, 331

"Politics of Publishing *Correspondence*" (JB), 268

Poston, Ted, 43–44

Prayer Pilgrimage, 219–20, 224–25

Price, William, 148

"Problems of Second Generation Chinese" (Wong), 357 (n. 60)

Protest politics: anti-war organizing and, 88–90; boycotts, 184, 215–20, 278, 300–303, 311–12, 392 (n. 42), 394 (n. 68); cultural workers and, 104–5, 281, 294–95, 311–12, 316–17; Demonstration for Democracy (Chicago), 93; demonstrations/protests at the UN, 281–84, 294, 388 (nn. 29, 40, 41); Group on Advanced Leadership (GOAL), 291, 303–4, 306, 310, 311, 312; Journey of Reconciliation, 242, 274; Lumumba assassination, 280–81; mass action, 91, 95, 173–74, 193, 217, 265, 296–306; MOWM and, 41–42, 91–99, 130, 141, 361 (nn. 24, 25, 27), 362 (nn. 32, 41, 43); 1942 rally (Chicago), 94–95; nonviolent direct action, 218, 259, 285, 305, 306, 309, 311, 319–20; Philadelphia boycott, 303, 392 (n. 42); popular insurgency, 102, 202–3, 209, 217–18, 239–40, 259–60, 263, 265; student strikes/sit-ins, 264–69; supermarket boycotts, 301–3; working-class leadership and, 96–99

Punching Out (Glaberman), 137

"Questions of the American Revolution" (Nicholas), 51, 52

Race and Radicalism (Record), 352 (n. 74)

Racism and the Class Struggle: Further Pages from a Black Worker's Notebook (JB), 327, 350 (n. 56)

Radicalism at the Crossroads (Gore), 352 (n. 74)

Randolph, A. Phillip, 41, 91–96, 97, 99, 243, 361 (n. 27), 362 (nn. 41, 43)

Record, Wilson, 352 (n. 74)

Reid, Frances, 332, 372 (n. 55)

Reid, Ira D., 74, 358 (n. 73)

Religious activism, 190, 193, 219–20, 224–25, 297–306, 348 (n. 8)

Republic of the Congo, 214, 281

Resilience: making a way out of no way, 12–13, 22, 341 (nn. 9, 10)

Reuther, Walter, 53, 172, 233–34, 275–76, 299, 300, 386 (n. 12), 387 (n. 15)

Revolution and Evolution in the Twentieth Century (Boggs and Boggs), 7, 328–29

Revolutionary Action Movement (RAM), 390 (n. 70)

"Revolutionary Answer to the Negro Problem in the United States" (James), 115–17

Revolutionary politics: American history/culture and, 112–17, 366 (n. 93); automation analysis and, 145, 235–38, 240–41, 263, 287–89, 307–8, 321–22, 382 (n. 110); black Americans and, 114, 260–64, 293–94, 321–22; critiques of black elite leadership, 172–73, 183–84; duality and, 79–80, 175–76, 212–13; mass action and, 111, 129, 135–36, 140–41, 144, 158–60, 234–35, 241, 293–94, 321–22; nonviolent direct action and, 218, 259, 285, 305, 306, 309, 311, 319–20; popular insurgency, 102, 202–3, 209, 217–18, 239–40, 259–60, 263, 265; as process of love and struggle, 7; racial assertion and, 217–18, 228–29, 279; revolutionary social forces, 129, 135–36, 140–41, 144, 158–60, 241, 293–94, 321–22; social transformation, 240, 262–63, 277, 278–79, 289; theoretical reflection/political practice and, 4–5, 6; theory of alienation and, 119–20; third-layer concept and, 135–37, 153, 369 (nn. 2, 7), 380 (n. 63); vanguard party concept and, 109, 111, 126, 129, 158–59, 201; visionary organizing, 336

Revolution journal, 322

Rhodesia, 214

Rivera, Diego, 27–28

Roach, Max, 294

Robeson, Eslanda, 192

Robeson, Paul, 191, 192

Robinson, Cedric J., 355 (n. 5). 359 (n. 95), 365 (n. 86)

Robinson, Jackie, 257

Romano, Phil (Phil Singer), 121–22

Roosevelt, Franklin, D., 38, 96

Rosenberg, Ethel and Julius, 138

Rosengarten, Frank, 363 (n. 52), 365 (n. 88), 381 (n. 76)

Rudwick, Elliot, 348 (n. 8)